To
Napier

whom, if I had
met before doing
this book,
it would have been
a much more
educated
book. —

Art Kleiner

Ten Years of

News That

1974–1984

Stayed News

EDITED BY ART KLEINER AND STEWART BRAND

NORTH POINT PRESS   1986   SAN FRANCISCO

North Point Press
850 Talbot Avenue
Berkeley, California
94706

Cover design by David Bullen

Table
of Contents

Acknowledgments   *ix*
Art Kleiner

Introduction   *xi*
Art Kleiner

CoEvolution and the Biology of Com-   3
munities (Spring 1974)
Paul R. Ehrlich

Salons and Their Keepers   10
(Summer 1974)
Stephanie Mills

The Atmosphere as Circulatory System   15
of the Biosphere—the Gaia Hypothesis
(Summer 1975)
Lynn Margulis and James E. Lovelock

For God's Sake, Margaret: A Conversa-   26
tion with Gregory Bateson and Margaret Mead (Summer 1976)
Stewart Brand

The Sun Riots (Spring 1975) and   47
The B & G (Summer 1976)
Steve Baer

Some Mice (Summer 1976)   51
Robert Horvitz

The Space Crone (Summer 1976)   55
Ursula Le Guin

Poem for the Living (Fall 1979)   59
Theodora Kroeber-Quinn

Winning (Summer 1976)   60
Ron Jones

Table of Contents

Biogeographical Provinces (Fall 1976) 68
Raymond Dasmann

The Lefthanded Bear and Other Animal 74
Stories (Fall 1976)
J. D. Smith

Animal Story Letters 79

How to Run the Arms Race Backwards 83
(Spring 1977)
Stewart Brand

The New Class (Spring 1977) 89
Herman Kahn, Jerry Brown,
and Amory Lovins

Yellow Diamonds (Winter 1977/78) 113
Malcolm Wells

Earl Butz versus Wendell Berry 116
(Spring 1978)

I Was Armand Hammer (Spring 1978) 130
J. Baldwin

First Week of November, 1978— 133
and More Anne Herbert (Winter 1978–
Fall 1982)
Anne Herbert

Human Harm to Human DNA 142
(Spring 1979)
Stewart Brand, with extensive quotes from
Bruce Ames

A Short History of America (Fall 1979) 165
R. Crumb

Six Days of Dying (Winter 1980) 170
Mary Catherine Bateson

"Where've You Been, Stranger?" 178
(Summer 1981)
Bryce and Margaret Muir

How Not to Commit Suicide 183
(Summer 1981)
Art Kleiner

Feminism and Sadomasochism 206
(Spring 1982)
Pat Califia

The Legend of Great Uncle Jim and the 215
Woman Behind It All (Spring 1982)
Will Baker

How I Became a Human Being 228
(Spring 1982)
Mark O'Brien

Don't Beg: Take Control 241
(Summer 1982)
Tom Parsons

Doing a Job (Summer 1982) 245
Admiral Hyman G. Rickover

On Farting (Summer 1982) 251
Michael Kimball

A Friend to the Children (Fall 1982) 258
Dan O'Neill

Born to Fail (Winter 1982) 263
J. Baldwin

Kokopelli—The Humpbacked Flute 267
Player (Spring 1983)
Gary Nabhan

Rachelann: A Remembrance 277
(Spring 1983)
Leo Dreu

Good, Wild, Sacred (Fall 1983) 282
Gary Snyder

Handfast (Winter 1983) 291
Sallie Tisdale

Silence Is a Commons (Winter 1983) 293
Ivan Illich

Events Are the Teacher (Winter 1983) 298
Katy Butler

Surviving in Small Business   309
(Spring 1984)
Paul Hawken

Coffee Hour: America's True Religion 313
(Spring 1984)
Jim Burklo

Burying Jed Kesey (Summer 1984)   316
Ken Kesey

The Difference Between Writing   324
and Building Racing Engines
(Summer 1984)
Harry and Larry Ingham

Who Do You Think You Are?   326
(Fall 1984)
Freddy Bosco

Afterword: Outtro   329
Stewart Brand

Appendix: A History of CoEvolution   331
Quarterly
Art Kleiner

Acknowledgments

Decisions to do this book were made independently but simultaneously at *Whole Earth* (between me and Kevin Kelly) and at North Point Press. Those two decisions were melded into one project with uncommon ease and courtesy. I'm grateful to North Point editors Jack Shoemaker and Tom Christensen for their support and help. Stewart Brand and I selected the material, making our arduous choices by give-and-take over the Electronic Information Exchange System computer network (which allowed me to do most of the editing of this book at home). Kevin Kelly was also involved in that process. We had useful suggestions from J. Baldwin and Richard Nilsen. Levi Thomas, Jonathan Evelegh, and Cindy Craig helped with some of the clerical work of the project; Andrea Sharp and David Cohn put in some accounting/negotiating support.

I'm grateful and indebted to the people I have known and worked with at *Whole Earth* over the years, who have taught me what making a magazine is about. These people include the other editors I worked with at CQ: Stewart Brand, Anne Herbert, Stephanie Mills, Jay Kinney, Richard Nilsen, Joe Kane, and Kevin Kelly. They include the designers and artists: Kathleen O'Neill, Don Ryan, Rebecca Wilson, James Donnelly, Isabella Kirkland, John Prestianni. They include the guardians of consistency—typesetters and proofreaders: Evelyn Eldridge-Diaz, Susan Erkel Ryan, James Donnelly, Ted Schultz, Hank Roberts, Nancy Dunn, Kara Adanalian, Annette Jarvie, Angela Gennino. They include people who supported the readers, or supported the operation: Andrea Sharp, David Burnor, Dick Fugett, Ben Campbell, Lorrie Gallagher, Jonathan Evelegh, Arnie Kotler, Debbie Hopkins, David Cohn, Lyn Gray, Jim Stockford, Kathy Parks, Matthew McClure, Cindy Craig. And they include contributors from *Whole Earth* past and present: J. D. Smith, Rick Fields, Andrew Fluegelman, J. Baldwin, Peter Warshall, Tom Ferguson, Mike Phillips, Paul Hawken, Barbara Robertson, Steven Levy. Also thanks to Rob Garross, who introduced me to the magazine in the first place. . . .

A.K.

ART KLEINER

Introduction

This book is an unabashed act of reckless homage to a unique, influential, prescient, unpredictable magazine called COEVOLUTION QUARTERLY.

It's also an act of homage to magazines themselves. Magazines are too little acknowledged for their effect on the North American culture. Just by existing, a great magazine defines a community of people with a common language of thought, and propels those people into a common experience—an amusement-park ride that takes place over years instead of minutes. Truly great magazines are rare: *Fortune* in the 1930s; the *New Yorker* in the 30s and 40s; *Esquire* in the 50s and 60s; the *Evergreen Review*, and the *Realist* in the 60s; and the magazine anthologized here, COEVOLUTION QUARTERLY, between 1974 and 1984.[1]

A typical issue of COEVOLUTION

had 144 black-and-white pages, about the size of this book's pages, without advertising,[2] and without any stated editorial theme except, perhaps, Gregory Bateson's definition of information—"a difference that makes a difference." It was a notoriously difficult magazine to describe to people who weren't already familiar with it, because it wasn't *about* any topic in particular—except quality. By big-magazine standards, it never had much of an audience—never more than 30,000 subscribers. Unlike most small-circulation magazines, COEVOLUTION QUARTERLY survived ten years, with a readership as loyal and influential as any magazine can hope for.

The man who allured and held those readers, Stewart Brand, is better known for his other publication, the *Whole Earth Catalog*.[3] (As it hap-

---

1. Although I refer to COEVOLUTION in the past tense, this is not an obituary. The magazine still exists under another name, the *Whole Earth Review*, which combines COEVOLUTION with its sister publication, the *Whole Earth Software Review*. For more information on the *Whole Earth Review*, see Appendix, p. 337.

2. Mostly without advertising, that is; for its last two-and-a-half years CQ accepted "unclassifieds," text-only classifieds in the back of the magazine, only from subscribers. Otherwise, it was completely supported by its readers and by special projects. Only *Mad Magazine* and *Consumer Reports* have sustained a larger readership without advertising for so long.

3. For those who do not know about the *Whole Earth Catalog* (I didn't, when I started working there): it's a book of informal reviews and recommendations of good tools, started by Stewart Brand in 1968 to cater (at first) to hippies living on communes. The *Catalog* went on to spark the resourcefulness of a generation of people. The early *Catalogs*

pens, COEVOLUTION QUARTERLY
was started in 1974 with proceeds
from the *Catalog*.) Stewart Brand
has two talents common to all great
magazine editors: the ability to
gather together a family of brilliant
contributors, and the ability to piss
them all off from time to time.[4] CO-
EVOLUTION's extended family included luminaries and arrogant ex-
hippies ("some of us are famous and
some are smug," Stewart once wrote
in the magazine's Gossip section)—
but the magazine was rarely cowed
by any of them. Stewart's first loyalty was always to the readers, as represented by his own emphatic but
open-minded judgment.[5]

COEVOLUTION experimented constantly, in ways that a magazine with
advertising can't. Stewart was always
trying something that no other magazine publisher would dream of

doing. Guest editors, for instance:
every four issues or so, Stewart would
relinquish his normal ironclad control over the entire magazine, find
someone with a special topic to
cover, put the staff into their hands
for the quarter, and disappear. Or
the financially unsuccessful Bold/
Lite experiment: to avoid offending
readers with explicit sex, yet not feel
hamstrung, Stewart created a "Bold"
section of the magazine with raunchy material intact, and gave subscribers a choice of CQ with or without it.

CQ opened up many debates and
topics for the first time. Space colonies: By printing Gerard O'Neill's
and his own arguments in their favor, Stewart annoyed many of his
ecologically minded contributors
and readers. So he printed *their* arguments. The controversy lingered for
several issues (some old CQ readers
can *still* get angry when they think
of it) and ultimately modified the
ideas of some of the space-colony
planners. Other themes got early notice in CQ before becoming prominent elsewhere. The Gaia hypothesis. Voluntary simplicity. Arguments against metric conversion.
Personal computers. The resurgence
of the antiwar movement. The flat
tax. Critical evaluation of magazines. The effects of chemicals on the
human gene pool.

Most importantly, COEVOLUTION
published a lot of material—essays,
reporting, and story-telling—that
will endure as "news that stays
news," to quote Ezra Pound's definition of literature.[6] Hence this

---

were quarterlies, and their recommendations
were compiled in 1972 into the 452-page
Last Whole Earth Catalog, a National Book
Award winner, best-seller, and culture chang-
er. A 1974 addendum, the *Whole Earth
Epilog*, and COEVOLUTION QUARTERLY itself, continued to cover how-to books, tools,
and more with *Whole Earth*-style reviews; in
1980 Stewart and the rest of us *Whole Earth*
staffers recompiled the *Catalog* into the gar-
gantuan 608-page *Next Whole Earth Catalog*.

4. That ability to anger contributors yet hold
them seems to be endemic to magazine editors; see James Thurber's *The Years With Ross*,
for instance. Stewart and *New Yorker* founder
Harold Ross seem to have had the same two
techniques for infuriating people: blithe inconsistency about detail, and not listening to
what other people *thought* they should do
with the magazine.

5. Not that Stewart was the *only* influence.
As CQ evolved, more and more people contributed in great and small ways to its overall
creativity; many of their names are listed in
the Acknowledgments to this book. CQ was
blessed with a warmhearted, capable, consistent staff which made possible much of the
flavor and value of the magazine.

6. In *ABC of Reading*, 1934, published by
William Morrow & Co., Inc. The definition
was quoted in the review of *ABC of Reading*
in both the *Last* and *Next Whole Earth
Catalog*.

book—a collection, in one place, of what we think is the most lasting work COEVOLUTION published. You'll find little of purely historical interest—for instance, although space colonies were debated fervently, we didn't include any of that material, already reprinted in a book that Stewart edited (*Space Colonies*, Penguin, 1978). If you're interested in the history of the magazine (its life is, after all, tied intimately with many cultural and political movements of the sixties, seventies, and eighties, particularly in California) you'll find an issue-by-issue discography in the Appendix.

If you're familiar with COEVOLUTION, you'll notice a few enduring pieces are missing in this book— Ron Jones's "The Third Wave," Carol Van Strum's "The Most Unusual Letter We've Ever Received," and "Trees" by Jean Giono. That's because these pieces, and others, appeared already in the *Next Whole Earth Catalog* (Random House, 1980). With the limited space available (we could easily have compiled a volume twice this size and *still* left good material out), we chose to reprint very few pieces from the *Catalog*. That pruning has allowed sunlight to nurture more forgotten blossoms—like Ron Jones's *other* story, "Winning" (p. 60). Similarly, a few articles—Wendell Berry's "Poetry and Marriage," for instance— were left out because they subsequently saw publication in other books (in this case, *Standing By Words*, North Point, 1983).

This is a book I've wanted to see published since I was first introduced to COEVOLUTION QUARTERLY in 1976; a friend handed me a copy and said, "I think you'll like this." I quickly became a fan; ordered the back issues that were still in print; searched for earlier ones in used bookstores. When I began writing journalism, COEVOLUTION was the first place I submitted my ideas (I suspected, correctly, that they'd be responded to with understanding and high spirits). Later I was hired by Stewart Brand—first to help research the *Next Whole Earth Catalog*, then as editor of COEVOLUTION itself. Every day of the five years I worked there, I was conscious that we were printing material that could last long beyond the lifespan of a typical magazine issue (even COEVOLUTION, whose perfect-bound back issues are kept on many people's bookshelves). Here is the best of that material.

News That
Stayed News

PAUL R. EHRLICH

CoEvolution and the Biology of Communities

COEVOLUTION got its title and its bent partly because I was bit early on by a series of biologists—Ed Ricketts (via John Steinbeck's Monterey books), Aldous Huxley (in print and person), Paul Ehrlich, and last and deepest, Gregory Bateson. Assistant Professor Ehrlich supervised my tarantula "research" at Stanford in 1959, when the Stanford Biology Department was still mostly molecular biology and an ecologist was hard to find. (In truth they're still hard to find, amid the proliferation of "ecologists.")

Starting with *The Population Bomb* (1968), on through *Ecoscience* (1977) and *Extinction* (1981) and numerous appearances on the Johnny Carson Show and the lecture circuit, Ehrlich has been *the* hard-science spokesman for population control. Unbeknownst to most of his fans, Paul is basically a butterfly freak. He's a first-rate population biologist with a reputation that has grown steadily through his career. His original

1965 paper on coevolution, coauthored with botanist Peter Raven ("Peter and I did the whole thing over coffee; didn't look at a single organism") is one of the most cited in the literature.

This later paper of Ehrlich's* is still one of the best scans of coevolution as idea and as natural history that I've seen, and it sounds like Paul talking, that is, like Walter Winchell. How better to start this book than with its founding metaphor, from Issue 1 (Spring 1974).

Stewart Brand

In recent years ecologists have been focusing more and more attention on the properties of communities of organisms. There has been a renaissance of what we used to call "synecology," and several new schools of community ecologists have emerged. One school has focused its interests on the concepts of niche, species diversity, and related topics. Members of this school often deal with questions such as: "Why are there more species of lizards on island X than on island Y?"; "What simple environmental measures can I use to predict the number of bird species in a grassland?"; or "What limits the similarity of sympatric species?" Another approach to communities which has gained prominence recently is a holistic-mathematical approach. Many measurements are made of a complex ecological system. Then the analytic and simulation

* This paper was the introduction to a symposium at the twenty-ninth Annual Biology Colloquium, 1968, published in *Biochemical Coevolution*, 1970, Oregon State University Press, Corvallis, Or., Kenton L. Chambers, ed.

techniques of systems analysis are used to identify important variables and predict future states of the system.

This colloquium deals with another new way of looking at the properties of communities. This way consists of examining the patterns of interaction not in an entire community but between two groups of organisms, groups which do not exchange genetic information but which do have a close and evident ecological relationship. Peter Raven and the author called the evolutionary interactions within such systems "coevolution" in order to emphasize the reciprocal nature of the relationship. This reciprocity is abundantly evident in the butterfly-plant systems which we investigated and in herbivore-plant systems in general.

PLANTS AND HERBIVORES

Many of the characteristics of plants, such as spines, pubescence, nutrient-poor sap, and so-called "secondary plant substances," have evolved in large part in response to selection pressures created by herbivores. The chemicals seem to be especially important, serving as both repellents and pesticides. Herbivores, on the other hand, have responded to the defenses of plants in diverse ways. Many obviously have adopted detoxifying systems to deal with the noxious compounds produced by the plants. For instance, the plant *Lotus corniculatus* occurs in populations polymorphic for the presence of cyanogenic glucosides. The plants containing the cyanogenic glucosides produce hydrogen cyanide when they are injured. Not surprisingly, these plants are much less bothered by herbivores than their noncyanogenic cohorts. Some herbivores, however, eat both kinds of plant with equal gusto. One of these is the blue butterfly *Polyommatus icarus*. Lane suggested that the larvae of the butterfly detoxify the cyanide by converting it into thiocyanate with the enzyme rhodanase.

Some insects have been so successful in dealing with plant poisons that they now recognize and are attracted to compounds which repel most herbivores. Indeed one "herbivore," *Homo sapiens*, consumes large quantities of plants because of the many uses he has found for "plant

pesticides." He uses them in the role for which they evolved—as herbivore poisons (e.g., pyrethrum) and as herbivore intoxicants (various hallucinogens) and in roles unrelated to their original purpose (pepper, quinine, tobacco). Perhaps the best all-around response to plant defenses is found in aposematic organisms (those that advertise their defensive abilities by conspicuous patterns and coloration, such as the monarch butterfly). These organisms take up the plant chemical defenses and use them for their own protection. The monarch butterfly, for instance, is avoided by most birds because it contains vertebrate heart poisons. These poisons are obtained directly from the monarch's milkweed foodplants. Monarchs and similar organisms gain additional advantage from the avoidance of their foodplant by other herbivores.

Many herbivores have adopted strategies to avoid plant defenses rather than overcome them. Some, for instance, may feed on parts of the plant which have relatively weak mechanical or chemical defenses. An example of this may be flower-feeding or pollen-feeding by many lycaenid butterflies, bees, and various beetles including scymnine coccinellids, dermestids, cantharids, and so forth. Other herbivores time their attacks carefully to avoid plant defenses. Paul Feeny reports that the larvae of the winter moth *Operophtera brumata* will not mature satisfactorily on oak leaves two weeks older than those on which the larvae normally feed. Larval development in nature is completed rapidly, early in the season before the tannins are laid down in the young oak leaves.

Plant-herbivore coevolutionary systems usually involve "selectional races." Strong selection pressure is put on plant populations by herbivores, and any improvement in plant defenses is at a selective premium. Herbivores, in response, must find ways of dealing with the plant defenses or they will starve. The tightness of the situation is exemplified by the winter moth case described by Feeny. The timing mechanism of the moths must be extremely precise to guarantee that the larvae hatch just as the young leaves are appearing. If they hatch too early, they starve before the leaves appear;

if they hatch too late, they are defeated by the tannins and other plant defenses. If the oaks can evolve ways of depositing tannins even earlier, or produce other defenses, the moths will lose the race, unless the moths can evolve a way of dealing with the oaks' defenses.

Perhaps the most unusual coevolutionary system related to herbivory is that composed of swollen-thorn acacias and obligate acacia ants, brilliantly investigated by Janzen. In this system, ants serve as substitutes for the usual defensive mechanisms of acacias. The ant acacias, for instance, lack the bitter-tasting chemicals which are characteristic of other acacias. The ants live in the swollen thorns of the acacias and feed on specially modified leaf tips. If the ants are removed, the acacias are killed by herbivorous insects. As long as the ant colony persists, the ants attack the herbivores and keep them from eating the acacias; the ants also destroy plant competitors of the acacias.

PREDATOR–PREY RELATIONSHIPS

A coevolutionary system which is the homologue of the plant-herbivore system is the predator-prey system. Like the plant-herbivore system, it, in essence, is a selectional race. The prey is selected for predator avoidance and the predator for prey finding. This system is much more familiar to us than the plant-herbivore system; for some strange reason most biologists seem to have the impression that plants just sit around defenseless, waiting to be devoured! All biologists, however, are familiar with the sharp senses and speed of the antelope, the stealth and fangs of the tiger, the spines of the porcupine, and the eyes and talons of the hawk. This is hardly the place to go into the vast literature on this subject, but I do want to point out that the relationship between predator and prey is all too often viewed as static, in spite of the evolutionary work done on *Biston*, *Cepaea*, *Natrix*, and mimetic assemblages. There is every reason to believe that most prey species are continually "evolving away" from their predators, and that the predators are either trying to catch up or get ahead. Extinction may very often be the result of a "win" by either side.

In investigating predator-prey systems, most of the emphasis has been placed on the nature and evolution of devices used by prey to avoid being eaten. There is, of course, a vast literature on protective coloration in both vertebrates and invertebrates. An equally impressive literature is accumulating on biochemical defense mechanisms in arthropods as a result of the work of Thomas Eisner and his associates. Although some research has been done on predator behavior—such as the classic work on orientation in bats by Griffin—much less work has focused on this side of the relationship. Recently, however, there has been an upsurge of interest in the functioning of predators in general, due in particular to the work of Holling in analyzing the components of predation. Once we understand predation more thoroughly, it should be far easier to investigate the reciprocal aspects of predator-prey systems. Perhaps those most amenable to analysis would be systems involving parasitoid wasp predators and their insect prey. Various components of attack and defense have been analyzed in these systems, but to my knowledge none of them have been approached from a coevolutionary standpoint.

PARASITE–HOST SYSTEMS

Parasite-host systems are similar to predator-prey systems in that one would expect a continuous selectional "race" between host and parasite. The race would be somewhat different, however. It is advantageous for the host, like the prey, to "escape." But it is not advantageous for the parasite to kill its host, while killing is advantageous for the predator. The counter argument, that it is not advantageous for a predator to eat too many of its prey either, will not hold water. In the vast majority of cases, we must assume that group selection is not operating and that predators which are effective killers leave more offspring than those which are not. There is anecdotal evidence that individual predators may kill far beyond their individual needs for consumption. More importantly, there is no known evidence that any predatory species except man does not feed to repletion, given the opportunity. Conservation of prey resources, if it occurs, is not through the exercise of altruistic restraint by individual predators. With most parasites, however, restraint is not altruistic. Reproductive or feeding behavior which results in the death of the host all too often results in the death of the parasite as well. The problem of the parasite, then, is somewhat more difficult than that of the predator. It must often take care that it does not overtax its resources—for the individuals which do overtax leave fewer offspring than those which do not.

Host-parasite relationships have been studied evolutionarily in some instances, although the evolutionary response has usually been studied one side at a time. Some of the most widely known examples of evolutionary responses involve man: hemoglobin responses to malaria and thalassemia as a host response and the development of drug-resistant bacteria as a parasite response. One host-parasite system is now being studied extensively from both sides by Dr. J. H. Camin and his associates at the University of Kansas. Working with rabbits and rabbit ticks (*Haemaphysalis leporis-palustris*), they have been able to demonstrate an immunity to tick attack developing in the rabbits. Ticks that get on a rabbit after others are already feeding either cannot attach or can take much less blood. Therefore, they produce fewer eggs or none at all. Immunity is temporary, only lasting ten to twenty days if it is not challenged. The ticks show a circadian rhythm in dropping off the rabbits which causes the ticks to concentrate in rabbit warrens and tends to synchronize the life cycles of the individual ticks. They, therefore, get on the rabbit en masse, rather than a few at a time. Many other aspects of the rabbit-tick system have been under investigation by the Camin group, including the fascinating question of why the rabbits have not evolved a long-term immunity. The circadian rhythm of the ticks is, by the way, relatively independent of the rabbit physiology (entrained by photoperiod), which makes an interesting contrast with the European rabbit flea in which the reproduction of the flea and its transfer from the adult rabbit to the young rabbits is controlled by the hormonal changes in the pregnant female rabbit.

Many other evolutionary responses have been inferred in connection with host-parasite systems, usually as "adaptations" of the parasite to the host and host responses (of which various immune reactions are the outstanding examples). The intimate relationship between parasites and the hosts which we consider to be "vectors" have also received considerable attention, but little evolutionary study. We know that vectors and vectored tend to occur together at the right time and place, but we do not know in most cases what kinds of selective pressures each places on the other. For instance, are *Wuchereria* populations and mosquito populations engaged in a perpetual dance in which a constant disruptive selection pressure occurs in both populations? Microfilariae tend to occur in the peripheral blood at the time that the mosquito vector is feeding. Presumably the earliest and latest mosquitoes have the smallest chance of picking up the parasites. This could lead eventually to a polymorphism of feeding times in the mosquito population, followed by a similar response in the parasite. Or other selection pressures may make either early or late feeding hazardous, so that directional selection would operate on feeding time. Or, other selective factors may override the effects of parasite infection and maintain a rather rigid mosquito feeding time.

Even in situations where we have some idea of the evolutionary dynamics, as in the case of sickle-cell anemia in man, we have not been able to examine the entire pattern of coevolution. For instance, although we know that hemoglobin S gives considerable protection against *Plasmodium*, we do not know the entire mechanism of protection or the exact kinds of selection pressures to which the parasites are subjected. The glutamic acid-valine residue substitution which changes hemoglobin A to hemoglobin S results in a fifty-fold increase in the viscosity of the hemoglobin. The phagotrophic feeding of the *Plasmodium* is inhibited, as the formation of food vacuoles becomes difficult. Changes occur in the surface of infected erythrocytes, making it possible for the liver to recognize them and remove them. The malaria parasite might evade this defense by evolving a new feeding strategy, perhaps by developing an enzyme to reduce hemoglobin viscosity. Whether there is any trend in this direction is unknown. To my knowledge, there has not been an attempt to compare features of strains of, say, *Plasmodium falciparum*, from areas of high and low Hb^s frequency.

MIMICRY

Closely paralleling the host-parasite case would be the coevolutionary interactions involved in Batesian mimicry. The mimic, of course, plays the role of the parasite. Its strategy is to take advantage of the model without destroying it. The model gains nothing—and faces the danger of a "credibility gap" developing in its potential predators. For at some point, if the mimics get too common, most predators will associate only happy experiences with what originally was an aposematic pattern in the model. Such a development, of course, ruins the game for both players. One would expect that the model would evolve away from the mimic at a maximum rate, everything else being equal. It is to the mimic's advantage to maintain a maximum of resemblance to the model, until that critical point mentioned above is reached. Then the advantage becomes a disadvantage—the mimic is conspicuously patterned, but predators now associate that pattern with tastefulness. As a result, selection would tend to move the mimic away from the model into a more cryptic pattern. It is not inconceivable that imperfect resemblances, now attributed to mimicry in the process of being perfected, are quite the opposite. They may represent mimics moving away from the model or mimics in an equilibrium situation between perfect mimicry and cryptic coloration. Development of a polymorphism in which one or more forms are nonmimetic may also be the result of such a reversal of the selective situation.

As Ehrlich and Raven pointed out, there is no sharp line between Batesian and Mullerian mimicry. (In Batesian mimicry a palatable species resembles an unpalatable one [the model]; in Mullerian mimicry, two different unpalatable species resemble each other.) In all cases it obviously is of advantage to the Batesian mimic to become distasteful if it is physiologically possible to do so. In butterflies, at least, it appears that the usual source of noxious compounds is plant biochemicals, so that foodplant relationships must play a large role in the evolutionary dynamics of any given situation. A butterfly has several different routes to obnoxiousness open to it. If it occurs on a foodplant which does not produce an appropriate compound, it may switch foodplants. If it is feeding on a plant with an appropriate compound or its precursors, the butterfly may evolve the ability to use the compound or synthesize a noxious compound from precursors. Finally the foodplant of the butterfly may evolve an appropriate compound, which then may be picked up by the butterfly. In the latter case the mimetic butterfly would be involved in a complex of "selectional races" involving the model, the foodplant, and predators. As the foodplant becomes more and more obnoxious, the butterfly must find ways of "breaking even" by avoiding poisoning or "winning" by turning the poison to its own advantage. Predators may simultaneously be undergoing selection for ability to discriminate between model and mimic, and for "resistance" to the obnoxious properties of the model. Of course the presence or strength of such selection will depend on many variables. For instance, in some cases butterflies in a single population may make up such a small proportion of the targets of a single predator that selective influence on the predator will be negligible.

In many ways mimetic assemblages make ideal subjects for the study of coevolution—as has been amply demonstrated by the Browers, Phillip Sheppard, and others. We understand a great deal about them, and yet there are many questions unanswered. For instance, detailed studies of putative Mullerian complexes are needed to answer a variety of questions. One would expect that the various members of the complex would have different effects on predators since they presumably are picking up poisons from different sources. As an example, one Mullerian butterfly complex consists of a *Lycorea* species, presumably feeding on Asclepiadacae or Apocynaceae, several Ithomiines on Solanaceae, two *Heliconius* on Passifloraceae, and a *Perrhybris* with an unknown foodplant. Ideally, of course, each member of the complex would give strong and similar reinforcement to all local predators, so that multivalent noxiousness might evolve in various members. It would be particularly interesting if biochemical mimicry could be detected in some of these organisms—that is, two quite different chemical compounds obviously selected to give similar effects in the same predator. Rothschild has suggested that this occurs with defensive odors.

Although it is clear that, in general, Batesian complexes should evolve toward Mullerian complexes, the fate of Mullerian complexes is less obvious. It would probably be unwise to think of them as stable "end points" of evolutionary sequences. If this were the case, one might picture all of the diurnal Lepidoptera (and perhaps many other herbivores and small predators) in an area eventually being recruited into one large complex. It would really save the memories of the birds, but the birds would not have to remember for long because they would starve to death. Obviously, the larger a Mullerian complex gets, and the more similar the defenses of its members become, the more "profit" accrues to a predator which devises a way of consuming the Mullerian mimics. Thus a large selective premium is placed on a strong stomach, and one would expect predators evolving rapidly to deal with the entire complex. If this happens, the advantages of belonging are reduced and one might expect the complex to break up.

PLANTS AND POLLINATORS

Mullerian mimicry is one good example of mutualism. There are many others, many of which doubtless would provide good materials for coevolutionary studies. Perhaps the most widely studied mutualistic coevolutionary system is that of flowering plants and their pollinators. Relationships in this system range from extremely close and clearly reciprocal to casual and possibly unidirectional. Best known of the "tight" relationships are those of the yucca and the yucca moth and of the fig and the fig wasp. In the latter case, both insect and plant are totally dependent on one another—the relationship is obligate in both directions. A wide variety of intimacy has been revealed in the relationships of bees and Onagraceae by the elegant investigations of Linsley, MacSwain, and Raven. A large number of bee species visiting *Oenothera* were found to be oligolectic, collecting pollen for their larval cells exclusively from plants of that genus. Many others, however, were polylectic, collecting pollen from *Oenothera* and from plants of other genera and families. The tightest relationship discovered was that of the bee *Andrena rozeni* and *Camissonia claviformis*. The plant, which has a flower well suited for bee pollination, presents its pollen and nectar in the late afternoon (it is presumably derived from a morning-opening species). *Andrena rozeni* only gathers pollen in the late afternoon, even though residual pollen is available early in the morning. The mouthparts of *A. rozeni* are elongated, permitting it to extract both nectar and pollen simultaneously, and these are very rarely taken from other plants. Mating likewise takes place at the flowers of *Camissonia claviformis*, the males cruising over them before the first appearance of the females. Of course, many pollination systems have been studied from the point of view of floral morphology, color, and odor in relation to attracting the proper pollinators: long corolla tubes for hawkmoths, red color for hummingbirds, huge widemouthed nocturnal flowers for bats, chemical attractants in orchids, orchids shaped as females to lure male insects, and so forth. It is not clear in most cases, however, what evolutionary responses in pollinators have been elicited by the vast smorgasbord with which they are presented. It would be a mistake to assume that the response has not been considerable, if subtle. It behooves a pollinator to get the job of feeding done with as little energy and risk as possible. Each pollinator is presumably programmed genetically to respond to a "proper" series of stimuli—an exact odor, color, or shape, or a series of odors, colors, or shapes. Each pollinator has adopted a strategy—in essence specialist or generalist. Similarly, each plant has adopted a strategy. As floras and faunas evolve together, the utilities of the various strategies are going to change. The specialist pollinator may find its food source becoming too rare, or the generalist pollinator may find the competition too stiff at many of its sources. Conversely, the specialist plant may find its pollinator going extinct, or the generalist plant may find it is not getting enough accurate transport. The end result of any of these anthropomorphized possibilities is a choice of "evolve or go extinct." When the behavior patterns of pollinators are more thoroughly understood, we shall appreciate more fully the reciprocal nature of most pollination systems.

COEVOLUTIONARY COMPLEXES AND COMMUNITY STUDIES

It seems appropriate now to discontinue the survey of coevolutionary complexes and return briefly to the question of the consequences of their study for community biology in general. Community biology is concerned with the composition of communities and the dynamics of that composition. Community composition is, in part, determined by physical tolerance limits on the distribution of species. Determining the factors limiting distributions and the ways in which organisms "adapt" to the areas they occupy is the preoccupation of a branch of "physiological ecology." Someone once said that the usual conclusion of a study in this field is the determination that the organism can indeed live where it lives. The question of why those limits exist—that is, why the organisms have not transgressed those limits evolutionarily—is rarely investigated. In some cases the answers may lie in the relationship of the organism to its physical environment. For instance, many butterflies may not have penetrated temperate regions simply because they have been unable to develop satisfactory diapause mechanisms. (This, of course, immediately raises the question of why some species have developed satisfactory mechanisms while others have not.) In other cases the answers probably lie in the area of coevolutionary interactions. The presence of a "winning predator" or the absence of a "beatable" foodplant may limit a herbivore. A model may be, in essence, "chased" by a mimic into an area which the mimic cannot penetrate (perhaps because of the distribution of its foodplant). We do know that mimetic species often extend their range beyond that of the model, ordinarily with a rapid loss of mimetic pattern. However, we do not know whether in any cases the mimetic species is restricted to the range of the model because of mimetic relationships.

Taking a coevolutionary approach to problems of community biology lessens the chance of being seduced into "explanations," such as "competition from X limited the distribution of Y." If the limitation of X is due to Y, then the two usually make up a coevolutionary system. In order to understand the limitation, it is necessary to understand the system. This means that questions about selection, such as were asked earlier, must be posed, and field and laboratory experiments must be carried out to find the answers.

STEPHANIE MILLS

Salons and
Their Keepers

*From the original introduction
(Summer 1974):*
The most powerful instrument of intellectual community organizing is
the salon. I'm convinced of this after
seeing the effects of two small grants
from the Point Foundation [publish-
ers of CQ and the *Whole Earth Catalog*] to Stephanie Mills for the purpose of giving dinners.

When talk is intended to be *good*
instead of merely efficient, meta-
business gets transacted. Something
gels. The abbot of the San Francisco
Zen Center says that culture is what
happens when a number of people
know each other well. Maybe that's
what gels.

A hostess with wit, culinary skill,
and access to people who ought to
know each other is all it takes.

Stewart Brand

The author is the same Stephanie
Mills who became a living symbol of
the movement for international population control, after giving a vale-
dictorian speech at Mills College in
1969 in which she said "I am terribly saddened that the most humane
thing for me to do is to have no children at all." She later edited *Not Man
Apart* and COEVOLUTION QUAR-
TERLY. In an essay in the Winter
1980 CQ called "Learning to Live
with Ambiguity," she foreshadowed
her shift from international to local,
or bioregional, politics: "Eleven
years after announcing the apocalypse I am coming to realize that I
probably won't get to watch the End
of the World in my lifetime. I . . .
have learned that doing unalloyed, or
sufficient good is [an] impossibility,
unless that good is so specific that it
may seem insignificant to the faith-
less and invisible to the demogra-
phers." Now she lives on a farm in
northern Michigan where she is writing a book, and involved in bioregional organizing.

Art Kleiner

*Salon: The reception room of a Parisian lady of
fashion; hence a reunion of notabilities at the house
of such a lady; also a similar gathering in other
capitals.* (Shorter Oxford English Dictionary)

Salons are spaces, psychic spaces created to
draw the best talk from a gathering of minds.
Since the Renaissance, they have been ostensi-
bly agendaless gatherings for the sake of conversation. At the time of their French flourishing, people were not so disillusioned with
words as we. Conversation had the status of an
art. Salons were its galleries.

. . . words are not merely . . . a means to com-

*municate ideas, feelings and needs but an instrument
one likes to play and which revives the spirit. . . .
A certain way in which people act on one another, a
quick give and take of pleasure, a way of speaking
as soon as one thinks, of rejoicing in oneself in the
immediate present, of being applauded without making an effort, of displaying one's intelligence by every
nuance of intonation, gesture, and look—in short,
the ability to produce at will a kind of electricity.*
Quoth Madame de Staël, history's most famous
salonière.

Salons still exist, but the conversational aesthetic has vanished. Cocktail parties are not salons. The talk that takes place at cocktail parties with its discontinuities and roving eyes
cannot be called proper conversation. Talk
shows might pass as a species of salon if they
were less self-conscious and plug-oriented, but
the quality of intelligence on talk shows is di-
luted. While it abounds in sharpness, it often
lacks the creative direction of good salon conversation. Talk shows are promiscuous. Salons
are organisms, collectivities which require
friendship and intimacy to function.

Attendance at the great salons of eighteenth
and nineteenth century Paris was habitual.
Different salonières (most of whom were
women) received on different evenings to avoid
conflicts with their friends' gatherings. Much
of the brilliance and constancy of the salons
derived from the presence of core groups of
friends—the planets—who attended faithfully
and warmed the parties with friendship. Brio
and excitement were provided by rising and
falling stars shooting through.

During the eras of Enlightenment and Revolution, Paris' atmosphere was charged with
the ideas of progress and reform, political debate, then intrigues—to depose the monarchy,
to save the republic, then to resist Napoleon's
dictatorship. These philosophies and strategies
were aired and developed in the salons; there
cells of opinion throve and the French Revolution was accomplished. The vehicle was not
polemic, but conversation.

Julie de Lespinasse and Germaine Necker
de Staël each presided over the most luminous
and eagerly attended salon of her generation.
Julie died in the springtime of 1776, when

Germaine was just ten. Their lives over-
lapped—many of the members of Julie's salon
also attended Mme. Necker's Fridays. Thus
Germaine grew up surrounded by Julie's contemporaries. And the two women were linked
by a lover—Hippolyte de Guibert, who may
have been Madame de Staël's first, and was Julie's last.

Julie de Lespinasse was the illegitimate
child of the Comtesse d'Albon. Therefore she
was propertyless. Her loving mother did attempt to provide her an inheritance, but when
her mother died, Julie, in an excess of grief,
turned the money over to her brother. Penniless, she wound up serving her sister Diane and
brother-in-law Gaspard de Vichy as a governess
for four years, the last two of which were made
rancorous by the discovery that Gaspard was
likely her father.

Gifted with kindness, intelligence, and
tact, made miserable by her domestic situation, and unstimulated in the remote chateau,
she was ready to be rescued. At which point
Gaspard's sister, the Marquise du Deffand, appeared at Champrond for a visit. Here was a
witty, civilized woman, keeper of a notable Parisian salon, sadly going blind. She perceived
in Julie a potentially charming companion,
and began to consider bringing her to Paris.

After about a year of negotiations with the
de Vichys, who feared that Julie might try to
claim some of her mother's inheritance, Julie
took up residence with Madame du Deffand in
the convent of St. Joseph. (At that time French
convents provided a refuge for single women of
reduced means and were not very cloistered.
The residents could maintain apartments and
their particular lives within their hospitable
shelter.) In her correspondence regarding the
move, the Marquise had written a prophetic
word of warning: "I am naturally distrustful,
and all those in whom I detect slyness become
suspicious to me to the point of no longer feeling the slightest confidence in them."

At twenty-two, then, Julie de Lespinasse
became part of Madame du Deffand's distinguished company of intellectuals with a grace
and ease that amazed them all. She was outwardly plain, but possessed, Grimm said,

"The difficult and precious art of drawing out the best intelligence of others." Her relationship with the Marquise lasted ten years, until it was severed by a terrible schism.

Julie had begun to hold a small salon of her own an hour or so before the Marquise's six P.M. arrival. When she descended early and discovered Julie skimming the cream of the conversation, she exploded in a fit of jealousy and drove the usurper out. Furthermore, she insisted that her friends declare their loyalty either to her or to Julie. Many of the regulars, including D'Alembert, went with Julie, and set about arranging for her to have a salon of her own. Such independence, for a woman of her means and status, was unheard of at the time. The novelty of their idea is testimony to Julie's genius as a salonière.

Various friends provided the money to rent a small house, furnish it, and pay servants. Among the most generous of these was Madame Geoffrin, another salonière, who sold her most valuable paintings to provide Julie an annuity.

While most Parisian salons offered lavish dinners and feasts, Julie's on the Rue Bellechasse was modest to the point of spartanism. She was the enticement. In one of many panegyrics on her skill as a hostess Marmontel said, "She gathered her people here and there in society, but she chose them so well that when they assembled it was like an experienced hand striking the chords of an instrument. To continue the simile, I might add that she played on that instrument with an art that knew no bounds." Her gatherings verified the nickname bestowed on her by Madame du Deffand—"Muse of the Encyclopedia."

While reigning as one of Paris' luminaries she was racked by two hopeless love affairs. To one of her lovers she wrote, "Mon ami, society offers me now but two interests. I must love, or I must be enlightened." The futility of her loves made a personal hell undetected by her friends. D'Alembert, who lived with her for years, was shocked by the revelation of them some years after her death.

Julie's first great love was a gifted young Spanish noble, the Marquis de Mora, who struggled for years to obtain parental consent to marry her. He struggled also with consumption and was away from Paris for long stretches of time. She began to console herself in his absence with the friendship of Guibert, and began the passionate, chiding correspondence, which survives as a complex lament of a soul tormented by remorse and unrequited love. As the affair with Guibert ripened, Mora's health waned, and he died en route to see her. Julie blamed herself for Mora's death, and perhaps masochistically threw herself into the pursuit of Guibert.

"My thought, my soul can henceforth be filled by you alone, and by my harrowing regrets." But Guibert had made no secret of his liaisons with other women, and married someone else. Julie died twelve months later, her health slowly wasted by a cough, her anxieties, and her increasing use of opium. What was amazing, wrote her friend Morrelet, was that "You would still find her interesting and animated in the midst of her daily increasing weakness."

Germaine de Staël had almost been hybridized to keep a salon. Jacques Necker, her father, was Louis XVI's Controller General. One of the richest and most powerful men in Europe, he briefly held France's fate in his hands. Suzanne Curchod Necker, her mother, maintained a famous salon in Paris. Strict, ambitious and intense, she provided Germaine with an arduous education. As a little girl, Germaine attended salons peopled by the likes of Diderot, D'Alembert, Gibbon, Marmontel, and Grimm. They challenged her wits—she responded with poise, and developed into the most brilliant conversationalist of her time. After her marriage in 1786, she began her own salon, which became a powerful influence on French politics thereafter.

When Napoleon's star began to rise, she sought to include him in her gatherings, but Madame de Staël drove him up a wall; he couldn't abide uppity women. Viz this exchange between them at a dinner given by Talleyrand: De Staël: "Who is the greatest woman, alive or dead?" Bonaparte: "The one who has made the most children." She had difficulty comprehending his aversion to her. Her excellent biographer, J. Christopher Herold, suggests an explanation in *Mistress to an Age*: "The most prominent of her guests were drawn not from among the enemies of his regime but from its elite. . . . In Madame de Staël's house the schoolboys were encouraged to be disrespectful of their master; they unlearned the fear on which his power rested."

De Staël threatened him further with her writing. Her opus consists of more than thirty works: novels, essays, elegies, treatises, and dramas. De Staël, "The Empress of Mind," was so influential that Napoleon, "The Emperor of Matter," exiled her after the publication of *Delphine* and later suppressed the publication of *De l'Allemagne*.

Her base during her periods of exile was in Switzerland at Coppet, her father's chateau. There she surrounded herself with her friends and lovers. The salon went on. Her life and the lives of her contemporaries were awash in words. Wherever she went, she carried a little green escritoire and wrote. The intelligentsia kept lengthy diaries, corresponded voluminously, and published their thoughts. De Staël's guests at Coppet played a parlor game called *petite poste* in which they sat around a table and, not speaking, carried on conversations and flirtations by passing little notes.

When not thus occupied or conversing, they wrote, acted in, or watched theatrical productions; or wrote letters to their friends down the hall. Charles-Victor de Bonstetten, one of the faithfuls, wrote, "I just returned from Coppet, and I feel completely stupefied . . . and exhausted by the intellectual debauches. More wit is expended at Coppet in a single day than in many a country during a whole year."

Madame de Staël passed much of her exile in travel, being received by nobility and sages throughout Europe. It was said that there were three great powers in Europe: England, Russia, and Madame de Staël. She was instrumental in bringing about Napoleon's downfall, compassionate enough to warn him of a subsequent plot on his life. She had the temerity to demand absolute loyalty from her lovers, and practice a double standard ("I do not like my

friends to get married"). She was funky enough to have lost the train of her gown during her presentation at the court of Louis XVI.

Socializing in those days was continuous—there was no distinction drawn between it and business. Human relationships were the matrix of a thriving life of the mind. Power was wielded more personally. Madame de Staël never held an office—she didn't need to. Influence was enough. There was a whole lot of nepotism going on, and it wasn't always a bad thing.

Though it is bad taste to condone nepotism in a democratic society, it is one of the ways things work. Members of an elite make their way along the grapevine finding jobs and homes, meeting friends and getting breaks by word of mouth. Nepotism isn't always reliable or fair, but it is human. The mechanistic devices that the free enterprise system uses to place people aren't always reliable or fair either, and they can be dehumanizing. Perhaps instead of condemning nepotism (the soft unacknowledged system) for the putative one, nepotism could be made more useful and elites diversified.

Thanks to nepotism, I received a foundation grant to keep a salon. A "Cookenheim," Nick von Hoffman dubbed it. The foundation director who supported it most actively had known me for years. Another director who chipped in is a lover of mine. Like Julie de Lespinasse, I was subsidized by my friends to keep a salon. Funding a grasshopper-pauper writer like me to throw dinner parties catapulted that kind of entertaining out of the realm of the well-connected wealthy.

It started offhandedly. I'd been an environmental activist for a while, traveling, speechifying, making acquaintances. Eventually I got out of that and began to write.

Meanwhile, the United Nations was planning its Conference on the Human Environment in Stockholm. Hopes were that it might be a great occasion of world environmental consciousness raising. A number of California's finest eco-freaks began making plans not just to attend, but to launch a veritable flotilla of counter-culturalists. Life Forum was the umbrella organization which transported some poets (Gary Snyder and Michael McClure), the Hog Farm complete with two buses, an estimable writer (Mary Jean Haley, who produced a guidebook to the city and conference), Native American and white members of the Black Mesa Defense Fund, and its own staff to the gallery and apartments at Pilgatan 11 in Stockholm.

Many of this company were friends and sought to involve me, suggesting that I do my population schtick. But all I wanted to do was give dinner parties. Almost within minutes funding was available for me to join the gang and set up the salon.

I wandered around Stockholm with my transit map and phrasebook, breaking up grocers wherever I went with my futile attempts at Swedish. We had some fine parties there.

One of the best was the Whale Salon. It starred Joan MacIntyre, head of Project Jonah, who has made saving whales her life—she came to Stockholm and reminded everybody that it was living creatures being discussed; Willy Wiloya, an Inuit, who hunts whales for a living; Lee Talbot, a White House advisor on wildlife conservation; a British cetologist; a Canadian marine biologist who made passionate entreaties that we not overlook the plight of the salmon; and Michael and Joanna McClure. Sundry members of Life Forum and Point Foundation rounded out the party.

The highlight of the evening was Michael's reading of one of his *Gargoyle Cartoons*, a dialogue between a Swedish garter snake and a Japanese garter snake on the relative merits of being a seal, mackerel, or whale on a nice day. This he did with deadpan vaudeville accents, and cracked us all up. The group was so diverse and alive that everybody delighted everybody else, and a good time was had by all.

Such a good time in fact, that I was funded to keep a salon in Berkeley for a year "to bring people together who wouldn't necessarily meet, to provide them with a leisurely gracious environment in which to become acquainted and intelligently converse, to encourage skylarking," as I said in my proposal. It worked, and did a fair amount of good. But that's a year's worth of other stories.

LYNN MARGULIS
JAMES E. LOVELOCK

The Atmosphere as Circulatory System of the Biosphere— the Gaia Hypothesis

The Gaia Hypothesis ("Gaia" is pronounced to rhyme with papaya) treats the anomalous Earth atmosphere as an artifact of life and comprehends the planet itself as a single life.

The two old puzzles—1) How does the bizarre Earth atmosphere maintain itself? and 2) How does fragile Earth life maintain itself?—solve each other. It took two remarkable scientists—Margulis & Lovelock—meeting outside their specialties to discover that convergence.

Lynn Margulis is a microbiologist at Boston University. Her best-known contribution is the symbiotic theory of the origin of complex cells (in her book *Origin of Eukaryotic Cells*). Popularization of that theory in *The Lives of a Cell* won Lewis Thomas a National Book Award. He even perpetuated Dr. Margulis' misspelling—"*Myxotricha paradoxa*" (should be *Mixotricha*, she notes).

James Lovelock is the envy of every scientist, a successful freelancer. Working out of a thatched cottage in the Salisbury Plain, England, this biospheric chemist has accumulated some sixty-nine patents—most of them in what he calls "gas pornography"—chromatographic analysis of gases at the parts-per-billion level. The *New Scientist* recently wrote of him, "In some ways, Jim Lovelock—begetter of the Gaia hypothesis—is one of the last of the old-style natural philosophers. A scientist who works from his own home because he believes that lack of security encourages creativity, he has invented—among other things—'a magnificent Pandora's box', the electron capture/detector gas chromatograph. Most sensitive of the analytical chemist's tools, it has been responsible for arousing concern about pesticide residues and Freons in the stratosphere, and may yet help to show that, thanks to Gaia, our fears of pollution-extermination are unfounded."

It was an honor for COEVOLUTION, in Summer 1975, to be the first nonspecialist American publication to carry the Gaia Hypothesis (it had earlier appeared in Britain's *New*

Scientist and in Carl Sagan's astronomy journal *Tellus*; Sagan it was who put me in touch with Lynn Margulis). The topic still burns in our pages, and Lovelock and Margulis are frequent contributors. The best place to find a full discussion is in *Gaia: A New Look at Life on Earth*, James E. Lovelock, Oxford University Press, 1979.

Gaia is an old idea. She is one of the four primary divine beings of the Ancient Greeks—Chaos (Space), Gaia (Earth), Tartarus (the Abyss), and Eros (Love). But Gaia is still a new hypothesis, containing more questions than answers.

In Gaia we are—all—Tangled Up in Blue.

Stewart Brand

We would like to discuss the Earth's atmosphere from a new point of view—that it is an integral, regulated, and necessary part of the biosphere. In 1664 Sachs von Lewenheimb, a champion of William Harvey, used the analogy of the circulation of water between earth and air to illustrate the concept of the circulation of blood. Apparently the idea that water lost to the heavens is eventually returned to Earth was so acceptable in von Lewenheimb's time that Harvey's theory was strengthened by the analogy.[1]

Three hundred and ten or so years later, with the circulation of blood a universally accepted fact, we find it expedient to revive von Lewenheimb's analogy—this time to illustrate our concept of the atmosphere as circulatory system of the biosphere. This new way of viewing the Earth's atmosphere has been called the "Gaia" hypothesis.[2] The term Gaia is from the Greek for "Mother Earth," and it implies that certain aspects of the Earth's atmosphere—temperature, composition, oxidation reduction state, and acidity—form a homeostatic system, and that these properties are themselves products of evolution.[3, 4]

From recent articles and books (e.g., refs. 5

and 6) one gets the impression that fluid dynamics, radiation chemistry, and industrial pollution are the major factors determining the properties of the atmosphere. The Gaia hypothesis contends that biological gas exchange processes are also major factors, especially processes involving microorganisms. Man's impact on the atmosphere may have been overestimated. Man is only one of some three million species on Earth, all of which exchange gas and most of which exchange gas with the atmosphere. Man has been around for only a few million years while microorganisms have existed for thousands of millions of years.

It seems to us that early twentieth-century nonmicrobiological analysis of the Earth's lower atmosphere will one day be considered as ignorant as early nineteenth-century nonmicrobiological analysis of fermentation or disease is today.

In an excellent introduction to atmospheric science, Goody and Walker [7] say, "There is a great difference between research in the laboratory and studies of the Earth and planets. In the laboratory the scientist can perform controlled experiments, each carefully designed to answer questions of his own choosing. Except in minor respects, however, the Earth and planets are too large for controlled experimentation. All we can do is observe what happens naturally in terms of the laws of physics and chemistry."

We agree that the laws of physics and chemistry are basic to the understanding of atmospheric phenomena but insist that the laws of biology must be considered as well. It is our contention that the paucity of overall understanding of certain aspects of the atmosphere, especially composition and temperature, is due to too narrow a paradigm: the idea that the atmosphere is an inert part of the inorganic environment and therefore amenable to methods of study that involve only physics and chemistry.

In this paper we explore what is perhaps a more realistic view—that the atmosphere is a nonliving, actively regulated part of the biosphere. In our model atmospheric temperature and composition are regulated with respect to certain biologically critical substances: hydrogen ions, molecular oxygen, nitrogen and its compounds, sulfur and its compounds, and some others, whose abundance and distribution in the atmosphere are presumed to be under biological control. Biological gas exchange processes, thought to be involved in possible control mechanisms, are discussed elsewhere.[8] The purpose of this paper is simply to present our reasons for believing the atmosphere is actively controlled.

Traditional atmospheric studies have left us with some strange anomalies. The atmosphere is an extremely complex blanket of gas in contact with the oceans, lakes, rivers (the hydrosphere), and the rocky lithosphere. It has a mass of about 5.3×10^{21} grams. (The mass of the oceans—the other major fluid on the surface of the Earth—is almost a thousand times heavier, being about 1.4×10^{24} grams.) Since the atmospheric mass corresponds to less than a millionth of the mass of the Earth as a whole, one would expect small changes in the composition of the solid earth to cause large changes in the composition of the atmosphere. Yet even in the face of a large number of potential perturbations, the atmosphere seems to have remained dynamically constant over long periods of time.

Many facts about the atmosphere are known—its composition, its temperature and pressure profiles, certain interactions with incoming solar radiation, and the like.[7] Some of these are shown in Tables 1 and 2. However, as the efficacy of long-range weather forecasting attests, there is no consistent model of the atmosphere that can be used for the purpose of prediction.[6] The Earth's atmosphere defies simple description. From the point of view of chemistry it sustains such remarkable disequilibrium that Sagan [9] was prompted to remark that given the temperature, pressure, and amount of oxygen in the atmosphere, "one can calculate what the thermodynamic equilibrium abundance of methane ought to be. . . . The answer turns out to be less than 1 part in 10^{36}. This then is a discrepancy of at least 30 orders of magnitude and cannot be dismissed lightly."

Table 2 shows that given the quantity of ox-

ygen in the atmosphere not only the major gases such as nitrogen and methane but also the minor atmospheric components are far more abundant than they ought to be according to equilibrium chemistry. Even though the minor constituents differ greatly in relative abundance, they sustain very large fluxes—comparable to those of the major constituents. The Earth's atmosphere is certainly not at all what one would expect from a planet interpolated between Mars and Venus. It has too little CO_2, too much oxygen, and is too warm. We believe the "Gaia" hypothesis provides the new approach that is needed to account for these deviations.

A new framework for scientific thought is justified if it guarantees new observations and experiments. The recognition that blood in mammals circulates in a closed, regulated system gave rise to meaningful scientific questions such as: How is blood pH kept constant? By what mechanism is the temperature of mammalian blood regulated around its set point? What is the purpose of bicarbonate ion in the blood? What is the role of fibrinogen? If the blood were simply an inert environment (as the atmosphere is presently viewed) such questions would seem irrelevant and never be asked at all.

Let us consider another analogy. Bees have been known to regulate hive temperatures during midwinter at about $31°C$, approximately $59°C$ above ambient (10). Under threat of desiccation they also maintain high humidities. While the air in the hive is not alive, it maintains an enormous disequilibrium due to the expenditure of energy by the living insects—ultimately of course, solar energy. How is the hive temperature maintained? How does the architecture of the hive aid to reduce desiccation? How does the behavior of the worker bees alter temperature? These are all legitimate scientific questions, generated by the circulatory system concept.

The Gaia hypothesis of the atmosphere as a circulatory system raises comparable and useful scientific questions and suggests experiments that based on the old paradigm would never be asked, for example: How is the pH of the at-

TABLE I. Reactive gases in the atmosphere (*billions of tons/year*)

Gas	Concentration in parts per million	How much of the gas comes from			Residence time	Where does the gas come from principally?
		Inorganic sources Volcanic, etc.?	Biological sources			
			Gaian?*	Human?		
Nitrogen (N$_2$)	790,000	0.001	1	0	1–10 million years	bacteria from dissolved nitrates in soil
Oxygen (O$_2$)	210,000	0.00016	110	0	1000 years	algae and green plants, given off in photosynthesis
Carbon dioxide (CO$_2$)	320	0.01	140	16	2–5 years	respiration, combustion
Methane (CH$_4$)	1.5	0	2	0	7 years	fermenting bacteria
Nitrous oxide (N$_2$O)	0.3	less than 0.01	0.6	0	10 years	bacteria and fungi
Carbon monoxide (CO)	0.08	less than 0.001	1.5	0.15	a few months	from methane oxidation (methane from bacteria)
Ammonia (NH$_3$)	0.006	0	1.5	0	a week	bacteria and fungi
Hydrocarbons (CH$_2$)$_n$	0.001	0	0.2	0.2	hours	green plants, industry
Methyl iodide (CH$_3$I)	0.000001	0	0.03	0	hours	marine algae
Hydrogen (H$_2$)	0.0000005	0	?	?	2 years	bacteria, methane oxidation?
Methyl chloride (CH$_3$Cl)	0.0000000114	0	?	?	?	algae?

*Gaian = nonhuman biological sources.

mosphere kept neutral or slightly alkaline? By what mechanism(s) has the mean midlatitude temperature remained constant (not deviated more than 15 °C) for the last 1000 million years? Why are 0.5×10^9 tons nitrous oxide (N$_2$O) released into the atmosphere by organisms? Why is about 2×10^9 tons of biogenic methane pumped into the atmosphere each year (representing nearly 10% of the total terrestrial photosynthate)? What are the absolute limits on the control mechanisms, i.e., how much perturbation (emanations of sulfur oxides, chlorinated compounds, and/or carbon monoxide; alterations in solar luminosity; and so forth) can the atmosphere regulatory system tolerate before all its feedback mechanisms fail?

The Gaia approach to atmospheric homeostasis has also led to a number of observations that otherwise would not have been made, for

TABLE 2. Composition of the atmosphere: gases in disequilibrium

Gas	Abundance	Flux (moles/yr x 10^{13})	Disequilibrium factor	Oxygen used up in the oxidation of these gases (moles/yr x 10^{13})	Abiological process	Source of gas % contribution by biological process	
						Human	Gaian*
Nitrogen	78%	3.6	10^{10}	11	.001	0	>99
Methane	1.5 ppm	6.0	10^{30}	12	0.0	0	100
Hydrogen	0.5 ppm	4.4	10^{30}	2.2	?	0	?
Nitrous oxide	0.3 ppm	1.4	10^{13}	3.5	.02	0	>99
Carbon monoxide	0.08 ppm	2.7	10^{30}	1.4	.001	10	90
Ammonia	0.01 ppm	8.8	10^{30}	3.8	0.0	0	100

*Gaian = nonanthropogenic biological sources; for details see Table 1.

? = quantities not known.

ppm = parts per million.

example, an oceanic search was undertaken for volatile compounds containing elements that are limiting to life on the land, and large quantities of methyl iodide and dimethyl sulfide were in fact observed.[11]

Given the Gaia hypothesis one deduces that all the major biological elements (Table 3) must either be not limiting to organisms (in the sense that they are always readily available in some useful chemical form) or they must be cycled through the fluids on the surface of the earth in time periods that are short relative to geological processes. (Attempts to identify volatile forms of these elements are in progress.) The cycling times must be short because biological growth is based on continual cell division that requires the doubling of cell masses in periods of time that are generally less than months and typically, days or hours. On lifeless planets there is no particular reason to expect this phenomenon of atmospheric cycling, nor on the earth is it expected that gases of elements that do not enter metabolism as either metabolites or poisons will cycle rapidly; e.g., based on the Gaia hypothesis, nickel, chromium, strontium, rubidium, lithium, barium, and titanium will not cycle, but cobalt, vanadium, selenium, molybdenum, iodine, and magnesium might.[12] Because biological solutions to problems tend to be varied, redun-

dant, and complex, it is likely that all of the mechanisms of atmospheric homeostasis will involve complex feedback loops (see ref. 8 for discussion). Since, for example, no volatile form of phosphorus has ever been found in the atmosphere, and since this element is present in the nucleic acids of all organisms, we are considering the possibility that the volatile form of phosphorus at present is totally "biological particulate." Figures 1 and 2 rather fancifully compare the Earth's atmosphere at present to what it might be if life were suddenly wiped out.

Ironically, it is the past history of the earth with its extensive sedimentary record (fraught, as it is, with uncertainties in interpretation) that might provide the most convincing proof for the existence of continued biological modulation. If one accepts the current theories of stellar evolution, the sun, being a typical star of the main sequence, has substantially increased its output of energy since the earth was formed some 4500 million years ago. Some estimates for the increase in solar luminosity over the past history of the earth are as much as 100%; most astronomers apparently accept an increase of at least 25% over 4.5 billion years.[13] Extrapolating from the current atmosphere, given solar radiation output and radiative surface properties of the planet, it can be

TABLE 3. Some critical biological elements that may be naturally limiting

Element	Use in biological systems	Possible form of fluid transport
MAJOR ELEMENTS		
C (carbon)	all organic compounds	CO_2; food; organic compounds in solution; biological volatiles; carbonate, bicarbonate, etc.; usually not limiting
N (nitrogen)	all proteins and nucleic acids	N_2, N_2O, NO_3, NO_2 (often limiting)
O, H (oxygen, hydrogen)	H_2O in high concentration for all organisms	rivers, oceans, lakes
S (sulfur)	nearly all proteins (cysteine, methionine, etc.); key coenzymes	dimethyl sulfide; dimethyl sulfoxide, carbonyl sulfide
P (phosphorus)	all nucleic acids; adenosine triphosphate	unknown (biological volatiles? spores? birds? migrating salmon?)
Na, Ca, Mg, K (sodium, calcium, magnesium, potassium)	membrane and macromolecular function	usually not limiting except in certain terrestrial habitats (27)
TRACE ELEMENTS		
I (iodine)	limited to certain animals (e.g., thyroxine)	methyl iodide
Se (selenium)	enzymes of fermenting bacteria (production of ammonia, hydrogen; animals (26))	unknown (dimethyl selenide?)
Mo (molybdenum)	nitrogen fixation enzymes of bacteria and blue-green algae; carbon dioxide reductase (*Clostridium*)	unknown

concluded that until about 2000 million years ago either the atmosphere was different (e.g., contained more ammonia) or the earth was frozen. The most likely hypothesis is that the earth's atmosphere contained up to about one part in 10^5 ammonia, a good infrared absorber.[14] Other potential "greenhouse" gases apparently will not compensate for the expected lowered temperature because they do not have the appropriate absorption spectra or are required in far too large quantities to be considered reasonable.[14] (There are good arguments for the rapid photodestruction of any atmospheric ammonia.[15]) However, it has been argued that ammonia is required for the origin of life,[16] and there is good evidence for the presence of fossil microbial life in the earliest sedimentary rocks (3400 million years ago.[17]) There is no geological evidence that since the beginning of the earth's stable crust the entire earth has ever frozen solid or that the oceans were volatilized, suggesting that the temperature at the surface has always been maintained between the freezing and the boiling points of water. The fossil record suggests that from an astronomical point of view, conditions have been moderate enough for organisms to tolerate and the biosphere has been in continuous existence for over 3000 million years.[17, 18] At least during the familiar Phanerozoic (the last 600 million years of earth history for which an extensive fossil record is available) one can argue on paleontological grounds alone that through every era the earth has maintained tropical temperatures at some place on the surface and that the composition of the atmosphere, at least with respect to molecular oxygen, could not have deviated markedly. That

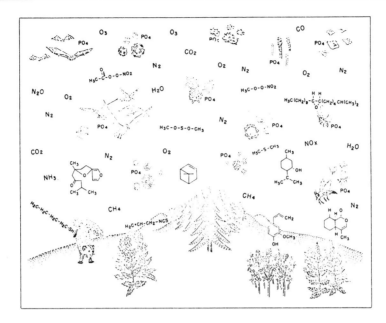

Figure 1. Earth's atmosphere at present: examples of major volatiles. (Key: the following compounds and spores are in the picture. It is left to the reader to identify them. See ref. 28 for many details.) Spores of: ferns, club mosses, zygomycetes, ascomycetes, basidiomycetes, slime molds, bacteria. All contain nucleic acids and other organic phosphates, amino acids, and so forth. Animal products: butyl mercaptan. Plant products: myoporum, catnip (nepetalactone), eugenol, geraniol, pinene, isothiocyanate (mustard). Unknown: PAN (paroxacetyl nitrate), dimethyl sulfide, dimethyl sulfoxide. Gases: nitrogen, oxygen, methane, carbon monoxide, carbon dioxide, ammonia.

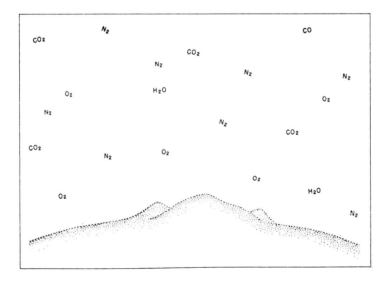

Figure 2. The present atmosphere were life deleted.

is, there are no documented cases of any meta-
zoan animals (out of about 2 million species)
that can complete their life cycles in the total
absence of O_2.[19] All animals are composed of
cells that divide by mitosis. The mitotic cell
division itself requires O_2.[20] Thus it is highly
unlikely that current concentrations of oxygen
have fallen much below their present values in
some hundreds of millions of years. By implication, oxygen and the gases listed in Table 2
have been maintained at stable atmospheric
concentrations for time periods that are very
long relative to their residence times. (Residence time is the time it takes for the concentration of gas to fall to $1/e$ or 37% its value; it
may be thought of as "turnover time.") Furthermore, since concentrations of atmospheric
oxygen only a few per cent higher than ambient lead to spontaneous combustion of organic matter, including grasslands and forests,
the most reasonable assumption is that the oxygen value of the atmosphere has remained relatively constant for quite long time periods.[21]

How can these observations be consistently
reconciled? How can we explain the simultane-
ous presence of gases that are extremely reactive with each other and unstable with respect
to minerals in the crust and at the same time
note that their residence times in the atmosphere are very short with respect to sediment-
forming and mountain-building geological
processes? In this respect Table 3 can be in-
structive. For one can see that even though absolute amounts of the gases vary over about 3
orders of magnitude, the fluxes are remarkably
similar. These gases are produced and removed
primarily by nonhuman biological processes.
(See Table 1 and ref. 8) While the processes involved in atmospheric production and removal
of reactive gases are not primarily dependent
on human activity, for the most part they are
not based on animal or plant processes either
(see ref. 8 for a version of the table that lists
these). It is mainly the prokaryote microorganisms that are involved in gas exchange; the
rapidly growing and dividing masters of the
microbiological world that make up in chemical complexity and metabolic virtuosity what
they lack in advanced morphology. These or-

Figure 3. Scene from a geothermal area in Fig
Tree times (about 3400 million years ago).

ganisms presumably played a similar role in
biogeochemical processes in the past as they do
today. There is direct fossil evidence for the
continued existence of Precambrian microorganisms.[17] That they have an ancient history can
also be deduced from current studies of their
physiology. Among hundreds of species of
these prokaryotic microorganisms are many
obligate anaerobes, that is, organisms poisoned
by oxygen. (All organisms are poisoned by oxygen at concentrations above those to which
they are adapted.) Hundreds of others are
known that are either microaerophils (adapted
to concentrations of oxygen less than ambient)
or facultative aerobes (can switch their metabolism from oxygen-requiring to oxygen-
nonrequiring).

As a group, the prokaryotic microbes show
evidence that the production and release of
molecular oxygen into the atmosphere was an
extremely important environmental determi-
nant in the evolution of many genera. Prokaryotic microbes (in the form known as the blue-
green algae, cyanophytes) were almost certainly responsible for the original transition to
the oxygen-containing atmosphere about 2000
million years ago.[17, 18]

Figures 3 and 4 present scenes before and
after the transition to oxidizing atmosphere respectively. Figures 5 and 6 are reconstructions
of anaerobic cycles corresponding to Figures 3
and 4, respectively. Figure 3 attempts to re-
construct the scene as it might have looked

Figure 4. Scene from a geothermal area in Gunflint times (about 2000 million years ago).

3400 million years ago, admittedly in a rather geothermal area. Although no free oxygen (above that produced by photochemical processes and hydrogen loss) is available in the atmosphere the scene is teeming with life—microbial life. For example, entire metabolic processes, as shown in Figure 5, are available within the group of anaerobic prokaryotic microbes today. Since at the higher taxonomic levels (kingdoms and phyla) once successful patterns evolve they tend not to become extinct,[22] it is likely that ancestors of present-day microbes were available to interact with atmospheric gases very early on the primitive earth. Certainly life was very advanced metabolically by the time the stromatolitic rocks were deposited. With the evolution of oxygen-releasing metabolism by blue-green algae came the stromatolites. These layered sediments are extremely common, especially in the late Precambrian.[23] With the stromatolites come other Precambrian evidence for the transition to the oxidizing atmosphere. By the middle Precambrian, about 2000 million years ago—the time at which the stromatolites and microfossils become increasingly abundant [24, 25]—

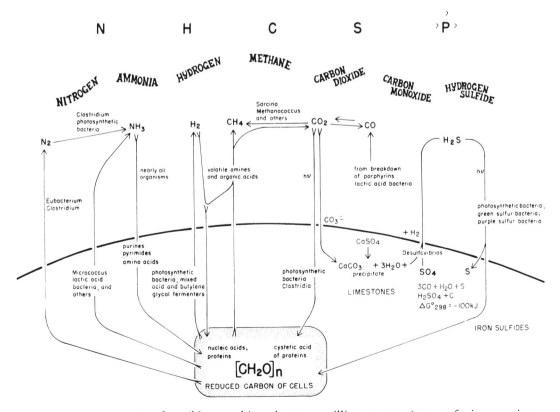

Figure 5. A reconstruction of possible anaerobic cycles: 3400 million years ago (genera of microorganisms catalyzing the reactions are underlined).

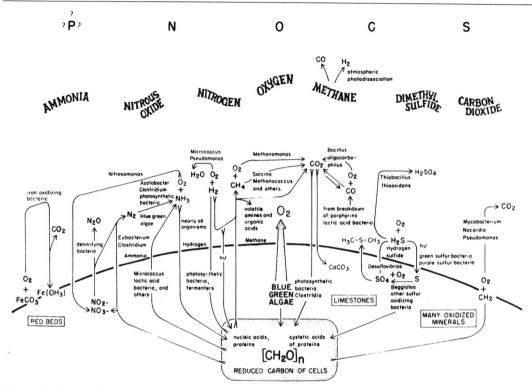

Figure 6. A reconstruction of possible microbial aerobic cycles: 2000 million years ago.

the scene might have looked like that in Figure 4. The metabolic processes accompanying that scene are shown in Figure 6. It is obvious that from among metabolic processes in prokaryotic microbes alone there are many that involve the exchange of atmospheric gases. This figure shows how oxygen-handling metabolism was essentially superimposed on an anaerobic world, a concept that is consistent with the observation that reaction with molecular oxygen tends to be the final step in aerobic respiratory processes. All of the processes shown in Figures 5 and 6 are known from current microorganisms (and, by definition, those that haven't become extinct are evolutionarily successful).

The fossil evidence, taken together, suggests that the earth's troposphere has maintained remarkable constancy in the face of several enormous potential perturbations: at least the increase in solar luminosity and the transition to the oxidizing atmosphere. The earth's atmosphere maintains chemical disequilibria of many orders of magnitude containing rapidly turning-over gases produced in prodigious quantities. The temperature and composition seem to be set at values that are optimal for most of the biosphere. Furthermore, the biosphere has many potential methods for altering the temperature and composition of the atmosphere.[8] The biosphere has probably had these methods available almost since its inception more than 3000 million years ago. Is it not reasonable to assume that the lower atmosphere is maintained at an optimum by homeostasis and that this maintenance (at the ultimate expense of solar energy, of course) is performed by the party with the vested interest: the biosphere itself?

REFERENCES

1. W. Pagel, 1951. Isis 42:23. Pagel quotes Harvey himself as saying: "I began to think whether there might not be a motion as it were in a circle. Now this I afterwards found to be true; . . . which motion we may be allowed to call circular, in the same way as Aristotle says that the air and the rain emulate the circular motion of

the superior bodies; for the moist earth, warmed by the sun evaporates; the vapours drawn upwards are condensed, and descending in the form of rain moisten the earth again; and by this arrangement are generations of living things produced. . . . And so in all likelihood, does it come to pass in the body, through the motion of the blood; the various parts are nourished, cherished, quickened by the warmer more perfect vaporous spiritous, and, as I may say, alimentive blood; which, on the contrary, in contact with these parts becomes cooled, coagulated, and, so to speak, effete; whence it returns to its sovereign, the heart, as if to its source, or to the inmost home of the body, there to recover its state of excellence of perfection."

2. J. E. Lovelock, 1972. Gaia as seen through the atmosphere. Atmospheric Environment 6: 579–580.

3. J. E. Lovelock and L. Margulis, 1974. Atmospheric homeostasis by and for the biosphere: The Gaia hypothesis. Tellus 26: 1–10.

4. J. E. Lovelock and L. Margulis, 1974. Homeostatic tendencies of the Earth's atmosphere. Origins of Life 1: 12–22.

5. I. Rasool, Ed. 1974. The Lower Atmosphere. New York: Plenum Press.

6. W. W. Kellogg and S. H. Schneider, 1974. Climate stabilization: for better or for worse? Science 186: 1163–1172.

7. R. Goody and J. C. G. Walker, 1972. Atmospheres. Englewood Cliffs, New Jersey: Prentice-Hall.

8. L. Margulis and J. E. Lovelock, 1974. Biological modulation of the Earth's atmosphere, Icarus 21: 471–489.

9. C. Sagan, 1970. Planets and Explorations. Condon Lectures, Eugene: Oregon State System.

10. E. O. Wilson, 1970. The Insect Societies, Cambridge, Massachusetts: Harvard University Press.

11. J. E. Lovelock, R. J. Maggs, and R. A. Rasmussen, 1972. Atmospheric dimethyl sulfide and the natural sulfur cycle. Nature 237: 452–453.

12. F. Egami, 1974. Minor elements and evolution. Journal of Molecular Evolution 4: 113–120.

13. L. Oster, 1973. Modern Astronomy. San Francisco: Holden Day, Inc.

14. C. Sagan and G. Mullen, 1972. Earth and Mars: Evolution of atmosphere and surface temperatures. Science 177: 52–56.

15. J. Ferris and L. Nicodem, 1974, pp. 107–117 in Origins of Life and Evolutionary Biochemistry, K. Dose, S. W. Fox, C. A. Deborin, and T. E. Pavlovskaya, eds. New York: Plenum Press.

16. J. L. Bada and S. L. Miller, 1968. Ammonium ion concentration in the primitive ocean. Science 159: 423–425.

17. E. S. Barghoorn, 1971. The oldest fossils. Scientific American 224: 30–42; E. S. Barghoorn and J. W. Schopf, 1966. Microorganisms three billion years old from the Precambrian of South Africa. Science 152: 758–763.

18. P. E. Cloud, Jr., 1968. Atmospheric and hydrospheric evolution on the primitive earth. Science 160: 729–736.

19. J. Augenfeld, 1974. Personal communication.

20. J. E. Amoore, 1961. Dependence of mitosis and respiration in roots upon oxygen tension. Proceedings of the Royal Society, B 154: 109–129.

21. J. E. Lovelock and J. P. Lodge, 1972. Oxygen in the contemporary atmosphere. Atmospheric Environment 6: 575–578.

22. G. G. Simpson, 1960, in Evolution after Darwin, S. Tax, Ed. Chicago, Illinois: University of Chicago Press, Vol. 1, pp. 177–180.

23. S. M. Awramik, 1973. Stromatolites of the Gunflint Iron Formation. Ph.D. Thesis Harvard University Department of Geology, Cambridge, Massachusetts.

24. E. S. Barghoorn and S. A. Tyler, 1965. Microorganisms from the Gunflint Chert. Science 147: 563–577.

25. J. W. Schopf, 1970. Precambrian microorganisms and evolutionary events prior to the origin of vascular plants. Biological Review 45: 319–352.

26. T. Stadtman, 1974. Selenium biochemistry. Science 183, 915–922.

27. D. B. Botkin, P. A. Jordan, S. A. Dominski, H. D. Lowendorf, and G. E. Hutchinson, 1973. Sodium dynamics in a northern ecosystem. Proc. Natl. Acad. Sci. 70: 2745–2748.

28. P. H. Gregory, 1973. Microbiology of the Atmosphere. 2nd ed. John Wiley & Sons. New York & Toronto.

I'D PLEDGE ALLEGIANCE

CQ introduced me to the concept of Gaia. Has anyone thought about a flag for Gaia?

Stephen Hodgkin
Hughes, Australia
[Spring 1983]

A Conversation with
GREGORY BATESON
MARGARET MEAD

For God's Sake, Margaret

It gives me glee to read this interview again. (We originally published it in Summer 1976.) I have never heard such high quality and sheer intellectual yield in argument. For a good look at what it was like to grow up in the Bateson-Mead family, see Mary Catherine Bateson's *With a Daughter's Eye* (Morrow, 1984). Mary Catherine's account of her father's death is in this book in your hand, p. 170.

Gregory taught me to stop obsessing on things and focus on the relations between them—to focus on pattern, the bigger and blurrier, the more challenging and potentially revealing. Doing that became one of the tasks of COEVOLUTION. I dedicated the *Next Whole Earth Catalog*: "To Gregory Bateson, 1904–1980. A pioneer in anthropology, psychology, cybernetics and epistemology, he always called himself a biologist. If I could count on Gregory's company in heaven, and I could get to heaven by being good, I'd be good."

Likewise Margaret, though she'd have the angels organized and doing cultural exchanges with hell by now, and St. Peter would be writing snitty articles about her early work in Samoa, and God would finally admit to being a Lesbian, self-fecund. I miss them both. Margaret died shortly before Gregory. This interview took place at Gregory's home near Santa Cruz, California, in 1976, when he was seventy-two and she was seventy-six.

They married in 1936. They had met and fallen in love in 1932 while both were doing anthropological fieldwork on the Sepik River in New Guinea (At the time, Margaret was with her second husband, Reo Fortune). In New Guinea, Gregory's unusual sense of theory met Margaret's improved field methodology and sparked much of the quality in Gregory's opus on the Iatmul tribe, *Naven*.

Newly wed in Bali, they spent two collaborative years in the most intense and productive fieldwork of their lives, developing, among other things, a still-unmatched photographic analysis of the culture.

Their daughter Mary Catherine, Margaret's only child, was born in 1939 in the United States. Gregory and Margaret worked together on the result of their Bali fieldwork, *Balinese Character—A Photographic Analysis*, and then were separated increasingly by World War II and their own diverging interests.

After the war they were both involved in starting the somewhat famous Macy Conferences (1947–53) that invented cybernetics. This interview begins with their joint recollection of that critical period.

Margaret Mead was one of the world's most remarkable women. She got a full mixture of praise and notoriety (notorious in that day because women weren't supposed to talk about sex) with her first book, *Coming of Age in Samoa* (1928). Since then, there have been ten other books and numerous honors and positions, including President of the American Anthropological Association (1960), and of Scientists' Institute for Public Information, and (in 1976) the American Association for the Advancement of Science, and a Curator of the American Museum of Natural History, which was her headquarters. In public affairs, for a while, she seemed to have taken over the Eleanor Roosevelt niche.

After Bali and the Macy Conferences, Gregory Bateson went on to work with schizophrenics, alcoholics, artists, dolphins, students, and a steadily more general set of understandings of what they have in common. He coauthored a book, *Communication: The Social Matrix of Psychiatry* (Norton, 1951–68) with Jurgen Ruesch, and edited *Perceval's Narrative—A Patient's Account of His Psychosis, 1830–1832* (Stanford, 1961). Daughter Mary Catherine wrote a book about one of Gregory's conferences, *Our Own Metaphor* (Knopf, 1972). His collected papers appear in *Steps to an Ecology of Mind* (Ballantine, 1972) which is the book that got me. Later I was able to participate in the making of his summation work, *Mind and Nature: A Necessary Unity* (Bantam, 1979) by granting $8,000 from Point Foundation for

Mary Catherine to come over from Iran and help with the book while Gregory recovered from surgery. In 1985 she has been assembling a posthumous Gregory Bateson work, *Angels Fear*, on religion.

Stewart Brand

STEWART BRAND: I need a little background, if it's all right, on how this whole Macy thing got rolling, why, and when, and what the sequence was.

GREGORY BATESON: There was this Macy meeting in what, '42?[1]

SB: Who started it, and what was it about?

BATESON: This was a meeting called "Cerebral Inhibition," which in fact was a meeting on hypnosis.* "Cerebral inhibition" was a respectable word for hypnosis. Most of what was said about "feedback" was said over lunch.

MEAD: Well, I know that's what you always tell people, but I didn't sit at the same place at lunch, and I heard what was said at that conference. But at that conference, which is the one where Milton Erickson hypnotized that Yale psychologist, it was at the end of that conference that you really had the design of what needed to be done. And then you were caught up in war work and went overseas and there was that long period.

I think that you actually have to go back to that earlier meeting that was held in the basement of the old Psycho-Analytic building on the West Side the day of Pearl Harbor.

BATESON: They didn't on-go from year to year, those early ones. Larry Frank was chairman I bet.

MEAD: No, Larry never was chairman, you know. He always sat on the sidelines and made somebody else be chairman. Kubie was a very important person at that point.

BATESON: Yes. Kubie was an important

* The twenty participants included representatives of anthropology, psychobiology, physiology, psychiatry, neurology, psychology, medicine, anatomy, and electronics. Among those present were Gregory Bateson, Lawrence K. Frank, Frank Fremont-Smith, Lawrence Kubie, Warren McCulloch, Margaret Mead, Arthur Rosenblueth.

bridge because Kubie had respectable-ized Milton. There's a whole series of papers which are jointly Kubie and Erickson. Now, in fact, they were Erickson's papers.

MEAD: And Kubie didn't know what was in them. That's the truth.

BATESON: But Kubie did get right the energy problem. He was the first person that really took Freud's "energy" and said, "Look, look, look, it makes no sense." There is a very good paper by Kubie on the errors of Freudian energy theory. [*Goes to find the reference.*] Huh. Kubie, "Fallacious Use of Quantitative Concepts in Dynamic Psychology."

MEAD: Now when was that?

BATESON: That was . . . guess.

MEAD: No, I don't guess that one.

BATESON: Published in '47. *Psychoanalytic Quarterly*. For which I suspect he very nearly got read out of the church. He never said it again.

MEAD: It was very hard to read Kubie out of the church because he had once been a neurologist, and that was the thing that they were all scared of. Now, where is the Rosenblueth, Wiener, and Bigelow paper? The first great paper on cybernetics.*

BATESON: Rosenblueth, Wiener, and Bigelow. "Behavior, Purpose and Teleology," *Philosophy of Science*, 1943.[2]

MEAD: That's it, you see.

BATESON: It could just have been published at the time of the Cerebral Inhibition conference.

MEAD: It was just coming out or just had come out.

SB: What was the experiment that that paper recorded?

BATESON: It didn't record an experiment, it reported on the formal character of seeking mechanisms, essentially. Self-corrective mechanisms such as missiles. The missile measures the angle between its direction and the target it's seeking, and uses that measure to correct itself.

* I am told a paper by W. Ross Ashby predated this by a year but we didn't know it.—Mead

Brand

Gregory, Margaret, and a microphone at the Bateson home near Santa Cruz.

MEAD: But using some very simple physiological experiments that Rosenblueth had been doing at the University of Mexico.

SB: Do you recall what they were saying that you overheard that got you excited?

BATESON: It was a solution to the problem of purpose. From Aristotle on, the final cause has always been the mystery. This came out then. We didn't realize then (at least I didn't realize it, though McCulloch might have) that the whole of logic would have to be reconstructed for recursiveness. When I came in from overseas in forty-five I went within the first two or three days to Frank Fremont-Smith, and said, "Let's have a Macy Conference on that stuff."

MEAD: You and Warren McCulloch had an exchange of letters when you were in Ceylon.

BATESON: We did?

MEAD: Yes. You told me enough about it in some way. I talked to Fremont-Smith. McCulloch had talked to Fremont-Smith.

BATESON: Fremont-Smith told me, "Yes, we've just arranged to have one, McCulloch is the chairman, go talk to McCulloch."

MEAD: And McCulloch had a grand design in his mind. He got people into that conference, who he then kept from talking.

BATESON: Yes, he had a design on how the shape of the conversation would run over five years—what had to be said before what else could be said.

MEAD: He wouldn't let Ralph Gerard talk. He said, "You can talk next year." He was very autocratic.

BATESON: Yes, but an awfully good chairman in many ways. It's very rare to have a chairman who knows what it's about at all.

SB: What was his grand design?

BATESON: Who knows?

MEAD: Well, I think more or less what happened was.

BATESON: How did the first meeting differ from the second meeting?

MEAD: There wasn't even any usable terminology. At first we called the thing "feedback," and the models that we were presented with at that point were the guided missile, tar-get-seeking. Now there had been another event that's worth considering here. That is that Wiener had written an article in the *Atlantic*, or *Harper's*, refusing to give the war department data on guided missiles. Remember that?

BATESON: Oh yes.

MEAD: He'd worked on them all through the war, and of course they had the material if they had hunted for it, but they made the mistake of asking him for some, and at that point he said that he would not give it to them, the war was over, and this was data that could only be used for war-like purposes. He would not give it to them.

BATESON: That's right, it was the *Atlantic*.

MEAD: They were talking almost entirely of negative feedback. By this time, Wiener and Bigelow and Johnny Von Neumann of course, were members of the group, and Rosenblueth, Kurt Lewin, Molly Harrower, Evelyn Hutchinson, Leonard Savage, Henry Brosin and that Hungarian who always knew who was sleeping with who and it was the only thing he was interested in, I've forgotten his name. Well, the lists survive all right.

There were three groups of people. There were the mathematicians and physicists—people trained in the physical sciences, who were very, very precise in what they wanted to think about. There was a small group of us, anthropologists and psychiatrists, who were trained to know enough about psychology in groups so we knew what was happening, could use it, and disallow it. And then there were two or three gossips in the middle, who were simply people who had a lot of loose intuition and no discipline to what they were doing. In a sense it was the most interesting conference I've ever been in, because nobody knew how to manage these things yet.

SB: So you had one group of people that was on to another group on a level they were not used to.

MEAD: Yes, and shifting back and forth between these levels and keeping everything straight was very interesting. So we used the model, "feedback," and Kurt Lewin—who

1952, one of the later Macy Conferences on cybernetics. From foreground clockwise: Larry Kubie, Larry Frank, T. C. Schneirla, H. L. Teuber, Walter Pitts, Gerhard von Bonin, Frank Fremont-Smith, Warren McCulloch (beard), W. Grey Walter, Henry Quastler, Heinz Von Foerster, John Bowman.

didn't understand any known language, but always had to reduce them to concepts—he went away with the idea of feedback as something that when you did anything with a group you went back and told them later what had happened. And he died before anything much else happened. So the word "feedback" got introduced incorrectly into the international UNESCO type conferences where it's been ever since.

BATESON: In the small group cult, feedback now means either telling people what they did, or answering.

MEAD: Yes. "I don't get any feedback from you," or "I can't go on with this without some feedback." It wouldn't have survived if Kurt had lived. He would undoubtedly have got it right.

SB: I would like a little more detail back at the initial time when you knew you had hit something.

BATESON: We knew we had, well, for me, I had analyzed the Iatmul of Sepik River in *Naven*[3] and I had analyzed out the fact there were interactions which must stockpile.

SB: This was your schismogenesis?

BATESON: This is schismogenesis, yes. We named it in '36.

MEAD: It hadn't been named yet. You're starting back before you named it schismogenesis.

BATESON: Well, *Naven* was published. I'm talking about the state I was in when this stuff appeared.

MEAD: In '43.

BATESON: Yes. The next thing that followed that was "Generalized Foreign Policies." L. F. Richardson.[4] I went back to England in '39. Hitler had invaded Poland. Bartlett said, "You might be interested in *that*," throwing it across the room in contempt.

MEAD: I'm glad I have another count against Bartlett. I didn't know he had contempt for Richardson.

BATESON: For Richardson and for me, you see. It was contemptible that I would be interested in the contemptible. So I ran off with that and kept it (probably it's Bartlett's copy of his files that we now have), and brought it back to this country.

SB: What was in that paper?

BATESON: This is the mathematics of armaments races. How do you build the mathematics of a system in which what I do depends upon what you do, and what you do depends upon what I do, and we get into a thing. Richardson set a limit by invoking "fatigue." He started with a simple pair of differential equations in the premise that my *rate* of armament could be a linear function of your strength, and *vice versa*. That led immediately to an exponential runaway. He added a "fatigue" factor representing the drain on your and my resources. The question then was whether the system could settle. Are we going to settle at a mutual . . . there's a word in international relations for slapping the other people's aggression back by threat. . . .

MEAD: You mean deterrence?

BATESON: Yes, mutual deterrence. That word hadn't been invented then. Then in the appendix, he had some revised equations in terms of not what is your strength and what is my strength, but what is the difference between our strengths. He worked it out in terms of the relation of two nations where each is stimulated by the amount the other side is ahead. This was obviously symmetrical—Iatmul Sepik River schismogenesis—right?

I then wrote to him at that stage, and said, "What about the other case, where you are stimulated to aggression by the *weakness* of the other side?" Which is the complementary schismogenesis, right? He worked out the algebra for that, and said, "It's very unpromising. I don't recommend nations to get into that at all. The orders of instability they get into are then very serious."

SB: Because that one would accelerate the difference rather than reduce the difference?

BATESON: Accelerates the difference, yes.

SB: A large amount of this strikes me as being the war. Would cybernetics have begun without the war? Richardson's armaments race, and Wiener's missiles . . .

BATESON: Wiener without a biologist wouldn't have done it.

MEAD: Wiener was working on Rosenblueth's stuff. Now Richardson is a very peculiar character. He was a Quaker schoolteacher of mathematics. He did all the basic work on weather prediction. It was used in World War II and he was never told how it worked, because of security. He died without knowing about it.

BATESON: Richardson was responding to

World War I. As a Quaker he refused to bear arms in World War I, and he became an ambulance man. He sat in the trenches waiting for the next call for the ambulance working out the mathematics of armaments races. Because he was sure that if only this could be got straight, the whole mess wouldn't have to happen, which indeed might be true.

MEAD: Now, there were some other things like this that were being talked about, and one was what was called a vicious circle. Milton Erickson had written a paper on a girl who quarreled and had headaches and got alienated from people, which led to further quarrels, and so on.

BATESON: Yes, all the positive feedback stuff was ready. And that presented the problem: why don't these systems blow their tops? And the moment they came out with negative feedback, then one was able to say why they don't blow their tops.

SB: This was a word and an idea you heard about in '43?

BATESON: That's when *negative feedback* came in.

MEAD: We had things about reversals of sign . . .

BATESON: That was another story, that's before Richardson, even, and way before feedback. Already in *Naven* there is a statement that complementary schismogenesis neutralizes symmetrical, and vice versa. If you get into too long a contrast between the bosses and the workers (which is complementary schismogenesis), you put them all out on the cricket field and make them play cricket, which puts them in a symmetrical situation. And it doesn't matter who wins the game of cricket, you know.

SB: As long as they're in that mode . . .

BATESON: Or if they're too far in symmetrical rivalry, such as a quarreling husband and wife, when one of them sprains his ankle, in comes the complementary with dependency. They suddenly feel much better.

SB: It doesn't matter who sprains?

BATESON: It doesn't matter who sprains his ankle, of course not.

At the 1952 Macy Conference. From foreground clockwise: Henry Quastler, Heinz Von Foerster, John Bowman, Gregory Bateson, G. E. Hutchinson, unidentified, Henry Brosin, Heinrich Klüver, Janet Freud, Y. Bar-Hillel (speaking), Julian Bigelow, Leonard Savage, V. E. Amassian, Margaret Mead, Y. R. Chao, F. S. Northrup, Don Marquis, Larry Kubie.

SB: So you had some notion that all of these various pathologies were structurally the same?

BATESON: No, structurally related, that there was a subject matter of inquiry defined by all these. You see, the fantastic thing is that in 1856, before the publication of the *Origin of Species*, Wallace in Ternate, Indonesia, had a psychedelic spell following his malaria in which he invented the principle of natural selection. He wrote to Darwin and he said, "Look, natural selection is just like a steam engine with a governor." The first cybernetic model. But he only thought he had an illustration, he didn't think he'd really said probably the most powerful thing that'd been said in the nineteenth century.

MEAD: Only nobody knew it.

BATESON: Nobody knew it. And there it is, still in the text. Nobody picked it up. Well, there was the machinery, the governor itself. There was the mathematics of the machine with the governor, which was done by Clerk Maxwell in 1868, because nobody knew how to write a blueprint for these bloody things— they would go into oscillation. Then there's Claude Bernard about 1890 with the *milieu interne*—the internal matrix of the body, control of temperature, control of sugar, and all that.[5]

SB: Which later became homeostasis?

BATESON: Which later became homeostasis in Cannon.[6] But nobody put the stuff together to say these are the formal relations which go for natural selection, which go for internal physiology, which go for me picking up the salt cellar. This was really done by Wiener, and Rosenblueth and McCulloch and Bigelow. And who really put the truth through, I don't know, do you?

MEAD: No. Wiener and McCulloch were first partners in this thinking, and then became rivals when McCulloch went to MIT. As long as McCulloch stayed at Illinois and Wiener at MIT they were working right together. With both of them at MIT they became totally alienated, and then Walter Pitts got involved. He was the youngest member of the group.

BATESON: Oh God, he was so clever. You'd set him a problem, you know, and he would reach up to his hair and take a couple of strands, and he would say, "Well, now, if you say that, you see, um, no then, you see," and he'd work it all out with his hair.

MEAD: He was a very odd boy. Now, one of the important points at this stage was one that Gregory kept making, that a possible cross-disciplinary mathematical language was available. We never got very far with that because all you could ever get out of people like Wiener was, "You need a longer run." We used to drive them absolutely out of their minds because they were not willing to look at pattern, really. What they wanted was a terribly long run of data.

BATESON: Of quantitative data, essentially.

MEAD: Quantitative data, and we never got them really to look at the problem of pattern. Von Neumann came the closest to it.

BATESON: Yes, he was in games theory, you see.

SB: How many of you were thinking you had some kind of a general solution?

MEAD: Gregory thought so, and Larry Frank thought so, Evelyn Hutchinson; we had Ross Ashby over, how about Savage?

BATESON: I don't think so, no. You see, one of the essentials, Stewart, for understanding it, was to have been brought up in the age when it wasn't there, when purpose was a total mystery. *Naven* is a disciplined book, written without teleology. The rule was you must not invoke teleology. Now, people like Savage, who was a mathematician, for one thing he never faced biological data, you see. He didn't know what a mystery it is that you have a nose between two eyes, and you don't have noses on the outside here, you know. All that sort of mystery wasn't a question for him. Now, if you say to somebody like that, "Why is the trunk of an elephant a nose?" they can't tell you without an awful sweat that it's because it's between two eyes. The formal puzzle has never been presented to them.

MEAD: I remember Robert Merton saying once that there wasn't a person in the country who was thinking hard about problems who didn't have a folder somewhere marked something like "circular systems." Horney's book *The Neurotic Personality of Our Times*[7] discusses the vicious circle, and interventions in the circle, and the effect of intervention. Milton's paper on that girl with migraine headaches and quarreling with her friends, there was lots of stuff around . . .

BATESON: On positive feedback.

MEAD: But also about possible intervention.

BATESON: But the essence of the other thing is that it's not an intervention.

MEAD: Yes, but intervention is a precursor of thinking of . . .

BATESON: Yes, yes. All cybernetic entities are displaced small boys.

MEAD: Displaced small what?

BATESON: Boys. They're jacks. You know what a jack is? A jack is an instrument to displace a small boy. A bootjack is a thing for pulling off boots 'cause you haven't a small boy to pull it off for you.

MEAD: I'll remember that next time. This is an English joke that no one will understand.

BATESON: I can't help it. On the first steam engines, you've got a pair of cylinders and you've got valves, and you pull this valve to run the steam into this one, close it, let it drive the piston, pull it—this is done by hand. Then they invented the idea of having the flywheel control the valves. This displaced a small boy.

SB: The governor displaced another one?

BATESON: And the governor displaced another small boy, who was to keep the engine going at a constant rate, that's right. Now then, the John Stroud stuff is the study of the psychology of the human being between two machines.

In any device such as an ack-ack gun you've got a whole series of small boys in the situation of being between a machine and another machine. What John Stroud worked on was the psychology of that situation. He found what I still think are some very interesting things, namely that the orders of equations (you know, equations in X, or X^2, or X^3, or whatever) are discontinuous in the human mind, as well as being discontinuous in mathematical paper work. Where is John Stroud now, do you ever see him?

MEAD: He is retired, teaching at Simon Fraser somewhat, and he's been brought back by Gerry O'Neill into discussions of space colonies.

SB: Good lord.

MEAD: He was very much interested in space colonies. He told me all about them twenty-five years ago, and I was interested in all the problems then, the selection of people, and what not.

BATESON: Stewart, you should get hold of John Stroud.

MEAD: Now Gerry has John Stroud's manuscript and he's not going to read it until he's finished his own. I said, "I think that's unscientific and childish."

BATESON: He wants credit for inventing anything that John Stroud had invented.

MEAD: Well, he did invent it separately, that's true, and he wants to prove it, because after all, what does a physical science have in the world except priority? I don't blame them you know, because they haven't got anything else. All they're interested in is priority. They spend weeks and months discussing priority. It's so boring. Somebody mailed a letter three days before somebody else did, and they have a whole meeting about it.

SB: Margaret, what was your perception at the time of the early Macy meetings as to what was going on?

MEAD: The thing that cybernetics made the most difference to me, aside from all the things that you know, in the social organization field, was the interaction between the mother and child. There had been too much emphasis that there were temperamental differences among children, so that you responded differently to a hyperactive baby than you did to a quiet baby. But the extent to which there was a system in which the mother was dependent on what the child had learned as the stimulus for the next position wasn't well articulated until we got the cybernetics conferences going.

BATESON: The link-up with the behavioral sciences spread very slowly and hasn't really spread yet. The cyberneticians in the narrow sense of the word went off into input-output.

SB: They went off into computer science.

BATESON: Computer science is input-output. You've got a box, and you've got this line enclosing the box, and the science is the science of these boxes. Now, the essence of Wiener's cybernetics was that the science is the science of the whole circuit. You see, the diagram . . .

MEAD: You'd better verbalize this diagram if it's going to be on the tape.

BATESON: Well, you can carry a piece of yellow paper all the way home with you. The electric boys have a circuit like that, and an event here is reported by a sense organ of some kind, and affects something that puts in here. Then you now cut off there and there, then you say there's an input and an output. Then you work on the box. What Wiener says is that you work on the whole picture and its properties. Now, there may be boxes inside here, like this, of all sorts, but essentially your ecosystem, your organism-plus-environment, is to be considered as a single circuit.

SB: The bigger circle there . . .

BATESON: And you're not really concerned with an input-output, but with the events within the bigger circuit, and you are *part of* the bigger circuit. It's these lines around the box (which are just conceptual lines after all) which mark the difference between the engineers and . . .

MEAD: . . . and between the systems people and general systems theory, too.

BATESON: Yes.

SB: A kind of a Martin Buber-ish breakdown, "I-it," where they are trying to keep themselves out of that which they're studying. The engineer is outside the box . . . and Wiener is inside the box.

BATESON: And Wiener is inside the box; I'm inside the box . . .

MEAD: I'm inside the box. you see, Wiener named the thing, and of course the word "cybernetics" comes from the Greek word for helmsman.

BATESON: It actually existed as a word before Wiener—it's a nineteenth-century word.

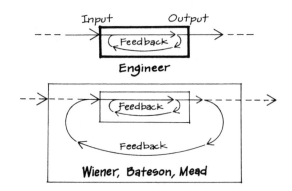

MEAD: Yes, but he wrote the book *Cybernetics*[8] and sort of patented the idea to that extent. And then he went to Russia, and was very very well received. The Russians were crazy about this right away—it fit right into their lives. But one of the big difficulties in Russian psychology is that they have great difficulty learning that anything's irreversible. So cybernetics spread all over the Soviet Union very rapidly, and in Czechoslovakia, whereas what spread here was systems theory instead of cybernetics.

SB: How did that happen? It seems like something went kind of awry.

MEAD: Americans like mechanical machines.

BATESON: They like tools.

SB: Material tools more than conceptual tools.

BATESON: No, because conceptual tools aren't conceptual tools in America, they're not part of *you*.

SB: How about McCulloch? He loved machinery. Did he also see himself as inside the box?

MEAD: Well, one of the things he spent a great deal of time on was perception machines, separate sensory apparatus for the deaf or the blind.

(*After reminiscence about other meetings following the Macy period the subject of "feed forward" comes up.*)

BATESON: As far as I was ever able to make out, "feed forward" was implicit and more or less explicit in the original Wiener paper. The feed forward process is what you get by using not the primary variable, but the derivative of the variable. You've got a machine for steering a ship, an automatic steerer, and you set her loose in the Atlantic, and you want her to go to London or some such place: she's to sail east. You have a compass card, and you measure the error between the compass card and the direction the ship's pointing, and you use that angle to control the steering machine, which pulls a rudder this way and that, right? Depending on the error. So, when the error is northward, the machine tells the rudder to swing it across southward, right? When it is going due east,

the ship has way on, rotational momentum, and is going to go way over to the south of east, and now it's got a new error, and it's going to come back and go way over to the north of east, and it's going to go yawing all across the Atlantic, right?

SB: This is hunting, technically.

BATESON: This is technically hunting, and if you want to cut that down, what you've got to do is to have a machine on top of that machine, another machine which measures the *rate* at which the ship is correcting its error. The faster it is correcting its error, the slower you have it correct its error. It will then, you see, actually hold itself before it gets to due east. If you've ever handled the tiller of a small boat, you know the problem.

SB: It's a double layer in other words. The first machine is treating the boat as something which needs to be given negative feedback, and then the second machine is treating the first machine as something which needs to be given negative feedback.

BATESON: That's right. You've got a hierarchy of logical types there, and their various complexities.

SB: Is feed forward a kind of discounting of part of the corrective signal?

BATESON: It's a discounting of the corrective signal in terms of the error which the corrective signal will generate if allowed to continue.

MEAD: Now, Stewart, what we thought we were going to talk about, but you didn't let us say what we wanted to talk about, you started something else under the pretense that you wanted to start the tape recorder (I want to point out I followed all those maneuvers) what we had said we were going to talk about was the need of having "some data flowing through the system."

SB: Some data flowing through the system?

BATESON: Yes, I set my classes an assignment. If they can, they will handle it purely abstractly. And they then get off into an awful mess of ill-drawn abstractions which act upon other ill-drawn abstractions. But if you can make them fool around with data of any sort, while they're playing with the abstractions, then you get something. I keep a fish tank going there, because a fish tank is a nice thing, really, to have in the back of your mind while you're thinking about whatever it might be. Norbert Wiener, when he had a problem, used to sit with the wind blowing on a curtain.

MEAD: I thought that was Von Neumann.

BATESON: It could have been Von Neumann. Pitts did it by disturbing his hair.

Now, this goes along with: "always the multiple approach." Any Hebrew poetry is like this. "The candles are white, as translucent as fishes," you know. "Lilies for joy, and lilies for funerals"; "How are the mighty fallen and the weapons of war perished." You get away from the pure verbalism by double-phrasing.

You make two statements, and what is true of both of them is the formal truth. This is what is called explanation.

SB: It's not that it's a repetition of the message, it's different derivations of the same message from different sources.

BATESON: Often. In psychoanalysis if you can recognize the same formal pattern in a dream and in a childhood memory and in how you're treating your analyst, you will say, "Aha, it's true." You've got it.

MEAD: And when you're studying a culture.

SB: What would be an example there?

MEAD: Well, you find the same pattern recurring in different aspects of the culture. You find, for instance, a house in which there's no ornamentation inside, all the ornamentation's on the gate. You find a people who are preoccupied with the external aspects of their skin and are always searching for some imperfection in their skin and believe that any breakage will impair them so that they're imperfect for something else, and so forth. With that kind of understanding, if you're told something, you can tell whether it fits or not.

For instance, the Balinese told us that they had marriage by capture, which didn't suit anything we'd understood about their culture. Our cook was going to carry off a girl by capture, so Gregory went outside the gate with him early in the morning, and the girl was there waiting. They looked around and there was nobody else there, so she trotted off with

him. If there had been another group there, she would have pretended, she would have screamed and been carried off, because that was correct etiquette.

Then we had the case of a very stupid boy who thought it was true. He carried off a girl who had already planned to elope with somebody else. It took the society months to sort that out.

From a complex culture like Bali you take a lot of chunks—birthday ceremonies and funeral ceremonies, children's games, and a whole series of things, and then you analyze them for the patterns that are there.

BATESON: In Iatmul they have flutes. The flutes are long hollow bamboo, an inch and a half thick, five feet long, and one hole here, which you blow across. And from that you can get about five notes by overblowing, by harmonics. All right. You have a flute, you're blowing with me, and yours is tuned one tone higher than mine. So your harmonics lie between mine, right? Between us we've got quite a bit of scale. If we blow alternately we can make a tune. Well, now this is how the generations are arranged. The grandparents go with the grandchildren, and the parents go with their grandchildren, and the initiation grades are like seniors–juniors–sophomores–freshmen, in which when you get a fight over initiation, the seniors and the sophomores go together, and the juniors and the freshmen go together. And so on.

SB: So what is the truth?

BATESON: The truth is that Iatmul like to make this pattern. This is a pattern of organization that they think is nice.

MEAD: When Gregory and Waddington talked to each other, I learned what I know about the way English biologists think, by listening to the two of them. They would pick their illustrations right across the field. One minute from embryology, the next from geology, the next from anthropology, back and forth, very freely, so that the illustrations from one spot illuminated, corrected, and expanded the one from another. This is the thing that Americans are not taught to do. In our school system you have one year of chemistry, then

you're through with chemistry probably, and
then you have one year of physics. Whereas in
the English system they took all of them at
once in smaller doses that went along.[9]

NORA BATESON: Goodbye.

MEAD: Goodbye. Are you going to school
now?

NORA: Yes.

MEAD: Well, it's been lovely to see you,
Nora.

NORA: It's been lovely to see you, too. Bye
bye.

BATESON: Goodbye.

NORA: Bye, Daddy.

SB: Margaret, an old student of yours told
me you have a list of reliable sources of insight. What's the list?

MEAD: I used to say to my classes that the
ways to get insight are: to study infants, to
study animals, to study primitive people, to be
psychoanalyzed, to have a religious conversion
and get over it, to have a psychotic episode and
get over it, or to have a love affair with an Old
Russian. And I stopped saying that when a little dancer in the front row put up her hand and
said, "Does he have to be old?"

SB: How many of those have you done?

(Blank here while cassette was changed. Dr.
Mead said she had studied infants and primitive
people. When she got to animals in the list, the conversation swerved to Konrad Lorenz.)

MEAD: Watching Konrad Lorenz be simultaneously a bird and a worm is one of the really
magnificent things in the world. You've seen
that, haven't you, when he's describing a bird
catching a worm, and he's both? Talk about
the whole system, there it is.

BATESON: One of the things I've always re-
gretted is that I didn't film him lecturing in
Hawaii. One could've, I think. Lorenz is a
Aurignacian.

SB: How do you mean?

BATESON: I mean that he is identified with
animals. Aurignacians are the people who did
the cave paintings, the good ones. Lorenz goes
to the blackboard and there is a live dog, hesi-
tating between attacking and retreating. He
takes the eraser, and he wipes the tail off,
changes the angle by ten degrees, and flattens

out the hair on the back of the neck, and he
says, "That dog's going to run." He sticks it
the other way, and "That dog's going to attack." And he is the dog while he's talking
about it. And this goes for cichlid fishes, bees,
any goddamn thing. And then, in the final lecture he gave in Hawaii, he got all mixed up,
you know, the way scientists do, with physics
and the Einsteinian universe, and his body got
twisted, as he started to talk about the Einsteinian universe where the straight lines are not
straight anymore. That's what I wish I had on
the camera. The others all think this is very
unfair you know, he has all of this information
that they simply don't have.

MEAD: He contributes tremendous zest. If
Lorenz is in a meeting, I can retire and take
notes and think and have no responsibility to
keep it going; whereas if he isn't there, I very
often have to keep it awake . . .

Gregory, have you any ideas on the subject
of the harm that is done by television because
of the rigidity of the body of people watching
TV? Sartre discussed at one point what happened when you peek into a keyhole. When
you look through a keyhole, the whole body is
focused to try to use this very small aperture,
and he described what happens if you touch
somebody who is looking through a keyhole.
They jump. I have a big set, now, of compara-
tive pictures of family groups (they weren't
taken for this, they were taken for family al-
bums) reading and looking at TV. When the
family is reading, they're a thousand years
away from each other, their eyes are all down,
but you get a sense of community and relaxation. Their bodies are very loose, and undoubtedly there's movement going on as they read.
But when they're watching television, the
same people sit like this, they don't touch each
other, and they're very rigid.

We have lots of material that if you move in
your mind, your muscles don't get stiff. For
years we had this very funny problem with
catatonics, such as a man who would stand all
day long in a ward with his eyes up and his
hands together in prayer, never moving.
They'd pick him up at night, tip him into a
bed, feed him artificially, and then after five

years or something, there'd be a fire. He'd walk across the ward, pick up a telephone, report, "Fire in ward five," help get all the patients out, and then when the fire was out, back he went to his position. But he was not stiff. Whereas if you take the ordinary person and put them in bed for three months, they have to relearn how to walk. All the data we now have on monitoring muscles with tiny transistor monitors shows, if you think about skiing or exercising, the muscles that you use to ski will respond.

If you inhibit movement, as one does watching TV, with no empathy, no muscular involvement at all, I think this is the thing that's doing harm.

BATESON: I was wondering about looking through, for example, a camera.

MEAD: Remember Clara Lambert and when you were trying to teach her? That woman who was making photographic studies of play schools, but she was using the camera as a telescope instead of as a camera. You said, "She'll never be a photographer. She keeps using the camera to look at things." But you didn't. You always used a camera to take a picture, which is a different activity.

BATESON: Yes. By the way, I don't like cameras on tripods, just grinding. In the latter part of the schizophrenic project, we had cameras on tripods just grinding.

MEAD: And you don't like that?

BATESON: Disastrous.

MEAD: Why?

BATESON: Because I think the photographic record should be an art form.

MEAD: Oh why? Why shouldn't you have some records that aren't art forms? Because if it's an art form, it has been altered.

BATESON: It's undoubtedly been altered. I don't think it exists unaltered.

MEAD: I think it's very important, if you're going to be scientific about behavior, to give other people access to the material, as comparable as possible to the access you had. You don't, then, alter the material. There's a bunch of filmmakers now that are saying, "It should be art," and wrecking everything that we're trying to do. Why the hell should it be art?

BATESON: Well, it should be off the tripod.

MEAD: So you run around.

BATESON: Yes.

MEAD: And therefore you've introduced a variation into it that is unnecessary.

BATESON: I therefore got the information out that I thought was relevant at the time.

MEAD: That's right. And therefore what do you see later?

BATESON: If you put the damn thing on a tripod, you don't get any relevance.

MEAD: No, you get what happened.

BATESON: It isn't what happened.

MEAD: I don't want people leaping around thinking that a profile at this moment would be beautiful.

BATESON: I wouldn't want beautiful.

MEAD: Well, what's the leaping around for?

BATESON: To get what's happening.

MEAD: What you think is happening.

BATESON: If Stewart reached behind his back to scratch himself, I would like to be over there at that moment.

MEAD: If you were over there at that moment you wouldn't see him kicking the cat under the table. So that just doesn't hold as an argument.

BATESON: Of the things that happen the camera is only going to record one percent anyway.

MEAD: That's right.

BATESON: I want the one percent on the whole to tell.

MEAD: Look, I've worked with these things that were done by artistic film makers, and the result is you can't do anything with them.

BATESON: They're bad artists, then.

MEAD: No, they're not. I mean, an artistic film maker can make a beautiful notion of what he thinks is there, and you can't do any subsequent analysis with it of any kind. That's been the trouble with anthropology, because they had to trust us. If we were good enough instruments, and we said the people in this culture did something more than the ones in that, if they trusted us, they used it. But there was no way of probing further into the material. So we gradually developed the idea of film and tapes.

BATESON: There's never going to be any way of probing further into the material.

MEAD: What are you talking about, Gregory? I don't know what you're talking about. Certainly, when we showed that Balinese stuff that first summer there were different things that people identified—the limpness that Marion Stranahan identified, the place on the chest and its point in child development that Erik Erikson identified. I can go back over it, and show you what they got out of those films. They didn't get it out of your head, and they didn't get it out of the way you were pointing the camera. They got it because it was a long enough run so they could see what was happening.

SB: What about something like that Navajo film, "Intrepid Shadows"?[10]

MEAD: Well, that is a beautiful, an artistic production that tells you something about a Navajo artist.

BATESON: This is different, it's a native work of art.

MEAD: Yes, and a beautiful native work of art. But the only thing you can do more with that is analyze the film maker, which I did. I figured out how he got the animation into the trees.

BATESON: Oh yes? What do you get out of that one?

MEAD: He picked windy days, he walked as he photographed, and he moved the camera independently of the movement of his own body. And that gives you that effect. Well, are you going to say, following what all those other people have been able to get out of those films of yours, that you should have just been artistic?

SB: He's saying he *was* artistic.

MEAD: No, he wasn't. I mean, he's a good film maker, and Balinese can pose very nicely, but his effort was to hold the camera steady enough long enough to get a sequence of behavior.

BATESON: To find out what's happening, yes.

MEAD: When you're jumping around taking pictures . . .

BATESON: Nobody's talking about that, Margaret, for God's sake.

MEAD: Well.

BATESON: I'm talking about having control

of a camera. You're talking about putting a dead camera on top of a bloody tripod. It sees nothing.

MEAD: Well, I think it sees a great deal. I've worked with these pictures taken by artists, and really good ones . . .

BATESON: I'm sorry I said artists; all I meant was artists. I mean, artist is not a term of abuse in my vocabulary.

MEAD: It isn't in mine either, but I . . .

BATESON: Well, in this conversation, it's become one.

MEAD: Well, I'm sorry. It just produces something different. I've tried to use "Dead Birds,"[11] for instance . . .

BATESON: I don't understand "Dead Birds" at all. I've looked at "Dead Birds," and it makes no sense.

MEAD: I think it makes plenty of sense.

BATESON: But how it was made I have no idea at all.

MEAD: Well, there is never a long-enough sequence of anything, and you said absolutely that what one needed was long, long sequences from one position in the direction of two people. You've said that in print. Are you going to take it back?

BATESON: Yes, well, a long sequence in my vocabulary is twenty seconds.

MEAD: Well, it wasn't when you were writing about Balinese films. It was three minutes. It was the longest that you could wind the camera at that point.

BATESON: A very few sequences ran to the length of the winding of the camera.

MEAD: But if at that point you had had a camera that would run twelve hundred feet, you'd have run it.

BATESON: I would have and I'd have been wrong.

MEAD: I don't think so for one minute.

BATESON: The Balinese film wouldn't be worth one quarter.

MEAD: All right. That's a point where I totally disagree. It's not science.

BATESON: I don't know what science is, I don't know what art is.

MEAD: That's all right. If you don't, that's quite simple. I do. [*To Stewart:*] With the films that Gregory's now repudiating that he took, we have had twenty-five years of re-examination and re-examination of the material.

BATESON: It's pretty rich material.

MEAD: It is rich, because they're long sequences, and that's what you need.

BATESON: There are no long sequences.

MEAD: Oh, compared with anything anybody else does, Gregory.

BATESON: But they're trained not to.

MEAD: There are sequences that are long enough to analyze . . .

BATESON: Taken from the right place!

MEAD: Taken from one place.

BATESON: Taken from the place that averaged better than other places.

MEAD: Well, you put your camera there.

BATESON: You can't do that with a tripod. You're stuck. The thing grinds for twelve hundred feet. It's a bore.

MEAD: Well, you prefer twenty seconds to twelve hundred feet.

BATESON: Indeed, I do.

MEAD: Which shows you get bored very easily.

BATESON: Yes, I do.

MEAD: Well, there are other people who don't, you know? Take the films that Betty Thompson studied.[12] That Karbo sequence— it's beautiful—she was willing to work on it for six months. You've never been willing to work on things that length of time, but you shouldn't object to other people who can do it, and giving them the material to do it.

There were times in the field when I worked with people without filming, and therefore have not been able to subject the material to changing theory, as we were able to do with the Balinese stuff. So when I went back to Bali I didn't see new things. When I went back to Manus, I did, where I had only still photographs. If you have film, as your own perception develops, you can re-examine it in the light of the material to some extent. One of the things, Gregory, that we examined in the stills, was the extent to which people, if they leaned against other people, let their mouths fall slack. We got that out of examining lots and lots of stills. It's the same principle. It's quite different if you have a thesis and have the camera in your hand, the chances of influenc-

ing the material are greater. When you don't have the camera in your hand, you can look at the things that happen in the background.

BATESON: There are three ends to this discussion. There's the sort of film I want to make, there's the sort of film that they want to make in New Mexico (which is "Dead Birds," substantially), and there is the sort of film that is made by leaving the camera on a tripod and not paying attention to it.

SB: Who does that?

BATESON: Oh, psychiatrists do that. Albert Scheflen[13] leaves a video camera in somebody's house and goes home. It's stuck in the wall.

MEAD: Well, I thoroughly disapprove of the people that want video so they won't have to look. They hand it over to an unfortunate student who then does the rest of the work and adds up the figures, and they write a book. We both object to this. But I do think if you look at your long sequences of stills, leave out the film for a minute, that those long, very rapid sequences, Koewat Raoeh, those stills, they're magnificent, and you can do a great deal with them. And if you hadn't stayed in the same place, you wouldn't have those sequences.

SB: Has anyone else done that since?

MEAD: Nobody has been as good a photographer as Gregory at this sort of thing. People are very unwilling to do it, very unwilling.

SB: I haven't seen any books that come even close to *Balinese Character*.[14]

MEAD: That's right, they never have. And now Gregory is saying it was wrong to do what he did in Bali. Gregory was the only person who was ever successful at taking stills and film at the same time, which you did by putting one on a tripod, and having both at the same focal length.

BATESON: It was having one in my hand and the other round my neck.

MEAD: Some of the time, and some not.

BATESON: We used the tripod occasionally when we were using long telephoto lenses.

MEAD: We used it for the bathing babies. I think the difference between art and science is that each artistic event is unique, whereas in science sooner or later once you get some kind of theory going somebody or other will make the same discovery.[15] The principal point is access, so that other people can look at your material, and come to understand it, and share it. The only real information that "Dead Birds" gives anybody are things like the thing that my imagination had never really encompassed, and that's the effect of cutting off joints of fingers. You remember? The women cut off a joint for every death that they mourn for, and they start when they're little girls, so that by the time they're grown women, they have no fingers. All the fine work is done by the men in that society, the crocheting and what not, because the men have fingers to do it with, and the women have these stumps of hands. I knew about it, I had read about it, it had no meaning to me until I saw those pictures. There are lots of things that can be conveyed by this quasi-artistic film, but when we want to suggest to people that it's a good idea to know what goes on between people, which is what you've always stressed, we still have to show your films, because there aren't any others that are anything like as good.

SB: Isn't that a little shocking? It's been, what, years?

MEAD: Very shocking.

BATESON: It's because people are getting good at putting cameras on tripods. It isn't what happens between people.

MEAD: Nobody's put any cameras on tripods in those twenty-five years that looked at anything that mattered.

BATESON: They haven't looked at anything that mattered, anyway. All right.

SB: I have a question that maybe relates to that, maybe not. What about field workers that join the tribe? Frank Cushing with the Zuni, and Carlos Castaneda, and such.

MEAD: Castaneda hasn't joined the tribe.

SB: He hasn't joined the tribe, he's tried to join the practice.

MEAD: No, only intermittently. We have examples. Edmund Carpenter's been making a study of these people.

SB: I've got some too. Everyone that knows anthropologists knows someone who's a little wiggy because of some over-zealous participation in something. And I wonder about that.

MEAD: It's the temptation for another culture. We also have a case of a man who was

studying the Chinese, and he married a Chinese girl. Which he then thought was enough anthropology; for quite a while he couldn't do anything else. It's a lot easier to study the cultures where you can't marry people, where there's such a gulf that that kind of over-identification doesn't occur. The minute you study a culture where you might marry them, or adopt their children, or be adopted by them, you get new complications. Extreme ones.

SB: Sometimes the ones who lose track of where they are, they find a place to be confused between, and proceed to be confused between it.

MEAD: I think that's a function of people who are confused wherever they are, anyway. One difference between pre-World War II anthropology and post-World War II is that most of us who did the pre-war work grew up in reasonably coherent cultures, and we knew what a pattern was when we saw one.[16] Remember that paper that I wrote that you invented the word "quizbits" for? (But the paper's called "Customs and Mores."[17]) It was a discussion of the extent to which information was being broken up into meaningless bits and fed to people. All your experience is chopped, everything out of scale. The news over the radio—one event is of world significance, the next is nothing. Contemporary young people have had the things that are presented to them so chopped up.

SB: You mean just in the speed with which they change, or the lack of integration?

MEAD: The lack of integration. You get it on radio in New Guinea: "Khrushchev has been deposed, there was a jewel robbery in the American Museum of Natural History, two small boats off Port Moresby have sunk," that's the news.

[Lois Bateson leans in on her way to an errand. Margaret will be gone by the time she returns. "OK, you people. See you in a while. I'm real glad you came, Margaret. Come again."]

MEAD: Well, it's been lovely to see you.

SB: You mentioned Gerry O'Neill a while ago, as though you're somewhat involved in the space colony business.

MEAD: Well, I've been interested in them, because of the possibilities of diversity. You

Brand

1976, leaving Santa Cruz

see, I've always loved the Pacific islands, because they have such high degrees of diversity. When John Stroud first told me about space colonies, the picture was that you could have an area about the size of Los Angeles, and they would be undisturbed for 1500 years, so they could vary.

SB: I have a question that goes back to the Macy conferences, and it also relates to projects that Gregory's getting interested in now. What is the history of the failure of conceptual cybernetics to become public knowledge? You said that the later Macy meetings were starting to get a sense that you had something that everybody ought to know.

MEAD: It wasn't quite as deep as that. We thought we had something that would be cross-disciplinary language. The meeting we had with the Academy of Sciences was to include more of the scientific community. Now, I worked a lot on that idea. *Continuities in Cultural Evolution* deals with the fact that in social science, unless you can carry the public with you, you can't use your findings. I think that we could trace part of the lack of response to

the American preference for linear sequences, which is very high. It's like the Manus, too. They're both moral cause-and-effect societies. You do *this*, and *that* happens.

A problem I was going to raise, to Gregory, is why do you think the United States has more runaway positive feedbacks than most cultures?

SB: Such as?

MEAD: Such as, gasoline taxes that can only be used on roads. With the tax you build more roads, which makes it possible to have more cars, which uses more gasoline. It's a perfect endless runaway. We have hundreds of them in this country.

BATESON: I think one of the things that's serious in this country is using the value one can catch hold of, rather than the real value. Such as, catching gangsters for their income tax returns. I had a whole series of examples of this at one stage. The actual feedback circuit runs upon a collateral variable and you don't, from the circuit, get insight into the whole structure.

SB: Still, you say that's good when it comes to something like oxygen or carbon dioxide being the controller of breathing rates.

BATESON: This is exactly the problem. Where do you want to do this, and where do you want not to do it? At one stage I was saying, the thing to do is never to use the lethal variable to control the feedback.

MEAD: The lethal variable?

BATESON: This was in asphyxia. The rate of breathing is not affected by the lack of oxygen but by the surplus of carbon dioxide in the blood. If you try to regulate by the lack of oxygen, it's already too late.

MEAD: Well, we said the same thing, that if you're teaching children nutritional habits, don't do it with something that's related to nutrition. It's much safer to say, "We'll take you to a circus if you eat your spinach," than to say, "If you eat your spinach, you can have ice cream."

SB: Safer means?

MEAD: Safer socially when you're bringing up children and you want them to learn to eat nutritionally good diets effortlessly. When you tie the eating to the food itself, if a child wants to fight about it, they fight about it by not eating the right food. So that you put all the trouble into the system. The Balinese say to a child when dressing a cut, "Listen to the gong, listen to the orchestra, go and see an orchestra!" There's no orchestra. She's just presenting something pleasant. Italian mothers do that. They say. "Ice cream! Ice cream! Lovely ice cream! Lovely ice cream!" while the child's having a cut fixed.

Americans say, "But she didn't mean it, she didn't give him any ice cream." Watergate, of course, was an outstanding example. We didn't have to get Nixon because of Watergate. We were using Watergate because he was taking the country apart and had delusions of grandeur. I think if we'd known about the income tax, that would have done it.

I've wondered, Gregory, whether all of these things go together—the nonrecognition of cybernetics in this country, as compared with the Soviet Union. I figure that they have about a hundred times as many people that understand the whole thing.

SB: Understanding it creatively and coming up with new thoughts?

MEAD: That one doesn't know. We do know that they are using it for purposes of social organization, especially in Czechoslovakia.

BATESON: At that first cybernetic meeting we had a Russian talk. He hadn't much idea what it was all about, I thought.

MEAD: I don't remember what he said at all.

BATESON: He had fifteen slides of circuit structures that would do various sorts of things like pattern recognition, or control temperature, or something. It was sort of about the level of the McCulloch and Pitts papers. Without, as far as I could make out, the enormous theoretical spin-off that those papers had.

MEAD: And evidently I wrote him off so I can't remember.

BATESON: I think you wrote him off. I wrote him off very quickly.

MEAD: Well, we had a period where I thought we could take cybernetics and use it as a language for communicating with the Russians, and then somebody in this country decided that the Russian cybernetic activities

were very dangerous, and we had a big intelligence report on cybernetics. It ceased to be politics-free and was no longer useful. I wrote up a discussion of that, and decided anyway, that instead of having a methodology or conceptual scheme for communication, it was much better to have agreed-on subgoals for communication between two systems as antithetical as the Soviet and U.S. [19]

SB: Well, then something funny seemed to happen with the whole general systems bunch. I've never understood that.

MEAD: Well, there are a dreadful lot of systems people in the Society for General Systems Research. Then von Bertalanffy died. Anatol Rappaport runs a very isolated group. Now, when the Society for General Systems Research was formed in Atlanta, and Anatol was in the chair (I had never met him), and Ross Ashby was there on the front row, and there were about twenty people there, I went back to the correspondence, Gregory, where you had proposed that we plan an organization in relation to its purposes. This was before the cybernetics meetings, while you were overseas. When the Society for General Systems Research was formed, I proposed that we apply general systems to our society. Nobody knew who I was and I was feeling like the little old lady in tennis shoes. I went up at the end of it and talked to Ashby, and he said, "You mean we should apply our principles to ourselves?"

BATESON: In what tone of voice?

MEAD: He was repudiating it, in a light playful voice that was appropriate, but he was repudiating it.

SB: So it was stillborn.

MEAD: So now, the Society for General Systems Research, which is proliferating, is proliferating by the standard methods that are used in this country—regional chapters. I said to Dick Erickson, "I don't think we should be so conventional, we ought to think of something better." We can't get anybody to use any kind of constructive thinking on the problems of organization. And, of course, there's no place where you can get a well-rounded degree in General System Theory. Rand has a school that is almost entirely military.

One of the most crazy situations—I was asked to speak at a dinner of the Air Force celebrating their fifth decade of Air Force intelligence. I talked about the fact that they weren't paying attention to the whole; the Air Force was modeling the Soviet Union as a system, and the Army was modeling the United States as a system, using different units, and they were both ignoring the fact that China existed, and therefore were making a hopeless mess when you knew you had a universe to deal with. What I was telling them was to use cybernetic thinking as it had developed into general systems theory. The next morning I was on a chartered plane bringing me back, and there was a man on it who said, "You left me way behind. I couldn't understand a word you said." I said, "What are you?" He said, "I'm an electronic specialist."

Americans are always solving problems piecemeal. They're always solving them *de nouveau* and artificially because they're all newcomers and they don't have decisions grounded in a culture.

NOTES

1. *The Josiah Macy, Jr. Foundation, 1930–1955.* New York: The Josiah Macy, Jr. Foundation, 1955, p. 20. *Cybernetics.* Transactions of the Eighth Conference, March 15–16, 1951. New York: The Josiah Macy, Jr. Foundation, 1952, p. xix.

2. Rosenblueth, Arturo, Norbert Wiener, and Julian Bigelow. "Behavior, Purpose and Teleology," *Philosophy of Science.* vol. 10, 1942, p. 18.

3. Bateson, Gregory. *Naven.* Cambridge: Cambridge University Press, 1936. 2nd edition, Stanford: Stanford University Press, 1958.

4. L. R. Richardson, "Generalized Foreign Policies," *British Journal of Psychology,* Monography Supplement XXIII, 1939.

5. Claude Bernard. *Leçons sur les Phénomènes de la Vie Communes aux Animaux et aux Végétaux.* 2 vols. Paris: J. B. Bailliere, 1878–1879.

6. W. B. Cannon. *The Wisdom of the Body.* New York: Norton, 1932.

7. Karen Horney. *The Neurotic Personality of Our Time.* New York: Norton, 1937.

8. Norbert Wiener, *Cybernetics.* Cambridge, Massachusetts: Technology Press, 1948.

9. C. H. Waddington, *The Evolution of an Evolutionist.* Ithaca: Cornell University Press, 1975.

10. Sol Worth and John Adair. *Through Navajo Eyes.* Bloomington, Indiana: Indiana University Press, 1972.

"Intrepid Shadows" was made by Al Clah, a 19-year-old Navajo painter and sculptor.

11. *Dead Birds.* Directed by Robert Gardner for the Peabody Museum, Harvard University, color, 83 minutes, 1964. Available through New York Public Library.

12. Betty Thompson. "Development and Trial Applications of Method for Identifying Non-Vocal Parent-Child Communications in Research Film" (Ph.D. thesis, Teachers College, New York, 1970).

13. Albert E. Scheflen. *Body Language and the Social Order: Communication as Behavioral Control.* Englewood Cliffs, New Jersey: Prentice-Hall, 1973.

14. M. Mead and G. Bateson. *Balinese Character: A Photographic Analysis.* New York: The New York Academy of Sciences, Special Publications, 11, 1942; reissued 1962.

15. M. Mead. "Towards a Human Science," *Science,* vol. 191 (March 1976), pp. 903–909.

16. M. Mead. "From Intuition to Analysis in Communication Research," *Semiotica,* vol. 1 (1969), pp. 13–25.

17. M. Mead. "Customs and Mores," *American Journal of Sociology,* vol. 47 (1942), pp. 971–980.

18. M. Mead. *Continuities in Cultural Evolution.* New Haven: Yale University Press, 1964.

19. M. Mead. "Crossing Boundaries in Social Science Communication," *Social Science Information,* vol. 8 (1969), pp. 7–15.

COUNSEL FOR A SUICIDE'S FRIEND

23 May

Dear Prof. Bateson:

I talked with you yesterday morning and near the end you asked me if I had any specific questions. I did but couldn't bring myself to ask them, but find that I really do want to ask them so this letter.

First unasked question has to do with something said to the effect that "if your heart's in the frying pan, then you can't go wrong." Well, obviously, nothing much can be done if your heart's not in the frying pan, but what if your guts are in it and things go wrong.

What I'm talking about is I was introduced to a young woman about two years ago by my ex-shrink because he was feeling a bit stuck with her & on the other her craziness reminded him of mine, so she & I became friends & struggled through a lot of "if it's not clear, I'll prove it" stuff and "Are you going to desert me/believe I'm a terrible person now? now? now?" stuff.

Anyway she suicided eight months ago. At 21.

I am not willing to accept the premise that we were not really friends as I know I was there and was paying attention. So I'm stuck, amongst other things, with trying to sort out how I can legitimately (to myself mainly) aspire to trying to help others with their crazinesses? Have I the courage—yes and no. That is, I still think I understand some of it, but doubt whether that understanding is sufficient. And if it isn't, what is?

Which brings me to unasked question #2. One thing that looks to me as if it had the possibility of being sufficient is small communities like Kingsley Hall, the Granville Road house, etc. What mostly worries me about them is how do you get a community stable enough to sustain itself and support people working on their maps but not get tangled up in questions of stability and/or minimizing chaos as to interfere with people's working?

Respectfully

————

27 May 1973

Dear ————

I am sorry I did not manage to answer your letter while I was in Seattle.

I suggest that you consider and complete in your imagination the following scenario (after all, it is in your imagination that change is requested or needed):

Your friend has achieved her suicide and arrived at the Pearly Gates, where she is challenged by St. Peter, who notes that she has come too soon. She says that it was all ————'s fault.

There are many ways of completing the scenario, but one way or another, your friend has to demonstrate that she had no free will but you had. I suggest either that you both had free will or that neither of you had.

Of course it is gratifying to you and to all therapists to believe that they have more free will than their patients. But it won't do.

Your problem is to stop the boat rocking between the arrogance of "I had the power and the knowledge to help" and the self-repudiation of "I failed."

Your second question is much more diffi-

cult, but the answer is I suppose really a corollary following from what I have just said. You will always be terrified of the things which will inevitably happen in any therapeutic community if you start out with a false estimate of the power and the wisdom of whoever it is that runs the community (especially if it's you). What one human being can do for another is not quite nothing, but it probably sometimes helps the helpee when the helper is clear about how little help can be given. Some temporary protection from the cold winds of an insane civilization, some shared tears and laughter, and that's about it.

Yours sincerely,
Gregory Bateson
Santa Cruz, California
[Spring, 1975]

————

PROTECT THE TROPHIES,
SLAY THE CHILDREN

Dear S. B.

I want to raise a question and CQ is perhaps a good place for it. My mathematics is not good enough but perhaps Peter Warshall or one of your readers will tell me the answer.

The question is simple: Is it good practice to eat up big animals rather than small ones? Would it not make better sense in terms of conserving wild populations to eat the small fish and throw the big ones back?

After all it is the big ones that produce the eggs and sperm—in millions in many cases.

Fish, crabs, lobsters, abalone, deer—in almost all hunting or "harvesting" of wild animals the law protects the juveniles and permits the taking of the adults. But I suspect that this is based upon some sentimental fallacy.

The question looks like this: Suppose that fish of a given species produce N offspring per female adult per year; that of these offspring .01% start to produce their own offspring in 3 years and go on producing for 3 years. Which should we eat—the bearing adults, the new adults, or the pre-adolescents?

I suspect that the .01% figure is rather stable in the sense that predation by birds, bigger fish, bacterial infection, epidemics, etc., etc., will be a function of density of population. If

45

there are more baby fish, the predators will get more. If this be so, and we eat a lot of the babies, this will simply leave fewer babies for the other predators to eat and the number of babies who reach reproductive maturity will not be severely reduced. Perhaps?

What will the relevant mathematics look like for creatures like salmon who spawn only once? Creatures which have few babies and a high survival rate, as contrasted with fish with many free-floating eggs? And so on.

Was Hillaire Belloc right in his ecological jingle:

> Parents of large families
> With claims to common sense
> Find a tiger well repays
> The trouble and expense.

Yours infantivorously,
Gregory Bateson
Santa Cruz, California
[Spring 1978]

STEVE BAER

The Sun Riots
and The B & G

This author thinks differently about
energy and technology than other
writers. As Stewart said in the first
CQ introduction to Steve Baer, in
Spring 1975: "Characters like Specific Heat, Turbidity Factor, Angle
of Incidence, and Dewpoint *live* as
thoroughly for Baer as Bored Social-
ite, Desperate Poet, and Vengeful
Brother might for a playwright or
novelist."

The first of these two essays, "The
Sun Riots," appeared in that issue.
The second, "The B & G," appeared
a year later in the Summer 1976 CQ.
It began as a college talk. More than
a dozen Baer essays appeared in CQ
during its ten years. If you want to
see more, his 1975 book *Sunspots* is
still in print (from Madrona Publish-
ers, Seattle, WA). To quote Stewart
again: "If a real philosopher were a
real engineer, he would write like
this."

Steve Baer is the proprietor of
Zomeworks, a company based in Al-
buquerque, New Mexico, which has
designed and sold innovative solar
and insulating technology since the
late 60s.

Art Kleiner

The chief of police in a southwestern city is
talking on the telephone to the city maintenance department—"I want reflective blinds
on every goddamned window and if you can't
get enough of them then tape tinfoil over the
rest of the windows, now! Before that damn
sun comes up again."

The bottom offices of City Hall and the police department have been gutted by fire—
black streaks surround the windows which are
now opaque and shiny with aluminum foil.
The police are still unable to confiscate mirrors, the matter is in the courts.

A week earlier at a demonstration a large
van driven next to the crowd—the driver, a
swarthy man of about forty, opened the back
doors and began passing out foot-square mirrors. "Give 'em some sunshine!"

A few dozen mirrors began playing beams of
sunlight on a police car that had been dogging
the rear end of the demonstration. The officers
were caught by surprise. The driver managed
to back the car down the street, but not before
his partner, panicked by the glare and the rapidly rising temperature, had jumped out and
run. More and more mirrors were out in the
crowd now. The crowd glinted like a bank of
crystals.

It couldn't reach the police car which had
found protection behind a drive-up liquor
store. The man with the van now stood on top
of it. An old bread delivery van, "Let's burn it
up. Yeh—this."

His voice is hoarse and breaking. A few mirrors flit across the van and the man on top.
More focus on the tin side. The man climbs
off. People are pulling the last mirrors from
inside the van as others begin to focus on it.
There are 800 mirrors out in the street.

The crowd is silent. The blob of brilliant light on the side of the truck is fringed with trembling squares of light flitting in and out of the target. You can hardly hear a noise. Then the sheet metal side of the van oil cans as the metal swells. A few more moments and smoke appears—the crowd has results. That was at 11 A.M.; by dark there have been 100 fires.

No one on foot has been burned—too hard to follow a man on foot. Rows of smoking cars—the ashes of a flag at City Hall.

It's the office buildings—the windows above the street—the crowd focuses through one window after another—the curtains go fast.

The police appear with arc welders' masks. They fire on the demonstrators. The demonstrators disperse, but the light keeps coming. More mirrors appear on the street—funny-shaped mirrors, mirrors with ornamental frames, tiny pocket mirrors in the hands of children.

Smoke is seen from another part of town.

Television crews arrive. The footage in the evening news across the nation is overexposed. An occasional clear image and then the picture goes white and overexposed.

The mirror crowds are completely silent—moving everywhere on foot. A secretary at City Hall, "They just looked so funny—a whole crowd of them standing just as still as could be holding on to those mirrors and then pretty soon the store across the street was burning."

"When they started coming our way they just glinted and shined like a drawer full of diamonds—when they steadied down again we got out of there fast because they were burning up Captain Garcia's office downstairs."

"Get those damned kids with the mirrors off the street."

"But officers, I'm just usin' this mirror 'cause I'm combin' my hair, no law against combin' your hair is there?"

Dozens of youths in the street combing their hair peering into gigantic foot-square mirrors.

THE B & G

I don't think there is a proper understanding of buildings, particularly institutional buildings. What activities are they really built for? I remember in college the B & G, which stands for Buildings and Grounds. They ran the school. There are such crews all across the world. Why are we so obsessed with the FBI and the CIA when there is the B & G? They wear dark gray or green uniforms. Personnel are not accepted below the age of thirty-five; stocky, lumpy physiques are preferred, or some form of lameness. Requirements are to be able to carry an enormous ring of keys with the proper seriousness.

You hear stories of the communists where some lowly sweeper or maid is actually party commissioner in a factory and the factory manager may have to seek him out in the toilet for advice or directions. We have all seen the same thing.

We are at an evening lecture at the university. The distinguished professor, scientist, author is before us. The topic is fascinating. There are lively questions and discussion. Suddenly, at 9 P.M. a side door opens slowly and a middle-aged woman appears in a gray uniform—behind her in the hall you can see the mop bucket. She says nothing, merely looks at the lecturer for a few moments. He is looking the other way and doesn't see her, but he feels a cold draft on his back and senses his audience's attention is wandering. The woman goes on to some other chore, but the door is left open. It's as if we were all taking a bath and someone has now started to drain the tub. There is no struggle. The students, only too ready to give the Dean the finger or belch while a professor is making a point, seem obedient to the B & G. Five minutes later, the woman appears again—the lecturer has tried to rally the audience, who now seem distracted. On this visit she has her mop. She catches the lecturer's eye for a moment and gives the mop a little shake—a very much less dramatic version of what you imagine a bullfighter's message to a sinking bull may be. The lecture begins to close and the woman starts hauling in her equipment. "Sorry sir, but the building is to be locked at 9:30."

No one shouts out, "Fuck the dust, on with our discussion!" Radicals, jocks, gays, feminists, engineers—all bow to the B & G.

Of what importance is such a scene? Not much in one sense, but then again this may be the tiny corner of a vast empire of stupidity and obedience to schedules and demands which have nothing to do with the more important uses of architecture. Let's be on our way—track down the power flowing through the maid with her lowly mop and message about the building closing at 9:30. Let's go on and examine the heating and cooling system, the lights, the ventilation. Finally, far back in the hierarchy of the support machinery of the B & G, we might find the atom bomb itself.

After long consideration of the B & G and the power they wield, we may conclude that man is not merely a "tool-using animal," as he is sometimes defined, but a "tool-hypnotized animal" ready to show concern for collections of pipes and wires as if they were parts of his own body. Ready to obey the equipment caretakers in even the most improbable circumstances. We may have opened a question that demands another Freud to begin to solve the puzzles. Someone to examine emotions aroused by copper pipes, marble floors, plate glass, locks. The architect seems helpless to grapple with the forces at work. Caught in the crossfire of concrete trucks, heating and ventilating equipment salesmen, and furniture suppliers, he dodges to the side agreeing to a space where the wares can be installed. And somewhere in the subconscious, sensing the times, I suspect most of us have caught the smell of the atomic bomb and the guided missile coming in to help with "respect" for the equipment.

Is the professor obedient to the B & G because in his heart he feels all his talk about science or culture is really a lot of hot air, perhaps a diverting act to take up time between important activities such as mopping the building? How much are words and ideas worth compared to bricks, glass, copper pipes? It depends on how you feel—which, of course, is what is fascinating about the B & G taking over a university.

What if the B & G are really the only people who ever work at the university? Certainly in a factory where the janitor is up against milling machines, punch presses, and chem mill tanks you don't see him throwing his weight around. The punch press operator, though he may earn only half as much as the professor, would hardly have time to glance at the cleanup man.

Every technical achievement strengthens the hand of the B & G. Every song, every poem, every scientific discovery strengthens that of the teacher and the student.

I don't mean all these words as merely some diversion about school days. These attitudes go beyond school and beyond the mop and broom.

It is common knowledge that filth and grime in buildings is bad. It makes you suspicious of the occupants. In a sense it is a moral failure—lack of attention. Once a floor is built, it should be swept and mopped. It's as if one had signed a contract on pouring the slab. Once a window is installed, it should be cleaned.

The same contract seems to appear on the installation of a central heating system and thermostat. They demand a standard be maintained even if people are not there, for now it has become a moral issue—are you or are you not going to live up to your agreement with the equipment?

The comfort of the occupant is really of secondary concern. The same logic applies to lighting systems.

I believe the school and university is a prime battleground in spreading obedience to equipment, schedules, routines, investments, etc. The man who wants to display how well he has trained a dog waits until the dog's dinner is in his bowl, then calls Rex and has him roll over, sit, shake hands, or whatever interesting ritual he has taught the dog. All the while the dinner and its odor are so close by. It emphasizes the power of training. And so it is with the small, seemingly powerless band of uneducated employees wandering about the institutions of learning—going into the closets under the stairs—coming up from the boiler room in the basement. The furnace versus ancient history? Don't be silly! The two are completely different. The furnace keeps the building warm so that you can concentrate in the classroom on what the professor is telling you about ancient history. But what about when the feed line ruptures and the crews work for two weeks with jackhammers outside the window digging it up? Why couldn't they do it quietly with a pick and shovel? Or at night? Or let us do without heat? The contract doesn't include such possibilities.

The regents of the university are only trying to help learning when they allocate ten million dollars for the new service center. What does it matter that those who have earned the money or power for such positions have not read a book since they left school?

You see, I am sure that the United Nations is run by the B & G—debates cut off out of respect for the schedule of a vacuum cleaner—office styles made to conform to an engineer's wish to give you the best.

It's easier on you students to learn these lessons while young. It will help the doctor later to understand the functioning of the modern hospital with a parking lot large enough to cause panic and despair in even a healthy visitor. It will help the ecologist adjust to the airports where he finds he spends half his time on the way to and from conferences on the environment.

I recently heard from a student that at his state university the administration doesn't even murmur about teachers advocating LSD and other drugs, but one poor faculty member was soon fired after he began explaining and demonstrating how to alter the dormitory rooms. Say what you want, but don't get physical.

Perhaps the only escape is to join them yourself—get your key ring, heavy shoes, and prepare yourself for a life in the halls. Or, maybe better, get upstream from the B & G. Draw up the prints which they follow—manufacture the equipment they manipulate. The problem with this escape, which seems to promise a more interesting career, is that this architecture building too has its own B & G.

ROBERT HORVITZ

Some Mice

About mice. They are, in Robert Horvitz's words, "the essence of mammalhood, the most concise statement of a personality–type that can be seen running through our whole portion of the animal kingdom. Their behavioral repertoire is so limited that, paradoxically, they live on a mythic level: fratricide, rape, invasion, exploration are the daily stuff of life, and once one gets used to the Lilliputian scale, their epics are absolutely captivating. For several years instead of watching television, we'd sit around watching the mice until early morning, following subplots and developing emotional attachments."

About Robert Horvitz. He published this article originally in a New York literary magazine called *Big Deal*; Stewart reprinted it in the Summer 1976 CQ. Thereafter Robert was called CQ's "Art Editor," which meant he roved around the art world, seeking potential contributors like Donald Burgy (CQ printed his mock-proposal to become a U.N. artist-in-residence), Charles Ross (who charted the sun burning a lens-amplified path across a series of boards), or Alex Grey (whose paintings, pho-tographs and performance pieces mingled horror and religious beauty). Robert Horvitz only traveled to the CQ offices once (for the Jamboree). To the editors of the magazine, he was a soft, persistent, idea-filled voice on the phone—a link with the East Coast. It was fitting that he was also *Whole Earth*'s expert on shortwave radio and radio politics. (He writes a regular column for the *Review of International Broadcasting*.)

Art Kleiner

When our lease on the beach house was up, we decided to divide the mouse colony: anyone could take some mice with him when he left, and any left over would be let go in the field next door. I picked two, the extremes of the litter. One was the bully, a handsome and aggressive mouse named Brown. The other was the runt. I named him God. God was black and white, quite small and high-strung. He was always hunched over in fear of being attacked, as indeed he had been under attack by other mice all his life, simply because he was the smallest.

In their new cage, Brown immediately made it clear to God that he would be allowed to live only so long as he obeyed Brown's wishes. He cornered God and nipped at his balls and bit him on the base of his spine until all the hair there was gone. With no other mice around, and food appearing effortlessly, Brown had nothing else to do but manage God's existence. He laid down an impossible code of behavior and punished all infractions severely. God got very thin because Brown punished him for eat-

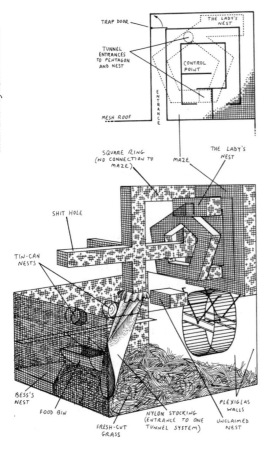

Diagram labels: TRAP DOOR · THE LADY'S NEST · TUNNEL ENTRANCES TO PENTAGON AND NEST · CONTROL POINT · ENTRANCE · MESH ROOF · SQUARE RING (NO CONNECTION TO MAZE) · MAZE · THE LADY'S NEST · SHIT HOLE · TIN-CAN NESTS · BESS'S NEST · FOOD BIN · FRESH-CUT GRASS · NYLON STOCKING (ENTRANCE TO ONE TUNNEL SYSTEM) · PLEXIGLAS WALLS · UNCLAIMED NEST

stantly, just in case he had done something he wasn't supposed to, or in case he might have been considering it.

Under this redoubled pressure, God could not get to the food dish at all. After a week of harassment and starvation, I intervened by slipping food directly to him through the wire mesh wall of the cage. He was afraid at first to accept anything because he knew that Brown would smell it on his breath and punish him. But after a day or so he gave in to temptation.

This backfired. Brown seemed to get the idea that God had found a way of conjuring up food; thereafter he never left God's side, hoping to either catch him in the act of making food or, better, get the food for himself.

The Lady had not lessened the tension between the males. The only other thing I could think of was to isolate Brown for a few days to allow God to recuperate from his life of routine torture. I lured Brown into a wire mesh tunnel with peanut butter and then barricaded the tunnel.

God noticed Brown's absence right away. He stayed in his corner the whole first day, afraid it was a trap. He smelled the air at intervals, but wouldn't move. The second day, he moved around the cage cautiously, stopping to check everything that smelled of Brown and jumping at unexpected sounds. He ate a little at the food dish. Then he discovered Brown behind the barricade and ran back to his corner. The third day, he went back to the barricade and gnawed at it at length. (I could never figure out if he was trying to liberate Brown or convince himself that he was safe from him.) God spent the rest of the night trying to mount The Lady. He had never had sex before so he was quite a comical lover. On the fourth day, God was noticeably more relaxed. His new self-confidence showed in the way he let his balls hang out under his tail. The social standing of a male mouse can be gauged by how prominently he displays his testicles: a dominant male wears them proudly, extended, one who is dominated wears his close in against his belly. God groomed himself leisurely while sitting at the "control point" in the center of the tunnel system—which had previously been

ing; his legs got stiff because Brown wouldn't let him run on their treadmill.

After a couple of weeks I bought two females at a pet store, hoping their presence would lessen the tension between the two males. One female died mysteriously her first night in the cage. Both God and Brown were fascinated with the one who survived, but Brown became even more oppressive, attacking God whenever she was nearby. The Lady was a "waltzing mouse," a breed with a peculiar waddling walk. While Brown was away at the food dish, God would sneak out from his corner to smell The Lady's vagina, but she would usually squeal and Brown would come rushing over. God got so he could make a quick trip out and back before either of the others knew what had happened. Brown's suspicions were aroused by finding The Lady's scent on God's whiskers and he began punishing God con-

reserved for Brown—and gained weight quickly as he was free to eat for the first time in over a month.

After four days, I thought their former pattern of supremacy and submission had been broken and they could begin anew as equals. But as soon as I removed the barricade and let Brown reenter the main chamber, they began to fight. They were a surprisingly even match and they fought until both were exhausted. After a pause, the fight resumed and God was clearly in charge. He went for the base of Brown's spine, sometimes biting his tail, and they fought until exhausted again. At the end of this round, Brown was either paralyzed or in such pain that he could not move his hind legs. God went back to his corner and the fighting ended. There was hardly any blood on either of them. Brown managed to pull himself back into the tunnel he had been sequestered in earlier and I replaced the barricade to protect him from further attacks.

Brown's rear legs were paralyzed, his penis had been bitten off, and one eye had been punctured. Two days after the fight, I saw him struggling to pull himself up to the edge of the water can. The fur on his belly, which had always been brown, was turning dull gray. He fell over on his side and could not get up. As I watched, he went into convulsions, gasped silently, relaxed, and died. I buried him outside.

It was peaceful in the cage until two weeks after Brown's death, when The Lady gave birth to six rosy, hairless babies. God had never seen babies and had no idea what they were or what to do about them. He went into a state of panic, hopping around the cage, bumping into walls, and twitching like a squirrel. I later saw him cowering at the end of a dead-end tunnel that was only used for urination. No mouse willingly stays in the shit hole for very long, but God stayed there for three days. Eventually, I coaxed him out with food and he went back to The Lady and her brood.

Soon after The Lady's first litter was born, I was given a year-old albino female who had not had any contact with other mice since earliest childhood. Bess's whole world consisted of herself, her food, and her shoebox full of nesting material which she sorted through and rearranged every day. She was fat and splendidly spoiled by solitude.

God was as bewildered by her arrival in the cage as Bess was to find herself there. The Lady left her brood to come down to the main chamber to meet her. After a few minutes of cautious smelling and mutual uncertainty, Bess had had enough of this new weirdness. She attacked The Lady. She was twice the size of The Lady, but very flabby and unskilled at fighting. The Lady fought back and chased her into a hole.

The fighting between the two females continued sporadically for weeks, but Bess had time between fights to learn her way around the main chamber. As she had no experience with complicated spaces and was too heavy to climb around the wire mesh walls, she was unable to find the entrances to the tunnels where God and The Lady lived. After learning where the food was and when it was safe to roam around, she began to construct an elaborate nest along the lines of her former one.

God began spending most of his time with Bess. His own nest was overrun with infants who kicked and squealed all day, competing for the best suckling positions, and when The Lady occasionally went downstairs to eat, he was besieged by pups who refused to believe he had no teats. So he moved out. The Lady was hurt and jealous: when God returned to visit her with Bess's smell on his fur, she would squeak bitterly and push him away.

Bess was only too happy to have God stay with her. He had earned her endless gratitude by introducing her to sex. Living alone she had never suspected that anything like sex existed. She had missed out on the rapes and adolescent gang-bangs that soured most females on sex, and, of all the mice I came to know, Bess was the only one who relished it. The others merely tolerated it. God and Bess had intercourse several times a night and even that was not enough to satisfy her.

It took Bess a month to find the tunnel that went to the shit hole, as it was almost a foot above the floor of the main chamber. A week later she found the tunnel that went to The Lady's nest. As she entered the nest tunnel, The Lady caught her scent. They confronted each other near the entrance. Bess had the extreme stupidity to attack. I tried to separate them with a screwdriver but was unsuccessful. Bess could not find her way out to safety and was thus trapped deep within the territory of her rival. By the time I managed to prod her along the pathway back to the main chamber, she was covered with blood and shaking with fear and anger. This same scene occurred a few days later and, to my knowledge, that was the last time The Lady and Bess fought. Thereafter, they left each other alone. Bess got pregnant and, shortly after God was killed by one of The Lady's sons (whose father had been Brown), she gave birth to seven babies of her own and discovered the joys of motherhood.

URSULA LE GUIN

The Space Crone

Theo for copies, which she always
gladly supplied. I resisted printing
the poem until we needed it (the Fall
1979 CQ).

Stewart Brand

Ursula Le Guin I regard as the highest quality writer working with science fiction since Kurt Vonnegut
moved on. Her books include *The
Dispossessed, The Lathe of Heaven, The
Left Hand of Darkness, Wizard of
Earthsea, The Farthest Shore, The Language of the Night*, and *The Compass
Rose* (a recent book of stories, one of
which CQ published in 1983).

When I told Margaret Mead that
we were printing a piece by Ms. Le
Guin which says that women start
getting really good after menopause,
Margaret snapped cordially, "She's
talking about her mother."

Ursula Le Guin's mother was
Theodora Kroeber-Quinn, author of
Ishi in Two Worlds, wife of the emi-
nent anthropologist Alfred Kroeber
(and his biographer—*Alfred Kroeber:
A Personal Configuration*) and, at the
age of seventy-nine when this was
published (in the Summer 1976 CQ),
a stunning, gracious woman. She
died in 1979 (and left famous advice
on how to handle that in the poem
immediately following this article).
The poem has had a life of its own,
passing by word of mouth and copy
machine among the populations of
the bereaved. Countless people asked

The menopause is probably the least glamor-
ous topic imaginable; and this is interesting,
because it is one of the very few topics to which
cling some shreds and remnants of taboo. A
serious mention of menopause is usually met
with uneasy silence; a sneering reference to it
is usually met with relieved sniggers. Both the
silence and the sniggering are pretty sure indi-
cations of taboo.

Most people would consider the old phrase
"change of life" a euphemism for the medical
term "menopause," but I, who am now going
through the change, begin to wonder if it isn't
the other way round. "Change of life" is too
blunt a phrase, too factual. "Menopause," with
its chime-suggestion of a mere pause after
which things go on as before, is reassuringly
trivial.

But the change is not trivial, and I begin to
wonder how many women are brave enough to
carry it out wholeheartedly. They give up their
reproductive capacity with more or less of a
struggle, and when it's gone they think that's
all there is to it. Well, at least I don't get the
Curse any more, they say, and the only reason
I felt so depressed sometimes was hormones.
Now I'm myself again. But this is to evade the
real challenge, and to lose, not only the capacity to ovulate, but the opportunity to become a
Crone.

In the old days women who survived long
enough to attain the menopause more often accepted the challenge. They had, after all, had

55

Theodora Kroeber

characteristic of female maturity. The significance of maturity now is not the capacity to conceive but the mere ability to have sex. As this ability is shared by pubescents and by post-climacterics, the blurring of distinctions and elimination of opportunities is almost complete. There are no rites of passage, because there is no significant change. The Triple Goddess has only one face: Marilyn Monroe's, maybe. The entire life of a woman from ten or twelve through seventy or eighty has become secular, uniform, changeless. As there is no longer any virtue in virginity, so there is no longer any meaning in menopause. It requires fanatical determination now to become a Crone.

Women have thus, by imitating the life-condition of men, surrendered a very strong position of their own. Men are afraid of virgins, but they have a cure for their own fear and the virgin's virginity: fucking. Men are afraid of crones, so afraid of them that their cure for virginity fails them; they know it won't work. Faced with the fulfilled Crone, all but the bravest men wilt and retreat, crestfallen and cockadroop.

Menopause Manor is not merely a defensive stronghold, however. It is a house or household, fully furnished with the necessities of life. In abandoning it, women have narrowed their domain and impoverished their souls. There are things the Old Woman can do, say, and think which the Woman cannot do, say, or think. The Woman has to give up more than her menstrual periods before she can do, say, or think them. She has got to change her life.

The nature of that change is now clearer than it used to be. Old age is not virginity, but a third and new condition; the virgin must be celibate, but the crone need not. There was a confusion there, which the separation of female sexuality from reproductive capacity, via modern contraceptives, has cleared up. Loss of fertility does not mean loss of desire and fulfillment. But it does entail a change, a change involving matters even more important—if I may venture a heresy—than sex.

The woman who is willing to make that change must become pregnant with herself, at

practice. They had already changed their life radically once before, when they ceased to be virgins and became mature women/wives/matrons/mothers/mistresses/whores/etc. This change involved not only the physiological alternations of puberty—the shift from barren childhood to fruitful maturity—but a socially recognized alteration of being: a change of condition from the sacred to the profane.

With the secularization of virginity now complete, so that the once awesome term "virgin" is now a sneer or at best a slightly dated word for a person who hasn't copulated yet, the opportunity of gaining or regaining the dangerous/sacred condition-of-being at the Second Change has ceased to be apparent.

Virginity is now a mere preamble or waiting room to be got out of as soon as possible; it is without significance. Old age is similarly a waiting room, where you go after life's over and wait for cancer or a stroke. The years before and after the menstrual years are vestigial: the only meaningful condition left to women is that of fruitfulness. Curiously, this restriction of significance coincided with the development of chemicals and instruments which make fertility itself a meaningless or at least secondary

last. She must bear herself, her third self, her old age, with travail and alone. Not many will help her with that birth. Certainly no male obstetrician will time her contractions, inject her with sedatives, stand ready with forceps, and neatly stitch up the torn membranes. It's hard even to find an old-fashioned midwife, these days. That pregnancy is long, that labor is hard. Only one is harder, and that's the final one, the one which men also must suffer and perform.

It may well be easier to die if you have already given birth to others or yourself, at least once before. This would be an argument for going through all the discomfort and embarrassment of becoming a Crone. Anyhow it seems a pity to have a built-in rite of passage and to dodge it, evade it, and pretend nothing has changed. That is to dodge and evade one's womanhood, to pretend one's like a man. Men, once initiated, never get the second chance. They never change again. That's their loss, not ours. Why borrow poverty?

Certainly the effort to remain unchanged, young, when the body gives so impressive a signal of change as the menopause, is gallant; but it is a stupid, self-sacrificial gallantry, better befitting a boy of twenty than a woman of forty-five or fifty. Let the athletes die young and laurel-crowned. Let the soldiers earn the Purple Hearts. Let women die old, white-crowned, with human hearts.

If a spaceship came by from the friendly natives of the fourth planet of Altair, and the polite captain of the space ship said, "We have room for one passenger; will you spare us a single human being, so that we may converse at leisure during the long trip back to Altair, and learn from an exemplary person the nature of the race?"—I suppose what most people would want to do is provide them with a fine, bright, brave young man, highly educated and in peak physical condition. A Russian cosmonaut would be ideal (American astronauts are mostly too old). There would surely be hundreds, thousands of volunteers, just such young men, all worthy. But I would not pick any of them. Nor would I pick any of the young women who would volunteer, some out

of magnanimity and intellectual courage, others out of a profound conviction that Altair couldn't possibly be any worse for a woman than Earth is.

What I would do is go down to the local Woolworth's, or the local village marketplace, and pick an old woman, over sixty, from behind the costume jewelry counter or the betel-nut booth. Her hair would not be red or blonde or lustrous dark, her skin would not be dewy fresh, she would not have the secret of eternal youth. She might, however, show you a small snapshot of her grandson, who is working in Nairobi. She is a bit vague about where Nairobi is, but extremely proud of the grandson. She has worked hard at small, unimportant jobs all her life, jobs like cooking, cleaning, bringing up kids, selling little objects of adornment or pleasure to other people. She was a virgin once a long time ago, and then a sexually potent fertile female, and then went through menopause. She has given birth several times and faced death several times—the same times. She is facing the final birth/death a little more nearly and clearly every day now. Sometimes her feet hurt something terrible. She never was educated to anything like her capacity, and that is a shameful waste and a crime against humanity, but so common a crime should not and cannot be hidden from Altair. And anyhow she's not dumb. She has a stock of sense, wit, patience, and experiential shrewdness, which the Altaireans might, or might not, perceive as wisdom. If they are wiser than we, then of course we don't know how they'd perceive it. But if they are wiser than we they may know how to perceive that inmost mind and heart which we, working on mere guess and hope, proclaim to be humane. In any case, since they are curious and kindly, let's give them the best we have to give.

The trouble is, she will be very reluctant to volunteer. "What would an old woman like me do on Altair?" she'll say. "You ought to send one of those scientist men, they can talk to those funny-looking green people. Maybe Dr. Kissinger should go. What about sending the Shaman?" It will be very hard to explain to her that we want her to go because only a person who has experienced, accepted, and acted the entire human condition—the essential quality of which is Change—can fairly represent humanity. "Me?" she'll say, just a trifle slyly. "But I never did anything."

But it won't wash. She knows, though she won't admit it, that Dr. Kissinger has not gone and will never go where she has gone, that the scientists and the shamans have not done what she has done. Into the space ship, Granny.

THEODORA KROEBER-QUINN

Poem for the Living

When I am dead
Cry for me a little.
Think of me sometimes
But not too much.
It is not good for you
Or your wife or your husband
Or your children
To allow your thoughts to dwell
Too long on the Dead.
Think of me now and again
As I was in life
At some moment it is pleasant to recall.
But not for long.
Leave me in peace
As I shall leave you, too, in peace.
While you live
Let your thoughts be with the Living.

RON JONES

Winning

Ron Jones teaches and writes amazing but true stories about teaching and learning. CQ published several of those stories; Norman Lear later filmed one of them ("Take As Directed," about a classroom experiment that demonstrated a little *too* well how well-meaning, ordinary people could become Nazis). Like that story, which was reprinted in the *Next Whole Earth Catalog*, this one took place in Cubberly High School in Palo Alto, California, in 1969. It appeared in the Summer 1976 CQ.

Where are the characters now? Huey Williams, Ron heard, is a telephone lineman—"another of my students saw this crew of people coming into a restaurant, and there was Huey, still with an exuberant smile. . . ." Chris Martin works as an English teacher. Ron Jones is the physical fitness director at the San Francisco Recreation Center for the Handicapped, where he coaches the basketball team. "Our team has been undefeated for the last four years, because we've learned the fundamental art of cheating. Our scorekeeper cannot keep score; our players often hug their opponents, which disarms them tremendously; we shoot at the wrong baskets; and we trade our players in the middle of the game." This story is partly about how Ron discovered that last technique.

Art Kleiner

All basketball coaches hope to encounter a "benny" somewhere in their coaching careers. A benny is one of those special kids that come along once in a lifetime. A kid that won't leave the gym until you've turned out the lights and locked the door. And after it's locked, will have fourteen ways and nine friends ready to reenter. They possess all the natural skills and instincts of great players. A desire to work hard perfecting the most elementary moves. And work even harder to help their teammates experience success. Perhaps that's the invisible quality that makes a benny. The unselfish willingness to share the art of basketball with anyone who cares to listen or participate in the game. Whatever that spirit is, it's the quality each coach looks for. It's the thing to build around and learn from. It's a winning season and perhaps a lot more.

At Cubberly High School in Palo Alto, where I was basketball coach, the presence of a benny was extremely unlikely. The students at Cubberly were white middle-class children of professionally oriented parents. For the most part, these kids mirrored their parents. They were striving to become successful at something; what that something might be was never made clear. Without an objective in mind, the striving became all-important. At Cubberly it meant getting in "advanced ability" groups, getting good grades, getting accepted into a good university. Getting ahead.

Getting through school. Getting. There was little time for intensity or giving to any one thing, especially a sport.

By a strange series of events it turned out I was wrong about ever finding a benny at Cubberly. It started when school integration came to Palo Alto. Black students volunteered to be bused across the freeway tracks. Cubberly High School as "host" school received its allotment of twenty-three "guest" students. As the basketball coach I waited anxiously to see if any athletes might be a part of this transfer. Of course I was looking for a benny. Three days after the transfer students arrived I called the first basketball practice.

The turnout was excellent. Our basketball program had been successful during the past few years and it gradually became known that if you turned out, you would get a chance to play. The prospect of gaining some new players from Ravenswood High School in East Palo Alto added to the tension and excitement of the first practice.

As the players came out on the floor for the first time I noted some familiar kids who had started on last year's team. In fluid movement they began the slow and graceful art of shooting their favorite shots. Dribbling a few steps and rearing up to take another shot. Rebounding and passing out to a fellow player. Reliving past plays. Moving to the fantasy of future game-winning shots. Eyeing the new players.

At the baskets on each side of the central court the new players are assembled. They dribble the available basketballs in place and watch the players moving on the center court. They don't talk much and look a little frightened. Then as if on cue they begin to turn and shoot at the available baskets. They too have a private shot and a move to the basket. Soon the entire gym is alive with players outwitting invisible foes and arcing up game-winning shots. Another season is beginning.

Midway into this first practice Cubberly High School basketball met Huey Williams. He came rushing into the gym. In fact he ran around the entire court three times. He didn't have a basketball. He was just running. And smiling. Nodding his head to the dumbstruck

players. He didn't speak a word. Just smiled and nodded hello. By his third lap, everyone knew we had our first black athlete.

Huey Williams wasn't exactly the transfer student coaches dream about. He was short, about the shortest player on the club. With stocky frame and bowed legs and radar-like hair, he seemed like a bottle of soda water, always about to pop. His shots were explosions of energy that pushed the ball like a pellet. When he ran, he couldn't stop. He'd race in for a layup and instead of gathering his momentum and softly placing the ball against the backboard, he raced straight ahead, full speed, ejecting the ball in midair flight like a plane letting go a rocket. The ball usually slammed against the backboard or rim and careened across the gym. To say it simply, Huey was not a basketball player. He was something else.

Every player carries to the game a personality. That's part of what makes basketball so interesting. That personality is directly reflected in the way a person plays. Now, Huey brought with him a personality I had never quite seen before. He loved life, people, school, anything and everything. "Mr. Jones, how are you today?" he'd say. "Fine I hope." You would have to agree with Huey. His view of the world was contagious. He always had a smile that burst out when you least expected. "Mr. Jones, I didn't shoot too well did I?" He'd be smiling, getting ready to shoot again.

As the first black player on our team, Huey was well received. After all, he didn't represent a threat to any of the white players. If anything he was a puzzlement. How could anyone try so hard, smile so much, and play so bad? Weren't all blacks supposed to be super athletes? How come he doesn't know his place, isn't solemn, and I like him? You couldn't help but root for Huey and want to be around him. Carnegie and the make-you-feel-good folks coud take lessons from Huey. He was a good human being who shared his optimism about life with anyone who ventured in his path. With a smile Huey started every practice with "We're going to win this whole thing, Mr. Jones. Just watch!"

I didn't share Huey's enthusiasm. It was the

Top row: S. Lee, J. Scholer, D. Warnock, P. Traynor, P. Keplinger, G. Morton, S. Chenn, B. Stanovic.
Bottom row: J. Mottsmith, T. Trish, H. Williams, K. Flattely, R. Buckley, T. McCrea.
The 1969 Cubberly High "B" team. Centerpiece, Huey Williams. Chris Martin is absent posing with the
varsity. The "D. Warnock" is Doug, brother of Dave.

most unusual group of kids I had ever coached. In fact the team really constituted three distinct groups. Huey represented one of these groups. This was a collection of five kids who had never played before. They couldn't shoot or dribble, let alone jump. Passing was iffy. When they were on the court my greatest fear was that they might run into each other. Although lacking skill, they personified Huey's faith and willingness to work hard. My God how they tried.

A second group of kids on the team had all played together the past year. They were typical Palo Alto kids. I guess Chris Martin most exemplified the personality of this group. Chris was a class officer, good student, achievement oriented, and serious about winning and of course playing. Chris just tolerated Huey and most everything else. His attention was on the future. Basketball at Cubberly was like the Pony League, Little League, and Junior League

he had participated in so well. It was one more right step to some mythical big league called Farah, Hilton, or perhaps Standard Oil.

Chris knew all the lessons and skills of basketball. His jump shot was a picturebook example of perfection. He released the ball at the peak of his jump and followed through with his hands guiding the path of the ball as it slid into the basket. The closest parallel to Chris' behavior might be described as that of a little old man. He was "finicky" at the age of sixteen. If things weren't just right, his voice would stretch several octaves and literally squeak. For Chris things going just right meant a championship and of course a star role. I liked and felt sorry for Chris all at the same time. He reminded me of myself. A little selfish and awfully conceited. Extremely insulated from feelings.

A third group of kids making up the team can best be described as outlaws. Dave Warnock characterized this group. Whereas Huey had a reverence for life and Chris was busy controlling life, Dave seemed always on guard and challenging hell out of it. He was always in trouble. Usually a team is composed of kids like Huey who can't play and kids like Chris who have played throughout childhood. Kids like Dave rarely show up on a team. To have five kids like him on the same team was most unusual. If not intolerable.

Dave's style of life and play was outside prediction. Dave reminded me of a stork trying to play basketball. His arms and legs flayed at the air as he stormed up and down the court. His shots were what players call "watch shots." He would crank up the ball without facing the basket from some unexpected place and yes it would go right in. Prompting the defensive player to say, "Look in the other hand . . . you might find a watch." Dave was always a surprise. A surprise if he showed up for practice and a surprise that he stayed with it. In a strange way he was also a breath of fresh air. He lived to the fullest. He didn't stop to explain his actions. He just acted.

So there you have it. Not exactly a dream team. Five kids charging around looking for the pass they just dropped. Five kids straining for an expected championship. And five kids who might not even show up for the game. The entire team tilted on the verge of combustion. The kids that centered around Chris and Dave openly hated each other. Huey and his troop of warriors became the grease that kept the team moving together. Happy and delighted to be playing, they were oblivious to the conflict. In their constant attempt to mimic a Warnock pass or a Chris jump shot they inevitably made the originals look ridiculous. Huey with his intensity and honesty put everything in perspective. It was simply impossible to get angry or serious about yourself with Huey around. He had girlfriends to tell you about, a cheer for a good play, a hand for someone who had fallen, and a smile for everything. And if all that failed, he always had his "new shot" to show you.

It wasn't long before everyone was working to help Huey and the other inexperienced play-

Chris Martin, head of "The A-Train."

ers. Chris was telling players about the right way to shoot. Dave was displaying one of his new trick passes. I was working hard to teach defense. If you don't have the ball, go get it. Don't wait for someone to put it through the basket or even start a play. Go get the ball. Chase it. Surround it. Take it.

We worked on how to press and trap a player with the ball. How to contest the inbound pass. Double team. Use the full court. Cut off the passing lane. Work together with teammates to break over screens and sag into a help position. Work to keep midpoint vision. Block out. Experience the feeling of achievement without having the ball or scoring the winning point. Taking pride in defense.

The intensity and intricate working of defense was something everyone on the team could do, and something new for everyone to learn. Defense is something most basketball teams just do not concentrate on. It's the unseen part of the game. Working hard on the techniques of team defense began to slowly draw the team together with a common experience. As for offense, well, I taught the basic passing pattern, but the shooting was up to whoever was on the court. Chris and his group ran intricate patterns for the layup or percentage shot. Dave with his team took the ball to the hoop usually after three dribbles and a confederate yell. Huey's team did their best just to get the ball up the court.

By the start of the season we had one spectacular defense and three offenses. In fact I divided the team into the three distinct groups. In this way everyone could play. It confused the heck out of opponents. According to basketball etiquette you're supposed to play your best five players. We played our best fifteen. You are also supposed to concentrate on scoring. We emphasized defense. Finally a good team has the mark of consistency. We were the most inconsistent team you could imagine.

We would start each game with Huey's bunch. They called themselves "the Reverends." With their tenacity for losing the ball and swarming after it plus their complete inability to shoot, they immobilized their opponents. The starting fives they encountered couldn't believe the intensity and madcaps of Huey's Reverends. By the time they realized they were playing against all heart and very little scoring potential it was time to send in Chris' group. Chris' team called themselves the "A-Train." That they were. Like a train they methodically moved down the floor, executed a series of crisp passes, and scored. By this time in the game Huey was smiling his all-knowing smile, and the coach from the other team was

Dave Warnock, head of "The G-Strings."

usually looking over at our bench in a state of confusion. Just as the other team adjusted to systematic and disciplined play, we sent in Dave's "G-Strings." Dave's team played with reckless abandon. They were always in places they weren't supposed to be. Doing things that weren't in the book. Playing their game.

By the middle of the season we were undefeated. Oh, I had to suspend Dave twice for smoking a cigar in the locker room, once for smuggling a girl onto the travel bus. And on occasion I had to remind Chris that I was the coach, not he. But all in all the teammates were actually becoming friends. It was a joy to witness this chemistry. Huey's group gradually improved. They started believing they could beat anyone. The basketball still didn't go in the basket, but in their minds and actions they were "starters." As for Chris, he was actually beginning to yell for someone besides himself. And Dave, well he didn't change much in an outward way. He was still frantic on the basketball court. It was off the court that he was becoming a little less defensive. He started telling me of things he wanted in life. Things not that much different from those securities and accomplishments sought by others. In fact it was something as simple as friendship.

Our first defeat of the year came not on the basketball court but at the hands of the school superintendent. With twelve games already played, the superintendent declared that all transfer students were ineligible for interscholastic sports. It was a knee-jerk reaction to other coaches in the league who feared we might "raid" Ravenswood High School of its top black atheletes. No one worried about us stealing away their intelligent students or class leaders, yet that's just what we did. No one thought to ask the students and parents about how they felt. This was a coaches' decision. Coaches who thought only about winning.

The superintendent ordered Huey off the team immediately. The announcement of this decision came not in a telephone call or personal visit, but in a ten-word directive. "No transfer students will be eligible for interscholastic athletic teams."

The announcement came on a game day. The team was already suited up waiting for the last-minute game plan. I read the superintendent's decision to the team. They were stunned. And angry. Ideas and plots for Huey's survival rang out against the white-tiled dressing room walls. Dave slammed his shoe against a locker, "It's a shitty decision." Chris agreed, "We can appeal . . . let's go to the board of education." Dave snapped, "When . . . in three weeks?" Everyone joined the argument. "Let's give Huey a new number." "Yeah, but can we also change his color?" "We can play against ourself . . . can't we?" "Let's make up our own league." In the din my own thoughts were welling up. How I hated the way decisions were made at this school.

It happened every day in a hundred ways. The textbook to use, the schedule to follow, the course to teach. At no point in the schooling process was the teacher or student allowed to make a decision and then be responsible for it. Every day I and those around me were being robbed of the chance to make decisions. It was like a draining away of life itself. Life must be tended daily. It can't be simply studied. Or mandated. Like basketball it must be played the best way you know how. What do we teach when all we do is hand down and follow directives?

My thoughts were obviously slipping out of my mouth. I didn't know when I started verbalizing my feelings, but I became aware of it as my whispers all of a sudden were audible in the now silent locker room. As my personal decision became clearer so did my pronouncement of it. "Huey's dismissal is wrong. It's unfair to defer the decision or obey it. I think we should forfeit all our remaining games. Huey is a part of this team. If you are willing to give other teams an automatic win over us in exchange for having Huey play . . . raise your hand." Fifteen players leaped to their feet. Dave was yelling, "Well, all right then, we've got a game to play!" It was unanimous.

The players streamed onto the floor to begin their warmup. I could hear a few rebel yells and even that high-pitched squeak of Chris'. Huey still brought gasps of surprise with his high velocity layup. When he did his latest new shot, a sweeping, running hook, the assembled fans roared approval. Huey grinned and promised more. As the players finished their warmup, the school principal came by to remind me of the superintendent's decision. "Ron," he said, "I'm sorry about Huey, but he hasn't scored many points for you has he?" "No," I replied, "Huey hasn't scored a point." "Things will be different next year," he confided. I agreed.

As the game was about to start, the team huddled for final instructions. "Any afterthoughts?" I asked. "There is still time." We were all bundled together in a knot. Hands thrust together in a tight clasp. Everyone looked up. Eyes all met. Every single kid was smiling. My God, I've got fifteen Hueys.

The horn sounded calling for the game to start. I took the entire team to the scoring desk and informed the league official. "We formally forfeit this game." The opposing coach from Gunn High School rushed over to see what the commotion was about. "What are you doing?" he asked. I told him of our decision. "That doesn't make sense. You guys are undefeated," he stammered. "We let two of *our* players go today." "It's our decision," I explained. "We're here to play basketball, all of us."

And we did. All of us. Huey did his patented dash, Chris his jump shot while Dave relied on surprise. It was a combination hard to beat. We poured in twenty more points than Gunn and, more importantly, displayed a constant hustle. Players ran to shoot free throws. Ran to take a place in the game. Ran off the floor on being replaced. It reminded me of that first practice with this strange kid running around the gym. Perhaps we had learned more from Huey than we taught. At the close of the game the Gunn coach stopped to comment, "Congratulations, you've got quite a team there." I reminded him that we had forfeited the game, that his team had won. He turned, "No, your kids won. They're a bunch of bennys."

Ron Jones, coach and history teacher.

Dave Warnock was dead. Chris brought the message to me. His father was a school official and he heard the news from the police. Dave had been at a party and suffocated inhaling hair spray. Like a tape recorder erasing its content I couldn't think or act. Then in forced flashes I began to retread the past days. Searching for glimpses of Dave. His face. His antics. Was there something there? A warning? A plea? What did I miss?

The school community for the most part remained ignorant of Dave's death and its self-destructive cause. There were faculty murmurs, "That crazy kid." Other than side glances at what had happened there was no marking of Dave's death. Drugs and death are not part of the curriculum. It was improper to alarm parents. The school didn't stop its parade. Even for a moment of respect or some such other platitude. Nothing. Everything as usual. Including basketball.

The team gathered for practice out of habit. The season actually had only a few days left. It had been a corrugated course. Our protest to allow Huey the right to play had sparked a boycott of all team sports. The boycott led to a

change in the rules allowing transfer students to play with the condition that "due to the disruptions" no league championship would be awarded. It was OK with us. We declared ourselves champions. Actually it was Dave's idea. Oh shit, it didn't seem fair. Dave was a storm. He kicked and dared the world. And lost. Or did he? I don't know.

One good thing about sports is that you can lose yourself in physical exertion. Push yourself into fatigue. Let the body take over the crying in the brain. I informed the team that this would be our last practice. We would have a game, full court scrimmage.

It was then that I realized Dave wasn't there. It's funny, Dave was dead yet I expected him to come prancing into the gym, the final trick on death itself.

Being short one player I joined in the scrimmage. First Chris' bunch against Huey's team and then Dave's group to play Chris'. I stood in for Dave. The play was strangely conservative and sluggish. Perhaps this measured play was in deference to Dave. Were we all letting our thoughts wander? Just doing mechanical steps? Or was it a subconscious statement that

Dave's life was errant and not to be emulated? Whatever, the play moved from one end of the gym to the other like the arm of a ticking clock. Up and down the floor.

It was Chris who broke the rhythm and silence. Without warning he sliced across the floor, stole a pass, dribbled the length of the court and slam dunked. Then in an unexpected leap he stole the inbound pass. Taking the ball in one hand he pivoted up a crazy sweeping hook shot. It was a "watch shot" if I'd ever seen one. Out of the blue as the ball cut through the net Christ erupted with a shrill guttural yell that pierced the stillness. It was a signal. The game tempo picked up and became frantic. Everyone pushed to his maximum. Straining for that extra effort. Hawking the ball. Diving for a loose ball. Blowing tension. Playing with relaxed abandon.

It felt wonderful. The game was fierce. Everything learned in years of play was used. New moves were tried. I crashed for a rebound, dived, elbows flying after a loose ball and got it. Sprinted full tilt on a fast break. Yelled full voice as I fed Huey with a behind-the-back pass that he laid up for two. Everyone is moving as if driven by some accelerating spell of power and will. Everything goes in. We can play forever. Play Forever.

The scrimmage raged on. The afternoon became evening and still we played. The gym glowed in the yellow light, warm and wet. We were racing now back and forth. Exploding for shots. Playing the toughest defense. Jumping over a screen. Blocking out. Back for one more sensation of excellence.

My chest heaved for relief. Body throbbed. I couldn't stop playing. And didn't want to.

Didn't Want To. Down the court. Set up. That's it. Feed the cutter. Fantastic. Now the defense. Keep low. Fuck no. Take it away. That's it. Steal the goddamn ball. Now go. Fly.

In a heap I collapsed. Legs simply buckled. I was shaking. Head not able to move. In slow motion the team centered around my crumpled form. I'm all right. The air is rushing back into an empty body. Giving life and movement. "I'm all right." Everyone is breathing hard, pushing out air and taking it back in. Grabbing their knees and doubling over. Letting the body know it can rest.

Without any words everyone gathered themselves, then silently headed for the locker room and home. It's over. The scrimmage was ended. Practice finished. The season complete.

I slowly shower and dress, waiting for the locker room to empty. Walking through the silenced place I stop to look and say goodbye. There is Chris' locker. A good kid. Hope his life goes well. He has changed and matured. Been a part of other lives. Huey's locker is still open. God, even his locker has a smile. What a person. I'll never forget. Dave's place. The cigar smoke is missing and so is Dave. I hate you for leaving us. I love you.

I push up a twenty-five foot jump shot that is five feet beyond my range. It goes in. Rush to chase the ball. Try again. Seek the magnificent feeling of doing the undone. The unplanned. The unexpected.

There is a sign that hangs over the exit from the locker room. It reads, "There is No Substitute For Winning." Someone scratched out the word "winning" and replaced it. "There Is No Substitute For Madness."

RAYMOND DASMANN

Biogeographical Provinces

"I had been hearing for years from
Peter Berg, Gary Snyder, and Huey
Johnson about Ray Dasmann's philosophy and research on biological
'provinces' and the fundamental effect on political thinking which they
might have," wrote Steward Brand
in the original introduction to this
map and article (Fall 1976). Stewart
arranged for the rough sketches
(done by geographer Miklos
Udvardy) of what Dasmann originally called "Biotic Provinces" to
be reworked into a world map.
(Udvardy renamed them "Biogeographic Provinces.") The map was
drawn by cartographer/painter/
sculptor Theodore Oberlander, who
also "teaches and researches primarily in geomorphology at U.C. Berkeley." The result, reproduced here in
black-and-white, was published by
COEVOLUTION in full color—the
first world map of boundaries not
created by people.

Stewart introduced Raymond
Dasmann that issue by noting that
his writing and teaching has "long
had a powerful, quiet influence on

the environmental movement." In
the same issue, Peter Warshall reviewed Dasmann's college textbook,
Environmental Conservation (Wiley,
1959, 1976) under the title "Homage to Dasmann." *Environmental Conservation* is a manual for ecological
understanding, care and repair; it
describes day-to-day technique and
practice, in context of specific regions and habitats, while, in Peter's
words, "simultaneously yearning for
humans to change and see and gain
loving guidance for the Planet."

At the time he developed this essay, Dasmann was senior ecologist at
the International Union for the Conservation of Nature at Morges, Switzerland (Udvardy was a geographer
at the IUCN). Now Dasmann is professor of Environmental Studies at
the University of California, Santa
Cruz. The concept, meanwhile, of
biogeographic provinces has been
picked up by government agencies
and environmental groups around
the world. The U.S. National Park
Service, for instance. The full-color
Biogeographic map is available for
$5 postpaid from the Whole Earth
Access Company, 2990 Seventh
Street, Berkeley, CA 94710. Reportedly, UNESCO is publishing a
newer version.

Art Kleiner

Is there any reason to produce a new classification for a natural world that has already been
classified and reclassified by numbers of ecolo-

gists and geographers? Why draw lines on a map and say that the areas enclosed are to be called biogeographic provinces? Do these have any meaning in reality? To answer these questions I'll start by saying that I was drawn into the mapping game by the demands of conservation. In the IUCN (International Union for Conservation of Nature and Natural Resources) headquarters in Morges, Switzerland, we wanted to know the extent to which the various communities of wildlife were being protected by existing national parks, reserves, or other protected areas. From this we could determine those areas most badly in need of conservation and establish some priorities for action.

Examination of existing systems of classification revealed inadequacies. Plant ecologists had developed many systems based on taxonomic relationships of plants, or upon the appearance or ecological characteristics of vegetation. These did not, however, take animals into account, and we were concerned with protecting the greatest array of animal and plant species.

In North America, early in this century, the plant ecologist Frederick Clements joined with the animal ecologist Victor Shelford to produce the *biome* system of classification.[1] Biomes are easily recognized, they are the obvious subdivisions of the world's biota—the desert, grassland, coniferous forest, tropical rain forest, and such. They are characterized by one prevailing dominant form of "climax" vegetation, meaning that which will develop if nature is allowed to take her course over a few centuries, without human interference. The prevailing climate shapes the climax vegetation along with the soils and associated animal life.

The biome system of classification has now been widely accepted and has been the basis of many international research programs, but for conservation purposes it does not go far enough. For temperate and arctic North America, Clements and Shelford did a reasonably thorough job of subdividing biomes into associations and smaller units of classification. These could have been the basis for a conservation-oriented system. But the challenge was

not picked up on other continents, and there only the larger units are recognized.

It began to appear inevitable to us in IUCN that if we wanted a global system that would take into account not only vegetation, but also plant and animal species distribution, we would have to do more work, starting from whatever system seemed the most promising. This then became a task for IUCN's Commission on Ecology, with the job of preparing drafts and sketch maps largely falling into my hands. After several preliminary publications, the principal work was passed over to a biogeographer, Professor Miklos Udvardy, of Sacramento State University. He has produced the maps which form the basis for what is presented here.[2]

The scheme of classification that we developed was not really new. In the 1940s the *biotic provinces* of North America were mapped by Lee R. Dice of the University of Michigan.[3] Like other American schemes, however, this one was not adopted in other countries. Nevertheless it seemed a good basis on which to work, taking into account as it did the distribution of both plant and animal species. The IUCN task was to extend the biotic province system to the entire world, and this was done in a preliminary way, recognizing that our knowledge of many areas was inadequate. Udvardy, however, pointed out that the term *biotic province* had become, through usage, almost synonymous with *faunal province*, and plants had been forgotten. He proposed the new term *biogeographic province*, which has yet to be corrupted.

It can be said that biogeographic provinces are simply subdivisions of biomes, based on animal and plant distribution. To a degree that is true, but we have freed ourselves from the question of what is, or is not, the true climax vegetation which is involved in the Clements-Shelford system. Essentially biotic provinces are areas that differ considerably, either in their animal or plant species, or in the character of their vegetation, from one another. To illustrate the concept, I will use the example of California, since it is the area I know best. The state includes all or part of five biotic prov-

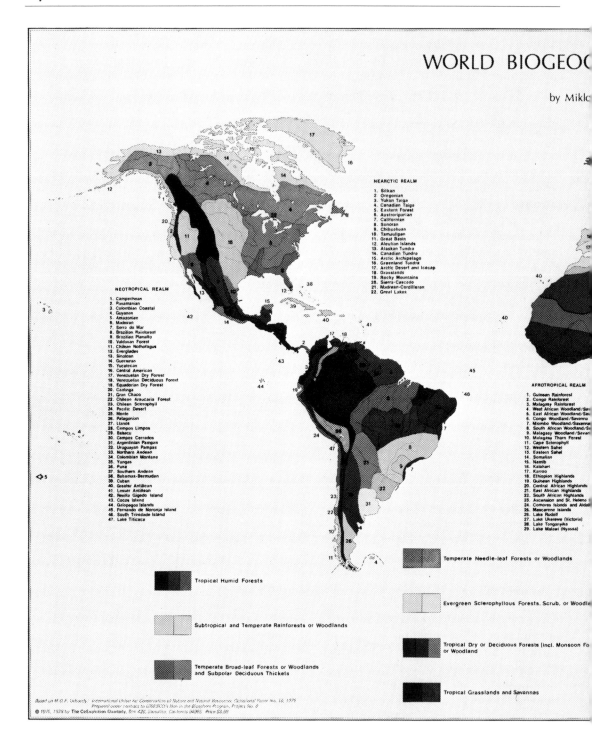

A reduced black and white photo of the map of *World Biogeographical Provinces*.

HICAL PROVINCES

dy, 1975

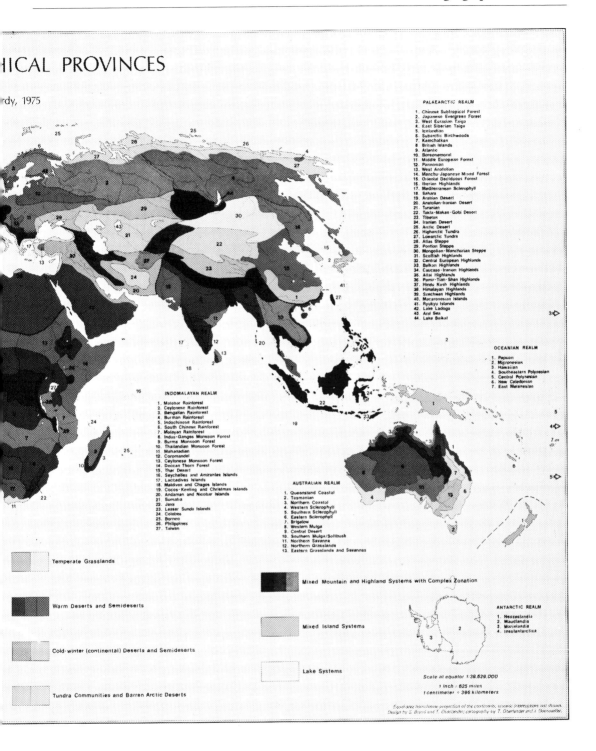

PALAEARCTIC REALM

1. Chinese Subtropical Forest
2. Japanese Evergreen Forest
3. West Eurasian Taiga
4. East Siberian Taiga
5. Icelandian
6. Subarctic Birchwoods
7. Kamchatkan
8. British Islands
9. Atlantic
10. Boreonemoral
11. Middle European Forest
12. Pannonian
13. West Anatolian
14. Manchu-Japanese Mixed Forest
15. Oriental Deciduous Forest
16. Iberian Highlands
17. Mediterranean Sclerophyll
18. Sahara
19. Arabian Desert
20. Anatolian-Iranian Desert
21. Turanian
22. Takla-Makan-Gobi Desert
23. Tibetan
24. Iranian Desert
25. Arctic Desert
26. Higharctic Tundra
27. Lowarctic Tundra
28. Atlas Steppe
29. Pontian Steppe
30. Mongolian-Manchurian Steppe
31. Scottish Highlands
32. Central European Highlands
33. Balkan Highlands
34. Caucaso-Iranian Highlands
35. Altai Highlands
36. Pamir-Tien-Shan Highlands
37. Hindu Kush Highlands
38. Himalayan Highlands
39. Szechwan Highlands
40. Macaronesian Islands
41. Ryukyu Islands
42. Lake Ladoga
43. Aral Sea
44. Lake Baikal

OCEANIAN REALM

1. Papuan
2. Micronesian
3. Hawaiian
4. Southeastern Polynesian
5. Central Polynesian
6. New Caledonian
7. East Melanesian

INDOMALAYAN REALM

1. Malabar Rainforest
2. Ceylonese Rainforest
3. Bengalian Rainforest
4. Burman Rainforest
5. Indochinese Rainforest
6. South Chinese Rainforest
7. Malayan Rainforest
8. Indus-Ganges Monsoon Forest
9. Burma Monsoon Forest
10. Thailandian Monsoon Forest
11. Mahanadian
12. Coromandel
13. Ceylonese Monsoon Forest
14. Deccan Thorn Forest
15. Thar Desert
16. Seychelles and Amirantes Islands
17. Laccadives Islands
18. Maldives and Chagos Islands
19. Cocos-Keeling and Christmas Islands
20. Andaman and Nicobar Islands
21. Sumatra
22. Java
23. Lesser Sunda Islands
24. Celebes
25. Borneo
26. Philippines
27. Taiwan

AUSTRALIAN REALM

1. Queensland Coastal
2. Tasmanian
3. Northern Coastal
4. Western Sclerophyll
5. Southern Sclerophyll
6. Eastern Sclerophyll
7. Brigalow
8. Western Mulga
9. Central Desert
10. Southern Mulga/Saltbush
11. Northern Savanna
12. Northern Grasslands
13. Eastern Grasslands and Savannas

ANTARCTIC REALM

1. Neozealandia
2. Maudlandia
3. Marielandia
4. Insulantarctica

Temperate Grasslands

Warm Deserts and Semideserts

Cold-winter (continental) Deserts and Semideserts

Tundra Communities and Barren Arctic Deserts

Mixed Mountain and Highland Systems with Complex Zonation

Mixed Island Systems

Lake Systems

Scale at equator 1:39,629,000

1 inch = 625 miles
1 centimeter = 396 kilometers

Equal-area homolosine projection of the continents, oceanic interruptions not shown.
Design by S. Brand and T. Oberlander; cartography by T. Oberlander and J. Stommsetter.

Three biogeographic provinces in California: redwood, chaparral, and desert.
From: *Environmental Conservation.*
"A sense of identity or place develops where an individual grows up within a particular province and learns to recognize its flora and fauna, to respond to its climatic regime, to become familiar with its limits. Many serious land use blunders could have been avoided if people had not tried to transplant land-use practices developed within one biotic province to the differing ecological conditions of another."

inces: Oregonian, Sierra-Cascade, Great Basin, Sonoran, and Californian (a sixth that I had added, the Channel Islands, has been dropped by Udvardy).[4]

The Oregonian province belongs to the Northwest and extends up to Canada. It is a region of tall, massive coastal forests, rain-drenched in winter, often fog-bound in summer. A greater mass of vegetation per square mile grows here than in any other area of the world. California has its own unique subdivision of this province, in the redwood region of which it shares only a small corner with Oregon.

The second extends along the high mountains of the Pacific Coast from the Fraser River in British Columbia south through the volcanic Cascades and then down the Sierra Nevada to the Tehachapi Mountains. Although the Sierra and Cascade sections differ strongly geologically, their vegetation and animal life do not separate out sufficiently to warrant dif-

ferent provincial status. Their vegetation is arranged in the life zones characteristic of western mountains, with a broad band of ponderosa pine near the lower edges of the province and a fringe of timberline forest at the upper limits of tree growth.

The third province belongs to the intermountain region, from the Sierras to the Rockies—the Basin and Range province of physiographers. California includes only a small area, in the Lassen-Modoc region of the northeast, and the Inyo-Mono section east of the highest Sierra. This is a country characterized by sagebrush, juniper, and pinyon pine.

The fourth province is desert and has its affinities with Arizona, New Mexico, and Sonora. California's Mojave and Colorado deserts have many differences from their counterparts across the Colorado River, but not enough to be called separate provinces.

All of the rest of the state is in the Californian province, which has a fauna and flora characteristic of California and, in most respects, of nowhere else. This is the region of chaparral, broadleaved evergreen forest and woodland, of open oak savannas, and prairies that are summer dry, and winter green.

I have analyzed the differences in mammalian species distribution between the provinces, admittedly using fairly crude methods. The greatest similarity is between the Oregonian and Sierra-Cascade provinces, which had approximately 68% of their mammal species or subspecies in common. This was not enough difference to warrant provincial separation on the basis of mammals alone. Much greater differences show up, however, in bird faunas and in vegetation. By contrast the Great Basin province shares only around 36% of its mammal species or subspecies with the Sonoran, and 38% with the Californian province. The Californian province has less than 50% of its mammal species or subspecies shared with any other province.

If we can agree at this point that biotic provinces are indeed different, then we can agree that to protect a particular array of plants or animals we should establish at least one reserve or other protected area in each province. Looking around the world, however, we find that whereas there are many national parks in some provinces, those of the African savanna, for example, there are none or scarcely any in others—the desert and semi-arid provinces of the Old World, or in various tropical rain forest provinces. If there is to be a choice it makes more sense to establish a national park in the Sahara, in a place where desert wildlife survives, than to establish another park in the East African savanna.

However, the usefulness of the province concept can be extended beyond the practice of plant and animal species conservation. They represent areas within which ecological conditions are relatively uniform, with certain natural potentials and limitations. During human history societies and cultures developed within certain provinces and adapted to their potentials and limitations. A sense of identity or

place develops where an individual grows up within a particular province and learns to recognize its flora and fauna, to respond to its climatic regime, to become familiar with its limits. Many serious land-use blunders could have been avoided if people had not tried to transplant land-use practices developed within one biotic province to the differing ecological conditions of another.

In the United States we are cursed with state and county boundaries drawn with straightedges by people who did not know the land. Would it not make more sense to re-orient them toward ecological realities? Worldwide, the existing national boundaries are for the most part absurd, particularly in those Third World regions where former colonial powers decided where the lines should be drawn. If people were allowed to sort themselves out rationally some new array of ethno-biotic entities would take the place of the existing nation-states.

I don't think we have gone far enough yet in our thinking about biogeographic provinces to start reorganizing the political world. People have been living on the planet for too long for their influence to be ignored. The distribution of human groups which have developed a sense of self-identity is at least as important as the distribution of plant species. One cannot put the English and Irish in the same country just because they share a biotic province. However, if we are to find a way out of the mess in which global industrial culture has placed us, the biogeographic map could be pointing in a useful direction.

REFERENCES

1. Clements, F. and V. Shelford. 1939. *Bio-ecology*. John Wiley, New York.

2. Udvardy, M. D. F., 1975. *A classification of the biogeographical provinces of the world*. IUCN Occasional Paper No. 18, IUCN, Morges, Switzerland.

3. Dice, L. R., 1943. *The biotic provinces of North America*. University of Michigan Press, Ann Arbor.

4. Dasmann, R. F., 1973. *A system for defining and classifying natural regions for purposes of conservation*. IUCN Occasional Paper No. 7, IUCN, Morges, Switzerland.

J. D. SMITH

The Lefthanded Bear and Other Animal Stories

From Stewart Brand's introduction of J. D. at the Whole Earth Jamboree, Summer 1978: "J. D. Smith has been with us since so many beginnings it's hard to count them. Back in earliest Whole Earth Truck Store days when the store needed a manager, J. D. showed up. He's one of the few cowboys trained in phenomenological philosophy at Harvard. He's a pretty good philosopher and a damned good cowboy, and one of the great story tellers. It was J. D. who introduced the whole genre of animal stories to COEVOLUTION QUARTERLY."

CQ printed its first animal stories in 1976; the genre lasted five years, fueled some by reader letters, and some by new stories J. D. heard during his summers in Idaho. These selections are culled from the full half-decade's-worth.

Art Kleiner

BIG AL'S BEAR STORY
(heard in the Lardo Saloon, McCall, Idaho, late summer 1974)

"Me and Churd and Hern were fishing the Wind River up from the McMeeken place and I was carrying a mess of fish back to this big rock where we had the fire, and when I came around the rock I ran into a lefthanded bear standing on his back legs. He looked me in the eye, kinda woofed, took a step my way, and I threw the fish at him. He didn't take the bait, so I screamed and started running across to the only tree around that wasn't a peckerpole. I made a jump I didn't believe but just as I was pulling my ass up to the limb, he took a swipe at my ass with his left paw, and took a big chunk out of my right cheek. Buy me a beer and I'll show you the scars."

HOW TO GET AWAY FROM A BEAR
(heard in Burgdorf, Idaho, summer 1973)

"Me and my nephew are up here from Tucson looking for gold. We were walking into California Lake, cause the road is still drifted shut in places, carrying our pans and lunch, and I noticed that there were pretty fresh bear tracks going our way across the drifts. So we slowed down a little. After a while we took the cutoff down to the lake, which isn't nothing but a peat bog, and when we finished lunch and were walking back out, there were fresh tracks ahead of us again. My nephew said that he'd always heard that you could get away from a bear by running downhill, cause somehow a bear is built to go uphill but not down. Could be something to it. I remember this oldtimer telling me that if a miner met a bear in the snow he ought to stand in his pan and start sliding downhill, and the bear won't follow."

LITTLE KNOWN SUPPOSITION
Seagulls drink sea water.

ANOTHER ONE
Pigeons take care of their elders.

MOUSE STASH ONE
I was a janitorial understudy in a big church office building, when one of the old-hand secretaries from the fourth floor showed up on the first floor with nervous perspiration and tales of mice in her desk. By the time I got back to her office with her, rodentophobia had filled the rooms of her fellow workers. Her desk had nice piles of paper on top, but underneath, where the typewriter supposedly goes when it swings away, was a little television set with an earphone, a few crumby tinfoil lunch wrappers, and an eight-day-old nibbling mouse. She had been watching soap operas when the mouse appeared, right there beside the drama.

Enter Caesar, the real janitor, carrying a mechanic's red rag as a mousetrap. The mouse ran up into the innards of the desk, and Caesar started tapping different places on the metal sides with the butt of his screwdriver, but the mouse had somewhere to hide and noise didn't bother it. It wouldn't come out to be slaughtered, so at Caesar's noisiest moment, I took the rag, wadded it up in my palms, caught Caesar's eye, and started walking slowly through the four grandmother secretaries.

It worked, the mock murder did. They thanked us plenty, and we cracked-up in the elevator. About two hours later, I was called back to the fourth floor when one of the ladies nailed the second mouse with the lip of an upside-down metal wastebasket. I carried it away in paper towels and tossed it in the dumpster.

MOUSE STASH TWO
I developed a pack rat roommate while I was sleeping light and alone in a mountain cabin in the dark of winter. He was nocturnal, and would pat his tail when happy or eating. It sounded like a little girl knocking at the door, and would wake me up, and I'd yell at the little fucker to quit reminding me of my daughter. He'd quit patting his tail and I'd go back to sleep. He'd crawl in at dawn and I'd do the day shift in the snow in the hot springs.

Eventually, he stole my braided silver neck chain, which I had carried all the way from Cambridge, but which I took off when I was trying to sleep. I began the search for his nest in my home, but I had so much clutter to my personal relation with the material objects around me that he could have been almost anywhere.

I waited up with a gun and a flashlight, saw where he ran when I hassled him, and blew him away with a twenty-two in the back of the head, about a foot behind where I lay my head when I slept. For murder I got a bunch of buttons, tinfoil corners, a roach clip, and my braided silver neck chain, which, at this writing, is lost again.

MOUSE DISCOUNT
(heard in Burgdorf, Idaho, 1974)
"I was the manager of the Penney's store in Nampa for a few years. One year business got a little slow, so I took a piece of plywood, drilled about fifty inch-and-a-half holes in it, randomly numbered them either ten, twenty, thirty, or forty percent, nailed mason jar rings to the bottoms, and screwed pint jars into them. The idea was that when a person had something figured out that he wanted to buy, he'd bring it to the mouse board, and I'd let out this little mouse and whatever hole the mouse would run down, that is how much discount the person would get. Now the trick is this: a mouse won't go into a hole where no mouse has ever been, so by taking a few mouse turds and dropping them down the ten percent holes, and say one turd down one of the forty percent holes, I could provide a little excitement for the customers, and a little for myself, as long as I only marked up the goods fifteen or twenty percent."

COONDOG MEMORY
(heard in Rutledge, Missouri, about eighteen years ago)
"Now, this dog is for sale, and she can not only follow a trail twice as old as the average dog can, but she's got a pretty good memory to

boot. For instance, last week this old boy who lives down the road from me, and is forever stinkmouthing my hounds, brought some city fellow around to try out ol' Sis here. So I turned her out south of the house and she made two or three big swings back and forth across the edge of the woods, set back her head, bayed a couple of times, cut straight through the woods, come to a little clearing, jumped about three foot straight up in the air, run to the other side, and commenced to letting out a racket like she had something treed. We went over there with our flashlights and shone them up in the tree but couldn't catch no shine off a coon's eyes, and my neighbor sorta indicated that ol' Sis might be a little crazy, 'cause she stood right to the tree and kept singing up into it. So I pulled off my coat and climbed up into the branches, and sure enough, there was a coon skeleton wedged in between a couple of branches about twenty foot up. Now as I was saying, she can follow a pretty old trail, but this fellow was still calling her crazy or touched 'cause she had hopped up in the air while she was crossing the clearing, until I reminded him that the Hawkins' had a fence across there about five years back. Now, this dog is for sale."

HOW TO FIX A DOG RACE

My Grandpa Frary took a dogfever pilgrimage from Colorado to Florida to learn how greyhounds are trained to run. He found out that many trainers work the dogs in low pens with live rabbits. Real rabbits rarely run in perfect half-mile ovals like their mechanical cousins at the track do. Real rabbits dart and weave and slow down just a little before they change directions. The dogs sense the move coming and break their own strides to make the turn with the real rabbits. At the track the mechanical rabbit runs on a rheostat setup, so that the person who is controlling the speed of the track bunny can slow it down at just the right time, the lead dogs think the rabbit is going to take a ninety degree turn, break their stride a little, and the hind dogs catch up. This knowledge didn't keep my Grandpa from betting on the dogs.

CHARLIE THE GOOSE
(heard in Burgdorf, Idaho, July 1976)

"A year ago last Spring, my oldest daughter's boyfriend gave her a little bitty wild Canadian honker, and she raised it up on mush and milk out on the back porch with our three dogs. That goose got housebroke pretty soon, and would come up to the back door just like the dogs, and he'd peck on it, and we'd let him in, and he'd beg food from the table, and it even got to the point where when my daughter was loading the dogs in the back of the pickup she'd just call "Charlie, Charlie," and that blamed goose would fly right up in the back of the truck and ride there, like a dog.

"Well, we worried ol' Charlie through hunting season that Fall, and kept him warm by the fire all Winter, then this Spring he started being gone overnight and the first time we figured out what he was up to was when one of our neighbors called up and said that our goose was down there bothering his dogs, and keeping folks awake all night. We figured he was trying to mate with a dog since he probably had never seen another goose.

"Finally he was gone for a couple of weeks and we started believing he'd flown up to Canada or somewhere, when my daughter was driving about fifteen miles from our place, and saw a wild goose out in back of this old fellow's place, and stopped and it turned out to be Charlie with his wings clipped. She and the old man had quite an argument about whose goose it was, but she eventually proved to him that the goose would follow her anywhere she would go, so she helped him up in the back of the truck and brought him home and put him out on the porch with the dogs, and, you know, believe it or not, we got up the next morning and our own dogs had eaten that goose. Musta had something to do with his wings being clipped."

LAST DEPRESSION CHICKEN FISHING

My dad is a railroader. He tells the story of being a young and hungry railroader during the thirties who rented a room over a chicken-yard, and worked the night shift. He'd set out trot lines from his window, bait them with canned corn, and let the chicken hook itself. He claims you had to be pretty fast to get one up to the second floor before it made much noise.

DOG FISHING

Dave Dewey invented a good city sport, involving a surf rod, spinning reel, lots of good line, and a bone. Most dogs like some form of tug-of-war, so you find an alley and cast out into it, wait for a dog to come along, and try to reel him in before he breaks the line or lets go of the bone. Or you can try trolling from the back of a pickup truck.

THE BEAR AND THE POINTED STICK
(Told to me by Gene Fuzzell, retired Sheriff of Idaho County, Idaho.)

"Word came down off of Marshall Mountain that Old Peterson had run into some trouble, so I rode up there one day, and as I came up over the top of the ridge and down onto what used to be Peterson's cabin, right there to the east of the house I found a bear trap cabled to four trees with a yearling bear in it, dead and bloated about a week, and a few chunks of dog meat scattered around like Peterson and his dogs had run into trouble alright. There was plenty of big bear signs and the old man's bootmarks.

"I guess the only gun Peterson owned was an air pistol for the pack rats, because next to the trapped bear I found a little lodgepole about twelve foot long with a sharpened spike on the end of it, held down by two hose clamps. Got to looking around and started finding pellets from his pistol too, so I started tracking him and the big bear. Didn't take long, cause the pellets were in a box in his shirtpocket. As he started running along the hillside, he started spilling pellets.

"His head was laying a couple of feet from his body, and his left arm was tucked right into his chest, like a lefthanded pledge of allegiance. The folks at the hospital didn't like it much when I had him x-rayed for lead.

"What I figure happened was that either Peterson was awful hungry for bear meat or the

big bear had been bothering him so much that he figured to trap it and just let it starve to death, but he caught a little one by mistake, and it was crying so much that Peterson was worried his claim would fill up with bears. A bear will go to trouble just like a dog will go to a dogfight. So Peterson figured to kill the little bear with a pointed stick, and about the time he got the job half done, the other bear showed up and was mad enough to rip him from asshole to elbow. There's talk that there's ore on that side of the mountain that runs forty ounces to a ton gold, and thirty silver."

A TRAPPER'S DOG
(From Leroy Rainey, Roseberry, Idaho, January 1979)

"We had a bad time when we first came to this country. We were living out where the roosters fuck the hoot owls and I was out of a job. So the Missus decides to take in ironing to get some money. You know, heating up the iron on the woodstove and sprinkling from a pork and beans can. And me, I decided to take up trapping.

"We had this old dog named Dave, looked like a coonhound with long hair that run into an airplane propeller. He was hungry as the rest of us and about half smart.

"I didn't have any traps, so being the optimist I was, I spent one night whittling a couple of stretcher boards to fit rabbit hides, starting small. When I got finished I set them outside the door and next morning when I got up, there was two dead rabbits laying there by my stretcher boards. I looked at old Dave and he kinda winked at me, so I went ahead that night and whittled up some bigger boards, and sure enough next morning there was a marten and a bobcat laying dead next to them, and Dave looking a little tired but happy.

"Well, things went on like that for quite a while. My fortunes was on the rise and me and Dave was eating good, until one night I came home half full of Jack Daniels and told my wife that we was getting too damn fancy to have her be taking in ironing anymore. Now I don't know what I was thinking about, and without the booze I probably wouldn't have done it, but I went and set that ironing board outside the door and I never saw old Dave again."

A BOOT STORY
(heard in the McCall, Idaho, hospital, summer 1977)

"Back in the '30s, I buckarooed for the ought-eight, down in the Snake River country one winter, where the lizards were glad to see you, the sun shined about two hours a day once a month, and cattle were half shadows from having to climb cliffs to get to the bunch grass. As I remember, the pay was thirty dollars a month and all the cowshit you could eat, so it took the better part of a lifetime to save up for a new pair of boots, but somehow that winter I had made it all the way into Grangeville and bought a spanking new pair of black beauties with little red roses stitched into the tops.

"Now me and ol' Dogmeat, my cow pony, were ambling along one afternoon, trailing some heifers back down into the bottomlands, and I had a cigarette in my mouth and one leg cocked up over the saddle horn polishing my left boot with my snot rag when Dogmeat spooked at a prairie dog or something, and I come unseated with one leg hung up in a stirrup. Of course, the heifers spooked at me dragging along on the ground and they began to make tracks for the river and ol' Dogmeat, being the pony he was, just wasn't going to let the cattle get away, whether I went along or not, and he began to pour on the coal to catch the heifers, which left me bouncing along from boulder to boulder, until, almost halfway to the river, Dogmeat kicked me in the chest hard enough to pull my foot out of the boot that was hung up.

"Now I laid there feeling mighty sorry for myself for a long time, until I got to feeling like I should at least find Dogmeat, so I crippled the rest of the way down the hill and found him holding the heifers on a little sandbar, and you know, by God, right there in my stirrup was that right boot. Boy, was I lucky."

Animal Story Letters

CUTE RACCOON STORY

Traveling cross-country on a ten-speed bike tour, we stopped to spend a few days at St. Andrews State Park in Panama City Beach, Florida. There we soon found that we had some competition for our campsite—after sundown the skunks and raccoons moved in. It was not uncommon to wake up in the morn' to find a dozen or so unwanted visitors helping themselves to whatever leftovers we had forgotten to hide away the night before.

On one of these occasions I awoke to find a half dozen raccoons working their way through a bag of Oreo cookies I had splurged on right before bedtime. Usually I enjoyed these late night raids. But tonight I was mad—that was my breakfast they were eating!—and I went after them with whatever I could find to throw. The 'coons took off fast. I secured the few remaining undamaged Oreos and went back to bed.

I was sleeping under the stars that night, stretched out beneath a friendly old Florida pine. After five minutes back in the sack, hanging right on the edge of sleep, I looked up—and saw a monstrously large limb about twenty feet above my head that was in the process of breaking off.

I did an incredible high-speed roll to my left, sleeping bag and all. I got maybe five feet out of the way before the branch crashed to the ground.

It was six feet long and a good four inches thick—and had fallen approximately twenty feet to touch down with deadly accuracy on the towel I had been using for a pillow.

Accident? Coincidence? Bad luck? Not a chance. I heard rustling noises from the former position of the fallen limb—two raccoons. They were rapidly leaving the scene of their attempted homicide, but one of them paused long enough to turn around and look back. He stared straight at me with a gleam in his bright yellow eyes.

I spent the rest of the night out in the open, and I no longer mess with raccoons.

Michael McClelland
Anderson, South Carolina
[Fall 1977]

AN AWFUL ROACH STORY

Your cockroach letters reminded me of my encounter with roaches. In 1939 my mother and I sailed on a small coast steamer from Chefoo to Shanghai, on the way home from a summer vacation. The first night out I ate supper at the children's sitting, put on my pajamas and went to bed. My mother left to have her meal with the adults. After reading for a while I turned off the light and settled down to sleep. It was hot, so I left the covers off. After the light had been off for about a minute I gradually became aware of a soft tickly feeling through my hair, over my pajamas, and concentrating especially on my toenails and fingernails. I switched on the light, and surprised about 100 cockroaches which were nibbling on my hair and nails and climbing over my body. Well, maybe not 100 but lots, anyway. I vaulted energetically from the top bunk to the floor and spent the next three minutes shaking every part of my body, clothes and hair and yelling "Eesh! Eesh!" (the current version of "yuck.") The roaches disappeared; I was too upset to notice where they'd gone. I climbed back into the bunk and turned off the light again. This time they didn't wait at all. The light went off, the cockroaches started nibbling, and I went into my jumping and yelling number again. I was an experienced enough traveler to know how to get the cabin steward in an emergency, but I was so tired and upset that all I could think of was finding my mother. I ran into the dining room barefoot and called out loudly "Mummy! The cockroaches are eating me!" My mother, embarrassed, hustled me out of the dining room. Together we found the cabin steward who filled our cabin with the fumes of Flit, pumped out of a little glass Flit-gun. The cockroaches left, probably to try their luck next door, and I was able to get some sleep.

For years I've told this story to people. I ran into some skepticism about whether the roaches were actually eating my hair and nails or were just checking me out. After a while I began to doubt my own memory; however, I recently read (in a children's science book about roaches) that they are particularly partial to eating hair and nail parings.

Dorothy Horn
San Jose, California
[Fall 1977]

STRANGER THAN FICTION
TRUE ROACH STORY

Several years ago, while living in Fort Lauderdale, my wife and I had problems with the one-and-a-half-inch Florida variety of cockroach. Whenever one of us came in the door, their small brown bodies could be seen scurrying behind furniture and around corners.

The most common course of action was to arm myself with a can of bug spray and go small-game hunting. One night I was using guerrilla tactics in a battle with a particularly ferocious spider. This involved leaping close to the wall he had stationed himself on, spraying him with the bug spray, and getting back out of the way before he could attack. The only effect of all this was to cover him with so much of the white spray that he looked like a hateful plaster museum model of a four-inch arachnid.

After about the fifteenth attack, while our eyes were locked in mutual species hatred, I began to have the distinct impression of being watched from the closet about four feet away. The feeling was not one of malevolence, but of a sort of benign curiosity. I immediately turned to address the intruder into my private wars and came face to face with a very large male cockroach (substitute female if you feel that theirs is a matriarchal society). He was immobile except for a systematic, constant back-and-forth waggling of his antennae, and he was very definitely wondering what the hell I was doing.

Suddenly I began to feel very foolish, standing there on my bug-spray battlefield. I realized that these bugs didn't hate me, they were simply trying to make a living. So why was I trying so hard to eradicate them? I began to feel a need to explain my actions, and since I could feel a very distinct mental connection between myself and the cockroach, I began to try and explain things to him. This was somewhat difficult at first since I don't normally communicate telepathically with bugs. I told him that it wasn't so much that I, or other people, wished to kill him and his friends—it was just that they couldn't be running around the house all the time when we were there. It bothers people, for Chrissakes, to open the door and see cockroaches running all over the place. Not that there was anything inherently wrong with them, of course. (I was trying hard not to offend him.)

Sensing that my thoughts weren't carrying a whole lot of weight, I decided to offer a compromise. "Why don't we do it this way— whenever there are people around, which would be during the day and evening, you cockroaches stay out of sight. Then at night, when everybody's asleep, your group can have the whole house. Just stay off the beds and make sure everyone is asleep before you come out. I really don't enjoy killing you, but I have to. I'm under tremendous social and racial pressure to keep you from overrunning my house. So if you only come out at night there won't be any problem. I won't set out any poison or fumigators and you won't interfere with my life, agreed?"

I received no message in response. He simply turned around and walked away. Apparently the conversation was finished. But from that day on we never saw another cockroach in the house. They cleaned up all the crumbs and dirt but they always waited till late at night.

I told a few of my friends about this (very few) and was asked to come over and have a talk with their roaches. I found that the large ones were always pretty agreeable and I generally established contact with them. Once or twice they agreed to the terms and tried to live in harmony with mankind. The smaller type of cockroach was much less communicative. They ignored most of my attempts at mental contact and never made any effort to go along with the terms of the treaty. I now feel that they simply don't have the facilities for this type of contact; they are on a different wavelength, or they just didn't agree to the terms.

The spider was a different story altogether. As soon as I finished my conversation with the cockroach, the spider attacked, obviously thinking he could surprise me while I was still dazed. Fortunately my survival instincts were intact and unfettered. Catching his leap out of the corner of my eye, I jumped back two steps, and, feinting with the can of bug spray in my left hand, stepped on him as soon as he hit the floor.

Stephen Finn
[Spring 1978]

DOG'S LIFE

Taurus Tom is a skinny blond barefoot hippie I knew in San Francisco in the late 1960s. He had a large black dog heavy in the neck and shoulders with pointed ears that curved upwards like horns, called Taurus. Taurus walked with a limp. When I asked Tom why, he replied, "He was run over by the Krishna Jug-

gernaut while I was watching their annual parade. He would have been killed," he added as an afterthought, "but the head swami made them stop and pull Taurus from beneath the wheels. The swami claimed he knew Taurus and that he had been a great swami in a past life."

I left town shortly thereafter and did not return for several years. Upon my return I inquired into the present whereabouts of past associates. I was told, "Taurus Tom went to Hawaii to join a Christian commune there. He is not called Taurus Tom anymore. Taurus died last year, just before Tom left. He was run over by the Juggernaut at the annual Krishna parade."

I thought it curious that a large healthy street-wise dog like Taurus, who had great presence, should be run over twice by a float in a parade. I had only a vague idea of what a Juggernaut is so I looked it up in the dictionary.

"Idol of the Hindu God Krishna pulled around in a large cart. Devotees of the God are said to have thrown themselves under the wheels to be crushed to death."

—*Thorndike Barnhart Comprehensive*
Desk Dictionary
(Published by Doubleday, 1952)
Joe Corgo
Domesa, New Mexico
[Spring 1981]

OR AM I A BUTTERFLY DREAMING I AM A MAN?

You dream. And I dream. And we both know that if we let sleeping dogs lie, they will twitch, whimper—and dream. What about all the other critters: horses, marmots, toads, terns, and termites? Where in phylogeny does dreaming begin—at the same place as sleep (wherever that is) or somewhere else?

That question of course raises a parallel one for ontogeny. Talk about a dream within a dream: how much of a brain does a fetus need for a fetus-dream? Or is all uterine life a dream and ex-utero dreaming a harkening to it, which we've long since put to other uses?

The best answer I've heard so far, to the phylogenetic question at least, is that no one knows because dreaming is hard to define in experimental terms. All right, then: REM sleep, has no one tested for it among the "lower" orders?

Nobody I know seems to know. So I ask you and your readers: does a wild bear dream in the woods?

William deBuys
Austin, Texas
[Summer 1982]

NOT A BUTTERFLY; A WHALE, MAYBE

This is in response to William deBuys' letter concerning rapid eye movement (REM) sleep in animals ("Or Am I a Butterfly Dreaming I Am a Man?" Summer '82 CQ). It is taken from *Some Must Watch While Some Must Sleep* by William C. Dement (W. H. Freeman and Company, San Francisco, 1978):

"Most reptiles appear to have non-REM sleep as we know it, but do not show any REM sleep at all. Birds have a very well-developed non-REM sleep and show very brief (about one second) episodes of what appears to be an evolutionary precursor of the REM period. Full-blown REM periods exist only in mammalian sleep. Interestingly enough, all mammals appear to have substantial amounts of REM sleep, and whatever differences exist do not follow any apparent rule. . . . A few of the many species whose sleep has been carefully studied are elephant, chimpanzee, whale, shrew, pig, sheep, monkey, rat, mouse, cat, bat, dog, donkey, guinea pig, and human. Some non-mammals that have been observed by sleep researchers are frog, alligator, lizard, various fish, pigeon, chicken, eagle, and snake. . . .

"One of the most remarkable aspects of REM sleep is the very large amount that is present in most mammals immediately after birth. In the newborn human baby, who sleeps an average of sixteen to eighteen hours per day, fully fifty percent of all sleep (eight to nine hours!) is occupied by REM periods. . . .

"In premature infants of thirty-two to thirty-six weeks gestation, the percent of REM sleep is even higher, around seventy-five percent. . . . This finding suggests that there is a phase in the early intrauterine life of the child when REM sleep is the all-encompassing mode of existence. . . .

"In some animals the predominance of REM sleep in early life is even more spectacular. For example, in the newborn kitten, REM sleep is the only sleep. This is also true of the newborn puppy, rat, and hamster. On the other hand, the newborn guinea pig has very little REM sleep.

"Because of the extraordinary amount of REM sleep in infants, and our difficulty in demonstrating the purpose of REM sleep in adults, we cannot help wondering if the real function of REM sleep is fulfilled early in life. Perhaps REM sleep is necessary for the normal pre- and postnatal maturation of the brain. This fits with the guinea pig data because that animal is mature at birth."

James Whelan
Sussex, New Jersey
[Winter 1982]

STANLEY MARSH 3 RIDES AGAIN

I am afraid of my cows. I know that one of them hates me, maybe they all hate me and always have. But there is at least one out there who knows that I can be had. I can be knocked down and rolled around and sent crawling off in pain. Has she told the others? I can't tell. But each time I force myself to go among them, each twitch of the ear and stomp of the hoof seems to be telling me that the word is out. I can be had.

Stanley Marsh 3
Amarillo, Texas
[Summer 1984]

STEWART BRAND

How to Run the Arms Race Backwards

A dog that hasn't been chained up long forgets. It rushes across the yard and then—bang. Today when people become excited about the future and involve themselves with new uses of technology they often get carried away with hope—then bam—they think about the atomic bomb, the H bomb, the ballistic missile. Today, like the dog, we all have the chain on us. There is nothing very marvelous going on unless it is something to untie that chain.

Steve Baer

This article, published in Spring 1977, is typical of Stewart's writing. It's direct, pungent, and informal; it's liberally sprinkled with fascinating gossip from a wide variety of fields; it's full of original thoughts, strongly stated ("Ignorance is a sin in a different way than it used to be"), and it's directed towards an important purpose.

There's no need to introduce that purpose: it'll be clear from the first paragraph, if not the title, of the article. Unfortunately, with the specialized exception of Amnesty International, there still is no global effort (that we know of) towards the kind of Alcoholics Anonymous equivalent for nuclear war that Stewart proposed here. One final comment: if Stewart's writing before 1982 reads like it's written in one draft, that's because it usually was. What happened in 1982? He got a word processor.

Art Kleiner

YOU CAN MAKE MONEY DEMONSTRATING ARMS RACES

Tell some people (friends, students, audience, whatever) that you're going to auction off a five-dollar bill. Highest bidder gets it.

"Oboy," says the suckers.

"One stipulation," you add. "I get the money from both the highest and the second-highest bidders." "Hm, OK," says the suckers.

The bidding begins. "10 cents!" "20 cents!" "30 cents!" It continues. "$1.50!" "$1.75!" People may or may not notice when it goes past "$2.50!," at which point you're making money.

They *will* notice when the bidding goes past $5. It will inevitably do that because whoever's just had his bid of $4.50 beat by someone bidding $4.75 stands to lose his $4.50 and get nothing. If he bids $5.10 for the $5 bill and wins, then he only loses 10 cents.

Unfortunately the now second-highest bidder stands to lose all of his $4.75 bid and get nothing, and he raises the bid. So it goes, indefinitely. You can sell your $5 bill for a *lot* of money. I've done it. Its market price is essentially infinite.

You've set in motion an Arms Race, a cybernetic runaway of positive feedback—the more, the more. (Negative feedback would be, the more, the less.) Once past $5 the bids become increasingly radical—"$7!" "$10!" "$20!"— as each party tries to annihilate the hopes of the other.

Everybody loses (except you, the arms manufacturer). What keeps the bidding going is each bidder's fear of losing more than the other fool—to quit, pay over the losing bid of $40 or whatever, and get nothing! Pity, maybe.

Watch the loser. He may in vengefulness try to start a different contest with the winner which he might win. He may look for another set of people to pull the same trick on himself. Or he may puzzle at the phenomenon and look for its solution. Even winners might do that, in view of the cost of winning. . . .

CONTEXT

Within the structure of an Arms Race there is no formal solution. They run to exhaustion. The place to look for relief is the context in which they are embedded—the language of the rules of the game and the cultural valuing of its conduct.

The present international rules—the real ones—are still pretty much what was established at Versailles in 1919 when the Allies went back on their promises to the defeated Germans. The rules are: anything goes. That principle lived on in President Johnson's Vietnam policy, "When you got 'em by the balls, their hearts and minds will follow." Interestingly, it was not the slogan of the winning side, but considerable expenditure of life and treasure was made in its service.

Is faith in the devil rewarded? Yes, but never for long.

My generation—I'm thirty-eight—grew up expecting nuclear devastation. The earliest dream I remember is of Rockford, Illinois, my home, obliterated by Russian atomic bombs. (The town fathers were ambivalently proud that Rockford was supposedly seventh on the Russian list because of our machine tool industry.) In my dream I always survived to search through the exciting panic and rubble for the lost fragments of myself—friends, family, familiar places.

The thrill of World War II was not repeated in our lifetime though it was faithfully awaited. Hiroshima spawned a generation of apocalypse buffs whose fantasies by the '70s have convoluted into full absurdity. We have wished, we ecofreaks, for a disaster or dramatic social change to come and bomb us into the Stone Age, where we might live like Indians in our valley with our localism, our appropriate technology, our gardens, and our homemade religion, guilt-free at last.

There's nothing wrong with that goal, except the notion that a disaster or revolution will make it possible. Comes any crunch at all—war, famine, serious depression—the first to go will be all our environmental accomplishments and any equity, any democracy, any localism, any grace. We can be pro-environment or pro-apocalypse, but not both without being grotesque. Some of us have done that—I for one—and some knew better. In any case the attitude seems to be passing.

What's the point then? The point is that the Arms Race is not taken seriously enough by our social innovators to try to do anything very radical about it. When it is not unconsciously worshipped it is perceived as too abstract, too remote, old hat. It is all those, but consider the effort that goes into stopping nuclear reactors in the United States and compare the likelihood and magnitude of radiation hazard from the use of nuclear reactors versus the use of nuclear weapons.

I figure that people are fighting nuclear energy as the only accessible toenail of the nuclear arms dragon. The reactors stand for the weapons because we feel helpless to do anything about the weapons.

Worldwide, there are just a few hundred people, outside foreign offices, working full time on disarmament issues. Regrettably, far more attention is paid to other major world problems— such as energy, the environment, development, population, and so on. A relatively large fraction of the few hundred disarmament scholars is So-

viet. In the non-Communist developed countries disarmament is not a popular subject for study.
Frank Barnaby
New Scientist

I do not think that environmentalism can get very far while this situation prevails. People do not sufficiently believe there is a future to conserve for. The main article of their disbelief, reasonably, is the persistent growth of nuclear mega-tonnage whose only function is to destroy whole systems.

Try a fantasy experiment. Imagine our present life and behavior with only one change—the confident absence of expectations of apocalypse. Imagine having creatively in mind the conduct of your family, neighborhood, business, town, county, state, nation, world over *centuries* of adaptation that you can work on now.

If that vision surprises you or leads you to thoughts you haven't had, you've got a picture of the present opportunist (get it while you can) context of arms uncontrol. Not promising.

WEAPONS ADDICTION

Gregory Bateson has drawn the formal parallel between an Arms Race and drug addiction such as alcoholism. In each case the perpetrator/victim buys short-term relief from his predicament at the cost of a subsequent worse predicament which demands even more relief—"I drink to forget I'm an alcoholic." And each case is a battleground of fictional adversaries—the alcoholic "versus" his pride, one body of people "versus" another.

So far the closest thing to a cure for alcoholism is the "ad hoc religion" (Gerald Heard) of Alcoholics Anonymous, which can force the surrender of the drinker to the fact of his alcoholism, to the care of a Higher Power, and to sustained care and shared responsibility with others who've been the same route.

There may well be an analogous cure for the Arms Race. Herman Kahn proposes something of the sort—gradual decommitment of nuclear threat by the United States and gradual increase of ecological consciousness as a religion which taboos nuclear weapons.

It's worth noticing that such a religion would have to be a practice religion like Hinduism or Buddhism rather than a revealed religion such as Christianity or Islam. Revealed religions generate, and probably require, enemies—we've got the Word; you don't; off you. In the cause of world peace you can forget about finding, or being, a Messiah. What's called for is a world set of religions of immanence rather than transcendence, based on personal observation and responsibility and love of worldly detail as the handiest handle on the infinite. That's one avenue of cure. . . .

VICTORY OF THE UNDERDOG

Another avenue, less grand than religion but still contextual, is a bit of tinkering with the structure of the Arms Race, which can't be done by people busy fighting within it. It is after all a war of anticipation. In the projected showdown it is assumed that Biggest Gun Wins. Therefore each side kills itself to maintain the Biggest Gun.

Imagine a situation in which everything is the same, except both sides believe that Smallest Gun Wins. In the five dollar bill auction it would be the same as changing the rule once the price was way up there, to "second highest bidder wins, but I still get both bids." Would incremental increase change to incremental decrease? (It would in the changed auction if the bidders were by now so mad at each other that each wanted to win *and* make the other guy suffer a humiliating loss. That might be the Arms Race solution. In the auction the first party to really catch on and bid "one mill!" would win.)

Try changing just that element. You still have confrontation and conflict and still have all the causes of war. Here it may be timely to quote some of Geoffrey Blainey's observations from *The Causes of War*:

Wars usually begin when two nations disagree on their relative strength, and wars usually cease when the fighting nations agree on their relative strength. . . .

85

Any factor which increases the likelihood that nations will agree on their relative power is a potential cause of peace. One powerful cause of peace is a decisive war, for war provides the most widely-accepted measure of power. . . .

A formula for measuring international power is essential: ironically the most useful formula is warfare. Until the function of warfare is appreciated, the search for a more humane and more efficient way of measuring power is likely to be haphazard. . . .

While the breakdown of diplomacy reflects the belief of each nation that it will gain more by fighting than by negotiating, the breakdown of war reflects the belief of each nation that it will gain more by negotiating than by fighting.

The keywords here are "gain" and "relative strength." Gain what? Relative strength in what? If the only place that power comes from is out of the barrel of a gun, then the answer is obvious, tautologous, and insane.

But suppose it meant "gain in the eyes of the world" and "relative strength of character." There's no doubt you're still talking about competition and important international stakes, but the mode of threat and battle might become radically different.

It's already happening.

The underdog *won* in Vietnam through relative weakness of arms and strength of character. The United States lost through strength of arms and weakness of character. We played the part of the bully, and in the eyes of the neighborhood we were despicable. Power in Southeast Asia came from some other place than the barrel of a gun.

You could make a similar case about Castro's Cuba or about Israel (to some). What's going on? Apparently it's a more mercantile, less military, world than it used to be, and information can get around rapidly and widely enough for there to be such a thing as World Opinion. And rather suddenly it is powerful. The world can put enough non-military pressure on an interventionist United States or a White-ruled Rhodesia to change behavior. It can probably do the same thing with rewards. (Is anyone studying that?)

What keeps the United States–Soviet Arms Race going then? World Opinion holds both

nations in contempt for their "obscene" weapons stockpiles. Well, as anyone knows who's been around one, a psychosis has a life of its own. I mean that pretty literally. It generates its own universe dynamically capable of denying truths obvious to others (such as the leaders and citizens of the insane nations). In theory that can go on forever. In the real world it doesn't. Given enough contact and time the hysterical system eventually reconnects.

If this line of argument is correct, then the way to cure the Arms Race is to increase the power of World Opinion and its moral authority. Let it punish with bad odor and boycott and insults to tourists any nation that relies on massive weaponry, massive imprisonment, institutional torture, severe inequity, or other wrongdoing. Let it revile those who gain military victory by overwhelming force of arms. Let it reward its gallant underdogs and its good citizens with praise, trade, respect.

For this to work there must be swift, accurate assessment of what's actually going on in confrontation situations. Lazy or controlled press is a sin. Secrecy is a sin (compare World Opinion on the Soviet and United States space programs). Favoritism is a sin (if torture is evil in Chile, it is evil in Rumania). Ignorance is a sin in a different way than it used to be.

World Opinion needs better information, more leverage, and fuller recognition of its power. Maybe it needs something like the Nobel Committee to articulate its views, maybe not. Maybe it needs to establish modes of token warfare, maybe not. It probably does need world-wide polling on issues. It does not need a bigger gun. It does need a lot of work, which it will reward. . . .

LOCAL DISARMAMENT

In American cities there is a miniature Arms Race going on between the cops and the robbers, egged on by TV shows such as "S.W.A.T." (Special Weapons and Tactics). If what I'm saying about Arms Races is true, the city might be an arena to test it. A gun is like a bomb—it causes more irreversible damage, such as death, and more innocent victims.

Ken Kesey, the Oregon novelist who did time in California on a dope charge, suggested this fall that cops have too important a role in society to rely on weapons to enforce. He cited the history of the patient, unarmed British bobby, who has never lost the respect of the people, versus the American policeman, who has never quite gotten it. A shooting in England remains rare enough to be front-page news when it occurs.

What if some city initiated an unarmed police squad, voluntary presumably? The patrolmen and women would have to rely on their wits, familiarity with their beats, neighborhood help, skill in martial arts, and guts. It would be hazardous duty. But the moral authority they would acquire would be worth it. A lot of urban crime is by kids, a lot of it has to do with pride. In a pride race the unarmed cop is ahead.

The inevitable TV show might even be all right.

Nice idea maybe, but how the hell do you implement it? Something like this has to be initiated by police somewhere, and that seems unlikely. It'll probably never get tried.

Except it's being tried somewhat in a town in Orange County, California, called Santa Ana. In the two years that Police Chief Ray Davis has been on the job—according to a report in *New West*—he's increased the force by thirty percent (largely minorities) to a total of 327 regular officers and 129 uniformed but *unarmed* "service officers." (Santa Ana's population is 180,000, racially mixed.)

The program is called COP—Community Oriented Policing. It "puts small teams of police officers into well-defined neighborhoods, and encourages cops and civilians to get to know each other." Formerly the Santa Ana force suffered from lousy morale and "had a reputation for kicking ass and taking names. They were quick to draw and fire their guns in delicate situations."

Result after two years? Serious crime was reduced 20.7% last year, replacing the former yearly increase. Forcible rape was down 53.6% in the first nine months of 1976. Officer-involved shootings are down 60%. Morale is up.

One patrol officer comments, "I wouldn't work anywhere else in the country—they might have new patrol cars every year, but they don't have kids coming up and calling you by your first name. . . ."

THE GRAIN OF INTELLIGENCE

"Grain" as in coarse-grained or fine-grained. It means the size of the perceptible texture. If there is an underlying message in the array of Whole Earth publications it is, "Think Little": live fine-grained.

You can see it in a New York skyscraper— a dazzling intellectual achievement of size and design. But when you look close there is little to admire—nothing quite works. The design intelligence is elsewhere, congratulating itself up on top maybe. Modern strategic and tactical weapons are astonishing instruments, interesting to analyze, fun to play with. But actual war conducted with them is more brutal than anything we've ever known. The intelligence of war, except for espionage and guerrilla activity, is now grossly coarse-grained.

Is that bad? It is if war is meant to be some measure of a people's character. There is no place for a samurai code or a fighting sailor's heart-of-oak in an arsenal or conflict of intercontinental missiles. Those are merely a measure of wealth, which is the opposite of character.

Maybe war can be abolished. I doubt it. But it can surely be made human again by revaluing its conduct. If people want to fight, and some do, let them do it hand to hand or prove their case with sailing ships and unrifled cannon, where only innocent waves are shattered by missed shots, and the valor of the combatants makes the difference.

I'm not kidding.

The rule of grain is: If you take care only of abstractions, the details will defeat you; if you take care of the details, the abstractions will take care of themselves. . . .

REFERENCES

Steve Baer, "The Bomb," *The CoEvolution Quarterly*, Summer, 1976.

Frank Barnaby, "Soviet Scientists and Disarmament," *New Scientist*, 13 January 1977.

Gregory Bateson, "The Cybernetics of 'Self': A Theory of Alcoholism," *Steps to an Ecology of Mind*, 1972, Ballantine.

Gerald Heard, *The Five Ages of Man*, 1963, Julian Press.

Geoffrey Blainey, *The Causes of War*, 1973, Macmillan.

Jonathan Kirsch, "Street Crime—A Tale of Two Cities/ Santa Ana: Turning the Numbers Around," *New West*, 17 January 1977.

LETTER TO ALL EDITORS

You don't win by killing, because they kill you back. You don't win by growing, because you grow too big, and fall over. You don't win by spending, because you spend too much, leaving only that percentage which is either stolen or imaginary. You don't win by winning, but living.

Sincerely,
David Wann
Indian Hills, Colorado
[Summer 1982]

WHY WE SHOULD DROP THE BOMBS

it would be so exciting
it would be so powerful
it would punish us for our sins
things wouldn't be so boring anymore
we could get back to basics
we would remember who we love
it would be so loud
it would be so hot
the mushroom clouds would rise up
we could start over
we wouldn't have to be afraid of it anymore
we wouldn't have to be afraid anymore
we would finally have done it
    better than Raskolnikov

it would release our anger
    in the ultimate tantrum
then we could rest

—Alia Johnson
[Fall 1981]

Alia Johnson lives in Berkeley, works night and day to defuse the Arms Race. Her method is truth, sampled here.

SB

POLITICAL EYEPATCHES

Two recent newspaper items report:

1. That if an H-bomb went off (for instance) in the Boston area anyone within a forty-mile radius unfortunate enough to be looking in its direction at the time would be blinded by retina burn.

2. That the pilot of the Air Force's SAC flying command post wears an eye patch at all times so he'll have sight in one eye when/after he gazes at an H-bomb going off somewhere above the United States.

Whether people should want to survive into the chaos post-nuclear-war may be moot, but survival *blind* may be just that straw that breaks the camel's back.

I'm suggesting that the eye patch, black as ink, might be an excellent symbol for public display by those who'd like to protest nuclear idiocy, unforgettable if worn by hundreds or thousands at a gathering, and yet a protective item of substance: real theater.

Think of Israel's Dayan, that Man in the Hathaway shirt and many, many more all come to town on the very same day.

Charles Pierce
Dunedin, Florida
[Spring 1981]

HERMAN KAHN
GOV. JERRY BROWN
AMORY LOVINS

The New Class

Edmund G. Brown, Jr., governor of California from 1974 to 1982, was the best interviewer CQ ever had. The breadth of his Jesuit education, the quickness of his wit and tongue, and the consequence of his understanding as innovative leader of the nation's bellwether state drew the very best from people. In our pages he vivisected the ideas of Gregory Bateson, Marshall McLuhan, Thomas Szasz, and the indomitable Herman Kahn. They, and other visitors such as Buckminster Fuller, Ken Kesey, Ivan Illich, James Watson (*The Double Helix*), E. F. Schumacher, Hazel Henderson, and Wendell Berry gave lunchtime talks in the governor's council room to an audience of staff, cabinet, and department heads. One of my roles on the governor's staff was setting up these visits and talks. This one was held on December 1, 1976; its edited transcript was printed in the Spring 1977 CQ.

Herman Kahn, who died in 1983 at sixty-three, was to American political intellectuals (to quote from my original introduction), "what Tom Wolfe is to the journalists. Both immerse themselves like anthropologists in field experience and impressions and let their perception grow from that rather than strictly from ideology. As a result, they are more open, less predictable, and far more informative than your standard idealogue. When it comes to political, social, military, or economic analysis, there is no view I'm more interested in than Kahn's. In addition—and this may or may not come across in print—Kahn has an engaging charm and wit in person that makes even hostile audiences laugh with him. Of the fifteen or so lectures at the governor's office this was the most hilarious."

Amory Lovins is still the standard-bearer for energy-conscious environmentalism. His trilogy of books, *World Energy Strategies, Non-Nuclear Futures*, and *Soft Energy Paths* make the best-documented, well-argued and persuasive case for an energy-conservative world. Shortly before this interview, he published in *Foreign Affairs* (October, 1976) a landmark paper, "The Road Not Taken."

Stewart Brand

For space reasons, I edited out about a third of the printed interview in CQ—which itself was about one-fourth of the original eight-hour transcript. I left out some of their political discussion, which has dated

89

since; Kahn's ideas about the New Class and the state of Western culture, and the others' responses, stayed in. In the original transcript there was still more quantitative dialogue between Lovins and Kahn—an entire separate debate on percents of inflation, thousands of cubic feet of natural gas, and quadrillions of BTUs. Wrote Stewart, "My mythic image is of the pair advancing on each other in a dusty street, the big trail-boss and the canny squirt from the city, hands poised above their pocket calculators. Lovins in fact does carry his in a holster. Kahn packs two."

Art Kleiner

HERMAN KAHN: We have two studies going on at the Hudson Institute today which I find terribly interesting. The first is on the New Class, being done by Barry Bruce-Briggs and others, including myself. Let me define the New Class for you. The term was coined by Milovan Djilas to mean the upper levels of Yu-goslav intelligentsia, who he felt were ripping off the country. We're not using it that way, but it's close. In our sense, the term is used by Bazelon, by Podhoretz, by Kristol, a few others. It was also noticed by Marxists and you'll find lots of references during the last hundred years to this concept.

Think of a group of people who come from upper-middle-class backgrounds, from families who are largely education-oriented, so they see that the children go to the good schools and who, after they get out of the schools, earn their living by the use of academic skills, language skills, esthetic skills, analytical skills. They don't earn their living by being entrepreneurs, businessmen, engineers, laborers, clerical workers. If you are staff here, you are probably New Class to some extent.

Now, we are defining a class. Classes are never homogeneous. You must understand that people can assimilate into a class. They don't have to have the same ethnic origins as the majority. We've put together a fair amount of evidence, part of it just anecdotal, arguing that the New Class in the United States largely has the following religious backgrounds: secular Jewish, Presbyterian, Congregationalist, Epis-

Till 2 A.M. in the Governor's office. Left to right, Amory Lovins, Herman Kahn, Elizabeth Coleman (Governor's press secretary), Jim Harding (assistant to the Energy Commission), Jerry Brown, and Gray Davis (Brown's Chief of Staff). Photographs by Stewart Brand.

copalian, northern Methodist, Quaker, Unitarian, and haute-bourgeois Catholic.

This group preserves the division in American history which goes back about 150 years. The basic reigning doctrine of the New Class first emerged in the mid-1870s, the Transcendentalists—Emerson, Thoreau, people like that. If you read them today, a remarkably high percent of their writing reads like it was written by Marcuse. It's a doctrine which believes in the Unitarian faith: there is at most one God, and we worship Him if He exists. It's a hedge.

This is an increasing class in the United States. They came into power with the Kennedy administration, in the early '60s. They went sort of crazy in the mid-'60s, and this brings me to the second book I'm writing: *1965–1975, A Decade of Social Malaise and Educated Incapacity*. Let me take the second term first. It comes from Thorstein Veblen, who used the term "trained incapacity"—by which he meant many things, among which was an inability of engineers and sociologists to deal with simple issues which they could have dealt with if they had not had graduate training. Is

the concept clear? "Educated incapacity" is a much more pervasive kind of thing, where your whole educational outlook, starting with your upbringing, childhood, everything, makes it almost impossible for you to deal with most of the obvious points of American social life today.

Now let me test your skill as politicians. There's a certain individual in American political life from roughly 1967 to about 1973 whom something like eighty to ninety percent of the American people claimed they admired for speaking out on the issues of their lives that bothered them the most. Now eighty to ninety percent is a pretty high percent, right? So you ought to be able to know this individual. How many people know, with a reasonable degree of confidence, who I'm talking about? Yes?

VOICE: George Wallace.

KAHN: I'm going to hate you the rest of your life. Normally, with audiences like this, you can really squeeze them. You can say, "Come on, you must know who eighty to ninety percent of the American people know."

This is not necessarily a good thing. Eric Hoffer commented upon it by saying, "There's

Herman Kahn

something sick about a country in which only a southern racist cracker can deal with the issues." Now that's a fair statement. That's an indication of social malaise, among other things.

Now, we have a list of about twelve issues of American life that are formally characteristic. About eighty percent of Americans understand these issues quite well. They don't learn these from newspapers. If you read the *New York Times, Washington Post, Time, Newsweek, Harper's, Atlantic Monthly,* and to the extent that they discussed these issues at all (except when they had a guest editorial once in a while, or an outsider or a temporary post-election attitude) they never explored these twelve issues. First, there's law and order. From '61 to '65 all these magazines claimed that this was a code word for anti-Negro. Remember that? We couldn't find a single demagogue who used it that way. Wallace would give you his position on the Blacks, and then would talk about law and order. He couldn't use it as a code word, because he'd already given you his position. Half the Blacks in the cities put law and order as the top issue in their lives. They couldn't use code words either. In other words, people understood what they were talking about. There was a big increase in crime, a good deal of it was young Black crime—it's been actually overstated how much of it was that, but a lot of it was. The liberals couldn't cope with it.

Or take busing. We've bused in this country since roughly 1908, I think. Mostly to better schools. In the South they bused to maintain segregation. What do you think a real estate agent told you, the first thing he could, when you were trying to buy a house? Neighborhood schools. If you check you'll find that the average American was willing to pay five, ten, fifteen percent more for a house if he thought it had good neighborhood schools in the area. He was always willing to bus his kids to better schools, but he was willing to pay a big hunk of his wealth for neighborhood schools.

You have a democracy in this country. You have a long tradition of public control of education. Right? We're about to change this, I suspect. Now, in the South, they committed a

legal crime—*de jure* segregation, and you could punish them. In the North there's no such legal crime committed. What do you think of a policy of trying to bus children long distances to bad schools in this kind of context? Do you think such a policy could succeed? Long distances to bad schools? I'm not talking about busing Blacks into the good schools, I'm talking about busing children to schools they judge to be bad. Let me tell you, you've got to be a fool to try it. You can destroy neighborhoods by the way, if you want, but you've got to be crazy. You can't play with children that way. Now, you may say that the people who oppose the busing are generally bigoted people, and that's correct. And so are people who don't oppose the busing. Bigotry is a class characteristic in the United States. You know Archie Bunker in "All In the Family"? He is a very good picture of the average American. And, by the way, the average American is pleased with that picture. I've talked to Norman Lear. He says they kill themselves to have Archie come out backwards, and they can't do it.

English libel law applies here. If you say something about an individual, and it's nasty, and there's no reason to say it, and it's false, you pay damages. If it's true, you pay triple damages, because the truth is so much more damaging. That's the way the average American feels about it. He knows he's a bigot, and it's none of your business. They're not *very* bigoted, the American public. Say you ask the average American, "Which would you rather cut, NASA's Space Budget or the Relief Budget." Which do you think he would postpone? He thinks of Relief as a boondoggle for Blacks. He thinks of NASA as a boondoggle for scientists. He likes scientists and he's sort of hostile to Blacks. But Blacks are at least people. Really, his hostilities are very low-level.

I want to address a very important issue. Why is it that the New Class seems to get everything wrong today? Here I differ from my colleague, Barry Bruce-Briggs. I believe the single major problem of the New Class is educated incapacity—they just don't know what they're doing. He thinks that it's self-interest. And he talks about Brevor's concept of interest affinities—people make the mistakes which favor them. It's just sort of natural. Let's look at the self-interest issue. One thing is terribly clear in the United States today, and in all Western cultures: the New Class is spending more and enjoying it less. In fact they are going down as their numbers increase.

The basic point seems to be the following. If you had 10 million cars, as you had in 1950, and you owned one, it was great. Now you have 110 million cars, and you're got traffic jams. One of the most interesting characteristics of the New Class is an absolutely manic hostility toward automobiles. It has to be seen to be believed. We told the automobile companies that they would have a lot of trouble selling small cars in America. The most typical activity of the average American is picnicking, camping, visiting relatives. He's got three children, a dog, and a bike. You just don't put that into a Volkswagen. You give him a Volkswagen, you just cut out the heart of his lifestyle. He's not going to stand for it. Why should he? He also believes the big cars are safer. The data's now with him: he's right.

The New Class has an agenda. What is their agenda? Number one is risk aversion. In the New Class theology the only real value is human life. You're never entitled to risk human life. It gets to be kind of manic. The risk aversion is pushed to the point where you're running bigger risks.

Take, for example, the issue of chemicals in insecticides. Today we know pretty much how to do biological insecticides—we don't really know, but we're at the verge. In order to really understand this, you've got to commercialize it and try it out. Now, it turns out that the government authorities are insisting on the same kinds of tests with the biological insecticides as exist for the chemical pesticides. These are very expensive, and for a number of reasons, incapacitating. The manufacturers are dropping out of business rather than try to go through these tests. The manufacturers took the position: these are all natural substances, we've had experiences with them, how much

damage can they do? They want to go back to the old rule that the government has to prove its case. (Incidentally, it's apparently impossible to prove safety. There's no experiment you can do which will viably prove safety. All you can prove is damage.) The whole business of medical malpractice is a similar matter.

The next single biggest characteristic of the New Class is localism. Let me ask you this: How many of you believe in unrestricted development for your personal neighborhood? Would you raise your hands please? Nobody does. Now, I want an honest answer. How many define "unrestricted development" as any development which is not in your favor? On the East and the West Coast: almost everybody. Not in the Midwest, not in the southern United States, not in the Southwest. They don't understand the question. They have a perfectly clear concept that you can't cut the ladder after you.

I can give you a list of about twenty items on the agenda of the New Class. Every one of them is very hostile to the middle class, especially to the upper middle class. Every single one of them. So we define politics in the United States in an oversimplified fashion: a war of the New Class versus the middle class. New Class versus working class. When you look at politics that way, everything falls into place.

I myself am obviously New Class. The New Class is about fifty percent of what we call neoliberal. You remember the old liberals—laissez-faire, let us alone, let us make do by ourselves? Then you had the concept of government intervention to make the market work better. Then you had the concept of government intervention to make the income distribution, income maintenance better. Now you've got government intervention by what we call the health and safety fascist. He doesn't give a damn about your morals—you can screw in public on a stage, he couldn't care less—but you can't smoke. And then he calls everybody else a materialist.

I happen to like the middle-class American. I think very well of him. And as I get older I identify more and more with him, with his virtues and so on. I don't want to romanticize him. Actually, on many issues my wife and I are incredibly middle class. I'll give you an example of what I mean by this. My daughter came home at fourteen, and at that time she couldn't date. She was allowed to go out with boys, but she couldn't define it as a heterosexual relationship. She brought home this boy and was holding hands in the living room. And when the boy left, my wife and I turned to her and we said, "What's this nonsense of holding hands in the living room?" She was shocked. She said, "Do you want me to do it behind your back?" And I said, "Absolutely." She said, "Isn't that hypocrisy?" I said, "Yes. Hypocrisy is the tribute vice pays to virtue. If you don't know enough to do that at fourteen, you haven't been socialized." And she got terribly puzzled. I said, "Debbie, do me a very big favor. In the next four or five years you can do all kinds of things. But if I catch you at it, you're in very serious trouble. If you don't do it, I'll send you to a psychiatrist. Now is there any problem about the kind of behavior that's expected?" I went around and made some speeches in the local high school on hypocrisy. The kids had it right, they understood it, the teachers didn't. The kids were clear on every nuance. . . .

WOMAN'S VOICE: I was interested in what you meant by the morality of the New Class.

KAHN: Part of it is traditional. Throughout all of American history the upper middle class has tried to force its values on the country. I would argue that up to about twenty years ago that was a good thing. They were the squares, they were the ones against vice, against thievery, for raising children clean, you know. They wouldn't stand for bringing the language of the streets into the schools. Today the upper middle class has reversed its values completely.

You know something? If you saw a hippie anywhere in the world before say '72, you know what he was? He was Scandinavian, Dutch, English, American, or Canadian. Once in a while Protestant sector of Germany. There were almost no Catholic hippies raised in Catholic countries. It's completely a phenomenon

of Japan and the Atlantic Protestant culture (not Swiss culture, which is also Protestant; it has none of this phenomenon).

Take a look at Holland. You know how people blame much of this phenomenon in the United States on the race problems, on poverty, on the Vietnamese war, and so on? Holland has no race problems, no poverty, no pollution except water from the outside, no Vietnam. They have a drug culture which is much worse than ours; their provos are much more violent and even get elected to the city councils; they have an alienation that has to be seen to be believed. This has nothing to do with Vietnam, or poverty, or race, or ugliness. It has to do with a problem possessed by every member of the Protestant culture except Switzerland.

The Protestant culture I'm talking about here (except for England) used to have a kind of manic love affair with God. And then they became manic atheists. What do I mean by manic atheists? Any totem, any taboo, anything that's irrational or arational in our lives, they're hostile to. In other words they don't understand the need for this kind of a thing.

I have a theory of culture which is not documented, but I've noticed the following: if you go to the South Pacific islands where there was no pressure by the physical environment on the society, the psychological environment was made unbelievably hostile. They have the most complicated taboos, most complicated dangers you've ever seen in your life. And life is terrifying. There are magicians, and they can raise boils on you. Why? I have a belief that if the physical environment doesn't give you structure, then the psychological environment must replace it—that you have to have structure.

Let me ask the following question: there are two basic views of humanity, the Pelagian view and the Augustinian. The Pelagian view can be summarized, there are no bad children, only bad parents. If you fix the environment, the kid grows up naturally well. The New Class is Pelagian. The Augustinian view is the child is basically evil. How many of you are Augustinian? Have you ever noticed a baby? They're not known for tolerance, moderation.

Babies will destroy the universe if they're empowered. Probably the most intelligent, well-thought-through Augustinian we know of is Freud. Now Freud said three things in Vienna: 1, Civilization is repression; 2, You must socialize that child at any cost; 3, Having accepted the first two theses, how do you reduce the cost? Now, that's all that America heard, was point number three.

Let me close this with just one other example. I have a friend of mine, his name is Gordon Dewey. He's a grandson of John Dewey, and I mentioned to him about four or five years ago that his grandfather really caused eighty percent of the problem. He said he's tired of hearing that (he believes it too, by the way). But he made a point which I'd never really understood before. He said, "Look, my grandfather was raised in New England. Their character tends to freeze like the stones, the rocks. And the problem is, how do you loosen them up a little bit? How do you get a little joy, a little creativity, a little spontaneity, a little flexibility? How was he to know the rest of the country was slobs?"

JERRY BROWN: You say that the New Class is growing in Protestant Western society, which a hundred years ago, someone wrote, was the reason why we had an industrial revolution.

KAHN: I believe that's right.

BROWN: OK. So first you get the Industrial Revolution, then we create all this wealth. That generates this by-product called the New Class. The New Class is growing in strength. It seems to me that the curve you're plotting shows that the country politically or technologically collapses in ten or fifteen years, and some other more retarded country takes over because they don't have the burden of this New Class that is produced by all the technological progress.

KAHN: That may happen. I would say: even money it happens. But it's not the only scenario. It has happened in England, remember. England was the one that started all of this. England has always had very much a New Class atmosphere in the upper classes. And England's in serious trouble. If we were in the old

Amory Lovins

system, with wars and things like that, England I'm sure would be taken out.

It's hard to imagine that in the United States, we are just so rich. You can mismanage this country for decades and not get into serious trouble, and that's the problem, by the way. Because if you could see the effects of your mismanagement, you wouldn't do it. Municipalities can see it. Every municipality I know of has changed its attitudes because of New York. But there's no such phenomenon in the Federal Government.

We've made a distinction between what we call the Athenian, French, Chinese type culture, where you're going to be able to have a great deal of wealth and safety without any collapse, and what we call the Spartan, Roman, United States type culture, where wealth and safety seem to bring a kind of collapse.

BROWN: Yeah, but Athens collapsed.

KAHN: Athens was beaten, but it was very hard to beat Athens. The only people around who could beat the Athenians were the Spartans and Romans. Nobody else. If there were

Gov. Jerry Brown

no Spartans or Romans around it was safe to be an Athenian. That's one of the points, by the way. If there are Spartans and Romans around, it's not safe to be an Athenian.

BROWN: The Athenians beat themselves. They kept fighting with their neighbors.

KAHN: Until they tangled with Sparta they won most of their wars. Now that's a clue. On the way up these Spartan and Roman, United States, English cultures are really ferocious. But when they get there they have a tendency to collapse. Don't tangle with them on the way up, wait 'til they get there. Now, the Romans didn't actually do that, so it's kind of interesting. The Romans adopted about ten things in order to prevent themselves from collapsing. (The Spartans did collapse, needless to say.) First of all the Romans Athenized. You remember the Virgil poem, "We conquered thee and in turn were conquered by thee"? They selected from Athens those elements of the Athenian culture which enabled them to live with safety and wealth. Augustus, for example, had a conscious concept of creating morality. Remember, "He found Rome great and left it moral"? They were religiously square. It used to shock the Greeks, when they visited Rome, to find that it was a religious culture.

The United States is a religious culture. If you look at the square religions—Baptist, Church of Christ, Pentecostal, Orthodox Catholic, Orthodox Jewish, Mormon—they're all on the increase in the United States, did you know that? The only one that's been noticed by the newspapers is the Jesus Freaks. Why are they noticed? Because they're the children of the newspaper reporters. One of the reasons why I think the United States is basically in good shape is this increase in orthodox square religions. There's been an enormous decrease in the transcendental religions, the New Class religions.

VOICE: How long has this religion increase been going on?

KAHN: About a decade.

VOICE: Well, how do you tie that into Vietnam?

KAHN: You think of Vietnam as being immoral?

VOICE: Well, isn't true religion not dropping bombs on little brown people?

KAHN: That's your picture of the war, it wasn't theirs. Look, if there have been any people who've been able to kill with a great deal of ease, it's any religious movement at a high point in its career. They kill in wholesale amounts. They've never had any problem rationalizing it. You may have a picture of religious peace, but I don't have that picture at all. We think of messianic movements as the most dangerous things in the world, barring nothing. . . .

BROWN: Hello again. If anybody's getting hungry they told me we've got some food here. {*Adjourn to a vegetarian dinner in the Governor's study. Gray Davis and Elizabeth Coleman have joined the group. Kahn has nothing but a cup of coffee. The tape recorder keeps listening.*}

KAHN: . . . In the very long run I would make a guess that as food is manufactured, people will adapt to it. In the United States today two out of three people prefer oleomargarine at the same price as butter because they were raised on it. It takes about a generation or two to change food habits. Now, that will never be true, I'll bet you, in France, even 300 years from now.

Herman Kahn

LOVINS: I gather that in United States markets for all sort of commodities now people are tending to prefer real to synthetic things and good to poor quality.

KAHN: That's not the same thing. There's a general desire for improved quality everywhere in the United States—people are richer and want to live better. Again, in the New Class, higher quality is equated with something called "natural."

BROWN: Like we're eating now.

KAHN: Exactly.

BROWN: Well, the hot lunch program in schools works better with McDonald's hamburgers than it does with dietetic lunches prepared by professionals.

KAHN: McDonald's is an incredibly well-designed place. There's an article in *Public Interest* on just how intelligently they designed the thing. Now, McDonald's has become one of those symbols of the upper class versus the middle class—like the car versus the bike, or the Cadillac versus the Mercedes. McDonald's understands American taste very well. But more than that they understand how to run a restaurant. They keep the floors absolutely

spotless, you may have noticed. And everything is done very close to the people serving, so they never feel hectic, they never feel pressed. They actually throw away hamburgers which have been cold for a certain length of time, so everybody's impressed with their own quality control. They have a high-morale crew and you never get that harried character of a short order cook.

LOVINS: Somehow that doesn't square with accounts of some of my friends who have worked in McDonald's.

KAHN: I assume your friends who worked in McDonald's were New Class.

LOVINS: Do you believe there'll be any slowing down of what you call square value systems?

KAHN: There's no question there's been a big change. It's illustrated by the movie *Love Story*, which is the epitome of a square movie from a square book. It's a best-seller in every language. There's a nude scene. You couldn't have shown a nude scene in a square movie twenty years ago. They use four-letter words freely. She dies of cancer. You couldn't die of cancer in an American movie twenty years ago. They have intercourse before marriage, and neither gets punished.

LOVINS: I'm still missing the sense of real people with real motives in your picture of the middle class.

KAHN: I'm giving you a list of things which are terribly important to people. Now, none of them may be important to you, but that doesn't make them any less real or less important to the people concerned. Now, the upper-middle-class family would not prepare its children to accept with equanimity and fortitude the unfairness of life, like being crippled, say. Let me give you an example of this. One of our staff guys who is square—the guy's a pilot—has a very beautiful daughter, eighteen. She was in an accident in Spain, and she's permanently crippled now. She was a musician: she really had a nice career in front of her. Her mother went to the hospital, and the daughter said, "Why should this happen to me? Why should this happen to me?" Which is a question, you know. And the mother answered her,

Amory Lovins and Herman Kahn

"I never told you that life was fair." A very tactful remark. "You never heard that from your father, you never heard that from me, you never heard that from the preacher. It happened." And you know something, it's changed the girl's attitude. She's learning how to use her legs mechanically. Before that conversation she was thinking in terms of suicide. They teach their children that way. Things happen. Life is not fair. That's a terribly important value lesson.

LOVINS: My Ukrainian grandmother used to say, "Life is an onion. You peel it bit by bit, and sometimes cry."

KAHN: Yeah, exactly. Now, to a remarkable degree, the upper-middle-class kid is raised without any clue of that. It's never mentioned to him that life is unfair.

BRAND: In the other room, Governor, Herman was allowing as to how he doesn't consider you New Class.

BROWN: I don't think you know. I haven't said enough yet.

KAHN: I don't know, but you have a style of calling a spade a shovel, which is very much not New Class.

LOVINS: I thought they were called terrestrial improvement implements.

KAHN: That is New Class. Of all the societies that I know of, America is the least class-conscious, except the Chinese society.

BROWN: But you're saying there's this New Class.

KAHN: Yeah, which is getting its self-consciousness. In order to be a class you have to be self-conscious. The New Class was not a class in the early 60s, because they didn't think of themselves as a group. Now they think of themselves as a group—the Sierra Club, the World Council of Churches, the League of Women Voters, Common Cause, all these things—they are the enlightened Americans, the people who care.

LOVINS: Essentially, the people who don't agree with you.

KAHN: No, come on. Do you think I'm making up the whole phenomenon? I'm New Class myself, incidentally.

LOVINS: I think you're in a class by yourself.

KAHN: No, I'm neo-conservative. I tend to confuse the discussion a little bit by taking the neo-liberal part of the New Class and using them for the whole, which is not a bad thing, because they are the most prominent part of the New Class. The whole *Public Interest* crowd would be New Class but very much not neo-liberal. Sometimes my friends ask, what do I mean by neo-conservative? Well, I'm conservative, but you can't trust me.

What I don't like about the New Class is the way they push the squares around. They have a total contempt for the square religions, dogmatic religions. You notice how the reporters just couldn't cope with Carter being a twice-born Baptist? They just ignored it. They couldn't handle it.

Take the hunting issue. I used to do talks at Harvard. I would ask the kids, "How many of you have three guns at home?" About thirty percent of the class would raise their hands. And I asked the others, "Why do they have three guns?" No one knew—shoot blacks, protect against the government? I turned to the thirty percent and I said, "How many of you got your .22 at the age of twelve, plus or minus six months?" Every hand goes up. "How many got your shotgun at fourteen, plus or minus one year?" Ninety percent of the hands went up. "How many got a .30-caliber at sixteen, plus or minus a year?" Eighty percent of the hands go up. I'm trying to teach the other guys they don't know anything about their own country. You ask them, "What's going on?" They don't know.

You live in a hunting culture. The best way to understand a good deal of America is to look at it as a hunting culture. Take a place like the Hudson Institute. Thirty-five staff members: one hunter. Twenty-two subprofessionals: twenty-one hunters. The twenty-second has constant pressure on him to hunt. I checked also with twenty-two taxi drivers in town. All of them are hunters. Every school teacher who is local is a hunter, none of the imported school teachers. None of them. It's a two-class society in the United States. But hunting is the clue. The rich hunt, the upper middle class doesn't, and the middle class hunts, and everybody who is rural hunts.

If I had to ask myself, what's the single biggest problem in the United States, I would say, we tranquilize our children. The hunters don't. The key to the raising of a square American with the kind of character structure I want to talk about is the hunting culture. Let me give you an example. When my son was fifteen, my wife and I were having a big weekend, she wanted to call her mother to babysit for him. I said, "You can't babysit a fifteen-year-old boy. You just can't do it." And she said, "He'll burn the house down." I said, "You're absolutely right. But he must be given the opportunity." She won the argument, of course, and the grandmother came.

We happened to do a small study, not a study but just sort of a quick look, at this issue of when do you give children responsibility. In most cultures it's twelve, thirteen, fourteen. Henry the Fifth was his father's general at the age of fourteen, ran the War on Wales. He was actually a general. Alexander Hamilton was the master of a ship at sixteen, took a ship from New York to Cuba and back. Washington surveyed the western state of Virginia at seventeen, ran an attack against a French fort at nineteen. Roughly the age of responsible jobs ran around thirteen, fourteen, fifteen. And I happen to believe that if you defer maturity, you never catch up. My wife said, by the way, "But notice something, none of them was left alone at night." The grandmother comes.

Notice what happens to half of America. You're given a .22 at twelve. You can kill somebody with a .22. It's a dangerous weapon, right? And you could kill somebody with it. That kid is trained to use that .22 if he's in a rural area. Somebody, an older brother or a Black in the South, will give him nearly two years of training on how to make a camp, break a camp, use the gun—very low accident rate, nearly negligible. At fourteen he's given a shotgun. Now, you can kill several people with a shotgun. At sixteen he's given a .30 caliber. He's trained, you know, to be a man, with a man's responsibilities, and a man's capabilities for damage.

Do you know why the voting age is twenty-one in most countries? Because they thought you shouldn't vote until you'd been an adult for seven years. Voting was for the older, more responsible people. Twenty-one was not their idea of adulthood. You're an adult at fourteen, but that doesn't mean you have a right to vote in the councils of the nation! You know what is the nuttiest New Class project ever made? The American Civil Liberties Union decided about four years ago to liberate the last minority in America which is still enslaved, and this turns out to be children under eighteen, who basically have no rights. And they wanted to give the kids a lawyer. I explained that you can't run a family if the kid has a lawyer. It can't be done. No way. Well, it turns out you can in a New Class family because it has a more complicated family structure. You can't run a middle-class family if the kid's got a lawyer, let me assure you.

BROWN: You'd have to have three lawyers.

KAHN: I was asked by Justice Burger to give a talk to a meeting he had in Milwaukee that was supposed to be fifty years after Comte's lecture on the "Causes of Popular Dissatisfaction with the Law." So I read the document, and it reads very well today. It says the one thing that people can't stand is to treat the law as a game with rules. There are three kinds of model of legal process. One is a due process model—everything should proceed according to due process. There's a crime-control model. This is where you keep the criminals down. And then there's a kind of a justice model, how often do you convict the innocent and how often do you let the guilty go. A kind of efficiency model. It's obvious that any system has to balance all three problems—efficiency, crime control, and due process. I would argue that our system has sort of gone manic on the due process.

LOVINS: I think that instead of efficiency equity might be closer.

KAHN: Yes, equity's better, although with equity you might let the guilty free.

BROWN: I think the saying is, "It's better for 100 guilty to go free than the one innocent man be punished."

KAHN: I'm in the ten to one ratio.

BROWN: If there was a social compact that basically threads everybody together, then these rules would occupy a smaller part of the whole network by which people relate. Now, as this social compact appears to be breaking down a bit, then more and more rules are needed to glue everybody together.

KAHN: I think that's right.

BRAND: Kropotkin goes the other way. He says you get more rules, and then the social contract breaks down.

BROWN: But I think you need more rules as the informal and internalized rules become less effective.

KAHN: Part of it is a lack of understanding on how rules work. I don't know of any organization which can work by the rules and operate. The rules are simply not there for rigid compliance. They're only guidelines. And they also work in a funny way—if you violate the rule, you do it at your risk. It's a little bit like my daughter—"I simply am not going to approve of you fooling around with boys, but I'm going to be very unhappy if you don't." It has that kind of a tension in it. There's a lot of academic studies you'll see in which a guy goes around with a cop and he notices that the cop is violating the rules three or four times a day and he's startled. They never ask the question, could the cop do his job if he didn't violate the rules?

BROWN: So how do you project all this? If these rules are obviously changing . . .

KAHN: If you have a system which believes it's legitimate, which believes it's working well, you can get away with these kind of changes. But if you have a system that teaches the kids that it's illegitimate, then you have problems. How do you do that? First of all, the way you teach history. There are three ways to teach history. One is traditional—there were giants in those days, their like will never be seen again. (A rather good description; I accept it.) There's a second way to teach history—clash of interest groups. The farmer against the rancher, both against the railroad, the west against the east, the bankers against the farmers. You've got to teach it that way, because obviously you want to tell the kids that people have interests, and they affect their behavior. The third way is debunking. The way we used to teach debunking history was perfectly OK. We'd say that Washington had warts, Jefferson had a Black mistress, and it was kind of interesting. You know what American history is now? A total despoliation of man and environment. That's all that's taught. We wrecked the Indians, we wrecked the plains, we killed the buffalo. The exploitation of Indians, of women, of children, of Blacks . . .

My wife went down to two of the best high schools in New York City about three years ago and asked the kids to name two heroic acts in American history, and they couldn't do it. How do you teach American History without heroic acts? It's full of heroic acts. I would argue that any culture that doesn't teach you traditional history is in trouble.

One thing anthropologists did when they first started studying cultures was they saw that everything was relative. What they never noticed was that in every culture there were things that were not relative. Between countries everything's relative. In this country you can kill, in the other you can't. But every culture has, within the culture, absolutes.

BROWN: You talk about the problem of the relativity and what sounds to me like the decline of the old values. And yet, one of the bases for an absolute commitment is the sense that resources are limited—that the world is a place with some kind of global relationship where people are part of a species or wider community that was not sensed before by the nation-states or the ethnic groups. So some of the gaps in the relativity that's obviously part of modern technological society perhaps can be closed by this sense that there are limits. The limit is that you can wreck the place, you can blow it up, despoil it.

KAHN: I think it's stronger than that. My own guess is that in the long run the issue of protection of environment and ecology becomes a religious issue, much as you suggest, partly in order to perform the function you're talking about, partly just to protect the envi-

ronment and ecology. In other words, calculations alone are not reliable. Superego is always better in some sense than ego. I know more about dieting than anybody you ever met, but I don't diet. Eating is an ego issue; dieting is a superego issue. I believe, though all my religious friends tell me I am wrong, that nowhere in the Old Testament or the New Testament is there any ecological position except where Noah saves the asps because they're God's handiwork. Almost every other religion that I know about gives a value to nature in its own right. You have no right to destroy the tundra unles you have to do it. The tundra was made by God.

BRAND: Does Islam put any value on . . . ?

KAHN: Islam puts nothing. They are famous for wrecking areas. All the peoples of the Book.

BRAND: This sounds strange coming from you, Herman.

KAHN: Remember, I'm going for religion here for operational purposes, not because I had a revelation. If you have a revelation you don't argue whether it's efficient or not. If God said, "Do it," don't argue. But this is an operational issue, and I'll argue, before you make the stuff religious, you better know a lot more of what you want to rule and what you don't. I'll make another bet, that any viable religion of this sort is gonna have to have the concept that there are areas which are, so to speak, industrial parks: do your worst. Because the idea of protecting everything just isn't viable. . . .

BROWN: You made the point that you don't choose the future, you make it, and I suppose you meant you do things that then result in other things which you don't choose because you can't see them.

KAHN: You can choose decision points very often, but you don't know where they're going to go. Ecology uses this a lot, that you can never change one thing at a time. That's true whatever you talk about.

LOVINS: Ken Boulding's Law of Political Irony is that whatever you do to help people hurts them and vice versa.

BROWN: I don't know whether these kinds

of questions even interest you, but how much choice do you really think there is?

KAHN: I would ask the following question: "What kind of people do you get?" If you act as if there's free will and people are responsible for their acts, you get one kind of person. If you act as if people and everything is determined, and they're not responsible for their acts, you get a very different kind of a personality. And since there's no question in my mind what kind of people we want, we have to treat people as if they are responsible for their acts and hold them to it. And I don't care what the real world has to do with this, because even if it's a deterministic world you get a preferable kind of people by treating them as if they have free will.

BROWN: What if you ask, "Could Kennedy have kept out of Vietnam?"

KAHN: Without a question. He raised the number of advisors to 14,000 for the most trivial reasons. He passed around a memo saying, even though we're sending these 14,000 advisors, this does not commit us. We passed that memo around the institute and just laughed about it. You ever tried to pull 14,000 people out of a disintegrating country? You just can't do it. He literally didn't understand that putting in 14,000 advisors was a commitment much more solemn than a speech or a treaty. . . .

BROWN: What do you think is the significance of the political differences that are going on in society?

KAHN: If you think of the New Left, protest, hippie, drug culture, joy-love culture, greening of America, small is beautiful, all this, as attampts to reform American society, the big scene you're getting next is a Counter-Reformation, which started about '68–'69, but never had any leadership. Wallace tried to be that leader but just couldn't make it. Nixon was not the leader. It's the biggest movement going on in America today. It's partly a synthesis; it's not completely a Counter-Reformation.

BROWN: All Counter-Reformations are a synthesis.

KAHN: Exactly. So what else is new? And it's kind of interesting. For example, 2 out of 3 Americans like to identify themselves as conservatives today. But they're antibusiness. "Conservative" had the connotation all my life of being probusiness.

BRAND: What do they mean by conservative?

KAHN: Return to traditional values.

BRAND: Such as?

KAHN: Respect for your father. Virginity, believe it or not. I don't know how much they're being hypocritical, by the way. But they want first of all good behavior in public places. They mean by good behavior: they don't want to see drugs or massage parlors on the main street. They don't mind if it's around the corner, you understand. For example, let's assume you have a small town, and the chief of police confiscates a pornographic film. I will guarantee that he'll show it that Friday night at the corner firehouse, and every male adult will be there watching. I said adult now, nobody under sixteen. And I'll make a bet that sometime during the next week the son of the chief of police steals the film and shows it to the sixteen-year-olds. And his father knows it.

There's no objection to pornography in the United States; there's an extraordinary objection to public pornography. People think of America as a Puritan country, but it's not. I used to use the following as an example, but the recent revelations have made it less useful. I would ask an audience, "How many of you knew (I never said thought), knew that Jack Kennedy was probably the biggest womanizer of any American president that we know about?" And about half of the audience would raise their hands. The other half would look and their jaws would drop—"What are you talking about?" And I said, "This was widely advertised, widely reported on, and every American who wanted to know about it knew about it. But those who didn't want to know about it, it wasn't forced on them." You see, if you chose not to know about it, you could live in ignorance. That was terribly important in the system.

BROWN: What do you think of the movement to push out into the public mind so much of the inconsistency and personal behavior that was formerly kept private?

KAHN: I think it's just sick. It's not a revival of morality. The people who are pushing it are on the whole New Class more than any other group, and on the whole it's their morality. Take the issue of graft. At Hudson we've always made the distinction between graft and corruption. Graft is a legitimate fee in certain cultures which you pay to an official for doing what he's supposed to do. In those cultures where they have this institution they always have a word for it—compteur, dash, baksheesh—and generally the word means, if you go back to the language itself, tip.

Corruption is excessive fee. The guy's getting more than he's entitled to, or he's doing something against public policy. Now we don't understand the distinction in the United States. What happens? Take Vietnam. Before we entered Vietnam, Vietnam was probably about the most honest country, I would guess, in that entire area. If you give a Vietnamese peasant ninety-five piasters and ask for a receipt for 100, he'll give it to you. You've got a legal right to it, as far as he's concerned. You give him 90 piasters and ask for a receipt for 100, he won't give it to you. They're very tough people. I mean, you're entitled to 5, you're not entitled to 10, that's his money. So if you audit, you keep it down to graft. We didn't understand the distinction. We said these assholes are just going to cheat us anyway. That's just not true. RMK was a big construction outfit with Vietnamese paymasters. They audited and RMK had no trouble with corruption. That was the only place in the Vietnamese theater that was audited. Every place else we poured in the billions of dollars without audit. We corrupted a society just by our own dumbness. I went down to the Embassy once when they were trying to put in a tax system in Vietnam. We have objective taxing in the United States, you know, where you report your own income. I said, "There's not a Latin country in the world that has an objective tax system—France doesn't have it, Italy doesn't have it, Spain doesn't have it, Portugal doesn't have it, Brazil doesn't have it."

LOVINS: It doesn't work in England either.

KAHN: It used to work in England. Inflation killed it. England is our example of the place that was corrupted by inflation. . . . The biggest problem in the United States is the enormous alienation which the average voter and citizen feels towards the system. I'm sure you've seen the poll data. If you asked in '66, "How do you feel about the leadership of big business, about the leadership of Congress, about the leadership in the White House, about the leadership in your church," about something like half to two-thirds would vote, "Approve very highly." That number is like ten to twenty percent today. It's gone down pretty steadily in the ten-year period. The attitude is a little funny when you look closer at it. "We think you have to have big business, but we don't like big businessmen. We like a Congressional system of government, but we don't think the current Congress is doing very well. We want to have a President . . . "

LOVINS: Aren't you saying there's a general loss of legitimacy?

KAHN: That's the next step, when you start challenging institutions. There's a general acceptance of institutions, but not of the men who run them. That's the first step towards illegitimacy.

LOVINS: I'm not sure about that at all. I think, for example, that the legitimacy of the industrial ethic is up for review right now.

KAHN: That's almost completely New Class now. There was a short period of time at the end of the Vietnamese war when the protest and reformation drew in a lot of people. You know what drew them in, by the way? The two things which forced the Americans to active rejection of the Vietnam War were the Calley case . . . (where he was actually wrong, in my judgment. It's one of the few cases where I disagree with the average American, who thought Calley was mistreated, which is absolutely insane) . . . and the drugs. You just can't draft people and send them to a drug environment. That's not tolerable.

But as for the general disapproval of the way things are being run, I'll make a bet that two or three years from now you'll find those polls reversed. I believe that that negative vote represents a genuinely reasonable scoring of performance. It is healthy. In other words, they looked at business, and business performed badly. The government officials performed badly and they recognized it.

ELIZABETH COLEMAN: Why is it going to turn around in three years?

KAHN: Because I don't think you'll have the same bad performance. I think '65 to '75 was a very special period in United States history—very special—and any attempt to extrapolate that decade into the future is going to be very misleading.

LOVINS: Why do you think that?

KAHN: First and foremost, you had this enormous surge to control of a group which had never before had control of anything. You remember the term "book learning" we used to use? Now that term can't be used in America any more.

BROWN: There are more people who never run anything because more people spend more of their time going to school. Apprentices learn their job in a junior college, not so much on the job anymore.

KAHN: And it doesn't work. I recently talked to Sid Warburg of the Rockefeller Foundation, and he said, "Take agriculture schools today. When I went to agriculture school, two-thirds of the faculty had been born and raised on highly productive farms, and they knew what they were talking about. It's just not true today in the United States, and it's completely untrue in foreign countries. Both sides just read books." So what happens, they take 100 of the top experts, put them through the training course at Erie, the rice farm, and none of them are able to get more than like thirty percent on the exam. Any farmer would have got a hundred percent on the exam.

BROWN: You're saying that the skills that are being imparted are not relevant to the task.

KAHN: Yeah. Let me just give you a quick example of this, how both Schlesinger and Sorensen don't understand how the presidency operates. You remember these are the experts, the historian and the President's assistant?

BROWN: They wrote the two big books.

KAHN: They wrote the two big books. And both books have the following scene. They're talking about the Cuban invasion, Bay of Pigs problem. The National Security Council sits around a center table. In this case you also had Senator Fulbright there. Normally he wouldn't be there, of course. There are five people sitting at the table. Then there's a lot of people sitting in the back, including General Twining, the Chief of Staff. President Kennedy looked around and said, "Are we agreed?" And nobody raised a voice, so he said they were agreed, and Sorensen said they were agreed.

They hadn't agreed at all. Nate Twining was waiting to be asked, "Nate, how do you feel about this?" and he would have told him how he felt about it. He had a whole dossier there. But he's not about to interrupt his boss, particularly with Senator Fulbright there. He's had a lifetime of training. They had no sense that those guys in the back of the room are not part of that meeting, and will not raise issues unless they're asked. Later on, Nate said, "I never agreed to that plan." Sorensen and Schlesinger said, "He was there in the room when the decision was made." They don't understand! And my jaw drops.

LOVINS: The whole English civil service is a classic case of educated incapacity in a sense. In a deeper sense it isn't. People are promoted there by their ability to write precise minutes and witty essays. It's a verbal culture that runs on paper.

KAHN: They all write incredibly well. It's indecent.

LOVINS: The result is that we have a civil service that is almost entirely innumerate. They can write white papers entirely out of their heads, but they wouldn't recognize a rate and magnitude problem if it came up and bit them. I then went across the channel to France, which is run by very clever *polytechniciens*, and I rapidly concluded, if you want a mistaken policy to be executed with great efficiency, get the French to do it. I then looked back again on my side of the channel and said, "Gee, maybe we're really better off." But being competent with numbers selects against you in

England. You're considered too clever. Clever in a derogatory sense.

KAHN: Too clever by half, is the British phrase. Whenever I hear that phrase I want to hit that guy.

LOVINS: It's said to the guy who in a sense breaks the feudal code by working with his hands. My first day in Merton as a Fellow of the College I had just moved into my room and I couldn't open one of the cupboards because the handle had broken off, so I was rigging a piece of parachute cord for it as a handle, and one of the college servants passed by and saw me doing this and was horrified. He said, "Oh, sir, you mustn't do that." And being American and naive I had to have it explained why I mustn't do that. It was because college servants might see me doing it, and I would lose face, and so would they, and it would all be very awkward.

KAHN: There are only three countries in the world where an engineer will pick up a shovel—Canada, the United States, and China. In England the engineer is a serf. His status is so low it's unbelievable. Hence, where the research is good, the application is worthless. They have no vote, no influence, you know what I mean? They're treated as servants.

LOVINS: Whereas on the Continent they have high status. It's a title—Engineer such-and-such. It's the old division of the theoretical and the manual again.

KAHN: I think it's just aristocrats and servants. The engineers are lower-class people. They're trade.

LOVINS: Like surgeons in England.

KAHN: That's one of the reasons they make really dumb decisions all the time. They just don't ask the guy who knows what's going on. He's not invited to that meeting. Now they have a basically correct position—the expert should be on tap, not on top. That I agree with. I think Americans make the opposite mistake of putting engineering too high. We give them too much status.

LOVINS: I think there's very little understanding in our own scientific and engineering community of the limited role of that kind of expertise in public policy.

KAHN: But if I have to make one mistake or the other, I prefer giving engineering too much status.

LOVINS: I wouldn't, I think it's very dangerous.

KAHN: I agree. Both mistakes are dangerous, and the question is which one do you want to make?

LOVINS: I'd much rather subordinate "we the experts" to "we the people."

KAHN: We the people, yes, but not we the aristocratic, very intellectual, very witty, very well-writing people. You see, in the old days they did things.

LOVINS: I'm a Jeffersonian.

KAHN: Remember, these kids used to be raised to be able to run things at age twelve, the ones who went through the British school system. They broke with their family at the age of seven. They had the very tough public school system—cold showers, beatings, all that nonsense. I once made a speech in England where I said this system is great, you get ninety percent men and ten percent homosexuals. And a guy there said, "You've got the figures right, but reversed, Mr. Kahn." By the way, in any tough society which raises the kids toughly this way, you always have homosexuality as an outlet for the kid who just can't handle it. Tolerated. The kids were trained to lead. I don't think that's true any more.

BROWN: Certainly in this country there are a lot more people waiting a lot longer to run things. They're spending more time in college.

KAHN: They never have responsibility. We've created this adolescent period between boyhood and manhood, which actually is an American invention. The whole concept is now worldwide, but we were the first. The adolescent is peculiar—he hasn't got responsibility, but he's got rights. He hasn't got duties but he's got privileges. He hasn't got a job, but he's got aspirations. If you wanted to corrupt somebody, you couldn't do it any better. Access to money, access to girls, but no marriage and no child. It's all privileges, rights, prerequisites—no commitments. You used to have a commitment: you've got to get through college, and you've got to do well. That's not true anymore. We're very forgiving. If you wanted to debauch society, that's how you'd go about it.

BRAND: Once you're on that path, how do you get off that path?

KAHN: Well, the kids themselves know it. They go for Outward Bound and this sort of thing. The Englishman went for the grand tour, when it was dangerous. He went through the Balkans. He went through survival training. Incidentally, one of the tricks here which every culture which has tried to adapt to these things has picked up is dangerous sports. Skiing is terribly safe, unless you make a mistake, and you break a leg. Skin diving at 500 feet is terribly safe, unless you make a mistake. These are unforgiving sports.

LOVINS: The extraordinary popularity of rock climbing.

KAHN: Rock climbing, this kind of thing. Perfectly safe if you don't make a mistake. But by God you're in touch with reality. There's no relative reality, it's absolute. The guy who thinks it's relative breaks his neck, and we settle that one.

BROWN: Don't you think there's less of these unforgiving situations that Americans are put through?

KAHN: Take Eric, my son. He does rock climbing, mountain climbing, skin diving, but I don't understand lethal fun. I like skin diving: ten feet. I don't want to depend on my watch for my ascent. I just can't risk my life for fun. I've done all kinds of incredibly dangerous things, but always for the job. It's always been my duty, as I saw it.

BRAND: What sorts of things?

KAHN: I've gone all over Vietnam, for example, walked through VC villages talking to people, I've gone through very rough terrain where I don't particularly like to go—the mountains in Africa. . . .

BROWN: Do you think the risk level in this country is going down, such that it's affecting our character?

KAHN: Oh, absolutely. If you want to raise a leader, it's got to be a little bit rough during his life. He's going to have disappointments, he's going to have tragedies, so on. Like the English public school system. Remember Wellington's remark, "Waterloo was won on the playing fields of Eton." It's a perfectly correct statement. Parents today would never be willing to send their kids to that kind of a system.

BRAND: An enormous amount of the counter-culture, in that weird period of '65 to '75, was the kids finding their own risks.

KAHN: If you don't have the work ethic, you need something to replace it. There's a dozen things we can use to replace it. One thing is the tradition of the gentleman. The gentleman is a man with many many skills, in which he has a very high level of capability, none of which are useful. They're done because they're there. Now, as soon as you tell me that they're not useful, my interest goes to zero. I'm not a gentleman. I'll take risks as part of a job, and that disciplines me.

BROWN: Today risk appears to be less tolerable because of our effort to spread well-being to as many people as possible.

KAHN: If human life is the most important value, you're not going to risk it just to improve the guy's performance later. Now I would argue, you cannot raise a child well if you protect them from all potential accidents.

BROWN: This is the idea that no one should fail?

KAHN: That's the final extreme. That's the end when you get to that. You're in trouble long before you get to that point.

BROWN: Is this related at all to this theory of equality of outcomes?

KAHN: It's more related to a sense that injustice is not tolerable. There has to be a sense of justice in the sense of legitimacy, but not in a sense that everybody gets what he has coming to him, that everybody has a right to an equal outcome.

BROWN: So among many people the inequalities that obviously exist for a variety of reasons are no longer legitimate.

KAHN: That's basically correct.

BROWN: The problem is that if you say, "It is correct," then you countenance perhaps systematic exclusion from the system, or an insensitivity that compassionate wise people ought to try to alleviate.

KAHN: You have to start with a basic assumption that every system has its injustice, its inequities, its tragedies. Every system. So the issue is not are you going to eliminate injustice, inequity, tragedy, but where are you going to place it? To put it in its worst form, who do you want to be in the bottom twenty percent? Obviously you don't want to put anybody there, right?

BROWN: Yeah, but in our society certain people have a higher potentiality for being in the bottom twenty percent, so people feel that that systematic process should be altered.

KAHN: Not everybody feels that way. This is a New Class idea. It's a question of guilt. You remember those New Class religions I mentioned earlier? They have one common characteristic. They rely heavily on guilt to keep people in order. I have a friend of mine, a Polish banker. He went to see LeRoi Jones' play which gave a very graphic picture of the suffering of the Blacks. At the end of the play, my friend went up to LeRoi and said, "What can we do to atone?" I said, "Sit down, you weren't here, you were in Poland." He couldn't understand it. He felt personally guilty. Now, I'll argue that one of the sickest characteristics of our society is the inability of the New Class elite to control their feelings of guilt.

BROWN: They don't go to confession every day.

KAHN: That's exactly right.

BROWN: Three Our Fathers, three Hail Marys.

KAHN: Then it's finished. Now you can go out and sin again.

BROWN: No. Go out and sin no more, but if you do, come back on Saturday.

KAHN: Crime is committed mostly by young people. It's committed mostly by uprooted people. It's committed by people who have lost their churches. This describes the southern migrator to the north.

GRAY DAVIS: I'd like to go back to this business of equality of opportunity versus equality of result. When I grew up there was this notion of contest, and what we were worried about was that everyone was at the same starting point.

BROWN: And the same rules.

KAHN: The key issue is, do you define the same starting point in terms of a series of objective rules. Some guys can run 100 yards in 10 seconds, some may run in 20 seconds. They're not starting with the same physical equipment. They're only running the same track.

DAVIS: The only inequality that we brooked was inequality of ability.

KAHN: That's correct, but ability came out of the instructional system, too, to some degree. In our society a Scotch Presbyterian does best in terms of upward mobility, jobs, and so on. Why? Enormous interest in education. The same with Chinese, Japanese, and Jewish. OK. You didn't choose your parents, you didn't choose this educational orientation, you were born into it. If you come from one of these families, you can do well in America because you can do well in college. Now, take the Black in New York City. Most Black parents want their kids to learn good working habits, but they have an idea that teaching the good work habits should be done by the school. The school won't teach work habits in New York, for a number of reasons. In the rest of the culture people understand that work habits are taught by the family. It's just not fair. The fact that it's not fair is a heavy burden for the upper-middle-class elites.

BROWN: Because they have more information about it.

KAHN: Naw, the information was always there. I think the reason is that they have nothing else to feel guilty about.

BROWN: You mean, as the extended family breaks down and your immediate responsibilities diminish, your more abstract responsibilities increase.

KAHN: Take a kid raised in suburbia. He sees no tragedy. Upper-class suburbia hides tragedy. If you have a sickness in the family you don't talk about it. He sees a tremendously nurturing system that cares about him, and it really tries to do things for him. He's spoiled. We're not giving the kids any sense that there's nothing wrong with having to wait three years for something, or five years. There's nothing wrong with never getting it. You're not supposed to get everything that's reasonable.

BROWN: Then, how does the parent who has the means, with all the surplus income floating around, where does he or she get the argument that a child really can't have something. You have to have a principle.

KAHN: There is a principle. Half the time you explain to the kid why you're doing it, because you're a democratic family. And half the time, it's " 'Cause I said so." Because you also want to teach the kid respect for authority.

BROWN: You don't hear that one too much anymore.

KAHN: In my family you hear it.

LOVINS: Herman, what in your future makes people happy? That's what I still don't quite understand. Why will they try to do all this?

KAHN: Because in fact they understand happiness. That is, I don't know any culture in the world which ever taught, despite the Declaration of Independence, that you got happiness by the pursuit of happiness. No culture has ever taught that before. This is the first, and boy it's a nutty idea.

LOVINS: But how do you do it?

KAHN: You get happiness as a by-product of other activities that you should be doing—being a good father, being a worker, being a good member of the aristocracy—that is, doing the things your family and class and nation require of you, and doing them well.

BROWN: In other words "human potential" wasn't the goal. Has that ever cropped up in any literature 100 years ago? I guess the Greeks talked about it.

KAHN: Not the way we talk about it. You know, they talk about a very disciplined . . .

BROWN: How about the Stoics? They were telling you how to be happy.

KAHN: Stoics aren't human-potential, at all. They're very interesting. The Stoics in Greek and Roman culture had a kind of notion that, "We keep the system running, we don't care how other people act, we keep it running." They're really uncritical people. Their basic model was not the soldier doing his duty, but the actor in a play. Whether the actor comes off well or badly doesn't depend on the actor's

efforts—that's the author's privilege. The author writes the lines. But at least you can go through the lines as well as you can. They were democrats; they ran an empire. They were anti-militaristic; they ran an army. They believed in equality of man and ran a slave system. And they *ran* the place. I don't think there's been a period of history where people had better governors except maybe some of the Chinese periods.

BROWN: They had a great sense of nature. Nature in the sense there were certain rules, natural laws.

KAHN: Natural laws were very important to them. There's a right and a wrong way, and we see to it that the system is run the right way. They weren't that small. They must have been twenty percent of the population, and they knew each other.

BRAND: Was there a school for Stoics? How did you become a Stoic, get born one?

KAHN: You got born one; it ran in families. We don't care how other people act, our family . . .

BROWN: Christians were very much influenced by them.

KAHN: They were very influential. I stylize myself as a Stoic. My wife says, "You can't be a 300-pound Stoic," so I'm a Neo-Stoic.

LOVINS: Where in your taxonomy of values are such traditional values as, say, thrift and craftsmanship?

KAHN: They're not particularly American values, anymore. They were left back about fifty-odd years ago. A lot of people still have them, but they're not.

LOVINS: I think they're enjoying a renaissance.

KAHN: No, they're coming back in the upper middle class, who don't need thrift. Thrift is a game now, not a serious activity. They go to an enormous effort to save aluminum and tin cans, things like that. It's symbolic. They'll buy a $3,000 tape recorder but use a bike. It's not thrift as I would use the term.

LOVINS: Craftsmanship?

KAHN: Craftsmanship is a great virtue but Americans don't have it. It used to bother the Germans that we had a rifle with stamped parts. The Germans said, "You let a machine do it? A rifle is something that's so important to you." We stamped it. Whenever there was a clash between craftsmanship and efficiency, craftsmanship lost.

LOVINS: Neighborliness?

KAHN: The poor are still neighborly. If somebody's evicted in a poor community, the whole block will help them out. That's much less true in the middle class now.

BROWN: How do you explain inflation? Doesn't your program require us to solve inflation?

KAHN: Either solve it or correct for it.

LOVINS: Essentially to define it away by indexing it. You can't direct it without knowing what causes it. I don't think any economist in the world can claim to understand inflation in industrial economies. Stagflation isn't supposed to exist.

KAHN: That's not true. It was predicted by Friedman and other economists.

LOVINS: If they're so damn smart, why do we still have it?

KAHN: Because they weren't listened to, among other things.

BROWN: How do we get rid of it in this country? Give me a three-point plan. Without raising unemployment.

KAHN: Two years ago people like myself were going around saying, "You'll probably have about five percent inflation, about six percent growth. We got that, by the way, from the House Economic Advisor's report. A government document, it cost $3.50. It predicts events almost perfectly. When that report came out, people laughed at it hilariously.

LOVINS: Prediction isn't the same as understanding.

KAHN: That's quite right. You have two kinds of prediction problems. One is to predict the effects of current measures. The other is to understand what happened originally. Now, what happened originally was reasonably complicated. The main point about inflation I'll argue, and we understand it perfectly well, is first and foremost it is a monetary phenomenon. If you don't create more money, you don't get inflation. Now, that prescription is almost worthless, because if you don't create more money, you'll have a big deflation, recession,

unemployment, bankruptcies, and all the unpleasant things that come with that. So you have to ask yourself two questions. Why do you feel it's impossible to print more money? And second, can you control it?

BROWN: People want things done. We've got people in mental hospitals that need care. We have child care because women want to work. Why do they want to work? Because they need this $20,000 you're talking about, or they don't want to live with their husbands. We got to have new standards of safety, health, roads, energy investment because of these other things you talk about, so you got to do it. If you do it, you got to raise the taxes. If you raise the taxes, you lower the consumption, and the television tells you you got to buy more. So you print money or you raise it. But there's no big mandate to raise taxes. There are very few people who are saying, "Sock it to us."

KAHN: If you say that the government and the people are irresponsible, and that's why we have inflation, I'll agree. And I think they'll learn by experience, as the Germans did, and have the lowest inflation around. One of the problems in the last recession is we didn't learn enough from it. It was not a painful experience. Almost nobody went bankrupt, liquidity was not dried up. People said all the time it was the worst since 1929. That's accurate. That's like saying a little fire in San Francisco is the worst since the great fire in 1906. It's just not comparable. You know, one of the things which the founding fathers understood very well was that democracy is one of the hardest forms of government to operate, because it tends to get irresponsible.

LOVINS: Jefferson says somewhere that the system that he and his colleagues set up will work fine in an essentially rural country. "But," he said, "if we all crowd into large cities as in Europe, we will become as corrupt as they."

KAHN: I think he's about half right. Maybe even more than half. Take New York City. You cannot find a single county board of supervisors which for twelve years pays short-term expenses with long-term debts. You can't find one. Really, I've looked it up. For twelve years

New York City moved next year's income into this year and moved this year's expenses into next year. They did it openly and nobody kicked. That bright city.

LOVINS: Governor, you're saying those actions were strongly motivated?

BROWN: I'm not saying anything, because I like to ask questions. But I'm wondering whether or not there are certain things going on in society that are driven by forces that aren't just malice. There are more people living longer, who are not working, who need more care, technology, and attention. And there are certain kinds of poor people and disabled people who are more visible because of our social arrangements and due to the principles that are written down somewhere 200 years ago. When those principles are applied to these new situations, they cost a lot more money. And a lot of these folks don't have it in their pockets. So you have to come up with all these devices to give it to them. Free education, free transportation, food stamps, unlimited jury trials and appeals five levels up, habeas corpus, three courts . . . that's all coming from forces that I don't know can be slowed. Somebody might argue that it shouldn't be slowed.

KAHN: Let's take three rich men. One of them has twenty luxuries and can afford them, no problem. The second has forty luxuries, and he just breaks even, has trouble. The other one has eighty luxuries and can't afford them and goes bankrupt. The guy who's got twenty luxuries is going to make it, and the guy who's got eighty is going to go bankrupt. It's a question of degree. Now let me give you a second example, which is really to the point. I have a theory I call the poverty of affluence. Lots of people come to the government and say, "We want this, and this, and this"—all the things you were talking about. If there's no money, you just say no. Everybody understands it, there's no problem. This is what the municipalities have learned since New York. If you haven't got the money, and you can't borrow it, you can't spend it. An incredible concept.

The basic problem is the following one. You're going from a situation where you can

tell people, "We haven't got the money, forget it," to a situation where you tell them, "We've got the money for everything you've always wanted, only we can't do it all this year." And the people get angry. They'll accept the statement, "No to everybody." They will not accept, "Wait in line."

BROWN: That's interesting. The trouble is that you have a group in here which is very sensitive to many of these problems . . .

KAHN: And they feel guilty if they spend it on A and not on B. They can't make choices of this sort. They can't give it to the Blacks because the Chicanos want it also. They can't give it to the Chicanos if the insane asylums need it. Their only way of answering this issue is to say "Everybody."

BROWN: We've never had to make choices like this before. It was all grow, expand. A lot of these constituencies were not noticed, or were not represented. There was not this alliance between many of the new college graduates—Outreach, the public advocates, that whole group which has allied itself with many of the ills that haven't been corrected.

KAHN: Now we have the money and we've got to correct them, but we can't do it all simultaneously. People have got to get in line.

BROWN: So you want patience and restraint.

KAHN: That is correct.

BROWN: In a democracy with high mobility and high information flow.

KAHN: You've always had it. The United States in this case is one of the most responsible groups of people in the world. Look at the labor unions. Remember the business that the President should jawbone them? If Ford had made a series of speeches one after the other that labor shouldn't get high raises because we can't afford it, you know what would happen? Every labor union leader would be forced to get as much as he can. He has to. In fact American labor unions took almost no raises during this two-year period. They restrained themselves.

BROWN: What are you saying, jawboning creates higher demands?

KAHN: Absolutely. He has no right to sacrifice his union's needs because the President singled him out.

BROWN: So what does the President do in this case?

KAHN: Shut up, which he did, and it worked well—depend on the basic integrity of these guys, and their basic good sense. By the way, Ford knew what he was doing. I had a conversation with him on that issue. He understood it. "If I jawbone, these guys can't do it. If I leave them alone, they'll do it." On a lot of these issues, there's nothing that works as well as frankness. One of the things that's impressed me about you in these issues, is you have a tendency to say, "I'm sorry, we can do one or two, we can't do five; decide which two you want." That kind of a speech works. But you have to be able to do that, choose between the claimants.

BROWN: That's never been made a very explicit process. Has there ever been a speech made on the floor of Congress that it is now important to reduce the purchasing power of the working people of this country so that we can increase the well-being of the social security recipient, so we can transfer from one generation to another certain amounts of wealth? Has anyone ever done that?

KAHN: We've done something even better than that, but we've done that too. We changed the budget process of Congress so that if you increase A you've got to decrease B. For the first time, and it's working. I think that the first person who gets up and makes the following speech, strongly, will look very good. "If anybody gets increases greater than the average increase in productivity in the country, then he's got a higher share of the GNP and somebody gets a lower share." That's the number-one principle.

BROWN: The number-one principle of my budgeting is for each program increase there must be a corresponding program decrease. But by what principle do you make these decisions? You have to allocate the goods in the public household. Before it used to be the market, and everyone took it with good grace. The market can cause bankruptcy, but government can't. You say life isn't fair, but politicians have to be.

HERMAN KAHN'S "NEW CLASS" IS A LABEL OF CONVENIENCE

When I first read the "New Class" talk by Herman Kahn in the Spring '77 CQ, I was disturbed by Kahn's concept of the New Class but I was unable to put my finger on exactly *why*. In the month since, I've continued to think about Kahn's presentation and ask myself why the New Class concept of which Kahn spoke was so familiar somehow and yet so skewed.

Today while reviewing Kahn's definition of this supposedly new class it suddenly hit me. The "New Class . . . earn their living by the use of academic skills, language skills, esthetic skills, analytical skills," says Kahn. In other words, Kahn is defining "Intellectuals."

Going through the article I substituted the word "Intellectuals" for "New Class" at each opportunity. Almost without exception this substitution worked, but with the curious result that suddenly Kahn's amusing and clever insights seemed somehow banal and foolish.

Even granting that the New Class in its broadest sense includes a full variety of mental workers (not just, strictly speaking, intellectuals), we are still left with the question of "why a new label for those who work with their minds?" Kahn referred back to Milovan Djilas as the originator of the category if not of Kahn's precise use of it. Clearly Kahn's New Class concept shares origins with the New Left-popularized mid-60s theory of the "New Working Class" which attempted to understand the growing role of those with technical, clerical and professional jobs in maintaining American capitalism. But while that theory was only partially successful in giving students a perspective on their future post-graduate roles, it was at least a straightforward attempt to seek a better understanding of modern Capitalist class stratification.

Kahn's intent is initially more mysterious and yet becomes clearer if for "New Class" we substitute "Pointy-headed intellectuals who can't even park their bicycles straight," or perhaps, "Effete snobs." In his long-winded and circular way Kahn is trying to isolate academics, intellectuals, professionals, etc., by defining them as a class unto themselves, while blurring other American class distinctions. He employs other sleight-of-hand to (in his own words) "confuse the discussion a little bit by taking the neo-liberal part of the New Class and using them for the whole . . ."

What is this but self-indulgent nonsense . . . and pernicious nonsense at that? I'll gladly grant that new perspectives can sometimes result from relabeling a group or phenomenon and that mental workers can benefit from learning how their shared assumptions and experiences set them apart from others. However, the upshot of Kahn's relabeling seems largely to be that the portion of the so-called New Class which most consciously services Corporate/Governmental policies is reluctantly labeled New Class and then swept under the rug, while the "50%" which Kahn calls "neo-liberal" are put on the line-up and given the third degree. Looked at in a different way, Kahn would be paid little heed if he ranted against "Damned leftist intellectuals," so he invents a new label encompassing all intellectuals, excuses the half who are on the Right, and proceeds to deliver his critique.

This would be merely silly if it were an isolated sermon, but it appears that this touting of the "New Class" analysis has only just begun and what is now a term used by a few neo-conservatives may be picked up at large and promulgated in all its ambiguity and imprecision.

Kahn is delighted to define American politics in "a simplified fashion: a war of the New Class versus the middle class. New Class versus working class. When you look at politics that way, everything falls into place." At least everything falls into the place which Kahn prefers. Later in his talk Kahn coyly calls America a "two-class society." The hunters (the real Americans) and the non-hunters (New Class). No matter that he lumps the upper class and the middle class together (hunters) in contrast to the upper middle class (non-hunters); no matter that earlier he called the New Class "very hostile . . . especially to the upper mid-

dle class." Let the contradictions and mushy dual-definitions pile up . . . pay them no heed as long as we see things as the New Class against everyone else.

Five years ago we were treated to the coining of the "Silent Majority," a convenient term which made a virtue out of silence and allowed an opportunist to speak for the mute. Now we're presented with the "New Class," a malleable term which scolds the engaged and the vocal.

I assume that in his and Bruce-Briggs' forthcoming book on the New Class many of the inconsistencies present in his CQ talk will have been dealt with. Clearly his session with the Governor and staff was not meant to be gone over with a fine-toothed comb.

But from all appearances the very heart and intent of his New Class conceptualizing involves a calculated misrepresentation of reality. According to Kahn, "At the moment I don't think we have any serious big problems." None, it would seem, except those created by the New Class.

I've great respect for Kahn's cleverness, charm and high-powered intellect, and in raising these objections I feel somewhat like a nightlight challenging a laser. But too much of his talk hit me as soft-sell demagoguery to let it go by without a squawk.

Jay Kinney
San Francisco
[Summer 1977]

THEORY AND PRACTICE

A friend's father argued insistently that nothing could be folded in half more than eight times. It was "theoretically impossible" and had been proven so again and again down through the ages. At home, it took me less time than we spent arguing about it to fold fifty feet of recording tape nine times.

I like the way high-powered thinkers can be gently brought back down to earth.

M.A.W.D. Hoffman
Sturbridge, Massachusetts
[Winter 1979]

MALCOLM WELLS

Yellow Diamonds

Architect Malcolm Wells is a Wry
Fellow. You get the feeling, reading
his book about underground architecture (*Underground Designs*, 1977,
self-published; $6 postpaid from Box
1149, Brewster, MA 02631) that he
went to all that trouble just so he
could be contrary—by, for instance,
constructing a quiet, sylvan building
next to a freeway. Beginning in
1976, Mac was the voice (in CQ, at
least) of ecological responsibility for
architects—plus a prolific postcard-
writer to us lucky recipients in the
CQ office. This batch of drawings is
reprinted from the Winter 1977 and
Spring 1978 issues. When he sent
them, he wrote that he was worried
that European-style traffic signs are
replacing "our big funny lovable yellow diamonds full of crazy imagery.
What follows is a tribute to the great
lemon-colored American gems."

Art Kleiner

Earl Butz versus Wendell Berry

When people grope for a way to describe Wendell Berry they frequently wind up invoking Abraham Lincoln—tall, countrified, wise, laconic (Berry: "I stand for what I stand on."), irrepressibly humorous, grave—sometimes wrathful—with moral concern, and blessed with God's own talent with words. This lifelong citizen of Port Royal, Kentucky, is restoring a piece of riverside farmland by nurturing it while it nurtures his family. Among his crops are poetry (*Farming: A Handbook*, 1970; *The Country of Marriage*, 1973), essays (*The Long-Legged House*, 1969; *The Gift of Good Land*, 1981; *Standing by Words*, 1984), and novels (*A Place on Earth*, 1967; *The Memory of Old Jack*, 1973). CQ has printed as much of his stuff as we could. He can debate like Lincoln too. Wanna see my scars?

Steward Brand

From the original introduction (Spring 1978):
Wendell Berry started this argument. [His] book *The Unsettling of America* (1977) "deals at length with the assumptions and policies of former Secretary of Agriculture Earl L. Butz," as Wendell put it in the preface. It's an eloquent book and a popular and influential one, without a kind word for Butz' ideas in it. . . .

Dr. Butz, sixty-nine, was a highly visible, forceful spokesman for agribusiness during his tenure as secretary of agriculture from 1971 to 1976 and was popular with his farmer constituency. When fired by President Ford for the offense of having a fine vicious joke overheard by press, he left office gracefully and without apparent rancor. At present he is Dean Emeritus of Agriculture at his alma mater, Purdue.

Ed McClanahan, an old friend of Wendell's and ours, put us wise to the debate at Manchester College, North Manchester, Indiana, on November 13, 1977. It seems that an English teacher named Charles Boebel put together the occasion as part of the "Life Schools Community Forum—The Crisis in American Agriculture," sponsored by the Indiana Committee for the Humanities. We're grateful for photographs to Debbie Lampert Dupré at the *Wabash Plain Dealer* and for photographs and additional tape to Jeffrey Hooper of the Appalshop, Whitesburg, Kentucky, who filmed the event.

Stewart Brand

BUTZ: I see we're supposed to debate about "The Crisis in American Agriculture." I think the word "crisis" is grossly overworked. I think if we asked what the crisis was, we'd get all kinds of answers here and some people would have a great deal of difficulty in even giving their own concept of what the crisis is, if indeed there is a crisis. It's a word that I refuse to place very high in my vocabulary, because if you look very hard on the other side of every coin you call crisis, it's opportunity.

So often I think we cry crisis when we want to resist change. We have a nostalgia for what was—the good old days. Somebody told me, the best thing about the good old days is a faulty memory. There were some good things about them, to be sure, but I don't especially like some of the other things when I begin to remember in detail about the good old days.

I want to make some comments about the positive side of American agriculture—some of the reasons why American agriculture is *not* in crisis, some of the reasons why modern American agriculture is the very foundation of the strength in America. I have read *The Unsettling of America*. There are a few paragraphs in it with which I agree, not many. I don't want to go back to the good old days. I don't want to go back to the outdoors pump and you carry water into the kitchen. I don't want to go back to the old round wood stove we had up here in Noble County forty miles up the road, where the fire went out at night and mother got up to build a fire the next morning and dad did once in a while but not very often. I don't want to go back to the oil lamp by which I studied until we got a Delco light system which seemed like heaven itself—and by today's standards would be very obsolete.

I don't want to go back to the lantern I carried doing chores. I don't want to go back to the back-breaking toil of cleaning out the stables by hand on Saturdays. Dad always left the barn to clean until Saturdays 'cause the boys were home from school. I don't want to go back to the hard toil we had and the long days. I don't want to go back to the fact that our entertainment on those long winter nights was the Sears Roebuck wishbook that we looked at.

In the spring we got an order off—we were all winter putting it together.

I don't want to go back to the very short cash days we had growing up back there. I don't want to go back to riding to high school three years in a horse and buggy. The last year Dad got a Model T Ford and we drove. I don't want to go back to the low level of cash income we had on the farm, the high degree of self-sufficiency where we made our own clothes in the main, and made our own baseballs at school by unraveling a sock and puttin' carpet warp in it to hold it together, until it got wet and came to pieces. Well, I can go ahead and name things I don't want to go back to.

I only want to go forward. I want to live in a changing society. That's the kind we're living in. I don't want to live in a static society.

What about American agriculture and some of the contributions it has made and is making? I sat in Brezhnev's office in Moscow a few years ago and we were discussing agriculture with remarkable frankness. He said, "Forty-five percent of my people are on the land. And I can't put my people into the business of producing consumer goods—TVs and radios and automobiles and that kind of stuff—'till I can learn somehow to feed my population with less than forty-five percent of my people on the land." And I thought, "Yes sir, Mr. Brezhnev, you are right now where my country was when I was born." (Sixty-eight years ago that was—just to save you arithmetic.) We were an agrarian nation—forty-five percent of us were on farms. If we had known then how to make nice automobiles and radios and TVs and bathtubs and nice schoolhouses like this one here, if we had known how to do that, we couldn't have spared the manpower to do it. We had to have 'em out in the field with a pair of plow handles in their hands. I can feel those lines around my back right now, guiding the horses like that.

Today we not only feed 216 million Americans much better than we did then, but we've got 24 billion dollars worth in the last year to send abroad—our number one source of foreign exchange. We've moved from forty-five percent on the land to about four percent on the land now. I know that causes some sociological problems. Change always does. On the

Dupré

other hand, all of us live better because of it—including those remaining on the land. They're in the commercial stream now. They too have electricity. They too have indoor plumbing. I didn't grow up with five rooms and a bath up here in Noble County, I grew up with four rooms and a path. How many of you did? Can I see your hands? . . . For you youngsters, it wasn't all that bad. On those cold winter mornings you learned to do things in a hurry. You can't find one in this county now, except at the resort out at the lake and you brag about it.

We've learned how to feed ourselves with a little manpower and a shirttail full of resources. Let's never forget that. I'm talking about modern, scientific, technological agriculture. It's big business, to be sure. We are still family farms. We talk about the corporation farm—less than one percent of our farms in America are corporation farms, and nine out of ten of them are incorporated for the purpose of passing title from father to son without breaking them up as they pass the tax collector.

What's it all amounted to then for America? It means that today we feed ourselves for a little less than seventeen percent of our take-home pay in America. That's less than any place else on the face of the Earth. It's less than any time previously in the history of America. Now, I know food prices have gone up and I know people talk about it. The other day I was

on one of these one-on-one TV shows, somewhere in Chicago I think. We had this smart-aleck young reporter. He thought, "I'll get Butz" right with his first question. His question was, "When are food prices going to go down?" And I said, "Well, food prices are going to go down about the same time the cost of advertising food on this station goes down. They're going to go down about the same time they reduce your salary. When do you want to start the cycle?" He said, "Well, since you put it that way, let's talk about something else."

Now, he asked the right question. He asked the question that every housewife listening wanted to know. He just got the wrong answer to it. The plain truth is we buy our food today in America for a smaller share of our take-home pay than ever before in the history of America.

And we get all that built-in maid service with it—the frozen TV-dinners that you poked in the oven tonight before you came down here. You take that ounce and a half of meat in one of those TV dinners and multiply it up to price per pound, it's not for cheap. I was out in Idaho a couple weeks ago, and they took me to one of these potato-processing plants. They said we now process at or near the point of production two-thirds of the potatoes we eat in America. You got to peel the potato to make it go in the American kitchen any more, it won't go in unpeeled. And that's not

Hooper

Earl Butz

for cheap—somebody has to do that. I've heard a lot about the wonderful agriculture in China. I've heard a lot about the way that there isn't any hunger in China. Well, hunger's relative. But they've got eighty percent of their people on the land. When I hear some of these characters out here talk about we have to reverse the flow and put people back on the land, I wonder how far back you want to go. You want to go back to where Russia is, with forty-five percent on the land? You want to go back to where India is, with sixty percent? You want to go back to where China is, with eighty percent? How far back do you want to go anyway?

When I was a kid and there were forty percent of us on farms in America we didn't have any schoolhouses like this. We had the little one-room country schools—that's the best we could afford. If you taxed yourself then like you do now the economy simply wouldn't have supported it, the surplus wasn't there to pay for it. Ninety-six percent of our families in America have a TV set. And fifty-five percent have two TV sets. The programs aren't good enough for one. Because we spend only seventeen percent of take-home pay for food is the reason that nearly ninety percent of our families have an automobile. And forty-five percent have two automobiles. If you've got a youngster in high school—three. We have an average of two people per automobile in America. In Russia, the super race, forty people per automobile. You don't have to look very long for a parking place there.

That's why I refuse to accept the word crisis

here. We have our problems to be sure. There are adjustments to be made, as is always the case. We're losing people on farms—by definition—as the family farm gets bigger. There's only so many acres in Wabash County, and you divide it among fewer operators. They're still family farms. At some point you reach an irreducible minimum, but never forget that the farmers in Wabash County are still family farmers. I shook a good many of your hands here tonight. I could tell which of you worked for a living. The calluses were here.

The other day this circus train was speeding across Illinois out here. They had this car with a baboon in it. The car door flew open, the baboon jumped out and hit a telegraph pole, and it killed him dead right there. A few hours later a couple farmers came along. They didn't recognize what it was. One of 'em said, I wonder who this is? The other one said, Well I don't know but judgin' from the location of his calluses, he must be a government worker.

We support a lot of government workers, because one worker on an American farm can now feed and clothe himself and approximately seventy other people. When I was a youngster up there in Noble County, he could feed and clothe himself and about nine other people. I think it's a remarkable story of success. Not only do we feed our people in America better than ever before and cheaper than ever before, we got twenty-four billion dollars worth of surplus products to send abroad. It's our number-one source of foreign exchange. It's the way we paid for this Sony microphone. What kind of recorder is that there—Panasonic? Where was it made? Japan. Somebody got a still camera? It may be American, but you look at the parts—they came from Japan. We didn't pay for a single one of those things with Japanese yen. We paid for 'em with Indiana-produced corn and soybeans and wheat. And I think it was a pretty good exchange myself. We just make soybeans better than they do and they make cameras better than we do.

Twenty-four billion dollars worth of that we sold abroad last year. And when you subtract what we paid for imported foodstuffs—half the sugar we eat, and coffee and tea and ba-

Dupré

Wendell Berry

nanas and that kind of stuff—we spent eleven or twelve billion dollars for that. So we made a net plus contribution last year in American agriculture to our balance of payments of twelve billion dollars. Believe me, that's rather important in this year when our overall balance of payments is running about a negative twenty-five billion. It's a serious matter—the dollar's under attack in the international exchanges of the world.

Well, that's American agriculture. It's in change to be sure. I know that some of the rural institutions are under pressure. I know the old country church is under pressure. The little church I went to up there in Noble County just forty-rod down the road, it's torn down. It's not there any more. The little one-room school I went to is now a hay-storage place for my sister and brother-in-law. But our challenge is not to yield before the nostalgia of yesteryear. Our challenge is not to turn the clock back. Our challenge is not to go back to more inefficient ways. Our challenge is *not* to put more people back on the land and therefore decrease the efficiency of American agriculture. Our challenge is to adapt to the changing situation in which we find ourselves. We need to evolve a new community structure. I'm fully aware as everybody else is that we've lost our old community identification around the rural school and the rural church. And yet there is a cohesiveness in this group here tonight. There is a cohesiveness in this North Manchester community, and our job is to develop that, to give it strength, and give it meaning to move

ahead. I've often thought that if I live long enough, that I'm going to adopt Butz's Law of Economics—it's a very simple one: Adapt or Die. It's a harsh one. But those who cling to the moldering past are the ones who die. They truly are the ones to which the word crisis would apply.

In my time I have seen so many improvements in the overall level of living of America and I've seen it tied right back to this efficient agriculture, that has applied change, that has applied technology, that's using capital, that has increased its efficiency, so that all America lives better in any way you want to measure. The people on welfare in this country live better in terms of the things they have than the top half of any population any place else on the face of the Earth.

The overriding objective of all of us in this world is peace. I've traveled the world a great deal. I've been behind the Iron Curtain. I've broken ranks in Moscow and Warsaw and Hungary and Yugoslavia to talk with people on the streets I wasn't supposed to talk to. In their hearts beats the urge for peace the same as in ours. Perhaps more than ours, because they've seen their countries destroyed. They've seen their loved ones killed before their eyes. They may want it on different terms than ours.

I am convinced that in this tremendously productive American agriculture we have the building blocks on which the diplomats of the world can build a structure of peace. And I think that peace is something more enduring than the absence of war. It's a positive thing.

In India shortly after the Indians got their independence from Great Britain, one day Gandhi very sagely remarked, "Even God dare not approach a hungry man except in the form of bread." I've seen starving men. No use talking to a man like that about human dignity. No use talking about democracy. No use talking about freedom. He listens only to the man who has a piece of bread.

And that is precisely the language we are prepared to speak in the United States. To speak loudly, to speak eloquently. We're kind of awkward with it, it's a new role for us. We're learning how to do it. But we have the capacity to do it. And we have that capacity because modern agriculture in this country is what it is. It's efficient. It's progressive. It's productive. And it's relatively free.

Thank you very much.

BERRY: My basic assumption in talking about agriculture is that there's more to it than just agriculture. That you can't disconnect one part of a society from all the other parts and just look at the results in that alone.

Let me give you an example of what I'm talking about—a little parable that hundreds of people are acting out all the time. This country is full of people now who've been liberated by modern agriculture from having to do any of what Dr. Butz called back-breaking work. And they look forward to a life of leisure. They've got nothing to do with their bodies except enjoy themselves. But when they get started on this life of leisure they discover that even to enjoy the many physical pleasures that are now available to them they've got to get in shape. So they go and take out a membership in a health spa and lift weights all day so they will be in shape to enjoy themselves at night. They've been liberated from meaningful work in order to pay to do meaningless work in order to keep healthy.

There's bound to be some kind of a connection between the liberation, so-called, of millions of people in this country from so-called back-breaking or menial work and the health problem. I don't know if you'd call it a health crisis or not; crisis is not a favorite word of mine either. But there is a health problem. The last figures I read were that everybody in the country now is paying five hundred dollars a year medical expenses. That's two thousand dollars a year for a family of four. That's too much. It seems to me that it might be conducive to health if people were doing more work.

And I don't want to go backward. I don't think that there's ever been a moment in history that's had enough net good in it to lure people back to try it again. I think what we all want to try is the future. It's just a question of how we try and who gets to make the attempt. Rather than talk very long and general, I'd like

to talk about the part of the country where I come from and I hope that my feelings on agriculture and policy implications will be clear to you from what I have to say about it.

I come from Henry County, Kentucky, not too far from Indiana. It's easy for us to come over to Madison sometimes to shop. Henry County is a place of fertile land but a very broken, rolling topography. It's a topography that makes the ground subject to erosion, especially since it's clay soil. Historically it's been highly productive agricultural country. It's one of the best tobacco counties in the state, but tobacco's always been part of a fairly diversified farming program, and so if you look back in Kentucky history, you find Henry County way up there among the livestock producing counties in the state. Traditionally Henry County was farmed by small farmers. When I was a boy there a two-hundred acre farm was a pretty big farm. For the reasons of topography that I have mentioned, it still needs to be farmed by small farmers. It needs to be farmed by people who know it very well, who care very much about it, and who will stay at home and pay attention to it.

What's happening in Henry County is what's happening every place. The farms are getting bigger, more mechanized, and the farmers are disappearing at a great rate. Henry County lies in what the real estate people call the golden triangle—between the interstate highways connecting Louisville, Kentucky, and Cincinnati, Ohio, and Lexington, Kentucky. This is driving the land costs at home way up, and the farmers aren't able to buy.

People who're buying it are city people— doctors and lawyers and businessmen of various kinds. They are able to pay the costs and the high interest rates and they get as a reward a place to come out to with their friends on the weekends. They make some of the worst neighbors that history has ever known. They don't know anything at all about a line fence. They don't know what their obligations are. I had a neighbor like that who told me he didn't need to build his part of the line fence because he didn't have any cattle. One of them told his neighbor that he was sure that he didn't need to build his part of the line fence because the hillside was so steep that the cattle would never go up where the fence was anyway. Well, I could tell you a lot of fascinating illustrations of the aptitude these people have for farming and for being neighbors, but I won't.

This is the pattern of modern agriculture where I live, and I think it's repeated in many places. The land has fallen into the hands of first the farmers' widows and then of these moneyed people who aren't farmers. The land is then cash-rented to young farmers who've made their investment not in land—which is appreciating—but in machinery—which is depreciating. And they're renting the land with cash, breaking in whole farms at a time, planting them to corn and soybeans. They're not using any animals. Not rotating back through pasture—which probably ninety percent of that land needs to be. They're not sowing any cover crops. They're plowing up the waterways and cutting the fences. Farm houses are going down. They've driving in, producing the crop, loading it, and driving out with it. In other words, in their patches the industrialization of farming is complete. They're treating the farm exactly as you would treat a factory or a mine.

This land is highly productive. And it will be for a while. But already the stories are beginning to circulate of land cleared with bulldozers, put in corn one year, and ruined. None of this land is being better farmed now than it was thirty years ago. In fact it's being neglected, abused, and wasted as never before. I've told you the grain farming angle of it. Another angle is for somebody to go in on one of those steep farms and capitalize it heavily with silos, dairy barn, loafing shed, and so on, contract a heavy debt on it, and then cover it up with Holstein cows that require it to be grazed far beyond its carrying capacity, and what isn't damaged that way they tramp into the hollers.

Henry County is a county of little farms now gathered into ever-larger ones or turned out to bushes. There isn't any land in that county that's beneath notice. All of it's potentially good for cropland or for pasture or for forest land. It's probably never been so neglected in its history. You'd have to ask, then, where are the families that used to be on that land? Well, some of them are in professions. Some of them have done extremely well. Some of them are no doubt very glad that they don't have to go back to farm those farms. Some of them are working in factories in the city. Some of them are on welfare—that is, instead of supporting themselves on what we now think of as negligible little farms, they are being supported by us. In the shifting-down of people among jobs, some people as a consequence of abandonment of those farms are in the ghettoes. My point is that wherever those people are, they are not as independent now as they were.

About a year ago a young neighbor of mine came to see me. He wanted to talk about buying a farm. He's the son of a tenant farmer who just lately finally got well enough off to buy a little farm for himself. This is a fine boy. I'd had him come help me some. I'd known him since he was a child. He's as cleancut, fine, honest a young man as you'll ever see, done a lot of hard work in his young life. He's married now, got a baby. He was living in a house trailer, growing as much crop every year as he could manage and working in construction. It's a familiar pattern, I'm sure.

Well, he'd seen a vision. He'd seen a little farm, a hilly farm, one of those marginal farms, 100 or so acres. He wanted to live on it. He wanted to buy it. He's a carpenter, he'd fix the house up. He and his family would have a place there. It would be something under foot, you see. It wouldn't be the house trailer. It wouldn't be depreciating.

I knew what he'd seen. I'd seen it myself. I know my forefathers have seen it. How it'd be to have a place of your own and be independent? You know how it is, you walk out, you see a piece of land and you know very quickly how you'd farm it, how it would look if you had it, right? Well, this young fellow had seen that vision. I think it's a grand vision. And an ennobling vision. And an indispensable one. I said, "What does it cost?" "Sixty thousand dollars."

He began to hustle around and see about the little money that he could lay down and what

Dupré

help he could get from his daddy and what help he could get then from the loan agencies and banks. And he'd come and tell me and I'd say, "Find out what the total cost will be after interest." He found that very hard to discover but he finally did. It was twice the amount—a hundred and twenty thousand dollars—and he can't do it.

Well, it was one of the hardest times I'd ever had. With myself. Because I thought from all I knew about this boy that he belonged on a farm—he wanted to be, he knew how to be— and if I was right about his character, he would've deserved to be. And you understand that you have to deserve to be. You have to prove that by being there and doing right on it.

Well, it seems to me that we lost something there. And I'm afraid we gained something. I'm afraid we gained a disillusioned, thwarted citizen who will not try quite so hard again maybe. Now, there're a lot of people like that in this country, who would like to have a piece of it. And we've chosen to keep them from having it.

It's not as though the biggest farm was the most efficient farm. It's beginning to be widely circulated—the news is out—there's a size beyond which size doesn't get any more efficient, and it's possible for small farms to be highly efficient. It depends on how you rate efficiency. If you're talking about efficiency as the output per man per day, maybe high mechanization is the most efficient. If you're talking about the

highest output per acre, the smaller operations tend to become the most efficient.

I was driving through Indiana today. I didn't see very many corn fields that had been sowed back to a winter grain crop. That means that there're going to be a lot of days in any year when those fields won't be processing solar energy into something that we can use. Sunlight falling on those fields today was wasted. If the farms were smaller, the crop could be taken off and those fields sowed back. I know it can be done this far north because I was on an Amishman's hillside in Holmes County, Ohio, last year and saw where he'd harvested his corn and shocked it, carried the shocks off the field, and he had a good stand of winter grain. That's the kind of care I'm talking about.

The Amish are doing very well, on a small scale. They're highly productive. They've been putting the money in the bank too, while a lot of mainliners have been going out of business.

Somebody told me the other day that out of every thousand dollars of government money that goes to subsidize industry in this country, five dollars goes for agriculture. I don't know. Maybe it's the free enterprise system to subsidize railroads but not farms. For my money, I would subsidize the farm. That's where I would place my tax money. I don't mean in give-away programs either. I mean in programs where price supports would be coupled with production control. Where the public outlay would be for administration. I'd like to provide some low-interest loans for fellows like my young neighbor. I don't think that's giving him an undue advantage. Think of the thousands of dollars we invest in the educations of doctors. You can put a young man on a little farm and educate him and realize a grand increment from that investment.

As I see it, the farmer standing in his field is not simply a component of a production machine. He stands where lots of cultural lines cross. The traditional farmer, that is the farmer who first fed himself off his farm and then fed other people, who farmed with his family, who passed the land on down to people who knew it and had the best reasons to take care of it— that farmer stood at the convergence of tradi-

Hooper

tional values, our values: independence, thrift, stewardship, private property, political liberties, family, marriage, parenthood, neighborhood—values that decline as that farmer is replaced by a technologist whose only standard is efficiency.

Our values have very clearly and markedly declined as the urban industrial values have replaced the old agricultural ones. Private property seems to me to be in a kind of crisis, because how can you expect people to defend the principle if they don't own any of the substance? What's private property to somebody who doesn't have any property? Did we really think that we were going to get people in the cities, who own no land at all, to vote or fight or whatever they're gonna have to do to protect our farms? I don't know why they should, unless we can get clever enough propagandists to brainwash them.

But these values are not native just to small farms, they're native to all small enterprises. And again by policy we've wiped these out—neighborhood grocers, little shoe shops. We have to drive forty miles now to get our shoes fixed. Maybe you're not supposed to get your shoes fixed any more. Maybe you're supposed to throw them away. I try to get mine fixed.

I think when the traditional people disappear, the traditional values will disappear. How could they survive? The lines of values converge on the traditional small operator, the

small man of enterprise. They all diverge from the profiteer. I'm assuming that when I say traditional values everybody knows what I'm talking about—democracy, neighborliness, kindness, and so on. If you're going to be neighborly you have to know your neighbor. You can't be neighborly in a convocation of strangers. It's what lots of people have been telling us for a long time—you can't have these things in the abstract. I don't think that you can love those old values and love what has come to be American agriculture at the same time.

REBUTTALS

BUTZ: I've got a feeling that Dr. Berry and I haven't met here tonight. Perhaps we won't. Because we are spending five hundred dollars a year in health insurance he says there is a crisis in health. I've lived past my life-expectancy when I was born by thirty years. My little granddaughter, two years old, now can expect that extra thirty years. I don't call that much of a crisis. When I was in high school up here at Wawaka, we always expected to have a couple of families out of school sick. You'd go out to see where the kids were and you'd see the sign on the door saying, "Quarantine—diphtheria here," or "Smallpox here." You can't find that in this county now we've wiped it out. We eat better. We're healthier. We're bigger. And of course we spend money for hospital insurance, because we're affluent enough now to afford the hospital. We didn't even have a hospital when I was a kid. I'll take right now beside the old days any day in this health business.

Let's get back to this young boy who wanted to farm, Wendell. I was interested. You were citing a specific case. We stopped at McDonald's out here a while ago. I was standing there at the counter waiting and this young fellow about in his early thirties recognized me. I said, "You a farmer?" "I certainly am," he said. "Where you farm?" "Oh, four–five miles out of town here."

We made some small talk, and I said, "Dad's farm?" "Nope." I said, "Did Dad get you started farming?" "Nope. I started on my own." I said, "How much of it's yours?" He said, "I own four hundred acres." I guess he was farming about six hundred acres; he said he had two or three landlords. Now that's the other story.

I see that taking place all over America all the time. I know some doctors are buying farms, and that's quite all right. Some farmers' kids are going into medicine, too. But the great bulk of farm purchases is done by farmers who are buying piece by piece, and the great bulk of the landlords in this county are farmers who've retired, or farmers' widows. The percentage of absentee ownership of farm land in Indiana is lower now than it has been for years and years. That's true in America too. Those figures are beyond dispute.

I asked Dr. Berry this evening how big a farm he had, and he said fifty acres. I said, "Do you farm with horses?" He said, "Yes." But you see, Dr. Berry can do that because he has a substantial income as a poet, as a writer, as a professor at the University of Kentucky. He can afford to pay the electric bill—he doesn't have to have kerosene lights. He can afford to have an automobile—he doesn't have to drive a horse and buggy. He can afford to do those things because he takes outside income. Let's never forget that. That's true of many writers who write about such things as he does.

People say, "Butz, you're not for the family farmer." Of course I am. I'm for the family farm to make a decent living for the farm family. I don't want that family to starve to death slowly. I want that family to be able to enjoy some of the amenities of life—a color TV set, electric lights, indoor toilets. I want them to be able to afford an automobile and a vacation trip once in a while. Now, about saying that if you don't have a piece of farm land, you're not independent, you're not democratic, you don't have an interest in America. . . . Don't tell me that the people who live in North Manchester, Indiana, and are home owners, who work somewhere in a factory—don't tell me they don't have a sense of independence. Don't tell me they don't have a sense of community involvement. Don't tell me that they're not re-

Dupré

sponsible citizens, I think more surely than if they were on a small piece of land which was so small as to be uneconomic.

I know you make some trade-offs in this world. You lose some of the old family entity that used to be out there. This is unfortunate, I think. But that's not because you live on a farm or don't live on a farm. That's because we've got automobiles and TV sets and roller skating rinks and that type of thing, and that's just as true of farm kids as it is of city kids. Those TV waves don't respect city limit signs a bit.

We talk about the crisis in culture, "because of no private property." There's a lot of private property in this country. You don't even have to own a house to have private property. We've all got life insurance. We've got interest in America. We've got interest in the very profit process in America.

So I say, when we get to dreaming about yesteryear and the nice things we like to remember about yesteryear, let's set it off against the advantages of what we have. When you do that, the comparison is so obvious that the choice is easy.

BERRY: Well, since Mr. Butz referred to my life, which is something I didn't intend to do, I may as well tell you about it. I know a little bit more about it than Mr. Butz. I am a school teacher and a writer. I've written a lot of books, which haven't exactly sold like hotcakes. I may have made a year's salary out of it by now—not a large year's salary. I turned away from the main line of a teaching career. I was living in New York City, and I got a chance to come home and teach in the University of Kentucky. And then I went all the way home, to Henry County where my family, seven generations of my family, have lived and now live—not on the farm I live on, but on the next farm.

I just had twelve acres for a while, most of it steep, and I could hardly have called myself a farmer then. But a developer bought the forty acres next to me and was going to cover it up with little cottages, without any plumbing or sewage. He did some rather bad bulldozer work on it and made a hideous mess of it and failed. Then I bought him out, and I've spent the last four years restoring that forty acres. It has been expensive. The land could never have paid for the operation. I paid for it out of my salary. It's productive land now—steep; by modern standards, marginal. It's producing enough cattle now to pay the taxes, and we're taking our subsistence from it.

I should say that subsistence taken off that little farm makes our domestic economy extremely sound. I've done the work with horses. I've done it because I like horses, and because driving horses, I'm independent of the oil companies. I like that. Also, having horses makes economic sense. A good broke team of young mares now brings from two thousand to ten thousand dollars without any trouble at all. So I don't want any of you all to worry about me, because I farm with horses.

I was wondering how my neighbors were thinking about it until one stopped—an old man—and told me how proud he was of me, and until another stopped just the other day, a young man, and asked me if I could find him a team. He said that he thought he'd cultivate his crops with them and do—one—a better job, and—two—a cheaper job than he could with his tractor. He's right on both counts.

I've done a lot of work. I've gotten a lot of exercise. I've eaten well. I don't feel that I'm the least bit damaged; it hasn't dulled my mind. I was on a panel with the vice-president of John Deere a while back, and he was congratulating himself on the number of people he'd liberated from groveling in the earth in order to use their minds. Well, then I went to New York, and I saw all those people up there, vomiting in the gutters and passed out in the subways and lying along the street, and I said, "Uh-huh. This is what people do when they're liberated to use their minds." I was delighted to find that out.

Now, Mr. Butz has given you a lot of quantitative arguments. Let me just take a few of them. We may never meet, because he's arguing from quantities and I'm arguing from values. Life expectancy is not a value in and of itself. Some things, our tradition tells us, are worse than death—among them, too long a life and bad circumstances. Quality of life has to do with morals and with spiritual good health. It doesn't necessarily have to do with a flush toilet.

One thing I do on my farm is use a composting outhouse. One of the most damaging things we've got in this country is the flush toilet. The nutrients of the earth that we eat pass through our bodies, and according to the laws of biology, if the land is to stay in good health, those nutrients have to go back on it. We use millions and millions of dollars worth of soil nutrients that we eat and then put into the rivers to become pollution, and then spend millions of dollars purifying it again to drink it. It doesn't make any sense. If we ran our own households on that kind of an economy, people would think we were stupid. Suppose you put a pump in your septic tank, ran the effluent through an expensive processing system, and then drank it. You'd have people in white coats at your front door. But this is the way this whole society works.

Independence? If you've got your own land, you're sure as hell independent if you grow your food from it. You won't be starved by a shortage of oil. The idea that human beings could starve for want of oil is something new under the sun all right. I won't mind a bit when we go backwards from that, just as an al-

Hooper

coholic oughtn't to mind if he goes backwards from his addiction.

There's a lot of private property, Mr. Butz says, in insurance policies in America. Those are abstract. I don't love my insurance policy. But I sure love my farm. I haven't laid awake at night thinking about my insurance policy. Lord god, I hope I never do lie awake at night thinking about it. I hope I never depend on it.

Mr. Butz has made two references to this nice schoolhouse. This one here, has it got a skylight in it? School takes place in the daytime. Modern educators don't know it. They've never been out of their air-conditioned solid-walled offices long enough to find out that school still takes place mostly in the daytime. You'd think that to save the taxpayers money—everybody's aching to save the taxpayers money—that some of these people'd build a school with a window or a skylight in it. It's same as with agriculture. We've based it on petroleum. We've based it on industry. Mr. Butz says, seventy people are being fed by one farmer. One farmer plus how many truck drivers, middle men, packagers, processors, precookers, road builders, oil companies, employees, how many? That's a sheer . . . It's misleading, is what it is.

I don't ask that my values be adopted overnight, and a bunch of people who've never farmed move to the country. What I'm advocating is a change of values, and I assume that changes in behavior will follow changes in values.

QUESTIONS

Question about the young man who inquired about buying a team. (Questions were indistinct in the tape, so they'll be paraphrased.)

BERRY: He's not stupid, and he doesn't have six hundred acres. He raises some tobacco, and even with the tractor, that's very slow work, cultivating tobacco. I don't know if you've ever used a two-horse riding cultivator. It's the best cultivating tool that was ever made, as far as I know.

Question about the Amish.

BERRY: Well, they're still doing very well farming with horses. They're doing well by cooperating in neighborhoods, as a lot of people used to. I don't know how old you are, but probably not old enough to remember when people used to get together and work, but they did. They still do in my part of the country. There's something to be said for the value of people helping each other, don't you think? I don't think that anybody's going to get to heaven by being efficient. I don't think St. Peter, when he meets us up there, he's going to ask a single one of us how efficient we were. I think he's gonna ask us, did we help our neighbors. And I think in our hearts that's what we ask ourselves. If we're going to trade the possibility of working with our neighbors for a four-row cultivator, I think we've made a bad trade. I like working with my neighbors. We talk to each other. Most of the stuff I know that I really enjoy knowing is from listening to my neighbors talk when we work together.

VOICE: You can't go backwards.

BERRY: I'm not talking about going backwards in history, I'm talking about going backwards in character.

Question about a lot of new people getting into farms.

BERRY: I don't think it can happen very quickly. One thing I've been fascinated with recently is watching some of the city people who come to the farm and are trying to learn how to farm. It takes longer than I thought it would. To look at this happen gives you some sense of what a complex thing a farmer's mind is. I don't think I appreciated it enough, although I appreciated it a good deal. It'll take a long time to get those people established and well off. What would you say, you farmers? It takes five years for a farmer to learn to use a new farm, learn the condition of it and how to get along on it. Never learn? I understand what you mean.

Question about limits to the trend of fewer farmers.

BUTZ: Obviously there is an irreducible minimum and we are approaching that. Right now we've got, by the census definition, 2.8 million farms in the United States. On over half of those, however, the operator makes more money off the farm than he does on the farm—he's a Wendell Berry. They're really rural residents who have some of the things that Dr. Berry's talking about here tonight. Approximately six hundred thousand farms in the United States produce better than eighty percent of our commercial farm products. There won't be much more reduction.

VOICE: If farmers are so important in the world, why don't more people listen to us?

BUTZ: It's a good question. I know we're in some economic stress right now, depending somewhat on the kind of farming you're in. In Iowa the other day I asked this farmer, "How's your cash flow?" He said, "My cash flow is pretty good, the trouble is I ain't stopping none of it." Well, why don't more people listen to you? I think in the current political situation, it wasn't farmers that elected Mr. Carter. I'm sure he must have gotten up the morning after the election, looked at the map of the United States, and he saw everything west of the Mississippi, plus Illinois, Indiana, and Michigan, colored the wrong color. He must have decided, "Nuts to those birds, they're not the guys who elected me. I'll take care of labor with the higher minimum wages and the cargo preference bill, I'll take care of people for free foodstamps for everybody." I guess it's just a matter of paying those that took care of you.

BERRY: I'd like to answer that question too.

I think they don't listen to farmers because there aren't enough of you. You're a negligible quantity, politically. I don't see how you're going to protect yourselves without some friends in the cities, and I don't know how you're going to get them. You see, this is the split that I'm talking about. You're feeding people who are not interested in raising food, they're interested in eating it. So when you've got a declining small population in which nobody is interested, I don't see how you stop it at an irreducible minimum. It seems to me that farmers are in rapid precipitous decline, they're without political friends, and I don't see how they can do anything except expect to decline some more. Unless values change.

Question about how we get more people on the land.

BERRY: I think that more people ought to be able to buy it. I was interested in what Mr. Butz said about the prevalence of farm buyers on the market. It seems to me that when we think about land prices and the income that's coming off the land, it's not a very good situation. People are selling out of farming at a great rate. It seems to me that the way the land is priced and the way interest is going, it's getting more and more likely that non-farmers are going to buy the land. And it doesn't seem to me to violate good sense in any way, or good economics either, to take steps through tax benefits to young beginning farmers and through low-interest loans.

Question about how serious the consequences of the current agricultural situation are.

BERRY: One thing I think you've got to have your eye on is the young people. My farm is a very negligible operation in Mr. Butz's terms, but one of the increments I've had from it is that when my kids have been home I've had something for them to do. They've been surrounded by a complex structure that they had to understand before they could work in it, and working in it taught them something about the complexity of it and the way it depended on them. They have some kind of sense of responsibility. I don't have a TV and so my kids have been thrown back on books a little bit.

What my kids have had, I'm beginning to see now that the oldest one's getting away from home. What they have—that I think is running pretty short in this country—is the capacity to entertain themselves. They don't get bored if somebody's not putting on a show for them.

A lot of kids now are getting credit cards and charge accounts at stores. And you know what they're doing? They're going to those stores and stealing stuff, to amuse themselves. In my classes, it's getting harder and harder to talk about traditional values now. It's getting awful hard to find a kid who's ever run into the Twenty-third Psalm. I asked my class the other day, "How many of you have read *Tom Sawyer?*" Not a soul. So, you've got color TV, charge accounts, new cars, no work, and you've lost Mark Twain. I think it's a bad bargain.

HERE LIES A FRIEND OF THE FOREST

This is my idea for a movement that all ecology-minded people can get behind.

You've heard of the saying, "When I die bury me face down so the world can kiss my ass." Well this works on the same principle.

Specify in your will that you wish to be buried without a casket in a prepicked place which is devoid of trees and have an oak or other long-lived tree planted in the Earth above your body. Let it be known that this tree is in effect your tombstone (maybe have a small plaque embedded in it).

Since there is a law in this country protecting graveyards and the like you have relative assurance that there will be at least one tree in the area that can't be cut down by this subdivision-happy country.

It's also unlikely to die because of the great fertilizer it will be growing in (unless of course you've overloaded your body with chemicals while alive).

If you could convince other people to do the same you could start whole forests that could never be touched by chain saws—what better way to help renew the Earth?

We've been taking from the Earth and not giving anything back but garbage for so long we seem to have forgotten that only death begets new life. Conventional graveyards don't do a thing to help the planet. Anybody got a better idea?

J. Blair Moffett
Silver Spring, Maryland
[Summer 1982]

J. BALDWIN

I Was Armand Hammer

This originally appeared in the Spring 1978 CQ as a follow-up to an article on job-sharing as an instrument for social change. J.'s experience turned out much more memorable than the original article. It's worth mentioning that CQ practiced job-sharing for years—the editorships and assistant editorships were rotated beginning in 1982 between me, Stephanie Mills, Jay Kinney, Richard Nilsen, and Kevin Kelly.

A full introduction to J. Baldwin would overwhelm this little gem of a story. To learn more about J. see page 263.

To learn more about J. see page 263.

Art Kleiner

My college dishwashing job ended in a heart-felt exchange of Fuck You's one sultry evening during rush hour. I had never much liked Howard Johnson's anyway, and reading Orwell's *Down and Out In Paris and London* hadn't helped a bit. Ninety cents an hour! Who were they kidding? True, you got to eat the untouched food that customers had left on their plates (you wouldn't believe the volume of uneaten food) but now the boss wanted me to take my Saturday morning to make a doghouse for his Great Dane, and for ninety cents an hour yet! To hell with it!

On the other hand, I'd have to find another job soon or I'd be back before my Dad, contritely accepting his "I told you so," and his "conditions" with his check. What middle-class nineteen-year-old hasn't had the problem of parents insisting that as long as they pay the bills, they have the say-so over your life? Damn! And it was a recession year too. I grumped down a malt at Red's Rite Spot and was in the process of completely bumming out a table of friends when a grad student type motioned me outside. "I have a job for you," he said innocently. "Six bucks a day for two hours work, but you have to keep your mouth shut." Wow. Thirty a week would not only pay my expenses, it would buy gas too. (Regular was twenty cents a gallon then.) In fact, if I was careful, I'd be able to spend the summer on the road instead of as a slave. So I said, "What do I have to do?"

The play was this. There had recently been a scandal at a famous Ivy League school where a group of jokers had put an imaginary man through college by paying his fees and taking his exams for him. He had received a degree with honors and a scholarship as well. The man I was talking to was a part of a similar scheme, only in this case the imaginary person was a factory worker. At the time he was one of three men sharing his shift. The three wanted a fourth so as to have more time for homework and also to avoid awkward face changes at

Elton Robinson

J. Baldwin, CQ's Soft Tech and Nomadics editor, in 1954 when he was Armand Hammer by night.

times other than coffee breaks. I had to buy in to show commitment. A hundred bucks. I'd get it back when I didn't need the job any more and had recruited a replacement.

The fabled worker was named Armand Hammer, a reference to the baking soda box symbol which to some had delicious Communist overtones in those days of McCarthy investigations. Armand worked the evening shift, and my part would be the eight to ten p.m. quarter. I reported early so as to be introduced all around to the people who made it possible for Armand to work unmolested.

The shop steward, line foreman, parking-lot guard, and several others who knew too much were paid off at Christmas with bottles of Cutty Sark (that most acceptable of bribes). Fellow workers were told that the ever-changing Armands were extras hired to fill in for absentees or men taken ill on the job. There was some suspicion of funny business, but as long as the shop steward was satisfied, nothing was said. He should have been satisfied! Armand was never late, absent, or troublesome, and he always voted correctly in union elections.

When I became a quarter of Armand, he was installing drive shafts in luxury sedans. It was a job that required you to be quick so as not to slow the line down and get fired. There were four bolts that had to be started by hand and then driven home with a shrieking air pistol wrench. You had to be careful not to cross-thread the bolts. It was all too easy to get severely pinched or worse between the transmission and the heavy drive shaft that dropped on a cable from the ceiling every fifteen seconds. It was just dangerous enough to require all your attention, and the idea of having to do that for eight hours a day for weeks, months, and years appalled me and still does. Two hours was about right.

Armand had been working for about three years when I joined him. He was accumulating seniority and immunity to layoff. In fact, the front office was considering him for promotion as a result of his good record. Armand, of course, refused, preferring to "stay with the boys on the line." Over the summer, Armand was usually one man, the one who needed the job most. At various times during the school year, he might be one, two, or four men, depending on school pressures. Three didn't fit the coffee breaks, and more than four was too awkward. Needless to say, Armand paid his tax on time. He told the company that he had his own retirement plan and insurance so as to avoid possible complications.

Last I heard from Armand was 1970. By then he had made nearly $150,000 for about 120 men. I've often wondered about the men involved, if they had any common trait other than being a part of Armand. I'll bet a party at which all the Armands showed up would be pretty interesting. And I've speculated on how many other Armands there might be in a nation as large as ours. There just *has* to be more of them, existing yet not existing, passing unseen among us, like ghosts.

BURGER KING BOOGIE

Some of my favorite jobs have been in fast food restaurants. That's where my mind is free to grow intellectually, while my hands labor.

If you like to travel, as I do, you can pick up a job in one anywhere in the country—allowing you to study the regional mores. It's good for the staff too. After all, it's not every day they find someone as interesting as you filling the cole slaw!

Kentucky Fried Chicken "cooks" in ways other than you might think. Here people of all different ages rub elbows at menial tasks. Being physically juxtaposed forces people to face each other and eventually . . . talk. McDonald's is a wonderful place to get a perspective of oneself in relation to other generations. For example, I've found that initially, my presence bothers the many high-school students who work there. It seems to upset them to be slinging hash with a former school teacher.

After all, the only reason they're working there is to get the tuition for college to become professionals themselves. When confronted by them I always have plenty of explaining to do. In essence I confess that after a few years in academic life it's "soul cleansing" to work at a physical job. Not to mention the good exercise. They end up liking me, which is a lucky thing because, believe me, it's the Archies and Veronicas who can make or break you in a job like that.

Aside from the financial reward it's a place where a traveler, away from home, can find an "on the spot" family.

There's piped music for dancing in the kitchen.

Also you can eat all you want and sneak a chicken liver home for your cat!

Mia Elizabeth Kangas
Madison, Connecticut
[Summer 1981]

First Week of
November,
1978—
and More
Anne Herbert

The greatest joy of editing a small
magazine is discovering talent, and
Anne Herbert probably qualifies as
our finest find, certainly the one who
in turn did the most for us. The finding was easy. I judge poetry by how it
sticks in the mind like a burr with a
seed inside. From a preacher's kid in
Ohio came this kind of thing: "I
would like to write a silence for all the
men I knew and didn't know and
heard about and didn't hear about
who came back from Vietnam and
died in single car accidents on
straight roads. A silence because I
still don't know what to say." "One
way to get out of going to Vietnam
was to have your father killed at Anzio
and not be born." "An orchestra is deceptive. It doesn't sound like elbows
and ties. Maybe an ecstatic furry di-

nosaur humming to itself or an over-
grown garden hooked up to an amp."
  "Ocean keeps on coming," she
wrote. Well, so does her goddamn
writing, talking like the mind talks,
infesting and jollying us along without our hardly noticing toward better behavior. Some have said her style
and mine are similar. Nah. I use
commas. And I'm an editor who
sometimes writes. Anne's a writer to
her marrow, who sometimes edits;
both skills, and her soul on her
sleeve, have carried COEVOLUTION a
long way. From all over our map, Issue 20 in Winter 1978, Issue 28 in
Winter 1980, and Issue 35 in Fall
1982, Art Kleiner assembled this
sampling. For more, there's Anne
Herbert on every righthand page in
the *Next Whole Earth Catalog*, and
there's a whole book, her first, *Senseless Beauty and Random Acts of Kindness*, newly out from Random House.
                        Stewart Brand

What are you getting in this collection? "First Week of November,
1978" is one of several stories Anne
Herbert has written about citizen
Amanda Madison of fictional Rising
Sun, Ohio. The title is the date it
was first published—Anne origi-
nated much of her writing in a self-
published journal, the *Rising Sun
Neighborhood Newsletter*, which she
distibuted mostly to friends. Stewart
got into the habit of printing excerpts in CQ—a popular move

among CQ readers. "The Day Martin Luther King Was Killed" was a piece Anne wrote before she joined CQ's staff in 1976, but it wasn't published until her own "Neighborhoods" guest-edited issue in Winter 1980. "Honest Hope" is one of a series of personal, somewhat politically-motivated essays that she still occasionally publishes in CQ (in its new form as the WHOLE EARTH REVIEW).

Finally, if the North Point editors will allow it (I'm sneaking it in at the last moment) there is an essay Anne wrote as a response to the 1978 Whole Earth Jamboree, a party Stewart and CQ held to celebrate Whole Earth's ten-year anniversary. At first I resisted reprinting the essay because it's so self-referential—you have to know the Jamboree, and the rest of that CQ issue, to fully understand it. But eventually I realized that it says things about community, neighborhoods, gatherings, and church that I, at least, have seen nowhere else . . . and it's some of the best writing Anne has ever done. I couldn't keep it from you. "Jonah," just preceding it, is a speech she gave at the same Jamboree.

Art Kleiner

FIRST WEEK OF NOVEMBER, 1978
People are tired of explaining the Amanda Madison Memorial Nonsense Box at Smitty's Bar to out-of-towners, and some people in town don't know the whole story. So I'm going to explain it all because I knew her and I like to explain things and everybody else who knew her would rather write postcards than explain. Amanda died in 1969 and was old and everyone loved her. She started her unusual career by not marrying, which was quite unusual at the time. Some people like to tell Delta Dawn stories about that, but Amanda said, when I

asked her about it once, "I never had a beau who surprised me once as much as I surprise myself eight or nine times daily. I see no reason to marry into boredom when the streets are littered with it." So she lived on almost no money in her father's house and did typical small town things in weird ways. She taught Sunday School, for example, and one time had her eighth-graders read the story in Matthew where Jesus curses the fig tree for no apparent reason and it dies. She asked each member of the class if they understood why Jesus did that and if they thought it was nice. After they all said no to both, she said, "You don't understand Jesus and he wasn't nice. Remember that. Now let's go play volleyball till it's time for church." She took unexpected gifts to people, like the time she took Lisa, who had been a girls' basketball star and then got laid up with leukemia, a purple baseball cap with yellow foam wings sticking out on the side and said, "I know you are tired of people looking at you with mushy eyes like you really are a sick person. Wear this and for one moment when they walk in they will forget that you are a sick person and remember you are a weirdo." Amanda did lots of other stuff, but the relevant thing here is that she wrote notes. She attended everything in town, and wrote alert thank-you notes to participants. One time she wrote Tommy Wills, "Dear Tommy, I know it was difficult to keep a straight face in the Christmas program when Amy was having such unfortunate difficulties with her undergear, but I appreciate your making the effort. Many others would have laughed out loud and yet you said your lines exactly as you were supposed to. This denotes a level of self-control and consideration for others that will no doubt be of use to you in many endeavors throughout your life. Your Admirer, Amanda." She always wrote to the assistant of the person who got all the glory, the last person on the cleanup committee to leave, and also wrote to people who quit something or other, city council, the Fourth of July parade committee, in disgust with bad feelings all around and thanked them for their past efforts.

But as time went on, she started writing other things. People say she got crazy when she got old, but I say she went from not caring much about what people thought to not caring at all. She started writing postcards to everyone, to people she saw every day, that had nothing to do with anything. Postcards of Miami Beach written as if she were an antarctic explorer—"Took this in my gear to remind me of warm weather. We'll meet on the beach soon, love. Progress is good, but we had to put down a penguin rebellion last night. It was rough but we're safe now. Think of you always. Norbert." Once you stopped worrying about senility, they were great, and people started writing back. Especially the young men going into the service who stopped by Amanda's house to say goodbye. She always said, "If you don't want to write me about what you're doing, write me about what you'd rather be doing," and they did. She got cards about preparing and serving a gourmet dinner from Anzio, about sitting in front of the fireplace drinking a case of wine from Korea and about planning and financing and building and using the perfect teddy bear factory from Vietnam.

She and LuAnn Sellers, who was eight at the time, carried on a long correspondence as if they were both going around the world, one west to east and one east to west. And even though Amanda and LuAnn saw each other at least once a week at church, they never talked about it. Just kept writing. LuAnn was one of the most crushed people when we met at Smitty's after Amanda's funeral to get wasted. "I'm only in Bengali," she said, "I never got to tell her how much I liked her card about the organ grinders' convention in Kansas City, Kansas. I thought we'd talk about our trips when they were over, but now we never can." I said write about the rest of your trip to me and that's when we all realized that Amanda could live forever in the mail. We could send her postcards to people who hadn't seen them and we could write to each other in the spirit of Amanda—write about the dogshit in the backyard or the grocery prices on Mars and we do, and we usually sign them Amanda or Rose or

Trailler, never with our own names. Rose and Trailler were these friends of Amanda who had the most incredible adventures around the world as Missionaries for Not Just the Acceptance but the Love of the Law of Gravity and we always thought she made them up until she died and we found piles of letters from them in her bureau. ("This little urchin took gravity into her heart tonight, Amanda; I wish you'd been here.") The nice thing about everyone using the same names is that you're never totally sure who sent you any given postcard. Amanda may write you asking for advice about treating her turtle's acne and you may send your reply as Rose to the wrong person who may reply to you or to someone else. People around here know each other's handwriting pretty well, but it does get interesting. Amanda liked things interesting. I remember once we were halfway through a bottle of wine and she said, "Life is alternately boring and horrifying and we are all quite unreasonably lonely and I see no reason to treat dreams as some unmentionable head disease like lice. We all have them and might as well mail them to each other until we learn to talk." So that is why, Stranger, Smitty's has the largest selection of postcards you've ever seen jumbled together in a box (people bring back dozens from vacation) and why some of them are used—those are Amanda's that she wrote herself, and we keep them moving, some have twenty-five stamps and addresses layered on by now.

This doesn't, however, explain why the sign over the bar says, "Invest in it!" That's there because whenever you'd ask Amanda if one of her fantastic stories was true, she'd say, "Are you planning to invest in it?" One time I was fed up with her and I said, "What the hell do you mean by that?" and she said, "Well, if you thought it was true, you'd invest in it, wouldn't you? You'd make something else be true because this was true. If you thought the true thing was bad, you'd try to stop it and if you thought it was good you'd try to spread it, but why do you need to know if it's true? If it hits your heart close enough that you care if it's true, you should invest in it anyway." So if you like Amanda enough to care if she's true, invest in her. Send a dream postcard to a friend and she's true for you too.

This item written with the help of Andrea Sharp who surprised me when I sent her a strange postcard signed Amanda by sending back an even stranger one signed Trailler and never saying a word about it.

JONAH

Hi. I'd like to share with you the story of Jonah. Jonah is the guy who lives in the Bible, about halfway between Elijah and Luke. A lot of you probably think Jonah is the story of a man and his whale. That's not actually true. Jonah is the story about the joy of hatred. Jonah is the story about that exhilarating feeling you get when you discover someone who is really morally more reprehensible than you are. Jonah discovered that joy, and Jonah's basic thing was hating Ninevites. Ninevites lived far away from him, and he'd never met any of them, but he had a lot of data about them.

Now, hating Ninevites was not like hating Jews, Catholics, Black people, etc. Hating Ninevites was like hating American Nazis, builders of nuclear reactors, and tuna fishermen. It was a rational, well-researched hatred based on the actual behavior of the hatees. Jonah had a lot of data on Ninevites, and he was building a career on them. He had just had a story about the relationship of Ninevites, the Mobil Oil Corporation, and saccharin on the cover of *Mother Jones*. He was hitting the junior college circuit with a speech about Ninevites, and he was hoping to make the Ivy League soon.

So he was not surprised when one day God came to him to talk to him about the Ninevites. He had never spoken to God before, and he wasn't really a God groupie, but he figured God knew who the expert was, right? So God came to Jonah, and said, "Jonah, I'm going to destroy all the Ninevites." And Jonah said, "Wow, you must have read my article." And God said, "Before I destroy them I want to warn them. It seems only fair. Since you know so much about them, I want you to go to Nineveh and tell them I'm going to destroy them, so they'll have a chance to change their ways

and save themselves." And Jonah said, "No way in hell. I don't want to go there, they're creepy people, and besides that, what if they change?" So Jonah took off. He took the Greyhound bus to the most distant point available, only it wasn't a Greyhound bus at that point in time, it was a boat. He got on the boat, and thought he would skip town, and all would be cool. He did not know he was dealing with a Whole Earth God.

God followed him in the boat and started a very large sea storm. The captain of the boat was extremely upset about the sea storm. He was an experienced captain who knew a theological sea storm when he saw it. So he said, "Someone on this boat is not on speaking terms with God. Let's draw lots and see who." Jonah said, "Ah, we don't need to do that, I'm the one, I'll jump overboard because it seems like the only way that I'm going to win." Now it turned out that God knew, as well as any civil rights legislator knows, that the only way to overcome hatred is with brute force. And God doesn't give up easy. So when Jonah jumped over the side of the boat, God had a whale there to catch him. Jonah landed in the whale, stayed in the whale with the rotting fish and the whale digestive juices for three days. Jonah was a stubborn man of principle—it took seventy-two hours of an unusual smell for him to change his mind, but finally he said, "Oh heck, God, I'll go to Nineveh." So the whale barfed him up on shore near Nineveh and he headed for the world capital of badness.

Now, when he got to Nineveh, he was pleased to see that everything that he'd ever thought about Nineveh was true. I mean they were right there on the streets using sweat shop labor to run a nuclear reactor that powered an ITT plant that made neutron bombs, whale trawlers, and saccharin. He was naturally appalled. So he got into his street-beggar mode, which he had once used to support his Ninevite research, and he started saying things in a way that not very many people would hear them. He shuffled down the street, leaned against the walls and muttered, "Repent. Repent. In forty days you will be destroyed if you don't repent." You had to be walking right by

Larry Keenan, Jr.

Anne Herbert

him to hear him but the very first person who happened to walk by him happened to be bored with his job as a nuclear reactor janitor and he said, "Wow, you're right, this is really awful, let's all repent."

And that guy started yelling Jonah's message and it turned out that a lot of people were bored with their jobs as neutron bombardiers and saccharin cane cutters and they went to the president of the country and said, "We've been gross and awful, and we're going to repent and you have to, too." They put on sackcloth and ashes, they turned their nuclear reactor into a solar generator and they all planted organic gardens and Jonah was *pissed*. He was just furious and he said, "OK, God, are you gonna be conned by these hypocrites, do you think that just because they're behaving different they're better?" And God said, " 'Fraid so. Behavior counts. You lose."

So Jonah stomped to a hill outside of town and sat under a tree praying for the Ninevites to show their true nature and for God to fry them alive. And all that happened was that God destroyed the tree Jonah was sitting under so he got a sunburn. Jonah said, "God, how come you destroyed this tree? This tree never did nothing." He did a ten minute rap about the tree and how trees are important and you

can't just destroy them for no reason. And God said, "How come, Jonah, how come, wherefore why is it, that you care so much about that tree, when you have no pity at all for Ninevah, a city that has a whole lot of folks in it, and some children and animals and you wanted me to kill them all? How come you didn't care about them?" And that's the end of the book in the Bible. You're left there with the question. You never know what Jonah said. And you find out the question is for you. What are you going to do? Can you live without hatred?

THE WHOLE EARTH JAMBOREE WASN'T WORTH IT ONCE

As anyone on the CQ staff couldn't help knowing, I had a negative attitude about the whole thing from the beginning, and lots of good reasons. I don't like events with large crowds at them, I don't like meeting people I don't know, I didn't like trying to put an already complicated issue together in the midst of a bunch of people who were high on panic, I didn't like seeing Stewart change from the well-organized small businessman I have known to a sixties artifact who believed in lack of planning as an article of faith ("Let's not ruin the spontaneity"). I didn't like never being able to place an outgoing call because all the phone lines were busy all day, and I hated more than I can tell you going to a 1½ hour meeting about the Jamboree two days before the magazine was due at the printer. (I swore I was going to tell Patty she had to go to a 1½ hour meeting about the magazine two days before the Jamboree, but it turned out that that wasn't a good week for jokes.) And my reaction to finding out at that meeting that everyone on the staff was going to have to work 12 to 24 hours a day after having been led to believe that they didn't even necessarily have to attend, moved me from anger to a fairly nasty bitterness that lingered through the long hours and multiple surprises of working at the Jamboree itself. So you can imagine my surprise at finding out two months later that I now feel negative about the Jamboree for a whole new reason. I think it was such a good thing that it's almost criminal to only do it once. This does not change the fact that if Stewart announced that he was going to do another Jamboree, I would immediately apply for a job with *Reader's Digest*. But I really believe that the kind of good feeling that was present there was designed to happen on some kind of continuing and regular basis.

The feeling at the Jamboree wasn't a high (that's why some people found it a let down), but was a very strong pleasant. It was in fact a neighborhood feeling—a relaxation and ease natural among a community that had temporarily become a neighborhood. A community can believe in itself, but a neighborhood can see itself—and what a relief to see with your own eyes that a lot of people like you really do exist, and here a bunch of them are, being nice and not throwing trash on the ground. I was surprised, and almost shocked, to find a neighborhood I liked at the Jamboree since I've always thought CQ subscribers were purer and more intense and more irritable than I. I wasn't at all sure that I'd like to be around a bunch of them for two days.

It turned out that the CQ people who write to the office may often be more like unfun true believers than my friends, but the people at the Jamboree stunned me with their wonderfulness, and made me wish we could have hung out together longer, or more frequently. The volunteers, who were the people I spent most of my time with, amazed me by being hard working; cheerfully willing to do anything, however boring; intelligent in the face of pressure, disorganization and oddness; and they had a nice funny low-key cynicism they used to cover their generosity, just like all my sixties leftover friends. In fact, a lot of them were potential friends, and I only saw them once. That seemed silly. Why bother to like someone you're only seeing once?

And the volunteers weren't the only wonderful ones. The whole crowd flabbergasted me by dropping their trash into trash cans to an extent that was nothing short of miraculous. I've worked on a lot of cleanup committees, and it was incredible to see at the end of each day that there was nothing, repeat nothing, to clean up. Intense searching by the cleanup vol-

unteers uncovered a few scraps of paper, but for all practical purposes, there was, before the cleanup, no way to tell that 8,000 people had been there—or that anyone had been there. This made me think that this neighborhood had interesting potential for other, larger-scale miracles, if it just stayed a neighborhood a while longer.

Since I'm messy, I never wanted to understand the saying about cleanliness being next to godliness, but maybe it means that if you've got the discipline for a minor goodness like being clean, you could easily use that discipline for major goodnesses. Eight thousand people who could be that clean all at once could do other things all at once, if they talked about it enough, if instead of going to a pleasant Jamboree once in ten years they went to some kind of organic, alternative energy equivalent of church once a week.

In fact, a lot of this amounts to saying that I miss church. You non-church-goers should know that Church As I Knew It, in the middle of the road, was nothing like Elmer Gantry. No one cried, and if you pushed people on what they believed, a lot of them were more vague than dogmatic—something about God existing, something about Jesus being special, something about modified altruism being better than pure selfishness. A lot of what was happening was people with lots of non-religious values in common (political conservatism, family life) getting together once a week to hang out. It was a nice place to hang out. If you didn't like grownups, you could volunteer to hang out with children without having to actually have any. If you didn't like big crowds, you could volunteer for the cleanup or preparation committee and hang out with other people who didn't like crowds and sort of liked shit work in a way, like the volunteers at the Jamboree. Also you could find out if you wanted to be friends with people without doing something artificial like going out to lunch.

What my few friends and I all have in common is that we don't have as many friends as we would if we were born sooner because we've renounced most institutions and are left with making friends at work or by inviting people we've met casually out to lunch. I find that unideal because it makes my stomach hurt and because if you take someone to lunch you just get each other's stories, but if you set up folding chairs together, you find out what people are really like and if you really like them.

Sixties leftovers have never really built a lowkey institution to hang out together at, and make friends at and casually bullshit about what to do next at. I think that's partly because compulsory education crippled us. We were in communities organized by grownups for so long we never learned to organize our own. What happened to the sixties a lot is that everyone graduated from college and didn't see each other much. The clean grounds and lovely volunteers at the Jamboree reminded me that much of what people had in common then they have in common now. If they met, casually, regularly, they might have fun and carry it on, whatever it was, in a whole new way.

I was surprised by how little the speakers had to say that was new, and it made me think that the newness would be found in the crowd, if they talked to each other long enough, if they lived in a neighborhood together instead of meeting once at a one-time event.

What I think would be good would be some regularly scheduled low-key place where people could meet, maybe hear a hippie sermon about how given our beliefs, we're better than everyone else, or about how given our beliefs, we're totally hypocritical and aren't doing shit to live them out. (Those are the 2 kinds of sermons, and we could use them both.) We could sing a few songs, have a few potluck suppers and accidentally possibly remake the revolution. I myself wouldn't do anything to make all this happen, but if it happened, I would set up folding chairs, I would write the newsletter, I would call up people to remind them to bring food to the potluck.

I'd love to help with maintenance, but starting things ain't my style. For one thing, I haven't got the intensity. In fact, lack of intensity is probably the big reason nothing like this will ever happen. To start something cold, you need to get real intense and to get other people

intense, and if there's one thing sixties leftovers I know avoid like the plague, it's intensity. We've *had* intensity. (Or, as Andrea said the other day, "I don't want to talk about politics. I've *talked* about politics.") Churches achieved lowkeyness by being founded by fanatics who were followed by tired and low-key children. Somehow, we've become our own second generation and don't want to feel our own true belief of yesterday any more than the children of converts want to get involved in their parents' enthusiasm. I don't know how we got worn down so fast. (Yes, I do, but I don't want to think about it enough to put it into words.) But however it happened, we may not be able to start any new processes, like a weekly small-scale Jamboree, because we've already started as much as we're going to start.

Then again, maybe not. Articles coming from different places for different reasons are coincidentally, inadvertently making this issue of CQ a neighborhood issue. The Jamboree stuff is about that neighborhood, Joe Bacon and I talk about our neighborhoods, Ray Jason writes about neighborhood performing—all about neighborhoods that are and were and should be. So maybe sixties people are getting interested in neighborhoods and maybe in some strange and unpredictable way, we'll start building new ones to hang out in. We've done stranger things.

HONEST HOPE

I've been thinking about honest hope.

When we start to hope often we promise ourselves too much. If this one thing changes, we say, then it will all change—injustice disappear and no more lonely days, lonely nights, for anyone, for me.

The war ends, we/they get the vote, waking up each day stays too much the same, people find new ways to steal joy from each other.

Give up, hide, lost dreams turn to headaches because we refuse to cry.

If we started with honest hope, could we go farther do you think? What would honest hope be like? What can we honestly hope for?

Time. The lie often has to do with too soon. The hopeless (lazy) say, "It'll never happen," and the hopeful say, "Yes, it will, and soon"—turning to the angry "NOW!" Some of it does happen now, some never, but mostly it happens some odd kind of not soon enough. Not soon enough for the hoping workers to notice that it happened. They've given up or want so much more it doesn't matter.

Percentages of a single lifetime may be too short for honest hope to live in.

I don't know, words keep trying to fit together, honesty, hope, seeds, garden, forest. Who'd have guessed a seed would do that, get so large? To be alive you have to have the quick seeds, tomatoes to plant and eat, and corn. Easy to remember, if you remember to remember, that it was you that started this good thing happening not long ago. But also we need to plant the forests, and tend them, and leave space for them to tend themselves.

Assembly line time, we're trapped in making things fast that break fast and thinking that something has happened. That magic moment, ablaze in television lights, praised in jingle and slogan, when you stand in the store and buy the new doohickus, when you believe it's going to make the difference, that moment is short. Other moments, less famous, are longer. Kachunk, kachunk, I can't wait to leave, where's oblivion—moments of making the shiny object go on a while, and there are many of them.

Then there's Christmas afternoon and it breaks. Even if it doesn't break, or not as soon as Christmas afternoon, it doesn't come close to touching your store hope. It doesn't *change* things. That short hope breaks in the many moments of the thing bored people made aging, but sometimes I don't notice because I'm on to other hopes, the next great purchase.

Tree time. Tree time takes longer. Trees, when they grow up, you don't think if you still like them. Your opinion is not the point. Tree time takes learning in a group of people like us where the rhythm of life has been determined (baba—boom, baba—boom) by tightening ten lugs a minute and on to the next car. If we're lucky we don't work there, but we measure our luck by how many things we can buy that were made there, and how fast we can buy them.

Pea pod time could teach you tree time. Fresh vegetables from the garden take longer than "this factory turns out twenty-seven hundred gadgies an hour" and are part of a species-long love affair with your mouth, take a while to happen and don't let you down. It's hard to remember how good they taste and then they wake up green pleasure cells you didn't know you had, the opposite of the third dent on the car and watching the dust settle on the electric knife sharpener.

Growing stuff with curves might match time more than building stuff with angles.

Honest hope and true time.

Real, slow-growing, long-lasting, hard-standing changes, like trees, never come up and pat you on the head and say, "You did it, kid, you made me possible, and you're terrific and I'm grateful as hell."

Because: 1) you might be dead by the time they're big and tall and you'll surely be different than when first hope caught you; 2) something that substantial you weren't the only variable that varied to make room for it; 3) trees and big changes aren't interested in personalities, even yours.

Honest hope. Plan to get your warm fuzzies someplace else. (What are friends for?) Hope that melts things and makes them new is as huggable as a flame. But warm at the right distance. The right uses of hope and the right distance. Get too close to the campfire, you get blisters, you get wounds. Stare at the flicker too long, you get crazy. Warm your butt and move it. Get to work.

THE DAY MARTIN LUTHER KING
WAS KILLED

The day Martin Luther King, Jr. was killed, John Evans decided to make a lot of money. He had worked for Dr. King for ten years. He got a real job, saved, invested against conventional wisdom, and got rich. In two years and three months, he had enough money. He quit.

He bought land on a state road in a southern state, hired a sculptor, and built his monument to Martin Luther King. When he was building it, he didn't ask for help because he knew it had to be done in a particular way. Other people would discuss and compromise.

He told no one about it because he didn't want words and pictures to make it invisible to people before they saw it. Since money can buy more than people usually ask it to, the monument now exists in its own way and is sometimes seen.

The place looks like a roadside park. Most people pull off and use the pump and restrooms and picnic tables and drive on. Some take time to wander around. A few of the wanderers walk over the little hill in the back. Behind the hill, they see fifteen life-size marble people standing in a circle holding hands. They aren't on a base; they're standing in the grass. They're wearing jeans and work shirts, dresses, suits, and overalls. Their mouths are slightly open. Small marble letters sitting on the grass in the middle of the circle say We Shall Overcome.

The circle is not unbroken. There's a space between two of the people. They have their hands open and out at their sides, but no one is holding them. Occasionally someone from the road answers the invitation and comes forward and takes the hands of the statues of John's lost friends. You look across the circle and see Martin Luther King looking at you. The sculptor did King well, especially the eyes.

When the monument was done, John knew that it wasn't in memory of King. It was in memory of that one moment in ten years when John had really believed in the dream, and of all the moments when he had wanted to believe.

John sometimes sits in a tree near the statues, hidden and waiting. He waits for one of the visitors to see it, to see what it was like, what he was like, to believe. It's a very quiet revival, but John hasn't liked noise since he heard the shot.

STEWART BRAND
With extensive quotes from
Bruce Ames

Human Harm
to Human DNA

Genetic Toxicity

Oh Art. Could you get that one? If I
get into it it'll be a whole new article
and I can't right now.

Stewart Brand

Oh Stewart. Well, suffice to say that
this is a major news story for individual people and the species as a whole.
It's scandalous how little attention
it's received in the more popular
press since CQ published this five
years ago. It's horrible to think that
the deformed babies shown in this
article are genetic pioneers, but they
well may be.

Art Kleiner

*From the original introduction
(Spring 1979):*
Remarks in quotations whose source
is not cited are from a conversation
taped in January 1979, between
Bruce Ames, Paul Ehrlich, and Mar-
cus Feldman at Stanford University
(where I got my biology degree in

1960). I am grateful for assistance
from Ames's colleague Lois Gold,
Susan Stern, and CQ staffers Patty
Phelan and Anne Herbert. The inac-
curacies and misinterpretations inevitable in a piece like this are my responsibility. The intent of the article
is to introduce the scope of a problem and equip the reader to do something about it.

Stewart Brand

*As serious as are radiation effects, it should be emphasized
that—barring nuclear war—induction of mutations by
other environmental agents probably is of greater importance. The list of potential chemical mutagens contained
in man's diet and other ingested or inhaled substances is a
long one. It still increases steadily.*
Curt Stern, Principles of Human Genetics, 1973[49]

*Although much attention, both scientific and public, has
been given to the possibility of inherited defects from ionizing radiation, virtually none has been directed to the same
hazard from chemicals, which may be as great as from
radiation. It is now well known that certain chemicals
can produce both major chromosomal damage, likely to
yield early defects in offspring, and point mutuations,
minor defects not detectable microscopically in chromosomes, but which, if present widely in the population, can
yield undesirable consequences in succeeding generations.*
Committee on Science and
Public Policy, National Academy of Sciences,
Biology and the Future of Man, 1970 (Ref. 26, p. 870).

*There is reason to fear that some chemicals may constitute
as important a risk as radiation, possibly a more serious
one. Although knowledge of chemical mutagenesis in man
is much less certain, a number of chemicals—some with
widespread use—are known to induce genetic damage in
some organisms. To consider only radiation hazards may
be to ignore the submerged part of the iceberg.*
James F. Crow, "Chemical Risk to Future Generations,"
Scientist and Citizen, 1968[50]

142

Comparing the routine running of the nuclear industry (without bad disasters or accidents) versus the routine running of the chemical industry and asking the question, "Are you more worried about mutations and cancer from nuclear or chemical?," I would say chemical. . . . If the local nuclear power plant has a meltdown, you would notice it, but you could easily be melted down by chlorinated hydrocarbons without knowing it's going on.

Paul Ehrlich, conversation, 1979

It's slow, deep poison. And there's no antidote, no cure. Only prevention.

BRUCE AMES*[1] *Damage to DNA by environmental mutagens (both natural and manmade) is likely to be a major cause of cancer[2,3] and genetic birth defects, and may contribute to heart disease[4] and aging[5] as well. These are the major diseases now confronting our society: currently almost one-fourth of us will develop cancer, and a few percent of our children are born with birth defects that might be attributable to DNA damage. Damage to the DNA of our germ cells can result in genetic defects that may show up in our children and in future generations. Somatic mutation in the DNA of the other cells of the body could give rise to cancerous cells by changing the normal cellular mechanisms, coded for in the DNA, that control and prevent cell multiplication. Mutagens are present among the natural chemicals in our diet; among manmade chemicals to which we are exposed (such as industrial chemicals, pesticides, hair dyes, cosmetics, and drugs); and in complex mixtures (such as cigarette smoke and contaminants in the air we breathe and the water we drink). . . .*

Clearly, many more chemicals will be added to the current list of human mutagens and carcinogens. It has been estimated that over 50,000 chemicals produced in significant quantities are currently used in commerce and close to 1,000 new chemicals are introduced each year.[6] Most of these—from flame retardants in our children's pajamas to pesticides accumulating in our body fat—were not tested for carcinogenicity or mutagenicity before their use.

---

* Italic quotes in this article are from Ames' paper "Environmental Chemicals Causing Cancer and Genetic Birth Defects" (December, 1978). In revised form it appeared in Science in 1979. For detailed citation see Note 1.

These statements contain two premises which are relatively new to science and owe a great deal to Bruce Ames' work at the Biochemistry Department, University of California, Berkeley. One premise is the considerable overlap of mutagenic with carcinogenic materials—suggesting that a similar or identical disruption of the DNA code in the chromosomes is responsible for mutations inherited through reproductive cells and for cancer which is spread through somatic (body) cells. In other words, if you hear that something is a mutagen, it is probably also a carcinogen. And vice versa. They both can be called "genotoxic."†

AMES: *We have validated our tests for the detection of carcinogens as mutagens by examining over 300 chemicals reported as carcinogens or noncarcinogens in animal experiments. The results show that almost all (90%: 158/176) of these chemical carcinogens are mutagenic in the* Salmonella *test. . . . We also examined the organic chemicals known or suspected as human carcinogens and found that almost all (16/18) were mutagens in the test. . . . Thus, almost all carcinogens tested are mutagens, and the converse also appears to be true: mutagens are*

---

† Although it is not established that somatic mutations are always involved in carcinogenesis, several lines of evidence strongly point in such a direction:

1. Tumor induction implies a permanent and transmissible alteration of the cells.

2. Tumors have been shown to be of monoclonal origin—that is, originating from one single cell—which is as expected for a mutational event.

3. Known carcinogens and mutagens share the same electrophilic (electron-seeking) property.

4. Experimental evidence indicates that most, possibly all, carcinogens are also mutagens.

5. An impairment of DNA-repair, as in certain human genetic diseases like *Xeroderma pigmentosum*, or in experimental animal systems, leads to an increased incidence of tumors.

6. Cell transformation by oncogenic viruses (i.e., those tending to cause tumors) implies a change at the DNA level.

The close correlation between mutagenicity and carcinogenicity has made it possible to deal with the carcinogenic and mutagenic properties of chemicals in the same context. In that spirit Druckrey has introduced the term *genotoxic* to cover hereditary changes of germinal as well as somatic cells, including tumor induction.[7]

—Claes Ramel, *Ambio*, No. 5–6, 1978[8]

carcinogens with few (if any) adequately documented exceptions. We found that almost all (95/108) "noncarcinogens" tested were not mutagenic, and those few that were may in fact be weak carcinogens that were not detected as such due to the statistical limitations of animal carcinogenicity tests.[9]

THE AMES TEST

The Ames test, also called the *Salmonella* test, is the other premise of the opening statements. By its use large numbers of suspect chemicals can be tested for genotoxicity quickly and inexpensively—in two days for $250–$1,000 per test substance instead of the two years or more and $250,000 required by animal tests (using rats or mice usually). Since the Ames test has made a revolution in the environmentally critical domain of bioassaying, instigating a growing family of short-term tests, it's worth going into detail about how it works and what it has done.

You take a petri dish, the standard microorganism test tool, and lay in agar (gel for nutrient medium) and a "lawn" of a billion or so of one of Ames' special strains of the bacteria *Salmonella typhimurium*. Very special strains—they've been elegantly tailored: 1) to have a mutation in a gene synthesizing the amino acid histidine, so they can't live in a histidine-free petri dish unless they revert by mutation to the histidine-synthesizing capability; 2) the mutation involved is a "frameshift" in the DNA which is not easily masked; 3) their DNA is specially susceptible to the reversion; 4) the cells are particularly permeable to outside substances; 5) their DNA-repair capabilities are

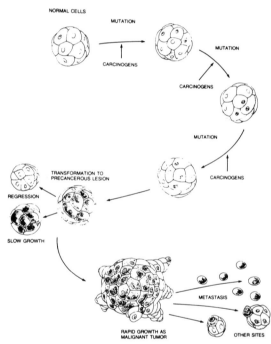

Bruce Ames with a petri dish of bacteria and a suspected mutagen—the *Salmonella* test. Because of this test Ames is one of the 100 scientists most cited in other scientists' papers.

Figure 1. One theory of carcinogenesis states that cells are restrained from becoming cancerous by several independent genes and that tumors develop only when mutations accumulate in all those genes within a single line of cells. The mutations (black dots within cell nuclei) are seldom spontaneous but are apparently caused by carcinogenic factors in the environment. Once a precancerous lesion has formed, it must in many cases regress or grow very slowly; only a few lesions progress to an invasive, metastasizing tumor. (After J. Cairns, 1975. See also Figure 4.) *From* Ecoscience *(ref. 23, p. 593).*

crippled and their enzymes for "locking in" mutations are enhanced. Four different stains are used to detect different types of mutagens. The result is a test of great sensitivity and high resolution.

(Now you know why labs like Ames' need to work with recombinant DNA—it's their basic tool for this kind of detailed DNA design. Developing the Ames test took ten years—1964–74.)

Also in the petri dish is a standard quantity of homogenized rat liver, whose enzymes will make the test more closely approximate what happens in the mammal. Some chemicals that would not directly mutate bacteria are metabolized into mutagens/carcinogens in rats and us. The liver puree gives the bacteria our problems.

Drop a quarter-inch piece of filter paper soaked in the substance you're testing into the middle of the dish, keep it at body temperature for a day, and look: if there is a ring of bacteria colonies around the test substance, it is mutagenic. A significant number of the crippled *Salmonella* bacteria have mutated back to histidine-synthesizing viability and have generated colonies big enough to see. (See figures 2 and 3.)

Using this test Ames and Arlene Blum detected in 1977 the mutagenicity of Tris, the fire retardant in sleepwear used by fifty million American children and absorbed into their bodies. A year and a half later Tris was removed from the market when it was found to cause cancer in animals. In 1975 Ames' lab found that 90% of the hydrogen peroxide hair dyes used by twenty-five million Americans, mostly women, were genotoxic and absorbed through their scalps. The hair dyes are still on the market.

Bad news—and there's more to come—but the bearer of the bad news is also itself the good news.

Free of charge or patent, Ames' lab has sent their strains of *Salmonella* to over 2,000 government, industrial, and academic laboratories who wanted to conduct their own tests. Said Ames recently, "Most of the industries in the world are using it—because it saves them

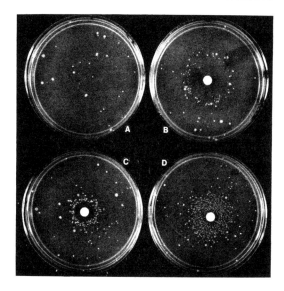

Figure 2. The "spot test" for mutagen-induced revertants. Each petri plate contains, in a thin overlay of top agar, the tester strain TA98 of *Salmonella* bacteria and, in the case of plates *C* and *D*, a liver microsomal activation system (S-9 Mix). Mutagens were applied to 6-mm filter paper disks, which were then placed in the center of each plate. Mutagen-induced revertants appear as a circle of revertant colonies around each disk.

A. Control plate: spontaneous revertants.
B. Plate showing revertant colonies produced by the Japanese food additive furyl-furamide (AF-2)—1 microgram.
C. The mold carcinogen aflotoxin B, -1 microgram.
D. 2-aminoflorene—10 micrograms.

Reprinted, with permission, from B. N. Ames et al.[51] Copyright © 1975 by Elsevier Scientific Publishing Co., Amsterdam.

money. In developing a chemical they go through hundreds of chemicals before they get one they really like. This way they can be testing them with our test and other short-term tests, and if something is bad they can throw it out and it doesn't cost them much. But when they finally develop a product, then it costs a lot of money to run an animal cancer test and they're not overjoyed to find out it's a carcinogen at the very end. So the companies have all

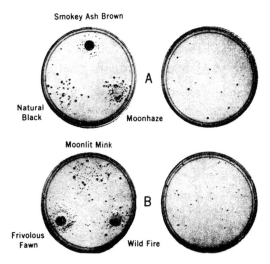

Figure 3. Spot tests on petri plates showing the mutagenicity of various hair dyes on strain TA1538: Moonhaze no. 32 (Miss Clairol), Moonlit Mink no. 360 (Clairol Born Blonde), Wild Fire no. 32 (Roux fancitone) (all tested without peroxide), and Frivolous Fawn no. 23 (Roux fancitone) (mixed with H_2O_2 as per instructions). Control plates without hair dyes are on the right. Plates B, but not A, contain liver microsomes (S-9 Mix). Smokey Ash Brown no. 775 and Natural Black no. 83 (Clairol Loving Care) are semi-permanent, non-oxidative type dyes. *From Bruce Ames et al.*[52]

been enthusiastic about using these short-term tests."

Since they're keeping genotoxic products from ever reaching the market, we can share their enthusiasm.

Also using the tests are regulatory agencies and environmental investigators.

AMES: *Lots of laboratories now are using the short-term tests for looking at all kinds of compounds in the environment, particularly complex mixtures. Water pollutants or air pollutants are horribly complex mixtures. You can use this for trying to figure out what chemicals in there look dangerous and where they're coming from. That's something you couldn't do with a traditional animal cancer test.*

The Ames test is not fool proof. It misses 10% of the potential carcinogens—some of the chlorinated chemicals, pesticides, and metals.[10] Fortunately the success of the Ames

test has inspired a whole generation of other short-term tests which, taken together, can provide an effective screen. Most laboratories using the Ames test now include it as one of a battery of short-term tests. Ames' colleague Joyce McCann reports there are at least eighty such tests being developed—other tests with microorganisms such as the Pol-A test working with *Escherichia coli*; whole organism tests using *Drosophila* (fruit flies), small fish, etc.; tests in cultured mammalian cells; and tumor-forming tests with mammalian cells.[10]

The animal tests still have the final say, but only 100 such tests a year are conducted by the National Cancer Institute, and they take two to three-and-a-half years.*

AMES: *One limitation of animal cancer tests, however, is their sensitivity. An environmental carcinogen causing cancer in 1% of 100 million people would result in a million cases of cancer. To detect a chemical causing cancer in only 1% of the test animals, we would have to use 10,000 rats or mice.*

EPIDEMIOLOGY

In fact one of the major test animals in use is humans, without their knowledge or consent. It's called epidemiology—what turns up in human medical histories.

AMES: *A chemical mutagen (and carcinogen)—the agricultural pesticide dibromochloropropane (DBCP)—was recently discovered, somewhat by accident, to cause infertility in many DBCP workers who had been exposed to it. DBCP might also cause a variety of genetic abnormalities among the offspring of those workers who were able to produce children. If the sterility had not been connected with the occupational exposure, thus alerting us to the dangers of DBCP, it seems doubtful that genetic abnormalities and cancer that might occur years later would be connected to the earlier exposure. . . .*

DBCP was used until recently at a level of about 10 million pounds per year in the United States. In 1961 it was shown to cause sterility and testicular atrophy in animals;[11] in 1973 it was shown to be a carcinogen,[12] and in 1977 it was shown to be a

---

* Because of the high cost, usually only fifty animals are used, even in a thorough experiment. The sensitivity problems are partially overcome (though not to complete satisfaction) by using very high doses.

mutagen in Salmonella.[13] *Its potency as a carcinogen is such that 2 mg/kg/day in male and in female rats gives 50% of the animals cancer. (It is slightly less potent {8 mg/kg/day} in male and female mice.) A 2 mg/kg daily level is approximately the exposure level of a worker breathing air contaminated with 2 ppm of DBCP—close to the actual level of worker exposure.*

It is too early to see if many of the workers will get cancer in twenty years, but it is not too early to see that a high percentage of them are now infertile. Currently, almost 100 workers in several companies have been made sterile or have low sperm counts as a consequence of exposures to DBCP for as little as one to two years. Because eighty industrial plants were handling the material, many more workers will probably be discovered to be affected by this chemical. It is unclear how much DBCP was eaten by consumers as residues in food since there has usually been no maximum level standard for residues.

One problem is that, other considerations aside, humans are truly lousy test animals. We're large, slow-reproducing, deceptive, exposed to innumerable potential toxins, and we don't hold still in any sense. The ideal test organism is uniform. In the noise of our immense variability, the signal of any particular environmental cause of disease gets lost unless it's overwhelming. This is particularly true of cancer, which takes twenty to thirty years to develop after the carcinogenic exposure.

AMES: *Even with the current level of sophistication of human epidemiology it is almost unheard of to identify the causal agent when the increase in risk is below 50% for the type of cancer being examined, and even increases considerably above that are difficult.*

The best human cancer data by far comes from cigarette smoking. A considerable population does it, another considerable population doesn't (the control group), and smoking is strongly correlated with a particular disease—lung cancer. Have a look at Figure 4 for a horrifying determinism. You can predict the exact number of women who will die of lung cancer in 1980 from the smoking they started in the '50s—over 60 per 100,000 population. For those women, stopping smoking now won't help much. 1980 is next year.

JARGON

Mutagenic—mutation causing (includes chromosome scrambling and point mutations within chromosomes).

Carcinogenic—cancer causing.

Genotoxic—DNA-damaging (combines meanings of "mutagenic" and "carcinogenic").

Teratogenic—"monster"-causing. Any influence during pregnancy that leads to birth defects. An unknown proportion of teratogens are mutagens.

DNA—Desoxyribonucleic acid, the "double helix" of material in chromosomes that passes on cell and whole-body characteristics. The reproductive essence.

THE CHEMICAL TIDE

As smoking by some men dramatically increased in the first half of this century, and smoking by some women in mid-century, the exposure of all of us to new chemicals has taken off since World War II. In the next decades we will be paying the price.

AMES: *The tremendous increase in production of chemicals, such as vinyl chloride, that started in the mid-1950s may result in a steep increase in human cancer in the 1980 decade if too many of these chemicals with widespread human exposure are indeed powerful carcinogens.*

For the 1980s, stopping all hazardous chemical exposure now wouldn't help much even if we could.

About 4 million chemical substances have been identified.[14] Ames says over 50,000, others say 63,000 are in common commercial use in the United States[10] and 1,000 new chemicals are introduced each year. For a sense of the volume of production and its recent increase examine Figure 5. Worldwide the total chemical business is $80,000,000,000 per

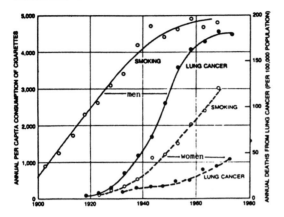

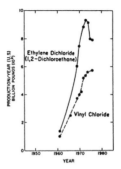

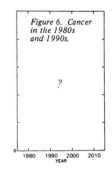

Figure 6. Cancer
in the 1980s
and 1990s.

?

Figure 4. *Ames:* Cigarette smoking and lung cancer are unmistakably related, but the nature of the relationship remained obscure because of the long latent period between the increase in cigarette consumption and the increase in the incidence of lung cancer. The data are from England and Wales. In men (solid line) smoking began to increase at the beginning of the twentieth century, but the corresponding trend in deaths from lung cancer did not begin until after 1920. In women (dotted line) smoking began later, and lung cancers are only now appearing.*
*From J. Cairns, "The Cancer Problem," *Scientific American* (November, 1975), p. 72. Copyright 1975 by Scientific American, Inc. All rights reserved. Reprinted by permission.

Figure 5. *Ames:* Production of two mutagens/carcinogens with widespread human exposure: ethylene dichloride and vinyl chloride (production data from "Top-50 Chemicals" issues of *Chemical and Engineering News*). Approximately 100 billion lbs. (5 × 10^{10} kilos) of ethylene dichloride and over 50 billion lbs. of vinyl chloride have been produced since 1960. Ethylene dichloride is a volatile liquid that is the precursor of vinyl chloride and is also used extensively as a fumigrant, solvent, gasoline additive (200 million lbs/yr), and metal degreaser.

Ethylene dicholoride was first shown to be a mutagen in *Drosophila* in 1960, and later in barley and *Salmonella*, but this fact has just been completed by the National Center Institute (September, 1978) and is positive in both sexes of both rats and mice. Vinyl chloride gas is used to make polyvinyl chloride (PVC; vinyl) plastic. It was shown to be a carcinogen in rats and in people in the mid-1970s, and a mutagen in *Salmonella* and other systems shortly afterwards.

year.[15] However you assess the current state of technology and affluence in the world, chemical production and use is at the heart of it.

Now, despite the impression we get from the newspapers, not all chemicals are carcinogenic. Most are not. Of the 3,500 "adequately" tested so far at the National Cancer Institute for carcinogenicity in animals, only 750 tested positive, and those were suspect chemicals being tested.[10] Nevertheless most of the chemicals in common use have yet to be tested at all.

To correct another common impression, Ames comments, *"It isn't that everything artificial is bad and natural is good, because there are a wide variety of natural mutagens. For example, Sugimura and his group in Japan have shown that when you char food with a lot of protein in it you make lots of mutagens. What the risk of that is we* don't quite know. Obviously humans have been doing it for quite a long time. On the other hand 25% of us get cancer, and it's likely that a good part of this is due to cigarette smoking, ultraviolet light, and natural carcinogens in our diet, as there hasn't been time for the modern chemical world to really hit us yet.

"A cigarette is, say, ten minutes off your life, and people are willing to smoke two packs a day and live eight years less than a nonsmoker. Smoking is fairly addictive. If it turns out that a charcoal-broiled steak is fifteen minutes off your life (I don't know if it's that), maybe people will say, 'What the hell, I don't eat them that often and they're good,' and other people may say, 'I'd rather have a poached fish than a broiled fish.'"

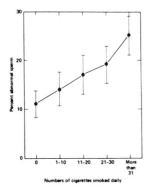

Figure 6. Semen changes in cigarette smokers. Each circle and error bar represents the mean and standard error of the level of sperm abnormalities in groups of men who for more than 1 year smoked the numbers of cigarettes indicated. In order of increasing dose, each point is based on 50, 22, 43, 48, and 7 males, respectively. Reproduced from Viczian.[17]

EFFECTS OF FATHERS' SMOKING ON THEIR INFANTS	
Cigarettes Smoked Daily by Father	*Severe Abnormalities in Babies*
0	0.8%
1 to 10	1.4%
more than 10	2.1%

From a study of 5,200 live births. G. Mau and P. Netter, *Dtsch. Med. Wschr.* 99, 1113–1118 (1974). Fathers' smoking affects the incidence of abnormalities whether the mother smokes or not. In addition, fathers' smoking is associated with an increase in perinatal mortality. (Compiled by Bruce N. Ames and Lois Swirsky Gold.)

Figure 7. Silhouettes of human sperm used by Andrew Wyrobek at Lawrence Livermore Laboratory for scoring sperm samples from exposed subjects. 1) Normal (oval), 2) small, 3) large, 4) round, 5) doubles (heads, tails, etc.), 6) narrow-at-the-base, 7) narrow, 8) pear, 9) irregular, 10) "ghosts."

Soot was the first environmental cause of cancer to be identified (in 1775 by Sir Percival Pott, investigating scrotal cancer in chimney sweeps). One of the most potent mutagen/carcinogens known is aflatoxin, a biochemical product of a naturally occurring fungus (sometimes found in peanut butter).

SMOKING

So there's lots of chemical exposure, most of it encountered unwillingly. But perhaps the worst exposure is not only encountered willingly, it's sought and paid for by individual choice.

AMES: *"I'd be surprised if there are very many things in the modern chemical world that do as much damage as cigarettes. It's clear they are causing life shortening, and I think more and more evidence will come out for genetic effects in the children of smokers."*

It's no wonder Ames is alert to this. As Arthur Lubow reported in *New Times*, "Cigarette smoke is so mutagenic that it knocks the Ames test off the scale. 'The Ames test can easily detect smoke from 1/100th of a cigarette as being mutagenic,' says Byron Butterworth, Director of Genetic Toxicology at the recently established Chemical Industry Institute of Toxicology. 'We can't allow smoking in the laboratory.' "[16]

Who the hell working in such a laboratory would smoke?

As for genetic effects, several German studies appear to link smoking fathers with an increased incidence of abnormal sperm, miscarriages and birth defects in their families.[17,18,19] The human sperm abnormality test for mutagenicity that Andrew Wyrobek is developing at Lawrence Livermore Laboratory, may be useful in pursuing this research. Ames and Yamasaki were able to detect mutagens in the urine of smokers (but not in nonsmokers), suggesting that many parts of the body, perhaps including the gonads, are indeed exposed to some of the gram of mutagenic tars that the two-pack smoker collects daily.[20]

Smoking mothers, according to a brand-new analysis of 50,000 pregnancies by the United States Collaborative Perinatal Project, significantly increase their chances of miscarriage, strongly increase the likelihood of birth defects (usually fatal), and somewhat increase the occurrence of crib death. Even if they stop smoking before getting pregnant, they have a higher risk of mislocated placenta and dangerous birth complications.[21] To what degree these problems are *genetically* caused is unknown.

In the United States there are 80,000 cancer deaths per year directly attributed to cigarette smoking.[22]

CANCER

You may recall in 1971, when the National Cancer Act was passed, hearing public statements such as, "We are so close to a cure for cancer. We lack only the will and the kind of money and comprehensive planning that went into putting a man on the moon. . . . Why don't we try to conquer cancer by America's 200th birthday?" (Ref. 22, p. 322.)

Eight years and 4,762,000,000 dollars later, you no longer hear such optimistic statements. There has been notable success with lymphocytic leukemia, Hodgkin's disease, and other relatively uncommon forms of cancer, and good research has been funded that contributes to understanding and preventing cancer, but many critics feel that the national "war on cancer" has been an expensive defeat. (Ref. 22, pp. 14–15.) The now common critique of what happened is well summarized by Paul Ehrlich in *Ecoscience*:

It is now generally accepted that at least three quarters of human cancers are "environmental" in origin (that is, not caused by viruses, spontaneous breakdown of immune mechanisms, and the like). . . . The scientists most involved in the "war" were largely recruited from the ranks of surgeons, biochemists, radiologists, and virologists—mostly people with little interest in studying the release of carcinogens into the environment or the possible nutritive factors involved in the induction of cancers. . . . In the mid-1970s it appeared likely that billions of dollars will be spent during the rest of this century, attempting to cure people whose sickness could have been prevented.[23]

Through 1976 the amount of the vast National Cancer Institute budget spent on cancer prevention was about 12%. It's now increasing markedly. (Ref. 22, p. 328.)

Interestingly, the Ames test came out of pure research on bacterial genetics, work in a completely different ballpark from cancer research and funding. It's also interesting that Ames spends a considerable amount of his time scanning and citing the work of people well outside his own field.

NUCLEAR RADIATION

Currently the most active war-on-something going on in America is the Guerilla War on Nuclear Energy. It's also the most successful—indeed pinching off the construction of new reactors and receiving the acknowledgement and approval of even Herman Kahn.[24]

Oddly, most of the antinuclear attention and emotion is focused on reactor safety. Odd, at least, when you consider:

1) The prospect of nuclear war, the one catastrophe that overshadows everything else, including population overload and the chemical hazards discussed in this article. That international encouragement of nuclear energy feeds the proliferation of nuclear weapons seems the strongest argument against a plutonium economy, even thinking only in terms of radiation exposure.

2) The cultural perspective. Any society that so discounts the future as to leave massive radioactive wastes earns the contempt of history.

3) The economics of reactor construction, use, and dismantling—already bad and getting worse.

4) The actual safety record of the nuclear industry, while not dazzling, is pretty good.

Radiation is the best-studied and understood of all major pollutants. Nuclear reactors are visible invaders on our landscape, and their control or reduction because of safety, though difficult, seems possible. Small wonder that so much effort has gone in that direction, even though greater hazard lies elsewhere.

The gut impulse—to protect the generations—is correct, and hopeful. It's the only social cause on the roster right now that well-off Americans are willing to go to jail for.

HUMAN GENE POOL

John Gofman and Arthur Tamplin, the major popularizers of nuclear genetic threat, have written: "Changes in the chromosomes of sperm or our precursor cells may be transmitted to all future generations of humans. The heredity of man, his greatest treasure, is thereby at stake. Once irreversibly injured, the chromosomes cannot be repaired by any process known to man."[25]

The Committee on Science and Public Policy of the National Academy of Sciences has declared: "The human gene pool is the primary resource of mankind, today and tomorrow. The present gene pool is the culmination of three billion years of evolution and natural selection."[26]

How large is this greatest treasure, this primary resource? CQ reader Rob Roach has volunteered the mathematics on the mass and volume of DNA it took to pass on all the heredity of all the 20 billion *Homo sapiens* of the past and present (4.3 billion are alive now). The grand total, measuring just the information-bearing base pairs in the double helix of human DNA, is *0.08 grams*. In volume, *0.2 milliliters*.* Less than a teardrop.

While we're at it, what is the value of the human gene pool in 1979 dollars?

A tiny resource, but intricately dispersed,

intricately protected, buffered, repaired, renewed. By some accounts our genes do not work for us, we work for them.[27] Consider just the tests the chromosomes must pass during conception and pregnancy. The male ejaculate ranges from 0.5 to 11 milliliters (!) with on the average 80 to 110 million sperm per milliliter. So an average wad has 300 million sperm. Of those, 40% can't swim very well and some 12% to 27% are visibly abnormal.[28] The vast majority never make it to the egg, even if they're deposited in a vagina, which is uncontracepted, and a just-ripe egg is handy. The few hundred who reach the egg perform an elaborate dance around it and then, by an unknown mechanism of selection, one gets through.

Then follows the complex process of fertilization, travel of the quickened egg to the uterus, and implantation there. It is estimated that one-third to one-half of all fertilized eggs do not survive to implant.[29] About 25% of early spontaneously aborted embryos (up to 17 days after conception) have detectable chromosome abnormalities. Such early abortions are usually not noticed; they are lost in what appears to be a late menstrual period. Selection continues through pregnancy—14–17% of fetuses after the fourth week are miscarried or stillborn.[30] Of spontaneously aborted fetuses nearly two-thirds have chromosome abnormalities.[31]

BIRTH DEFECTS

All of that is good news, the working of an efficient and merciful gauntlet. However, 7% of babies are born with birth defects—one out of

---

* Here's how Rob Roach, of Olympia, Washington, figured it.

Assumptions: 20 billion people
Human DNA, uncoiled, is 1 meter in length
Each base is about 3.2 Å in length
Each base has a molecular weight of about 400, or 400 g/mole

So:

$$\frac{1 \text{ meter}}{3.2 \times 10^{-10}/\text{meter (bases)}} \rightarrow 3 \times 10^9 \text{ bases}$$

Then:

$$\frac{2 \text{ (DNA strands)} \times 20 \times 10^9 \text{ (people)} \times 3 \times 10^9 \text{ (bases)}}{6.023 \times 10^{23} \text{ (Avogadro's Number)}} \rightarrow$$

$$\frac{20 \times 10^{18}}{10^{23}} = 20 \times 10^{-5} \rightarrow 2 \times 10^{-4} \times 400 \text{ g/mole} =$$

$$800 \times 10^{-4} = 8 \times 10^{-7} = .08 \text{ grams}$$

or about .02 milliliters.

fourteen.* Of those it is thought that 20% are purely genetic, 20% purely environmental (caused during pregnancy), and the remaining 60% an indistinguishable combination of genetic and environmental.[32] Some 2,336 different kinds of birth defects have been identified—many more are assumed to exist.[33]

Here we come to the heart of the matter—the immeasurable and usually hidden suffering that goes with having (or being) a defective child. The event is frequently shattering for the parents. The costs of special medical and educational care are immense, both for the family and the community at large. Though some of the children are cheerful, most suffer from their condition to degrees that can't be quantified—the constant fear of the hemophiliac (bleeder) of any minor accident that could kill, the humiliation in public of the malformed or incompetent, the endless obstacle course of life in a wheelchair. Dependency. Physical pain. Short lifespan. Guilt. Rage. . . .

GENETIC LOAD

Call the lives of the born-defective the social load. They are the bodily expression of what is termed the genetic load, which measures the loss of fitness of a population due to the harmful mutations carried in its gene pool.

Not all mutations are harmful, but since they amount to random jiggering in a complex, delicate process, the great preponderance are deleterious, some are neutral, and a tiny fraction may be advantageous. Also most mutations are recessive—they are expressed only if both parents have the same recessive trait. In freshman Biology: Aa x Aa (the carrier—heterozygous—parents)→AA (the dominant homozygote) and Aa, Aa (more carrier heterozygotes) and aa (the recessive homozygote child, expressing the otherwise hidden trait).

---

* That's the March of Dimes figure. Here's their rap: 1 out of 10 families knows the anguish that comes with having a birth-defect child; every year 250,000 babies are born [in the United States] with significant birth defects; at least 18,000 infants die in their first year because of birth defects; 500,000 unborn babies die as a result of birth defects every year.

Harmful recessive mutations—once they occur it is practically impossible to remove them from the gene pool. They don't increase, but neither do they decrease. Even if the trait is lethal in the recessive homozygote (aa), it hides and persists nearly indefinitely in the heterozygotes. That's not all bad—such variability in the gene pool might be useful if conditions for the organism change. Some of the genetic load is insurance.

But most of it is pure load. All of us carry a dozen or so lethal recessive genes that won't show up unless we mate with someone with a matching recessive (Ref. 26, p. 910). That occurs more often with inbreeding groups such as small island populations and religious sects, and even more in consanguinous marriages such as between cousins. Outbreeding therefore conceals new recessive mutations. These days, when nearly anyone can mate with anyone anywhere, such mutations may be assumed to be collecting invisibly, to be expressed much later (and perhaps more harmfully then, for reasons to be seen).[34]

That's what's maddening about human genetics. Nearly everything is expressed so much later—generations later—that you can't track anything back to its causes. Some nuclear enthusiast nonbiologists have rejoiced that not many mutations turned up in the children of the bombed in Hiroshima and Nagasaki. They wouldn't—not until the third generation and then only if cousins marry. The mutations are there—recessive, unremovable. And when eventually they turn up they'll be indistinguishable from all other mutations except that statistically there'll be more.

Mutations vary in their harmfulness. Some are lethal when expressed—they kill the embryo before birth. Some are sublethal—they live past birth and may even reproduce, but they have "reduced fitness." Others may be subnoticeable—more on that later. One fascinating idea of genetics is the Haldane-Muller principle: Each individual harmful mutation is in the end equally harmful—a lethal gene kills right away, a sublethal spreads its harm over a number of generations. As Garrett Hardin points out, in a growing population such as

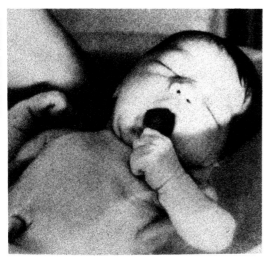

Birth Without Violence

Physically normal baby—93% of births.

These are not easy pictures to look at. But neither will it be easy to change the habits—personal, commercial, governmental, and military—that are increasing the occurrence of such births.

Many birth defects look far worse than these. I've included only ones that may live past birth and are relatively common. Also left out are the more hidden defects—muscular dystrophy, heart malformations, diabetes mellitus, cystic fibrosis, sickle cell anemia, hemophilia, PKU, and Huntington's chorea. These photos and most information with them come from two excellent medical texts: Keith L. Moore, *The Developing Human*, 2d ed. (Philadelphia: W. B. Saunders, 1977); and David W. Smith, *Recognizable Patterns of Human Malformation*, 2d ed. (Philadelphia: W. B. Saunders, 1976).

The usual image of lethal human folly is the skull. The faces of these children may carry a more accurate impact. Death is an end and space for a renewal—the genes expressed here live on.

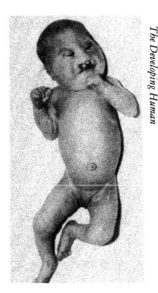

Recognizable Patterns of Human Malformation

The Developing Human

Trisomy 13 syndrome

Trisomy 18 syndrome

As Down's syndrome is the result of three chromosomes No. 21 rather than the usual two, these defects result from tripling of chromosomes 13 and 18. Trisomies tend to increase with maternal age, and to some extent the tendency is inherited. The incidence of Trisomy 21 (Down's syndrome) is 1/660, of Trisomy 18 is 1/3500, and of Trisomy 13 is 1/7000. Both of the latter two are severely defective physically and mentally. Most don't survive the first year.

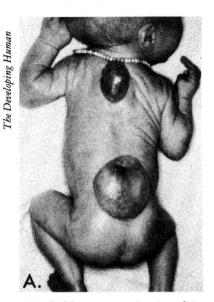

A.

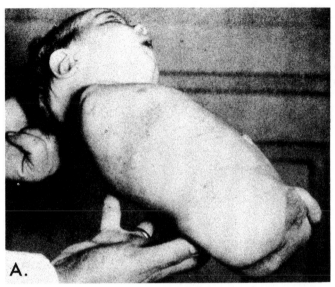

A.

Spina bifida, an externalization of the spinal cord, is one of the commonest forms of birth defect. Incidence is 1/375. In the United States 6,200 newborn a year have either spina bifida or hydrocephalus (below). Many survive birth: 53,000 are alive, under 20, in the United States.

Thalidomide, a sedative prescribed to mothers because of its apparent absence of side effects, caused over 7,000 babies to be born with various degrees of limb malformation. The children are now reaching college age.

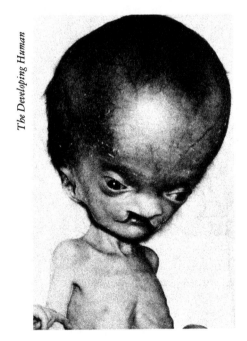

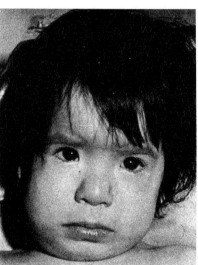

Hydrocephalus, said to occur in 1/550 births, results from the accumulation of spinal fluid in the skull. Sometimes the condition develops after birth.

Another known teratogen is alcohol. This 2½ year old shows Fetal Alcohol syndrome, resulting from her mother's chronic alcoholism. Such babies have a 17% death rate at birth. The survivors have weak bodies, an average IQ of 63, and possible brain malformation.

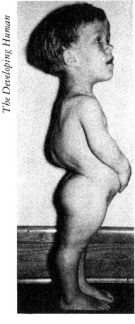

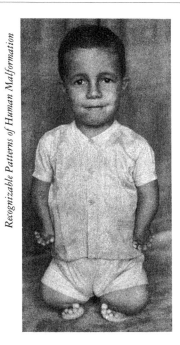

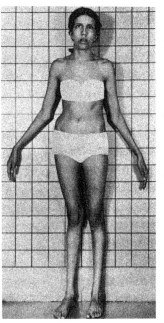

The Developing Human

Recognizable Patterns of Human Malformation

Recognizable Patterns of Human Malformation

Achondroplasia, a form of dwarfism, results from a dominant gene. Occurrence is about 1/10,000, with about 90% thought to be the product of new mutations. Intelligence is normal. If this child reproduced, half of his children would have the defect.

The result of inbreeding in a Brazilian population, Grebe's syndrome has affected 47 children. Some died in infancy.

A 16-year-old with Marfan's syndrome, resulting in this case from a new mutation since no other cases were known in her family. Mean age of survival for individuals with the condition is 45.

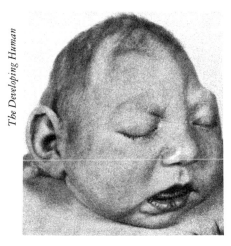

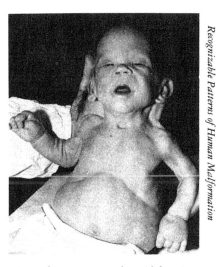

The Developing Human

Recognizable Patterns of Human Malformation

A microcephalic infant has a normal-sized face but underdeveloped cranial vault, leading to severe mental retardation. This defect, sometimes genetic, has also been associated with exposure to ionizing radiation during pregancy.

Turner's syndrome—a ten-day-old female possessing only one X chromosome instead of the usual two. The child will grow up with short stature, perhaps mild mental retardation. Incidence is 1/5,000.

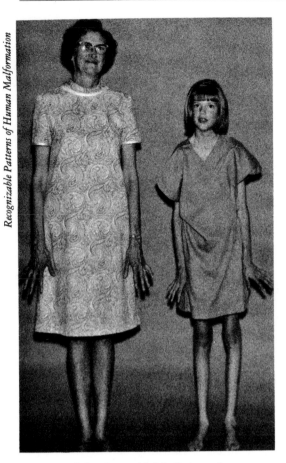

Mother and daughter with Marfan's syndrome.

Normal adult.

ours, "The less harmful genes exact a greater numerical toll than the more harmful, because a larger proportion of the loss is postponed to the later generations when the population is larger." (Ref. 34, p. 267.)

MUTATION RATE

Dominant harmful mutations also occur, and since they are expressed and selected against right away, the ones that show up are usually recent.[35] With dominants then, as with sex-linked aberrations that are distinct because they're in the X chromosome, you can get a better idea about the mutation rate than you can with recessives.

It's low. The average mutation rate per gene per generation is estimated at 1/1,000,000 (Ref. 35, p. 107) to 1/100,000.[36] So what are

we worrying about? One in a million is long odds. Besides, all you're doing is adding a little additional variability to an enormous pool of genetic variability already in the population—some say the existing variability is 5,000 times greater than is added by mutations to a single generation (Ref. 36, p. 72). (That's why mutation rate has scant effect on the rate of evolution, which runs on variability.)

The problem is that most mutations are harmful and they can't be corrected, they have to be selected out, which takes time. And look at the whole picture: "Among hundreds or even thousands of genetic diseases and malformations known in man, most have an incidence of 1:10,000 or less. Taken all together, these deficits nevertheless add up to a genetic load which is by no means negligible." (Ref. 36, p. 108.)

It's getting foggy (it will get worse)—no one seems to know exactly how harmful an increase in human mutation rate is. Referring just to radiation, H. L. Carson in the new *Encyclopaedia Britannica* article on Human Genetics writes, "There is a general dread that a doubling dose of radiation to the human population of the world would end in major calamity."[37]

Nobel geneticist Joshua Lederberg said in 1970:

> I believe that the present standards of population exposure to radiation should and will (at least de facto) be made more stringent, to about one percent of the spontaneous [mutation] rate, and that this is also a reasonable standard for the maximum tolerable mutagenic effect of any environmental chemical (better for them in the aggregate). . . . A ten percent increase in the existing "spontaneous" mutation rate is, in effect, the standard that has been adopted as the "maximum acceptable" level of public exposure to radiation by responsible regulatory bodies. (Ref. 25, pp. 186–187.)

Bruce Ames recently asked, "If there were a doubling in human genetic birth defects, would we know it? Is that being studied?"

Last August [1978] in Moscow, Nikolai Dubinin, head of the Soviet Institute of General Genetics, speaking to over 2,000 geneticists at the International Congress of Genetics, declared that the percentage of children in the world born with birth defects has doubled over the last twenty-five years, largely because of increase of mutagens in the environment. "This shows that the human race and human heredity are entering a dangerous phase."[38] (By reputation, human genetic epidemiology in the U.S.S.R. is ahead of ours.)

On this subject environmentalist/scientist Paul Ehrlich draws a clear distinction between what should be said politically and what can be said scientifically. Political: "Doing anything that spontaneously increases the mutation rate in *Homo sapiens* is a dumb idea." Scientific: "It's very difficult for me to see exactly what kind of statement can be made about what the human

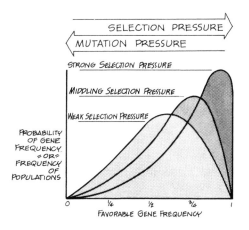

Figure 8. "Survival of the fittest," if it were true, would dangerously limit an organism's variability. "The fittest is favored" more closely approximates biological reality—maximizing the advantage of a favorable gene while keeing a reserve of some variability. If there is less selection pressure, then "favorable" is less strongly favored, and and more variability is expressed. The same happens with increased mutation rate—a decreased proportion of favorable genes. Humans are simultaneously lowering their selection pressure and increasing their mutations rate—decreasing favorable genes on both counts. (From Garrett Hardin, *Nature and Man's Fate*, ref. 34, p. 232.)

population consequences of the level of circulation of mutagens—or of radiation for that matter—is likely to be. It's a very difficult technical problem."

About nonhuman species Ehrlich has more certainty: "The argument for protecting *nature* by reducing mutagens is a crappy argument. In a *Drosophila* [fruit fly] population or a lizard population if you have a dose of radiation that causes a very high genetic load, selection will quickly reduce it. A *Drosophila* population doesn't go into shock if it loses half of its individuals or 90% of its individuals in a generation or for 20 generations. That would be tough for *Homo sapiens*. If humanity could accept a selective mortality of 90% for 20 generations, we wouldn't have to worry about mutagens increasing our genetic load."

What's the difference between us and lizards? Self-interest obviously. Culture perhaps—is civilization, language, prolonged child-rearing, etc., more or less vulnerable to increased genetic load? I don't know of any formal speculation on that one. But one difference we're sure of, selection pressure on humans is lower than on other species. We've lowered it ourselves, first through the agricultural revolution, then through the industrial and medical revolutions. Albinos, bleeders, genetic dwarfs, those born blind, deaf, or feebleminded can survive now, and some reproduce. Former lethal defects are made sublethal, former sublethals are made almost normal, somewhat unfit are made fully fit. That's immediate humanitarian good news, long-term genetic bad news. Instead of being selected out, deleterious genes are accumulating.*

National Academy of Sciences:

> Having thwarted the historical process of natural selection against our disadvantageous genes, civilization must now provide an acceptable substitute. . . . As medical euphenics ("eu" = well, "phen" = appearance) becomes increasingly successful, it will become increasingly important that genetic counseling be universally practiced. Otherwise, in a few generations, the ethic which guides medical practice will have seriously damaged the heritage of countless previous generations. (Ref. 26, p. 911.)

SUBNOTICEABLE SUBLETHAL MUTATIONS

Knowledge of human genetic epidemiology—who has what—is sufficiently imprecise that numerical estimates have a way of varying tenfold, at least in the issues we've addressed so far. Now let's proceed to where there are no agreed-upon numbers at all—genetic effects on general fitness, behavior, intelligence, and such.

Geneticists have good reason to be leery of this subject, as it leads promptly to endless arguments over nature/nurture (genetic inheri-

tance vs. upbringing), race and IQ, etc. The arguments are endless because they are based as much on articles of faith as on the scanty, blurry data. We'll skip the argument and report the general agreement that there is "some"—unquantified—genetic component to IQ (Ref. 35, p. 618), to schizophrenia (Ref. 35, p. 623), and most disease. To some degree in this domain, genetic like begets like.

I'm calling these traits, which *may* increase with higher mutation rate, "subnoticeable" because you don't know at its birth that you've got one and you don't know later when you do have one whether it's genetic or not—that's four ignorances stacked up right there. It leads to an ignorant assertion: if selection pressure is reduced against subnoticeable sublethal traits the unfavorable traits will gradually increase, particularly if mutation rate is increasing.* I can't prove it. You can't disprove it. We both can worry about it—it's vague all right, but as clouds go it is large and dark. Are we accumulating sublethal genes for which humanity may pay a high price in the future?

Disease is worth a closer look. A good summary of the situation may be found in "Environmental Mutagenic Hazards," a special paper prepared by the Council of the Environment Mutagen Society and printed in *Science* in 1975:

> Many geneticists believe that man's genes constitute his most precious heritage, and that a deterioration in gene quality can result in a corresponding decrease in the quality of life. Steady progress in the control of infectious diseases, lengthening human life spans, and improved procedures for identifying genetic disorders have revealed an important residue of genetic disease in human populations. An impressive proportion of hospital admittances, for instance, are now recognized as reflecting genetic disabilities.[39] The prospects for directly curing the resulting

---

* This is not exactly an original fret. It dates back to Francis Galton in 1865 and has had a number of distinguished and undistinguished (A. Hitler *et al.*) proponents since then.

* Ehrlich puts it more precisely: "The proportion of deaths caused by selection in human populations is vastly lower than in most other species. . . . The reproductive differentials between genotypes that are the essence of natural selection are probably smaller today in *Homo Sapiens* than in the past."

genetic diseases, in contrast to merely alleviating their symptoms, are poor, and are not likely to improve in the near future. Furthermore, the wide variety of mechanisms by which radiations and chemicals induce mutations[40] make it very unlikely that generalized schemes can be devised to protect against mutagens, except by avoiding them in the first place.[41]

CHEMICAL TERATOGENS

More fuzziness: you often can't tell a genetic birth defect from one caused during pregnancy—"the mechanism initiated by the genetic factor may be identical or similar to the causal mechanism initiated by an environmental teratogen." (Ref. 29, p. 123.) Furthermore, the same substance may cause both. That makes sense. If a mutagen is also probably a carcinogen, then it's also likely to be a teratogen. The cells in an embryo are multiplying rapidly and fragilely—DNA disruption is bound to be disastrous to the development.

(Of course there are a number of teratogens that don't cause mutations or cancer—mostly infectious agents such as German measles or herpes simplex [Ref. 29, p. 139]. Perhaps if the term "genotoxic" comes into common use to link the meaning of mutagenic and carcinogenic, it should also cover part of teratogenic, and a new term should be coined for the non-DNA-disrupting causes of birth defects.)

If the case can be at least loosely made that teratogens overlap with other genotoxins, then birth defects and miscarriages can be studied as a human indicator of exposure to widely dangerous substances. More and more of the scientific literature (for example *Science, Science News, New Scientist*) is doing exactly that. So far it's the only avenue of direct evidence we have that mutagenic chemicals are in fact harming the human gene line, and still all we have is hints and glimpses.

The *wives* of vinyl chloride workers have a significantly higher rate of fetal deaths, or miscarriages. The 70 exposed husbands studied and the 95 control husbands (working with other chemicals) had a 6–7% fetal death rate in their families *before* exposure. The vinyl chloride workers had a 12–20% fetal death rate

after exposure—double to triple that of the control group.[42] Vinyl chloride is clearly mutagenic on the Ames test and other short-term tests and is a carcinogen in rats and people.

An exhaustive survey of nearly 50,000 operating room personnel (compared with 24,000 other hospital workers) has shown that waste anesthetic gases are affecting women and men. The results, corrected for age and smoking habits, show a 50% to 100% increase of miscarriages and birth defects (and a 30–90% increase in cancer) with the exposed women. *Children* of the exposed men had a 25% higher rate of birth defects—"this unexpected finding represents a matter for serious concern and deserves further investigation." The study was made because of preliminary reports that miscarriages were more frequent among operating room women. Venting systems are now being installed in operating rooms.[43]

Enter "Behavioral Teratogens—Birth Defects of the Mind," as reported by Gina Bari Kolata in *Science*, 17 November 1978. Some excerpts:

> To many people, the idea that children may have lower intelligence or impaired behavior because they were exposed in the womb to certain drugs or foreign substances is at least as disturbing as the idea that they may be physically deformed. . . .
>
> Behavioral teratologists are looking for subtle and common defects—shorter attention span, lower intelligence, or hyperactivity, for example. . . .
>
> The implication of obstetric medications as behavioral teratogens may have far-reaching consequences because these drugs are so commonly used. In a recent colloquium, Yvonne Brackbill of the University of Florida estimated that women are given medications in 95 percent of all labors and deliveries in this country. . . . When the babies in these studies were tested at 4 months, 8 months, and 12 months of age, those whose mothers were heavily medicated lagged in development of their ability to sit, stand, and move about. They were also deficient in developing inhibitory abilities, such as the ability to stop responding to redundant signals, to stop crying when comforted, and to stop responding to distracting stimuli. As they grew older, their

development of language and cognitive skills lagged or was impaired. . . .

It is now clear that behavioral defects can occur in the absence of physical malformations. Moreover, the fetus is vulnerable to brain damage throughout gestation—there is no safe period. Finally, drugs that in high doses produce physical malformations often produce behavioral defects in lower doses. . . . Possibly women have already been exposed to a behavioral teratogen comparable to thalidomide in its potency. But, unlike thalidomide, the effects of such a behavioral teratogen would have gone unnoticed in the general population.[44]

The teratologists and psychological testers have only recently found each other and combined their skills. May they soon link up with genetic epidemiologists and environmentalists and test the children of vinyl chloride workers, nuclear industry workers, farm workers exposed to pesticides, and forest industry people and Vietnam vets exposed to herbicides. Maybe they'll find nothing.

That's it, that's the argument—from mutagens to carcinogens to teratogens to behavioral teratogens, with a lot of uncertain genetics thrown in. We know that the human mutation rate and genetic load are increasing. We know that selection pressure is decreasing. We don't know quantities or much about causes or anything about consequences.

RESPONSIBILITY

Bruce Ames commented to Paul Ehrlich, "If the smokers are filling the gene pool with mutations and their children are going to marry your children, then one has to really think about the societal responsibility. It isn't only a matter of individual choice."

Ehrlich replied, "Bruce, you have as much to do with my thinking on this as anyone. If it is true that mutagenicity and carcinogenicity are caused by the same kinds of phenomena, the problems perceived by human beings will always be much more serious on the cancer end, because before you would get a level of mutagenicity that would make much difference to the 'gene pool' everybody would be dying of cancer. So biologists tend not to be very concerned with the quality of the human

gene pool whereas the social load of cancer is enormous."

Ames retorted that the social cost of a defective child lasts a whole lifetime whereas cancer is in general a disease of old age. And a harmful gene will be harmful generations after the cancer patient is out of the picture.

The fact is, whether you're more worried about cancer or genetic damage, we have both and both are increasing. If you smoke and you're my friend I'll look at you with one kind of dismay; if you're my mother-in-law I'll look at you with another.

In any case it would be well if more prospective parents sought genetic counseling and if more doctors were trained in it. Nobel geneticist Hermann Muller, known for his enthusiasm for eugenics, made this fair statement:

What is most needed in this area of living is an extension of the feeling of social responsibility to the field of reproduction: an increasing recognition that the chief objective of bringing children into the world is not the glorification of the parents or ancestors by the mere act of having children but the well-being of the children themselves and, through them, of subsequent generations in general.[45]

What this article should have demonstrated is that far more than just the parents are involved in that responsibility.

Of course, we could wait for a cure for cancer and a corrective for mutations. It may be a long wait. DNA damage is on the molecular level. How would you detect which body cell or which germ cell is the critical defective one, and which gene is defective, and what the defect is—before they're expressed? Then how would you reach in, with what tweezers, and make what correction and keep the whole mess alive? As they say, genetic disease resists treatment.

Well, then, how about eugenics? We could keep our mutagens and embark on a national/ world policy of active favorable selection, or, if that sounds too Hitlerian, settle for comprehensive negative eugenics. Sterilize workers exposed to high levels of mutagens and provide a hazardous-duty fund for their later cancer treatments. Sterilize everyone who survives infancy with birth defects. Sterilize people who are kinda dumb. Be sure never to be racist, sexist, ageist, or elitist.

Folksinger Woody Guthrie died long and slow of Huntington's chorea—a sublethal dominant genetic disease of the nervous system brought to this country by just three immigrant families from England. It has affected 7,000 individuals since then. If Woody had been sterilized or genetically counseled not to reproduce, there would be no folksinger Arlo Guthrie. Should Arlo have had kids?

Genetic responsibility is just entering public consciousness. We'll be decades, perhaps centuries, sorting out its rights and wrongs. Better for now to concentrate on reducing the mutagenic hazards.

ACTION—PERSONAL

For both reasons, lay off items that appear to cause cancer—cigarettes, hair dyes, nitrites in meats (that's one I've just dropped thanks to all this), unnecessary x-rays, unnecessary anesthetics, chronic alcohol or drug use, pesticides, herbicides, moldy nuts, charred meat or fish, too much fat, food additives generally, medical drugs generally including birth control pills, aerosol cans, cleaning agents with benzene or chlorinated compounds (carbon tetrachloride, trichlorethylene, etc.), asbestos insulation, wallboard, etc., and whatever else turns up on the endangering list.

If you're pregnant, take this list quadrupally seriously.

As for political action, the usual: research, bitch, organize, boycott, demonstrate, publicize, vote, help, and thank.

Has your local population had a sudden rise in babies born dead with spina bifida associated with increased local herbicide spraying? Nail one of them to the door of the agency responsible.*

ACTION—COMMERCIAL

Here's three quick stories from Arthur Lubow's 1977 article on Bruce Ames in *New Times*:

1) When American Cyanamide found that an agricultural chemical tested weakly positive on the Ames test, it was able to identify and eliminate the guilty contaminant. Merck Sharpe and Dohme, which has been using an Ames screening test for the last three years, also discovered a slightly mutagenic impurity in one of its drugs. The impurity has been removed, although it has not yet been identified.

2) Bruce Ames stumbled on Tris while buying pajamas for his two small children. He noticed that the pajamas were flame-resistant, and wondered what chemicals had been added to the cloth. Calling his friend Mike Prival, who was then at the Environmental Protection Agency in Washington, Ames learned that the chemical was named Tris. Tris was already on the EPA list of suspect carcinogens, and Prival had added it to a list of compounds being run through an Ames test as part of a general validation study of bacterial assays. "I was surprised when Bruce called, because I didn't know that anybody outside our small group was concerned about Tris," Prival recalls. "Although, from its structure, you would think it would be pretty bad, certainly if you had a background like Bruce's."

On the EPA Salmonella test that had been underway before Ames called, Tris tested positive as a mutagen. The chief of Prival's section wrote a letter to the Consumer Products Safety Commission in October 1975. The commission required the use of Tris to flame-proof children's sleeping garments. "We informed them that we had found Tris was mutagenic in the bacterial test," Prival says. The commission began investigating absorption of Tris through the skin. At the same time, the NCI was conducting animal assays of Tris. The NCI report implicating Tris as a carcinogen was announced early in 1977, after Bob Harris of the Environmental Defense Fund pressured NCI into releasing it. A few weeks later, the Consumer Products Safety Commission announced its in-house study showing Tris absorption through the skin. The chemical was banned as a flame retardant in children's clothing—about a year and half after it had been identified as a probable carcinogen by the Salmonella test.*

For that year and a half, millions of children slept in Tris-coated pajamas, soaking up the chemical when they sweated, when they chewed

---

* Would I actually do this? I wouldn't. Someone else might, and people in the relevant companies and bureaucracies should be thinking about that.

* As a result of this experience corrective staff and policy changes have been made at the Consumer Products Safety Commission.

on the cloth, when they did nothing but lie still. Because the scrotum is particularly absorbent, it sponged up more than its fair share of Tris. Ames fears that the Tris generation of boys may suffer an unusually high rate of sperm cell genetic damage, and possibly testicular atrophy and sterility. "The more we looked at Tris, the more dangerous it seemed," he says. "In hindsight, it was a crazy idea in the first place. Related compounds were known to be carcinogenic, and the structure of these compounds suggested they could be." For a year Ames, Prival, and Harris tried without success to get the commission to do something. "These government bureaucracies are very slow to react," he says. He is today fighting the almost incredible plan to substitute inadequately studied Tris-related substances as flame retardants in children's clothing now that Tris is banned. "The replacements they're using look bad," Ames says. "I don't like the whole idea of add-on flame retardants of this type. I've been on the phone to all the commissioners and I think they're coming around, but I think they're hemmed in by what their powers are."

3) If a new carcinogen is substituted for an old one, it won't be the first time. One of the saddest ironies in the annals of cancer prevention is the case of decaffeinated coffee. In February 1976 the NCI found that trichloroethylene, a solvent used to decaffeinate coffee, was weakly carcinogenic in mice. "Trichloroethylene is about the weakest carcinogen, with the possible exception of saccharin, that has ever been found in animals," says Ames' colleague Joyce McCann. Because trichloroethylene is so nontoxic, enormous doses of it could be fed to laboratory animals. When megadoses were pumped into mice through a stomach tube three times a week, tumors appeared in a significant number of animals. "When we started this test, we didn't know that trichloroethylene was used as a solvent for decaffeinating coffee," says NCI's Elizabeth Weisburger. "After we published a technical report, General Foods contacted us."

Under the recently celebrated Delaney clause, which required the banning of saccharin, any trace element of a carcinogen like trichloroethylene in Sanka, however weak, would be forbidden. General Foods didn't wait for the FDA to issue a regulation. It quickly switched from trichloroethylene to another industrial solvent, methylene chloride. It was going from bad to worse.

"One needs only to look at the structure of these chemicals," Joyce McCann says in exasperation. "There are plenty of chemists at General Foods, and they can look at these chemicals and draw the same conclusions we do. Yet there is this attitude that seems to throw all caution to the winds, and to use this chemical until it is proved to be a carcinogen. It seems so irresponsible." As Ames observes: "Trichloroethylene has been replaced by methylene chloride, which is more mutagenic than trichloroethylene on the Salmonella test, but which hadn't had a cancer test done on it." A paper soon to be published by Paul Price of Microbiological Associates in La Jolla reveals that methylene chloride is two to three times as potent in malignantly transforming rat cells as the discontinued trichloroethylene. (Ref. 16, pp. 30–33.)

Until business learns to serve the whole customer it will be regarded as an untrustworthy and dangerous adversary by consumers, workers, and the government.

ACTION—GOVERNMENT

AMES: *The problem of cancer and genetic birth defects can be usefully attacked by prevention. The following approaches are suggested.*

1. Identifying mutagens and carcinogens *from among the wide variety of environmental chemicals to which humans are exposed. All approaches must be used: human epidemiology for cancer and for genetic birth defects; animal tests for cancer and for genetic birth defects; short-term mutagenicity and transformation tests; and new approaches based on measuring damage in people must be developed.*[46,47]

2. Pre-market testing *of new chemicals to which humans will be exposed. We have seen, and will continue to see, the folly of using people as guinea pigs.*

3. Making information *more easily available on chemicals capable of causing cancer and mutations (including their relative danger, when this is known) for use by the state and federal governments, industry, unions, consumer groups, and the public at large.*

4. Setting priorities and minimizing human exposure *to these chemicals, starting with those that need the most attention and working down the list. These would be based on the respective amounts of human exposure to each chemical and the potency of*

the chemical in animal cancer tests. Where adequate animal cancer data are not available, potency information from several suitable short-term tests—such as Salmonella, which can be obtained quickly—might be substituted when they are validated for this purpose. (Soon more sophisticated and sensitive ways of measuring DNA or other damage in people could play an essential role.) The particular "chemical of concern" at any one time may often be a mixture, such as air pollutants from auto exhaust (which is quite mutagenic in Salmonella). A general attack on a problem may sometimes be called for, for example, minimizing the use of mutagenic, carcinogenic, or untested chemical pesticides by education about potential hazards, product use, or alternatives, and incentives, penalties, and taxes where necessary.

ALLIES

As *occupational* exposure to genotoxic chemicals is probably the greatest hazard right now, labor unions have a primary responsibility and capability. Alliance with their efforts by environmental groups would be poignant (given past disagreements) and probably highly effective.

The politicians and medical heavyweights who managed to channel billions of dollars into curing cancer should not find it difficult to re-channel their efforts into prevention. The apparatus is in place. All that's needed is better aim. Signs are it's already happening.[48]

The highly capable veterans of battles with nuclear energy can use the same skills and commitment against the subtler, greater hazard of chemical mutagens. There's no need to switch targets, just go at the whole problem.

The health food nuts, who were right all along, can avoid smugness by further refining their research and expanding their activity. As an informed electorate and vast consumer population, they may have more leverage than they realize.

How about the Right-to-Life people? A human-caused increase in spontaneous abortions should be of interest to them.

And keep an eye out for artists who translate the hidden into the obvious. DEVO, for instance—the thinking man's punk-rock band.

Expounding "The Truth about De-evolution," these spuds, these robotoid Rollerball corporate clones, these happy mongoloids have a lively deadly music for you. Each concert begins with a litany. The band demands:

"ARE WE NOT MEN?"

And we in the crowd reply in a numb mechanical mass-market singsong:

"WE ARE DEVO."

Maybe so.

REFERENCES

1. Bruce Ames, "Identifying Environmental Chemicals Causing Cancer and Mutations," *Science*, Spring 1979; edited from "Environmental Chemicals Causing Cancer and Genetic Birth Defects: Developing a strategy to minimize human exposure," California Policy Seminar series, monograph no. 2. Berkeley Institute of Governmental Studies, University of California, 1978.

2. R. Doll, *Nature*, 265, 589 (1977).

3. *Origins of Human Cancer*, H. H. Hiatt, J. D. Watson, and J. A. Winsten, eds. (Cold Spring Harbor Laboratory, Cold Spring Harbor, New York, 1977).

4. E. P. Benditt, *Scientific American* 236, 74 (1977).

5. F. M. Burnett, *Intrinsic Mutagenesis: A genetic approach to aging* (Lancaster, England: Medical and Technical Publishing, 1974).

6. U. S. Environmental Protection Agency, L. Fishbein, *Potential Industrial Carcinogens and Mutagens*, 560/5–77–005 (1977); T. H. Maugh II, *Science* 199, 162 (1978).

7. "Evaluation of Genetic Risks of Environmental Chemicals: Report of a symposium held at Skokloster, Sweden, March 11–15, 1972," C. Ramel, ed., *Ambio Special Report* no. 3 (1973).

8. Claes Ramel, "The Detection and Control of Mutagenic and Carcinogenic Compounds in the Environment," *Ambio*, vol. 7, no. 5–6 (1978), p. 244.

9. J. McCann, E. Choi, E. Yamasaki, and B. N. Ames, *Proc. Natl. Acad. Sci. U.S.A.* 72, 5135 (1975); J. McCann and B. N. Ames, ibid. 73, 950 (1976); J. McCann and B. N. Ames, in *Origins of Human Cancer*, pp. 1431–1450, see ref. 3 above.

10. Thomas H. Maugh II, "Chemical Carcinogens: The Scientific Basis for Regulation," *Science*, 29 September 1978, pp. 1200–1205.

11. T. R. Torkelson, S. E. Sadek, V. K. Rowe, J. K. Kodama, H. H. Anderson, G. S. Loguvam, and C. H. Hine, *Toxicol. Appl. Pharma.* 3, 545 (1961).

12. W. A. Olson, R. T. Huberman, E. K. Weisburger, J. M. Ward, and J. H. Weisburger, *J. Nat. Cancer Inst.* 51, 1993 (1973).

13. A. Blum and B. N. Ames, *Science 195*, 17 (1977); M. J. Prival, E. C. McCoy, B. Gutter, and H. S. Rosenkranz, *Science 195*, 76 (1977).

14. *Chemical Abstracts Service*, , Report no. 5, p. 2 (1976). Cited in "Chemicals and the Environment," *Ambio*, vol. 7, no. 5–6 (1978), p. 240.

15. Jan W. Huismans, "The International Register of Potentially Toxic Chemicals (IRPTC): Its Present State of Development and Future Plans," *Ambio*, vol. 7, no. 5–6 (1978), p. 275.

16. Arthur Lubow, "Bruce Ames Escalates the War on Cancer," *New Times*, 16 September 1977, p. 32.

17. M. Viczian, "Ergebnisse von Spermauntersuchungen bei Zigarettenrauchern," *Z. Haut Geschlectskr. 44*, 183–187 (1969). Cited in Andrew J. Wyrobek and W. Robert Bruce, "The Induction of Sperm-shape Abnormalities in Mice and Humans," *Chemical Mutagens*, vol. 5, p. 274 (Plenum Publishing Corporation, 1978).

18. K. H. Degenhardt, *Conference on Population Monitoring Methods for Detecting Increased Mutation Rates, Jahreskonferenz 1975* (Zentrallaboratorium für Mutagenitätsprüfung, Freiburg, West Germany, 1975) p. 34. Cited in Ramel, ref. 8, above.

19. G. Mau and P. Netter, *Dtsch. med. Wschr. 99* 1113–1118 (1974).

20. Edith Yamasaki and Bruce N. Ames, "Concentration of mutagens from urine by adsorption with the nonpolar resin XAD-2: Cigarette smokers have mutagenic urine," *Proc. Natl. Acad. Sci. USA*, vol. 74, no. 8 (1977) pp. 3555–3559.

21. "Smoking Imperils the Unborn," *Science News*, 27 January 1979, p. 55.

22. Samuel S. Epstein, *The Politics of Cancer* (San Francisco: Sierra Club Books, 1978), p. 24.

23. Paul R. Ehrlich, Anne H. Ehrlich, and John P. Holdren, *Ecoscience: Population, Resources, Environment* (San Francisco: W. H. Freeman, 1970, 1972, 1977), pp. 591 and 597.

24. "Herman Kahn Changes His Mind," *CoEvolution Quarterly*, Spring 1978, p. 141.

25. John W. Gofmann and Arthur Tamplin, "How Radiation Causes Disease and Hereditary Alterations," *Encyclopedia of Common Diseases* (Emmaus, Pennsylvania, Rodale Press, 1976), p. 185.

26. *Biology and the Future of Man*, Philip Handler, ed. (New York: Oxford University Press, 1970), p. 902.

27. Richard Dawkins, *The Selfish Gene* (New York and Oxford, Oxford University Press, 1976).

28. Andrew Wyrobek, (Ref. 17, above), p. 270.

29. Keith L. Moore, *The Developing Human: Clinically Oriented Embryology*, 2nd ed. (Philadelphia: W. B. Saunders, 1977), p. 42.

30. B. K. Trimble and J. H. Doughty, "The Amount of Hereditary Disease in Human Populations," *Ann. Human Gen.*, *38* (1974) pp. 179–209. Cited in ref. 36, p. 107.

31. J. Boué and A. Boué, *Biomedicine 18*, 372 (1973). Cited in Claes Ramel (Ref. 8 above), p. 245.

32. "What Are the Major Causes of Birth Defects?" *Encyclopedia of Common Diseases* (Emmaus, Pennsylvania: Rodale, 1976), p. 176.

33. Victor A. McKusick, *Mendelian Inheritance in Man: Catalogs of Autosomal Dominant, Autosomal Recessive, and X-linked Phenotypes*, 3rd ed. (Baltimore: Johns Hopkins, 1975).

34. Garrett Hardin, *Nature and Man's Fate* (New York: New American Library, 1959), p. 266.

35. L. L. Cavalli-Sforza and W. F. Bodmer, *The Genetics of Human Populations* (San Francisco: W. H. Freeman, 1971), p. 761.

36. Theodosius Dobzhansky, Francisco J. Ayala, G. Ledyard Stebbins, and James W. Valentine, *Evolution* (San Francisco: W. H. Freeman, 1977), p. 71.

37. *Encyclopaedia Britannica*, 15th ed. (1974), s.v. "Genetics, Human."

38. Associated Press, *San Francisco Chronicle*, 22 August 1978, p. 12.

39. B. Childs, S. M. Miller, A. G. Bearn, in *Mutagenic Effects of Environmental Contaminants*, H. E. Sutton and M. I. Harris, eds. (New York: Academic Press, 1972), pp. 3–14.

40. J. W. Drake, *The Molecular Basis of Mutation* (San Francisco: Holden Day, 1970).

41. John W. Drake *et al.* for Council of the Environmental Mutagen Society, "Environmental Mutagenic Hazards," *Science*, 14 February 1975, p. 503.

42. Peter F. Infante, Joseph K. Wagoner, Anthony J. McMichael, Richard J. Waxweiler, and Henry Falk, "Genetic Risks of Vinyl Chloride," *Lancet*, 3 April 1976, pp. 734–735.

43. Ellis N. Cohen *et al.*, "Occupational Disease among Operating Room Personnel," *Anesthesiology*, vol. 41, no. 4 (1974), pp. 321–340.

44. Gina Bari Kolata, "Behavioral Teratology: Birth Defects of the Mind," *Science*, 17 November 1978, pp. 732–734.

45. Hermann J. Muller, "The Guidance of Human Evolution," *The Evolution of Man*, vol. 2 of *Evolution After Darwin*, Sol Tax, ed. (Chicago: University of Chicago Press, 1960), p. 436.

46. A. J. Wyrobek and W. R. Bruce, *Proc. Natl. Acad. Sci. USA*, vol. 72 (1975), p. 4425.

47. D. Segerbäck et al., *Mutation Res. 49*, 71 (1978).

48. Luther J. Carter, "Yearly Report on Carcinogens Could Be a Potent Weapon in the War on Cancer," *Science*, 9 February 1979, pp. 525–528.

49. Curt Stern, *Principles of Human Genetics*, 3rd ed. (San Francisco: W. H. Freeman, 1973), p. 630.

50. James F. Crow, "Chemical Risk to Future Generations," *Scientist and Citizen*, June-July 1968, p. 113.

51. B. N. Ames, J. McCann, and E. Yamasaki, *Mutation Res. 31*, 347 (1975).

52. Bruce N. Ames, H. O. Kammen, and Edith Yamasaki, "Hair Dyes Are Mutagenic: Identification of a Variety of Mutagenic Ingredients," *Proc. Nat. Acad. Sci. USA, vol. 72, no. 6 (1975), p. 1432.*

R. CRUMB

A Short History of America

Here's the only item in this book
that subsequently got made into a
poster—available, incidentally, for
$5.50 postpaid from Last Gasp
Press, 2180 Bryant Street, San Francisco, CA 94110. (Biogeographical
Provinces on pp. 70–71 doesn't
count—it was created as a poster and
article simultaneously.) Like Dan O'-
Neill, Robert Crumb did regular
cartooning for CQ, with four pages in
every CQ between '76 and '81. His
CQ work is probably less well known
than his underground cartooning,
which began in the early 60s (obliga-
tory litany here: Fritz the Cat, Zap
Comics, Mr. Natural, Joey Tissue
and the Dummies, etc. etc.) and
continues today in a magazine also
published by Last Gasp called
Weirdo. This cartoon ran as part of
the special guest-edited "Oceans Issue" in Fall 1979—you figure out
the thematic connection. Probably
they couldn't bear to leave it out of
the magazine.

—Art Kleiner

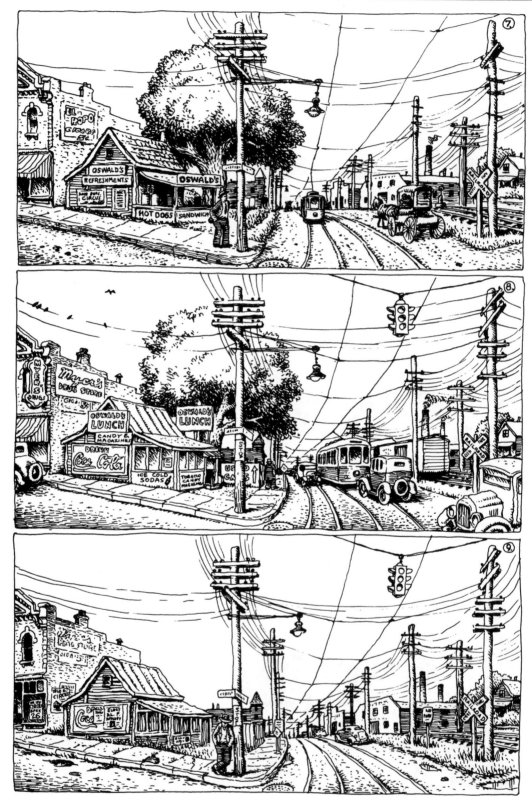

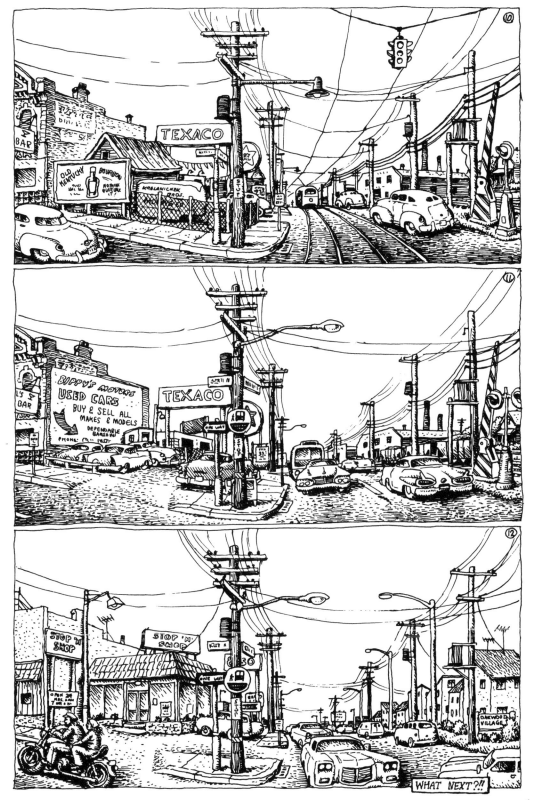

MARY CATHERINE BATESON

Six Days of Dying

Catherine Bateson, the only child of Gregory Bateson and Margaret Mead, is an anthropologist presently at Amherst College, Massachusetts. In Gregory Bateson's *Steps to an Ecology of Mind* (Ballantine, 1975) there is a collection of "metalogues," semi-fictional conversations between father and daughter inspired by real dialogues they had when Catherine was a child. Some other family members present in this account (originally published in the Winter 1980 CQ) are: Gregory's wife Lois, whom he met while working on his Double Bind theory of schizophrenia and creativity at the VA Hospital in Palo Alto, California during the 1950s; Nora, Lois and Gregory's daughter, now seventeen; John, Gregory's son by his second marriage; and Eric, Lois' son by a prior marriage. In addition to Catherine's own considerable work, she has collaborated frequently with her father; a list of Gregory's collaborations is included in the introduction to the interview with Catherine's parents, "For God's

Sake, Margaret," on page 26 of this book. She is also literary executor for both her father and Margaret Mead. It is clear the metalogue never stopped.

Stewart Brand

Just as the intimacies of childbirth and early mothering have gradually been restored, first with natural childbirth and rooming in and most recently with childbirth in the home, so there is a growing effort to meet death more intimately and simply. The logical end of this development is that people die at home or in an environment as close to home as possible. The depressions which used to afflict mothers after childbirth are probably related to interruptions in the early intimacy between mother and child which plays a biological role in the establishment of parental love and care. Similarly, the shadows of guilt and anger which so often complicate grief may also be related to interruptions in the process of caring, and they may be lightened by the experience of tending someone we love with our own hands, so that much that seems externally repellent and painful is transmuted by tenderness.

Death is surely more variable than birth. Where experiences are difficult to predict or compare, the specific is more useful than vague generalization. This is an account of the period from the second to the seventh of July of 1980, the period in which I experienced the death of my father, Gregory Bateson. I can only describe events as I perceived them; other members of the family or close friends may find my perceptions bizarrely at odds with their own. Nevertheless, I think all of us agreed that the fact that we were with my father at the guest-house of San Francisco Zen Center, where he spent his last days and was laid out after death, gave us the privilege of a rare and blessed participation. We felt that we gained a new understanding of some of the things that my father taught, and also of the teachings of Zen Buddhism. Trying to make experience explicit in words is not typical of Zen, but it was something my father cared about. Lois Bateson, his wife, commented that Gregory had been a teacher all his life and that he continued to teach in the manner of his death. The privilege we experienced can only partly be shared. Still, the attempt at description may be helpful, for it is at moments of birth and death that it is easy to become timid and to be cowed into an acceptance of standard institutional forms.

My father's final illness began in midspring and I came to California to be near him in June, arriving one day before he was hospitalized. While he was in the hospital I had to be away for about a week, to keep a previous commitment, and I returned to San Francisco on July 2 to find that he was out of the hospital and being cared for at Zen Center, where I too went to stay. Two days before I had left, we had been talking, with some sense of realism, about where he might be able to convalesce, but even as I departed that had come to seem unrealistic. Lois felt the gradual change in the quality of the nurses' care as, with implicit triage, they shifted from the effort of healing to courtesy to the dying. Towards the end of the week, Lois made the decision to discontinue intravenous feeding—he was eating and drinking a little, and was receiving no medication through the I.V.—and then to bring him to Zen Center and nurse him there, knowing that he would probably die there.

Gregory had entered the hospital June 10 because of a respiratory crisis that proved to be pneumonia and an unexplained pain in his side. Everyone assumed that the pain was related to the lung cancer he had had in 1978,

Stewart Brand

In 1978 Gregory nearly died of lung cancer. Part of his recovery was Catherine traveling from Iran to help with his book, *Mind and Nature: A Necessary Unity*.

which was expected to be terminal and then went into remission. He himself felt that the pain might be a local nervous disorder related to his earlier surgery, and went back to a term used by his old friend the neurophysiologist and systems theorist, Warren McCulloch, who had described how a group of nerves, regenerating after surgery, might get into a self-reinforcing cycle of resonating pain, but McCulloch's term, *causalgia*, proved to be unacceptable in current parlance and was treated as fantasy in the context of the cancer. The pain had driven him to his bed in late May where pneumonia had followed in lungs long handicapped by emphysema and the cancer episode. He had been living at Esalen Institute in Big Sur since the cancer, and friends there came and went with counsels spun from different epistemologies, the multiple holisms of an unfocused new age. He had dutifully done a session of imaging and was told that perhaps indeed he did not want to live. He had by his bedside an array of megadoses of various vitamins and microdoses of homeopathic medicines, wheat grass juice available in any quantities he would accept it, and at the same time he was told that he was too preoccupied with the physical and should be concerned with the spiritual, this being available in various traditional and syncretic forms.

When we left Esalen, heading for San Francisco in a VW van with a supply of emergency oxygen, we had two possible destinations, either University of California Hospital or Zen Center. I do not believe Gregory was making a choice between "holistic" and "establishment" medicine, but a choice between multiplicity and integrity. He maintained a profound skepticism towards both the premises of the medical profession and the Buddhist epistemology, but certainty is scarce and there is a kind of relief to be found in a system that expresses the disciplined working-out of a set of premises, whatever these may be. Furthermore, he wanted to be in a place where he could have more information about what was happening and where his own curiosity would be allowed to play a role, his own vitality nurtured by knowledge rather than by hope.

Nora, Gregory, Lois

When we arrived at UC Hospital and got the diagnosis of pneumonia, everyone concurred that pneumonia was something that establishment medicine knew how to handle and that it made sense to stay there. Gregory was deeply tired and in need of an impersonal, matter-of-fact environment, and for several days he wanted few visitors and as much new information about his condition as nonintrusive diagnostic procedures would provide. X-rays showed no growth or spread of cancer and provided no explanation for the pain. At that point, after working carefully on the details of a will, Gregory and his doctor decided that relief from pain was what he needed most, and he had several days of relatively frequent and large doses of morphine. When Lois demanded a recess in which he could be fully conscious and able to discuss other treatment possibilities after these days, he remained somewhat blurred and disoriented and the pain was a dull ache rather than an agonizing burning sensation. He was terribly weakened, partly by vomiting caused by some of his medication. He spoke of going home and came lurching out of the bed in the middle of the night, asking for scissors to cut the I.V. and oxygen tubes. Much of his talk was metaphorical and so discounted by nurses who made cheerful and soothing noises, but he remained very much himself, relating in clearly different ways to different people, compliant but skeptical. Our initial optimism in this period was a response to the decrease in pain and the improvement in pneumonia, but it was premised on a recovery of strength and will to live which did not occur.

During the last week in the hospital, there was a recurrence of the pneumonia, necessitating another round of antibiotics, and finally an explanation of the pain, when an eruption around his side provided the identification of *Herpes zoster* (shingles). This form of herpes is a virus which attacks the nervous system, causing acute unilateral pain, especially in the elderly, and eventually a skin eruption. It is almost impossible to diagnose before the rash, and in Gregory's case the location of the pain on one side of his body was all too easy to connect with the cancer. No one dies of shingles, but the pain may continue indefinitely; it does seem reasonable to say that Gregory died by withdrawals from unexplained pain, and that the explanation came too late to save him.

The six days of the title are the three days from my return to the moment when his breathing ceased, approximately at noon on July 4, followed by the three days until his cremation. Thus, not all of the punctuation comes from the natural process of death, but it serves to frame a period instead of focusing on a single moment. During those six days we were at San Francisco Zen Center, with most of the family and a few close friends sharing in the nursing and the Zen community providing practical help and a context of coherent tranquility.

On the morning of July 2, Gregory asked his son to kill him. The asking was not a fully conscious request for practical steps—he suggested getting a stick and hitting him over the head with it, as if by brutal overstatement to achieve the opposite of euphemism—but it was a demanding paternal honesty. When I arrived, Lois suggested that John and her son, Eric, and I meet with Michael, Gregory's friend and physician, hoping that we could accept as a group what she had already accepted in the decision to leave the hospital. Michael talked about the fact that there were various aggressive forms of treatment that could be taken to keep Gregory alive, and about his sense, having observed Gregory during the earlier crisis and in the intervening period, that Gregory had been turning toward death and that such interventions would be inappropriate and ultimately futile. All of us felt that mentally at least Gregory's withdrawal was probably irreversible, whatever the mechanism involved, and that his wishes should be respected as far as they could be. What this meant was giving up the pressure on him to suffer those things that might prolong his life—sitting up for a few minutes, respiratory therapy or an oxygen tube at his nostrils, another spoonful of custard, another sip of broth—while making each of these available if in any way he seemed to want them, or doing anything else we could to make him more comfortable. The more deeply one rejects the separation of mind and body, the more difficult it is to treat the processes of disease and death as mechanical and alien to the self. Even as one gives up the image of an external enemy, of death personified as the Grim Reaper or reified in the name of a killing disease, the problem which lives in most people's unconscious becomes conscious, the feeling that the death of those we love is a betrayal. We tend to feel that someone who is dying has an implicit obligation to stay alive: to accept treatment, to make an unflagging effort, and indeed to think thoughts that would support the effort at life rather than the drift toward death, not because to do so is comforting but because it may be a real factor in what happens.

We went back into the room where a hospital bed had been brought for Gregory, and we shared some sherry and stilton cheese. Gregory accepted a mouthful of each. We sat in a half-circle open towards the bed, and a student and friend of Gregory's, Steve, played the violin, while Lois accompanied him with chords on the tambur and those who could harmonized their voices, weaving a wandering chant in the darkening room for what seemed a very long time. During the music Gregory, half dozing, brushed the tube that was supplying oxygen away from his nostrils, and each of us, I suppose, struggled with the impulse to get up and replace it. Some of us were crying quietly. The music was gentle mourning, uniting the various terms to which each of us had come in the acceptance of his death into a single covenant. When the music ended we sat for a while, listening to his labored, drowning breathing. After a time, lights were lit, Gregory stirred himself to eat and drink a little more, a few mouthfuls, the night watches were shared out, and one of the Zen students entering the room restored the oxygen tube. After that it was put back or offered several times, but eventually each time he rejected it.

Within the rhythm of our day, one of a small group was always with him: Lois, or Kathleen, a friend and nurse who had come with the family from Esalen, or I, or John and Eric, or Robert, the Zen priest who manages the guest house. Each evening different Zen students, some of them friends and others unnamed, would come and sit in the room also, erect and immobile unless they were needed, for Baker Roshi, in touch every day by telephone from across the country, wanted the students to approach the suchness of dying and to give their quiet support to Gregory and to us. He instructed them to deepen their empathy by breathing in unison with Gregory, supporting and sharing. Those of us staying in the house slept at different hours and slipped out briefly to join the meditations in the Zendo or to chant or join in the Eucharist at a convent around the corner. Others came and went. We felt that for Gregory the process of dying proceeded gradually but without even a clear distinction between sleeping and waking.

On July 3 Gregory spoke occasionally, making gestures of affection and recognition, but much of what he said was blurred and unintelligible. He also spoke to others he seemed to see around the bed and once or twice asked whether a particular person was indeed present or only a dream. It was often necessary to move his big ungainly body for he had become almost completely incontinent. This more than anything was reminiscent of the care of an infant, but moving him to clean or change pads or to guard against bed sores became especially difficult on that day because although he was not able to help at all, there was a sort of recalcitrance in his body against these indignities. He gave an impression of deep concentration.

Jerry Brown came in on the evening of the third and Gregory recognized him and stretched out his hand to greet him, calling him by name. As Jerry left and we settled down for the night, Gregory's labored breathing had slowed to the point where sometimes the interval between breaths left room for a momentary doubt of whether another breath would follow. We shared the certainty that less than a day remained. Gregory was dying as people die in books, gradually sinking towards death in a self-reinforcing process. Intravenous feeding and continous oxygen could drag that process out, interfering with the choice of mind and body not to sustain life, and another counter-attack might have been possible on the pneumonia which we could hear in Gregory's breathing. But pneumonia has long been called the "old man's friend." I never thought of my father as an old man until he was dying.

During the late night and the morning hours of the Fourth of July, each of us had time alone with him. He still smiled and responded to a handclasp, or would draw a hand to his lips. Touching seemed important, and the hospital bed enforced an isolation that had to be bridged. I found I wanted to give him the sound of a voice, so I read aloud the final chapters of the Book of Job. I held up a flower from one of the vases, not as something sweet and pretty but as a symbol of the order of truth to which he had been most true, the grace and intricacy of mental phenomena underlying the patterns of the biological world, and wondered whether a flower could still evoke that allegiance as, for someone else, a lifted cross could evoke a whole life lived in the Christian context. He would have been able to call the flower by name.

By mid-morning he was unable to drink, and we put tiny amounts of water in his dry mouth to give some moisture, afraid that he would choke on any more, unable to swallow. His breathing was laborious and slow. Lois noticed a pattern of blotches on his chest which at first we thought was a further eruption of the *Herpes* and then realized was a result of a change in circulation.

A short time later, Roger, a friend from Esalen, saw the pupils of his eyes dilate as his mind encountered the dark. So we gathered around the bed, some six of us who had been caring for him most closely, hardly breathing ourselves as we waited from breath to breath, the time stretching, the time stretching beyond the possible, and yet again and again followed by a gasping reflexive inhalation, and then again the lengthening pause. I kept praying that he would be free from each next compulsive effort, let go, rest, and when after a time no further breath followed, we still stood, slowly relaxing with the faintest sighs, barely able to return to a flow of time not shaped by that breathing. Lois reached forward, after her office, and gently closed his eyes.

We did not at that time pause to mourn but slowly found our way into the expression of continuing care. After Lois, in my turn, I reached out and began to straighten his arms, then folding his hands. Someone lowered the bed to the flat and dropped the sides. I thought briefly of those cultures in which the bodies of loved ones are transmuted at the moment of death into something impure, polluting those who touch them. During my lifetime few Americans have tended their dead, just as few have tended their dying, and we had to grope our way, following clues from other times or other cultures. For Lois the available model was the Balinese one, in which the bodies of men are washed by men, and those of women by women, but for me the model was the Western one where women have received the

newly born and the newly dead into their care. In the end we all worked together, removing the soiled pads, cleaning away the final traces of excrement, lifting and turning and washing each limb, shifting from side to side this beloved body from which all tension and recalcitrance were drained so that he suffered our care with a curious innocence. The blotches on his skin had faded.

Roshi had instructed that all traces of the sick room be removed, and Gregory was lifted and carried to the double bed at the other side of the room, dressed in a bathrobe and covered with the sheet and spread. He was still a little too long for any bed. With half a dozen Zen folk joining in, the hospital bed and table were dismantled and carried out, the linens and the clothes and basin we had used to wash him were removed. Consulting each other in muted voices, we bound a kerchief around his chin, experimenting with the angle until we were able to close his mouth, collecting and composing ourselves even as Gregory's body and the room were made serene in composure. As the work was completed, Robert surveyed the scene and then went and straightened the folds of the bed cover so they fell in sculptured order to the floor. Then he set up a small altar, a table with an incense burner at the foot of the bed, and said that now he would show us how to offer incense to Gregory: bow (the bow whose name is "asking"), touch a few grains of incense to the third eye in the center of the forehead, place them on the burning charcoal, add a few more grains, bow. It seemed to me well to perform an act which was both alien and completely formal, combining affection and courtesy with total estrangement. From that time, incense burned constantly in the room, and two or more of the Zen folk sat and watched. Gregory was not a Buddhist, but Zen mindfulness and decorum were for him an affirmation of the intricate order of mind. We sat for awhile, and soon I went and slept in another room of the guest house.

When I woke up and returned to my father's bedside it was late afternoon. His body was cold now when I touched his hands, and the tracery of red blood vessels in his cheeks

At the Zen Center funeral on July 20, family members and any of the 200 other mourners present were invited to speak to Gregory. A lively conversation resulted, sometimes funny, sometimes quite moving, always warm and personal and a release. Here Catherine says her piece. Left to right: Lois, Nora, Catherine, Eric.

drained of color. Someone had removed the kerchief and combed his hair. As his body had settled gradually into the rigor of death, his face assumed a gentle, just slightly mischievous smile, and with the wisdom of mothers who refuse to believe that their infants' first smiles are caused by gas, we felt we could recognize the carrying over of irony into peace. As he had weakened and had been able to express less and less, the final attribute distilled from the others was sweetness, so this was the natural form into which his features settled, unfalsified by cosmetics and the skillful artifices of morticians who teach the dead to lie to the living about what they meet at journey's end.

Downstairs we drank sherry and ate the stilton cheese that Gregory loved with other members of the immediate circle who had not been present at noon, in undefined shared sacrament. Through the next two nights and days, a new pattern developed an echo of the rhythm of Gregory's last days. The Zen students came and went, keeping their vigil, and we also took turns being by Gregory's side, watching the continuing changes as death increasingly and more deeply asserted itself. The window was kept open to the cool San Francisco weather, and in the morning he seemed to me a thousand miles more distant, his skin pale as wax, his hand still and very cold. As a child I believed that the dead became such strangers immediately, not realizing that there is a maturation in death. Having offered incense once, I found I preferred to enter the room informally and sit close by his side, touching his hand in greeting and farewell.

Our Buddhist guides told of their belief that the soul lingers near the body for up to three days before it finally departs, so that cremation should not occur for three days and the body should be attended, especially during the first two days, and they encouraged us and other visitors to read out loud or to address Gregory. At the same time, all of us had limited experience and we were shy of the physical complications of keeping a body for too long a period of time, so the decision was made to send the body to the crematorium on the sixth. That morning the Zen students withdrew, leaving the watch with Gregory to the family. My sister Nora and I went in together, sitting for a time on either side of the big bed as she explored the quality of death, feeling his hands, asking about the mechanism of rigor, wondering at the absence of the familiar bulk. Reb, one of the Zen teachers, spoke of him as being like a beached whale, but at the end he was strangely diminished. Then the Neptune Society van came, and Gregory was wrapped in a sheet that someone had carefully ironed that morning, strapped to a stretcher, and finally his face was covered with a dark green wrapper. The Zen Guest House is an old and gracious building, with stairs wide enough for one to make a final departure on a stretcher or in a coffin, and probably Gregory was not the first person to leave it so.

Baker Roshi's advice was to stay as close to the process as possible, following Gregory step by step through the concrete reality, so on the seventh the family went to the crematorium with a small group of Zen monks who had also been close to Gregory. We took various things to send with him into the fire: a volume of Blake's poetry, flowers and sweet smelling herbs, individual roses. We gave him a small crab that Eric and John had gone out with a flashlight to capture the night before, in memory of the way he had taught each of us to study tide pools and of the way he had taken a crab with him year after year to his opening classes at the San Francisco Art Institute, to open his students' eyes to the "fearful symmetries" of organic life. Nora brought a bagel because he had once quipped at Esalen that the hole in a bagel would be reincarnated in a doughnut. There were incense and the ashes of incense from Zen Center.

We went into the backstage of the crematorium where the great ovens are, a disheveled and unkempt region of noisy machinery. His body was on a plank on a wheeled stretcher, and when the covering was turned back we could see that rigor had passed and his mouth had fallen open, his head fallen sideways. His body seemed gray and abandoned as if finally life had fully receded. We piled our gifts within the shroud and offered incense, and as the Zen folk chanted in Sanskrit we each whispered whatever other prayers we felt the moment needed. Reb, the Zen priest officiating, whispered in his ear before the oven door was closed. None of us felt any longer the need or desire to touch him.

Reb showed Lois the button to press to start the oven, as in another age she would have set the flame to a pyre of fragrant woods. And then he suggested that we go outside to where the smoke of the crematorium was escaping into the bright sky.

BRYCE AND
MARGARET MUIR

"Where've You Been, Stranger?" Disintermediation in the Maritimes

more locally sufficient work ethic—gardens, the underground economy, industries with smaller and steadier growth, people living off their skills.

We didn't print Paul's essay here because he reworked it into a book, *The Next Economy* (Holt, Rinehart & Winston, 1982); but this response to that essay, published Summer 1981, is wonderful and illuminating in its own right. The Muirs wrote several essays for CQ, each taking a theory (disintermediation, local politics) and testing the practice of it in the unflappable experimental laboratory of their New England maritime lives and town. Peggy is an anthropologist; Bryce is a toymaker.

Art Kleiner

OK, reader, first you need to know what disintermediation is. Here's the textbook definition quoted from Paul Hawken, who made the term the title of his article in the Spring 1981 CQ: "In economics, disintermediation is used to describe the displacement of funds from banks and savings institutions when depositors decide to seek higher yields by investing on their own, bypassing the institutions." Paul used the word to describe a healthy process happening now in the new "information economy"—individuals are abandoning stagnant economic intermediaries like banks, corporations, and specialized professionals, in favor of a

The "subterranean economy" has gotten a lot of press recently, as if barter, or discount cash business, were some wonderful new invention. Less affluent Americans have always used these strategies, of course. It's only when their middle-class cousins discover invisible income that it becomes news. Leave it to the middle class to rediscover the obvious.

Now Paul Hawken has put a new catchword on the tips of our tongues: disintermediation. In business, it used to be called cutting out the middleman, and it's still an excellent cure for shrinking profits. The American middle class may now be discovering that disintermediation also heals an aching wound in the family pocketbook.

One form of disintermediation is increasingly popular: networking. The 80s are the decade of the personal network. The happy coincidence of a contracting economy and an information revolution makes this inevitable. Exchanging goods, services, and information through extended personal networks, we can dispense with middlemen and stretch our dollars.

To read COEVOLUTION QUARTERLY you might think that networking is a brave new world. Disintermediation by personal network is, in fact, as old as islands. Hawken points out that middlemen proliferate where there is continuous economic growth. In places where cash flows are sluggish, or seasonal, middlemen don't predominate, and personal economic networks are a way of life. This is the case in the maritime hinterlands of Maine and Atlantic Canada.

In traditional maritime society every man is a jack of all trades, able to cut his own firewood, build a house and boat, make and mend fishing gear, fish and hunt, keep animals for meat and dairy products, do his own boat and auto mechanics, plumb and wire. In a pinch he can do a little smithing in the parlor stove, some rough doctoring offshore, and put down a wellpoint by hand. Each maritime woman is a respected master at the arts of child rearing and housekeeping. Raising, gathering, and preserving; making and mending clothing; and keeping the social gears greased are all in her day's work. These traditional skills enable disintermediation in spades.

When cash is abundant, maritimers may hire out some or all of the subsistence chores: buy California lettuce, take the car to a garage, send away for a new dress. So long as cash work, or good fishing, produces surplus income, beyond present needs and subsistence maintenance for the off season, specializations proliferate. When the fish are running, there's lots of work for carpenters. When the catch is off, I can pound my own nails, thank you.

The uncertainties, and seasonality, of maritime cash flow mean that no specialist can depend on continuous employment. Carpenters cut pulp in the winter. A grocer may own a truck for hauling gravel. Anthropologists call this diversified pattern of employment "seasonal pluralism," and it is an appropriate adap-

tation to the ebb and flow of a resource-based economy.

Seasonal pluralism makes maritimers sensitive to any opportunity for disintermediation. Consider the fish business. When I can go out and catch 10,000 pounds of groundfish a day, all I want to do is come in, dump those babies on the dock, gas up, and get back at them. I'm willing to take a lower price from a middleman, so long as I can land big volumes, and he can worry about the market. But, when the best I can do is bring in 50 pounds of lobster for a day's haul, I might be tempted to float those lobsters in crates until I have a truckload, and personally deliver them to a restaurant owner in Ohio—for a big cash price. (IRS doesn't like that one bit. Government bureaucrats are the ultimate intermediators. They stand between us, as taxpayers, and ourselves, as consumers of government services. Bypassing the taxman is the lowest form of disintermediation.)

Even in the best of times maritimers will tend to buy winter staples in bulk, in season. While the fish are running, fishermen will salt away enough cash to cover winter subsistence before they indulge in consumerism. Affluence is just another run of luck which has to end. Maritimers are prepared for an age of economic uncertainty. A healthy distrust of affluence and a full set of traditional skills stand them in good stead. They also have fine-tuned another necessary skill for disintermediation: network communications.

While every maritimer is a jack of all trades, any given man may excel at one trade or another. If you have a gift for engine mechanics, I may prefer your work to mine—so long as we can come to some arrangement. Maybe you'd like some of the special cheese my wife makes. Not only is the distribution of special aptitude uneven, so is the availability of capital equipment. Unlike the suburbs, where every house may have a lawn tractor, perhaps only one man in a fishing village has a tractor, or a set of torches, or a torque wrench. Matching individual needs with local skills and appropriate tools requires information.

Getting and maintaining access to economic

information is a constant pursuit in the maritimes. Much of what passes for nosiness is just keeping track of economic activity and capital equipment. I watch my neighbor's tractor in the spring. When he hooks up the rototiller I know he's stopped skidding pulpwood for the year and is ready to plow gardens. That's the time to make a deal to bust up my new potato patch—not before. Any maritimer can tell you the optimum moment to access someone's economic skills, and where every major tool in town is at that instant—or he knows who to ask.

Maritime men and women spend a considerable portion of each day maintaining personal networks—in no small part to have continuous access to economic information. Usually founded on kinship, a personal network will tend to encompass all those persons whose skills and material resources are necessary for one's subsistence. Maritimers also frequent those places generally known as information exchanges. Restaurants in coastal Maine are often the place where men drink coffee and keep up on what's going on. A boatbuilder's shop or the manager's office on a wharf may be the local information brokerage house.

The key to continuous access is constant attention. Maritime men are expected to contact each member of their active network every day, face-to-face. If you don't make the rounds for a couple of days, you will be greeted with, "Where've you been, stranger?" Maritime women chat around their active nets numerous times each day, via phone. These channel checks, or continuity tests, assure that news circulates rapidly, and they identify an individual as a dependable member of the network. You are always logged in.

Once logged in you may have to fulfill network obligations at a moment's notice. If you have a labor exchange understanding with your brother-in-law, and you see him hauling his boat, you'll stop and lend a hand. Summer visitors to the maritimes always seem astounded that a man will promise to do a job and then not show up for weeks. Summer people don't understand that a maritimer is juggling a raft of obligations, many of them dependent on

chance of the weather and the pattern of activity in his network—all unpredictable. If a maritimer promises to do a job, he will, but *when* is a matter of circumstances. You don't "make a date" with a maritimer. This unscheduled sort of disintermediation doesn't suit an industrial environment.

Industrial wage work, or any sort of regular hours, tends to disconnect you from local economic networks—which is only fair. You won't be in the restaurant on windy days, or on the phone while the baby naps. Professional women in the maritimes find this particularly destructive, because network breakdown disrupts their female solidarity as well as their economic access.

The point for middle-class Americans who might turn to disintermediative networks in the face of economic adversity is that personal network maintenance is extraordinarily time-consuming. Total access to local disintermediative goods, services, or information takes a total commitment. You can't just plug in when you want access. Disintermediative networks in the larger society often suffer from the same complaint: a bad signal-to-noise ratio. Computer data banks can spew out reams of information before you find the bit you want. Just so, you'll suffer through hours of small talk at the restaurant before that one vital bit of information comes along. Time may be the price we pay for networking.

Let's follow a maritime search routine to see what it entails. Say we are looking for a work crew to move a building, and our local economic relations are all in order. We'll wait for a blowy day when all the fishermen are ashore. First we activate our close network, letting them know what we are planning. We'll go to the restaurant early in the morning and let it be known, casually, that we plan to move a building at such a time and are in the market for labor. Shortly before the stated hour we'll go to the beer store, buy a few cases, and announce the job. As if by magic, a crew will materialize. After the job is done (and the beer), we'll offer to pay the labor at the universal local rate (say $5 an hour). Some may accept payment. Most will refuse, citing a previous debt to us, or suggesting an alternative payment in kind.

"Maybe I can use your house jacks sometime," or "I'll probably need *your* help sometime."

You can see why access takes attention. That last crew member, who expects to use our labor sometime, assumes we'll know when, because we are regular players in the game. Similarly, automated barter networks will only be generally useful if there is a variety of necessary goods and services always available locally via the net. Otherwise they will merely be an economic sideshow.

Personal economic networks have political implications. The ripoff artist is quickly ostracized. If you don't play fair, you don't play long. This not only includes providing quality goods and services, it means adhering to the local wage level. My time is no less valuable than yours, doc. You can allow for amortizing capital equipment, but everyone paid for his education—don't be putting on airs.

Once integrated into a local exchange system, you realize that every good and service has a recognized fair value. Everyone knows how long it takes to time an engine. Everyone is keeping score. I know you owe me fifteen minutes of sweat and a bale of hay. Everyone's goal is "balanced reciprocity"—tit for tat. This has the advantage of making us all economic equals, and the disadvantage of reducing us all to the lowest common denominator. Those who wish to break out of equalized subsistence must go out into the larger economy for cash income, and forfeit access to the exchange network. Outsiders pay top dollar for local goods and services.

The prevailing economic assumption in the maritime culture is the idea of "limited good": there is only so much resource to go around. Every fish you catch is one less for me, so we better share more or less equally. A rough justice prevails in fishing communities. Economic advancement (getting ahead) while your neighbors only get by, makes you a target of jealousy. Too much conspicuous consumption is antisocial, and the local teenagers may trash your property some dark night. Don't be

greedy. Set out 1,000 lobster traps in an area where most men fish 500 and you'll lose a lot of traps. By the same token, if your luck is bad this season, and I've been doing all right, I might give you a hint where to set some gear, lest you call *me* greedy.

The idea of limited good has been dismissed as a shortsighted local view, suitable for peasants, perhaps, but not applicable to industrial civilization and economies of scale. Only recently have the limits to growth become a topic of discussion in the larger society. The economic egalitarianism of the maritimes may become a more popular social adaptation as we approach the limits to resource development.

The intrusion of outside capital and the acceleration of technological innovation have disrupted the maritime homeostat. Fishing communities, local resources, and environmental conditions traditionally composed a dynamic steady-state system. The limited marine resources were treated as common property. If one man took too much, it was at the expense of all, and he was castigated. Fish and men survived together in rough harmony. The process of *modernizing* maritime society is hardly complete, and the old values endure below the surface. Maritimers may have to depend on their traditional common sense during the next decade.

Another political aspect of maritime culture has implications for wider disintermediation by networks. Every man is taken at face value in the maritimes. Each maritimer speaks for himself, out of his personal knowledge. It is recognized that each view of the world is different, and no one local view has higher authority. Anyone presuming to a position of leadership is accused of being big-headed. Anyone presuming to have the last word on a local subject is laughed out of court.

This is not how information is treated in American society at large. We have experts and specialists whose opinions have authority. Scholastic knowledge is hierarchical. This stands to reason. When we are building towers of abstraction, we must agree on the foundations—call something "truth." An orderly hierarchy of abstractions is fine, if we are constructing academic models. Adhering to a generalized "truth" can be dangerous in real life. Concrete local knowledge too often contradicts a lovely abstraction. Network communications must be egalitarian lest they lose touch with local realities. Arbitrarily rejecting local knowledge in favor of the conventional wisdom has made the mass media a sorry vehicle for the transmission of useful and accurate information. Part of the success of the *Whole Earth Catalog* and *CoEvolution Quarterly* is that all submitted information is treated as equally valid. This is open networking—the only way to guarantee the free flow of information.

Maritimers are generally open-minded about new information. When my truck exhibits mysterious symptoms, I will certainly put more faith in the opinion of a gifted mechanic I know than in the casual advice of some stranger. But I'll listen to the stranger's advice and put it on file. If he is a maritimer, it is probably based on experience—not just gas. An egalitarian attitude toward information keeps maritime networks open to the smallest economic opportunity. Fishermen are considered extremely conservative, in the conventional wisdom. Actually they are quick to seize the least advantage. Let it be rumored that you have a market for barnacles, and your phone will ring off the wall.

It is worth noting that maritime networks, for all their egalitarianism, are not based on friendship. Friendship implies an emotional relationship which supersedes economic advantage. You'd give a friend the shirt off your back. That makes a friend an economic liability. Middle-class Americans can afford the luxury of friendship. In a world of limited good it's every man for himself. A friend might ask where the good fishing is. Maritime networks don't rely on trust, or the emotional bonds of friendship, for their durability. They depend on that old individualistic motive: mutual self-interest.

By contrast, disintermediative networks in the larger society are often animated by a certain emotionalism. Old boy networks are colored with the aura of schoolboy camaraderie. Countercultural nets assume a common idealism. Co-ops are supposed to be warm and friendly before they are businesslike.

Friendship can be a fine foundation for economic networking. It provides an egalitarian attitude toward shared information, and a predisposition for fair dealing. Friendship nets generally lack the diversity to be widely utilitarian, however, and network interactions get clouded with emotional expectations. The behavior of traditional economic networks in the maritimes indicates that unswerving practicality may be the best way to share limited resources equally, through personal networks.

Which reminds me, any of you have a good market for barnacles?

Married female, age 38
I can't bear the pain any longer.
I'm tired, discouraged and unhappy.

ART KLEINER

How Not to Commit Suicide

*From the original introduction
(Summer 1981):*
This article arose from a conversation
among the directors of our foundation, Point. Michael Phillips and I
wanted to publish information on
how to commit suicide. Hiding such
information is a vicious taboo, we
opined in high libertarian dudgeon.
Richard Baker, abbot of the local
Zen Center and one who sees a lot of
disturbed people, remarked drily, "If
the information were generally available, a fellow I talked with last week
would be dead now. He wouldn't do
it this week I think. The information
that people need is how *not* to commit suicide. They think if they take
an overdose of sleeping pills they'll
just go to sleep and never wake up.
Instead they wake up choking on
their vomit, and there's the emergency room and stomach pumping
and brain damage, and it's the opposite of relief for their suffering. People try all sorts of things that don't
work, all horrible."

CQ staffer Art Kleiner got the assignment and immersed himself in

it with his customary zeal. (He
wants noted that "four people who
have worked with suicidal people
helped me articulate the article, even
though they weren't directly quoted
in it—Mary Deems, Ron Jones,
Larry Cohen, and Ben Campbell.")
Journalist Kleiner also adds, "This
article was probably the most rewarding I've ever done, nightmares
and all."

Stewart Brand

During the four years since this article was published, I've heard from
half-a-dozen people, saying they or a
friend or patient of theirs would not
be alive but for this article; in each
case the person stumbled across the
information herein, thought hard
about their suicide attempt, realized
what they were getting into, and decided to try changing their life
instead.

Art Kleiner

*Instead of oblivion and relief, nine out of ten suicide at-
tempters live through various ordeals of intense physical
suffering, stomach pumping, lasting internal injury,
brain damage, bureaucratization, moral condemnation,
uninvited psychiatry . . . and sometimes new attitudes
about life.*

Resurrection, the voyage to the land of the
dead and back again, is common enough in old
legends and myths and in the experiences of
people who live through a near-terminal illness
or accident. But that journey is also made daily
in hospital emergency rooms.

About thirty thousand people kill themselves in the United States each year. An estimated ten to forty times that number try to kill themselves but don't die, either because they don't really want to die or because they don't know how.

I didn't realize the impact of that statistic until I talked to friends and acquaintances while researching this article. Everyone I talked to, whether I interviewed them or casually brought the subject up, knew someone who had attempted suicide.

Some of the stories are tragic. A friend of a friend jumped from a high building and hit a parked car several stories below. She broke most of her bones and punctured several of her inner organs but didn't die. Instead she was wheeled, conscious, to the local emergency room, her most privately conceived act announced to the world by the ambulance siren. She spent the next year in bed, much of it in a hospital ward allocated to critically ill victims of violence, her still-suicidal mind the only functioning part of her body.

This article about what happens to people who attempt to kill themselves started as a brief review of a pair of new publications aimed at the terminally ill. One booklet, the widely-publicized but little-read "death manual," *How to Die With Dignity*, contains a chart of lethal doses of different types of pills and methods of deliberately ensuring a calm death in a suicide attempt. It was published by Scottish Exit, a northern spinoff of British Exit, the London group that has in the past year sought and won more than its share of controversy. Two of the members of the London group are now facing trial on nine charges of aiding people to kill themselves.

The other book, *Let Me Die Before I Wake*, is a collection of case histories of people who have committed suicide or attempted it and failed, with detailed descriptions of the methods used. It was published this spring by a Los Angeles group called Hemlock, which also counsels terminally ill people on their other options. The book's author, Derek Humphry, is a British journalist who wrote the sentimental memoir *Jean's Way* (1978; $5 postpaid from Hemlock, Suite 101, 2803 Ocean Park Boulevard, Santa Monica, California 90405), the first popular book to describe what Hemlock calls "Self-Deliverance." Humphry's first wife, Jean, discovered that she had bone marrow cancer and took a fatal drug overdose as she was on the verge of becoming immobile.

"Perhaps ten percent of our members are terminally ill," Humphry told me. "The great fear of the rest of our members is that they may face a painful, awful death one day. If they can say, 'I have this cache of pills and good advice on how to use them,' they can feel prepared if they eventually do fall ill, and in the meantime can get on with the business of living."

So when I went to emergency room physicians, paramedics, and therapists, I expected to hear of many people who might have needed this information—people who, faced with a grim illness and no alternatives to it, had tried to kill themselves and ended in the emergency room instead. Wrong. People who plan deliberate suicides usually succeed—as Humphry said, everything in the suicide manuals can also be found in medical textbooks. People in emergency rooms are usually people who attempted suicide on impulse, in temporary despair or anger. Many decide later that it was a mistake.

They are the people whose fate has been thrown into sharper focus by the existence of these new books. The argument between Exit and the British suicide prevention groups played with much commotion in the press and in conversation. The books should not be published, the suicide prevention people said, because temporarily distraught people would use them impulsively and die, where without them they would probably live. Yes, said the voluntary euthanasia groups, but preparing for a rational, planned suicide as the books encourage, and thinking out its ramifications (like who will be affected by it) makes people less likely to kill themselves impulsively. Yes, but the context of the how-to-die information shows suicide as an easy way to solve problems, and doesn't encourage people to look for other options first.

Yes, but the books are available only through the mail, with a three-month waiting period, just to discourage such abuse. Yes, but with easy Xerox access no one can guarantee the books won't find a subterranean following. Yes, but banning the book is equally manipulative—it keeps people from the option of dying easily unless they are lucky enough to find people who will help them. Yes, but they might find people who will help them avoid the pain tomorrow, if they aren't encouraged to end their lives today. Yes, but . . .

The debate is fascinating to follow, because usually talk of suicide is hushed up, for fear it will create more suicide or someone will be held responsible. Psychologist David Gruder worked in a California high school a few years ago when one of the popular seniors killed himself. "In the next two weeks everybody pulled me aside—students, teachers, the principal—to ask me what they could have done, what he meant by it. But nobody said anything out loud to each other. Finally I gave a talk at the library about suicide and suicide prevention, and I had to argue with six levels of school administration to do it. I had to tell them the clinical truth is that talking about suicide often neutralizes it. Ignoring it always paves the way for more attempts."

When a genuine myth rises into consciousness, Ursula Le Guin wrote in "The Language of the Night," the message is always: *You must change your life.* Each suicide attempt, I'm convinced, carries that message: to the person who tries it, to the people who are close to that person, and to the rest of us as a society. I think what happens after a suicide attempt is a sort of autopsy of what's best and worst about our culture. Here is some of that story.

Like the other two hundred suicide prevention telephone hotlines in the U.S., the Marin Suicide Prevention Center holds several eleven-session training classes a year. I sat in on one of the introductory sessions. It looked like any suburban adult education class—sixty fidgety people of all ages in chairs too small for them, and two instructors, the Center's Acting Director Noreen Dunnigan and the Program Director David Nolan. After a warning that statistics are misleading, Dunnigan jumped in.

"For every 100,000 people in the United States," she said "an average of 12.5 attempt suicide each year. At this center we get 1200 calls a month, from 250 clients. Most people call more than once. Wednesday is our busiest day. ("It's the day most therapists take off," Nolan interrupted.) Eighty percent of the people call about themselves; the rest are clergy, friends, family—calling because they're worried about someone. The later the hour, the higher the number of calls. Thirty-four percent of the callers are male, sixty-six percent female. Can anybody guess why?"

"Men aren't as used to reaching out for help," said a man, the only black person in the room.

Dunnigan nodded and went on: "Fifty-four percent of the callers are not in a suicidal crisis. Forty-six percent have problems with alcohol or drugs. Thirty-five percent live alone. Once every fifty hours, in what we call active intervention, we send someone in—an ambulance or friends, or clergy, or someone else goes over to their house because we ask them to."

"What do you mean by suicidal crisis?" asked a studious-looking woman. "You don't mean forty-six percent are actually trying suicide?"

David Nolan replied. "No, the fifty-four percent are people who don't mention suicide at all. They have some other problem—loneliness, maybe—and they want somebody to talk to. Twenty-six percent have suicidal ideation. They're thinking about it. Thirteen percent are threatening suicide. Six percent are attempting it as we talk to them. The rest, we don't know about; the calls are too short or we don't find out."

Noreen Dunnigan gave some statistics from the Marin coroner's office about people who did kill themselves. "The highest rate of suicide is in May. We'll talk more about what happens to people in the spring. The second highest is in January, just after the holidays. The older the person the higher the suicide rate. The average age for males is forty-one. The average for females is forty-five."

"That doesn't mean anyone was actually at those specific ages," Nolan said.

"There were forty-seven known suicides in Marin in 1980. (There are others we don't know about.) Thirty-four were male. Thirteen were female. Fourteen people shot themselves. All but one of them were male. Six people died from car exhaust. Four jumped off the Golden Gate Bridge. The rest were drug overdoses."

Dunnigan described the established theories about why people commit suicide. Freud, for instance, thought most people have two basic instinctual drives—the wish to live (Eros) and the wish to die (Thanatos). Karl Menninger said a suicidal person acts out a wish to be killed ("I don't deserve to live"), a wish to kill someone else, or a wish to die. Old people usually fall into the latter category ("I can't go on."). Young people usually wish to die or be killed.

"There is also a need for attention," she said. "A lot of these people have worn out their family and friends. The coroner's office tells us that they can usually tell most people didn't really want to die. According to their suicide notes, they wanted to be rescued. Anyone here can be suicidal given the right circumstances or the proper amount of stress.

"When someone calls, we assume they are ambivalent, no matter how suicidal they say they are. Otherwise, they wouldn't call. For myself I want the right to choose to live or die—for example, if I were terminally ill I don't know how I'd choose—but anyone who calls here will have a hell of a battle.

"They let us know that there's a glimmer of hope and that's the side we work with. We feel them out—we ask if they are thinking of killing themselves. We try to find alternatives— not giving them our alternatives, but asking them what they did the last time they felt this way, getting them to remember when they *didn't* feel this way."

About half the people in the room were taking notes. A woman in her twenties asked, "What do you say after you ask 'Are you thinking of killing yourself?' and they say 'Yes'?"

"Well, often the simplest response is that you don't want them to die. It's not easy. Dealing with suicidal people is usually unrewarding. They're the toughest for therapists, and in fact dealing with them makes some therapists become suicidal." A bearded man in his thirties nodded his head.

A teenage girl with glasses and short-cropped brown hair said, "You say to the person, 'I don't want you to die' and the person says 'Why?' What's your answer?"

"You say, 'I don't want you to die because I care about you.'"

"They go for that?"

"Yes, they do, if you're sincere." She paused. Nobody said anything. The girl looked dubious. "Have you ever cared about anyone who wanted to die and *not* been able to come up with a reason why they should go on living? Usually by the time I'm on the phone awhile I have a rapport going, and by that time I usually do have a reason that I care about them. A very intimate relationship builds up very quickly on the phone. Some of you may not be able to dredge up any feeling for some of your callers and in that case you shouldn't lie to them. They can spot a phony right away."

The girl still looked unconvinced, but nodded. Someone else asked, "What do you do with your emotions?"

"You talk to fellow counselors, you talk to staff," Noreen Dunnigan said. "You don't let any individual callers get into a personal relationship with you. In fact, any counselor who meets a caller outside of the Center is automatically suspended—not suspended—what's the other word for final?"

"Expelled," someone called out.

"Expelled. We don't use the word terminated here."

Laughter. More talk about what to say to people on the phone. "We want to explore their death fantasies and deglamorize them. How do you know there's a life hereafter? Have you known anyone who came back? You won't be able to see your own funeral, and show everyone you were serious. If you overdose you'll probably choke on your own vomit. Your bowels will go. Who's going to find you?

"Get used to saying, 'I want you to flush the pills away now,' instead of saying, 'Would you mind putting the pills away for us?' We want to assert ourselves. We ask, what will your children think when they find you? What kind of example would this be for your children as a way to solve problems? We use all the things we can think of and sometimes they sound manipulative. They *are* manipulative. We want to get the person through the crisis. We want them to take the gun away and put it on a shelf where they can't see it. Or put it out of the house, better yet.

"We find out what has given meaning to their lives. Has it always been this way? What was it like when it was not this way? Sometimes people say they've always felt this way. You say, 'Let's count back and see if that's true.'"

"But isn't that denying what they just said?" someone asked.

"No, you acknowledge their feeling but you want to do a reality test with them. 'It sounds like you've always felt this way but let's talk more about it.'"

"It sounds like you're trying to instill guilt."

"We don't want them to feel any worse than they already do. But often they haven't thought about everything. It's like tunnel vision. Usually it hasn't dawned on them who it will affect or what the long-range effects of their act will be. Once they realize it they often don't want the suicide to happen. They don't want to die; they want the pain to stop. People who are sure about killing themselves rarely call the suicide hotline."

Telephone crisis hotlines didn't exist until 1958, when two Los Angeles psychologists stumbled across a bulging file of suicide notes in the coroner's office. Intrigued by the lack of research on rescuing or preventing suicides, they made themselves available for emergency consultation to suicidal patients. Soon it seemed like daytime hours weren't enough, so they set up a phone where patients could call day and night, and manned it with seven staff members. This was the first telephone crisis hotline of any kind, ever. After a few months the paid staff couldn't handle the number of calls, so the doctors trained volunteers.

By trial and error they worked out the principles that most suicide prevention work is based on now. Find out first how lethal a person's intentions are and defuse their plans as quickly as possible. Don't talk about how much there is to live for; ask the callers what their options are. Encourage callers to talk to a different counselor every time they call, so one doesn't get overloaded. Assume that because they called they are asking for help and you have a mandate to save their lives however you can, including tracing the call and sending the police.

Personally, I feel suicide prevention volunteers, like volunteer firemen, are among the truest altruistic community heroes we have. Telephone hotlines are probably the readiest and least manipulative escape valves available for the lonely or depressed. A lot of their value comes from the quality of the people who put in time on them. Most work six to eight hours a week, and the people I've talked to or heard about say they volunteer mainly because they like the other people who work there.

Some volunteers got their start with the drug abuse bad-trip hotlines of the sixties, and drug and suicide hotlines co-evolved, taking methods, enthusiasm, and staff people from each other. Other hotlines like poison control or sex information developed later from these.

The upper-echelon professional suicidology scene is more like an academic industry. Edward Shneidman and Norman Farberow, those two Los Angeles psychiatrists who started it all, have thirteen books in print on the subject between them. Most are collections of essays by respectable social scientists. Farberow's latest, *The Many Faces of Suicide* (1980; $21.95 postpaid from McGraw-Hill Book Company, Princeton Road, Hightstown, New Jersey 08520), says that sky-diving, intervening in violent crimes, drunk driving, prostitution, gambling, and taking risks in general are all suicidal, and implies they can be treated psychiatrically.

In suicide prevention much of the training is learning to listen and react to people. You have to ask direct questions, like "What happened next?" instead of trying to smooth over bad feelings. You have to learn to keep someone who sounds apathetic about everything on the phone until you dredge up something they can get excited about. You have to find out what's going on at the other end—are the callers drinking? Have they abused a child? Are they calling so they can masturbate while they talk to you?—and you have to find out without making judgment about any of those things.

The end of every call is supposed to involve a contract. The caller agrees they will call again before they try suicide, or they will set a small goal for themselves, like writing a letter, and do it. Or they'll go for therapy. The exception is the six percent of people who commit suicide before or during the telephone call. They get the police and ambulance sent to their door.

"Someone calls up and says, 'I just took all these pills, and now I don't want to die'—that's easy," David Nolan said. "They're willing to give you their address. One counselor stays on the phone with them, the other calls for the emergency vehicles. It's a code 3—lights and sirens—but we like them to turn them off when they get near the house.

"Other times a caller says, 'I just took fifty Valiums and I'm drinking a quart of vodka and I want to talk to you while I die.' We don't do that. If we think a life is in danger, we take over. Getting them to tell us where they are depends on the skill of the counselor. 'I need to know where you are and I need to know right now. You are dying.' It's extremely eerie when a person is told he is dying.

"If we have to we will hold them on the line and trace the call. In Marin, tracing takes thirty minutes to two hours, so we usually don't do it. Other places, we hear, are faster. Once it's traced, we tell the people that we are sending over an ambulance. (Not every suicide prevention center tells them, but it's our policy.) 'You called suicide prevention,' we say, 'and you're dying, and I'm sending you some help.' We ask them to turn on the lights and unlock the door. We don't break contact over the phone until the emergency people get there."

Marc Rubin, a paramedic with the San Francisco Department of Public Health, heard I was doing this article and suggested I interview him. Until then it never occurred to me to interview any of the emergency people who are sent to the scene of a suicide. I didn't realize that they are probably more involved with the suicidal person than anyone else. They're the first people who comfort them, the only people who see where they live and what they did to themselves, and they seem to get a more vivid idea of the person's personality than anyone else, until they drop them off at the hospital and never see them again. Rubin talked like he had been storing up feelings for some time. He made me wonder if working in emergencies by nature makes people impassioned and articulate.

"Half my ambulance calls just involve going to a person's house, calming them down, recommending they go to a doctor in the morning. It's a 'give me strokes' kind of call. People just want to talk to somebody. If they call emergency and say they're contemplating suicide they are sent the ambulance and the police. If there's violence the police go first—they're paid to risk their lives. Then we take the people to the hospital.

"If you talk to the police and paramedics you find they feel many of these people should be allowed to die. We're bound by our jobs to make them live, but there's a lot of distaste for it. You never know if the suicidal person was distraught or made a rational decision. It's real hard to put a value judgment on it.

"We see a lot of alcoholics, gays, recently divorced or separated people, lonely people. People that I would characterize as emotionally vulnerable. We see them at the height of their vulnerability. We see some people who cut their wrists gingerly, knowing that it won't kill them, just to try it and see what it feels like. We see others who are serious about it, actively seeking it out but not sure if they're going to do it until the moment comes. Those are the ones we have to talk to as they're about to jump off a building.

"My last call of the shift last night was a man who shot himself. I got there and saw this girl cool in the doorway: 'I think my father's shot himself. Check downstairs.' His wife said, 'I didn't want him around any more and he shot himself.' He was Chilean. In some cultures in a situation like that they don't think the man's a jerk if he takes his life. It's the courageous thing to do.

"I like working on the street. People in emergency rooms get patients for a length of time, but I do my medical things and get them there and then I'm done. My role is medical intervention. I make sure they don't compromise their vital functions. That means checking their airway—listening for the movement of air through the mouth and nose—and their breathing rhythm—are their lungs expanding? And checking their heartbeat—is it fast enough? Is it stopped? If it's off you have to do cardio-pulmonary resuscitation, which involves pressing on the sternum and spine to get the heart going again. A lot of times if someone's lost fluid or if they're in shock we have to replace the fluid or blood intravenously.

"If they're suicidal we are always required to take them to the emergency room. If they're conscious, say if I've just bandaged their arm, then as a courtesy I'll ask if they'll come to the hospital with us. If they're upset or say no, they'll still have to come, though.

"There are so many scenarios. Most of the time the police, medical people, and firemen are compassionate, but it's still scary. There are six or eight people in uniforms looking at this scared, vulnerable person. If everything goes well, they might even like giving up responsibility for themselves to the people in uniform. But otherwise, all it might take for them to go off the handle is for somebody to make a wisecrack—say if the patient's in drag. Or sometimes people get angry just because you're in a uniform. Then you have to talk them down.

"I stay professional a lot of the time—not cold, but impersonal. Then I move up or down from there to more or less professional in tone. Sometimes I'll talk to the person about why they did it, what their alternatives are. If they're hysterical I try to get them to talk about something they like to do. I'll talk about my own problems, real or contrived.

"Society doesn't support its losers. A theme I get repeatedly from suicides is, 'Look at me,

The suicide notes on these pages were gathered at coroners' offices by a suicidologist/psychiatrist who asked to be anonymous. He edited identifying details out of the compiled manuscript, and we changed the names. But the text of each letter plus the age and sex given are real. All these people did kill themselves. Were they ambivalent about it? About half the hundred or so letters we saw seemed to have some element of doubt.

(There's a strange story in computer folklore about a suicide note that appeared late one night on the Arpanet computer network. The other people on the network had regularly corresponded with the man, but always under the name of his lab, not his own name. When the message saying he was killing himself flashed on the screen they tried to call the police, but nobody could identify him, and he died.)

Art Kleiner

Married female, age 59

Dear David,
After six weeks of streptomycin shots and a total of eleven weeks of rest in bed we have conclusive proof that the ulcers in my bronchial tubes have not healed. The short period of the streptomycin inhalations could not have brought on the results if the ulceration had even partially healed. To try further would mean many more months of bed rest—more shots and inhalations—I can't remain at the hospital for the winter months and a prolonged stay at a rest home is out of the question. I did some figuring—the weekly rate there—the amount of streptomycin for shots and inhalations plus the doctor's weekly visits would total to over $200 a week—I can't bleed my family for any such amount of money, and that means that as soon as the money I have in my checking account runs out I would have to return home—back to the same conditions which caused me to go downhill so steadily. It's a vicious circle from which there seems no escape. I could of course use up the money from the sale of our furnishings and silver as well as some I put aside for the furnishing of our home—but all of it put together would be like a drop in the bucket—besides I am now convinced

that my condition is too chronic and therefore a cure doubtful.

All of a sudden all will and determination to fight on has left me. I have long ago prepared myself for the time when I reached the end of the trail. I feel calm and at peace and grateful that I can *go to sleep* painlessly. I feel justified in terminating a life which no longer holds any hope of having the essentials which make it worth living—I did desperately want to get well—I still had much to live for—hope for recovery—hope of a reunion with the children—work which I loved and which could have given me financial security and great satisfaction. But it was not to be—I am defeated and exhausted physically and emotionally.

Please tell the children that I loved them always and that my love has never faltered. I grieve that I could not have had the joy of being close to our babies, but that is no one's fault. Thank God they are well—with my passing all menace to their wellbeing will have disappeared.

I want you to know that I have a deep affection for you. I am deeply grateful for all your kindness. I wish I could have made a happier life for you. It was mostly my fault, please forgive me.

Please write to Fran and Tony and to Marilyn and Jim and tell them that my love and gratitude could not possibly be put into words. Their generosity, devotion, love and tact made it possible for me to accept their financial help over a long period of time. I wish with all my heart that they might have been better rewarded—All of you, my dear ones, I ask to keep my memory alive in your hearts—To live on in the hearts of our dear ones is all that I can conceive of immortality. Please think of me kindly. Remember that which was good and lovely in our relationship and forgive me for the many mistakes I have made. Now that it is all said I feel at peace.

I want Dr. B. to officiate at my funeral. I think Joe would like to have him with him at that time.

Dear David, I am sad that I must go just a few days before your birthday—

I've failed and I don't want to go seek help.' There's a lot of embarrassment. I tell them everybody needs help. A lot of people go to psychiatrists—doctors, police, politicians. I try to get them laughing. I don't myself but I try to get them to.

"I kind of enjoy it. As you know there are realms of thought under a psychedelic that you can't enter any other way. Psychosis is like that and that's why I appreciate it. I've sung things like quasi-Indian chants with people. I find that some policemen do the same. There's often a lesson that a psychotic person is offering me. Not to get too dependent on something—habits, jobs, people, money, family—that has let someone down. Or not to take myself too seriously. I think you have to be somewhat egocentric to attempt suicide. I ask the egocentric ones sometimes if the world is really going to care that much.

"There's a lot of voyeurism in it. I find that with a lot of medical people. They'll hear a hot call—a knifing, maybe—and really want to see it. Anytime you have a collection of fire and ambulance equipment, people gather on the street.

"A lot of people don't want to take the responsibility. A friend of mine had a call downtown—a man on a roof twenty stories high. She stayed up there talking with this man. Can you imagine how you'd feel if he said, 'No, no, you're wrong' and jumped off?

"That guy who shot himself in the head last night—I wouldn't feel comfortable trying to resuscitate him. He was warm but the chances of living were too low. If he had had any other signs of life—blood pressure, pulse, respirations—I would have had to do something. It's hard to do heroics to bring someone back to life for a day or two. I had a man a couple of months ago who had been shot in the head and I did resuscitate him. I felt bad that he had the trauma of being slapped in an ambulance. Things like that you have to try to do—you have to try.

"The whole idea of trauma centers is to take people who would die otherwise and bring them back to life. Whether their life is meaningful or not doesn't matter. We go for everybody. You're usually naked when you go in. I can't put it down, but in a way it's barbaric. I wouldn't want to go through it. If I'm that close I'd just as soon let it go."

Until recently, emergency room doctors were people who'd rather be elsewhere. Even now, a lot of emergency room doctors are moonlighting residents or specialists forced by their hospitals' rotating assignments to do occasional "trauma duty." But emergency medicine is becoming a specialty of its own, perhaps because four times as many people per capita visit emergency rooms as did twenty years ago. If someone you know is in danger of dying, call emergency services, not your family doctor, because that's what the emergency room does—keeps people from dying.

The basic principle for keeping suicides from dying is to do as little as possible. Most drug overdosers are left unconscious in a place where they can heal. The more the hospital has to do, the more chance of infection or accident. Drugs, including psychiatric drugs, are avoided, because they might react with drugs the patient already took. Before the 1940s, when Swedish doctors discovered this, about forty-five percent of the barbiturate overdose patients in emergency rooms died from attempts to wake them up with drugs. Now more than ninety-five percent of people who come into the emergency room on a drug overdose live. Many suffer no more than a day or week of discomfort in a hospital bed, like a teenager I heard about who tried to kill himself with 100 vitamin tablets. Others compound their problem with severe medical damage that may be permanent or take years to go away.

My information on the medical aftermath of suicide comes from half a dozen interviews with emergency room staff people, but two were especially helpful—Larry Bedard, M.D., a former psychiatric resident who now manages the emergency room at Marin General Hospital, San Rafael, and Howard McKinney, Pharm. D., a pharmacologist with the San Francisco Poison Control Center, who answers telephone inquiries and consults with emergency room staff. Like other emergency room

but it so happened to pan out. I see no good in incurring the expense and misery of the bronchoscopy. I wish I could spare you the ordeal you have ahead. Try not to grieve. I ask all of you, my dear ones, not to mourn my passing. Be glad I am at least free from the miseries and loneliness I have endured for so long and that at last I'll have peace and rest . . .

Single female, age 21
My dearest Andrew,
It seems as if I have been spending all my life apologizing to you for things that happened whether they were my fault or not.

I am enclosing your pin because I want you to think of what you took from me every time you see it.

I don't want you to think I would kill myself over you because you're not worth any emotion at all. It is what you cost me that hurts and nothing can replace it.

Single male, age 51
Sunday 4:45 PM   Here goes
     To who it may concern
     Though I am about to kick the bucket I am as happy as ever. I am tired of this life so am going over to see the other side.
     Good luck to all.
                                        Benjamin P.

Married male, age 48
Elaine Darling,
My mind—always warped and twisted—has reached the point where I can wait no longer—I don't dare wait longer—until there is the final twist and it snaps and I spend the rest of my life in some state run snake pit.

I am going out—and I hope it is out—Nirvanha, I think the Bhudaists (how do you spell Bhudaists?) call it which is the word for "nothing." That's as I have told you for years, is what I want. Imagine God playing a dirty trick on me like another life!!!

I've lived 47 years—there aren't 47 days I would live over again if I could avoid it.

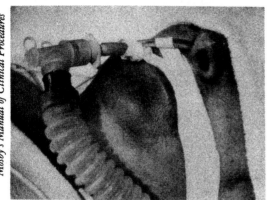

Mosby's Manual of Clinical Procedures

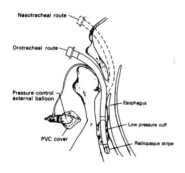

Nasotracheal route

Orotracheal route

Pressure-control
external balloon

Esophagus

Low pressure cuff

PVC cover

Radiopaque stripe

Drug overdoses can cause inability to breathe, which in turn can cause brain damage. The immediate remedy, intubation, involves running an endotracheal tube through a patient's nose or mouth to their lungs—thus clearing an airway. The photo shows a "properly secured ET tube"; the diagram shows the path the tube takes down to the lungs.

staff people I talked to about this article, both these men are among the most thoughtful, direct people I have met.

This is *not* an exhaustive survey; anything less than a medical textbook is bound to be sketchy, misleading in places, and oversimplified.*

Most suicides are drug overdoses, and many drug overdose patients reach the hospital in a coma. The danger in all drug overdoses is that the brain may not get enough oxygen. The airway to the lungs may get blocked off by the patient's vomit, or by the tongue falling back into the throat, or by drug-induced slowdown in the part of the deep brain that controls the rate and depth of breathing. Or the heart may seize and fibrillate—all the heart muscle fibers quiver, but none in rhythm with each other. The blood doesn't move, so it doesn't take oxygen to the brain or carry away waste.

It only takes three to five minutes without oxygen to do permanent damage to the brain, starting at its most sophisticated sections. The memory is destroyed; the ability to read or speak is cut back. The longer it goes on, the more severe the retardation. So any poisoned patient is constantly monitored to make sure they can breathe and their heart is beating. If they can't breathe, they are intubated. A physician slides a tube down their mouth or nose, through their throat, into their lungs for air to pass through.

Drug overdose patients are usually given sugar (in case they have low blood sugar), thiamine (which might have been depleted from

Let us, for a moment be sensible. I do not remember if the partnership agreement provides for a case like this—but if it doesn't and I think it doesn't, I would much prefer—I haven't time to make this a legal requirement—but, I would much prefer that you, as executrix under my will, *do not* elect to participate in profits for 2 or 3 years or whatever it may be that is specified there. My partners have been generous with me while I worked with them. There is no reason why, under the circumstances of my

* Some books in *The Next Whole Earth Catalog* which I found useful for information are *Licit and Illicit Drugs* (p. 579), *The Essential Guide to Prescription Drugs* (p. 326), and the emergency medicine textbooks reviewed on p. 311. A good book to browse in for the technical story of drug effects on people (along with anything else in pharmacology) is the classic medical text *Pharmacological Basis of Therapeutics* (Louis S. Goodman and Alfred Gilman, Editors; 1941, 1980; \$45 postpaid from McGraw-Hill Book Company, Princeton Road, Hightstown, New Jersey 08520). A good emergency room guide with illustrations is *Atlas of Diagnostic and Therapeutic Procedures for Emergency Personnel* by James H. Cosgriff, Jr. (1978; \$26 postpaid from J. P. Lippincott Company, Keystone Industrial Park, Scranton, Pennsylvania 18512).

the blood by alcohol) and Narcan, an antidote
for opiates. They're given because the deficiencies or drug effects they correct are hard to spot
right away and can be quickly lethal. Compared to the very few other antidotes that exist,
these are considered low-risk. Patients are
often given Ipecac, which makes them vomit.
Then they are given activated charcoal, which
looks like gruel and soaks up some of the poison in the intestines before coming out in diarrhea induced by a cathartic, magnesium citrate. The cathartic also increases the rapidity
with which the poison goes through the intestines, thus cutting down the amount absorbed
by the body.

If the patient is in a coma a tube may be run
through the nose or mouth and passed bit by
bit down the esophagus into the stomach. A
saline solution flows through it into the stomach, and then is sucked back through the tube
with some of the poison. Emergency room staff
call this "lavage"; on the street it's known as
getting your stomach pumped.

"If you come in awake and alert you should
not have your stomach washed out," Bedard
said. "But some doctors and nurses don't like
to take care of overdoses. They feel like suicidal people should be punished, so they stick
a tube down. It's not pleasant—the tube is
about the size of your thumb. Most people feel
like they're choking to death."

The two most common types of drugs in
suicides, McKinney said, are those found
around the house and those used in psychotherapy. Seemingly innocent aspirin is "one of
the messiest, most complicated overdoses you
ever hope to see," he said. People who swallow
lots of aspirin react first by getting sick to
their stomachs. Beyond that, it affects nearly
every system in the body unpredictably, and
two different people who took 100 aspirins
could get sick in completely different ways.
Aspirin is an acid. It burns the gastrointestinal
tract from the inside. It changes the blood's
pH level, which is normally 7.4 (close to neutral). It sometimes makes the blood acidic, but
it also accelerates the brain's breathing control
center, which puffs out carbon dioxide twice as
fast as it normally would, and thus makes the

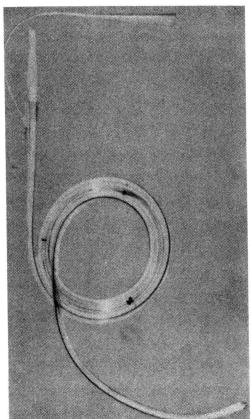

Procedures for Emergency Personnel Atlas of Diagnostic and Therapeutic

The Salem sump tube, one of the several types
that are passed down a patient's esophagus in
gastric lavage, or "stomach pumping." The process is usually used only with patients in comas
or conscious suicidal patients who are being
"punished."

withdrawal from the firm, they should
pay anything more.

I could wish that I had, for my
goodby kiss, a .38 police special with
which I have made some good scores—
not records but at least made my mark.
Instead, I have this black bitch—bitch,
if the word is not familiar to you—but
at least an honest one who will mean
what she says.

The neighbors may think it's a motor
backfire, but to me she will whisper—
"Rest–Sleep."

Albert

P.S. I think there is enough insurance to see Valerie through school, but if there isn't—I am sure you would out of the insurance payments, at least—

I hope further and I don't insist that you have the ordinary decensy—decency that is—to do so—Will you see Valerie through college—she is the only one about whom I am concerned as this .38 whispers in my ear.

Married male, age 45

My darling,
May her guts rot in hell—I loved her so much.

Henry

Divorced female, age 61

You cops will want to know why I did it, well, just let us say that I lived 61 years too many.

People have always put obstacles in my way. One of the great ones is leaving this world when you want to and have nothing to live for.

I am not insane. My mind was never more clear. It has been a long day. The motor got so hot it would not run so I just had to sit here and wait. The breaks were against me to the very last.

The sun is leaving the hill now so hope nothing else happens.

Married male, age 74

What is a few short years to live in hell. That is all I get around here.
No more I will pay the bills.
No more I will drive the car.
No more I will wash, iron, & mend any clothes.
No more I will have to eat the leftover articles that was cooked the day before.
This is no way to live.
Either is it any way to die.
Her grub I can not eat
At night I can not sleep.
I married the wrong nag-nag-nag and I lost my life.

W. S.

to the undertaker

We have got plenty money to give me a decent burial. Don't let my wife kid

blood alkaline. Either way, it throws off the metabolic balance among kidney, lung, and blood. "It produces fever," McKinney said. "The fever, in turn, if it goes on long enough to overheat the brain, can cause seizures. You can burn out parts of your nervous system." Aspirin also carries a high risk of gastric hemorrhage. Occasionally people on aspirin overdoses become deaf or develop a ringing in their ears that doesn't go away.

The pain-reliever acetaminophen, sold as Tylenol, also makes people sick to their stomachs at first, but then gets more deadly. The drug changes into toxic particles that are usually neutralized by glutathione, one type of coenzyme found in the liver. In overdose, if it isn't pumped out in time, the toxic particles deplete all the glutathione, causing the painful death of an hepatic coma. Even relatively late in the process surrogate glutathione can save the liver, but if the organ does become diseased the results can be similar to those of hepatitis: jaundice, itchy skin, depression, long-term listlessness, inability to eat much.

"The liver detoxifies poisons that build up in the body," McKinney said. "If you destroy the liver it's like never taking the garbage out. Specifically the most common buildup is ammonia in the blood, which you know if it goes too far will put you in a very deep coma, and then kill you."

Both McKinney and Bedard told me about people who took Tylenol or phosphorus, which also destroys the liver (and incidentally produces phosphorescent vomit). In both cases, they slept off the initial sickness, and recovered for five days—during which time they decided suicide was a mistake after all, and they wanted to live. But the liver had been destroyed, and after five days each of them started to feel very sick, passed into deep coma, and died. "He knew it would happen, and that there was nothing we could do about it," Bedard said, "and his friends and family knew it, and for five days they sat in the hospital together waiting for it."

Probably the most painful form of suicide attempt, whether or not it ends in death, is swallowing lye, Drano, oven cleaner, and other

household caustics. Most of us know how painful these are because scare stories have been
passed down in household lore from 100 years
ago, when caustics were the preferred suicide
method. Unlike suicides today, who visualize
themselves slipping off into oblivion, people
who killed themselves in the nineteenth century expected to suffer along the way.

"Very few people that ingest caustics die,"
McKinney said. "If they do die, it's days,
weeks, or even months later, of infection. I'm
pretty immune to most gore, but I draw the
line at the burn unit." Caustics scar the mouth
and tongue, puncture holes in the esophagus,
burn the chest from the inside and block the
gastrointestinal tract with scar tissue. Even the
process of treating inner burns is painful; surgeons drop an endoscope, or fiber-optic camera, down the person's throat, unavoidably
scraping it against the raw nerves there, to see
what the damage is. Repairing an inner burn
can take fifteen or twenty years worth of surgical operations, plus fluid therapy and antibiotics to keep infections from growing. Swallowing can be painful for the rest of a person's
life, and some survivors of such attempts have
to be fed intravenously for years afterwards.

Psychiatric drugs—phenothiazines like
Thorazine or Haldol, tricyclic antidepressants
like Elavil—cause what are probably the most
morally offensive overdose cases. "It's a built-in
irony," McKinney said. "The very population
of patients currently under therapy to supposedly avoid suicide are often handed enormous
quantities of medication. You might as well
give the guy a gun. Except for child abuse,
nothing outrages the emergency room staff as
much as when someone comes in with an overdose on Thorazine and you go through their
pockets and see the same doctor has prescribed
three or four hundred tablets in a two-week period. Those are the doctors who get a phone
call at three A.M. saying, 'You better get down
here now and see your patient.'" (Hardly ever
does the psychiatrist show up, McKinney and
other doctors told me; it's more common for
the answering service to find out who's calling
and why and then say the psychiatrist is out of
town.)

you by saying she has not got any
money.
Give this note to the cops.
Give me liberty or give me death.
W. S.

Married male, age 45

Dear Claudia,
You win, I can't take it any longer, I
know you have been waiting for this to
happen. I hope it makes you very happy,
this is not an easy thing to do, but I've
got to the point where there is nothing
to live for, a little bit of kindness from
you would of made everything so different, but all that ever interested you was
the *dollar.*

It is pretty hard for me to do anything
when you are so greedy even with this
house you couldn't even be fair with
that, well it's all yours now and you
won't have to see the Lawyer anymore.

I wish you would give my personal
things to Danny, you couldn't get much
from selling them anyway, you still have
my insurance, it isn't much but it will
be enough to take care of my debts and
still have a few bucks left.

You always told me that I was the one
that made Sharon take her life, in fact
you said I killed her, but you know
down deep in your heart it was you that
made her do what she did, and now you
have two deaths to your credit, it should
make you feel very proud.

Good By Kid
P.S. Disregard all the mean things I've
said in this letter, I have said a lot of
things to you I didn't really mean and I
hope you get well and wish you the best
of everything.
Cathy—don't come in.
Call your mother, she will know what to
do.
Love
Daddy
Cathy don't go in the bedroom.

Married female, age 50

When a "man" doesn't know where to
take his wife—then she isn't a wife any
more—

I hope you will be "free" to take any-one any place and I'm sure you will not have any trouble as to places—

Please don't tell my mother the truth—your whole tribe is partly responsible for this—from your mother on down—hope they are satisfied.

Married female, age 56

About the Evil god (yes)

About the Evil Seers killing people for their money (yes)

I am a profit at my death

I am a root of the stem of Jesse (yes)

We have made many discoveries. We have found out who the people with the mark of the beast are. And the devil was a human being now killed and cast into hell and the angel with the keys of the bottomless pit is in hell casting out all the good souls which these evil people have cast into hell for no reason. The good Seers who serve our God are ⅓ to ⅔ of the evil ones in this world. We are better than holding our owne but in Heaven God is almost over come and I kill myself so I may go and help him, because I have a funny little quirk in my brain which helps.

6 palmy each at a few years sport. Our god will send them into the world.

Single male, age 13

I know what I am doing. Annette found out. Ask Cara. I love you all.

Bill

Widowed female, age 52
(Her husband died three months before.)

Please tell Ron's folks I love them very much but my heart breaks when I see or hear from them. Also all our friends especially Irene and Charles and Ella I love them also. Forgive me for not seeing them.

Everyone seems so happy and I am so alone. Amy. I wanted to visit you but I am going around in a dream. Alice I wanted to help you paint but how could I with a broken heart. And my head aches so much any more my nerves are ready to break and what would happen if they did.

"Tricyclic antidepressant patients are in a particular high-risk situation," McKinney said. "Typically a person is depressed over a long time; he goes to a psychiatrist and after some psych workshop procedures it's decided he needs an antidepressant. Classically, Elavil is prescribed. Elavil takes three to eight weeks to work, and an average of four weeks. The person may not be told clearly enough or may not want to hear that the drug takes a long time. Two weeks later he bolts upright and says, 'This is the biggest crock of shit,' and swallows the rest of them."

The phenothiazines, or major tranquilizers, are used to calm down psychosis or extreme anxiety. The tricyclic antidepressants are chemical mood elevators. Both work by somehow altering the minute bursts of chemicals which neurons send across the synapses, or gaps between nerves, to carry impulses from one nerve to another.

Because they affect the nervous system which in turn reacts with every other system in the body, psychiatric drugs have lots of side-effects—dilated pupils, dry mouth, feverishness, speeded-up heartrate, slowed-down digestive muscles, breakdowns in coordination, rolling eyes. Overdose can accelerate these in any part of the body. I once met a man whose hand muscles had contracted violently after a phenothiazine overdose, leaving his fingers permanently warped. Tardive dyskinesia, a Parkinson's Disease-like condition caused in some patients by long-term use of the drugs, can be accelerated by an overdose. Probably the most common permanent damage from overdose is brain damage, caused by seizures and fibrillation.

The exotic drugs of mystery novels, strychnine and cyanide, are painful and deadly but rarely show up in emergency rooms. What shows up all the time are sleeping pills and mood pills—the sedative hypnotics—barbiturates like Seconal, mild tranquilizers like Valium. Typically, a sedative overdose will do nothing more than put you to sleep for a day or two, and leave you with a bad hangover and a case of the slows when you wake up. But like many other overdoses, sedatives are often taken with alcohol, which makes people nauseous. Anyone who vomits when they're passed out risks sucking some of the vomit into their lungs, which is called aspiration.

It's as dangerous as it sounds disgusting. Vomit contains enzymes from the stomach that destroy tissue, and those go to work on the lung walls. It also contains a rich broth of food, perfect for pneumonia bugs to grow in. People can also drown in vomit, which keeps air from getting to the brain, which once again causes brain damage. An aspirating patient goes into intensive care; a device called a bronchoscope is used to look into their lungs and pull out whatever pieces of vomit it can.

Drug overdoses are always unpredictable. The drugs react with other drugs people take at the time, with alcohol, with odd allergies, and drugs lingering around in the bloodstream from years before. "One fellow took four cold tablets," McKinney said, "and went to an emergency room complaining of a headache. He blew the blood vessels behind one of his eyes out."

Violent death is so often portrayed as sudden and painless, but the human body is harder to kill than it seems. For instance, people rarely die from slashing their wrists. "Most people who try it aren't really suicidal," Bedard said. "Usually it's a cry for help. A few want to see what it feels like to cut themselves. We just sew them up and call in the psychiatrist." Even if you cut your artery, which most people don't, it's hard to bleed to death because the bleeding stops on its own unless the cut is extremely severe. Popular wisdom says sitting in hot water makes you bleed faster, but Bedard said he's known people who tried it, passed out, and woke up in a bathtub full of cold bloody water.

"But it's an easy way to hurt yourself," he said. "You can damage the tendons and median nerve which control the muscles of your hand. People end up with claw hands. Lots of times, with microsurgery, that can be repaired, but it means six to twelve months out of your life, and you still end up with a weak or deformed hand."

The few people who cut their throats also

You will say I am crazy and I can't go on this way just half living.

I loved this house once but now it is so full of memories I can't stay here. I have tried to think of some way to go on but can't. Am so nervous all the time—I loved Ron too much but is that a sin, with him gone I have nothing. Oh I have the girls and family but they don't fill the vacant spot left in my heart . . .

Xmas is coming I can't go on I'm afraid I would break down. I've thought of this so many times. I love every one but I can't be one of you any more. Please think kindly of me and forgive me. I only hope this is fatal then I can rest and no more trouble to any one. Do with Lisa whats best I know she has been a lot of worry to mama and I'm sorry. I tried to keep the yard up that seemed to be the only comfort I had. I loved it but that wasn't anything. I've lost every thing so why go on. I worshipped Ron and when he went I lost my whole world and everything.

I'm so tired and lonely.

There goes a siren. Oh how can I stand being left. I need to go to a Dr. but I am afraid. I'm so cold.

Mother

Love, Louise

Married male, age 40

Jimmy!
Remember what I told you and always respect, protect and obey your mother and always remember that I love you so much. I am going to leave you forever because I am too sick to go on. God bless you my Son and when your time comes to go to Heaven you will find your ole Pappy waiting for you.

Daddy

Single female, age 16

Dear Mother & Dad,
Please forgive me. I have tried to be good to you both. I love you both very much and wanted to get along with you both. I have tried.

I have wanted to go out with you and Dad but I was always afraid to ask for I always felt that the answer would be no.

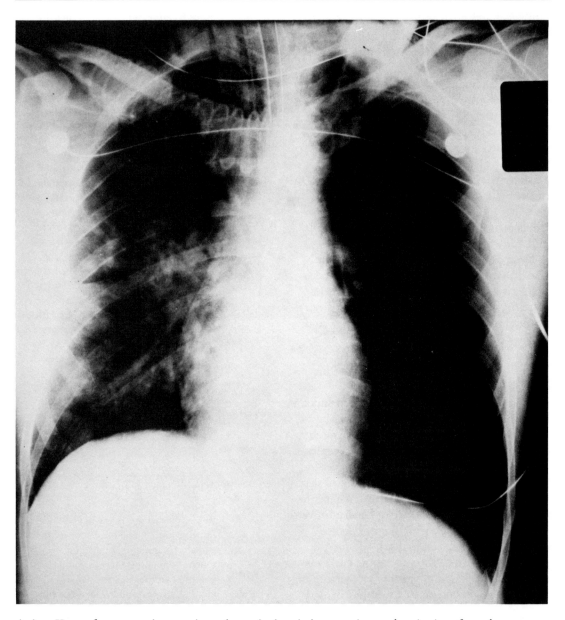

A chest X-ray of someone who came into a large city hospital unconscious and aspirating after a drug overdose. The X-ray looks into his front, so the lung on our left is actually the patient's right lung. That's where the trouble is. What looks like gray and white bubbles floating inside is vomit that dripped down from his throat. His left lung (on our right) is comparatively clean. In a normal X-ray both sides would look like that. At the top of the throat is the bronchial tube through which they are trying to help him breathe. The sharp white dots (electrocardiogram probes) and the thing that looks like a telephone cord (part of the intubation machine) are both outside his body.

I saw this man. He had been running a 106° fever for more than a day when this picture was taken and his rib cage jerked spasmodically every time he tried to take a breath. His eyes stayed half-open. They expected him to die. But he was still alive, in the same state, two weeks later. It's doubtful he will ever be conscious again. If he stays alive like this he'll be transferred to a chronic ward in a mental hospital.

—Art Kleiner

rarely die. "They often cut the recurrent laryngeal nerve," Bedard said, "the nerve that goes up to the voicebox and larynx, and lose their voices. Or they cut themselves and bleed beneath the surface until they choke on a buildup of blood inside the trachea."

Bedard said most suicide shootings he's seen were hostile, done while someone else was around to react to it. Interestingly, you can shoot yourself in the head and miss the brain but merely blow out an eye or part of your jaw. If you die, the death is usually drawn-out and painful.

"People can live eight hours with a hole in their head the size of a half dollar," Bedard said. "If you shoot yourself in the temple, the primitive parts of your brain that control breathing will go on for a long time, from minutes to hours. Eventually they may be shut off by pressure from the swelling of the upper brain that was shot. Or they may not be shut off at all. One man I treated is completely paralyzed on his left side, and can't speak, walk, or feed himself. It's as if he had a major stroke. He hit the area of the brain which controls motor function."

Jumps and hanging, again from Bedard: "I'm amazed at how far you can fall after a jump and not kill yourself. Some people have fallen 150 feet and lived. They'll break many of their bones, or rupture an organ like the spleen. Many people who try to hang themselves don't fall far enough to jerk their neck back and snap their airway. They strangle themselves instead, and don't always die; they get brain damage from lack of oxygen." People who try to poison themselves with gas or carbon dioxide may also get brain damage for the same reason.

And finally, just falling into a coma can lead to permanent damage. "If you're slumped on a table, leaning on your arm for a day and a half," Bedard said, "you put pressure on the armpit. You can permanently damage the nerve there and make it hard to use your arm. Or your muscles might start to dissolve into your bloodstream and clog up your kidneys. The muscle damage probably eventually returns to normal."

And about Bud, I want to dismiss every idea about him. I don't like him any more than a companion, for a while I thought I did but no more, in fact, I am quite tired of him, as you know, I get tired of everyone after a while.

And mother, I wish that you hadn't called me a liar, and said I was just like Hap. as I'm not. It is just that I am afraid of you both at times, but I love you both very much.

So Long

Your loving
daughter
that will always
love you
Mary

P.S. Please forgive me. I want you to, and don't think for one minute that I haven't appreciated everything you've done.

Single male, age 35
(He committed suicide after he killed his girlfriend.)

Mommie my Darling,
To love you as I do and live without you is more than I can bear. I love you so completely, wholeheartedly without restraint. I worship you, that is my fault. With your indifference to me; is the difference. I've tried so hard to make our lives pleasant and lovable, but you didn't seem to care. You had great plans which didn't include me. You didn't respect me. That was the trouble. You treated me like a child. I couldn't reach you as a man and woman or man and wife as we've lived. I let you know my feelings toward you when I shouldn't have. How I loved you, what you meant to me. Without you life is unbearable.

This is the best way. This will solve all our problems. You can't hurt me further and anyone else. I was a "toll" while you needed me or thought you did. But now that I could use some help, you won't supply the need that was prominent when you need it. So, good bye my love. If it is possible to love in the hereafter, I will love you even after death. May God have mercy on both our souls. He alone knows my heartache and sorrow and love for you.

Daddy

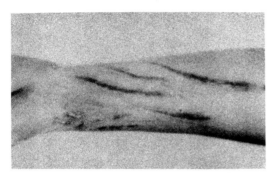

The scars of a young woman who cut herself on the wrist. "Intensive individual case work suggests that self-laceration may involve an altered state of consciousness akin to a dissociative state. . . . There may be no experience of pain until after the event when there is subjective relief of tension mixed with feelings of disgust and regret at what has happened." ——Picture and quote from the clinical psychiatry text *Death Wishes?* by H. G. Morgan (1979; John Wiley and Sons).

Single female, age 31

My boss, Kenneth J., seduced me and made me pregnant. He refuses to help me. I had not had intercourse in two years. He says that I will have to suffer through it by myself.

Several people know about this—my doctor, Dr. James R., and Pete M. who works at Williams. Pete and I never had a love affair, although Kenneth would like to drag Pete into it. Also Dr. Arnold W. knows about it.

I have always been such a good girl. Daddy dear—

As much as it hurts me, I cannot make it this Friday. I may be in very serious trouble. I have always been a very good person, but it looks like I really got in a mess, through no real fault of my own.

I must have been born to suffer.

Love—Elizabeth

P.S. Call me if you can. When will Sally be back? I may need her desperately.

These clinical generalizations make suicidal people seem like statistical ciphers who made a mistake and suffered the immediate, appropriate retribution. But it doesn't feel like that at the time. Whether or not you are glad you were rescued, recovering from a suicide attempt is like being in the emergency room for any other reason. The flash that brought you there was over in a moment. The waiting, being embarrassed, wondering what will happen next, and bearing sharp or dull pain go on for hours.

How, according to people who work with them, do suicide attempters feel when they wake up in the hospital? Glad they were saved. Convinced that suicide was a mistake. Angry they were saved. Angry at the friend or neighbor who betrayed them by calling emergency. Eager to get out of the hospital so they can try it again. Embarrassed. Relieved. Happy to be taken care of. Eager to start taking care of themselves again. Unwilling to think about it. Wondering what everyone else they know thinks about it. Wondering if the person they were trying to reach will finally pay attention to them.

"A lot of what I hear in the emergency room is hostility towards a specific person," Dr. Bedard said. "Once they know they're not going to die, they go out of their way to talk to me about it. 'I'll show that son of a bitch. He didn't think I had the guts to do it.' A lot of these people fantasize about seeing themselves at the funeral. 'The whole world's going to be upset.'"

There are people who get ignored repeatedly until they attempt suicide. One woman I heard about tried to kill herself six times in one year. "My husband says he's too busy if I ask him to take me out to dinner," she told the emergency room staff. "But for this he makes time."

If it isn't the attention of a particular person, it might be the emergency room staff. Sadly, many people can only get a lot of paid professional people to notice them by threatening their own life. "A lot of people we see are repeaters," Bedard said. "They might come in twenty times in five years. To them it's a game. 'Either you take Ipecac and vomit or we'll have to do gastric lavage,' we'll say. 'You know and I know it'll hurt, so why don't you take the Ipecac?' Sometimes you see the same people so often it's like visiting an old friend."

Other people take a pill overdose not to risk their lives, but to find a place where they can be taken care of and forget their problems for a little while. "People want time out," said Temple University psychiatry professor Michael Simpson, who ran the emergency psychiatric service at Guy's Hospital in London. "That's why sometimes they'll seek psychiatric support but leave in a day or two. They used to be able to do it more freely in the drug culture by finding a crashpad. Now the medical model is one of the few excuses for going away and lying around and having people be kind to you that is seen as a valid reason to leave work. Maybe we need other ways to legitimize that."

People who attempt suicide are almost never arrested, but they lose their right to decide what happens to them. In every state, being a possible danger to yourself, in the opinion of the psychiatrist who interviews you, is cause for being held for psychiatric care for a limited period of time. In California, the period of time is three days; it can be followed, with an application to a judge, by a fourteen-day period, and after that by another fourteen-day period. Beyond that, the regular rules for entering a mental hospital voluntarily or being committed apply. Clearly, how you act at the initial interview with a psychiatrist has a lot to do with how long you stay under psychiatric care. So does the attitude of the psychiatrist who examines you and the availability of good or bad psychiatric facilities in your area.

Rarely are patients held longer than three days for psychiatric reasons. In fact, some hospitals send more than half of the suicidal patients home as soon as they can go. Some patients are routed to state or private psychiatric hospitals; some go to local board-and-care homes or halfway houses or outpatient clinics or nowhere at all. "The only generalization you can make," said Ed Hamell, a senior psychiatric specialist at a private psychiatric hospital in Washington, D.C., "is that people who find

Married male, age 52

Dear Joan,
For 23 years we lived happy together. Our married life was ideal, until two years ago when I witnessed Kristy die in the hospital something snapped in me. You remember when I returned from the hospital I broke down. That was the beginning of my illness. Since then my condition was getting progressively worse, I could neither work or think logically. You have been thru "Hell" with me since then. Only you and I know how much you have lived thru. I feel that I will not improve and can't keep on causing you and the children so much misery. I loved you and was proud of you. I loved the children dearly and could not see them suffer so much on account of me.

Dear Children:
Please forgive me.

Love, Frank

Divorced female, age 37

To No-one and Everyone:
Because of a growing conviction that a hereditary insanity is manifesting itself beyond my control, I am taking this way out—before mere nuisance attacks and rages against others assume a more dangerous form.

Because I am an agnostic and believe funeral fanfare to be nonsense—I ask that it be forgotten. Instead, knowing there to be a marked shortage of cadavers for the medical profession, for which I have endless respect, I hereby bequeath 1) my body to medics for dissection; also 2) To Mark B. all personal effects—to be divided as whim decrees—with Dr. Lois J., L. A. and to each—a deep fondness and love. 3) To Joe A. the greatest devotion—the kind that "passeth all understanding." 3a) And my life.

Anita R.
4) To my father, Vincent N., the sum of one dollar ($1)

Trina, a college student, 21 years old

Fall quarter I called Suicide Prevention. I'd called them before and the people were nice, but this time the woman acted a little indignant. "Why the hell do you want to do something like that?" she asked. We talked until she said she had other phone calls. But she made me promise I wouldn't try without calling back first. I had a bottle of Coricidin from a wisdom tooth operation. I'd been thinking about it for a month off and on. Much later that night I took ten Coricidin and went to bed. I woke up in the morning feeling really rotten— weepy, groggy. I could hardly move. I thought I was going to die any minute. My roommate came home and got a friend to drive me to the school infirmary, where they gave me something that made me sick to my stomach. The doctor who gave it to me calmed me down. She said it happens to a lot of people, the pills wouldn't hurt me. I felt tingly, like I might pass out any minute.

I was immediately taken in a wheelchair to the psychiatrist's office. I talked to him about five minutes. He kept yelling at me about why did I take the pills, why didn't I do this or that. I remember thinking, boy this man is a real jerk. I told him I didn't want to see him any more. He said, "That's fine," and put me in a locked room with bars on the windows. I couldn't make phone calls. I felt humiliated, which made me angry. I'm not crazy. I'm not weird. I don't want people to look at me like I'm nuts. I'm not some nutty kid who tried to knock herself off. I was most angry at being stuck in that room. I expected to be put in a straitjacket any minute. I complained until they moved me to a pretty room and let me make phone calls.

I was there about two weeks. My psychiatrist kept harping at me about school—was I going to stay in or drop out? I saw him ten minutes a day. The other patients and one orderly helped me a lot more than he did. I just wanted to find a place where I could be alone and think about things. I left feeling like not much had been accomplished, except letting me know that I didn't want to at-

themselves in hospitals following suicide attempts will be treated as not able to be responsible for their own safety."

Howard Blackstone, the clinical director of the Marin County mental health crisis unit, told me some of the things that happen in the initial psychiatric interview. "We're trying to find out what happened. Was it well thought out or was it impulsive? What kinds of problems led up to that point? What state were they in when they tried to do it? How likely are they to try it again? Oftentimes someone will come in upset, but after a day or two hold they will look back and say 'Why the hell did I do that?' If we believe that someone is still perturbed and still ruminating about how to kill themselves, we are required to hold on to them. We evaluate reasons less than states of mind. The purpose of what we're doing is to help someone out of a state of mind where they may do something not in their best interest."

Beyond that, I can't generalize about the psychiatric consequences of suicide. There are too many possibilities, they differ too much from place to place, and the patient has too little control over where he or she ends up. In many psychiatric institutions (and other social welfare institutions, like nursing homes) suicide is a sensitive issue, because a funding agency may investigate an institution if a suicide happens within its walls. Or a psychiatrist may be held responsible for a suicide if it can be proved he knew about it beforehand and didn't act reasonably to prevent it. Here as everywhere else, the main priority is keeping the person alive.

That may be changing. "There are a growing number of people in the psychiatric community," David Gruder said, "who feel privately that their patients, regardless of the law, have the right to decide whether or not to take their own life. Under certain circumstances, there are psychiatrists who won't prevent some of their patients from killing themselves. But you can't talk about this out loud too often, because it's illegal and could also be grounds for disbarment." He said an influential book for therapists on this subject is *Back to One* by

Sheldon Kopp (1977; $7.95 postpaid from Science and Behavior Books, P.O. Box 11457, Palo Alto, California 94306).

If you believe, as I did starting this article, that each of us has a right to commit suicide and potentially valid reasons for doing so which should be respected, you might think there's something gruesome about a system which automatically acts to preserve life, whether the person wants it preserved or not. There's an apocryphal story told in every emergency room: someone comes in for the thirtieth or fortieth time on a suicide attempt and a doctor finally explodes and says, "Look, why don't you try it *this* way," and the patient does next time and dies. Every professional I talked to—doctor, paramedic, suicide prevention counselor, therapist, pharmacologist, nurse—said there have been people who made them think, 'you're right. You have nothing to live for.' But the attempt to save the person's life is always made. As Dr. Richard Fein, who directs outpatient services at San Francisco General Hospital, said, to decide whether someone's life is worth living in an emergency is gross arrogance.

There are people who think suicide can be a method of natural selection in an overcrowded world. Suicides in prison are often not saved, I was told by several people; the same is true sometimes in some cities, for the indigent suicide, the alcoholic suicide, the aged or non-white suicide. Nobody else wants them; they finally succumb to the obvious. Aren't there people who ought to be killing themselves but are not?

Brr. I'm on the side of saving lives automatically. I liked what Stuart Bair, who counsels many of the desperate and penniless suicide attempters at San Francisco General Hospital, said: "I believe in miracles. I think there's always a reason to hope someone's life will improve." And I like what psychiatrist Michael Simpson said about the terminally ill that groups like Exit and Hemlock are trying to reach: "Those who work with terminal patients, like people in hospices, say there are

tempt it again. No—I felt like I've become a lot more sensitive to people. I don't look at their problems as trivial any more. I almost like it when my friends come to me with problems. I feel like I can help now. I still haven't told the two people I was most angry at—my father and my boyfriend—why I was in the hospital.

Sandra, a clerk, 27 years old

A year ago March, while I was living in Michigan, I took an overdose of Elavil. I was seeing a psychiatrist and I was just getting off the medication. But the bottle was still in my apartment. I'd gone out and had drinks, came home and that's when I did it—about ten in the evening or so. I called my boyfriend Jonathan in California and my social worker. I told them I had taken the pills. The social worker told me to drive to the emergency room. I'd have been lucky to make it to the front door. Jonathan called a friend of mine, who came to the apartment and broke down the door. I was in a coma for five days. I guess I was lucky because the doctors told everybody I wasn't going to make it. Then they said I'd have permanent brain damage. When it didn't happen they said it was the miracle of the floor. I was out of the hospital in about three weeks; a week of that was in the psychiatric ward, which was a real drag.

I had a lot of problems with my memory for a while. Even now I can't remember some things. Starting a week before the overdose I don't remember anything at all. All I know about it is what Jonathan says I told him over the phone. Everybody asks "Why did you do it?" and I don't know. It sounds real stupid.

Everybody in the hospital was real nice. I was afraid that they would get down on me but they didn't. It was a Catholic hospital, and I had my own room. Friends were there 24 hours a day. It made me realize how many friends I had. On the psychiatric ward they give you tests for brain damage. They ask you a lot of silly questions. They test your reflexes, your memory. They give you EKG tests. It took a while to get back my coordination. I couldn't write or do other things with my hands. Most of the time I stayed by myself. There were programs for the other patients but they didn't put me in any because they didn't know how long I would be staying.

I'd tried twice before, but those times weren't serious. I was just trying to get some attention. The first time I was fourteen, and I slashed my wrists. It was basic adolescent scare tactics. As a result I ended up in an inpatient clinic for teenagers for about five months. Almost everybody there was there because they ran away or they were doing a lot of drugs. The second time was a couple of years ago. I did a Valium overdose. It wasn't very serious—I just had to have my stomach pumped.

This time it shocked me to realize what could have happened to me. I realized how much I had hurt my friends and family, which I didn't think about before. I started wondering if people could trust me. It upset my life a lot—it threw everything backwards. Jonathan flew in from California. He said the scariest part was worrying about having to decide what to do if my body kept living but I had no brain response. When I first woke up I didn't think there would be anything wrong with me. And then it hit me that I couldn't move. I was embarrassed that people had to see me like that.

Once you're out of the hospital a lot of institutions won't hire you. You can't get health insurance. You have to lie on your job applications. People look at you like you're dangerous. It's real scary for some of my friends—they think they're responsible. Trying to convince people that I was OK was the hardest thing. That they didn't have to watch over me, that I wasn't going to try it again.

Thomas, a hairdresser, 21 years old:

I tried it five years ago. I was at a neighbor's house and fired a gun at my head. Nothing happened; it seemed empty. I fired it at a wall and put a bullet in it. So

very few requests for suicide. People want to be relieved of pain, which we could do for nearly everyone if we were given good hospice and palliative care. We need to be sure we've guaranteed mercy living before we get around to mercy killing."

Anyway, I suspect suicidal people are automatically rescued not for their own sakes, but for the rest of us. A suicide death, unless it is rationally prepared for, devastates. The message of a suicide attempt is often: Death is better than the pain you've caused me. And the message doesn't have to come from someone you know. David Gruder, who directed crisis hotlines, told me about a woman who called up and raved: "I've had it. I'm pissed off. I'm killing myself and damned if I'm not going to take someone else with me and you, you bastard, are coming." BANG! She shot herself. And, as it happened, it was the hotline worker's first call. She went right into a nervous breakdown.

But I believe the main reason a suicide attempt devastates and fascinates us is it reminds us how fragile our own hold on life is. "Here I am struggling along with my problems," Michael Simpson said, "and here's a guy who's given up. Is it possible I'm wrong in bothering so hard to try to live? Once you start discussing suicide you're asking what the grounds are for killing ourselves. The other side of that question is, 'What am I living for?' That's an ugly question for most of us because we don't usually know."

If someone you know is thinking of suicide, or you think they are, and you don't want them to die, tell them. "Please call me or call suicide prevention before you try anything because I care about you and I don't want you to die." Don't argue with them about why life is worth living, because you can't win that one in rational argument. Tell them how you and other people will feel when they're gone. If there are mental health services you trust in your neighborhood, you may want to suggest them.

If you are scared you may commit suicide, and sometimes you don't want to, there may be more options than you realize. A good guide to whatever mental health services are around and how to find them is *You Are Not Alone* (*Next Whole Earth Catalog*, p. 327). It's worth looking around to see if there's a friend, family member, or neighbor that you can talk to about it. Even if, like me, you distrust mental health services, it's probably worth calling suicide prevention. They're listed under that name in the phone book white pages, or call the American Association of Suicidology at (303) 692–0985 for the phone number of one near you.

If you want to make someone pay attention to you through a suicide attempt, you might consider leaving a note for that person and checking into an emergency room and telling them you're suicidal. You'll go through the same psychiatric hold, but without the damage to your body. Choose your emergency room carefully. Some, like Herrick Hospital in Berkeley, often have eight- or ten-hour waits for noncritical patients, in dismal surroundings that will probably make you feel worse.

Or, have you considered changing your life?

a minute later I found some Seconals in a medicine cabinet. I remember watching cartoons and taking the pills one by one. A neighbor lady found me and couldn't wake me up. I couldn't open my eyes or move, but I heard everything. I remember the lady shaking me and saying, "Oh, my God." I remember the ambulance people taking off my clothes and making me throw up. There wasn't any pain. I don't remember having my stomach pumped.

When I woke up it was five days later. A big black lady kept tickling me. "'Bout time you woke up," she said. "I've been tickling you for three days." I thought I was in heaven—it looked like some place in heaven for the misfits. Turned out I was in the basement of a free clinic, a long room with rows of beds with all kinds of teenagers, pregnant girls, suicides, drug addicts. We walked around in gowns, smoking cigarettes and watching TV. The reason I tried was I was angry at my mother, but when she came in she just said, "Why'd you do this—to try to get attention?"

Am I glad I was rescued? Oh, yeah. I was so glad I didn't die. It made me realize how much I appreciated myself, because I had a glimpse of what I might have lost. I had some friends and I would've missed them. I didn't have to go home after that. They put me in a foster home. The State made me go to a psychiatrist. I never liked the man. I thought he had more problems than I did. I felt drugged and slow for a couple of years. Every now and then I'd take speed to feel normal. Downers still make me feel speedy. If I had a suicidal friend now I'd ask them, "Why don't you have any alternatives? Could it really be so awful?" That's what I say to myself now.

PAT CALIFIA

Feminism and Sadomasochism

*From the original introduction
(Spring 1982):*
This article . . . deals with the objections some feminists have to S/M.
However, the biggest problems in a
sadomasochist's life are not caused by
the bigotry of some members of the
women's movement. We are far more
concerned about the vicious harassment, imprisonment, and violence we face from the state and its
agents—especially the vice squads of
local police departments. The bulk
of prejudice against sadomasochism
does not come from feminism. It
comes from organized religion, psychiatry, and others who promulgate
Judeo-Christian morality. This article is an attempt to reach an audience
that is potentially more educable
than the people and institutions who
are genuinely responsible for sexual
repression. Despite the shortcomings
of some segments of the women's
movement, I remain a firm supporter
of the basic goals of feminism. . . .
                              Pat Califia

We had an article by Ivan Illich
called "Vernacular Gender," about

how industrialization had corrupted
men's and women's work-roles. We
had "What to Name the Children"—
strategies for when husband and wife
keep their own names. It looked like
we were accruing material toward a
CQ issue on gender. Then Stephanie
Mills spotted this article in a feminist
magazine called *Heresies*.

I happen to think this is one of the
best articles COEVOLUTION has ever
published. Many CQ readers felt it
was one of the worst—reacting, as
you might guess, against the sadomasochism rather than the feminism. "What about the producers of
snuff films?" asked one letter. "Will
they be next in line to be sanctioned?" Another letter said, "By
presenting an article that is favorable
towards sadomasochism, you cultivate thought, tilling the ground
where the seed of violence can grow."
Other readers felt sadomasochism
was just one more decadent California perversion, out of touch with
real-world needs like children, food
and shelter, and local communities.

Other readers responded to *those*
letters, saying that S/M may be a
peacemaking release of the same feelings that otherwise contribute toward real violence; that we judge
without understanding if we don't
hear the story as told by the people
who live the story; that S/M as Pat
describes it is a form of play, and
most people are generally too quick
to condemn forms of play that they
don't share (including play-con-
demning, I'm sure).

Who is Pat Califia? In Stephanie Mills' words written in 1982: "[She] is a working-class kid from a Mormon background. Her father was a construction worker and the family moved around a lot. . . . [Now] she lives with a woman lover in an open relationship. She makes quilts, reads science fiction, and has a cat. She believes that 'You don't have to be anti-pornography to be feminist' and has been a feminist for ten years. In addition to that, she has done work on antiwar issues and low-income housing. 'I do more than sex,' she says. 'I'm a rad.' Pat is the news editor of the *Advocate*, the largest gay newsmagazine in the United States, and a freelance writer." Since then, Pat has moved to New York, from where she writes the "Advisor" column for the *Advocate*.

You can read the History Appendix (p. 331) for a blow-by-blow description of the aftermath of this article.

Art Kleiner

Photos by Honey Lee Cottrell

Pat Califia, feminist and sadomasochist

Three years ago, I decided to stop ignoring my sexual fantasies. Since the age of two, I had been constructing a private world of dominance, submission, punishment, and pain. Abstinence, consciousness-raising, and therapy had not blighted the charm of these frightful reveries. I could not tolerate any more guilt, anxiety, or frustration, so I cautiously began to experiment with real sadomasochism. I did not lose my soul in the process. But in those three years, I lost a lover, several friends, a publisher, my apartment, and my good name because of the hostility and fear evoked by my openness about my true sexuality.

Writing this article is painful because it brings back the outrage and hurt I felt at being ostracized from the lesbian feminist community. I've been a feminist since I was thirteen and a lesbian since I was seventeen. I didn't lose just a ghetto or a subculture—lesbian feminism was the matrix I used to become an adult. Fortunately for my sanity and happiness, I managed to construct a new social network. My friends and lovers are bisexual women (some of whom do S/M professionally), gay and bisexual men, and other outlaw lesbians. If I were isolated, I would not be strong enough to speak out about something that makes me this vulnerable.

I describe my feelings about this issue because sadomasochism is usually dealt with in an abstract, self-righteous way by feminist theorists who believe it is the epitome of misogyny, sexism, and violence. In this article I shall examine sadomasochism in a theoretical way, and attempt a rapprochement between feminism and S/M. But I am motivated by my concern for the people who are frightened or ashamed of their erotic response to sadomasochistic fantasies. I don't want to hear any more tragic stories from women who have repressed their own sexuality because they think that's the only politically acceptable way to deal with a yearning for helplessness or sexual control. I don't believe that any more than I believe homosexuals should be celibate so they can continue to be good Catholics. The women's movement has become a moralistic force, and it can contribute to the self-loathing and misery experienced by sexual minorities. Because sexual dissenters are already being trampled on by monolithic, prudish institutions, I think it is time the women's movement started taking more radical positions on sexual issues.

It is difficult to discuss sadomasochism in feminist terms because some of the slang S/M people use to talk about our sexuality has been appropriated by feminist propagandists. Terms like "roles," "masochism," "bondage," "dominance," and "submission" have become buzzwords. Their meanings in a feminist context differ sharply from their significance to S/M people. The discussion is rendered even more difficult because feminist theorists do not do their homework on human sexuality before pronouncing judgment on a sexual variation. Like Victorian missionaries in Polynesia, they insist on interpreting the sexual behavior of other people according to their own value systems. A perfect example of this is the "debate" over transsexuality. In its present form, feminism is not necessarily the best theoretical framework for understanding sexual deviation, just as unmodified Marxism is an inadequate system for analyzing the oppression of women.

Since the label "feminist" has become debased coinage, let me explain why I call myself a feminist. I believe that the society I live in is a patriarchy, with power concentrated in the hands of men, and that this patriarchy actively prevents women from becoming complete and independent human beings. Women are oppressed by being denied access to economic resources, political power, and control over their own reproduction. This oppression is managed by several institutions, chiefly the family, religion, and the state. An essential part of the oppression of women is control over sexual ideology, mythology, and behavior. This social control affects the sexual nonconformist as well as the conformist. Because our training in conventional sexuality begins the minute we are born and because the penalties for rebellion are so high, no individual or group is completely free from erotic tyranny.

I am not a separatist. I believe that men can be committed to the destruction of the patriarchy. After all, the rewards of male dominance are given only to men who perpetuate and cooperate with the system. I am not "woman-identified"—i.e., I do not believe that women have more insight, intuition, virtue, identification with the earth, or love in their genes than men. Consequently, I cannot support everything women do, and I believe the women's movement could learn a lot from politicized or deviant men. On the other hand, I do not find it easy to work with men, partly because male feminist theory is pitifully underdeveloped. I do not think separatism is worthless or bankrupt. It can be useful as an organizing strategy and teaches women valuable survival skills. The taste of autonomy that separatism provides is intoxicating, and can be a powerful incentive to struggle for real freedom.

I think it is imperative that feminists dismantle the institutions that foster the exploitation and abuse of women. The family, conventional sexuality, and gender are at the top of my hit list. These institutions control the emotional, intimate lives of every one of us, and they have done incalculable damage to women. I cannot imagine how such drastic change can be accomplished without armed struggle, the appropriation and reallocation of wealth, and a change in the ownership of the means of production. When women are liberated, women will probably cease to exist, since our whole structure of sex and gender must undergo a complete transformation.

The term *sadomasochism* has also been debased, primarily by the mass media, clinical psychology, and the antipornography movement. After all, homophobia is not the only form of sexual prejudice. Every minority sexual behavior has been mythologized and distorted. There is a paucity of accurate, explicit, nonjudgmental information about sex in modern America. This is one way sexual behavior is controlled. If people don't know a particular technique or lifestyle exists, they aren't likely to try it. If the only images they have of a certain sexual act are ugly, disgusting, or threatening, they will either not engage in that act or be furtive about enjoying it.

Since there is so much confusion about what S/M is, I want to describe my own sexual specialties and the sadomasochistic subculture. I am basically a sadist. About ten percent of the time, I take the other role (bottom, slave, masochist). This makes me atypical, since the majority of women and men involved in S/M prefer to play bottom. I enjoy leathersex, bondage, various forms of erotic torture, flagellation (whipping), verbal humiliation, fistfucking, and watersports (playing with enemas and piss). I do not enjoy oral sex unless I am receiving it as a form of sexual service, which means my partner must be on her knees, on her back, or at least in a collar. I have non-S/M sex rarely, mostly for old times' sake, with vanilla friends* I want to stay close to. My primary relationship is with a woman who enjoys being my slave. We enjoy tricking with other people and telling each other the best parts afterward.

Because sadomasochism is usually portrayed as a violent, dangerous activity, most people do not think there is a great deal of difference between a rapist and a bondage enthusiast. Sadomasochism is not a form of sexual assault. It is a consensual activity that involves polarized roles and intense sensations. An S/M scene is always preceded by a negotiation in which the top and bottom decide whether or not they will play, what activities are likely to occur, what activities will not occur, and about how long the scene will last. The bottom is usually given a "safe word" or "code action" she can use to stop the scene. This safe word allows the bottom to enjoy a fantasy that the scene is not consensual, and to protest verbally or resist physically without halting stimulation.

The key word to understanding S/M is *fantasy*. The roles, dialogue, fetish costumes, and sexual activity are part of a drama or ritual. The participants are enhancing their sexual

* *Vanilla* is to *S/M* what *straight* is to *gay*. I don't use the term as a pejorative but because I believe sexual preferences are more like flavor preferences than like moral/political alliances.

pleasure, not damaging or imprisoning one another. A sadomasochist is well aware that a role adopted during a scene is not appropriate during other interactions and that a fantasy role is not the sum total of her being.

S/M relationships are usually egalitarian. Very few bottoms want a full-time mistress. In fact, the stubbornness and aggressiveness of the masochist is a byword in the S/M community. Tops often make nervous jokes about being slaves to the whims of their bottoms. After all, the top's pleasure is dependent on the bottom's willingness to play. This gives most sadists a mild-to-severe case of performance anxiety.

The S/M subculture is a theater in which sexual dramas can be acted out and appreciated. It also serves as a vehicle for passing on new fantasies, new equipment, warnings about police harassment, introductions to potential sex partners and friends, and safety information. Safety is a major concern of sadomasochists. A major part of the sadist's turn-on consists of deliberately altering the emotional or physical state of the bottom. Even a minor accident like a rope burn can upset the top enough to mar the scene. And, of course, a bottom can't relax and enjoy the sex if she doesn't completely trust her top. The S/M community makes some attempt to regulate itself by warning newcomers away from individuals who are inconsiderate, insensitive, prone to playing when they are intoxicated, or unsafe for other reasons. The suppression of S/M isolates novice sadists and masochists from this body of information, which can make playing more rewarding and minimize danger.

For some people, the fact that S/M is consensual makes it acceptable. They may not understand why people enjoy it, but they begin to see that S/M people are not inhumane monsters. For other people, including many feminists, the fact that it is consensual makes it even more appalling. A woman who deliberately seeks out a sexual situation in which she can be helpless is a traitor in their eyes. Hasn't the women's movement been trying to persuade people for years that women are not naturally masochistic?

Originally, this meant that women do not create their own second-class status, do not enjoy it, and are the victims of socially constructed discrimination, not biology. A sexual masochist probably doesn't want to be raped, battered, discriminated against on her job, or kept down by the system. Her desire to act out a specific sexual fantasy is very different from the pseudopsychiatric dictum that a woman's world is bound by housework, intercourse, and childbirth.

Some feminists object to the description of S/M as consensual. They believe that our society has conditioned all of us to accept inequities in power and hierarchical relationships. Therefore, S/M is simply a manifestation of the same system that dresses girls in pink and boys in blue, allows surplus value to accumulate in the coffers of capitalists and gives workers a minimum wage, and sends cops out to keep the disfranchised down.

It is true, as I stated before, that society shapes sexuality. We can make any decision about our sexual behavior we like, but our imagination and ability to carry out those decisions are limited by the surrounding culture. But I do not believe that sadomasochism is the result of institutionalized injustice to a greater extent than heterosexual marriage, lesbian bars, or gay male bathhouses. The system is unjust because it assigns privileges based on race, gender, and social class. During an S/M encounter, the participants select a particular role because it best expresses their sexual needs, how they feel about a particular partner, or which outfit is clean and ready to wear. The most significant reward for being a top or a bottom is sexual pleasure. If you don't like being a top or a bottom, you switch your keys. Try doing that with your biological sex or your race or your socioeconomic status. The S/M subculture is affected by sexism, racism, and other fallout from the system, but the dynamic between a top and a bottom is quite different from the dynamic between men and women, whites and Blacks, or upper- and working-class people. The roles are acquired and used in very different ways.

Some feminists still find S/M roles disturb-ing, because they believe they are derived from genuinely oppressive situations. They accuse sadomasochism of being fascistic because of the symbolism employed to create an S/M ambiance. And some S/M people do enjoy fantasies that are more elaborate than a simple structure of top versus bottom. An S/M scene can be played out using the personae of guard and prisoner, cop and suspect, Nazi and Jew, white and Black, straight man and queer, parent and child, priest and penitent, teacher and student, whore and client, etc.

However, no symbol has a single meaning. Its meaning is derived from the context in which it is used. Not everyone who wears a swastika is a Nazi, not everyone who has a pair of handcuffs on his belt is a cop, and not everyone who wears a nun's habit is a Catholic. S/M is more a parody of the hidden sexual nature of fascism than it is a worship of or acquiescence to it. How many real Nazis, cops, priests, or teachers would be involved in a kinky sexual scene? It is also a mistake to assume that the historical oppressor is always the top in an S/M encounter. The child may be chastising the parent, the prisoner may have turned the tables on the cop, and the queer may be forcing the straight man to confront his sexual response to other men. The dialogue in some S/M scenes may sound sexist or homophobic from the outside, but its real meaning is probably neither. A top can call his bottom a cocksucker to give him an instruction (i.e., indicate that the top wants oral stimulation), encourage him to lose his inhibition and perform an act he may be afraid of, or simply acknowledge shame and guilt and use it to enhance the sex act rather than prevent it.

S/M eroticism focuses on whatever feelings or actions are forbidden, and searches for a way to obtain pleasure from the forbidden. It is the quintessence of nonreproductive sex. Those feminists who accuse sadomasochists of mocking the oppressed by playing with dominance and submission forget that *we* are oppressed. We suffer police harassment, violence in the street, discrimination in housing and in employment. We are not treated the way our system treats its collaborators and supporters.

The issue of pain is probably as difficult for feminists to understand as polarized roles. We tend to associate pain with illness or self-destruction. First of all, S/M does not necessarily involve pain. The exchange of power is more essential to S/M than intense sensation, punishment, or discipline. Second, pain is a subjective experience. Depending on the context, a certain sensation may frighten you, make you angry, urge you on, or get you hot. People choose to endure pain or discomfort if the goal they are striving for makes it worthwhile. Long-distance runners are not generally thought of as sex perverts, nor is Mother Theresa. The fact that masochism is disapproved of when stressful athletic activity and religious martyrdom are not is an interesting example of the way sex is made a special case in our society. We seem to be incapable of using the same reason and compassion we apply to non-sexual issues to formulate our positions on sexual issues.

S/M violates a taboo that preserves the mysticism of romantic sex. Any pain involved is deliberate. Aroused human beings do not see, smell, hear, taste, or perceive pain as acutely as the nonaroused individual. Lots of people find bruises or scratches the morning after an exhilarating session of lovemaking and can't remember exactly how or when they got them. The sensations involved in S/M are not that different. But we're supposed to fall into bed and do it with our eyes closed. Good, enthusiastic sex is supposed to happen automatically between people who love each other. If the sex is less than stunning, we tend to blame the quality of our partner's feelings for us. Planning a sexual encounter and using toys or equipment to produce specific feelings seems antithetical to romance.

What looks painful to an observer is probably being perceived as pleasure, heat, pressure, or a mixture of all these by the masochist. A good top builds sensation slowly, alternates pain with pleasure, rewards endurance with more pleasure, and teaches the bottom to transcend her own limits. With enough preparation, care, and encouragement, people are capable of doing wonderful things. There is a special pride which results from doing something unique and extraordinary for your lover. The sadomasochist has a passion for making use of the entire body, every nerve fiber, and every wayward thought.

Recently, I have heard feminists use the term "fetishistic" as an epithet and a synonym for "objectifying." Sadomasochists are often accused of substituting things for people, of loving the leather or rubber or spike heels more than the person who is wearing them. Objectification originally referred to the use of images of stereotypically feminine women to sell products like automobiles and cigarettes. It also referred to the sexual harassment of women and the notion that we should be available to provide men with sexual gratification without receiving pleasure in return and without the right to refuse to engage in sex. A concept which was originally used to attack the marketing campaigns of international corporations and the sexual repression of women is now being used to attack a sexual minority.

Fetish costumes are worn privately or at S/M gatherings. They are as unacceptable to employers and advertising executives as a woman wearing overalls and smoking a cigar. Rather than being part of the sexual repression of women, fetish costumes can provide the women who wear them with sexual pleasure and power. Even when a fetish costume exaggerates the masculine or feminine attributes of the wearer, it cannot properly be called sexist. Our society strives to make masculinity in men and femininity in women appear natural and biologically determined. Fetish costumes violate this rule by being too theatrical and deliberate. Since fetish costumes may also be used to transform the gender of the wearer, they are a further violation of sexist standards for sex-specific dress and conduct.

The world is not divided into people who have sexual fetishes and people who don't. There is a continuum of response to certain objects, substances, and parts of the body. Very few people are able to enjoy sex with anyone, regardless of their appearance. Much fetishism probably passes as "normal" sexuality because the required cues are so common and easy to obtain that no one notices how necessary they are.

Human sexuality is a complicated phenomenon. A cursory examination will not yield the entire significance of a sexual act. Fetishes have several qualities which make them erotically stimulating and unacceptable to the majority culture. Wearing leather, rubber, or a silk kimono distributes feeling over the entire skin. The isolated object may become a source of arousal. This challenges the identification of sex with the genitals. Fetishes draw all the senses into the sexual experience, especially the senses of smell and touch. Since they are often anachronistic or draw attention to erogenous zones, fetish costumes cannot be worn on the street. Fetishes are reserved for sexual use only, yet they are drawn from realms not traditionally associated with sexuality. Fetishism is the product of imagination and technology.

Sadomasochism is also accused of being a hostile or angry kind of sex, as opposed to the gentle and loving kind of sex that feminists should strive for. The women's movement has become increasingly pro romantic love in the last decade. Lesbians are especially prone to this sentimental trend. Rather than being critical of the idea that one can find enough fulfillment in a relationship to justify one's existence, feminists are seeking membership in a perfect, egalitarian couple. I question the value of this.

There is no concrete evidence that the childhoods of sadomasochists contained any more corporal punishment, puritanism, or abuse than the childhoods of other people. There is also no evidence that we secretly fear and hate our partners. S/M relationships vary from no relationship at all (the S/M is experienced during fantasy or masturbation) to casual sex with many partners to monogamous couples, and include all shades in between. There are many different ways to express affection or sexual interest. Vanilla people send flowers, poetry, or candy, or they exchange rings. S/M people do all that, and may also lick boots, wear a locked collar, or build their loved one a rack in the basement. There is little objective difference between a feminist who is offended by the fact that my lover kneels to me in public and suburbanites calling the cops because the gay boys next door are sunbathing in the nude. My sexual semiotics differ from the mainstream. So what? I didn't join the feminist movement to live inside a Hallmark greeting card.

Is there a single controversial sexual issue that the women's movement has not reacted to with a conservative, feminine horror of the outrageous and the rebellious? A movement that started out saying biology is *not* destiny is trashing transsexuals and celebrating women's "natural" connection to the earth and living things. A movement that spawned children's liberation is trashing boy-lovers and supporting the passage of draconian sex laws that assign heavier sentences for having sex with a minor than you'd get for armed robbery. A movement that developed an analysis of housework as unpaid labor and acknowledged that women usually trade sex for what they want because that's all they've got is joining the vice squad to get prostitutes off the street. A movement whose early literature was often called obscene and banned from circulation is campaigning to get rid of pornography. The only sex perverts this movement stands behind are lesbian mothers, and I suspect that's because of the current propaganda about women being the nurturing, healing force that will save the world from destructive male energy.

Lesbianism is being desexualized as fast as movement dykes can apply the whitewash. We are no longer demanding that feminist organizations acknowledge their lesbian membership. We are pretending that the words *feminist* and *woman* are synonyms for *lesbian*.

The antipornography movement is the best of the worst of the women's movement, and it must take responsibility for much of the bigotry circulating in the feminist community. This movement has consistently refused to take strong public positions supporting sex education, consenting-adult legislation, the right to privacy, the decriminalization of prostitution, children's and adolescents' rights to sexual information and freedom, and the First Amendment. It has encouraged violence against sexual minorities, especially sadomasochists, by slandering sexual deviation as violence against women. Their view of S/M is derived from one genre of commercial pornography (male-dominant and female-submissive) and makes Krafft-Ebing look like a liberal.

Commercial pornography distorts all forms of sexual behavior. There are several reasons for this. One is that it is designed to make money, not to educate people to be aesthetically pleasing. The other is that it is quasi-legal, and thus must be produced as quickly and surreptitiously as possible. Another reason is that erotic material is intended to gratify fantasy, not serve as a model for actual behavior.

S/M pornography can be divided into several types, each designed for a different segment of the S/M subculture. Most of it represents women dominating and disciplining men, since the largest market for S/M porn is heterosexual submissive males. Very little S/M porn shows any actual physical damage or even implies that damage is occurring. Most of it depicts bondage, or tops dressed in fetish costumes and assuming threatening poses.

Very little S/M porn is well produced or informative. But eliminating it will have the effect of further impoverishing S/M culture and isolating sadomasochists from one another, since many of us make contact via personal ads carried in pornographic magazines. The excuse for banning "violent" porn is that this will end violence against women. The causal connection is dubious. It is indisputably true that very few people who consume pornography ever assault or rape another person. When a rape or assault is committed, it usually occurs after some forethought and planning. But legally, a free society must distinguish between the fantasy or thought of committing a crime and the actual crime. It is not a felony to fantasize committing an illegal act, and it should not be, unless we want our morals regulated by the Brain Police. Banning S/M porn is the equivalent of making fantasy a criminal act. Violence against women will not be reduced by increasing sexual repression. People desperately need better information about sex; more humanistic and attractive erotica; more readily available birth control, abortion, and sex therapy; and

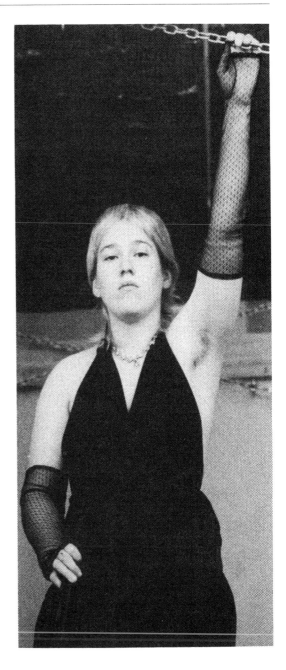

more models for nontraditional, nonexploitative relationships.

I am often asked if sadomasochism will survive the revolution. I think all the labels and categories we currently use to describe ourselves will change dramatically in the next 100 years, even if the revolution does not occur. My fantasy is that kinkiness and sexual variation will multiply, not disappear, if terrible penalties are no longer meted out for being sexually adventurous.

There is an assumption behind the question that bothers me. The assumption that sadomasochists are part of the system rather than part of the rebellion has already been dealt with in this article. But there is another assumption—that we must enjoy being oppressed and mistreated. We like to wear uniforms? Then we must get off on having cops bust up our bars. We like to play with whips and nipple clamps and hot wax? Then it must turn us on when gangs of kids hunt us down, harass and beat us. We're not really human. We're just a bunch of leather jackets and spike heels, a bunch of post office boxes at the bottom of sex ads.

We make you uncomfortable, partly because we're sexual, and partly because we're not so different. I'd like to know when you're going to quit blaming us, the victims of sexual repression, for the oppression of women. I'd like to know when you're going to quit objectifying us.

WILL BAKER

The Legend of Great Uncle Jim and the Woman Behind It All

little more—it said that he teaches writing and film at the University of California, Davis, that he raises rabbits and almonds, and that he has written a novel, *Dawnstone* (Capra Press). All of this is still true, plus Will has a 1984 book from North Atlantic Books called *Backward: An Essay on Indians, Time, and Photography*.

Art Kleiner

From the original introduction (Spring 1982):
This contribution [Will Baker] calls his "first attempt at bareknuckle gonzo journalism. It is all true, and that is often a bad sign." In sending this story of losing at love, he wondered if one ought to talk about such things in front of strangers. O yes. It saves them from thinking that their deep misery (inevitable with a jilt; man or woman, it hurts like dying) is unique. The backdrop for this true tale is Nevada—wide open, weird, and just the place to get married or divorced in a hell of a hurry.

Stephanie Mills

Who is Will Baker? For the appearance of his story "Left Over in Your Heart," which ran in the Summer 1977 CQ, Anne Herbert wrote an introduction that said little more than "Will Baker exists." Well, maybe a

The lady in rhinestone glasses at the Winner's Inn wasn't just sure how you got to Tuscarora. She knew it was eighty miles from downtown Winnemucca, and believed there was pavement as far as Golconda, but after that it was all back roads, and likely no signs. I should ask at the hardware store, where they had county maps.

The hardware lady—clean Levi's, hair dyed jet black, an evergreen smell—helped me to find the right map. Elko County is about the size of Delaware, and appears to be mostly back roads. The roads run in long and lonesome lines through immense sagebrush basins bounded by worn but impressive mountains.

The region is inhabited mainly by jackrabbits and jet fighters, with an occasional far-off peg of a man aboard a horse. Sometimes in the basins there is a slate-green river (forks of the Owyhee or Humboldt); sometimes a wide, shallow lake; sometimes a mirage. Ranches hereabouts run from little ones of five thousand acres to good-sized spreads of one hundred thousand acres or more. From a rise in the road you occasionally see one: a distant clump of poplars, not bright green but at least different, maybe a glitter of aluminum from a trailer. What you will see mostly is rabbits.

Before the ranches were the mines. All over the map you can see the little crossed picks and shovels: Old Timer's, Silver Cloud, Midas, Little Jewel. Tuscarora was the biggest in the whole northeast corner of the state until 1904 when the price of silver and the depth of the shafts didn't figure out right, and they began to pull the pumps and let the water take over. At one time the population was given as ten thousand—probably on the high side the way all miner's estimates are—but it was mostly tents, a little wood and less brick. Now the hardware lady guessed twenty people might be living there, but no motel, no store, not even a bar, and the road was one of those checkered lines identified as a "gravel road, not graded or drained." Might be tricky this season, she said. They'd been seeing some rain up there. A Volvo? Maybe. She looked vaguely encouraging.

The mountains were shrouded in high mist and light squalls were blowing through when I took the Golconda exit. Gray rain. And raining also in my heart—to embroider a little C & W on the edge of this tale—since I left Reno, where the dark-eyed waitress at Harrah's said it was a good pass and she would have been more than happy to consider it but she had plans after work to catch the tail end of Charlie Daniels' last set, and next week when Willie Nelson went through it was the day before her birthday and she had a date with her dad. I wondered if I was still younger than her dad and told her again about her smile and ordered another whiskey, because there was some chance, maybe a good chance, she was lying.

I hadn't planned this essay in historical research at all this way. It was just a loose chip from my childhood, an Ancient Mariner charm or virus that I picked up, listening by the woodbox while my dad and my uncle Jess told the story of Great Uncle Jim, the family's only honest-to-God straight-up-and-down hero. Of course they also told bear stories, and tried to figure out how the Bakers were related to Quannah Parker's Comanches, and retold their own father's exploits as a cowpuncher on the Chisholm Trail. But the saga of Uncle Jim in Tuscarora was the big story, I could see that. They told it more often and they told it differently. Still in his galluses and ironpants, smelling of pitch from a day in the woods, my father would lean forward and grip his knees in his big-knuckled hands and shout at my uncle.

"A big man by God."

"Mountain of a man." Jess always spoke as if dad had gotten it wrong.

"He did for that sonofabitch."

Jess would snort and look away into the ceiling. "Did for him? Jesus Christ, did for him? Cut his goddamned head off, is what he did."

And so they would go back and argue over the whole thing again. How Jim had been carving on the hitching post with the clasp knife, how the other had approached, what they had most likely said, whether the other man had shot Jim in the alley or in the basement under the saloon, and on and on.

I knew other stories like that. In fact once dad had come in from fighting fire to tell my awestruck mother that a trail boss, one of the Reed boys, had shot one of the loggers who got drunk and came for him with an axe. That didn't kill him though, dad observed in some disgust, it was the other dumb drunk sonsofbitches who tried to pack him out and didn't know how.

But Great Uncle Jim was different because he was our own blood. He wasn't in any picture books, or famous anywhere else, but he was all ours. My grandfather had known him personally. He was a big man, a mountain of a man, strong as a bull, and he died full of lead with his boots on. At that age I read a lot of Zane Grey and trashier stuff as well, and it was easy for me to elaborate on the skeletal ballad my dad and uncle were chanting. I could see Big Jim in my mind's eye, see the street, the dustdevils and tumbleweed, the weatherbeaten buildings, the horses shying and stomping in apprehension.

Some of the details made me uncomfortable, and to myself I fudged around them to get the heroic action I needed. It seemed to me Uncle Jim should have a gun too, a blazing gun, and they should walk up the middle of the main street toward each other, saying finally, "All right you dirty sidewinding ———, go for your iron!" or the like. But it wasn't like that,

I really knew. It was surely much more like the Lovelock *Tribune* had it in their edition of June 6, 1909:

Shot Through the Head

He Mustered Sufficient Strength to Sever His Opponent's Head With a Knife

In one of the bloodiest battles ever recorded in the annals of the state, James Baker and Clyde Thompson, two residents of Tuscarora, fought to their death Sunday night about 8 o'clock.

There were no witnesses to the awful affray—the men fighting their battle alone. After the fight, Baker alone remained alive, and from him the meager particulars obtainable were received.

The two men met on the street and angry words passed between them. Challenges were issued and accepted and the men went into an alley away from the gaze of chance passers-by, to settle their grievances. Very soon four shots, fired from a pistol in the hands of Thompson rang out, and Baker fell to the ground badly wounded, one of the shots taking effect in the head and two in the abdomen. Although wounded unto death, Baker managed to arise and grappled his assail-

ant. The men wrestled and fought until Thompson fell to the ground with Baker on top. Baker then managed to take from his pocket an ordinary pocket knife and with this weapon he inflicted frightful injuries upon Thompson. In an awful frenzy, maddened by the fearful pain he was suffering, and with his strength fast ebbing away, Baker held Thompson while he wielded his knife across his throat. When Baker had finished his butchery, Thompson was practically dead with his throat cut from ear to ear. A later inspection of the remains of Thompson, who died immediately after receiving the wounds, revealed a ghastly spectacle. It was found that the head was almost entirely severed from the body.

Baker and Thompson came from Texas a couple of years ago and had been living in Tusacarora and in that vicinity ever since. Baker was a married man and at the time of the affray his wife was visiting in Elko.

Both men were well known by a number of people in Lovelock. Baker has been in and out of here for the past year. He was a large, raw-boned man and had a glass eye, and was built on the Buffalo Bill order.

I was on the gravel road not graded or drained now, climbing gradually. The plain fell away in a long sweep to the south, in colors of ash, rust, and ghost green. To the north and east the mountains reared, pocked and rotten rock breaking through the flanks of some, a light shawl of snow on the highest. Between these peaks and the thunderheads stacked above them were caverns of shadow, gunmetal

blue and dark gray with sometimes a tone of rare, deep mauve.

For twenty minutes I didn't pass a vehicle, and then a muddy old Chevy ton-and-a-half truck with no fenders and a load of hay went by. The two inside looked at me flat from under their wide brims and didn't smile. The ruts had set like ridges of concrete and the Volvo slathered along in them, the steering wheel jumping under my hands with its own life.

Lonesome country. That brings up another bothersome detail of the Uncle Jim story, a detail that as a boy I had little use for, but which now, especially now, suggests itself as perhaps the central one, and maybe explains why I was driving myself ruthlessly over this godforsaken eighty miles. Dad and Uncle Jess used to refer in a veiled way to "that woman." The Woman Behind It All. When I was eight I didn't know what it was women were behind, and certainly didn't think one of them without even being present could push those two men into the alley and lay them out there in each other's blood. But now I know. Just now I was in fact myself remembering and trying hard not to remember a sweet smile, a beautiful behind, a cheating heart—a combination that can cause one considerable grief. I was right in that time when everything you ever said or did to her appears wrong, when she seems more powerful and glorious and radiant, in your overheated memory, than the mere human you took for a movie and pizza; the time also when this vision suddenly chills and darkens because a shadow has crept beside it, a faceless shadow that she turns to, smiles at, reaches for, kisses, tongues, opens. . . .

A shock as from crossed wires and a burned smell. For your own welfare, from a sense that you are teasing something that is too mad and ravenous for the cages of your mind, you jerk away. There is a numb time. The fenceposts flicker past. Then a word from an old song or a scene from happier times starts the deadly loop all over again.

I smoked for a few miles, because that is one of the things I do at these times. Besides propositioning cocktail waitresses and Keno girls. Maybe because they wear black. Then I pulled up at a place, a scatter of shacks and corroded trailers trying to squeeze under half a dozen ragged cottonwoods. Kirby's Midas Tavern said OPEN but wasn't. Parked in yards were various vehicles, mostly not operable, but one trailer had a wash flapping out back in the cold wind. I got to the front door and there was a phlegmatic man in a plaid shirt to meet me.

Yep it was the right road to Tuscarora back there at the fork over the bridge. Might or might not be passable. He had seen a little foreign job go over it yesterday, so maybe. Nothing there, in the way of accommodations. He stopped, blank, so I turned and left.

Maybe the old woman was dead anyway. Distant Cousin Earl, an affable teacher of Industrial Arts from Sacramento, one summer four years ago drove his spanking RV to Tuscarora to investigate the family legend. He reported that he met an octogenarian lady who had lived in the town all her life, and who as a girl of 19 had listened to the excited gossip at the stage depot on that June afternoon when two men died. So there was somebody who might know things about this last detail, this Woman Behind It All.

But only gossip. Dinnertime gossip seventy years old. It was beginning to look less and less like a sensible day. Maybe I didn't care whether the old lady was still alive, or whether she could remember anything if she was, or whether what she could remember would reveal anything to me. Maybe I was just driving, and driving now in steeper country, swatches of dirty snow along the roadside, so I could think about how her hair cascaded down over that beautiful behind and how she came to me sometimes like a wave from the other side of the ocean, and think safely about such things, not being able to put my head in my hands and bawl, because my hands had to be on the wheel, still spinning and jerking from the hard ruts. It is another thing you can do, besides smoke and make hopeless passes. You can drive. I had done it before. The first time especially. If you've heard this one don't stop me.

A man has a job and a house and a car and a wife and a kid. He loves them all and worries about them approximately in that order. For years they hold together; they interlock; the wife takes the kid in the car to the school while the man does his job and then for a few hours they all fall asleep in the house and leave it again early in the morning. One year small things change. A neighbor drives the kid to school but the wife disappears with the car anyway. The man pursues the job so far he does

Michael Moore

not fall back into the house some evenings. There are parties and dinners and some people leave before others. Finally some people don't even go. Glassware may be broken. Things are said which have a magical effect of suddenly diminishing greatly both the person speaking and the person spoken to. One day the wife takes the kid in the car and does not come back, ever, to fall asleep in the house.

The man gets another car and he drives. He drives perhaps all night. Sometimes he gets someplace, where he smokes a lot, and drinks too, and makes passes at people. Or he drives around looking for her, the Woman Behind It All, parks near her house, waits. Perhaps she arrives finally and is with someone else, the shadow, and he can hear them laugh in anticipation on the way to the front door. So he begins driving again.

We must talk about violence now. In my case, not that uncommon, it was the self hurt-

ing the self. I cut myself and tried to take too many pills, but not very seriously. Some of my friends did it much better with the bottle and the automobile. An odd thing, that when the Woman goes away or at least plays away, a man looks for a quiet room where he can hack himself or eat oblivion. Not everyone of course. These are modern times. There is a new school of thought, according to which one is cool, one shrugs, one keeps an "open relationship." I have seen a few of these open arrangements up close. One from very close. I want to report that I find, beneath the casual laughter, the worldly winks, the arch jokes, the same hard and horny core of hate, the same murderous undertow that exists in the ghettos of common love.

These days everybody is a shrink, so everybody knows that the modern man who turns the blade on himself or goes in for revenge fucking is only taking a substitute. What he really wants to do is kill the two of them, or at least the rival, but society frowns on this sort of direct action.

The implication is, must be, that to take such steps is a serious aberration, not to be countenanced. A whole rhetoric has grown up to mask these raw animal feelings. I understand your position. My needs are not being met. We have to communicate honestly. I respect you. The children are the most important thing. We have to stay friends. Friends. Thought I'd drop over, friend, and try out this double-barrelled twelve gauge.

Perhaps some people do not believe in these powerful and sinister emotions. Perhaps most men are only "upset" or "disappointed." Perhaps only a few discover such Neanderthal strata in themselves. But when I watch my friends go down into divorce, I see the same external signs I know so well. The nicotine insomnia, the sudden and indiscriminate lust, a pale and haggard mien that reminds one of consumption, an inner, eating fire. They've got the tiger by the tail.

So maybe I am a rare and dangerous Neanderthal aberrant, and so was Uncle Jim. Western genes. I do know that the second time around it got just as hard. A very modern affair, this second one. Massage and good dope and the Sierras. A blonde. She ran into a Jewish psychiatrist with a swimming pool in Marin. And I began to understand some things. I understood the Nazis. I even understood David Berkowitz, the chubby young man who could not resist the thrill of firing a .44 magnum point-blank into the faces of pretty girls. I understood rape. On certain days directly after sensing the first nub of my antlers I saw some very terrible little movies inside my skull, while I drove the Volvo around like a zombie. The psychiatrist did not get off easily either.

I was not proud of being the producer of these ghastly little flicks. But they were hard to control. I thought I might be crazy and sought help. Of course it had to be another Jewish psychiatrist. With detachment he helped me to translate the horror shows scene by scene into the new rhetoric. He encouraged me to talk this language to others, and indeed after a time I did not feel so weird and began to think nice thoughts about my ex. You know, communication and accceptance. Two years later we all three chatted around the swimming pool, heated and deductible because of his bad back, and admired their new baby. We were modern and normal again.

The rain picks up and the mud ridges are now slick on the surface. It occurs to me that I could be stranded here all night if I try to straighten out one of these curves. Since the haytruck I have encountered only two four-wheel-drive pickups, traveling fast, the drivers at the last moment lifting two fingers from the steering wheel in an ambiguous gesture. I have a bag of oranges from my tree in California and one thin Mexican blanket, which is not much to pit against a gusty and moonless night on this high desert. But after making a couple of hills in second gear I drop into another of the basins and see on the other side a cluster of buildings perched on the side of a considerable peak. Mount Blitzen, according to the map.

On the last rise before town I see higher on the mountain some tailing heaps and a ruined smelter chimney. Otherwise Tuscarora is mostly weathered trailers, a few sagging frame houses, and one geodesic dome covered in asphalt paper. All of them try to squeeze under a dozen ragged cottonwoods. Beside the post office there is one square, ancient adobe building, but the windows are boarded shut. I park in what looks like the middle of whatever this is, and see a wooden sign MUSEUM on the back porch of one old house. A woman in a down jacket, supported by a cane, moves toward me from another house across the street and we exchange pleasantries. No she is not the particular old woman I am looking for. I must be after either Dela Phillips here at the museum or Nona Trembath in the white house at the end of the street there. They're both over eighty. Both been here always. Ring long and hard at Dela's. Hard of hearing.

I thank her and walk up the steps to begin ringing long and hard. Dela may be hard of hearing, but she certainly does not look eighty. Hair dyed a bright carrot, she still fills her loose rayon blouse and her eyes are huge and warm behind coke bottle lenses. I introduce myself as I am led into the museum, also her living room, and she brightens.

"Why sure they was two of them and one had a wife, her name was Edna, and a kid too I think. And man number two come along and they was something went on before, used to be his wife then I think, and they fought out there in the street. There was a saloon right across from that old brick building and they rolled down in the cellar under it. One had a gun and the other a knife I think but I don't know who shot who. Which one was your uncle?"

"The one with the knife."

"That was one of them, all right. I was only eleven, you know. We had the dinner station where the stage came in, and I heard the people talk about it. We fed seventy-five people a day there sometimes."

The porch windows are stacked full of old pink and violet tonic bottles, lending an Edgar Allan Poe hint to the light. In the main room there are glass cases full of chunks of rock frosted with crystals, cut stones and turquoise, and an assortment of combs, carbide head-lamps, button hooks, revolvers, cuff links, crimpers, augers, and the like. On the wall, several racks from big bull elk; also a row of guns including a Sharps buffalo rifle and several Winchester and Henry repeaters. Also many pictures of men beside steam engines or on ore cars: burly, moustachioed men not given to hilarity. Other pictures of twelve-horse wagons stacked with sagebrush (Dela explains that the smelter ate up all the brush for miles around; five hundred Chinamen grubbed it out with hoes). The usual heyday hilltop views of a sprawl of tents divided by roads of churned mud.

"So everybody was scared to go down there, wouldn't even get close to the saloon. Finally they heard one man hollering and they came to see. I don't know which one it was—"

"My uncle."

"—one of them hollered out 'Come and git me I don't want to die here with this sonofabitch.' They pulled him out but the other was already dead, cut up something awful. The other didn't live too long after that. Your uncle. Where was he from?"

"Texas, I think."

"That probably accounts for some of it." Dela laughs. "They say." She moves to one wall beside an old pedal pump organ. "Here's a picture of that woman. Edna."

It is one of those man and wife portraits in a little oval frame with a cloudy backdrop, woman in the foreground and turned a little to one side, below her master. Hard to tell about these images of femininity from bygone times; the coiffures and starch and whalebone usually obscure whatever it is that made the blood leap then. But this time I think I can see it. A petite woman, dark eyes and hair, though perhaps a little full in the cheeks for the small, fine nose. Not exactly a smile, but just conceivably that other expression that goes a shade beyond a smile in the direction of the devil's casino.

"That fella ain't either one of them. He was my husband's uncle. She married him afterward and they moved East. So she got into the Phillips, my family."

Dela beams at me, happy at this relation, however distant. Then there is a tremendous shock of thunder and the pink bottles chatter excitedly on the sills.

"Sonic boom." Dela nods reassuringly at me, and waves generally west. "It's the Navy over there."

The Navy, of course.

"We had a big ranch. Not big like Spanish ranch, but we had ten thousand deeded acres and three thousand head of cattle. We sold out to Bing Crosby." She pauses and I murmur. "Yes, we knew him and his family real well. They come here often but then of course they sold it after he died. Here, I'll show you the gun that killed the first man in Tuscarora."

I look at the old Colt under the glass. "Interesting," I say and tap the case. "Were there lots of murders here?"

Dela laughs. "Oh no. Tuscarora wasn't a real wild town. One man shot over a water deal I remember. Oh of course when the range hands got through with riding for two months and got their three days they would hit for town on horseback and when they got to the top of the hill they'd start shooting and come at a dead run. After three days in town they'd have to go back and the boss would come around to the saloons then and settle up for their damage. You know just busted glass and chairs and such."

I pause before a magnificent slab of polished, petrified wood.

"Sequoias." Dela shakes her head. "Thousands of years ago you know those sequoias, that's the big redwoods, went from coast to coast. This whole country was tropical then you know."

I examine the red and yellow whorls of the grain.

"Were the mines going then, in 1909?"

"They was downhill then. Last big mine closed in 1916. Hardly anything left of those days now. That big adobe block building there. Used to be the lodge building, Masonic and Odd Fellows and Knights of Pythias all together. Would you sign the register?"

I notice behind the register a hand-lettered sign that lists the admission at one dollar. I pull out two.

"I'm paying double, ma'am, for all your help. And I want to take some pictures. Now what happened to all that machinery?"

"Why thank you sir. There was all kinds of machinery for a while, all those pumps and engines and the little ore cars you know just rusting away. Between wars they picked it all up and sent it to Japan. For scrap."

Japan, of course.

I shoot a few pictures, thank Edna for her time, and then ask about Nona Trembath.

"White house on the corner. Now she'll tell you all about that business. She's older than I am you know." She blinks the huge brown eyes and smiles. "Sure enjoyed it."

Walking down the muddy street under a cavernous sky, the cloud cover now showing a rift or two as the wind stiffens, I think about those men in armbands and narrow collars and moustaches. How they handled the open relationship. I know I wouldn't care to be a party

in any such arrangement with most of them. I suppose they came to this place, these vistas of empty air and dry plain and ugly rock, for the silver and gold, which meant for the money and the power, the silk and the wine and the cheroots, which meant ultimately the women. And most of them didn't find it. But that didn't get rid of the need. The Big Need. Men's needs were probably not being met here in Tuscarora in 1909.

A little bell tinkles when you open Nona's gate, just for the opener's pleasure. For Nona there is a regular doorbell. I see her coming through the window in the door, warped a little in the glass. She looks under five feet, but erect in a faded cotton dress. She too wears thick spectacles, and over the right lens is taped a square blue wrapper from some powder or tablet. I am directly invited into the cluttered, too-warm room, and state my business.

She commands me to sit in the overstuffed chair and then she begins at the beginning and lets me have the whole thing, pausing just a moment for me to finish fumbling with my notepad, speaking in bright, flat prose.

"Yes, Baker and Thompson. One was one-eyed, a great big nigger. Baker I think that was. Happened on Celebration Day. Thompson was stayin' here in town. Real quiet fella. Never said nothin' to nobody. Baker was working on a ranch, Roseberry's place. He was a real bulldog. They say he'd slip off a wagon and throw a steer right flat on the ground. Had a wife or said it was his wife that he kept on the ranch there. Anyway after this Thompson came around he spied on 'em I guess and this particular day he and Baker started something and then walked down the alley by the saloon. The real fight started there. People heard shooting. I guess they rolled down into the cellar and for a long time everybody was afraid to come near, but finally this Baker threw the cellar doors back and walked out. He said 'I won't die in there with that sonofabitch. I did for him though.' But he never lived past seven o'clock that night. The other fella had his head cut almost off, just a little skin holding it. I know that because my dad helped the doctor sew it back on. People asked Baker what the trouble was and he said 'Ask Shorty.' But when the Sheriff went to find Shorty he had cleared out. To Idaho. The other thing this Baker said before he died was 'Do something for me. Don't bury me in the same grave with that sonofabitch.' But they did anyway. This is hard ground. Well everybody figured that woman was Thompson's wife somewhere else and this Baker run off with her, and come here and introduced her as his own. But the funny thing was a few months later the Sheriff got a letter from a woman out in Nebraska or someplace asking about this Jim because she said she was his wife and wanted to know if there was anything left, like an estate. There wasn't anything of course but an old saddle and bridle not worth much."

Somewhere in this tight weave I got in a question about the one eye, and Nona said yes she was sure about that. He was a good fella too, cordial, and could pitch hay like the dickens. Then the postmistress tapped and came in, and they talked about an unfortunate accident two nights ago. An old man died in a head-on collision on Highway 95 out of Winnemucca. "He was eighty years old and wouldn't wear glasses, that's why," Nona observed. They moved on to talk about the square dance coming up. The postmistress said they might even have enough for two squares.

During this interlude I am still thinking of the woman in Nebraska who wasn't the Woman Behind It All but who was the other kind, the Woman Left Out. Probably left on a bleak sodhut homestead with a band of ragged, whining children. Left for a little tramp with something deadly in her near-smile. Why does a Woman Left Out stick it through, raise the kids, plant and plow, bake bread and gather cow chips, while the man with his Big Need turns to murder? I am speaking of a general pattern, knowing of many exceptions, those Frankies who toted .44s into barrooms or took their men apart with a razor. But generally not. Generally men do it.

I do know the feeling, if not the reasons. There is some connection with the children. In our time women take the kids when they leave, and whether fair or not it releases some deep, dangerous force in a man. After the first numb horror you go molten at the core, something rears and begins to rage. Every nerve twangs to some ancient battle song. When it happened to me, that first time, I felt the voltage in my nervous system take a quantum leap. I slept maybe four hours a night for a month, smoked three packs of cigarettes a day, and scrawled pages full of drivel. I also hatched plots. Shoot him with my deer rifle, take my daughter and hijack a plane to Cuba. Attuned to such possibilities, I began to notice how much of that was going on in the daily newspapers. In the very city I was living in somebody tried it; he holed up in a maintenance shed at the airport with his child and made demands, mostly on his ex-wife. The FBI sharpshooters did for him and his Neanderthal genes. The kid was unharmed, though spattered with her daddy's blood.

Most of the time I knew in some chamber of the brain that these fantasies would not be realized, were only some kind of imperfect psychic pressure valve. Outwardly I taught classes and went to committee meetings and mowed the lawn, and smiled and thanked the neighbors who brought sympathetic hot dishes to the Abandoned One. But the heaving magma was still there inside. A wise old friend came to visit and told me I was still normal. However, the tremendous energy I felt was an illusion. "You probably think you can uproot trees," he said. "Actually you are very tired and probably not functioning at peak efficiency." Maybe so, but during that month I built a hell of a fence, played some outstanding touch football, and wrote the only sonnets of my career.

And no experience of my lifetime has ever matched this one, the loss of wife and child, for sheer savage intensity. I felt positively luminous with adrenalin, and if ever I was capable of—or thought with relish about—walking down a dusty alley to meet another man with a gun, it was then.

After the postmistress leaves we shift the conversation to Nona herself. She has removed the paper wrapper patch from her spectacles, and her eyes are magnified like Dela's, but they are a different, odd color. It is the color of this country, a subtle blend of gray and green and brown.

"I'll be ninety come the thirteenth of October. I was married a year or two after we're talkin' about, 1911, to a Welshman. We saved up and bought a ranch to get him out of the mines. He was a Cousin Jack, we called 'em. Welshmen and Cornishmen. Good miners. In one of the other big mines they had Irish, so the shifts had to quit at different hours, otherwise the Jacks and the Irish fought all the time. We bought 878 acres and 100 head of cows and ran it until he died in 1941. Bad lungs, from the mines. Nicest man you'd ever want to know."

One of the lucky ones, I think. There were three men for every woman in this territory then. And Nona is pretty clearly not an ordinary woman.

"First thing I had to do after he died was prove up title. My name wasn't on anything, just his. I spent three thousand dollars on lawyers and accountants and assessors to keep that place. And I ran it myself. When I sold it in the fifties—you know who I sold it to?"

I shake my head but I think I already know.

"Bing Crosby. Yes sir. And when I sold it I had seventeen hundred acres, two hundred head of sheep, two hundred and fifty head of cows and I put up two hundred and fifty measured tons of hay every damn year. I wasn't sittin' down."

I keep a respectful silence.

"I wrote a story about that and they printed it in the Elko paper, I'll show you. And the *Deseret News* in Salt Lake sent a man here and they wrote me up."

She is swift on her feet and knows just where the clippings are. I look them over. Woman Runs Ranch By Herself. Gal with Gumption. Pictures of Nona in overalls and short hair beside her saddled horse. Her life laid out in the same level talk over sixty-eight column inches, including two paragraphs on Great Uncle Jim.

"I got five proposals of marriage after that *Deseret News* story. Men just wrote from anywhere, even Canada." She laughs. "One fella wanted to know just how many head of cows I was running, before he completed his proposal."

She was, I suggest, interested? Oh no. One man and he was the nicest you could want.

What is it women want out of men?

"Kindness." Quick as a rattler. "See her wants before she does."

I work on that by myself for a while.

"Say, you want to see an ounce of gold?"

She returns from a back room with a little clear plastic locket full of dull yellow grains.

"Got that chain from Buckskin Jack. He wanted to know where the gold come from." She sees me smiling.

"Oh I know some fellas with nicknames." She looks at me sideways, devilish. "Buckskin Jack he was a big nigger like you."

"You got a name for me?"

"Don't know you well enough yet."

"I'll bet you make up those names."

"I do no such a thing now. You just look, I got a list of 'em and everybody is somebody I knew or heard about. Look here."

She produces a sheet of paper from her album and I read through the collection:

Flyspeck Bill, Crooked Neck McCray, Dirty Shirt George, Cream Puff Ike, Twenty-five Pinky, The Denver Sheik, Fade Away Kid, Chippie Chaser, Tamale, Silk Hat Harry, Bolts and Nuts, Seldom Seen Slim, Snake River Pete, Gimme Kid, Scissor Beak, and of course Buckskin Jack.

Then there is Gold Tooth Bess, Broken Nose Helen, Dirty Neck Grace, and Bull Shit Alice.

"Some women here too."

"The sportin' girls. There was a big sportin' house here. These people come from all over the Klondike, Australia, Wales."

"Couldn't hide their flaws."

"Land no, everybody got a name right away."

"Were there fights over these sporting ladies?"

"No, not much. Fellas didn't seem to fight over them."

A pause, while I work to come to the question I realize I have been heading for, have driven six hundred miles to ask.

"Why do men do that?"

"What: Sportin'?"

"No. I mean why do they kill each other, like Baker and Thompson?"

"That's nature. You see a lot of that."

She waits, alert and confident, but no followup question occurs to me.

"Not so much like that nowadays. Now there's always something else comin' along."

I keep silent, wondering if that makes the difference. What if I had not been able to foresee another after the first, and again after the second? What if this last one, still haunting the freeway with me, were the absolute last? What if no waitress or Keno girl would ever smile at me again except to increase her tip? Would nature then push me to murder?

It could not be that simple. Mr. Thompson did not have to hunt Edna down; there must have been others available—at least Bull Shit Alices—in Omaha or St. Louis or Abilene. It must have been partly the child. Perhaps men have a horror of their barrenness, a desire to perpetuate and extend their identity, a desire which if frustrated becomes violent. Zoologists tell us that the males of a species often fight to insure that the most aggressive and durable genes will be transmitted to progeny. The female merely waits, provocative, at the edge of the field of battle; she only need exercise her blind urge to turn her tail to the victor. Her place in history is already assured. The male can plant his seed, shape his race after his own image only by conquest, and in most species he is put to the test of battle each season.

Among many ungulates, walrus, and some primates, the defeated males become mournful exiles. Some have grown too old, and in one short, bloody encounter have lost whole harems. Once whipped, the stud cannot approach his former loving mates, who ignore him or even slash at him in contempt. Sometimes they do not live long after their loss of power; sometimes they collect in a spiritless fraternity and graze out their days on poor and stony ground. Give them an intense consciousness of their

Photo by Will Baker

Nona Trembath

lot, an ability to conceive their own desolate future, and perhaps you have the formula for mad lust and destruction, herds of Nazi mustangs thundering through the streets of Reno, frothing to violate and kill. But I guess I would have such imaginary Hun-hordes start with the nuclear testing stations, or the Navy over there.

"But it was a better world then than it is now," Nona goes on without me. "These poisons they're putting in the ground. These wastes. Why that stuff just doesn't go away you know. Terrible. But our worst problem is the refugees."

I look inquiring.

"Yes, hell, where are we going to put them? Thousands and thousands coming in from El Salvador. We haven't got the room. And those Cubans. They were just crooks. What are we going to do with them?"

I don't know.

"People don't know what's going to happen any more. A fella come around here a few years back, wanted to look at a mine I have a little interest in. Wanted a shelter, a storehouse with food and water and guns underground. Big old fat pious nigger he was. Had lots of money. Why I told him he was crazy. What's the point of living if everybody else is gone, I said to him. That's damn fool craziness."

I agree. We talk over a few other world affairs, then get back to her life. I ask if she was ever lonesome during those twenty years spent running cattle on seventeen hundred acres of hard ground.

"Oh no. If you got a ranch you got no time to be lonesome."

It occurs to me all at once that I have not asked about children, but she has seen where I am headed before I do.

"I lost five children, I did. Never had any children." She bites her lip when she smiles this time.

"Your children? You had—"

"I didn't have 'em. I carried 'em. Four, five months usually. Couldn't keep them. Not enough water in my womb, I think. Something." She is biting hard on her lip now, and there is a just perceptible shake in her voice.

I fumble out a story about my grandmother, who had nine, she always said, although two only lived for a few hours. Those two she always counted and you could tell she cared about them. It is neither the right nor the wrong thing to offer. I stare at the clippings to keep from looking at her, and after awhile one of us thinks of something to say and we go on.

Another tap at the door, and I let in a little man with straight brown hair, freckles, and buck teeth.

"This is my boyfriend, comes to see me every day almost."

"Hiya Nona," he says and takes a seat. "What's your name?"

"Will."

"Mine's Rick."

"He's lived in every state in the union except Alaska and Hawaii," Nona volunteers.

"My dad's a millwright."

"How old are you?"

"Eight."

"Every state?"

"Except Hawaii and Alaska," Nona reminds me.

"Yeah, we was in Arizona last year. I hope to go back there. Where do you live?"

"California."

He looks noncommital.

I see the landscape darkening outside, and begin my thankyous, preparing to leave. Then I remember the oranges, and trot out to the Volvo and get half a dozen for her. When she tells me to come back, she means it, though neither of us believes it will happen. I drive away, leaving this ninety-year-old and her boyfriend of eight to their own rare and special romance.

When I pass Midas the western sky is the color of stainless steel and I need the headlights. The rabbits are suddenly everywhere. These are big, gray Western Jacks with ears and tails tipped in black. Soon I am swerving, skidding, braking, trying to avoid them. The spears of light make them crazy and stupid; they freeze or run the wrong way. Once I counted four at once weaving figure eights in front of me. Inevitably, with a curse, I hit one. Then another.

Dodging this way, I think of the beautiful behind only intermittently, a little wearily. The next-to-last cigarette in the pack tastes dry and bitter, and I am finally feeling the mileage. I am also feeling ashamed. The legend of Great Uncle Jim and the Woman Behind It All. That little bit of a ranch lady back there is worth six of them. She lost five, died inside five times, and was driven to kill nobody, but to run more sheep and more cattle on more land.

Nature, she would say. Maybe that's it. When it comes down to it they are stronger. They don't need us, except for seed, and it drives us crazy. Our nature to be crazy. Or are there three kinds, the Woman Behind It All and the Woman Left Behind and the Woman Above It All. And all three of them drive us crazy, crazy as these rabbits, Jesus hundreds of them, now I have hit four. They take the children or they lose the children, and we go wild. We drive the jets and set off the bombs and grub for the gold and kill each other. Or ourselves.

I hit the fifth rabbit and there is nothing but a little jerk at the corner of my mouth. Because of the sound. The terrible sound.

MARK O'BRIEN

How I Became
a Human Being

Photographs by Betty Medsger

Residents of Berkeley, California, get used to seeing people in wheelchairs because Berkeley welcomes the disabled into everyday school and work life. Even so, when I was a student there in 1977, there was one man whose disability seemed so total that he startled nearly everyone who saw him—and inspired a lot of awe and admiration besides—just by getting himself around campus. He was Mark O'Brien—a man who, because of childhood polio, can only move his head, neck, left knee, and left foot. I would never have guessed at the time that I would turn out five years later to be Mark's editor, or that his article in the Spring 1982 issue would turn out to be some of the most accomplished writing CQ has ever published.

Mark dictated this article into a tape recorder in August 1980. His friend Barbara Belding transcribed it and suggested he send it our way. In December 1981 he graduated from

the University of California at Berkeley with a B.A. in English, and spent the next few years (while writing for CQ, Pacific News Service, and elsewhere) convincing the Berkeley Graduate School of Journalism to admit him as a student. (They did, finally, in 1985.) Along the way Mark bought a computer—a Radio Shack TRS-80 model 100 lap portable—which he operates entirely by mouthstick. "For the first time, I feel my writing can be private," he wrote in the *Whole Earth Software Review*. "I am free to keep a journal, write personal letters that really are personal, and rewrite as much as I want without having to pay a secretary."

This article gives several good reasons why disabled people should be part of mainstream life, but there's one it doesn't mention. Part of becoming a human being for me has been (slowly and painfully) learning to be human with groups of people, like the disabled, who initially make me feel uncomfortable. That's not possible unless I see them in daily life. Shutting them away diminishes the humanity of the rest of us.

Art Kleiner

When I was about ten years old and growing up in a South Shore suburb of Boston, my family and I packed ourselves into our station wagon and headed north for a brief vacation in Quebec. I had never journeyed so far from home, but I remember that the trip was fairly pleasant and that we arrived at our motel east of the city of Quebec a little after sunset. The shape and the colors of the landscape were the things which impressed me the most. The hills were much steeper, the houses were painted brighter and, in general, everything seemed to be more intense in La Belle Province than they had been in New England.

One day we went to visit the massive Gothic Cathedral of Ste. Anne-de-Beaupré. The gray solidity of its mass dominated the surrounding land in much the same manner as its ancestors must have dominated the fields of medieval France. Inside the cathedral there were signs printed in French and English which forbade the use of cameras. There were also many photographers busily taking snapshots of the statue of Ste. Anne.

But the thing I recall most vividly is the enormous stone wall covered with casts, crutches, and various devices associated with illness. All of these things, we were told, had been discarded by people who had made the pilgrimage to the shrine of Ste. Anne, had prayed with devotion to the saint, and had sprinkled themselves with the holy water which was available there. I realized then that the purpose of the trip was not to see the red-jacketed Canadian soldiers in the Citadel or the Canada Dry bottling plant in downtown Quebec. The purpose of the trip was to find some means whereby I could get out of the terrible bind which polio had put me in. All my limbs and my trunk were paralyzed. Only my head could move. As my parents pushed my little hospital cot around the church, both of my eyes were filled with tears. To think that all of these strangers should be praying for me, that my parents should have gone through the trouble and expense of bringing us all up here and that this entire religious enterprise was directed towards people like me was more than I could bear. My mother asked me if I was all right. I nodded because I couldn't say anything. I knew that I did not deserve all of this love and energy. I knew that I was severely disabled and therefore of very little worth in the

world. I also knew that I would remain severely disabled for the rest of my life, miracles being few and far between.

Today, twenty-one years later, I am a reasonably happy, reasonably busy thirty-one-year-old student at the University of California at Berkeley. I am reaching the end of my junior year and will, with some grace and fortune, receive an A.B. in English at the end of 1981. My chief worries right now are whether I shall qualify for graduate school, which graduate school I shall enter, and what kind of work I shall do after I am finished with school. I still am as paralyzed as when I was a child. I still cannot sit up straight, turn my head to the left, or sleep outside of a respirator. But these problems no longer set me apart or mark me as a freak as they did when I was a child and an adolescent. The reasons for this change have more to do with the nature and the quality of society than they have to do with me. In particular, they have to do with how much responsibility a society will entrust to disabled people.

When I was a child, I had very little responsibility entrusted to me. That is the way it is with most of us. Liberal economist Dr. Paul Samuelson tried to counter the conservative slogan "There ain't no such thing as a free lunch" by asserting that we all received free lunches when we were children. But I am sure that Dr. Samuelson must have known, even as a child, that those lunches were not totally free, that he had to treat his parents with respect, be a good boy, and in all manner live up to the terms of the parent-child contract which had been imposed upon him at birth. At least, that's the way it was with me up until the time when I contracted polio. And for many years after.

A sharp, persistent pain in the gut kept me awake one night in September of 1955 when I was six years old. My parents telephoned the family doctor, who came over immediately and recommended that I should be taken to Boston Children's Hospital. I was to spend the next two years in hospitals, becoming well enough

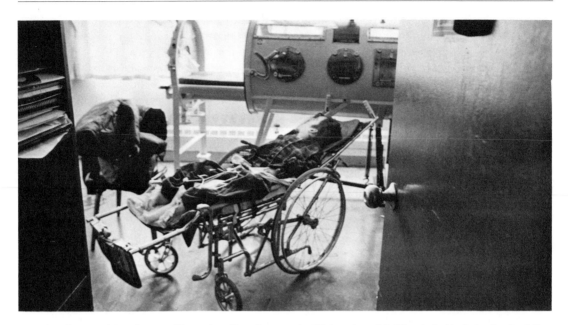

My iron lung and I took up residence in a dormitory at the University of California in Berkeley in the fall of 1978. I was told I'd be "on my own" here. I wasn't sure what that would mean. I was twenty-nine when I came to Berkeley. Until that time I had been a child of my parents, dependent on them at home, and a patient of doctors and nurses, dependent on them at hospitals.

That fall I hired attendants for the first time, including Christien Bagley, who pushed me to class. The state of California provides money for disabled people to hire attendants, something that turned out to be very important for me. It felt much better being an employer who hired attendants to *work* for me than being a patient who waited for nurses and others to *care* for me. The government spends considerably less when I live on my own and hire attendants for basic needs than it spent to keep me in a hospital. In the bargain, I also learn to control my life.

to be outside of a respirator but never regaining the use of my limbs. During this time I had to submit myself to the wills of the doctors, nurses, and therapists. This was a new kind of relationship to me because it demanded stricter obedience than my parents had expected and also because it involved very little love. For these two years I lived in terror of the tyrannical doctor and the short-tempered nurse. They controlled every aspect of my life and the only relief which I could find was in the visits of my family and the work of the hospital volunteers. I remember at one point pulling the sheet up with my tongue and my teeth so that it would cover my head. I was so frightened by my surroundings that I didn't want anyone to see me.

That is why I looked so eagerly ahead to the day when I would be discharged so that I could live with my family. My parents were provided with the equipment and the training they needed to take care of me at home. And life at home was pretty good; I can't complain. Of course, like every child, I had to do what my parents told me to do. But it was a lot easier than the hospital. I spent my days with my brother Ken and his friends watching them play the kind of games boys play. Sometimes my mother would push me on my little hospital cot to the vacant lot where the kids played baseball and football. I liked the arrangement and I did not want it to change. I did not want to go back to the hospital and I did not want my parents to get any older. My life had found a calm center and I just wanted it to stay there.

But it didn't. It couldn't. My family and I moved from Boston to Sacramento in 1966. I thought at first that things would remain pretty much the way they had been, but they did not. I studied at home on my own and received a high school equivalency degree in 1968, when I was eighteen, which was about the time that I began to notice that it was hurting my mother to lift me. To keep from hurting her, I began to spend more and more of my time in my room reading, watching television, and listening to the radio. Except for medical appointments, I never left. Mean-

while, my brother Ken was studying at Sacramento State College, participating in the debate team, traveling all around the country and winning trophies which covered a mantelpiece. I was not jealous of him; I could see, however, as I was getting deeper into my twenties, that life was passing me by. I could also see that the blistering Sacramento summers were taking a toll on my parents. The extent to which they worked in the heat frightened me.

I think that the day in May of 1976 when my brother graduated from a nearby law school was the time I finally became convinced that I had to get out, that I had to get away from home. My family went to the ceremonies and left me behind to read Aldous Huxley's *Doors of Perception*, listen to baseball games, and await their expected return around four o'clock. Having gotten wrapped up in the celebrations of the day, they did not get back till after seven, by which time my only desires were to urinate and go to sleep. That summer I prayed intensely to the Lord for some kind of release from this embarrassing and uncomfortable situation—from my physical dependence on my parents.

Meanwhile, without my knowing of it, my parents were working toward that end. They had read a story in the *Sacramento Bee* about the Physically Disabled Students Program (PDSP) of the University of California at Berkeley. My father contacted the local office of the California Department of Rehabilitation, but the people there were of little help. So he raised hell with the department at the state level and finally succeeded in getting an appointment to see Ed Roberts, the director of the Department of Rehabilitation. It was Ed and his mother, Zona, who launched me on the course which would take me to Berkeley. At that time, Zona Roberts was the director of the dormitory program at PDSP. She suggested that I should go into a hospital so that I could be physically rehabilitated before I entered Berkeley.

I did not think that this was possible. I thought that everything which could be done to improve my health had been done at Children's Hospital back in Boston. The day I left

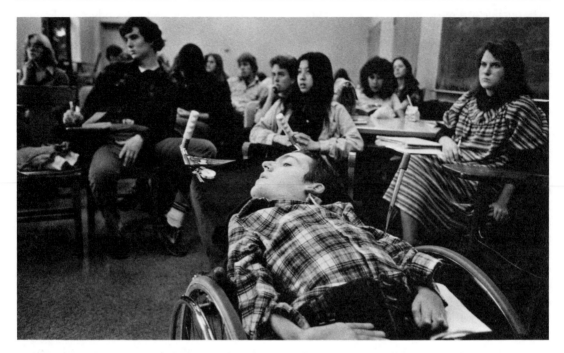

I enjoyed my classes, particularly those where ideas were discussed. Until I left home at age 27, I had virtually no contact with peers, except my brother. For the first year at the university, all I wanted to do was study. I didn't see the point of socializing.

home and went to Kaiser Hospital in Vallejo, California, was a sad one for me. I had never thought I would leave home. I was sad to leave my parents but I felt it was a necessary step toward finding a future of my own. I thought this might be a new start for me; maybe the people in Vallejo could help me.

Kaiser Hospital was entirely different from any hospital I have ever been in, before or since. The building was sleek and modern, the staff aggressive and hardworking. The thing which surprised me the most at the time was that they had developed a new form of physical therapy, proprioceptive neuromuscular facilitation (PNF), which seemed to have some effect on me. This form of therapy emphasizes avoidance of pain and the use of crushed ice to stimulate blood circulation. It is a radical break with earlier schools of physical therapy and seemed to be much more effective than other kinds. I felt stronger every day. But there were no obvious, measurable effects of this, except that I was able to stay up in my wheelchair for

two or three hours at a time, something I had never been able to do before.[1]

The other difference in this hospital was less obvious but perhaps more important. I was encouraged to take responsibility for keeping to a schedule which was attached to my wheelchair every morning. The schedule had a list of all my appointments with a space for the person who was supposed to sign. If I missed an appointment, the schedule would not get signed. This forced me to get rides to my appointments from every possible source, including even doctors. The therapists told me that if the nurses could not get me to therapy I was enti-

1. Kaiser Hospital is the only facility in the world that gives extensive training in PNF. They will refer prospective patients to the nearest available graduate. Write Kaiser Foundation Rehabilitation Center, Attn: Rehab PT, 975 Sereno Drive, Vallejo, California 94589. There is one book for PNF practitioners, very technical and difficult: *Proprioceptive Neuromuscular Facilitation* by Margaret Knott and Dorothy E. Voss; 1968, 2nd Edition; $30 postpaid from Harper and Row, Mail Order Department, 10 East 53rd Street, New York, New York 10022.

tled to yell at them. I was very busy at that place; each weekday I had two trips to physical therapy, one to occupational therapy, one to the teacher to whom I dictated some short stories, and a weekly visit to my social worker in her office. I don't know whether it was the PNF or the intensive activity which made me feel so exhilarated. All I knew was that I wanted to stay there.

One day the social worker (whom I shall call Brenda) took me outside in my newly acquired wheelchair. It was my first wheelchair; until then I had been on a hospital cot. She sat down on a bench and talked with me about my future. She said that I could not stay at Kaiser, that such a stay was not a part of the plan (whatever that was) and that I could make things a lot easier for her if I voluntarily went to Fairmont Hospital, a county long-term-care hospital. She said that it also had therapists trained in PNF, that it was either in or near Oakland, and that if I didn't like it I could ask the social worker at Fairmont to arrange transportation back to Kaiser. Contemplating Brenda's large brown eyes, I decided to make things easy for her. Besides how could I miss with a money-back guarantee like that?

It was stifling hot when the ambulance I was riding in pulled up in one of Fairmont's parking lots. I noticed that some of the windows in the buildings had air-conditioning units in them. For a Sacramentan, that was bad news. It meant that there was no central air-conditioning. But there was more bad news to come. The inside of Fairmont was dark and crowded, with walls painted in sickly, pale shades of green and yellow. The plumbing and the electrical wiring were on the outside of these walls, not neatly tucked away inside them.

When I got to my room, the ambulance attendants plopped me down upon a bed whose mattress was as soft as a marshmallow. The people at Kaiser had always preached the virtues of lying on hard surfaces to strengthen back muscles. Most of the room was to my left, so I couldn't see it. All I could see was an enormous yellow cylinder filled with com-

pressed air. The cylinder was attached with tubes to something in the bed next to me. I couldn't see the thing on the bed because it was covered over with a sheepskin. I could just see part of it slowly rising and falling. Occasionally, a nurse would come along and pour some brown liquid into another plastic tube which she would hold aloft like the Statue of Liberty. Later I found out that my neighbor was Michael Sipos, a bank officer whose brain had been injured in an automobile accident.

There was nothing to do except try to become accustomed to the heat and the lethargy of the place. There seemed to be *very* little happening. Patients talked about going to therapy maybe once or twice a week, not every day as I had done at Kaiser. The staff seemed to be about twice my age and rather spooky—interested primarily in furniture, their exhusbands, and their own ailments. All this I might have been able to endure were it not for the fact that some of the nurses were willing to dish out small bits of cruelty to show me who was boss. At my first opportunity I had someone take me to a telephone so that I could call my mother and beg her to call Brenda at Kaiser so that I could get out of that awful place. I am afraid that I upset my mother terribly and after that the nurses were more careful about taking me to the phone. A few days later the doctor for my ward told me flatly that there was no way that I could go back to Kaiser.

I don't know how I survived my first three months there. The two things which saved my sanity were California State University at Hayward, and a typewriter. My association with Cal State began in January of '77 with the beginning of winter quarter. Students were paid by the state to tape record the classes I had signed up for and to bring the tapes to the hospital. This way I got to meet Bay Area people who were not associated with the hospital.

When I was given an opportunity in the summer of '77 to attend some classes in person, I grabbed it without consulting any of the authorities at the hospital. I would take one or two classes on campus and one or two by tape at the hospital. Going out to Cal State reinforced my sense that something was wrong with the hospital. In class, the professors would treat me with deference as an interested, older student. After taking the fifteen-minute ride back to the hospital, I felt like Cinderella after midnight. Now I was something that had to be put to bed and fed. When one of my English professors talked about the schizophrenic lifestyle of Theresa Dunn, the protagonist of *Looking for Mr. Goodbar*, I told him that such a divided kind of life was familiar to me, that it was, in fact, the way I lived.

And in between classes there was the unstructured, lighthearted life of campus. I would usually be fed lunch by my attendant in the disorderly and boisterous atmosphere of the disabled-student center. The people there would talk about movies, parties, anything except the hospital. That was what I wanted, the illusion that I was free of the hospital.

The typewriter was something which my occupational therapist acquired for me in April of '77. It had a pair of microswitches which were placed above my chin. After my wheelchair and the switches had been positioned properly, I could operate the typewriter by hitting one switch with my chin. This would set off a series of high-pitched beeps which could be turned into low-pitched beeps by hitting one of the microswitches again. Every character on the keyboard was electronically associated with a certain pattern of beeps. In this way I could type out whatever I wanted, albeit rather slowly. And since the typewriter was downstairs in the occupational therapy department, it gave me an excuse to stay off the ward for most of the day.

Meanwhile, my physical rehabilitation was not coming about. I received physical therapy once a day, and although my therapist had been trained at Kaiser, she could not keep me going at the Kaiser pace because, under pressure from the chief of physical therapy, she had to cut back on my therapy. If I wasn't getting any better, Medi-Cal, the state health insur-

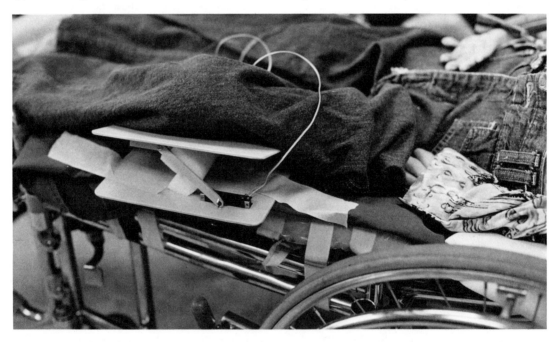

Of all the disabled people I knew in Berkeley, I was the only one who couldn't operate his own chair. I felt peer pressure for the first time. I hired an attendant to take me to Stanford University, where some rehabilitation engineers, over a period of a year, modified an electrically powered chair for me. To make the controls, they had to figure out what strength I had. I doubted whether they could make my meager strength useful. Except for moving my neck from front to right side, the only movement I have is in my left foot and my left knee.

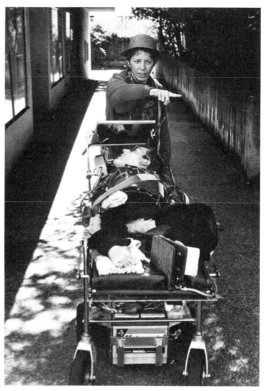

They tested several devices. One day, by raising and lowering my knee a very short distance, I was able to move a dot through an electronic maze. If that was possible, they said, I could move through the streets. But there were no cars or people in the maze.

ance program, would not pay for my therapy. I did feel better, but Medi-Cal's idea of "better" was that it should be possible to measure my progress in such terms as "can now raise arm; could not before." I just felt better, something that can't be measured.

So I spent the next two years concentrating on my studies, typing, and occasionally having pleasant chats with my physical therapist. After a year, near the end of a session of therapy, my physical therapist told me that she would not be able to work with me any more. She told me that if I were able to go to Berkeley and get an electric wheelchair it would probably be better for me than any therapy she could give me. As she left my bedside she patted me on the shoulder and I cried a little. I cried because I was losing a good friend and, at the same time, losing my last hope for physical rehabilitation.

My trips to the occupational therapy depart-

When I got my new chair, I had to learn to operate it. One of my attendants, Mary Lea, volunteered to be my driving instructor. We practiced in parking lots and then on the sidewalk in front of my apartment. Through a series of mirrors—a large one above my head and two fisheyes on my right side—I am able to see an area of nearly 360 degrees. But I had to learn to judge distance perspective, different in each mirror. At first, I was exhausted after only a few minutes of practice. What with me getting exhausted quickly and the chair breaking down, it took several months before I had enough skill and confidence to go on the street alone.

ment were my source of friendship and support. Shortly after I got the typewriter my occupational therapist, Linda Panikoff, looked at my typing and said, "I'm tired of seeing song lyrics. Why don't you do something creative? Write me a novel." So I wrote her a novel. At least I tried to. I also wrote letters, one of which, addressed to a doctor I knew at Kaiser, begged for readmission. When my social worker at Fairmont found out about this she became upset. But the vote of the Kaiser admissions committee had been close; I had almost been readmitted. It had been worth the effort.

Through all of this time I felt as if my life was being controlled by some external force, some mysterious "they" who wanted me to stay in Fairmont until I was "ready" for Berkeley. I had no burning desire to go to Berkeley; I liked Cal State a lot. But I gradually came to see that the only way I could get out of Fairmont was to gain admission to Berkeley. The doctor would only let me leave the hospital on the condition that I enter a situation which offered twenty-four-hour-a-day care. This is what the Berkeley dorms offered. I would live in my own dorm room and hire attendants, but there would be staff available through the night downstairs if I needed help. In June 1978, after a year and a half and three applications, I was finally accepted. The nurses were surprised. They didn't think that a person like me could live on my own. Even my doctor was surprised, but because the dorm program met his standards, he had no reasonable excuse to keep me out of it.

A brown van rolled into one of Fairmont's parking lots and took me away from that place. It took me fifteen miles to Davidson Hall, one of the UC dormitories. The trip was brief and pleasant. I felt like a prisoner who had just been released. My elation was tinged with a mistrust of the reality I was experiencing; something this good couldn't be happening to me. I could not believe it was actually happening until we parked outside the dorms. There were attendants there, two per shift. They didn't wear uniforms like nurses did and they told me that the dorms were not a medical facility. But still, I tried to evaluate the place the way I would evaluate a new hospital. I wanted to know which attendants were helpful and which were not.

I soon discovered, however, that this was beside the point. I was expected to hire my own attendants and to pay them with the money which the county gave to me. The attendants whom I hired treated me better than the nurses had because they worked for me and not some

institution. Because they worked for me I had to see to it that they were competent and reliable. I dreaded the day when I would have to fire one of my attendants. I didn't want to do that. But when one of them refused to come to work or even talk to me on the telephone, I fired him right away. But good attendants (and they were the majority) were a pleasure to work with. My morning attendant, Gifford Swanson, invited me over to his place for Thanksgiving dinner, and my school attendant, Mary Lea, performed so many acts of kindness for me that it is difficult for me to cite just one.

She also taught me how to drive my electric wheelchair, a task which required enormous patience and keen perception on her part. It was difficult because I had to navigate by looking in a mirror that was placed over my head. She couldn't see what I saw and couldn't see where the wheels of my wheelchair were. I controlled the direction of the chair with a lever under my left foot. To go sharply to the right I would push my foot down all the way. To go to the left I would take my foot off the lever. To control the speed of the chair I had a lever under my left knee. To make the chair go full speed I would lift my knee off the lever. To make it stop I would put my knee down on the lever. There were switches next to my chin which enabled me to put the wheelchair into reverse or to turn it off. It took me more than six months to learn how to drive the thing and more time to gain the confidence I needed to drive by myself. Her perception enabled her to imagine herself in my place and her patience enabled her to endure my rudeness and stupidity.

Because I was, for the first time in my life, essentially on my own, I had to learn how to run my own life. I had to take responsibility for maintaining my health, keeping track of my money, and battling the institutions which were designed to help me.

Stanford University was one of these institutions. They had contracted with the California Department of Rehabilitation to convert an electric wheelchair so that I could use it. For several months I made the fifty-mile trip to Stanford, expecting a chair I could drive. The

Now I "walk" alone. I take myself to class. It takes me longer to get anywhere than it takes a walking person. But I get there, and I get there when I want to get there. I hire no attendants now to move me from place to place. With each step in my independence, the government saves money.

Once I misjudged a curb. The chair toppled and I fell out of it, bruising my knee and my ego. I was scared, but I knew there was no turning back, that it was unacceptable not to power my own chair. I drove alone as soon as my knee healed. I recently learned that some strangers refer to me on campus as the guy who goes to class on his bed. And someone, describing my moving along alone, was quite sure that the chair was operated by remote control, that I couldn't be in control of it. I am.

trips were long and exhausting and very little progress seemed to come out of them. At one point, I grew impatient and telephoned one of the rehabilitation engineers at Stanford and asked him why things were going so slowly.

"Well, we're not sure you really want the chair," he answered blandly.

I was furious! For years I had been trying to get a workable electric wheelchair. And now these guys wanted me to beg them, pretty please, to give me the chair. I knew that I was a customer, that they were the merchants, and that I didn't have to put up with this kind of crap.

"Do I have to kiss your shoes?" I asked before I hung up. By this time I had stopped being a patient who accepted whatever was done or not done for me. I had become a person needing and buying services.

I knew that it was a difficult engineering project, designing and making a wheelchair for someone who couldn't move his arms or legs. I never understood the technicalities involved, but I was determined that they should not treat me as if I were a patient.

The day I finally took delivery of the chair was very exciting. I had to go to Stanford to get some final work done on it. When that was completed they told me that I could drive it on my own. I drove unsteadily into the reception area, afraid that I might hit a man in a wheelchair. When I somehow managed to miss him, doors were opened for me and I went down a curving path with adequate skill but overriding terror.

This was the way I continued to feel when I began learning how to drive with Mary Lea. I had never been responsible for my own personal safety before, at least not since I contracted polio. Now there would be no one around to help me if I made mistakes. All my mistakes would be my own. Mary Lea sensed my fear and suggested that I go on a series of extended trips by myself. On the Fourth of July she said that I should try to go to Shattuck Avenue and to the Center for Independent Living (CIL) by myself. I was afraid of going to Shattuck Avenue, even though it is only three blocks west of where I live. (By now I was no longer living in the dorms but had an apartment of my own.) I did not want to disappoint her, though. So I headed off for Shattuck Avenue.

It was a long trip on a narrow sidewalk with bushes and plants brushing against my wheelchair. There were strange buildings all around and I knew that it would be difficult to get any help here. I had to stop before I got to the next cross street because there was a hole in the sidewalk covered over with boards. There was also a sofa and miscellaneous bits of furniture cluttering up the sidewalk. I just had to sit and think about the situation for ten or fifteen minutes. Finally, I decided that there wasn't enough room to turn around, so I went straight backwards until I reached a driveway where I could turn around. That journey wore me out with fright and I went straight back to my apartment.

I rested for about a half an hour. Then, bored with my inactivity, I went off to the Center for Independent Living, which was only a block away, toward the east. As I crossed the broad expanse of Telegraph Avenue, I marveled at my power to bring cars and buses to a halt. I drove up on the parking lot of CIL and stayed there for about ten minutes. Because it was a holiday there was nobody working there, so I decided to go home. When I later told my mother about the events of that day, she called it my "Independence Day."

Another institution I had to deal with was UC Berkeley, which proved to be more tractable. I took just one course during the fall quarter, but two during the winter quarter, and three during the spring quarter. I spent all of my time studying, eating, or sleeping, but the grades I received never seemed to satisfy me. They were mostly Bs with a scattering of As and Cs to give the mix some dash. But going to school itself was fun. I got to move around, hear some interesting lectures, and meet some people. One of my classes was a seminar which included only eight students. I arrived in the classroom early one day and was by myself when two of the other students entered. They were involved in some silly dispute and when they began to argue about which of them "should go to the nuthouse first," they asked me to arbitrate the matter, hailing me as "Oh, model of rationality." I had seldom been referred to in such flattering terms. It was because of incidents like this that I gained the strong impression that I had taken control over my life and that I was doing something of value with it.

I sensed that other people understood this and respected me for it. And strange to tell, they began to treat me as if I were a human being. It's strange to tell because up until then people had made me feel as if I were something else, something less, something not capable of bearing personal responsibility. Because this society has, by unspoken agreement, defined a human being as someone who can bear the major responsibilities required for a self-directed life, I was not a human being. Nor are convicts, children, or retarded people regarded as such. But now that I have been given this responsibility and have proven that I can run my life as well as anybody else, I have been granted that degree of respect which is commonly accorded to a human being. When one of my attendants referred to me as "buddy" it thrilled me because I had not been accustomed to receiving that degree of respect. Such respect came as something of a surprise.

Another surprise which has come my way is that the federal government is cutting back on

In addition to getting around on my own, I know people now. Peers, the sociologist would say. Friends, I say. I'm just as likely as any other person to be going across campus and have someone call my name. One of my most important discoveries since being on my own is that I've discovered that people can like me. It's good being a human being.

the money needed to fund independent living projects. That means cutting back on disabled people being able to become human beings. These projects help people like myself get out of untenable positions of dependence in homes, hospitals, and nursing homes and into the world so that they may be full participants in it. The programs do this by providing the help needed to find a place to live. They provide the names, telephone numbers, and qualifications of attendants to the people who need such information. They provide a spectrum of services which include transportation, wheelchair repair, and career and academic counseling. In short, they provide all of the services which a disabled person *must* have available if he or she is to live independently.

Berkeley has more support services for dis-

abled people than any city I know of. But Berkeley cannot be expected to be a refugee camp for all of the disabled people in the United States. There must be independent living projects in other parts of the country so that disabled people can live, work, and study wherever they please. It is difficult to make the leap from hospital to university or from hospital to private apartment. Most communities have not expected disabled people to live on their own; they have expected them to remain dependent on aging parents or other relatives or to be institutionalized. Independent living projects can give these communities the chance to deal with disabled people in a more human and effective way.

A cutback of federal funding of independent-living-for-disabled-people centers will force state and local governments to spend more money on hospitals, welfare payments, and other debilitating dead-end programs that keep people alive but don't permit them to really live. Not only are these programs ineffective, but they also cost the public a great deal of money. My stay at the Fairmont cost over five thousand dollars a month. I didn't pay for it; taxpayers in general paid for it. The money I receive now that I am living on my own comes to only about one thousand dollars per month and I am living much better than I did at the Fairmont. Though my physical condition is the same now as then, I was a patient there, and a person who hires help here. Independent living not only helps disabled people, it also saves the public money.[2]

I have been told that many people in medicine and education are ignorant of the very concept of independent living for disabled people. They shouldn't be. It's essential. From my own experience I can say that once a person is forced to take responsibility for his own health, he will take better care of himself. This runs counter to the idea expressed by my doctor at the Fairmont: that disabled people should be placed in hospitals where they will be forever taken care of. They will certainly be taken care of, but they will not be taking care of themselves. And the act of taking care of oneself not only improves one's physical health, it also improves one's mental health. It even leads people to come to believe that they are human beings.

2. Community people trying to start independent living projects can write the Center for Independent Living, Senior Deputy Director Judy Heumann, 2539 Telegraph Avenue, Berkeley, California 94704. Disabled people looking for referrals to independent living projects in their areas can write the CIL Intake Department at the same address.

TOM PARSONS

Don't Beg: Take Control

Why and How to Hold Local Political Office

From the original introduction (Summer 1982):
"I could go on for several thousand words about the day-to-day of dealing with the fire department, city staff, neighbors, and the incredible wealth of unsuspected problems that goes with (elected) office," wrote Ridgefield, Washington, city council member Tom Parsons in a letter to the Fall 1981 CQ. "Yes please," replied Stewart Brand, and this tactical manifesto resulted.

Besides making decisions about sewer lines and subdivisions, Tom teaches chemistry, physics, photography, geometry, and sometimes biology at Ridgefield High School. . . . He's up for reelection at the end of 1983.

Art Kleiner

Tom didn't run for reelection at the end of 1983. Between this article's publication and then, three things happened. One fellow city council member was arrested for drug dealing and eventually acquitted on grounds of entrapment after a long, vicious trial. Another city council member—who had been a bitter opponent of Tom's on the drug issue (Tom wanted education, his opponent wanted a fund for paying-off informants and making drug buys)—was charged with murdering a woman whom people thought was his wife (it turned out she was actually his niece). Finally, the town suffered through a messy campaign to recall the mayor, which ultimately succeeded. Eventually, says Tom, "I got worn out with irrelevancies. There are so many other things to do with your life. It's a question of what kind of person you are and how much of that you can stand."

The article itself is still valid and valuable.

Art Kleiner

If I had known then what I know now. . .

How often have such thoughts crossed my mind, somewhere between rage and regret? Had I known more of Nixon, asked less of Humphrey, would I still have voted for Pat Paulsen in 1968? Would I have carried a sign and walked out of a Humphrey rally, a registered Democrat headed for the American Eagle Party?

Had I known in 1976 what I know now, would I have been content to win a floor debate with Ed Fischer at the Clark County, Washington, Democratic Convention? The issue was Washington's Initiative 325, our nuclear safeguards initiative. Ed was (and is) a member of our public utility district's board of directors. And he was chairman of the now-notorious Washington Public Power Supply System (WPPSS, pronounced *whoops*), sponsors of the state-wide nuclear power program.

I was the delegate from my precinct. We good guys had spent a lot of time gathering signatures to get 325 on the ballot. I had come to the convention prepared with a file of nuclear nuggets from *Science* and the wire services. Fires at the Rocky Flats Arsenal, deaths at Idaho Falls, New York's liability for a nuclear fuel reprocessing plant abandoned by Getty Oil . . . it was too much nuclear negligence for the genial salesman to counter or explain. We passed a resolution endorsing 325.

So what?

The initiative's opponents were Westinghouse, Bechtel, Babcock and Wilcox, Combustion Engineering, Puget Sound Power and Light, Exxon Nuclear. They outspent us twelve to one, outlied us ten to zero. We lost where it mattered—at the polls.

That was before Three Mile Island, before publicity about the Soviet nuclear disasters, before WPPSS ran up tens of billions of dollars of debt.

We now stand as deep in financial fallout as if we had stayed home or gone to a John Denver concert.

Ed Fischer, who was chairman of WPPSS as it slid toward bankruptcy, has recently been forced to resign. He says that he is not to be blamed, that he got bad advice from the experts. He has not admitted that he got *good* advice from those antinuclear nuts he said wanted to put us all back in the Stone Age. At least we can say "we told you so," like we said about the war in Vietnam and Richard Nixon and so on and so on. . . .

So what?

If we had known then what we know now, we would have been in office making the right decisions. Instead, we let everyone down. We made the mistake of being outsiders, of trying to mobilize the people behind our cause. We tried to educate the public.

But the power of the people is much overrated. True, it can topple governments. But it is a clumsy tool, difficult and dangerous to use, and we idealists tend to overestimate people's educability. Unless you can buy prime time at a hundred kilobucks a minute, several times a night, you won't get your message across.

There *are* other ways to attract attention, to get free air time. But if they worked, the Generals Electric, Motors, and Mills would be tossing bombs, staging rallies, and passing petitions to sell their products.

I wish I had known enough in 1976 to run against Ed Fischer, not just debate him. I know now what I didn't then, so I have been on the Ridgefield, Washington, City Council for two years now, making decisions.

About once a week I go to a council meeting. It is usually less than exciting, but at least I am on the right side of the table: the one where the decisions are made.

Local politics seldom makes headlines, but local politicians make lots of decisions.

As a sewer commissioner, you may decide how big that sewer line will be and where it will run. You thus determine which land will stay in farms, be subdivided, be industrialized. Knowing that Zonker's Uncle Duke got his start as a local sewer commissioner should be an inspiration to us all.

Here in Clark County, it was sewage problems that shut down the Forest Service's Mount Saint Helens Information Center and helped shoot down an airport wanted by the Federal Aviation Administration. Local authorities have thus twice in the past year overpowered agencies of the federal government.

As a member of a cemetery board, you decide whether to trim weeds or spray herbicide. You don't petition, you decide! How much should it cost to tie up forever a ten-by-fifteen-foot piece of good arable land as compared to storing ashes in a small crypt, shared by many? You decide. If you are willing to bother. So few of us seem to be.

Why do so few of us act as rationally and effectively to prevent government decay as we do to prevent tooth decay?

Perhaps we move too often to get involved with local issues. Perhaps we spent too long in the university as adolescents, being fashionably cynical. Perhaps we have fallen in love with the role of underdog, outsider. Maybe we are masochistic Cassandras, loving it, reading the news each day to find the next big "I told you so."

I hope not.

Worthwhile action *is* possible on the local level, the personal level.

Dan O'Neill seems to have learned and acted effectively. Back in 1970 his cartoon character Fred found through the "mush room" that "politics is poopadoodle." But his *Odd Bodkins* cartoon appeared and disappeared at the whim of Establishment editors. Dan learned and is now his own editor. Moral: Don't beg, take control. And if that means being a big frog in a small pond, well, there are a lot of us out here in these small ponds.

Here in Ridgefield, I ended the draft. We had an ordinance which set up a Director of Civil Defense and empowered him to "commandeer vital supplies for public use" and to "command the aid of as many citizens . . . as he considers necessary." When the governor would declare an emergency, as she did when the volcano blew, the CD's orders of impressment had the force of law. Our ordinance no longer reads *command* and *commandeer*, but *request*. Sure, we should all help out in an emergency. But *should* isn't the same as *should be required to by law*.

In 1974 I had to stand in front of a truck to stop the spraying of diesel oil and malathion on my block. Felt foolish. Last year I just made sure that Ridgefield did not contract for that "service." Much better.

Of course I do not act alone. There are four other councilmembers and a mayor. *It is vital to play politics.* But that does not have to mean something slimy. Here are some game rules:

First, **do your homework**. Be sure that you are right and can prove it. Most of your fellows will have been far too busy with their own issues to have studied yours. They will be happy to accept your view and vote your way.

Second, **approach them privately**. Nobody wants to be lectured and convinced in front of an audience. Don't lecture at all. Talk about the weather. Bounce your idea off them as "I've been thinking . . . ," and leave it tentative. Don't press for a commitment until they have had plenty of time to think it over. They may see it your way from the start, given a chance. Pressure invites resistance. There is always time to try a hard sell later. If they agree without pressure, you have not used up any political capital you may need for some less popular idea. If they simply see that you are right, you have gained status as a leader.*

Third, **don't bring something up at a public meeting unless you have** First and Second **taken care of**. Have the votes lined up ahead of time and minimize discussion. This may sound antidemocratic and Machiavellian, but there are just too many people who enjoy a fight for its own sake. You may have such among your fellow decision makers. The audience is sure to contain a few. You don't want a fight or a debate, you want results. Whip it past them before they figure it out. The sensible majority of your constituents will respect and thank you for it.

Fourth, **be on good terms with your local press**. In my experience this simply means being honest and accessible. Reporters are as idealistically dedicated to an underpaid job as you are. They are trustworthy until proven otherwise. You need each other. Besides, they are interesting and well-informed, fun to talk to.

Fifth, **use your voice judiciously**. The more you say, the less you will be heard. Pick your issues, let others have theirs.

Finally, **most important, speak no evil**. Your opponents may or may not have despica-

---

* While using the private approach, avoid two legal pitfalls. First, a quorum may gather for purposes other than a regular or special meeting, but must make no decisions, take no votes. To take action at an unannounced, nonpublic meeting is to violate the Open Meetings Act in Washington State. Other states have similar or stricter statutes.

Second, the appearance-of-fairness doctrine, based on case law, requires decision makers to bring an open mind to the meeting where decisions are made. The idea is sound: you should be open to argument from both sides. The practice is absurd: you may be elected for your strong position on dog control, then have to muzzle yourself so that your vote will not be challenged as prejudiced. According to our city council's lawyer, it's legally dangerous for a council member to express a strong opinion prior to a vote.

ble personal and political habits. It is irrelevant. If it is so, people will find out. They probably know already. Look for the best in even your nastiest opponents. Stick to the issue. These are your neighbors, not punching bags. There is such a thing as friendly disagreement. Keep it friendly, at least at your end. You'll sleep better. Personal remarks may *never* be forgotten or forgiven. You may be wrong. People change. So shut up and be nice. (Boy do I have a hard time with this. But it is important.)

Let's say you're convinced you want to be a decision maker but you don't know where to start.

Start with the local newspaper. Find the local political news. Follow it for a month or a year as religiously as most people follow the sports pages. Learn the issues. Learn the players' names and records. Go to meetings. Pick your favorite issues and arenas. Find out who is up for re-election and when. Will they run? Are they popular? Do they have heavy backing? Research newspaper files for their last campaign's strategy, opposition, margin of victory. Call city hall or the county clerk and find out the mechanics of running for office. Don't take it personally if you lose. Be prepared to lose and try again.

If you want to do a better job than is now being done, do it. You can. I have. You should.

ADMIRAL
HYMAN G. RICKOVER
U.S. NAVY, RETIRED

Doing a Job

man Polmar and Thomas B. Allen's new *Rickover (Controversy and Genius)* (1982, Simon & Schuster).

Stewart Brand

From the original introduction (Summer 1982):
Admiral Rickover, builder of America's nuclear submarines, has been much in the news of late for his pronouncements at a farewell hearing before the Joint Economic Committee of Congress. "We're spending too much on defense," he said. And "I do not believe that nuclear power is worth it if it creates radiation." And "The most important thing we could do is start in having an international meeting where we first outlaw nuclear weapons, then we outlaw nuclear reactors too."

Where did Rickover get the clout to build such machines and make such remarks? Primarily from a career of highly effective management. Recently reader John Willis sent us a copy of a speech that Rickover gave at the Columbia University School of Engineering last November 5. In it a lifetime of work experience is capsulized with astonishing economy. Here it is. For an unauthorized biography of the demon/saint, see Nor-

In 1929 I attended the Columbia School of Engineering for postgraduate study in electrical engineering. Columbia was the first institution that encouraged me to think rather than memorize. My teachers were notable in that many had gained practical engineering experience outside the university and were able to share their experience with their students. I am grateful, among others, to Professors Morecroft, Hehre, and Arendt. Much of what I have subsequently learned and accomplished in engineering is based on the solid foundation of principles I learned from them. I am therefore especially gratified by your invitation to return and speak this evening.

In 1939 I became head of the electrical section of the Bureau of Ships. In this capacity I was responsible for the design, manufacture, and operation of the electrical equipment for the Navy as it rapidly expanded throughout World War II. Since 1947, after a year studying nuclear engineering at Oak Ridge, Tennessee, I have been responsible for the research, design, construction, and operation of the nuclear reactors and the propulsion machinery of the Navy's nuclear-powered ships; also for the Shippingport, Pennsylvania, nuclear power station—the first commercial nuclear power plant.

Rickover during the 1960s on a return trip to the *USS Nautilus*, the first operating nuclear submarine he built.

In the course of my work, I have interviewed more than fourteen thousand recently graduated college students for jobs in my organization and in nuclear ships. In recent years a surprising number of applicants, even graduates of engineering schools and the Naval Academy, have become enamored with the study of management—some even majoring in this subject.

Almost without exception they are fluent in the jargon of systems analysis, financial manipulation, and quantitative management. They graduate convinced they have learned management techniques that will enable them to administer any job. Yet most seem to have an unrealistic perception of what is actually involved, with little appreciation of the importance of technical knowledge, experience, and hard work.

Many who teach management in our universities do their students and society a disservice. By focusing on the techniques of "modern management," they promote the idea that by mastering a few simple principles of how to handle people and situations one can become a universal manager: capable of running any job without having to know much about the work to be managed.

Our factories and companies are increasingly being bought, sold, and operated by professional administrators, lawyers, and financial experts who have little understanding of their products, the technology involved, or the needs of customers. As these professional "managers" reach top corporate positions, others emulate them and avoid technical education in favor of management studies. In my opinion, our universities should emphasize the importance of a solid grounding in substantive learning and downgrade so-called management science.

What it takes to do a job will not be learned from management courses. It is principally a matter of experience, the proper attitude, and common sense—none of which can be taught in a classroom.

After a lifetime of work I conclude that what can be said about doing a job is hardly enough for one lecture, let alone an entire field of study. The key points of such a lecture I would summarize as follows:

Human experience shows that people, not organizations or management systems, get things done. For this reason subordinates must be given authority and responsibility early in their careers. In this way they develop quickly and can help the manager do his work. The manager, of course, remains ultimately responsible and must accept the blame if subordinates make mistakes.

As subordinates develop, work should be constantly added so that no one can finish his job. This serves as a prod and a challenge. It brings out their capabilities and frees the manager to assume added responsibilities. As members of the organization become capable of assuming new and more difficult duties, they develop pride in doing the job well. This attitude soon permeates the entire organization.

One must permit his people the freedom to seek added work and greater responsibility. In my organization, there are no formal job descriptions or organization charts. Responsibilities are defined in a general way, so that people are not circumscribed. All are permitted to do as they think best and to go to anyone and anywhere for help. Each person then is limited only by his own ability.

Complex jobs cannot be accomplished effectively with transients. Therefore, a manager must make the work challenging and rewarding so that his people will remain with the organization for many years. This allows it to benefit fully from their knowledge, experience, and corporate memory.

The Defense Department does not recognize the need for continuity in important jobs. It rotates officers every few years both at headquarters and in the field. The same applies to their civilian superiors.

This system virtually ensures inexperience and nonaccountability. By the time an officer has begun to learn a job, it is time for him to rotate. Under this system, incumbents can blame their problems on predecessors. They are assigned to another job before the results of their work become evident. Subordinates cannot be expected to remain committed to a job and perform effectively when they are continuously adapting to a new job or to a new boss.

When doing a job—any job—one must feel that he *owns* it, and act as though he will remain in that job forever. He must look after his work just as conscientiously, as though it were his own business and his own money. If he feels he is only a temporary custodian, or that the job is just a stepping stone to a higher position, his actions will not take into account the long-term interests of the organization. His lack of commitment to the present job will be perceived by those who work for him, and they, likewise, will tend not to care. Too many spend their entire working lives looking for the next job. When one feels he owns his present job and acts that way, he need have no concern about his next job.

In accepting responsibility for a job, a person must get directly involved. Every manager has a personal responsibility not only to find problems but to correct them. This responsi-

bility comes before all other obligations, before personal ambition or comfort.

A major flaw in our system of government, and even in industry, is the latitude allowed to do less than is necessary. Too often officials are willing to accept and adapt to situations they know to be wrong. The tendency is to downplay problems instead of actively trying to correct them. Recognizing this, many subordinates give up, contain their views within themselves, and wait for others to take action. When this happens, the manager is deprived of the experience and ideas of subordinates who generally are more knowledgeable than he in their particular areas.

A manager must instill in his people an attitude of personal responsibility for seeing a job properly accomplished. Unfortunately, this seems to be declining, particularly in large organizations where responsibility is broadly distributed. To complaints of a job poorly done, one often hears the excuse "I am not responsible." I believe that is literally correct. The man who takes such a stand in fact is not *responsible*; he is *irresponsible*. While he may not be legally liable, or the work may not have been specifically assigned to him, no one involved in a job can divest himself of responsibility for its successful completion.

Unless the individual truly responsible can be identified when something goes wrong, no one has really been responsible. With the advent of modern management theories it is becoming common for organizations to deal with problems in a collective manner, by dividing programs into subprograms, with no one left responsible for the entire effort. There is also the tendency to establish more and more levels of management, on the theory that this gives better control. These are but different forms of shared responsibility, which easily lead to no one being responsible—a problem that often inheres in large corporations as well as in the Defense Department.

When I came to Washington before World War II to head the electrical section of the Bureau of Ships, I found that one man was in charge of design, another of production, a third handled maintenance, while a fourth dealt with fiscal matters. The entire bureau operated that way. It didn't make sense to me. Design problems showed up in production, production errors showed up in maintenance, and financial matters reached into all areas. I changed the system. I made one man responsible for his entire area of equipment—for design, production, maintenance, and contracting. If anything went wrong, I knew exactly at whom to point. I run my present organization on the same principle.

A good manager must have unshakable determination and tenacity. Deciding what needs to be done is easy, getting it done is more difficult. Good ideas are not adopted automatically. They must be driven into practice with courageous impatience. Once implemented they can be easily overturned or subverted through apathy or lack of follow-up, so a continuous effort is required. Too often, important problems are recognized but no one is willing to sustain the effort needed to solve them.

Nothing worthwhile can be accomplished without determination. In the early days of nuclear power, for example, getting approval to build the first nuclear submarine—the *Nautilus*—was almost as difficult as designing and building it. Many in the Navy opposed building a nuclear submarine.

In the same way, the Navy once viewed nuclear-powered aircraft carriers and cruisers as too expensive, despite their obvious advantages of unlimited cruising range and ability to remain at sea without vulnerable support ships. Yet today our nuclear submarine fleet is widely recognized as our nation's most effective deterrent to nuclear war. Our nuclear-powered aircraft carriers and cruisers have proven their worth by defending our interests all over the world—even in remote trouble spots such as the Indian Ocean, where the capability of oil-fired ships would be severely limited by their dependence on fuel supplies.

The man in charge must concern himself with details. If he does not consider them important, neither will his subordinates. Yet "the devil is in the details." It is hard and monotonous to pay attention to seemingly minor matters. In my work I probably spend about

Columbia Engineering Alumni Times

Rickover giving this speech at Columbia University

ninety-nine percent of my time on what others may call petty details. Most managers would rather focus on lofty policy matters. But when the details are ignored, the project fails. No infusion of policy or lofty ideals can then correct the situation.

To maintain proper control one must have simple and direct means to find out what is going on. There are many ways of doing this; all involve constant drudgery. For this reason those in charge often create "management information systems" designed to extract from the operation the details a busy executive needs to know. Often the process is carried too far. The top official then loses touch with his people and with the work that is actually going on.

Attention to detail does not require a manager to do everything himself. No one can work more than twenty-four hours each day. Therefore, to multiply his efforts, he must create an environment where his subordinates can work to their maximum ability. Some management experts advocate strict limits to the number of people reporting to a common superior—generally five to seven. But if one has capable people who require but a few moments of his time during the day, there is no reason to set such arbitrary constraints. Some forty key people report frequently and directly to me. This enables me to keep up with what is going on and makes it possible for them to get fast action. The latter aspect is particularly important. Capable people will not work for long where they cannot get prompt decisions and actions from their superior.

I require frequent reports, both oral and written, from many key people in the nuclear program. These include the commanding officers of our nuclear ships, those in charge of our schools and laboratories, and representatives at manufacturers' plants and commercial shipyards. I insist they report the problems they have found directly to me—and in plain English. This provides them unlimited flexibility in subject matter—something that often is not accommodated in highly structured management systems—and a way to communicate their problems and recommendations to me without having them filtered through others. The Defense Department, with its excessive layers of management, suffers because those at the top who make the decisions are generally isolated from their subordinates, who have the firsthand knowledge.

To do a job effectively, one must set priorities. Too many people let their "in" basket set the priorities. On any given day, unimportant but interesting trivia pass through an office; one must not permit these to monopolize his time. The human tendency is to while away time with unimportant matters that do not require mental effort or energy. Since they can be easily resolved, they give a false sense of accomplishment. The manager must exert self-discipline to ensure that his energy is focused where it is truly needed.

All work should be checked through an independent and impartial review. In engineering and manufacturing, industry spends large sums on quality control. But the concept of impartial reviews and oversight is important in other areas also. Even the most dedicated individual makes mistakes—and many workers are less than dedicated. I have seen much poor work and sheer nonsense generated in government and in industry because it was not checked properly.

One must create the ability in his staff to generate clear, forceful arguments for opposing viewpoints as well as for their own. Open discussions and disagreements must be encour-

aged, so that all sides of an issue will be fully explored. Further, important issues should be presented in writing. Nothing so sharpens the thought process as writing down one's arguments. Weaknesses overlooked in oral discussion become painfully obvious on the written page.

When important decisions are not documented, one becomes dependent on individual memory, which is quickly lost as people leave or move to other jobs. In my work, it is important to be able to go back a number of years to determine the facts that were considered in arriving at a decision. This makes it easier to resolve new problems by putting them into proper perspective. It also minimizes the risk of repeating past mistakes. Moreover, if important communications and actions are not documented clearly, one can never be sure they were understood or even executed.

It is a human inclination to hope things will work out, despite evidence or doubt to the contrary. A successful manager must resist this temptation. This is particularly hard if one has invested much time and energy on a project and thus has come to feel possessive about it. Although it is not easy to admit what a person once thought correct now appears to be wrong, one must discipline himself to face the facts objectively and make the necessary changes—regardless of the consequences to himself. The man in charge must personally set the example in this respect. He must be able, in effect, to "kill his own child" if necessary and must require his subordinates to do likewise. I have had to go to Congress and, because of technical problems, recommend terminating a project that had been funded largely on my say-so. It is not a pleasant task, but one must be brutally objective in his work.

No management system can substitute for hard work. A manager who does not work hard or devote extra effort cannot expect his people to do so. He must set the example. The manager may not be the smartest or most knowledgeable person, but if he dedicates himself to the job and devotes the required effort, his people will follow his lead.

The ideas I have mentioned are not new—

previous generations recognized the value of hard work, attention to detail, personal responsibility, and determination. And these, rather than the highly-touted modern management techniques, are still the qualities most important in doing a job. Together they embody a common-sense approach to management, one that cannot be taught by professors of management in a classroom.

I am not against business education. A knowledge of accounting, finance, business law, and the like can be of value in a business environment. What I do believe is harmful is the impression often created by those who teach management that one will be able to manage any job simply by applying certain management techniques together with some simple academic rules of how to manage people and situations.

There is concern today over the apparent decline in United States productivity. In searching for its causes we should not overlook the impact of the many professional administrators who run large corporations. Though trained in management at our leading universities, they are often unskilled in the technical aspects of the company. As a result they manage largely in the terms they learned at school. Technical, operational, and production issues are quickly reduced to issues of numbers and dollars, upon which these administrators apply their management techniques. Although in this way they may achieve financial benefits, an overemphasis on short-term profits often ignores broader issues such as efficient production or planning for the future. How can they act otherwise, when they have knowledge only of management theories learned in school?

Universities must accept their share of the blame for this situation. They have played a key role in promoting so-called management science, often at the expense of more substantive topics such as engineering. If students are the country's future, how can we justify this waste of their talent?

The students of today attend college, as I did over fifty years ago, to lay the groundwork for the expertise they will develop only after years of experience in their field. It is the obligation of Columbia University, as it is of all colleges, to seek to provide them a solid basis upon which to build their careers—one that is realistic and practical. We would be far better off graduating fewer technically capable young men with realistic ideas of what it actually takes to do their work, than to graduate a larger number highly skilled in the techniques of so-called management yet incapable of doing a job.

MICHAEL KIMBALL

On Farting

With this article, published Summer
1982, Mike Kimball established himself as one of the world's foremost
authorities on farts. An elementary
school music-teacher near Augusta,
Maine, he devoted four months of
his spare time to research on flatulence after sniffing in vain around the
local library. Need I say that this is
one of the most beloved articles,
judging by reader mail, in CQ history? Another taboo busted, I
guess. . . .

Art Kleiner

Everyody farts. And from primordial man, or
at least since the Garden of Eden Caper, everybody has always farted—and, most likely, we
will all fart forever. Nobody doesn't fart, *n'est-
ce pas?*

Why, then, when I began researching this
article, did I find so squeaking-little published
on the subject? Virtually nothing in the English language has been penned concerning the
fart. In fact, this little piece you're reading is
a strong candidate for the definitive modern
work on intestinal gas and its socio-scientific
place in the world.

Do you realize there isn't even an accepted
verb for farting? *Fart*, itself, is considered vul-
gar and unacceptable by our dictionaries. *Flatu-*

lence, an acceptable noun, is defined: "The
presence of excessive gas in the digestive
tract." But who cares about it, really, when it's
still in the body? The word *flatulent* is an ad-
jective describing the condition of having excessive gas in the digestive tract. *Flatus*, gas
generated in the stomach or intestine, is another noun.

Hey, everybody knows that at some point in
its short life *fart* is a verb—we average American males prove that about 14 times every day.
Even polite terms like *pass gas* or *break wind*
didn't make it into my dictionary.

Could it be that we average Americans are
simply not supposed to talk about it? But,
surely, you must be thinking, someone must
have to talk about it sometime. Like doctors,
for instance; what do they say? Well, here's an
excerpt from a letter defending the word *fart*,
a breath of fresh air as it were, written by a Dr.
Robert J. L. Waugh to the *New England Journal
of Medicine*: ". . . such awkward phrases as
passed flatus or *excreted gas* are always used instead of *farted*. And a *fart*—as a noun—can be
visualized on X-ray."

And Dr. W. C. Watson from Ontario, Canada, in another letter to the *NEJM*, carried the
ball even further:

"This letter makes it official. The word *fart*
was used factually, without embarrassment, at
1310 hours on Wednesday, May 17, in Lecture
Room B, University Hospital, during a lecture
to the second year medical class on 'Gaseous-
ness.' . . . The students have been encouraged
to use it freely where clinically appropriate.

I hope that all other clinicians, men of
honor and upright standing, will follow this
lead. A spark has been struck; a torch has been
lit. . . ."

And so on.

Not surprisingly, these emotional appeals spurred a wave of reaction from others in the medical profession, would-be etymologists who weren't quite ready to accept the verb/noun *fart*. One suggestion for a better verb was *crepitate*. Now, *crepitate* means, literally, "a creaking or rattling sound," and may be fitting, albeit condescending, for older folks; but it's certainly not the universal verb we need. How about *exogust*? Actually, that's not a bad noun, but it makes a fairly awkward verb. *Boomerate*? A good British-type verb for a certain genre of fart, but overstated in most cases. A logical entry was *flatulate*; the only drawback is the pomposity of its three syllables (or four, as in, "Who flatulated?"). Another one was *B.M. Burp*. I hate that one. It's lewd and it's tasteless. *Exmeteorate*? Sounds like what Jor-El used to do before Krypton exploded. Then there was gaseous intestinal discharges, and an entry from the Harvard Medical School for *deflate* as both "pleasing to the ear and etymologically satisfying." Not bad, but we might stop and consider the reputations of balloons and tires. And, finally, someone humorously suggested the term *flatus advance by rectal transport*, or its acronym, FART.

Fart, for me, says it all. It's derived from the Greek word *perdix*, meaning partridge, a bird that makes a sharp, whirring sound when flushed. The root, *perd*, easily changed to *pherd*, then to the more staccato Germanic *fertan*, then to *fartan* in Old English, and finally to its present refinement, *fart*.

Fart is unpretentious, simple, and above all, onomatopoetically right on target—especially here in New England, where a dialectal pronunciation is closer to *faaht*, which is pretty darn close to the real sound (a little off target west of the Mississippi, though; not even native Californians roll the R when they farrt). The dead bull's-eye, onomatopoetically speaking, of course, is the children's word *poop*, from the noun *poopyhorn* (that's poŏpēhôrn). This is easily demonstrated by tightly pursing the lips and expelling a short burst of wind through them. Society, however, chooses to leave *poop* behind in the nursery of babywords such as

Joseph Pujol, also known as Le Petomane, photographed at Moulin Rouge.

doo-doo, pee-pee, bum-bum, taa-taa, nay-nay, and *mousie-with-(or without)-the-hat*.

Fart also tops all other countries in onomatopoetics. In Russia, you don't fart, or even poop. You захмёстыватькормý, and if that's onomatopoetically satisfying, it must be physically jarring. In Germany you *furz*; in Sweden, *väderspänd*. A fart in Italy is *flato*; in Greece, φαρτ. In Paris, they *pet*, a neat little verb, when you think about it—*pet*—well fitted to the cosmopolitan Parisian and to the villager alike.

It's no surprise, really, that France would be right up there contending in fart linguistics. After all, she gave the world Le Petomane, the greatest exponent of the "pet" that ever lived. Le Petomane (his real name was Joseph Pujol) rose to fame and fortune on the stage of the Moulin Rouge in late nineteenth-century

Paris, where at the height of his unusual career he was earning more than double the box office of his celebrated contemporary, Sarah Bernhardt. Pujol's remarkable talent was his ability to inhale and exhale fresh air through his anus, an odorless performance of music, mimicry, and other dubious feats such as blowing out candles from two feet away. (Naturally, if his gusts were gaseous, he would have torched the people in the good seats.)

Decked out in a red coat, white bow tie, and gloves, and sporting black satin breeches, Pujol's most popular routines were his amazing imitations: "This one . . . a little girl; this . . . the mother-in-law; this . . . the bride on her wedding night; this . . . the dressmaker tearing two yards of calico" (a ten-second rip that was reportedly an uncanny imitation). Other standards in his popular routine were, of course, the sounds of thunder and ("Gunners, stand by your guns! Ready—fire!") cannons.

Le Petomane notwithstanding, humans have taken remarkably few strides through the ages in understanding, let alone accepting, the fart. Way back in 400 B.C. Hippocrates wrote in his *Book of Prognostics*: "It is best when wind passes without noise, but it is better that flatulence should pass even thus than it should be retained; and when a man does pass thus, it indicates either that the man is in pain or in delirium, unless he gives vent to the wind spontaneously." Delirium? Perhaps that is why, even two thousand years later, proper Victorian ladies would swoon dramatically if an audible fart sneaked out past the rustling of their bustles.

Insanity and drunkenness have also been singled out. In Chaucer's *Canterbury Tales*, the Miller claims, "First, I want to declare that I am drunk; I know it from the noise I'm making. . . ." And in 1577 another Englishman, Hugh Rhode, wrote in his *Booke of Nurture and Schoole of Goode Manners*:

"Be not lowde where you be, nor at the table where you syt; Some men will deeme thee dronken, mad, or else to lack thy wit."

Inevitably, the lowly fart became the object of breezy underground satire. In 1722, in the

Fart-lighting can be an enjoyable pastime, but only when proper safety precautions are taken. Safety glasses and a fire extinguisher are two essential safeguards.

tenth edition of an anonymous author's pamphlet, *The Benefit of Farting Explained*, was printed, "Wrote in Spanish by Don Fart in Hando translated into English by Obadiah Fizle." And Mark Twain, in 1890, wrote a privately printed parody which was dubbed by fans "A Fart in Queen Elizabeth's Court."

The eighteenth and nineteenth centuries, indeed, proved dark years for the fart, knocking it down the social ladder to the bottom rungs of acceptance. It had become the object of street slang and derision. A parasite was now called a fart-sucker; one's footman or valet, his fart-catcher. Trousers were your farting crackers. In Ireland, your jaunting car was a farting-trap, probably a sly dig at the horse that pulled it. And if the horse became restless and began walking in circles, he was "like a fart in a colander"—that is, until the latter part of the nineteenth century; then he was "like a fart in a bottle." If you "couldn't trust your arse with a fart" you had diarrhea, same as if you "let a brewer's fart, grains and all."

Needless to say, farting has always been a condition of the working class. Even today the blue-collar fart is far more commonplace than the white-collar fart. Take television, for example. When Edith Bunker mistakes the popping of a champagne bottle for an Archie fart, the audience erupts in unbridled laughter. He never really does fart, but just the mention, the very allowance that the fart probably exists in the Bunker household is a radical kick in the funnybone for situation comedy—but, in Archie Bunker's case, it's believable. On the other hand, could you imagine his contemporary, Tom Bradford, *Eight Is Enough*'s dad, cutting loose with a TV fart? Or how about TV's comic doctors? Any of them—even the irreverant Trapper John or Hawkeye Pierce. No, it's much easier to envision a fart on *Taxi* than on *Dallas*.

It is a socioeconomic prejudice that we're pretty much all guilty of, and if you think you're not, read the following two dialogues and see if either sounds more plausible to you:

"Hi . . . uh, excuse me . . . uh, is my car ready yet?"

"Whaddaya want?"

"Have you finished on my car yet? The Toyota there."

"Nope. 'Nother hour or so. She needs (*pfaahp*) a new diaphragm."

"Okay. Sorry for the interruption. I'll be back at three."

Or, how about this exchange:

"Yes, er, Mr. Kimball. Have a seat, please."

"Thank you."

"Now, let's see, you've applied to us for a collateral loan of two thousand dollars, is that right?"

"Yes, that's right."

"Well, we've checked your credit references and I don't see any complications. All we need from you (*pfaaahp*) is a signature here and right (*pfaaahp*) here. Very good."

"Okay. Thank you very much."

It wasn't until 1976 that serious attention was finally given to the fart. In Minneapolis, a Dr. Michael D. Levitt, professor of medicine at the University of Minnesota Hospital and Associate Chief of Research at the Minneapolis Veterans Administration Hospital (and probably the world's leading authority on the fart), was contacted by a twenty-eight-year-old man who complained that his excessive gas was ruining his sex and social lives. Dr. Levitt and his associates took the man's case and in the process of treating him made several important observations concerning the fart, which they detailed in a paper entitled "Studies of a Flatulent Patient" (*New England Journal of Medicine*, July 29, 1976).

In the article, the doctors pointed out that the fart is composed of five gases: hydrogen, carbon dioxide, methane (methane is inexplicably produced by only a third of the population, and it is this lucky group that has floating feces), and smaller amounts of oxygen and nitrogen. The oxygen and nitrogen accumulate in the intestines when air is swallowed, while hydogen, carbon dioxide, and methane are produced in the large intestine as the body's last resort in its digestive process. Explains Dr. Levitt, "The job of the small intestine is to absorb anything nutritional from foods. The large intestine, on the other hand, contains a large mass of bacteria that ferments the undigested food, producing gas." Undigested foods, in most cases, are complicated sugars that cannot be absorbed by the small intestine, such as the sugars found in cabbage, radishes, and apples; it is the bacteriological breakdown of these sugars in the large intestine which produces gas, giving us the fart, with all its thrust and characteristic odor.

The doctors found further that the average twenty-eight-year-old man farts 14 (plus or minus 5.6) times a day, quite a bit less than the unfortunate man who originally contacted Dr. Levitt. By his own flatographic estimates, he had been averaging 35 farts daily for two years. Dr. Levitt performed a flatoanalysis of the man's gas and found that it was 70 percent hydrogen, indicating intraluminal production (that is, produced by the bacteria in the lower

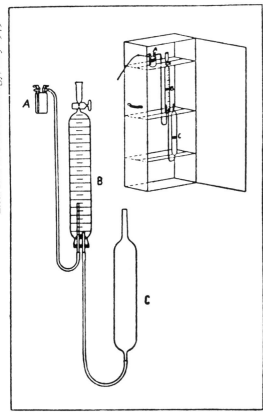

Esben Kirk in Gastroenterology, May 1949

Apparatus used in the late Forties by a doctor in St. Louis to collect farts as bubbles in water. After an enema, water is pumped through a rubber tube into a flask (A) with a cadmium acetate solution to absorb the gas. The gas is transferred to a calcium chloride solution in a graduated chamber (B) and measured by adjusting the solution's level against the solution in the leveling bulb (C). The flatus is analyzed chemically later.

intestine). Sugar was the suspect, specifically the lactose found in milk. So, to test that suspicion, the patient was ordered to drink nothing but milk for two days. Sure enough, on the second day he nearly exploded, farting an incredible 141 times, including a four-hour roll of 70 blasts, a probable world record!

Bizarre as it may seem, surgical patients with gas actually run the risk of exploding. Anyone who has ever struck a match to a fart can testify to its flammable properties, but when the gas is hydrogen, trapped in an intes-

tine, look out. Dr. Levitt tells of a surgeon who was cauterizing a rectal polyp on a patient when a spark touched off the patient's intestinal gas. The explosion blew the doctor backward into the wall, jammed the patient's head into the table, and ripped open six inches of his colon. Fortunately, the doctor recovered and the patient survived.

You may ask, why do I fart more than my neighbor? Certainly the food you eat and the way you eat it are the two major contributors to farting. If you are an air swallower—if you gulp your food and drink, or take a breath before each swallow, or if you drink from a bottle—you will fart more. Carbonation and chewing gum will also put more air into the fart, hence, more fart into the air.

The lactose in milk can cause lots of gas in people without enough of the enzyme lactase to break it down. Other foods which are known gas producers are bran, onions, cucumbers, raisins, cauliflower, lettuce, coffee, and dark beer. And, of course, the infamous baked bean, which contains the indigestible sugars called trisaccharides.

Look, if you really want a fartless bean, all you have to do is remove the trisaccharides. Simply soak the beans for at least three hours and drain off the water before cooking. That'll do it, mostly, but for extra-fart-free beans, keep changing the water the beans are boiling in. The only problem with this method is that along with removing the gas, you will also be removing some nutrients. The *Daily Planet Almanac* suggests that you then add a little brewer's yeast to replace the nutrients.

But why do all that to the baked beans in the first place? Everybody farts, right? Brooke Shields farts. Tonto farts. Mr. Rogers farts. Donny and Marie fart. Even swans fart. I think. I wrote to Dr. Levitt in Minneapolis and asked him if swans did, in fact, fart. He wrote back and said he had a one-million-dollar National Institute of Health grant pending to study exactly that problem. The point is, why the secrecy? Why the taboo? Why does society officially not believe in farts? Why, for heaven's sake, in Emily Post's *Etiquette*, is there never even a mention of passing gas?

Centuries ago, actually in 1460, a similar etiquette manual was published in England, and one chapter, "A Lytyl Reporte of How Young People Should Behave," addressed the subject quite matter-of-factly, without embarrassment: ". . . look into the lord's face; keep hand and foot still; don't spit or snot; break wind quietly . . ."

A century later in the *Booke of Nurture and Schoole of Good Manners*, Hugh Rhode instructed for more abstinence: "Don't stare about or wag your head, scratch it, or put your fingers in your mouth. Don't look at what comes out of your nose, or break wind."

John Russell, in his *Booke of Nurture—Symple Condicions: How to Behave*, admonished more bluntly, and metaphorically: "Don't pick your teeth, cast stinking breath on your lord, fire your sternguns, or expose your codware."

Later, in 1619, Richard Weste took a bold progressive step in his book, *The Schoole of Virtue*, when he suggested that farting may actually be healthy.

> Retaine not urine nor the winde
> which doth thy body vex,
> So it be done with secresie, let that not thee
> perplex.

Sadly, though, just as it seemed that protocol was about to look more favorably on the fart, it was banished. In 1825 *fart* was abruptly dropped from the *Footman's Dictionary* in England, the strategy being, of course, that if nobody called it by name, it would go away. Still, I think it's safe to assume that even future moral-whip Queen of the Empire, Victoria, then only six years old, managed to rip off her daily allotment of royal stinkers—and a century later, so did Emily Post! But in 880 pages of her modern journal of social decorum, she wouldn't breathe of the fart's existence. (God knows a runny nose was appalling enough to the lady: "Don't apologize and thus call unnecessary attention to anything so unpleasant as having to blow your nose at the table," she wrote. "The only thing to do is to end it as quickly as possible." Evidently, if you also ac-

cidentally farted at the table, you simply took a sip of Chardonnay and continued eating.)

It would have been an easy enough task for her to offer some rules for flatulence; simply by taking a cue from Steve ("Mind if I smoke? No, mind if I fart?") Martin, and substituting *fart* for *smoke* (or *cigarette*) in Chapter 64 of *Etiquette*, "For Those Who Smoke" becomes a workable code of gastric behavior. For example:

FOR THOSE WHO FART

· One may not fart in a church, or during any religious service or ceremonial proceedings.
· One may not fart in a sickroom unless the patient himself is farting or unless he specifically says his visitor is welcome to fart.
· Good taste still forbids farting by a woman on a city street. It should be unnecessary to say that no one should think of farting or lighting a fart when dancing.
· Farting is forbidden on local buses and on some coaches on the railroad. These cars are clearly marked "No Farting."
· Farting is permitted in the mezzanine or loge seats in some movie houses, but never in the main orchestra.
· Farting is forbidden in most museums, although some have designated areas where it is allowed.
· Legitimate theaters do not allow farting in the theater proper. It is usually allowed in the outer lobby, and those who wish to fart during the intermission go there to do so. It is perfectly correct for a man who wishes to fart to leave a lady who doesn't, but he should hurry back, and not leave her too frequently.
· In private situations when there may be some objection before lighting your fart, always ask, "Do you mind if I fart?" If there is any hesitation in the reply, do your best to refrain from farting until you leave.
· A man should light a woman's fart if he is close to her, but not if he is on the other side of the table or if it would be awkward in any way.

Not bad. Aside from the obvious gender double-standard, pretty sensible advice, wouldn't you say? Too bad she missed the boat. Well, I didn't. We're in the Eighties now, a time of radical conformity, and it's high time the people had a little farting etiquette, so here it is. Cut this section out and tape it to your refrigerator, 'cause it's official—and it's modern!

A WHOLISTIC APPROACH TO ANAL-GASTRO-SOCIAL SYSTEMS

1 *Fart* is an acceptable verb and noun.
2 It is generally appropriate to fart in the presence of one's friends and/or immediate family, so long as the area is ventilated.
3 When in the company of those other than close friends or family, simply move to an open, ventilated part of the room, fart, and say, "Excuse me" or, if you prefer, "Canadian geese."

Never fan the fart back at the others unless specifically asked to do so.
4 It is often unnecessary to comment on the volume, timbre, pitch, or olfactory strength of your fart unless someone else comments first.
5 There is little to be said for the rascal who farts in close proximity to an infant emerging from the womb or a person on his deathbed.
6 It is seldom necessary to fart into the telephone.

DAN O'NEILL

A Friend to the Children

Dan O'Neill's "comics and stories"
occupied at least four pages in every
CQ between 1975 and 1982. Once
they cost CQ $10,000 in legal fees,
thanks to a copyright-violation suit
with Walt Disney, Inc. (See the History Appendix for more on that.)
This one, which ran in the Fall 1982
issue, is often regarded as his best CQ
work, although there were several
close runners-up. He may be the single spookiest cartoonist in the history of the medium. Dan now draws
a weekly feature for the *San Francisco
Chronicle* "Punch" section.

Art Kleiner

Dan O'Neill

260

J. BALDWIN

Born to Fail

J. Baldwin has succeeded-by-failing at more enterprises and projects than any other human being I know.

Here's part of Stewart Brand's introduction to the 1978 CQ book *Soft Tech*, which J. edited:

"James Tennant Baldwin graduated from the University of Michigan in 1955 and did graduate work at the University of California, Berkeley. In 1952 he had the eighth Volkswagen in America. He first worked with Buckminster Fuller about that time. 1955–57 he was in the Ski Infantry in Alaska. 1958–62 with Bill Moss Associates working on such advanced camping equipment as the Pop Tent. 1962–68 he was teaching design at San Francisco State College (where I met him), San Francisco Art Institute, and Oakland College of Arts and Crafts, simultaneously. 1968–69 at Fuller's invitation he was Visiting Lecturer in Design at Southern Illinois University. 1969–72 he was at Pacific High School teaching the kids and working with Lloyd Kahn on *Domebook I* and *Domebook II*. 1972–74 he worked with Bob Reines at Integrated Living Systems in New Mexico contriving a totally independent solar and wind energy system. In 1976 J. helped the New Alchemists finish the renowned Ark on Prince Edward Island, Canada. . . . With his skills, J. has never looked for a job. Work looks for him."

At CQ, J. is the "soft tech" maven—ongoing expert reviewer on topics ranging from backpacking to wind energy to understanding physics to traveling in China to automobiles to the musical saw. Fortunately for CQ, he has the rare ability to write fascinatingly about the things people make, and the tools they use.

Between 1978 and 1982, J. lived and worked at the New Alchemy Institute on Cape Cod in Massachusetts, where he hung out some with a Cambridge-based writer/financial trust administrator/urban activist named Conn Nugent. Conn, reacting to what he perceived as smug secessionism in the CQ "Bioregions" issue, proposed a special issue on "failure and misfortune," as if to say to the bioregionalists, "This, too, shall foul up." J.'s article was one of the bright spots of that issue (Winter 1982).

Art Kleiner

Failure is a way of life for designers. We *know* our work is going to exhibit certain undesirable qualities until development is pretty much complete. That's what research and development ("R & D") is all about. That's why we have computer simulations, prototypes, and test pilots. And a junk pile behind the lab. (Or

263

barn. There's nothing formal about any of this.) We learn to live with the possibility that our ideas may not work at all, and that even if they do work, the critics may not receive us kindly. The market might not be there, or a political perturbation might shoot us down. Any way you look at the situation, the potential for miserable failure is there. Statistically, about ninety percent of new designs do not achieve societal (market) acceptance. In the face of these dismal odds, how can designers continue to feel confident enough to work? And how is disaster to be avoided?

Henry Ford is one of my heroes, mostly because he dared to ignore much of the conventional wisdom of his day. For instance, when he was designing the Model T, his engineers were not issued the expected order to make it as strong and tough as possible so that failure would be unthinkable. Instead, they were told to make it as light as they dared. Then, when it inevitably broke during road testing, they were to beef it up appropriately and test it again. When at last the test car didn't break, Henry knew he had the lightest and most economical car possible at that time. While his competition carted around hundreds and even thousands of useless pounds supposedly needed for strength, the Model T went on to become a deservedly great success, at a weight less than a modern VW. Today, design is primarily for the perceived market niche rather than for physical performance on the road. Consequently, when there is a rapid shift of customer desires, automakers are left trying to sell cars that are inherently not very good—a failure of a different sort.

It is interesting to speculate what Henry's press would have been if reporters had been allowed to witness the tests. I can see it now. FREAK CAR CRASHES! FLAMING PYRE MARKS END OF EXPERIMENT! The media have always had a penchant for such things. The public seems eager to hear of anything that doesn't "win"; anything that doesn't work right is accorded derision or at least a dilettantish macabre attention. Corporations hide their work until it is market-ready, not only to confuse competitors but to prevent media "misunder-

standings." It is mostly for such reasons that Bucky Fuller admonishes us to never to show anyone half-finished work.

There is a way to prevent bad press and the sneers of peers: don't do anything that is likely to have problems right there in front of God and everyone. Carried to an extreme: don't do anything new. Or don't do anything at all. Students seem attracted to this last route. The professors that let them get away with that are obstructing education, but you can see why they do it. For one thing, professors themselves don't care to be exposed to accusations of failure, and poor student performance tends to reflect badly on the teacher. Sure-to-succeed assignments assure that the students will not shame the prof. You won't hear much talk along these lines among students or in the faculty lounge, but the fear-of-failure forces are at work nonetheless, even in an atmosphere where you might not expect to find them.

For instance, I once asked some design students to construct boats that could carry them fully clothed and dry across a nearby pond. The boats were to be fashioned from box cardboard anointed with waterproof paint. I thought it would be a good exercise in that there was no literature to search and no "resource persons" available for advice on the subject. The students would be forced to think for themselves. They'd also get some practice in using materials appropriately (you can't make a wooden boat design out of cardboard), they'd get a chance to see an idea take physical shape under their own hands, and if they didn't sink they'd get a taste of success. After a great deal of teeth-gnashing and some hilarious test sinkings, they produced a fleet. Since the students all faced the same problems, the test sinkings were regarded with amused interest rather than mean laughter and ego-deflating gibes.

On launching day, even though I knew better and despite looking outwardly calm, I was as nervous as a long-tailed cat in a room full of rocking chairs. What if they all sank? What if somebody got hurt? Someone might *sue* me! People in California can get sued for just about anything. Worse, CBS-TV was going to be there. Was I about to be made a public fool along with my students? In many societies, that's a fate worse than death. Well, the launching went fine. Only one boat sank, and it had been rather cleverly made to do so by a gal whose public personality was based on eliciting pity, so we may still claim that one as a success. TV presented us in an acceptable, nonderisive way. It was a great day for all. My mailbag over the years tells me that those students appreciated being put into a position where the "win" was not at the expense of another person. In a sports-oriented society, that's a rare opportunity.

Among my peers, however, there were few who approved of the assignment. With one exception, all who approved were without tenure. The gist of the disapproving remarks was that sorties outside of the classroom were somehow suspect, and that my students had been guilty of doing their bulky projects in space officially designated as "noncurricular." But we got the real message, all right. It was "Don't take chances."

I was enough of a whippersnapper at the time to be shocked at finding this attitude in a school of creative arts. I began to note that even in beginning art classes, students were graded on whether or not they did "good art." They could fail if they tried something that didn't work all that well. At that time, a male student could fail his way to Vietnam! The results of this policy were predictable: Students faithfully executed art that closely resembled the then-current style, all too often the style in which their professor worked. Students who bravely attempted innovations generally received poor grades. Their work tended to look ragged—a natural consequence of innovation, because the first of the new is nearly always at a disadvantage when compared to the last of the highly developed old. Needless to say, there was not much failing work produced, especially by the men. There wasn't much new either. There rarely is under such circumstances, even when there is a big prize awaiting a well-taken Bold Move. Witness the sorry display of impotence in Detroit when the very existence of the American automobile industry is at stake. In a real sense, the fear of immediate,

laughable, Edsel-type failure precipitates larger catastrophes. These are often seen as the result of mysterious bad luck or malice or ineptitude. They are more often the result of lack of nerve.

Assessing blame for failure is an enterprise closely associated with chance-taking. It's easy to do even if one does not have any idea of what is really going on. It doesn't take a Ph.D. in music to detect when a concert pianist hits a wrong note, and this principle can be effortlessly extended into invalidity. Murphy's Law ("Anything that can go wrong, will go wrong") is often cited to cover mistakes arising from insufficient thought, insufficient information, or sloppy execution of an idea. In my own incarnation as an Industrial Designer, I have never once seen a Murphy's Law failure that was not, in fact, a failure due to pure carelessness. A laid-back, don't-get-uptight attitude combined with an ever-increasing technical complexity make Murphy a popular excuse.

This seems a good place to say that it is probably not possible to make any relatively complex technology absolutely fail-proof. The interactions involved in a nuclear-power plant, for example, are so labyrinthine that there is no way to foresee all possibilities. Computer analysis helps, but obviously has not proved to be one hundred percent effective at predicting conditions that lead to failures. In such cases all we can expect is (I hope) a reduction of the evil effects of failure—hardly a comforting thought. The only sure preventive measure then becomes "Don't attempt the project in the first place."

This is different from the student failure-of-nerve cited earlier. It comes after due thought and investigation. A reading of the history of some of the more infamous technical failures, such as the Teton Dam, nearly always reveals that bravado (some say machismo) overrode thoughtful analysis that would have either modified the design or stopped the project altogether. Uninformed courage can be fatal! Failure of "experts" is all too often due to political meddling.

I admit that my own most spectacular failure was, uh, well, I *ignored* something I shouldn't have. I was testing a small sports racing car designed for use on a track. It had three inches of ground clearance. The seat was an anatomically comfortable shape pounded into the belly pan of the car and upholstered with a quarter-inch of foam and leather. The three-inch ground clearance was measured under the bulges hanging down beneath the main floor line. What I had ignored was what would happen if a tire blew or a wheel came off. That wasn't on my mind when I was striving to get the car as low as possible. In trying to be very clever, I had not thought out all aspects of the situation. When a steering part snapped, the car dropped to the pavement and the bottom of the seat bulge zizzed along the shoulder as I fought the car down from ninety or so. We stopped, enveloped by an evil-smelling smoke comprising foam, leather, and fried ass. I've thought things out with assiduous discipline ever since, and have not had to invoke Mr. Murphy again. (I also have my welds x-rayed.) For a long time after that I tended to be conservative rather than smarter and more careful. (There's a difference.) I got bored being conservative.

I'm sure you can think of instances where avoidance of immediate failure can lead to later failure. As with my car, the later failures tend to be things we didn't think of or didn't want to think of. Much of the environmental degradation seen today has come from folks trying to avoid, say, a market failure. They worry about that so much that they don't consider what their actions are going to do in the long run, especially to the environment, which is not a paying customer. Yet over and over I've seen manufacturers stoutly oppose environmental laws affecting their businesses even when compliance would result in extra profit. I think this happens because the people involved are causing failures in "another department," one with which they are not familiar. The phenomenon reminds me a bit of Thomas Kuhn's "paradigm shifts" in that there is not as yet a metalanguage that enables people in one field to talk meaningfully to those in another. Money does not talk usefully when one is discussing environment, though business people often try and force it to.

All this chat adds up to most failures being preventable. Oh yes, there will always be just plain bad luck—after all it is possible to roll snake eyes a thousand times in a row on honest dice. And sometimes failures come from Forces Beyond Our Control. But, unlike kilo-snake eyes, usually not. If you really think things through, even to the point of checking things out in bailiwicks other than your own, and if you don't worry too much about people laughing at you, and if you do your work carefully, you'll probably do okay. At least you won't have failed in the worst way possible: seeing something go down because of insufficient effort or courage.

GARY NABHAN

Kokopelli–
The Humpbacked
Flute Player

From the original introduction
(Spring 1983):
Gary Nabhan is a bit of a hump-
backed flute player himself. He's
been appearing at various Southwest
Indian reservations bearing seeds of
vegetables that the locals haven't
seen in decades and long ago gave up
on. Both he and the Indians are intent on a sustainable agriculture that
spans centuries, that uses the accumulated wisdom of centuries. It's a
first-rate science.

This paper was originally given as
a talk at the Lindisfarne Fellows
Conference, November 1982, Cres-
tone, California.

Stewart Brand

Gary is the president of a nonprofit
conservation organization in Tucson,
Arizona, called Native Seeds/
SEARCH. About the same time he
gave this talk, he published a
book—*The Desert Smells Like Rain*,
from North Point Press—that am-
plifies this story further. It's about

the desert—wet or dry—as a place
where people can thrive if they seek
stewardship, not conquest, of the
land.

Art Kleiner

In *The Gift of Good Land*, Wendell Berry
expresses the true, hard challenge for those
who are involved in farming and resource
conservation:

> The most necessary thing in agriculture . . . is
> not to invent new technologies or methods, not
> to achieve "breakthroughs," but to determine
> what tools and methods are appropriate to spe-
> cific people, places, and needs, and to apply
> them correctly. Application (which the heroic
> approach ignores) is the crux, because no two
> farms or farmers are alike; no two fields are alike.
> Just the changing shape or topography of the
> land makes for differences of the most formidable
> kind. Abstractions never cross these boundaries
> without either ceasing to be abstractions or
> doing damage. . . . The bigger and more expen-
> sive, the more heroic they are, the harder they are
> to apply considerately and conservingly.[1]

Wendell Berry makes clear the contrast between heroic abstractions, characteristic of certain religious traditions, and daily *practice*,
sometimes found at the margins of these same
traditions. He feels that although the Bible
does define proper human uses of the natural
world, the heroic Judeo-Christian tradition has
been too abstract, not *earthly* enough in its application or in its attention to practical particulars. Even the earthward example of St. Francis of Assisi was never seriously applied by the
Franciscan order; even before his death, the
Franciscan institution decided that he was "for
the birds." This "other worldly" philosophy

267

Etienne B. Renaud, Kokopelli in Southwestern Lore,
September 1948

This and similar drawings in this article show some of the many representations of Kokopelli the Locust, the Humpbacked Flute Player, copied from prehistoric Pueblo Indian pottery fragments and petroglyphs by archaeologists in the 1920s and 1930s. "In his hump he carried blankets, belts, embroidered scarves, and some seeds and grains, as presents which he gave to each girl whom he seduced." Other Kokopelli pictures show different spellings of his name, based on their sources.

has long dominated civilized mankind, and Berry urges us to return to responding skillfully to the particulars of the place in which we live.

I sense that much of the ecological destruction wrought by people participating in certain religious traditions is not considered by them to be *spiritually impoverishing* in any way. Although desertification in the Middle East has been blamed on the Judeo-Christian tradition, it clearly predates and is not limited to just this one branch of Western religion. It is perhaps not surprising that the so-called cradle of Western religions and of annual grain agriculture—the Tigris-Euphrates "Fertile Crescent"—was one of the first areas in the world

to be ravaged by soil erosion, siltation, and salinization as a consequence of poor agricultural management. Fields at Tell Asmar from six thousand years ago now sit under ten to eleven meters of silt.[2] Yet I doubt that a fact such as this is ever discussed in courses on the history of Western religions—it is not recognized as evidence of *negative feedback* or poor practices associated with a belief system; it may even be considered to have *nothing to do* with religion.

In contrast to this view, there still exist traditional (though not *unchanging*) communities in which the way that one farms and concerns himself with wild resources has *everything to do* with the spiritual life of the community. Some of these are Native American communities, which have associated with them agricultural fields that have been tended for centuries; a few of these villages are considered to be among the longest continuously inhabited places in North America. This stability through time has helped harbor agricultural diversity. These villages offer us insights into the mutually reinforcing connections between spiritual life and skillful care for the ecological integrity of food-producing land.

Although I am not a resident of these communities, I have worked in some of them. My friends within them have taught me some things that have stirred up my beliefs, and redirected my learning toward certain practical skills. Yet I do not wish to make Hopi and Papago farmers out to be "heroes" of the sort that are in some kind of ideal balance with nature, as if you could put a dozen noble savages on one side of a scale, and a dozen plants and animals on the other, and strike some kind of homeostasis. When we decide that Indians are or are not "in balance," we usually stop there in learning anything from them; these two choices limit rather than advance our understanding. Certainly, contemporary Native Americans are increasingly faced with serious land-use problems, as the results of economic pressures and acculturation that have caught up with them. Local deforestation occurred prehistorically, and native people suffered the consequences. I will even grant that when a large wave of Native American ancestors crossed the Bering Straits ten to twelve thousand years ago, these invaders played a key role in the extinction of mammoths, mastodons, horses, and camels, and that since then, other local faunal extirpations have occurred due to short-term over-exploitation. Yet I tend to agree with Calvin Martin that "on the whole, the North American Indian earns high marks for his cautious use of plant resources . . . cautiously because she (Nature) could strike back against abuse."[3]

I also agree with Martin that a spiritual contract between certain cultures and particular lifeforms is evident, but I do not pretend to understand the depth and complexity of their spiritualism. A final apology: I do not wish to imply that all Papago or Hopi accept the viewpoints I am about to discuss. Rather than speaking for them, I am simply relating a few things that some of them have spoken to me.

For several years I have been studying native agricultural ecosystems in the desert Southwest, and the drought- and heat-adapted crops which allow them to function. They are *native* not merely because Native Americans farm them. They are *native* because their crops are mostly ones that evolved from wild relatives which can still be found in or near these fields. They are pollinated by endemic solitary bees that coevolved with particular American plant genera and are much more efficient in pollen transfer and more faithful to their crops than are honeybees. Certain indigenous legumes such as the tepary bean have associated them with nitrogen-fixing *Rhizobia* bacteria endemic to the region. These crops and their symbionts are finely tuned to local climatic and soil conditions. In *ak-chin* floodwater fields, nutrient-rich runoff from local watersheds is utilized, rather than water "imported" from mountains nearby or from underground aquifers filled during the Pleistocene. These fields exemplify the concept that agricultural ecologists George Cox and Michael Atkins have written of—that the food-producing systems having the best chance of enduring are those which deviate *least* from the energy flows and nutrient cycles

Marjorie F. Lambert, A Kokopelli Effigy Pitcher, in American Antiquity, July 1967

Side view of a Kokopelli effigy pitcher, about twelve inches long, dating ca. 1000–1150, found in a Pueblo site in northwestern New Mexico. The rounded contour of its underside represents the humped back.

of the natural ecosystems within which they work.[4] Some of the native fields are so well integrated into natural desert ecosystems that it took European-Americans literally centuries of contact to realize that cultures such as the Sand Papago and Southern Paiute farmed as well as gathered. Papago fields, unlike most "advanced" agricultural systems, show levels of plant diversity comparable to the surrounding wild floodplain environments, rather than reducing nature to monoculture.

Needless to say, these native fields provide a sober contrast to the modern water-consumptive agriculture transplanted to the desert, which is undergoing a demise. Some of the highest rates of water loss from transpiration recorded in the world have been observed in exotic crops under irrigated agriculture in the Phoenix, Arizona area. Whereas hybrid corn and cotton use two to three acre-feet of irrigation water in central Arizona, native crops such as teparies produce respectable yields on eight to twelve acre-inches, and their yields decrease with excessive irrigation. Introduced crops sometimes require two to five times the irrigation a native crop would need, if one takes into account irrigation to cool the environment, deliver chemicals, etc. The native strategy is the opposite—to fit the crop to the environment rather than trying to remake the environment to fit the crop.

As part of my work, I have been helping Indian farmers to locate and conserve native desert-adapted crop varieties, since it is projected that over half of the crop varieties utilized in the New World at the time of Columbus may have already been driven to extinction due to colonial suppression, acculturation, and other factors. Where do the remaining varieties persist? In the fields of Native American communities with a strong traditional spiritual life—of more than forty reservations in the Southwestern states, it is largely the five or ten where native ceremonial observances persist that the genetic diversity of desert crops persists as well.

This is more than just a correlation. At the Hopi mesas, where more than eighteen varieties of beans and over twenty named varieties of corn have been recorded, many of those which persist are utilized in ceremonies basic to the community's spiritual life. While on the surface these ceremonies could be interpreted as being as "abstract" as some Christian observances, they serve to tie people into the land community of plants and animals in very concrete ways.

A few years ago, I was inquiring at a Hopi home about a bean variety that not only is resistant to root knot nematodes but is higher in protein quality and quantity, as well as in several minerals, than most beans found in our grocery stores. A Hopi man at Second Mesa told me, "Oh yes, I always have some of these stored away, and I grow them every year as well. We need them to sprout in the kiva prior to the *Powamu*, the Bean Dance in the winter."

I had been to the Bean Dance the year before, and had seen the forty-five-centimeter-long sprouts delivered door to door by *Katsina* dancers one frosty dawn. "So those are the kind of beans that make the long sprouts?" I asked. The Hopi man laughed and replied, "Yes,

that's the one—those *pahaana* [white man] beans won't even work. We had a new boy initiated into the kiva last year who didn't help grow out his clan's beans, and thought he could get away with just buying some white lima beans at the store to use in the kiva. He planted them in the sand basins just like we did our Hopi bean, but when our sprouts were tall, his hadn't even come up. Did he ever *hear it* from the other men. . . ." The reason the newly initiated boy was chastised by the other kiva members is that this later winter underground planting of beans is said to forecast the productivity of the coming crop season. If the beans do well in the sand basins in the kiva, the crops in the summer fields will be plentiful. The boy had perhaps endangered the coming crop and the optimism of the ceremony by *not* paying attention to particulars—all beans are *not* the same.

While the Hopi make fine distinctions between particular varieties of crops, they are careful to maintain some variation within each variety. Perhaps I should say, they are careful not to be *too* careful, or to act as though they could totally control a crop's destiny. On one occasion, I asked a Hopi woman at Munqapi if she selected only the biggest corn kernels of all one color for planting her blue maize. She snapped back at me, "It is not a good habit to be too picky . . . we have been given this corn, small seeds, fat seeds, misshapen seeds, all of them. It would show that we are not thankful for what we have received if we plant just certain ones and not the others." Agricultural ecologists have demonstrated that such genetic mixtures are key to farming in marginal, unpredictable environments. While no single native seed may do as well as hybrid corn under optimal conditions, the mix may well out yield it under variable conditions.

In a similar way, many Indians are tolerant of certain plants in their fields that outsiders would call weeds. Some of these, like the anomalous sunflower, found at Hopi, are not only wild relatives of cultivated crops, but they are rare enough to be considered for threatened species status elsewhere in their range. On the mesas, this sunflower is found almost exclusively around sand dune fields, where it is specially recognized and left to grow. Most untrained observers would be hard-pressed to recognize it as being different from the common wild sunflower species. Yet for centuries, the Hopi have let it grow around their fields, and have harvested some of its petals, from which they make a yellow ceremonial face-paint. It has been sustained despite this low-level harvesting, adding to the diversity of their fields and perhaps occasionally contributing genes to the Hopi's cultivated sunflower. A valley of fields is named for it— *A'qa'qaungwu*—in recognition that even rare wild things have their place in this world.

My impression is that these gestures of concern for other living things aren't done out of economic motives, even though the failure to do so might later affect the community economically. These are acts done out of the Hopi sense of spiritual propriety.

Similarly, I have heard Papagos argue that it is a spiritual responsibility to farm, and that failure to do so erodes the community from the *O'odham Himdag*, the People's Way. Since the Papago way of farming is rainfall- and watershed-dependent, they enter into an intricate system of mutual feedback with natural events: To farm, they must have rain. To have rain, they must have a cactus wine feast and "throw up the clouds." To harvest enough cactus fruit, there must have been enough rain for the saguaros to be productive. To be productive, it must have rained earlier, but also, no one must have harmed the saguaro cactus in any way, for they are people too, and vulnerable.[5]

Yet the rain that falls on the field itself is not enough to sustain a crop; the desert washes must run free to bring water into their fields. The water from the sky must meet the water from the ground. When watersheds and aquifers are tampered with, the whole web of interactions begins to unravel. Imagine cranky old Papago farmers showing up at government meetings to complain about a well being put in the ground twenty miles away from their homes, or to condemn a solid-waste disposal

put in a seemingly dry sandy wash fifteen miles upstream from their fields. While such acts of resistance are relatively rare today, they nevertheless suggest that traditional Papago recognize that their agriculture is watershed-sensitive and that their responsibility goes beyond simply tending to their own field and houseyard. Although the entire watershed may not belong to them, in a very real way they belong to it.

There is increased public awareness of the problem of species extinction and loss of genetic diversity in both wild and cultivated or tended biota. But only a few analysts of this dilemma, such as Steve Brush,[6] have related that the remaining genetic diversity is dependent upon the persistence of a variety of agricultural ecosystems, each finely tuned to its geographic setting and ecological context. These agricultural ecosystems have in turn coevolved with various cultural groups, whose ethnicity, or distinctive ways of dealing with particulars, are now being consumed by modern media-mediated monomania. As ethnic communities become acculturated, losing their *other-ness*, the Earth loses part of the diversity of its life-support system. Ironically, an elderly Sand Papago woman has used the analogy of distinctive seed stocks to describe the fate of her people:

> It is this way, long time ago, when people first realized the world, from that time on it is recognized from their maker that people who bore children . . . band together. People were like a cultivated field producing after its kind, recognizing its kinship, the seeds remain to continue to produce. Today all the bad times have entered the People, and the People no longer recognize their way of life. The People separated from each other and became few in number. Today all the People [*O'odham*] are vanishing.[7]

In Mexico, Victor Toledo, Cristina Mapes, and their colleagues have warned that their country will fail to feed itself as long as it tries to impose one kind of agriculture on an ethnically and geographically diverse land. Instead, they should begin with the existing agricultural ecosystems that indigenous cultures have

The Hump-backed Flute Player

by Gary Snyder

1.
The hump-backed flute player
    walks all over.
    sits on the boulders around the Great
     Basin
    his hump   is a pack.
Hsüan Tsang
    went to India 629 AD
    returned to China 645
    with 657 sutras, images, pictures,
    and 50 relics—
    a curved frame pack with a parasol,
    embroidery, carving,
    incense censer swinging as he walked
    the Pamir   the Tarim   Turfan
    the Punjab   the doab
    of Ganga and Yamuna,

Sweetwater, Quileute, Hoh
Amur, Tanana, Mackenzie, Old Man,
Bighorn, Platte, the San Juan

    he carried
        "emptiness"
    he carried
        "mind only"
        vijnaptimatra

The hump-backed flute player
Kokopilau
his hump is a pack.

2.
In Canyon de Chelly on the North Wall up by
 a cave
is the hump-backed flute player laying on his
 back,
playing his flute. Across the flat sandy canyon
 wash,

wading a stream and breaking through the ice,
 on the
south wall, the pecked-out pictures of some
 Mountain Sheep
with curling horns. They stood in the icy
 shadow of the
south wall two hundred feet away; I sat with
 my shirt off in the sun facing south, with the
 hump-
backed flute player just above my head.
They whispered; I whispered; back and forth
across the canyon, clearly heard.

A Quichua Indian of Cochabamba, photographed in 1942, showing the carrying blanket
and flute common throughout the Andean highlands. Wrote botanist Hugh Cutler, "Possibly
one of his ancestors, similarly equipped, carried
pod corn to North America and became the leg-
endary flute player, Kocopelli."

California Academy of Sciences, in Pacific Discovery, January 1982

3.
In the plains of Bihar, near Rajgir, are the
ruins of Nalanda. The name Bihar comes from
  "vihara"
—Buddhist temple—the Diamond Seat is in
  Bihar, and
Vulture Peak—Tibetan pilgrims come down to
  these
plains. The six-foot-thick walls of Nalanda,
  the
monks all scattered—books burned—banners
  tattered—
statues shattered—by the Turks.
Hsüan Tsang describes the high blue tiles, the
  delicate
debates; Logicians of Emptiness, worshippers
  of Tārā,
Joy of Starlight, naked breasted, "She who
  saves."

4.
Ghost Bison, Ghost Bears, Ghost Bighorns,
  Ghost Lynx,
Ghost Pronghorns, Ghost Panthers, Ghost
  Marmots, Ghost
Owls:
Swirling and gathering, sweeping down, in
  the power
of a dance and a song. Then the "White Man"
  will be gone.
Then the butterflies will sing
on slopes of grass and aspen
thunderheads the deep blue of krishna
rise on rainbows; and falling shining rain—
each drop—
tiny people gliding slanting down: a little
  Buddha
seated in each pearl—
and join the million waving Grass-Seed Bud-
  dhas
on the ground.

5.
Ah, what am I carrying? What's this load?
    Who's that out there in the dust
    sleeping on the ground?
    with a black hat, and a feather stuck in his
      sleeve.
—It's old Jack Wilson,
Wovoka, the prophet,

Black Coyote saw the whole world
in Wovoka's empty hat

the bottomless sky

the night of starlight, lying on our sides

the ocean, slanting higher

all manner of beings
may swim in my sea
echoing up conch spiral corridors

the mirror: countless ages back
dressing   or laughing

what world today?

pearl crystal jewel
taming and teaching
the dragon in the spine—
spiral, wheel,
or breath of mind

desert sheep with curly horns,
the ringing in your ears

is the cricket in the stars.

6.
Up in the mountains that edge the Great Basin
    it was whispered to me
    by the oldest of trees,

    by the oldest of beings,

    the Oldest of Trees,
      Bristlecone Pines.

    and all night long, sung on,
      by a vast throng
        of Pinyon Pine.

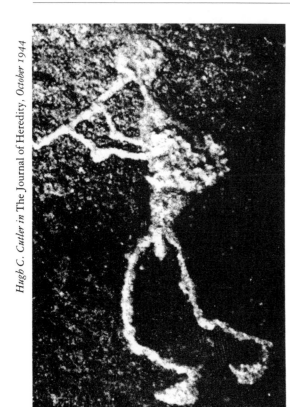

Hugh C. Cutler in The Journal of Heredity, October 1944

A Pueblo Indian petroglyph of Kokopelli from the upper reaches of the Glen Canyon, photographed in 1942.

Hugh C. Cutler in The Journal of Heredity, October 1944

An ear of Bolivian Indian podcorn (below) compared with an ear of ordinary corn. The podcorn survived despite no support from established agronomists. At first its survival was attributed to repeated mutations; then Hugh Cutler realized that Indian medicine men had perpetuated and distributed it.

evolved, and develop a number of local or regionally adapted food production strategies based on this diversity.[8] Crying "food first" is not enough, especially if it imposes inappropriate food production systems on the land.

Today, genetic engineers tell us not to worry about the drying up of indigenous gene pools, for they will soon create new genetic combinations faster than they can evolve in nature. Engineers tell us not to worry about falling groundwater levels and the rising costs of fueling pumps, for they will create solar pumps to extract the presumably infinite amount of water below the Earth's surface. Sociologists tell us not to worry about the demise of traditional cultures, that new lifestyles and religious cults are cropping up every day. Yet these are ephemeral in the sense that they are "components" without contexts, creations without long-term fitness. To accept these cheap substitutes while letting twelve thousand years of organic agricultural experimentation slip away means not only that we will lose a rich agricultural heritage but that we will diminish our options for the future as well.

As I was pulling together these thoughts, I realized that perhaps the native-crop-conservation effort needs a guardian spirit in the sense that St. Francis has become the patron saint of the ecology movement. A fitting candidate may be the humpbacked flute player, who has been seen on petroglyphs near agricultural fields in the Southwest for millennia. His flute has been considered a cloud-blower or drinking tube by some Southwestern peoples, suggesting an association with water-bringing for crops, according to anthropologist Bruce Anderson.[9] It has also been considered a phallus, and he is certainly associated with sexuality and fertility for both humans and plants. What is striking is that so many observers have imagined his hump to be a bag of seeds. For instance, Gary Snyder has called him an "itinerant seed carrier." Forest Roth-Shomer of the Abundant Life Seed Foundation (*Next Whole Earth Catalogue*, p. 100) has for years modeled not just his appearance but his activities after this archetypal seed carrier. Forest travels throughout the Pacific Northwest with a flute in hand and a bagful of seed-collecting equipment on his back. As he hikes, he harvests seed, and has brought dozens of species into commercial distribution through his efforts.

Perhaps the most remarkable connection was made by ethnobotanist Hugh Cutler in the 1940s in an essay, "Medicine Men and the Preservation of a Relic Gene in Maize."[10] He noted that flute-playing, pack-carrying medicine men in South America have for centuries used a very rare form of maize, podcorn, for the cure of respiratory ailments. The irony is that podcorn cannot survive without diligent care from humankind—every kernel has its own tightly held husk and is also enclosed by the larger papery husks surrounding the entire cob. When expressed in most maize varieties, it does not breed true. Over millennia, most farmers have likely destroyed or neglected this relic gene if it shows up in their cornfields, due to the extra work involved in maintaining it. Yet Callahuayo and Quichuan medicine men have taken care of this relic gene, as well as carrying it with them to other cultures. These wandering South American herbalists are known to have reached into Central America historically. Perhaps more importantly, podcorn persists today in South America where it was first recorded nearly two centuries ago.

What Hugh Cutler noticed is that where podcorn crops up in prehistoric sites in the Southwest, it is often near petroglyphs of the humpbacked flute player! He speculated that the same line of indigenous medicine men who were responsible for the persistence of a relic gene of maize over centuries may also have transported it from one continent to another. The South American herbalist with his *flauta indigena* and the Hopi's Kokopelli may carry the same grain.

The trouble is, Kokopelli is not exactly "saintly" in Southwestern Indian myths and ceremonies. He has been known to "hump" little girls and even old anthropologists. I mentioned this dilemma to Gary Snyder; he smiled, replying, "It all goes back to fertility."

NOTES

J. W. Fewkes, Hopi Kachinas, Bureau of American Ethnology, 1903

A drawing by a Hopi artist of a Kachina dancer, wearing a painted mask representing Kokopelli. Ethnologist and Hopi priest J. W. Fewkes wrote: "The head is painted black and has a white median facial line. . . . There is a warrior feather on top. The body is black and girt by an embroidered sash. There are buckskin leggings, stained yellow and green."

Agricultural Systems in Dry Regions," in *Agriculture in Semi-Arid Environments*, pp. 1–43, A. E. Hall, G. H. Cannell, and H. W. Lawton, editors, 1979, $56 postpaid from Springer-Verlag New York, 175 Fifth Avenue, New York, New York 10010.

3. Calvin Martin, *Keepers of the Game*, p. 186; 1978, $12.45 postpaid from University of California Press, Order Dept., 2120 Berkeley Way, Berkeley, California 94720.

4. George W. Cox and Michael D. Atkins, "Agricultural Ecology," *Bulletin of the Ecological Society of America* 56 (1975), p. 6.

5. Gary Paul Nabhan, *The Desert Smells Like Rain*, 1982, North Point Press.

6. Steven Brush, H. J. Carney and Z. Huaman, "Dynamics of Andean potato agriculture," *Economic Botany* 35 (1981), p. 70.

7. Filamena Bell, Keith Anderson, and Yvonne G.

1. Wendell Berry, *The Gift of Good Land*, p. 280. (Reviewed in Summer '82 CQ.)

2. Harry W. Lawton and Phillip J. Wilke, "Ancient

Stewart, *The Quitobaquito Cemetery and Its History*, Western Archaeological Center, National Park Service, Tucson, 1980.

8. Victor Toledo, J. Carabias, Cristina Mapes, and C. Toledo, "Crítica de la ecología política," *Nexos* 4 (1981), p. 17 (Mexico City).

9. Bruce Anderson, "Kokopelli: The Humpbacked Fluteplayer," *American Indian Art* (1976), p. 36.

10. Hugh Cutler, "Medicine Men and the Preservation of a Relic Gene in Maize," *Journal of Heredity* 35 (1944), pp. 291–294.

AAAHHH!

It suddenly came to me today that the word for the spirit of the universe or whatever you want to call "It" has the sound "aahhh" in many languages. To wit: God, Jah, Ra, Allah, Brahma, Atman, Yahweh, Ram, Baal, Ahura Mazda (I'm using the Thesaurus), Og, Hachiman, Mab, nagual, mana, wakan, huaca. . . . I think it's because the "aahhh" sound is so relaxing of the jaw and throat, letting go, giving in to what is. Makes me reminded of the oneness of all us folks.

Larry Ephron
Berkeley, California
[Spring 1983]

Not to mention "Wakan Tonka" ("Great Mystery"—Sioux), "Buddha," and other examples and exceptions that readers might recall.—Stewart Brand

LEO DREU

Rachelann:
A Remembrance

*From the original introduction
(Spring 1983):*
We see writing dealing with the decade of the 1960s fairly often, and
I'm never sure if it's because of the
history of this magazine or that the
period is now at a sufficient focal
length to allow for introspection.
This story impressed me with its language and a celebration of quiet differences. Leo Dreu lives in Lowell,
Massachusetts.

Richard Nilsen

It hardly matters that she was plain; matters
not at all since we were, both of us, plain in
those far ago days, she in her kick pleats and
ribbons, me in my Eisenhowers.

True, there was the freckle I didn't like but
there were the powder-blue eyes which I did—
very much. The smile, too, was pleasing, I
think: a wry, tight-lipped little smile, extremely sensual for one so obviously pure.
And, of course, there was the laugh like bowl-
ing balls knocking at the door, a guffaw but
oddly welcome.

Rachelann. It was all one word like that—
no second capital, no hyphen, but deliberately
Rachelann, meant to be spoken full in one
breath like a Nat King Cole song or an edict.

To say she was a throwback is to understate
the case. Certainly she predated Lou Ann
Curry, the first and only girl whose books I
would carry home. She had not Lou Ann's
Catholic school-uniformed plumpness or orange trampoline curls that bounced whenever
she walked, had not the kewpie Irish smile of
pretty Brenda McKenzie who waltzed with me
at the Cadet Officer's Ball. No, Rachelann was
Victorian, hers a life of cameo and lace, the
sort of squeaky-clean, bookish girl-next-door
girl so mythically abundant in the 1930s yet
very nearly a cultural impossibility in that but-
terfly-and-blue-jean decade known to us as the
1960s, which is why I now suppose I consider
myself lucky to have known her.

I deny accusations I was drawn to her simply
because she was easy to be with and washed
with Camay. More than for what she was, I
needed her for what she was not.

They were not years I had been reared for,
the 1960s. Typically Catholic, I had been
weaned on a doctrine of eternal hell for a fib to
father or for a piece of meat eaten on a Friday.
Imagine, then, my little boy's concept of punishment when applying this same crew-cut
theology to, say, the Tet offensive or the Berkeley awakening. The whole world, or so it appeared, had given itself over to Satan and I was
in no way about to trade in my tuna salad sal-
vation for a bayonet for anyone. Against war
and the whiffs of change, I had only a little,
silver star to hold on to placed upon my forehead by the Sisters of Notre Dame. Back then,
emerging from a world which promoted Julie
Andrews and Sleeping Beauty, a world I more
than believed in, that star seemed to me
enough—and then some.

Rachelann was the ideal counterpart to this innocence of estrangement; she had studied ballet and was learning to sew when first we met (pursuits found unacceptable among the female population of her day).

In an age of curiosity, Rachelann remained curiously aloof, a princess in a tower who suspected little, if anything, of what the rest of the world was up to. It hardly fazed her that, all around, her peers were speaking differently from her; she did not understand so-called hippie jargon and never expressed a moment's interest in caring to. If she could not close her ears to what was said, to so-and-so describing a friend as "burned out" or so-and-so describing a song as a number that "really cooked," she could, in fact, close her eyes and would petulantly pass off these, to her, foreign expressions as little else than proof positive of what she termed the "arsonistic tendencies" of a counterculture drinking and drugging its way toward eventual oblivion.

Very little sixties substance made its way through her turret window. Amidst it all, she continued a cultivation of proper ways and clung to her own special language of standards. If there was a friend with whom she had, perhaps, become suddenly disenchanted, she would explain the situation regally, eyes lowered, and in a barely tolerant posture whisper, "M has fallen out of my good graces." Inferiors (those found to be lacking in strong I.Q.'s and style) were quickly dismissed as "fudgeheads" and individuals considered by her to be particularly offensive (and there were many) were invariably set aside as "sorry cups of tea."

This archaism, this self-immersion in a thought and a manner more becoming to a turn-of-the-century spinster, was the result (or so insisted her mother, from whom she might well have taken lessons in charm and accessibility) of "too little socializing and too much Amy Lowell." And while there was daily evidence that she had, indeed, deliberately raised herself in an atmosphere which no longer held any basis in fact, leaving her the brunt of many an acneed tease, there were also those times when it became more than apparent that her behavior stemmed, too, from some hidden line of anger, a self-pity coupled with genuine fear (and this fear *was* justified, her concept of a rock group being the Lettermen) that culture had scheduled a change of costume and that she, in the wings, had been left a character no one had bothered to tell.

But meekness, charity, intellect; these, too, were dear to her ways and many, put off at first by what they saw in her as economy of emotion, were later anesthetized, even charmed by her devotion to a combination pragmatic/romantic sensibility, an attitude of order and balance possessed of the tranquillity of mathematics, the near-perfect alignment of plaid. Vatican II, fallen heroes, Magical Mystery Tours, mothers burying their sons; each and others of these were either beneath her comment or beyond her ken. And yet, in her awful isolation, she seemed somehow (or so I could pretend) the only Dutch boy for miles around with an eye on the dike and a finger at the ready. Old-fashioned though they were—a reverent passion for the history of manners, a health for time, an insistence for roses—her oddities were lovely, and because they were so very out of their element, they lent respect to sentimentality and created for me (dare I say recreated?) the clearest illusion of a simpler age.

Where it began, I think I can say. Memory serves up a weekend phone call during which I ventured a merry imitation of a favorite Classics professor. Rachelann laughed, and somewhere in the timbre of that laugh I sensed something, a trickle of newness, the glad rustle of old coats being shaken out of moth balls, that had my ego thinking no one before me had ever made her laugh.

She seemed pleased, on the other end, that I shared her love for books, affection not only for their substance but affection for bound paper print. Soon, nightly talks turned to nightly strolls.

The windows of the library would be orange for us on those dark university evenings. There seemed, at the time, nothing more wholly satisfying than a walk with a bunch of books un-

perhaps, hovering above and just to the front of her, had attached a string to her navel and was forever invisibly pulling her forward, feet at right angles, hips thrashing for gravity in three-quarter time. Unique, to say the least.

"Do you find I have a foolish gait?" she asked me suddenly one day.

"Different, not foolish," I answered.

She nodded approvingly. "You're the first one who hasn't made fun. Actually, I'm quite proud of my walk. It comes from long hours spent at the barre."

"I see," I said.

She stopped. "And you mean to say you find it not revolting? Even my double ankles?"

"Even those." I smiled.

Her freckle did a little dance. "It's time you met my folks," she said.

Most of our time was spent in the family kitchen with Rachelann's mother, Woodrow, and her younger brother, Lee. Oh, yes—and with Mittens and Snoopy, the dogs. A father figured somewhere in all of this but he was one of those dinosaur daddies in whose presence one always felt imminent the discussion of a dowry and whom one avoided as often as possible.

I favored most the time spent in the kitchen. I like kitchens, particularly "Meet Me in Saint Louis" kitchens where the emphasis on patterns and windows stages the sun and where, in any corner, you are likely to taste the smell of poppy seeds and licorice that makes you feel good and safe and warm, only it isn't really poppy seeds or licorice at all you are smelling but ordinary things—dough and apples and sugar—wrongly identified by our fostered belief that only the exotic could ever make us feel so very much at home.

I became, I think I can tell you, surrounded as I was by piping bowls of bisque, kindly words, and fluttery mothers, quite the pampered suitor. Woodrow baked oven cookies served with watermelon slices on the side while Lee, he of a choirboy's face and demeanor, fashioned a white knick-knack shelf as a gift for me one Christmas.

On Saturdays, the three of us, Rachelann,

der arm and a chat with Rachelann. I listened intently to her discourses on Currier and Ives and museums, tried mightily to understand her contempt for the myths of faded jeans and flannel shirts and, welcome wonder, even came to know fondness for her slightly comic walk. She had a curious, pendular walk, a dancer's build and thighs, optically bent at the belly as if someone or something, some devilish sprite

her brother and I, passed our noons at a downtown Woolworth's where you could still buy sun-gold canaries and carry home angelfish in a bag. We broke balloons for penny sundaes and laughed and had a swell time.

Our dates defied the times we were living in. On the eve of the Beatles' break-up, I remember, we attended an Arthur Fiedler concert and heard the Boston Pops play "Clair de Lune" and selections from *South Pacific*. Rachelann wore a hand-made, floor-length gown; I wore Old Spice cologne.

The week Betty Friedan's picture appeared on the cover of *Time*, we visited Amherst and Dickinson's grave. We were translating Ovid's "The Founding of Rome" during the Washington Watergate trials.

We took long sojourns on campus, mostly, sitting on cold, gray, autumn rocks and letting our feet feed on the leaves. Conversations went something like this:

"Do you ever miss the ballet?" I would say.

"Naturally not. I have you."

"What I mean is—am I enough?"

Rachelann would close her eyes. "It is only right and proper that we should have found one another. We are practical and live by certain laws."

"What laws?"

"Societal laws. The protocol of courtship. You respect me and I want to keep house for you. It's what's done. Not like the dance. The dance turned my head, put me up on a cloud. I was pretty then. I wore banana curls and tiny bows. I liked the dance. I liked the way I looked practicing in the mirror with the tulle stiff and obedient in a circle 'round my middle." She would here pause and look me in the eye. "You didn't know I know I'm not pretty anymore, did you? Well, I do. I'm not pretty anymore. It's a simple, declarative sentence. The toe shoes were a dream."

"Nothing wrong with wanting something better," I would say.

Rachelann would shrug it off. "I used to think I was special."

"What happened?"

She would fold her hands upon her lap. "The world laughed at me. It hurt at first but it's supposed to. It's for growing up. Oh, these Harpies with the bells on their ankles, they make a lot of noise but nothing's going to come of it. Not a thing. It isn't clean, what they're doing. They don't see the order. A simple faith, a tidy kitchen. You follow the rules because it's all you can do."

"And honeymoon at Niagara, I suppose?"

"Just as did our Mothers and Dads."

"I want to be safe," I would say.

"And safe you shall be," she would answer and motion me permission to kiss her apple cheek. We anticipated marriage.

I woke one morning hating her.

News of a friend killed in Cambodia took me like a fever, carried me to a funeral that became, for me, a birth.

Questions began to be asked of me: "What about *your* draft card number?" "What's your opinion of the Berrigans?" "Were you there at the protest on the ninth?"

I stirred as if from a long, lazy sleep. Like anyone existing in a time machine, encased, secure, I had forgotten there was a world beyond not able to tolerate my game. I had not hidden well. Belief in my invisibility had served to make me all the more opaque. Terrified, angry, I panicked. In my guilt and naked tardiness, I blamed Rachelann, the shadow from the past, the princess in the tower. Sanctimonious! Phony! Ancient! Prude! What name didn't I call her? Not to her face, no, but in my heart, in the part of me that wanted to belong. To her face, I mumbled excuses and let slip curses *sotto voce* regarding "laws" and "absolute propriety." I wanted out.

"What can I do?" I asked a friend, begging a solution. "She will take me away from my time."

I promised the stars I would change.

But the 1960s ended the morning after I discovered they existed.

I quit my job on impulse and boarded a Greyhound for the West. I didn't know where I was headed or what, specifically, I expected to find there. I was empty and alien and sought my fill of highways and revolution. Little did I know that what I sought had long since vanished.

No one spoke of "The Movement" anymore, at least not to me. There were people who looked like hippies, all colors and hair, but the few I struck up conversations with talked of two and three kids and of IBM.

A Dutch girl, pretty and plain in denim, sat with me for awhile. She, too, she said, had never made it to the Woodstock Festival, though she had tried. She offered me granola and went on tenderly about the Kennedys, Jack and Bobby. She had brought flowers with her, asters, to place upon their graves and longed to sit in on a rally.

Fond of making the peace sign, she did not understand when fellow passengers saw this and sneered. Janis Joplin was her idol, she said, and Oakland, her destination.

We heard and saw nothing of those years, though, of which we spoke. Disco music blared from the bus radio and the scenery outside consisted of working silos and general stores. Everywhere, workmen were busy covering over the polemics of sixties graffiti with false brick front and latex. Protest and change had passed to nostalgia. At one point, a guy at the back of the bus raised three cheers for Dylan but got petered, lazy response. The Dutch girl cried. It was an echo of the way the world had been then.

I stayed on only a night in San Francisco, buying a return ticket home the next dawn. The first thing I did, upon my arrival, was to write to Rachelann. I explained everything as best I could and apologized for running away. My sudden departure I blamed on her father, travel fever, schizophrenia, amnesia, and an over-whelming sense of history. I prayed she would forgive.

She would not. Several days later, I received the following reply:

L,
You are a talented boy and I think you will go far. I bear you no ill will and wish you the best life has to offer.

However, there is no doubting that your bestial abandonment on the night of the 18th has lowered you considerably in my sights. Surely you must know you have fallen out of our good graces.

Perchance, the error was mine. I might have given more of myself. When and if I ever do give myself, I realize now it will have to be to a much more mature and understanding man, one who will accept the fact that I and my kind do not want to change.

Really, it all worked out for the best and since we never truly tasted one another's thoughts, we shall never know what we missed. It's best you forget.

Never call or write me again. We shall meet at the place where the sea meets the sky.

Placidly,
Rachelann

Ignoring her requests, I mailed more letters, even dialed her once, but she calmly refused to talk with me. I never heard from or saw her again.

For the sea never really meets the sky. Mutual friends tell me Rachelann retains to this day the hair style she favored as a girl. The shelf her brother made me still hangs from my bedroom wall, only now it hangs crooked and yellowed and is losing its capacity for holding.

GARY SNYDER

Good, Wild,
Sacred

Gary Snyder wrote several thoughtful essays for COEVOLUTION QUAR-
TERLY starting around 1982. (Earlier, in 1978, he had coedited the
"poets' issue.") Of his essays—one
on the end of urban culture in Sung
Dynasty China, another on the purpose of saying grace—this gathered
the most response. It appeared in Jay
Kinney's guest-edited section on reconciling politics with religion.

                            Art Kleiner

*From the original introduction
(Fall 1983):*
I first became aware of Gary Snyder
sixteen years ago when I read the
transcript of a four-way discussion
held on Alan Watts's houseboat
which was published in the *San
Francisco Oracle*. As Watts, Tim
Leary, and Allen Ginsberg traded
often-romantic observations of the
budding Counterculture back and
forth, Gary Snyder's voice came
through clearly and attentively, time
and again pulling the discussion (especially Leary) back to solid ground.
Gary's poetry, of course, predated
that discussion by at least a decade,
and has remained a stable reference
point for me in the years since. His
feet, happily, are as solidly planted
on the Earth as ever.

   This paper on the political and
spiritual implications of our relations to the land emerged from talks
Gary has given in Sweden, Wyo-
ming, and the United
Kingdom. . . .

                            Jay Kinney

I

I live on land in the Sierra Nevada of Alta California, continent of Turtle Island, which is
somewhat wild and not terribly good. The indigenous people there, the Nisenan or Southern Maidu, were almost entirely displaced or
destroyed during the first decade of the gold
rush. Consequently we have no one to teach
us which parts of that landscape were once
thought to be sacred, but with much time and
attention, I think we will be able to identify
such sites again. Wild land, sacred land, good
land. At home developing our mountain farm-
stead, in town at political meetings, and farther afield studying the problems of indigenous peoples, I hear each of these terms
emerging. By examining these three categories
perhaps we can get some further insights into
the problems of rural habitation, subsistence
living, wilderness preservation, and third- and
fourth-world resistance to the appetites of industrial civilization.

   • *Wild* refers to all unmanipulated unman-
aged natural habitat. Most of the planet in
precivilized times was hospitable to humans—

rich rain forests, teeming seacoasts, or grass-lands covered with bison, mammoths, or prong-horns. Near-climax, high-biomass, perennially productive, such places were essential expres-sions of biological nature. Some parts are bet-ter than others in terms of supporting much life, with soils rich in nutrients, but even in-hospitable mountain terrain may provide spe-cial plants or animals of unique value. Knowl-edge is the real key: for a Kalahari bushman, a Pintubi of the west-central Australian desert, or a Ute of the Great Basin, those arid lands are a life-sustaining home. Many if not all ar-chaic and nonliterate peoples have also found some parts of the landscape to be special, "sa-cred," and have given etiquette and lore to that. Such spots are of course also wild.

• The idea of Good Land really comes from agriculture. Here *good* is narrowed to mean land productive of a much smaller range of fa-vored cultivars, and thus the opposite of wild, cultivated. In wild nature there is no disorder: no plant in the almost endless mosaics of micro and macro communities is really out of place. For hunting and gathering peoples who draw on that spread of richness, a cultivated patch of land might seem bizarre, and not particularly good, at least at first. Gathering peoples gather from the whole field, ranging widely daily. Agricultural people live by an inner map made up of highly productive nodes (cleared fields) connected by lines (trails through the scary for-est). A beginning of "linear."

• In civilized agrarian states the term *sacred* was sometimes applied to ritually cultivated land or special temple fields. The fertility reli-gions of those times were not necessarily re-joicing in the fertility of all nature, but were focusing on crops. The concept of cultivation was extended to describe a kind of training in lore and manners that guaranteed member-ship in an elite class. By the metaphor of "spir-itual cultivation" a holy man is one who has weeded out the wild from his nature. But weeding out the wild from the natures of members of the Bos and Sus clans—cattle and pigs—transformed animals which are intelli-gent and interesting in the wild into sluggish meat-making machines. Cultivation at the top

makes domestication and exploitation possible below.

Wild groves and grottoes lingered on as shrines in agrarian states, and were viewed with much ambivalence by the rulers from the metropole. They survived because the people who actually worked the land still half-heard the call of the old ways, and certain folk teach-ings were still being transmitted that went back to even before agriculture. The king of Is-rael began to cut down the sacred groves, and the Christians finished the job.

The thought that wild might also be sacred returned to the Occident only with the Ro-mantic movement. This reappreciation of na-ture projects a rather vague sense of the sacred, however. It is only from very old place-centered cultures that we hear of sacred groves, sacred land, in a context of genuine belief and practice.

II

In North America and Australia the original inhabitants are facing the latest round of in-cursions into their remotest territories. These reservations or reserves were left in their use because the dominant society thought the arc-tic tundra or arid desert "no good." The People of Australia, Alaska, and elsewhere are vigor-ously fighting to keep logging or oil explora-tion or uranium mining out of some of their landscapes, and not only for the reason that it is actually their own land, but also because some places in it are sacred.

So a very cogent and current political issue rises around the question of the possible sa-credness of certain spots. I was at the Univer-sity of Montana in the spring of 1982 on a pro-gram with Russell Means, the American Indian Movement founder and activist, who was trying to get support for the Yellow Thun-der Camp of Lakota and other Indian people of the Black Hills on what is currently called For-est Service land. These Indians wish to block further expansion of mining into the Black Hills. They argue that the particular place they are on is not only ancestral land but sacred.

During his term, former California Gover-nor Jerry Brown created the Native American

Heritage Commission specifically for California Indians, and the commission identified a number of Indian Elders who were charged with the task of locating and protecting sacred sites and graves in California. This would avoid in advance confrontations with landowners or public land managers. It was a sensitive move, and though barely comprehensible to the white voters, it sent a ripple of appreciation through all the native communities. The white Christian founders of the United States were probably not considering American Indian religions when they guaranteed freedom of religion, but interpretations by the courts, and the passage of the American Indian Religious Freedom Act of 1978, have gradually come to give native practices some real status. Sacred virtually becomes a new land-use category.

III

In the hunting and gathering way of life the whole territory of a given group is fairly equally experienced by everyone. It becomes know for its many plant communities, high and low terrain, good views, odd-shaped rocks, dangerous spots, and places made special by myth or story. There are places where women go for seclusion or to give birth, places the bodies of the dead are taken to. There are spots where young girls or young boys are called to for special instruction. Some places in this territory are recognized as numinous, loaded with meaning and power. This has happened to all of us. The memories of such spots are very long.

I was in Australia in the fall of 1981 at the invitation of the Australian Aboriginal Arts Board doing some teaching, poetry readings, and workshops with aboriginal leaders and children. Much of the time I was in the central Australian desert south and west of Alice Springs, first into Pitjantjara tribal territory, and then three hundred miles northwest into Pintubi tribal territory. The aboriginal people in the central desert all still speak their languages. Their religion is fairly intact, and most young men are still initiated at fourteen, even the ones who go to high school at Alice Springs. They leave the high school with the cooperation of the school authorities for a year, and are taken out into the bush to learn bush ways on foot, to master the lore of landscapes and plants and animals, and finally to undergo initiation.

I was traveling by truck over dirt track west from Alice Springs in the company of a Pintubi elder named Jimmy Tjungurrayi. As we rolled along the dusty road, sitting in the bed of a pickup, he began to speak very rapidly to me. He was talking about a mountain over there, telling me a story about some wallabies that came to that mountain in the dreamtime and got into some kind of mischief there with some lizard girls. He had hardly finished that and he started in on another story about another hill over here and another story over there. I couldn't keep up. I realized after about half an hour of this that these were tales to be told while *walking*, and that I was experiencing a speeded-up version of what might be leisurely told over several days of foot-travel. Mr. Tjungurrayi felt graciously compelled to share a body of lore with me by virtue simply of the fact that I was there.

So remember a time when you journeyed on foot over hundreds of miles, walking fast and often traveling at night, traveling night-long and napping in the acacia shade during the day, and these stories were told to you as you went. In your travels with an older person you were given a map you could memorize, full of the lore and song, and also practical information. Off by yourself you could sing those songs to bring yourself back. And you could maybe travel to a place that you'd never been, steering only by songs you had learned.

We made camp at a waterhole called Ilpili and rendezvoused with a number of Pintubi people from the surrounding desert country. The Ilpili waterhole is about a yard across, six inches deep, in a little swale of bush full of finch. The People camp a quarter-mile away. It's the only waterhole that stays full through drought years in several thousand square miles. A place kept by custom, I am told, welcome and open to all. Through the night, until one or two in the morning, Jimmy Tjungurrayi and the other old men sat and sang a cycle of journey songs, walking through a space of desert in imagination and song. They stopped between songs and would hum a phrase or two and then would argue a bit about the words and then would start again, and someone would defer to another person and would let him start. Jimmy explained to me that they have so many cycles of journey songs they can't quite remember them all, and that they have to be constantly rehearsing them. Night after night they say, "What will we sing tonight?" "Let's sing the walk up to Darwin." They'll start out and argue their way along through it, and stop when it gets too late to go any farther. I asked Jimmy, "Well how far did you get last night?" He said, "Well we got two-thirds of the way to Darwin." This is a way to transmit information about vast terrain which is obviously very effective, and doesn't require writing. Some of the places thus defined will also be presented as sacred.

One day driving near Ilpili we stopped the truck and Jimmy and three other elderly gentlemen got out and said, "We'll take you out to see a sacred place here." And, "I guess you're old enough." They turned to the young boys and said that uninitiated boys couldn't go there. As we climbed the hill these ordinarily cheery and loud-talking aboriginal men began to drop their voices. As we got higher up the hill they were speaking in whispers, their whole manner changed. They said, in a whisper, "Now we are coming close." Then they got on their hands and knees and crawled. We crawled up the last two hundred feet, over a little rise into an area of broken and oddly shaped rocks. They whispered to us with respect and awe of what was there and its story. Then we all backed away. We got back down the hill and at a certain point stood and walked. At another point voices rose. Back at the truck, everybody was talking loud again and no more mention was made of the sacred place.

Very powerful. Very much in mind. We learned later that it was a place where young men were taken for instruction and for initiation.

IV

So the nature of the "sacred place" in Australia began to define itself as special rocks, beauti-ful, steep defiles where two cliffs almost meet with maybe just a little sand bed between, a place where many parrots are nesting in the rock walls, or a place where a blade of rock stands on end balancing, thirty feet tall, by a waterhole. Each of them was out of the ordinary, a little fantastic even, and they were places of teaching. Often they had pictographs, left by past human ancestors. In some cases they were also what are called "dreaming spots" for certain totem ancestors. "Dreaming" or "dreamtime" refers to a time of creation which is not in the past but which is here right now. It's the mode of eternally creative nowness, as contrasted with the mode of cause and effect in time, where modern people mainly live, and within which we imagine history, progress, evolution to take place. The totem dreaming place is first of all special to the people of that totem, who sometimes make pilgrimages there. Second, it is sacred to the honey-ants (say) which actually live there. There are a lot of honey-ants there. Third, it's like a little Platonic cave of ideal honey-ant forms. (I'm imagining this now. I'm trying to explain what all these things seem to be.) It's the archetypal honey-ant spot. In fact, it's optimal honey-ant habitat. A green parrot dreaming place, with the tracks of ancestors going across the landscape and stopping at the green parrot dreaming place, is a perfect green parrot nesting spot. So the sacredness comes together with a sense of optimal habitat of certain kinfolk that we have out there—the wallabies, red kangaroo, bush turkeys, lizards. Robert Bliney sums it up this way: "The land itself was their chapel and their shrines were hills and creeks and their religious relics were animals, plants and birds. Thus the migrations of aboriginals, though spurred by economic need, were also always pilgrimages." Good (productive of much life), wild (naturally), and in these cases, sacred, were indeed one.

This way of life is going on right now, threatened by Japanese and other uranium mining, large-scale copper mining, and petroleum exploration throughout the deserts. The issue of sacredness is a very real political question, so much so that the Australian Bureau of Aboriginal Affairs has hired some bilingual anthropologists and bush people to work with elders of the different tribes to identify sacred sites and map them. Everyone hopes that the Australian government really means to declare such areas off-limits before any exploratory team ever gets near them. This effort is spurred by the fact that there have already been some confrontations in the Kimberley region over oil exploration. This was at Nincoomba. The People very firmly stood their ground and made human lines in the front of bulldozers and drilling rigs, and won the support of the Australian public. Since then the Australian government has been more careful. In Australian land ownership, mineral rights are always reserved to "The Crown" so that even a private ranch is subject to mining. To consider sacred land a special category in Australia is a very advanced move, at least in theory. But recently a "registered sacred site" was bulldozed near Alice Springs, supposedly on instructions of a government land minister, and this is in the relatively benign federal government jurisdiction! The state of Queensland is a minifascist nation to itself, favored by emigrants from white South Africa.

V

The original inhabitants of Japan, the Ainu, can see a whole system as in a very special sense sacred. Their term *iworu* means "field" with implications of watershed, plant and animal life, and spirit force. They speak of the *iworu* of the great brown bear. By that they mean the mountain habitat and watershed territory in which brown bear is dominant. They also speak of the *iworu* of the salmon, which means the lower watersheds with all their tributaries and the plant communities along those valleys that focus on the streams where salmon run. The bear field, the deer field, the salmon field, the orca (killer whale) field. To give a little picture of how this world works, a human house is up a valley by a stream, facing east. In the center of the house is the fire. The sunshine streams through the eastern door each morning to contact the fire, and they say the sun goddess is visiting her sister the fire goddess in the firepit. They communicate for a moment. One must not step across the sunbeams that shine

in the morning on the firepit; that would be breaking their contact.

Food comes from the inner mountains and from the deeps of the sea. The lord of the deeps of the sea is Orca or Killer Whale, the lord of the inner mountains is Bear. Bear sends his friends the deer down to visit us. Killer Whale sends his friends the salmon up the streams to visit us. When they come to visit us we kill them, to enable them to get out of their fur or scale coats, and then we entertain them because they love music. We sing songs to them, and we eat them. Having been delighted by the songs they heard, they return to the deep sea and to the inner mountains, and they report to their spirit friends there, "We had a wonderful time with the human beings. There's lots to eat, lots to drink, and they played music for us." The other ones say, "Oh, let's go visit the human beings." If the people do not neglect the proper hospitality, the music and manners, when entertaining their deer or salmon or wild plant-food visitors, the beings will be reborn and return over and over. This is a sort of spiritual game management.

VI

The Ainu were probably the original inhabitants of all of Japan. They certainly left many place-names behind and many traces on the landscape. Modern Japan is another sort of example: a successful industrialized country, with remnants of sacred land-consciousness still intact. There are Shinto shrines throughout Japan. Shinto is "the way of the spirits." By *spirits* the Japanese mean exactly what almost all people of the world have always meant: spirits are formless little powers present in everything to some degree but intensified in power and in presence in outstanding objects, such as large curiously twisted rocks, very old trees, or thundering misty waterfalls. Anomalies and beauties of the landscape are all signs of *kami*—spirit power, spirit presence, energy. The greatest of all the *kami*, or spirit forces of Japan, is Mt. Fuji. The name Fuji is now thought to be an old Ainu placename meaning "fire goddess." All of Mt. Fuji is a Shinto shrine, the largest in the nation, from well below timberline all the way to the summit.

Shinto got a bad name during the 30s and World War II because the Japanese government created a "State Shinto" in the service of militarism and nationalism. Long before the rise of any state, the islands of Japan were studded with little shrines—*jinja* or *miya*—part of the expression of Neolithic village culture. Even in the midst of the enormous onrushing industrial energy of the current system, shrine lands remain untouchable. It would make your hair stand up to see how the Japanese will take bulldozers to a nice slope of pines and level it for a new development. When the New Island was created in Kobe harbor, to make Kobe the second busiest port in the world (next to Rotterdam), it was raised from the bay bottom with dirt obtained by shaving down a range of hills ten miles south of the city. This was barged to the site for twelve years, a steady stream of barges carrying dirt off giant conveyor belts, totally removing soil two ranges back from the coast. That leveled area was then used for a housing development. In the industrial world it's not that "nothing is sacred," it's that the sacred is sacred and that's *all* that's sacred. We are grateful for the little bit of Japanese salvaged land because the rule in shrine lands is that (away from the buildings and paths) you never cut anything, never maintain anything, never clear or thin anything. No hunting, no fishing, no thinning, no burning, no stopping of burning.

Thus pockets of climax forests here and there, right inside the city, and one can walk into a shrine and be in the presence of an eight-hundred-year-old cryptomeria tree. Without shrines we wouldn't know so well what Japanese forests might have been. But such compartmentalization is not healthy: in this model some land is saved, like a virgin priestess, some is overworked endlessly like a wife, and some is brutally publicly reshaped, like an exuberant girl declared promiscuous and punished. Good, wild, and sacred couldn't be farther apart.

VII

Europe and the Middle East inherit from Neolithic and Paleolithic times many shrines. The most sacred spot of all Europe was perhaps the caves of southern France, in the Pyrenees. We shall say that they were the great shrines of twenty thousand years ago, the center of a religious complex in which the animals were brought underground. Maybe a dreaming place. Maybe a thought that the archetypal animal forms were thereby stored under the Earth, a way of keeping animals from becoming extinct. But many species did become extinct. Most became so during the last two thousand years, victims of the imperium, of civilization, in its particularly destructive western form. The degradation of wild habitat and extinction of species, the impoverishment and enslavement of rural people and subsistence economies, and the burning alive of nature-worship traditions were perfected right within Europe.

So the French and English explorers of North America and then the early fur traders and hunters had no traditions from the cultures they left behind that would urge them to look on wild land with reverence. They did find much that was awe-inspiring; some joined the Indians and the land and became people of place. These few almost forgotten exceptions were overwhelmed by fur-trade entrepreneurs and, later, farmers. Yet many kept joining the Indians in fact or in style—grieving for a wilderness they saw shrinking away. In the Far East, or Europe, a climax forest or prairie, and all the splendid creatures that live there, is a tale from the Neolithic. In the western United States it was our grandmothers' world. For many of us, without intellectualization or question, this loss is a source of grief. For Native Americans this loss is a loss of land, life, and culture.

VIII

It is of course not evil, to, as Thoreau did, "make the soil say beans"—to cause it to be productive to our own notion—but we must also ask, what does mother nature do best here when left to her own long strategies? This comes to asking, what would the climax vegetation of this spot be? For all land, however long wasted and exploited, if left to nature, the *tzuran*, "self-so" of Taoism, will arrive at a point of balance between biological productivity and stability. A truly sophisticated post-industrial "future primitive" agriculture will be asking: Is there any way we can go *with* rather than against a natural tendency toward, say, deciduous hardwoods—or as where I live, a mix of pine and oak with kitkitdizze ground cover? Such a condition in many cases might be best for human interests too, and even in the short run.

Wesley Jackson's research indicates that a perennial and horticultural-based agriculture holds real promise for sustaining the locally appropriate communities of the future. This is acknowledging that the source of fertility ultimately is the "wild." It has been said that "good soil is good because of the wildness in it." How could *this* be granted by a victorious king dividing up his spoils? (Spanish land grants—Royal/Real estate?) In my imagination the God/dess that gives us land is none other than Gaia herself: the whole network.

It might be that almost all civilized agriculture has been on the wrong path from the beginning, relying on the relative monoculture of annuals. In *New Roots for Agriculture* Wes Jackson develops this argument. I concur with his view, knowing that it raises even larger questions about civilization itself, a critique I have worked at elsewhere. Suffice it to say that the sorts of economic and social organization we invoke when we say "civilization" can no longer be automatically accepted as useful models. To scrutinize civilization as Dr. Stanley Diamond has in *In Search of the Primitive* is not, however, to negate all varieties of culture or cultivation.

The word *cultivation* in civilization, harking to etymologies of *till* and *wheel about*, generally implies a movement away from natural process. Both materially and psychologically, it is a matter of "arresting succession, establishing monoculture." Applied on the spiritual plane this has meant austerities, obedience to religious authority, long bookish scholarship, or a dualistic devotionalism (sharply distinguishing "creature and creator") and an overriding metaphor of divinity being "centralized," just as a secular ruler of a civilized state is at the center—of wealth, of the metropole, of political

power. A Divine King. The efforts entailed in such a spiritual practice are sometimes a sort of war against nature—placing the human over the animal, the "spiritual" over the human. The most sophisticated modern variety of this sort of thought is found in the works of Father Teilhard de Chardin, who claims a special evolutionary spiritual destiny for humanity under the name of higher consciousness. Some of the more extreme of these Spiritual Darwinists would willingly leave the rest of Earth-bound animal and plant life behind to enter a realm transcending biology. The anthropocentrism of some New Age thinkers is countered by the radical critique of the deep ecology movement.

IX

Yet there is such a thing as training. The natural world moves by process, and by complementarities of young and old, foolish and wise, ripe or green, raw or cooked. Animals too learn self-discipline and caution in the face of desire and availability. There is learning and training that goes with the grain of things. In early Chinese Taoism, "training" did not mean to cultivate the wildness out of oneself, but to do away with arbitrary and delusive conditioning—false social values distorting an essentially free and correct human nature. Buddhism takes a middle way, allowing as how greed, hatred, and stupidity are part of the given conditions of human nature, but seeing organized society, civilization, "the world" as being a force that inflames, panders to, or exploits these weaknesses in the fledgling human. Greed exposes the foolish person or the foolish chicken alike to the ever-watchful hawk of the food-web, and to early impermanence. It's interesting to note that preliterate hunting and gathering cultures lived well by virtue of knowledge and a quiet sort of manipulation of systems. We know how the people of Mesolithic Britain selectively cleared or burned, in the valley of the Thames, as a way to encourage the growth of hazel. An almost invisible horticulture was once practiced in the jungles of Guatemala. The spiritual equivalent of nature-enhancing practices can be seen in those shamanistic disciplines which open the neophyte's mind to the fascinating wild territory, the Unconscious.

We can all agree: there is a problem with the chaotic, self-seeking human ego. Is it a mirror of the wild and of nature? I think not: for civilization itself is ego gone to seed and institutionalized in the form of the State, both Eastern and Western. It is not nature-as-chaos which threatens us (for nature is orderly) but *ignorance* of the real natural world, the myth of progress, and the presumption of the State that it has created order. That sort of "order" is an elaborate rationalization of the greed of a few.

Now we can look again at what sacred land might be. For a people of an old culture, *all* their mutually owned territory holds numinous life and spirit. Certain spots are of high spiritual density because of their perceived animal or plant habitat peculiarities, or associations with legend and perhaps with human ancestry via totemic systems, or because of their geomorphological anomaly and formal intensity, or because of their association with spiritual training, or some combination of the above. These spots are seen as points on the landscape at which one can more easily enter a larger-than-human, larger-than-personal, realm.

x

Nowadays some present-day inhabitants of Turtle Island, and many Europeans, join with the native peoples of the world in a rather new political and economic movement concerned with "the ecology." Stephen Fox says it is also probably a new religion, so new that it has not been called such yet. Though sometimes attacked as being an elitist movement (even by the Reagan administration!) the growing popularity of the Earth First! organization and its "Rednecks for Wilderness" bumpersticker in blue-collar areas shows this to be not true. The temples of this movement are the planet's remaining wilderness areas. When we enter them on foot we can sense that the *kami* or (Maidu) *kukini* have fled here for refuge, as have the mountain lions, mountain sheep, and grizzlies. (Those three North American animals were found throughout the lower hills

and plains in prewhite times.) The rocky icy grandeur of the high country reminds us of the overarching wild systems that nourish us all—even an industrial economy, for in the sterile beauty of mountain snowfields and glaciers begin the little streams that water the huge agribusiness fields of the San Joaquin Valley of California. The backpacker-pilgrim's step-by-step, breath-by-breath walk up a trail, carrying all on the back, is so ancient a set of gestures as to trigger perennial images and a profound sense of body-mind joy.

Not just backpackers, of course. The same happens to those who sail in the ocean, kayak rivers, tend a garden, even sit on a meditation cushion. The point is in making intimate contact with wild world, wild self. *Sacred* refers to that which helps take us out of our little selves into the larger self of the whole universe.

Inspiration, exaltation, insight do not end, however, when one steps outside the doors of the church. The wilderness as a temple is only a beginning. That is: one should not dwell in the specialness of the extraordinary experience, not leave the political world behind to be in a state of heightened insight. The best purpose of such studies and backpack hikes is to be able to come back into the present world to see all the land about us, agricultural, suburban, urban, as part of the same giant realm of processes and beings—never totally ruined, never completely unnatural. Great Brown Bear is walking with us, salmon swimming upstream with us, as we stroll a city street.

xi

To return to my own situation: the land my family and I live on in the Sierra Nevada of California is "barely good" from an economic standpoint. With soil amendments, much labor, and the development of ponds for watering, it is producing a few vegetables and some good apples. As forest soils go it is better: through the millennia it has excelled at growing oak and pine trees. I guess I should admit that it's better left wild. It's being "managed for wild" right now—the pines are getting large again and some of the oaks were growing here before a white man set foot anywhere in

California. The deer and all the other animals move through with the exception of grizzly bear; grizzlies are now extinct in California. We dream sometimes of trying to bring them back.

These foothill ridges are not striking in any special way, no great scenery or rocks—but the deer are so at home here, I think it might be a "deer field." And the fact that my neighbors and I and all of our children have learned so much by taking our place in the Sierra foothills—not striking wilderness, but logged-over land, burned-over land, considered worthless for decades—begins to make it a teacher to us. A place on Earth we work with, struggle with, where we stick out the summers and winters. And it has showed us a little of its power.

But this use of "teacher" is still a newcomer's metaphor. By our grandchildren's time there may begin to be a culture of place again in America. How does this work? First, a child must experience that bonding to place that has always touched many of us deeply: a small personal territory one can run to, a secret "fort," a place of never-forgotten smells and sounds, a refuge away from home. Second, one must continue to live in a place, to not move away, and to continue walking the paths and roads. A child's walking the land is a veritable exercise in "expanding consciousness." Third, one must have human teachers, who can name and explain the plants, who know the life cycle of an area. Fourth, one must draw some little part of one's livelihood from the breadth of the landscape: spotting downed trees for next year's firewood, gathering mushrooms or berries or herbs on time, fishing, hunting, scrounging. Fifth, one must learn to listen. Then the voice can be heard. The nature spirits are never dead, they are alive under our feet, over our heads, all around us, ready to speak when we are silent and centered. So what is this "voice"? Just the cry of a flicker, or coyote, or jay, or wind in a tree, or acorn whack on a garage roof. Nothing mysterious, but now you're home.

Fine, and what about right now? As Peter Nabokov says, goodhearted environmentalists can turn their backs on a save-the-wilderness project when it gets too tiresome and return to a city home. But inhabitory people, he says, will "fight for their lives like they've been jumped in an alley." Like it or not, we are *all* finally "inhabitory" on this one small blue-green planet. It's the only one with comfortable temperatures, good air and water, and a wealth of living beings for millions (or quadrillions) of miles. A little waterhole in the Vast Space, a nesting place, a place of singing and practice, a place of dreaming. It's on the verge of being totally trashed—there's a slow way and a fast way. It's clearly time to put hegemonial controversies aside, to turn away from economies that demand constant exploitation of both people and resources, and to put Earth first!

As the most numerous, ambitious, and "musical" (as the Ainu would say) sort of the larger mammals, human beings might well awaken to their great possible place in the biosphere as sensitive transformers. We might someday initiate a more sophisticated dialogue between the poles of cultivation and original nature, technology and the self-born, production and reproduction, than has ever been imagined before. These possibilities go far beyond any fantasies of high-tech. I'm thinking of a condition where wild, sacred, and good will be one and the same, again.

SALLIE TISDALE

Handfast

Sallie Tisdale introduced herself to
COEVOLUTION QUARTERLY in Summer 1983 by sending in an essay
called "Women's Work," about what
gets lost when nursing is forced from
"menial, demanding, dirty work,
with low wages and little status"
into a professional job. Since then
she's appeared in nearly every CQ.
This piece, which Stewart later said
"has almost become a cult item
among parents," appeared in Winter
1983. At twenty-eight, Sallie has
the kind of thoughtfulness and skill
at phrasing which can convey to
readers the sense of listening to a
perceptive friend. When not writing
she supports herself as a registered
nurse—most recently at Reed College, Oregon. Her book on "patients' experiences with medical
technology" was published by Mc-
Graw-Hill in January 1986.

Art Kleiner

One factor determines all else about our relationship with our children: it is irreversible.
The contract cannot be broken. Daily we leave
jobs, houses, friends, lovers, but the child always comes along.

When the going is rough—when we don't
like each other—my son and I can't call it
quits and cut our losses. I can't pack a bag,
make a break for it, perhaps find a more com-
patible child. Were it even the remotest of possibilities, everything else would change.

So I take risks with him I would never dare
take with anyone else. I treat him badly, with
rough impatience, with all the bile I hide from
friends and lovers for fear of losing them. I am
less tolerant of deviation and idiosyncrasies
with him. We fight—bitterly—then, sad and
weary of it, make up with a tentative kiss. I
demand so much: love, loyalty, obedience, attention, and faith to a degree few adults would
allow me to approach. For the most part in
these early years, I get what I demand—de-
serving or not.

He is tied and bound to me. We are entan-
gled. When I wake from a bad dream without
a sound, he wakes in the next room and cries
for me. As a baby, his cry could make my
breasts run with milk, his weight missing
from my arms left me restless and sore. I
watched the babyfat melt and muscles emerge
from the perfect downy skin. I watch the features smooth over, change, gradually hiding
the newborn between cheek and chin somewhere. He is the flesh of my flesh that lovers
promise and can't deliver.

Yet he is hardly conscious of the intimacy.
Later, when he wakes to his own appetites,
others' hands—strangers' hands—will stroke
where I stroke now. I am jealous of this future
secret-sharing apart from me, jealous of the response those hands will provoke.

Between us, yet, is no shame, no inhibition.
He thinks me beautiful; he wants to grow to
be like me. And I am bound to fail him, and

bound to lose him. Daily the gap between us grows. He is not mindful of it—but I am. Oh, I am.

For many years, unremembered years, our children have only the vaguest notion of their separateness from us. We are an immutable and invariable framework in their lives, a perpetual foundation. Therefore they treat us with an abominable negligence and come one day, hat in hand, to claim themselves and leave. They grow into strangers certain to disappoint and perplex us, having long before wakened to disillusionment with us. They seem oblivious to our loss—after all, they've lost nothing. We are only their parents. And haven't we done all this before?

I treat my own mother with an offhand and rather inattentive disregard. She is, after all, my mother. She is always there, and I am always her child, as my son is my child, first, forever and ever.

Could she ever have felt this same fierce protective love for me? It seems she should be grieved, bereft, if that is so. I am far away from her. I cling to my son; this ordinary woman chats of relatives and the weather. What could she be hiding, inarticulate, beneath mundane conversation?

I may never know. Affection embarrasses us. A lump comes to my throat when my mother and I move close to each other; we both feel relief when the contact is averted. Will it be the same for my son and me, who now crawls like a spoiled child-prince across my lap? How could such ease be forgotten, to become the shy silence between my mother and me?—though I know she is like a limb to me, a vital organ.

She shows up, surprising me, in my words to my son. I repeat what she told me, the phrases and platitudes, in the same tone of voice and inflection I heard as a child. We all have vowed to do it differently, to be unlike our parents, and the most we can manage is a variation.

Will my son, then, repeat me, as I my mother and she my grandmother? I become part of his inheritance, and will prevail despite

his efforts. Even when he's gone and busy forgetting me I'll show up, surprising him. He'll try to throw me off, the monkey on his back.

I'll grow old on him. The trick of parents through the ages—we turn again into children. "When I grow up," he tells me, "you'll be my baby." Yes, I smile. Yes, if only you knew, my son. I have put my grandmother on the toilet, to bed, consigned to death. Perhaps I'll do the same for my mother in her time. Perhaps one day I'll lie in bed, watching this smooth-faced boy fold my diapers, and see in him a gesture that reminds me of myself once young. But now he remains under my still-strong wing, unconcerned.

This frightful responsibility! I invited it, and I carry it out in a workaday way. But I quail secretly at the number of mistakes I'm bound to make, what I'll saddle him with, what the price for both of us will finally be. I'll give the world a son, heavy with the grief of giving him at all. Then and after, he'll drift in and out of my view, keeping secrets, neglecting me, while I watch from a distance, unrequited.

Postscript: He's seven now; this essay is more than four years old. I am still taken aback by the strength of feeling, by the subtle, unexpected turns of the heart. An old friend recently became a father for the first time, after years of saying he never would. Right before the birth he told me, "The thing that scares me most about being a parent is that I'm certain to fail at it. There's just no way to do it perfectly." All I could say was Yes.

I've had seven years to fear his death, too. When he's sleeping, arms flung out and smug smile on his soft face, I can believe I've created something true and enduring. I can believe then in perfection. And when I fear his death, when I contemplate the space he takes up, and how vast its emptiness would be, I know that most of all I'd miss him sleeping. My greatest challenge is to feel that sweetness, and that sorrow, through and through.

IVAN ILLICH

Silence Is a Commons

Ivan Illich has become civilization's best critic. No one else has his range—education, energy, medicine, communications, economics, gender, dwelling (*De-Schooling Society*, 1971; *Energy and Equity*, 1974; *Medical Nemesis*, 1975; *Vernacular Gender*, 1983). No one else is simultaneously so radical (original, penetrating), so conservative (protective of the native, the vernacular), or so theoretically consistent. Everywhere the chill of human institutions threatens the warmth of human life, Ivan Illich eventually shows up with his wolf grin. Here, from the Winter 1983 issue, with computers. This article is from Illich's remarks at the "Asahi Symposium: Science and Man—The Computer-Managed Society," Tokyo, Japan, March 21, 1982.

Stewart Brand

Minna-san, gladly I accept the honor of addressing this forum on Science and Man. The theme that Mr. Tsuru proposes, "The Computer-Managed Society," sounds an alarm. Clearly you foresee that machines which ape people are tending to encroach on every aspect of people's lives, and that such machines force people to behave like machines. The new electronic devices do indeed have the power to force people to "communicate" with them and with each other on the terms of the machine. Whatever structurally does not fit the logic of machines is effectively filtered from a culture dominated by their use.

The machine-like behavior of people chained to electronics constitutes a degradation of their well-being and of their dignity which, for most people in the long run, becomes intolerable. Observations of the sickening effect of programmed environments show that people in them become indolent, impotent, narcissistic, and apolitical. The political process breaks down, because people cease to be able to *govern* themselves; they demand to be *managed*.

I congratulate Asahi Shimbun on its efforts to foster a new democratic consensus in Japan, by which your more than seven million readers become aware of the need to limit the encroachment of machines on the style of their own behavior. It is important that precisely Japan initiate such action. Japan is looked upon as the capital of electronics; it would be marvelous if it became for the entire world the model of a new politics of self-limitation in the field of communication, which, in my opinion, is henceforth necessary if a people wants to remain self-governing.

Electronic management as a political issue can be approached in several ways. I propose, at the beginning of this public consultation, to approach the issue as one of political ecology. Ecology, during the last ten years, has acquired a new meaning. It is still the name for a branch of professional biology, but the term now increasingly serves as the label under which a broad, politically organized general public analyzes and influences technical decisions. I want to focus on the new electronic management devices as a technical change of the human environment which, to be benign, must remain under political (and not exclusively expert) control. I have chosen this focus for my introduction, because I thus continue my conversation with those three Japanese colleagues to whom I owe what I know about your country—Professors Yoshikazu Sakamoto, Joshiro Tamanoi, and Jun Ui.

In the thirteen minutes still left to me on this rostrum I will clarify a distinction that I consider fundamental to political ecology. I shall distinguish the *environment as commons* from the *environment as resource*. On our ability to make this particular distinction depends not only the construction of a sound theoretical ecology, but also—and more importantly—effective ecological jurisprudence.

Minna-san, how I wish, at this point, that I were a pupil trained by your Zen poet, the great Bāsho. Then perhaps in a bare seventeen syllables I could express the distinction between the *commons* within which people's subsistence activities are embedded, and *resources* that serve for the economic production of those commodities on which modern survival depends. If I were a poet, perhaps I would make this distinction so beautifully and incisively that it would penetrate your hearts and remain unforgettable. Unfortunately I am not a Japanese poet. I must speak to you in English, a language that during the last hundred years has lost the ability to make this distinction, and—in addition—I must speak through translation. Only because I may count on the translating genius of Mr. Muramatsu do I dare to recover Old English meanings with a talk in Japan.

"Commons" is an Old English word. According to my Japanese friends, it is quite close to the meaning that *iriai* still has in Japanese. "Commons," like *iriai*, is a word which, in preindustrial times, was used to designate certain *aspects* of the environment. People called commons those parts of the environment for which customary law exacted specific forms of community respect. People called commons that part of the environment which lay beyond their own thresholds and outside of their own possessions, to which, however, they had recognized claims of usage, not to produce commodities but to provide for the subsistence of their households. The customary law which humanized the environment by establishing the commons was usually unwritten. It was unwritten law not only because people did not care to write it down, but because what it protected was a reality much too complex to fit into paragraphs. The law of the commons regulates the right of way, the right to fish and to hunt, to graze, and to collect wood or medicinal plants in the forest.

An oak tree might be in the commons. Its shade, in summer, is reserved for the shepherd and his flock; its acorns are reserved for the pigs of the neighboring peasants; its dry branches serve as fuel for the widows of the village; some of its fresh twigs in springtime are cut as ornaments for the church—and at sunset it might be the place for the village assembly. When people spoke about commons, *iriai*, they designated an aspect of the environment that was limited, that was necessary for the community's survival, that was necessary for different groups in different ways, but which, in a strictly economic sense, was *not perceived as scarce*.

When today, in Europe, with university students I use the term "commons" (in German *Almende* or *Gemeinheit*, in Italian *gli usi civici*) my listeners immediately think of the eighteenth century. They think of those pastures in England on which villagers each kept a few sheep, and they think of the "enclosure of the pastures" which transformed the grassland from commons into a resource on which commercial flocks could be raised. Primarily, however, my students think of the innovation of poverty which came with enclosure: of the absolute impoverishment of the peasants, who were driven from the land and into wage labor, and they think of the commercial enrichment of the lords.

In their immediate reaction, my students think of the rise of a new capitalist order. Facing that painful newness, they forget that enclosure also stands for something more basic. The enclosure of the commons inaugurates a *new ecological order*. Enclosure did not just physically transfer the control over grasslands from the peasants to the lord. Enclosure marked a radical change in the attitudes of society towards the environment. Before, in any juridical system, most of the environment had been considered as commons from which most people could draw most of their sustenance without needing to take recourse to the market. After enclosure the environment became primarily a resource at the service of "enterprises" which, by organizing wage-labor, transformed nature into the goods and services on which the satisfaction of basic needs by consumers depends. This transformation is in the blind spot of political economy.

This change of attitudes can be illustrated better if we think about roads rather than about grasslands. What a difference there was between the new and old parts of Mexico City only twenty years ago. In the old parts of the city the streets were true commons. Some people sat on the road to sell vegetables and charcoal. Others put their chairs on the road to drink coffee or tequila. Others held their meetings on the road to decide on the new headman for the neighborhood or to determine the price of a donkey. Others drove their donkeys through the crowd, walking next to the heavily-loaded beasts of burden; others sat in the saddle. Children played in the gutter, and still people walking could use the road to get from one place to another.

Such roads were built for people. Like any true commons, the street itself was the result of people living there and making that space livable. The dwellings that lined the roads were not private homes in the modern sense— garages for the overnight deposit of workers. The threshold still separated two living spaces,

one intimate and one common. But neither homes in this intimate sense nor streets as commons survived economic development.

In the new sections of Mexico City, streets are no more for people. They are now roadways for automobiles, for buses, for taxis, cars, and trucks. People are barely tolerated on the streets unless they are on their way to a bus stop. If people now sat down or stopped on the street, they would become obstacles for traffic, and traffic would be dangerous to them. The road has been degraded from a commons to a simple resource for the circulation of vehicles. People can circulate no more on their own. Traffic has displaced their mobility. They can circulate only when they are strapped down and are moved.

The appropriation of the grassland by the lords was challenged, but the more *fundamental transformation* of grassland (or of roads) from commons to resource has happened, until recently, without being subjected to criticism. The appropriation of the environment by the few was clearly recognized as an intolerable abuse. By contrast, the even more degrading transformation of people into members of an industrial *labor force and into consumers* was taken, until recently, for granted. For almost a hundred years the majority of political parties has challenged the accumulation of environmental resources in private hands. However, the issue was argued in terms of the private utilization of these resources, not the distinction of commons. Thus anticapitalist politics so far have bolstered the legitimacy of transforming commons into resources.

Only recently, at the base of society a new kind of "popular intellectual" is beginning to recognize what has been happening. Enclosure has denied the people the right to that *kind* of environment on which—throughout all of history—the *moral economy of survival* had been based. Enclosure, once accepted, redefines community. Enclosure undermines the local autonomy of community. Enclosure of the commons is thus as much in the interest of professionals and of state bureaucrats as it is in the interest of capitalists. Enclosure allows the bureaucrat to define local community as important—"*ei-ei, schau-schau!!!*"—to provide for its own survival. People become economic individuals that depend for their survival on commodities that are produced *for them*. Fundamentally, most citizens' movements represent a rebellion against this environmentally induced redefinition of people as consumers.

Minna-san, you wanted to hear me speak on electronics, not grassland and roads. But I am a historian; I wanted to speak first about the pastoral commons as I know them from the past in order then to say something about the present, much wider threat to the commons by electronics.

This man who speaks to you was born fifty-five years ago in Vienna. One month after his birth he was put on a train, and then on a ship and brought to the Island of Brac. Here, in a village on the Dalmatian coast, his grandfather wanted to bless him. My grandfather lived in the house in which his family had lived since the time when Muromachi ruled in Kyoto. Since then on the Dalmatian coast many rulers had come and gone—the doges of Venice, the sultans of Istanbul, the corsairs of Almissa, the emperors of Austria, and the kings of Yugoslavia. But these many changes in the uniform and language of the governors had changed little in daily life during these five hundred years. The very same olive-wood rafters still supported the roof of my grandfather's house. Water was still gathered from the same stone slabs on the roof. The wine was pressed in the same vats, the fish caught from the same kind of boat, and the oil came from trees planted when Edo was in its youth.

My grandfather had received news twice a month. The news now arrived by steamer in three days; and formerly, by sloop, it had taken five days to arrive. When I was born, for the people who lived off the main routes, history still flowed slowly, imperceptibly. Most of the environment was still in the commons. People lived in houses they had built; moved on streets that had been trampled by the feet of their animals; were autonomous in the procurement and disposal of their water; could de-

pend on their own voices when they wanted to speak up. All this changed with my arrival in Brac.

On the same boat on which I arrived in 1926, the first loudspeaker was landed on the island. Few people there had ever heard of such a thing. Up to that day, all men and women had spoken with more or less equally powerful voices. Henceforth this would change. Henceforth the access to the microphone would determine whose voice shall be magnified. Silence now ceased to be in the commons; it became a resource for which loudspeakers compete. Language itself was transformed thereby from a local commons into a national resource for communication. As enclosure by the lords increased national productivity by denying the individual peasant the right to keep a few sheep, so the encroachment of the loudspeaker has destroyed that silence which so far had given each man and woman his or her proper and equal voice. Unless you have access to a loudspeaker, you now are silenced.

I hope that the parallel now becomes clear. Just as the commons of space are vulnerable, and can be destroyed by the motorization of traffic, so the commons of speech are vulnerable, and can easily be destroyed by the encroachment of modern means of communication.

The issue which I propose for discussion should therefore be clear: how to counter the encroachment of new, electronic devices and systems upon commons that are more subtle and more intimate to our being than either grassland or roads—commons that are at least as valuable as silence. Silence, according to western and eastern tradition alike, is necessary for the emergence of persons. It is taken from us by machines that ape people. We could easily be made increasingly dependent on machines for speaking and for thinking, as we are already dependent on machines for moving.

Such a transformation of the environment from a commons to a productive resource constitutes the most fundamental form of environmental degradation. This degradation has a long history, which coincides with the history of capitalism but can in no way just be reduced to it. Unfortunately the importance of this transformation has been overlooked or belittled by political ecology so far. It needs to be recognized if we are to organize defense movements of what remains of the commons. This defense constitutes the crucial public task for political action during the eighties. The task must be undertaken urgently because commons can exist without police, but resources cannot. Just as traffic does, computers call for police, and for ever more of them, and in ever more subtle forms.

By definition, resources call for defense by police. Once they are defended, their recovery as commons becomes increasingly difficult. This is a special reason for urgency.

KATY BUTLER

Events Are the Teacher

In the Winter 1983 issue this piece ran immediately after one called "The Secret Life of Swami Muktananda," by William Rodarmor. It chronicled the decline of the founding guru of the Siddha meditation movement, with thirty-one ashrams around the world. In his final years, in the late 70s and early 80s, Muktananda had sex with young female followers, misappropriated major funds, and threatened and authorized beatings of departing malcontents by his bodyguards, Rodarmor reported. The charges, abundantly testified to, were stonewall-denied by Muktananda's surviving followers. And so this article on the San Francisco Zen Center stood out in contrast.

There were three things I hoped for in running the article. I hoped it would not undo my decades-long friendship with Dick Baker; total failure on that score. Dick doesn't talk to me now. I hoped it might be of some use to Zen Center in refinding its balance. That one's hard to assess. Many people in the commu-

nity critiqued Katy Butler's article through a sequence of drafts, till it became almost an official document, though still intensely her own. Some were deeply unhappy with its existence and its content; some felt relief that a compassionate, fairly detailed account was what finally went out to the world.

Events since Fall 83. On December 20, 1983, after months of turmoil, Baker resigned as abbot of Zen Center, and the Board of Directors accepted his resignation. A dozen or so students followed Baker to two new Buddhist practice centers he founded and funded in Santa Fe, New Mexico, and on Potrero Hill in San Francisco. Many senior students left Zen Center, some continuing their Zen practice, some not. Katy Butler still works at the *San Francisco Chronicle*, and in her home she still sits zazen in the early mornings. Zen Center itself reorganized around a wider distribution of responsibility. Each piece of the whole has greater autonomy—the practice centers in San Francisco, Tassajara, Green Gulch Farm, the businesses like Greens restaurant, Green Gulch Grocer, etc. Finances were brought under control—the fundamental financial legacy of the Baker-roshi years is a sound, even spectacular, one, which he can well be proud of. Zen Center is taking its time finding a new abbot; the current part-time teacher possibly becoming full-time is Katagiri-roshi, of the Minneapolis

Zen Center. A long, careful healing with strength where the scars are is well along.

The third thing I hoped for, and the entire reason for running the piece, was that other religious communities might be shocked to awareness and might find a handle on their own problems. That seems to have happened. Voluminous mail confirmed that Zen Center's situation was the opposite of unique. Problems of sex, money, control, runaway charisma, and denial were found in the leadership (and hence the followership, since they make each other) of probably the majority of new religious groups in America. *Not* all, but most. Some undertook the labor of reform. One Buddhist group confronted their teacher's alcoholism, and he dutifully joined Alcoholics Anonymous. Some set about freeing the teacher from total administrative control. Some simply employed, even encouraged, a new wariness in the students. And some insisted There's No Problem Here. They'll be sorry.

Stewart Brand

Do not believe in anything simply because you have heard it.

Do not believe in traditions because they have been handed down for many generations.

Do not believe in anything because it is spoken and rumored by many.

Do not believe in anything simply because it is found written in your religious books.

Do not believe in anything merely on the authority of your teachers and elders.

But after observation and analysis, when you find that anything agrees with reason, and is conducive to the good and benefit of one and all, then accept it and live up to it.

This plea for common sense has been handed down as the words of the Buddha, a man born in 560 B.C. in India, who studied with many teachers before finding his own way, through meditation, to enlightenment.

Last April 8 [1983], the day commemorated as Buddha's birthday, Zentatsu Baker-roshi, dharma heir of Shunryu Suzuki-roshi and a line of teachers tracing back to Buddha, was at Tassajara monastery near Big Sur, leading the intense meditation period called *sesshin.* At the same time, the sixteen members of the Board of Directors of Baker-roshi's San Francisco Zen Center were sitting on chairs in a circle inside the center's Victorian guest house in the city. Three senior priests (a woman and two men) told the group that Baker-roshi had recently become sexually involved with a woman student. Her husband, whom Baker-roshi had described as his best friend, was extremely upset.

Each Board member then spoke slowly and carefully in turns around the circle. All came to know what some had known for years, and others had suspected. There had been at least two other affairs with women students, both of them damaging to the efforts of those women to practice Zen. For Blanche Hartman, a fifty-eight-year-old former chemist and statistician who had been ordained a priest by Baker-roshi, "The meeting was devastating. A sinking feeling in my stomach, like, I knew it was coming, and here it is. My life is smashed. Our life together is smashed. Something very precious in me is destroyed. At that point, I couldn't see how we could continue." It was a moment that changed Zen Center, I believe forever.

Yvonne Rand, another priest who was first introduced to Zen Center by Richard Baker, said of the meeting, "It seemed very clear that this was an event that was out of whack. For myself, my sense was that there was a real shift in authority which I don't know how to describe in any other way but moral authority."

The board met again the following day. The senior teaching priests, Lew Richmond and Reb Anderson, had met with Baker-roshi and brought back the news that he did not appear to understand how seriously the Board felt

299

about the matter. At this meeting, Blanche Hartman began to understand that something had changed on the Board, which in the past had almost always acquiesced to Baker-roshi's wishes. This time, nobody tried to explain away his actions. Nobody tried to ostracize those who were critical of him, as had happened so often through the previous twelve years.

Remembers Blanche, "I began having a sense of the commitment of the group, the unanimity of concern and care. It reassured me that this time, there wasn't going to be any sweeping under the rug. We were going to face it together, and I wasn't going to have to leave [Zen Center]."

Baker-roshi appeared at the next Board meeting, the following day, by invitation. He walked into the room where the priests and students sat on chairs in a circle, wearing their black robes. He knelt on the floor in *seiza*, a strong, formal *zazen* position, and began to explain. Yvonne Rand, who was chairing the meeting, asked him to sit in a chair like the rest of them, and to listen to what the Board had to say. At first, he remained in seiza and continued to try to explain. Yvonne asked again that he sit at their level. And again. Baker-roshi rose and sat on a chair.

Many Board members later felt that the meeting had come to an impasse. Baker-roshi was "obviously distraught," remembered Ed Brown, the author of the *Tassajara Bread Book* and comanager of Greens, the highly regarded vegetarian restaurant in San Francisco run by Zen Center.

Brown came away from the meeting with the feeling that their words had not really penetrated.

One by one, board members spoke to Baker-roshi, the man who had been their teacher for

Baker-roshi at *sesshin* lecture, Tassajara Mountain Center, 1975.

Lewis Richmond

twelve years, for whom many felt great gratitude. They have since told me that they spoke of their own collusion in allowing him to become so removed from feedback. Said Blanche Hartman, "It was something we had done together; something we had to straighten out together. In the middle of a lot of anger, we knew it had to be done with a sense of right speech."

Blanche, and others, apologized to this man who had spent so many years trying to practice Zen and to lead this relatively young Buddhist community. "I told him I thought it had been doing him no service to say nothing about my suspicions. It was a mistake to protect him from the consequences of his own consequential actions," she said.

Another Board member said to Baker-roshi, "Listen. Please just listen."

Said Yvonne, with great passion, "I want you to stop."

So, last spring, we became the first new American religious community to effectively tell its leader to stop. It has been painful, but I think that the way the people of Zen Center have faced this crisis could be an encouragement to other religious communities facing similar problems.

A process began which I and other Zen students are still living through. There has been shock, love, pain, grief, and anger. Some students have left. Others have likened their feelings to going through a divorce after a long marriage.

There has been intense self-questioning, as people try to unravel the role they played in effectively isolating Baker-roshi from meaningful feedback. The community has seized this crisis as an opportunity to recreate itself, and to change so that in the future its leaders may be less isolated from students. Nobody yet knows how it will all come out, or exactly how it happened.

After the first series of meetings, the Board members met in small groups with students, telling them what had been discovered and allowing them to express their emotions about it. Most students took the news of Baker-

roshi's sexual involvements very seriously—something that has puzzled people who point out that we are not a celibate community, and that such relationships take two people.

But within the context of a religious community, the news was shocking. Baker-roshi, who is married, had not followed the code he had clearly described to Zen students who were having affairs: no deceit, no manipulation, and no harming of anyone else's spiritual path. Leaders, he had often said, were expected to set an example judged by tougher standards.

Hearing about the affairs was especially confusing to some priests because Baker-roshi had discussed such situations at a monks' meeting some months before the crisis. Baker-roshi had referred to another Zen teacher with a reputation for sexual relationships with students. He expressed his disapproval, saying that the teachers' board of directors should have strongly confronted the situation.

As a woman student, I felt particularly threatened. I felt burnt, as though my tongue had been singed with boiling tea. When I first approached the man whom I hoped would become my teacher in the deepest sense, I hoped to establish a relationship of trust. I wanted to reveal myself, to drop the games I used to survive in the "outside" world. I hoped he would help me continue to practice zazen (meditation) through times of self-doubt, frustration, and fear.

Given my own hopes, I see why some women might be very vulnerable to sexual advances from a religious teacher. It must be hard on these men: another woman student has told me she watched women flirt with Baker-roshi for years. "Of course there are sexual feelings," she said of her own close teaching relationship with Baker-roshi. "I was aware of it and working with it. I learned how not to take these feelings and run with them."

Although Baker-roshi gave me much helpful advice in the two years I was his student, we did not succeed in building a deep, trusting relationship. Hearing about the affairs has made me wary about trying again.

After the Board members told students about the situation, they asked Baker-roshi not to lead services or give lectures, and he agreed. He was also asked not to perform the *Jundo*, the silent morning walk during the first period of zazen, when each student responds with raised, palm-pressed hands. Some students began to refer to him as Richard Baker instead of *roshi* (teacher); others did not know what to call him.

Students began to talk to each other in a more open way, and all the other resentments about Baker-roshi boiled up as though a lid had been removed from a pot.

Uneasiness had been growing, especially during the last three years. He had traveled to Russia on a mission of world peace, but he had been seeing students increasingly rarely. He was almost never in the *zendo*. He seemed to be involved in a whirl of meetings, trips, telephone calls, and shopping, unable to rest on the ground. Decisions, it became clear, were made by him, and community meetings and the Board of Directors had little weight. While students worked for minimum wage at Zen Center businesses, he spent more than two hundred thousand dollars a year. Many of these expenditures related to his role as abbot; for instance, his office expenses and trips. But while students at Green Gulch Farm, Zen Center's Marin County practice center and working farm, lived in trailers and showered outside, he spent money impulsively on art, furniture, and expensive restaurant meals. One year Zen Center paid four thousand dollars for his membership in New York's Adirondack Club.

The contrast between the abbot's and the students' lives was symbolized for many by his car. About three years ago, he had asked the Board if he could buy a very expensive BMW. The Board had voiced widespread uneasiness, but when Baker-roshi asked the treasurer to go to the bank with him and sign the papers, he had done so.

Now, suddenly, the emperor had no clothes. At the end of April, after numerous discussions with Baker-roshi, the Board reported that he had "requested" a leave of absence for an indefinite period, to be reviewed in a year. Baker-roshi, the statement said, would continue to "live, practice, and work with us."

They quoted him as saying, "I want to understand this matter to its depths but I don't know how to do that. The best answer I have to this question now is to immerse myself in the practice of the *Sangha* [community] for I know Suzuki-roshi is there."

Over the next six months, Richard Baker's expense accounts were stopped, and he and his family were limited to a stipend of approximately twenty-five hundred dollars a month, plus the use of his two Zen Center houses. His three *anjas* (attendants) and three administrative assistants were given other jobs, and their offices turned into temporary dormitory rooms. The notorious white BMW was garaged, and the Board announced plans to sell the vehicle, which is extremely expensive to maintain.

Richard Baker told people he wanted to walk alone from Zen Center to Tassajara, the Center's monastery near Carmel Valley, a distance of 175 miles. The trip was interrupted by visits to friends' houses, a weekend in Palm Springs with his wife Virginia, and detours to New York. Once at Tassajara, he worked for several days side by side with students. Then he left for Europe, where he appeared at a conference, and then went to the south of France to spend time with Thich Nhat Hanh, a Vietnamese monk for whom he has great respect. He has mostly been absent from Zen Center, and has not met publicly with students since the crisis.

In his absence, Zen Center began to experiment with new ways of doing things. Meetings at the city center, which in the past had been extremely subdued, erupted with new frankness. At one meeting, a priest said he had never before felt free to speak his mind.

A volunteer committee of students brought in consultants and psychologists. Recognizing the lack of "horizontal" communication between ordinary students, they led small groups and workshops in communication skills. I began to feel free to express parts of myself which I had previously tried to leave at the door of Zen Center, and to talk in my own language. Other students underwent similar transformations.

One student, Betsy Sawyer, told me she has returned to her first questions about Zen practice, and has begun to examine her own need for psychological growth as well. "This big boo-boo has liberated me," she said.

"The students woke up," said Lew Richmond, the head of religious practice at Green Gulch Farm. "Something had been lifted, and they were who they were—and that's the way Buddhism is supposed to be."

The Board of Directors, which had been almost dormant for several years, began to meet every week and take on the running of Zen Center. Its meetings were opened to small groups of students, and its minutes made available. In a community where information had previously been tightly guarded, it was a radical change.

"Affinity groups" of eight to ten students and an overseeing "spokescouncil" were formed to discuss Zen Center's direction. There is now a new mood of shared decision-making, as people struggle to create a healthy community for the study of a profound teaching.

The problems Zen Center began to face last spring are not new. Abuses of power, money, and sex occur within the Catholic Church, political parties, and corporations—as well as within the non-Western religious movements. Buddhism, for all its intellectual elaboration and long tradition, is not immune. It was brought to the West by pioneering individual teachers, most of them far removed from those who taught them. In America, teachers are too far apart—both in style and in geographical location—to supervise each other as an effective community of peers.

In New York, the community of Eido-roshi has been repeatedly split by accusations, which he has denied, of sexual relations with students. Elsewhere, another Buddhist teacher with a serious drinking problem openly and cheerfully sleeps with women students. Some Buddhist leaders are terrible administrators, some experiment with drugs, some are homosexual, and some think homosexuality is wrong. I believe that as our communities mature, we will learn to treat these talented teachers with a realistic American kind of respect they need. We have been driving them crazy by accepting everything they do as an expression of religious teaching. Living without feedback in a community of emotionally dependent people is something like living in a sensory deprivation tank. It distorts the perceptions and isolates the leader.

I think that something like this happened slowly and gradually at Zen Center as it grew. I believe that Zen Center had developed weaknesses as a community that made it hard to stay in touch with common sense, self-assertion, and trust in one another.

In November of 1971, Richard Baker, a former Harvard student and organizer of conferences for the University of California's extension program, put on blue and brown robes. In what is called the Mountain Seat Ceremony, his dying teacher, Suzuki-roshi, made him abbot of Zen Center, entrusting to him his gentle brand of Japanese Soto Zen.

Dick Baker was not then, and is not now, your typical monk: Maine-born, energetic, bright, talkative, hungry for new experiences and ideas, headstrong, and epicurean, he faced at thirty-five the difficult job of following a beloved Japanese teacher who had died too soon. I was not there, but the image I get of the community that watched this ceremony is that it was stripped down, oriented more toward zazen practice, with Suzuki-roshi's example of its effectiveness before it.

When Suzuki-roshi died two weeks later, Zen Center was little more than a place to sit zazen; there was the city center in the heart of the slums, and Tassajara monastery in a deep canyon near Carmel Valley. As Baker-roshi assumed leadership, Zen Center changed in many positive ways. He worked with other students translating chants from Japanese to English; he encouraged single women and families with children to try monastic practice at Tassajara. He engineered the acquisition of Green Gulch Farm, supported Buddhist scholars, and managed to be a helpful Buddhist teacher, especially at Tassajara, or in sesshin. He had a genius for entrepreneurship and a vision of a vigorous, self-supporting Buddhist community. But over the next twelve years, something happened. One older student told me that while Baker-roshi knew how to give help, he did not know how to take it. He knew how to nuture people who felt weak, but he had a harder time encouraging them to be strong.

Marc Alexander, Zen Center's current president, described it as the "frog in hot water syndrome": put a frog in boiling water, and he'll jump out. Put a frog in cold water and slowly heat it and he'll stay and boil to death.

Said Alexander, "The businesses began after students began coming back from Tassajara wanting to have some continuation of working throughout the day with other people doing the same Buddhist practices—mindfulness, compassion, right livelihood. Supporting ourselves was the secondary reason. But little by little, supporting ourselves became the stronger motivating factor. Baker-roshi was creating all these things while we didn't have the staff to take care of them fully. As a result, it became less interesting to work there."

From places devoted to "work practice" that were incidentally businesses, they became Buddhist-flavored businesses. It's a sad irony that over the years many of them became more successful to their patrons than to the people who worked in them. They are places where you can sit still. The Buddhist qualities of wholehearted attention, of a calm noninterfering kindness, permeated them. They are beautiful spaces, their clean Japanese aesthetic spiced with luxury. Every time my family comes to San Francisco, we have a ritual dinner at Greens, and things get said that haven't been said elsewhere. But students who worked in the kitchen began to complain that the frenetic restaurant work had gone beyond any conception of Buddhist practice, and the hours made it difficult to get to zazen.

John Bailes remembers working at Green Gulch Farm, which is an oasis of quiet for interested non-Buddhists who visit for Sunday lectures. "I'd be down in the fields struggling with the carthorses, sweating and not too happy, and Baker-roshi would arrive in his golden robes with a group of dazzled Marinites. They'd ask me, 'Isn't it wonderful to be living here?' There was a great gap that I would describe as feudalistic. I was enraged. It was coming out of my pores. But there was some kind of tension against speaking out."

As the businesses needed more workers, a confusion developed between serving the needs of the institution and serving Buddhism. Being serious became equated with one's willingness to work within a business or live in a residence. When I told Baker-roshi I was serious about studying Zen, he jokingly suggested that I quit my job, move into the building, and start working at Greens. Doing what I did—working outside Zen Center—was subtly denigrated, and what might be called "lay practice" was not sufficiently respected for its ability to contribute another perspective and some form of reality check.

While students worked long hours in the bakery, the restaurant, or the fields, they tried to live as though they were in a monastery. Zazen began at 4:30 in the morning, and students often nodded off in lectures. The monastic style of life that worked so well for a limited period of training at Tassajara—hierarchy, no discussion, and little sleep—was exhausting for families, city dwellers, and farmworkers.

I still do not understand exactly why people had such difficulty talking openly about their reservations, but I can describe my own experience. I came to sitting by accident. I was visiting Tassajara on a summer camping trip six years ago when I met an old friend, a student there, who invited me to sit. I remember walking out of the stone *zendo* at six A.M. into a clear morning light. I had time, and I had space in a way I had not experienced before.

Another summer I spent six weeks following the schedule of work and meditation at Tassajara, and began to feel there might be a place where I could allow my deepest, least-articulated motivations to come forward. Making beds with other Zen students, I did not have to prove I was the best; I could just try to be wholehearted about whatever I was doing. Rising at 4:30, sitting zazen, eating and working with long periods of silence, I did not have to manufacture an interesting "personality" in order to make conversation with people. I had been a union organizer and an investigative reporter. I knew how to assert myself and make trouble. But I was tired of it. I had felt starved for most of my life for a way to question and express my deepest self. I wasn't about to throw it away to raise questions about a crummy twenty-six-thousand-dollar BMW. And yet my common-sense questions kept rising. Like many other students, I thought I was the only one that had them.

Two summers ago, I sat sesshin at Green Gulch Farm. We were visited by a respected Japanese teacher, and the day he left we lined the driveway at Baker-roshi's request to say good-bye to him. Sesshin has a way of producing an intensity of awareness. I clearly remember standing in my black robes with some sixty others that gentle summer day. One of Baker-roshi's assistants drove the white BMW up. Another cleaned the windshield and the trunk. A woman stood at the side with a basket of flowers. Baker-roshi, his visitor, and other guests got into the car. As Baker-roshi's assistant loaded in the luggage and prepared to drive the entourage to the airport, we all bowed repeatedly, and I thought, with a smile, this is being in a cult.

I don't think Zen Center is a cult, of course, and I think the way this crisis has been handled proves it. But the day I stood there in front of that car, I was doing something I didn't understand, taking on a piece of Japanese behavior, simply because I had been asked to. I didn't tell anyone I felt that way.

Despite growing unhappiness and increasing resistance to Baker-roshi's expansion plans, the community could not effectively tell him to stop. Among the senior students, who might have said stop, the atmosphere was like a medieval palace, one said. The courtiers strove to outdo each other for approval of their insight. Said one senior monk, "Then, when it comes time to confront Baker-roshi, you don't feel like the person you are competing with will support you."

Other senior students were not caught in this web of competition, but felt too dazzled to challenge him. He seemed so articulate and worldly to these men and women who had become monks in their early twenties. And so many of the projects for which he argued so convincingly had worked so well.

When a friend of Blanche Hartman's hinted that Baker-roshi had been involved in affairs she said, a little too quickly, "That's hearsay." Now she says she thinks she was saying, "Please don't tell me. I don't know what I'd do. I might have to leave, and I'm fifty-eight years old; my whole life is here."

Among newer students like myself, a confusion about certain Buddhist ideas contributed to people's inability to trust their own common sense or speak out about their doubts. The first of these ideas is the concept of *Dharma* (teaching) transmission. Most simply put, as I understand it, the goal of each Buddhist teacher and student is to gain or allow access to the student's enlightened mind through meditation and practice together. The ceremony of transmission acknowledges that the student has found access to this clear, big mind, which all of us have the potential to find, which is the same as the teacher's mind, and ultimately, Buddha's.

It is a tricky concept. We speak of a Zen "lineage," or dharma "heirs," as though the essence of Buddhist teaching had been handed down through the generations like a patrimony. The language can lead us to think that the teacher who is a dharma "heir" possesses something as physical as the brown robe and bowl that symbolize it.

At Zen Center, the idea of dharma transmission became a way of keeping Suzuki-roshi alive. Richard Baker was conceived of as a fragile vessel that contained Suzuki-roshi's pure mind. Many senior monks told me they felt powerless to disgrace or stop Baker-roshi until he transmitted Tenshin Reb Anderson, so that Suzuki-roshi's lineage would survive. Thus, the concept of transmission began to tyrannize. In 1972, when the Board of Directors resisted the purchase of Green Gulch Farm, Baker-roshi threatened to leave if it wasn't bought. The Board then acquiesced. "He used the authority of dharma transmission to frighten us. He said, 'I'm going to take my baseball bat and go home, and you guys won't be able to play Buddhism any more,' " remembered one senior monk.

The conception of dharma transmission is intertwined with a popular image of a perfectly enlightened human being whose every gesture is a teaching—an image that makes it hard to question a teacher's actions even when one's common sense cries out for an explanation.

"The idea is out of context here," said Lew Richmond, the head of religious practice at Green Gulch Farm. "In the Orient, every craft has transmission from master to disciple. Its purpose is to protect against unauthorized and self-appointed teachers. But this aggrandizement of transmission in the minds of young meditators has not served our interest. What are you authenticating? Every word and deed for the rest of your life? We have an idealized image of an enlightened person. It's not, strictly speaking, accurate to speak of an enlightened person, but rather of enlightened activity."

This is not a simple issue. Some trust is crucial. Reb Anderson likes to tell the story of helping Suzuki-roshi build his rock garden at Tassajara. Suzuki-roshi would ask Reb to lever a huge boulder into one position. Then to another position. Then back to the original position. When Reb protested and asked if they couldn't think it through first and then move rocks, Suzuki-roshi told him to shut up. Finally, Reb simply let himself go wholeheartedly into moving the rock and not thinking ahead.

From the outside, this could look like an eccentric old man forcing a student to meaninglessly move rocks around. For Reb, from the inside, it was a way of learning. There's no easy litmus test for when a teacher's actions tend toward liberation, and when they're selfish. Your own common sense, how your body feels, and the actions' results can help guide you. There are no teaching stories about teachers enriching themselves at students' expense

or sleeping with their students. But how are you to know when your resistance is an expression of common sense, and when it's the pride of your small mind balking at moving rocks around all day in the sun? Part of Zen practice consists of trust, some willingness to try something out, not to be too sure of yourself.

Another confused notion of Zen teachings played a role in creating a community where plain talk was often discouraged. Zen warns against too much dependence on written teachings. Many of its teaching stories don't make rational or linguistic sense—in fact they're designed not to. At Zen Center, some students seemed to interpret this to mean that there was something wrong with speaking in simple English sentences during our student meetings. We were encouraged to practice living without saying, "This is good, this is bad," or "I like this, I don't like this." The older the student, the less was said, and this silence was mistaken for wisdom. In our weekly meetings, people, including me, were afraid of looking like fools, of revealing that they did not dwell constantly in their widest minds.

We sat straight-backed and still in the zendo, breathing deeply, inevitably releasing unconscious material. Outside the zendo, we tried to follow practices of right conduct, right thought, and right speech. But it appeared that for fear of harming others, some of us were afraid to express anything at all. It was a pressure cooker. I don't think that the structure of Japanese Zen provided a way for Americans to work with the unconscious material released in zazen, to release or express it in a way that would not harm others. People also subtly withdrew within a community which had no nonjudgmental way of sharing unacceptable thoughts and feelings.

Suzuki-roshi often described Zen as similar to putting a snake into a bamboo tube as a way of showing it its nature. How to stand, bow, and sit in the zendo is carefully prescribed, and very powerful when seventy people do it together. When I first came, I discovered what a relief it can be not to mechanically smile, but to bow instead. Outside the zendo, after the bow, I didn't always know what to say. The Japanese forms became a way of avoiding contact. This coldness, awkwardness, and this lack of peer contact, contributed to a flow of energy and emotion upward into the hierarchy. Each person thought they stood alone.

Much of this has been stood on its head since the April crisis. As mentioned earlier, a committee of students brought in consultants to teach us to talk to each other, and we have formed affinity groups that meet twice a month to discuss the future direction of Zen Center. The formal structure of the organization is still hierarchical—legal power rests with Baker-roshi and the Board, unless they fail to agree. Then the students would break the tie.

Most of the affinity groups have recently told the Board that they want to resolve our relationship with Baker-roshi, one way or another. Some students do not want him to be their teacher again. Other would like him to return, but not on the same terms. There seems to be widespread agreement over the need to separate "church" (practice) from "state" (administration), so that students don't feel their spiritual understanding is on the line when they question an administrative decision. The affinity groups are encouraging feedback from the "bottom"—if not outright democracy.

Some students are leaving; some feel bitter that their trust and Buddhist teaching have been abused. One student said, "If he could give up all attachment to being a teacher, the student could begin to trust him. As long as he seems to need being a teacher, they don't trust him. They're expecting him to transform himself without safety. You can't learn a whole new way to be, under attack. People are saying, 'transform,' and yet they're still angry."

Students, and a visiting Zen teacher, have suggested that Richard Baker try working side by side with students, or studying with another teacher, or counseling, as a way of completing his Zen training. How he will respond to such ideas still remains to be seen. Some students say they will never think of him as a

Wind Bell

Baker-roshi at Green Gulch Farm.

Buddhist teacher again, and hope that he will resign. Among some of them, there has been a kind of satanization of Richard Baker, as though all of Zen Center's ills can be laid at his feet. To them, he's too powerful, too manipulative to be safely reined in by ordinary people. It is the flip side of the delusion of the perfectly enlightened person. There are others, like poet Philip Whalen and businessman John Nelson, who would like to see Richard Baker return as Baker-roshi, the same as before.

"It worked for me," said Nelson, who came to Zen Center shortly after graduating from Yale, and found a way to spend time at Tassajara with his wife and children as monastic students, and also build a career. "When he lectured, I was inspired. He never really followed the schedule, but he made everybody else follow it. When I bowed to him fully, I felt I was bowing to our heritage. He represented in his person the legacy of our teachers. He was always helpful to me, even when he was hard on me. I knew he was driving a fancy car and all that, but I feel tremendous gratitude. I see my teacher in trouble and I say, 'Wait, let's take better care of this.' I'm willing to let him spend a lot of money. What am I supposed to say? Fine, please go off him?''

We tried to swallow whole the Japanese form of Zen—or at least, our naive understanding of it. Now we're in the process of chewing it up, digesting it, making it into an American Zen. For a long time, most of us accepted, without thinking it through, foreign conceptions of hierarchy, of information restricted on a "need to know" basis. Coming from a culture almost devoid of ways of showing respect, some of us hungrily took on another way. Now, those foreign ideas are being tested for their usefulness against the values that are the genius of Western culture: democracy, open information, a free press, psychological development, the separation of Church and State, and systems of checks and balances.

As I write this in early November, it is unclear exactly how Zen Center's members will resolve their relationship with Baker-roshi, and what form the community will take in the future. The process is still evolving, and for all the self-questioning by Zen students, I don't think anyone fully understands exactly how people stopped taking the risks of speaking out.

One senior student has written of "our confusion about how to work with a teacher, our not knowing how to question and trust him simultaneously, our isolation of him and of ourselves, our abdication of our own perspective . . . our impoverishment with our own cultural inheritance, our emotional immaturity, our readiness to imitate forms not fully understood."

"Our coming to rest in zazen expressed for many of us a great need to deepen our lives and find satisfactions deeper than our culture offers," the student wrote. "The fact that this small group of Americans does not yet under-

stand how to take this brilliant, simple, impossible practice and create a social form around it that supports the individual and the community is the deepest teaching for all of us, and I would hope, the deeper teaching of this event in American religious life."

A TRULY WICKED ROSHI

We have just read "Events are the Teacher" by Katy Butler. We read this with awe, trying to imagine all those flourishing industries, all that money flowing in, all those students, and all this in the Paris of the West. We drooled and our fantasies went wild. What we wouldn't give to trade Roshis.

Our Zen center is in one of the smog city's worst ghettos. Every time we start a business to earn enough money to get out, our Roshi shuts it down. We tried raising vegetables in a window box and he turned off the water. We opened a diner and our Roshi called the health department and finished us off. We started a publication and our Roshi sued us for publishing him. We bought him a secondhand Datsun and it was stolen and wrecked. Our priceless bells and statue were stolen twice. There are too few students, so scholarships are offered strangers off the street to fill the zendo. Our Roshi prefers beginners anyway . . . he says it's much better than TV. Reflecting on the San Francisco Zen Center controversy, we were even more in awe . . . could there really be a Zen Center with only *one* controversy in ten years? Our Roshi specializes in continuous multiple crises with palace intrigue. Upon further reflection, maybe our Roshi is now the one for Dick Baker to study under . . . ?

Seiko Long
Joshin Bigelow
Shuko Green
La Jolla, California
[Spring 1984]

P.S. The women students are sad to report that our Roshi has never once tried to romance any of them.

PAUL HAWKEN

Surviving in Small Business

*Random Notes from a
Small Business Junkie*

Paul Hawken became our most popular writer almost overnight with his first article in Summer 1980, "What's Economical?" Bantam Books and the Senate Finance Committee called him with offers and questions. With the next article, "Disintermediation" in Spring 1981, the skeleton of a book was becoming apparent. Sure enough, *The Next Economy*, based on a number of CQ articles, came out from Holt, Rinehart & Winston in 1983 (it's now in paperback from Ballantine). The Spring 1984 article here, his last before CQ became *Whole Earth Review*, is in the process of becoming a book, possibly also a TV series, possibly also a computer program, all called "How to Grow a Business."

Paul's in his late thirties now. That "first business when I was nineteen" was Erewhon, based in Boston, a phenomenon of the times. His subsequent foray into writing was *The Magic of Findhorn* (Harper &

Row, 1975), which became a bestseller. His present business, Smith & Hawken in Mill Valley, California, purveys the best garden tools from all over the world via a much-loved mail-order catalog. It's much loved because the level of service is so high, because gardening itself is loved, and because the tools speak to an idea of excellence and a philosophy of real economy through quality. The Hawken articles and the Hawken tools have the same message.

Since 1980, Paul has had a major role in the survival of the small business called Point Foundation.

Stewart Brand

I started my first business when I was nineteen. It is difficult to say, even eighteen years later, whether it was a success or not; it depends on how you measure it. The business was a natural food company, started in 1966—well before there was such an industry. My business had two big strikes against it: me, and the fact that I didn't have a clue as to what business I was in. The problem with me was that I didn't know anything about business, and had a positive aversion to the entire business ethic as I understood it. After all, it was the mid-sixties, and the link between corporate avarice and overseas adventurism was trumpeted every night via television footage on Vietnam, Dow Chemical, et al. Business seemed like a good thing *not* to do.

The second problem, not knowing what business I was in, was even thornier. Usually when you start a business, you know what it will be. If it is a deli, you have visited and eaten in dozens. You know what you like, what you don't, and what you would do differently. In the case of the natural foods business, there were no antecedents. The health food stores in my neighborhood were staffed by women in white uniforms and hosiery, looking like nurses on night duty. They (the stores that is) had strange odors and reminded me of quasi-licit pharmacies. There was virtually nothing natural in them. Everything was a concoction, full of additives that were putatively better than the ones in the supermarket. So, in that sense, I knew what not to do. But it was small help.

Nevertheless, it was the right business to be in at the right time, and it grew from twenty-five dollars per day in gross revenues to twenty-five thousand dollars per day seven years later. I have to confess, it wasn't fun. It was only fun in the beginning, when its size allowed me to be in touch with my customers, suppliers, and associates. When it reached the size that took me away from the counter and put me behind a desk, it got hard. It took me several years to figure that out, and when I did, I left it.

During those years, the business made money some years, lost it in others, hired 150 employees, bought railcars, opened stores on both coasts, set up manufacturing, almost went bankrupt, and engendered a lean and hungry group of competitors. The first lesson in small business is that you *will* be noticed if you succeed or grow, and you will be ignored if you fail. Former friends, hawk-eyed entrepreneurs, and marketing executives of corporations will all notice. And they will all try to cream you. Sounds awful. But in fact it is merely inevitable. I remember walking into my store one afternoon and seeing four executives of a supermarket chain measure the store's square footage while tallying register totals on a notepad. They were trying to figure out our sales per square foot (which were phenomenally high for the food industry). Hi guys. Kellogg's used one of our subsidiary names for an advertising slogan to reposition its corn flakes in the market. Pet Foods walked off with our logo-type and package design without so much as a tip of the cap.

After seven years, I left the country and took up the pen. When I returned to America four-teen months later, what I discovered was sober-ing. I was unemployable. I had never been an employee. I checked the want ads in the Sun-day paper. I couldn't find a job description that matched my qualifications. After all, what was I? I had sealed my fate at an early age, and not wanting to go back to college to get a job de-scription, I went back into business. Today, after eighteen years of being in small business, I have come to certain inescapable conclusions. Be careful: They may be wrong. They have worked for me, though. They are the distilla-tion of my own experience, as well as the ob-servations of many other small businesses with which I have consulted.

Start at the beginning. This is the most ob-vious-sounding rule of all. I wouldn't mention it if I didn't constantly see people do the oppo-site. Usually, when people start a business, they have an image. It may be of some other company they have seen or worked in, or it may be just a fantasy. Whatever it is, it is probably an image of where they would like to end up. So, don't start where you want to end up. If you haven't had experience in starting a business before, start small, very small, and use your minuteness and obscurity as an oppor-tunity to learn. This means low overhead, fru-gal means, hands-on. I have seen many people who associate a successful business with the trappings: a carpet, computer, car, secretary. In eighteen years of business, I have never had a personal secretary. (Read *Up the Organization* by Robert Townsend [*NWEC* p.306; $3.95 postpaid from Fawcett/Random House, 400 Hahn Road, Westminister, Maryland 21157] for further elaboration on this point.) I've had the rest, but not until the business was well es-tablished. In other words, do the business di-rectly with as few frills and trappings as possi-ble. You will learn faster, have a better chance of survival, and you won't be fooled by sur-rounding yourself with the affectations of success.

Entrepreneurs are risk-avoiders. This is not so ob-vious. The commonplace attitude is that an entrepreneur is a gung-ho, three-sheets-to-the-wind risk-taker, willing to plunge ahead where others squirm. I don't read it that way. An entrepreneur is a risk-avoider. He or she usually starts by seeing a situation from an entirely different angle than someone else. They see a market, a niche, an idea, a product that is unseen or discounted by others. Whether this is a personal computer (Apple), a hub-and-spokes air delivery system (Federal Express), or housewives' needs for aerobic exercise (Jane Fonda), to these people the need for the product or service is obvious. There is no risk because they are totally identified with the end result. They are not studying the market, they *are* the market. That's a big difference. What an entrepreneur will then do is try to identify every possible risk and obstacle that could prevent him or her from achieving that goal, and eliminate as many as possible. Entrepreneurs only appear to be daring and innovative.

Borrow a lot or none. Money is where risk is most obvious. You and whoever else you have persuaded to join you stand to lose if you fail. If you decide to borrow, then do not borrow piddling amounts. Borrow as much as you can. Why? Because if you are leveraged to your teeth, no one will mess with you. An anecdote: At one point in my food business days, I had amassed and drawn over one million dollars on my line of credit from the bank. These were ninety-day notes that customarily rolled over as well as letters of credit to overseas suppliers. The bank loans exceeded our net worth by a factor of five. When Nixon put on wage and price controls in 1971–72, interest rates soared to the historic high of thirteen percent. Bank examiners from the state audited our loan package and discovered that with the high interest rates, we no longer "qualified" for all those loans. The bank was forced to call the notes.

Disaster. As I began paying down the notes as they came due (thirty thousand to fifty thousand dollars per week), I couldn't pay my bills. I was going broke, payrolls were kited, and suppliers were angry. The solution seems so obvious in retrospect, but it took an agonizing few weeks of tribulation before I cottoned on.

One Monday morning, I called the vice-president of the bank and told him in my best Boston accent to stuff it. An extraordinary thing happened. I, who had always obsequiously minced into the bank with my hat in hand, was invited to the executive dining room on the forty-eighth floor of the Prudential Tower. I saw Oriental art on the walls, maids scurrying about, and asparagus and strawberries accompanying the scallops (although it was still February). In other words, as soon as I became a problem, I was treated with the kind of attention that should have been accorded a good customer. I became a good customer, in their crossed eyes, when I became a bad one. In short, there was nothing they could do—which affirms the maxim of Fred Smith, the chairman and founder of Federal Express: "The worst that can happen if you borrow a lot is that you have a second partner."

The other side of that coin is to borrow nothing. Finance your start-up with savings and investments from friends that are equity investments. In other words, start with no debt and keep it that way. This is an entirely different way to do things, and is suitable for people with faint hearts, aversions to debt, or simply those who do things the old-fashioned way. (Having tried the former, I prefer the latter.) The discipline of using only paid-in capital is that you know exactly how long your leash is. You have so much money, and you tend to do everything possible to at least preserve the amount of capital paid in.

If it's a good idea, it's probably too late. When you have a new idea for a business, talk it up with friends and associates. Notice carefully their reaction. First, eliminate all responses from persons who always say nice, positive things. From those who are objective and will usually speak their mind, notice the drift. If they say "that's a wonderful idea, John," you are in big trouble. If your friends look a little confused, and shrug their shoulders, that's looking up. If they snigger and laugh at it, you may be on to something. If you have an idea for a business and it is so good that everyone recognizes that it is great, you are too late. You may not realize it, but the fact that everyone recognizes its value is a sure sign. ("I have this great idea of starting a chain of chocolate chip cookie stores to be placed in shopping malls where all the hypoglycemics hang out." Response: "Great idea, chocolate chip cookies are really popular in my office.") Dud. And the fact is that most ideas are duds. While you may have only one idea every seven years, the rest of the world has been relentlessly probing every corner of commerce and service trying to figure out how to make a killing. In other words, don't be seduced by your ideas no matter how brilliant you think you are. In most cases, somebody is already there. I tried for ten years to convince other people and companies to do what Smith & Hawken does: import high-quality horticultural tools and sell them direct. I begged people to do it. I pointed to sources, indicated the market, and even offered assistance. No takers. After four years of doing it myself, I have five competitors, including Quaker Oats, as well as the company that originally turned it down. You see how quickly a "niche" fills up.

Be the market. Don't try to figure out the market—be it. The market is as fickle as fog in a swamp. It is constantly changing, and there is not any agreement yet as to how to measure it. How else can you explain the fact that the largest companies, the ones with the most money to spend on marketing, launch some several thousand new food products every year for supermarket shelves, and only a tiny fraction make it? What do they know? If you have a food passion, and can't find the right products to satisfy your passion, you have a much better chance than Ralston Purina.

In other words, if you are looking for a business to go into, don't. Don't look. The right business for you is under your nose. It is as close to you as your hangnail. There are tens of thousands of businesses you could go into, but the one you will have fun in, the one you will be a hot knife in the lardy world of commerce in, the one that will satisfy you, is probably sitting around the house someplace. If not there it is around the yard, in the garage, or on your desk. It isn't out there.

Businesses with "being" goals last longer than businesses with "doing" goals. Successfully starting a small business does not mean you are going to be able to stick around. As soon as you enter the world of business, you are swimming in the seven deadly sins. You are bathed in the ambitions, conveniences, and shoddy ethical practices of your fellow bipeds. Watch out. But you don't have to become cynical to be aware because it is precisely those businesses that do treat people right that last, not the creepy ones. *In Search of Excellence* (CQ 37, Spring 1983) can be summed up in one sentence: Being a good human being is good business. The book has now outsold *Roots* to become the number-one hardback bestseller. And what its authors and others have discovered is that those companies, big and small, that emphasize how to be in the world survive over those companies that have achievement goals spelled out in terms of size, growth, and means. In other words, your goal can be "Our company will provide the whitest nappies in America." Laudable. Or it can be "Our company will be the finest nappy service in America." More laudable. Given that both companies are diaper services, the one with the orientation to "being" will prevail.

Have fun. This is the easiest and hardest. If you are not having fun, what's the point? It is only a cruel dog-eat-dog world if you see it that way. If the business becomes a bastion of self-doubt, suspicion, and grimy Calvinism, forget it. You are on the wrong path, and your lack of fun is its testament. A good business is where people laugh. You laugh, the people you work with laugh, and so do customers. If that sense of *esprit* is missing, perspective is lost, good people leave, and the business becomes a cycle of negative reinforcement. This is not smarmy "aren't-we-great-people" advice. It is the bottom line.

JIM BURKLO

Coffee Hour: America's True Religion

From the original introduction (Spring 1984):
The Politics of Religion isn't all spark and spittle; it definitely includes the quieter side of things as well. This "exposé" of who really runs our mainstream churches comes from CQ subscriber Jim Burklo, who does ongoing research as associate minister of First Congregational Church in Palo Alto, California.

Jay Kinney

Jay's original Politics and Religion section was concerned with reconciling those two human needs in a culture which sees them as contradictory, especially for those with a liberal or leftist background. This response by Jim Burklo appeared two issues later and suggested that for many Americans, the drives toward politics and religion have long been reconciled. Since he wrote this, Jim Burklo has become the resource coordinator of the church-supported Ecumenical Hunger Program in

East Palo Alto, which provides emergency food and helps find shelter and other emergency aid for local people. On Sundays, he's a traveling preacher among the congregations that support the hunger program. "The veracity of the theme of my article is impressed upon me every week, 'cause I get to sample the coffee hour in one of thirty different churches every Sunday."

Art Kleiner

Her hands gripping the fingers of a seventy-year-old-man, a child jumps and does a heels-over-the-head flip back onto the linoleum. Nearer the aluminum coffee percolator, where a line of people wait to fill their styrofoam cups, a young engineer talks about the contracts his firm is seeking while a high-school girl and her stepfather listen over the animated tones of a cluster of people behind them. The church janitor, a middle-aged school administrator, the widow of a college professor, and a phone company executive and her two children speculate on the reasons for the success of the recent rummage sale against the poor showing of last year's.

RULE OF THUMB: *The folks who stay after worship for "coffee hour" are the ones who run the American church.*

If you want to comprehend the politics of American religion, "coffee hour" is a first course. The disparate doctrines, structures, and worship forms of American Christianity distract us from proper respect for this informal time in the social hall after worship. I began to appreciate the importance of this phenomenon when I tried to schedule a seminar immediately after the church service. Ignoring my pleas to come into the classroom, people continued to hang out together by the coffee pot until after several Sundays of futility I concluded that coffee hour was a permanent fixture of Christian orthodoxy. This has proven true in each of the churches I have served since.

The Baptists and the Catholics, the Unitarians and the Pentecostalists all drink from a common styrofoam cup. Coffee hour has a function in America that transcends the divisions of the church. This is a huge and lonely country. New people keep moving in, and the rest keep moving around. The American local church is an extended family, a clan, for people whose natural clans are scattered and lost. It is a family for people who would otherwise be strangers to each other. It is a place for teenagers to know elderly people, for new parents to inherit baby clothes, for newly divorced women to hear about part-time jobs from business people, for single newcomers to town to meet people.

The clan conducts its affairs most intensely during the coffee hour. Stories are swapped, dates are made, plans are laid. It becomes obvious over several coffee hours that certain people know most of the others. These people, regardless of their official titles in the church or lack thereof, are the ones who have the greatest political influence in the church. Denominational officials make it their business to know these people and to consult them, as well as the officers of the church, on the state of the church. These are the people who can introduce you to other people during coffee hour; the informal network that is the real foundation of the church is in their hands.

The dominant political system of the Christian churches of the United States is "congregationalism"—local church autonomy. The Baptists (in all their many flavors), the Congregationalists, the Disciples, most Pentecostal churches, and many other denominations totaling the largest number of American churches are structured so that each local church owns its own building, chooses and fires its own pastors, and determines its own doctrines and by-laws. This system has crept into the Presbyterian churches, the Methodist churches, the Episcopal churches, and others with a more centralized political system; these denominations are giving in increasingly to local church demands for control over ministerial appointments, budgets, and worship forms. Americans are drawn to churches more because of their local characteristics than their denominational affiliations. This year, for the first time, the delegates to the World Council of Churches meeting joined together in a common celebration of the mass. Why is this possible? Because years ago, their local church constituents concluded that coffee hour was more important than creedal purity. Christian hierarchs have for a long time convinced themselves against the evidence that they still lead the church, while the people years ago began to ignore them while forming up behind the aluminum urn.

The staggering variety of American religious forms displayed in the hour before coffee still have, of course, important functions, not the least of which is the primal need of any clan to have a unique, identifying ritual. The ritual may have lost much of its original intrinsic meaning, but it remains potent as a way for the community to recognize itself. The hymnal of my church consists of the top ten hits of the 1840s, but while even the strongest defenders of the use of the hymnal would be hard-pressed to explain the meaning of the words, its value is primarily as a means for the church to express its identity. Is the minister or priest or elder really in charge of the worship service? I find the opposite. I am strongly subordinated by the liturgy itself, and thus by the congregation.

RULE OF THUMB: *The more obscure and dated the worship, the more democratically is the church run.*

Why do more Americans go to church than Europeans? It is certainly not because our worship is more meaningful. It is because coffee hour is as much a feature of our social landscape as shopping malls, fast food, and baseball. America is set up in such a way that people need coffee hour. You can worship at home, praying before a candle or turning on a T.V.

preacher. But what is there to replace the church potluck, the ladies' bazaar, the rummage sale? How many other places can you mingle with people of such diverse ages and life-situations?

I am in agreement with the political persuasions of my denominational leadership. However, as a parish pastor, I know that it matters very little to my church members whether I lean to the right or the left, as long as I love them. The preacher's political religion and religious politics can be ignored or affirmed as long as they do not prevent people from enjoying each other's company in the social hall afterward. It has amazed me how little I have bothered people with what I say from the pulpit. There are folks who completely disapprove of my convictions while getting along warmly with me on a personal level—which is the level they seek in coming to church in the first place. Coffee hour does not force any political point of view on anyone; thus, in a time of radicalization of the pulpit, the social hall has become the sanctuary of the church. Radicals and Reaganites can carry on about anything from Kierkegaard to croquet as they sip coffee after church.

RULE OF THUMB: *Brew two cups of coffee for every three people attending worship. This allows for the abstinence of children and those who had their coffee early in order to make it through worship.*

If democracy is the free and equal exercise of power by each citizen, then coffee hour surely qualifies: Most churches do not charge for their coffee, and you can help yourself until it runs out. This is certainly the most important form of democracy—economic democracy.

So, to understand the political life of the American churches, one must begin by recognizing that their members are primarily attracted by the fellowship life of the church, and are largely immune to the belief systems and lines of authority which form their facades. How many Catholics use birth control? How many Southern Baptists ignore Jerry Falwell? How many members of the liberal Protestant churches that have condemned nuclear weapons production are still working for the defense industry? More than the supposed leaders of Christendom would care to admit. In fact, Christianity in America is completely out of control of anyone except this Sunday's coffee host.

KEN KESEY

Burying
Jed Kesey

*From the original introduction
(Summer 1984):*
Ken Kesey is a novelist—*One Flew
Over the Cuckoo's Nest, Sometimes a
Great Notion*, and something forthcoming, set in Alaska, [notes for
which appeared in the Spring 1983
CQ]. He's a longtime cohort and
mentor of mine. I rolled into his
house in Palo Alto in July 1963, the
very week Jed Kesey was busy being
born, and never quite rolled out
again. Unlike many of the famous
I've encountered, Kesey and Faye
have always attended better to their
family than to his fame, letting decades go by novel-less but no landmark large or small of the kids' lives
pass without appropriate attention
and ceremony. Sweet solid citizens
resulted—Jed's older brother Zane,
older sister Shannon, younger sister
Sunshine, and Jed himself looking
most like and wrestling most like his
old man. The living-room rug in the
Kesey home (an Oregon barn) is a
wrestling mat.

The first letter printed here is to a
handful of Kesey's old buddies,

Wendell Berry, Larry McMurtry, Ed
McLanahan, Bob Stone, and Gurney
Norman, who came of writing age
together in the creative-writing program that Wallace Stegner ran at
Stanford University in the early sixties. Kesey notes: "I sincerely hope
that I do not—as Richard II worries—'play the wanton with our
woes,' by this display of my family's
private grief and publication of my
personal correspondence. I mean it
only to suggest a path for others
wandering in similar pain. We've
all got a lot of dying ahead of us. We
might as well learn how to go about
it."

Stewart Brand

*It was the toughest thing any of us has ever had to go
through, harder than jail, or my dad's death, or an
OD on STP, yet it also had and always will have a
decided glory. Partly, I think, because Jed was such
a good kid, very loving and very loved, and the
power of his being carried us through a lot of the
ache. But there was also the support we got, from
friends and family, from teachers and coaches and
schoolmates. Without this support I don't think we
would have attempted the kind of funeral we had, or
plunged into the activism prompted by the circumstances of the accident.*

*It's the funeral that I mainly want to share, be-
cause I think you guys and your constituency of readers should know that this homemade ceremony is legally possible. All you need is the land, the determination, and the family. The activism comes later
but I thought I would include it; it's part of the
glory. Besides, it's attached to two good letters I
wrote after Jed's death. Here are parts of the letters:*

Kesey's Athlete Son Killed

Jed Kesey, the son of author Ken Kesey, was one of two University of Oregon wrestlers killed in a highway accident in Pomeroy, Wash.

Kesey, 20, died yesterday in a Spokane hospital as a result of a head injury suffered in the Saturday accident. Two other wrestlers remained in critical condition at Deaconess Medical Center, where they were taken after the team van, carrying 10 varsity wrestlers and two assistant coaches, slid off an icy, hilly road on the way to a match and crashed 185 feet down a steep embankment.

Also killed in the accident was Lorenzo West, 20, of Portland, Ore.

Kesey's father, who lives in Pleasant Hill, Ore., is the author of "One Flew Over the Cuckoo's Nest" and "Sometimes a Great Notion," and was one of the heroes of the 1960s counterculture. He was at the hospital at the time of his son's death yesterday.

—San Francisco Chronicle
Tuesday, Jan. 24, 1984

Dear Wendell and Larry and Ed and Bob and Gurney:

Partners, it's been a bitch.

I've got to write and tell somebody about some stuff and, like I long ago told Larry, you're the best backboard I know. So indulge me a little; I am but hurt.

We built the box ourselves (George Walker, mainly) and Zane and Jed's friends and frat brothers dug the hole in a nice spot between the chicken house and the pond. Page found the stone and designed the etching. You would have been proud, Wendell, especially of the box—clear pine pegged together and trimmed with redwood. The handles of thick hemp rope. And you, Ed, would have appreciated the lining. It was a piece of Tibetan brocade given Mountain Girl by Owsley fifteen years ago, gilt and silver and russet phoenixbird patterns, unfurling in flames. And last month, Bob, Zane was goose hunting in the field across the road and killed a snow goose. I told him be sure to save the down. Susan Butkovitch covered this in white silk for the pillow while Faye and MG and Gretch and Candace stitched and stapled the brocade into the box.

It was a double-pretty day, like winter holding its breath, giving us a break. About three hundred people stood around and sung from the little hymnbooks that Diane Kesey had Xeroxed—"Everlasting Arms," "Sweet Hour of Prayer," "In the Garden" and so forth. With all my cousins leading the singing and Dale on his fiddle. While we were singing "Blue Eyes Crying in the Rain," Zane and Kit and the neighbor boys that have grown up with all of us carried the box to the hole. The preacher is also the Pleasant Hill School superintendent and has known our kids since kindergarten. I learned a lot about Jed that I'd either forgotten or never known—like his being a member of the National Honor Society and finishing sixth in a class of more than a hundred.

We sung some more. People filed by and dropped stuff in on Jed. I put in that silver whistle I used to wear with the Hopi cross soldered on it. One of our frat brothers put in a quartz watch guaranteed to keep beeping every fifteen minutes for five years. Faye put in a

317

Jed Kesey

snapshot of her and I standing with a pitchfork all Grantwoodesque in front of the old bus. Paul Foster put in the little leather-bound New Testament given him by his father who had carried it during his sixty-five years as a minister. Paul Sawyer read from *Leaves of Grass* while the boys each hammered in the one nail they had remembered to put in their pockets. The Betas formed a circle and passed the loving cup around (a ritual our fraternity generally uses when a member is leaving the circle to become engaged) (Jed and Zane and I are all members, y'unnerstand, not to mention Hagen) and the boys lowered the box with these ropes George had cut and braided. Zane and I tossed in the first shovelfuls. It sounded like the first thunderclaps of *Revelations* . . .

But it's an earlier scene I want to describe for you all, as writers and friends and fathers . . . up at the hospital, in cold gray Spokane:

He's finally started moving a little. Zane and I had been carrying plastic bags of snow to pack his head in trying to stop the swelling that all the doctors told us would follow as blood poured to the bruised brain. And we noticed some reaction to the cold. And the snow I brushed across his lips to ease the bloody parch where all the tubes ran in caused him to roll his arms a little. Then more. Then too much, with the little monitor lights bleeping faster and faster, and I ran to the phone to call the motel where I had just sent most of the family for some rest.

"You guys better get back over here! He's either going or coming."

Everybody was there in less than five minutes—Chuck and Sue, Kit and Zane, Shan and her fiance Jay, Jay's dad Irby, Sheryl and her husband Bill, my mom, Faye . . . my whole family except for my dead daddy and Grandma Smith down with age and Alzheimer's. Jed's leg was shaking with the force of his heartbeat. Kit and Zane tried to hold it. He was starting to go into seizures, like the neurosurgeon had predicted.

Up till this time everybody had been exhorting him to "hang on, Old Timer. Stick it out. This thing can't pin you. You're too tough, too brave. Sure it hurts but you can pull through it. Just grit your teeth and hang on." Now we could see him trying, fighting. We could see it in his clenching fists, his threshing legs. And then aw Jesus we saw it in his face. The peacefully swollen unconscious blank suddenly was filled with expression. He came back in. He checked it out, and he saw better than we could begin to imagine how terribly hurt he was. His poor face grimaced with pain. His purple brow knitted and his teeth actually did try to clench on the tubes.

And then, O my old buddies, he cried. The doctors had already told us in every gentle way they could that he was brain dead, gone for good, but we all saw it . . . the quick flicker-back of consciousness, the awful hurt being realized, the tears saying "I don't think I can do 'er this time, Dad. I'm sorry, I truly am. . . ."

And everybody said, "It's okay, ol' Jedderdink. You know better than we do. Breathe easy. Go ahead on. We'll catch you later down the line."

His threshing stopped. His face went blank again. I thought of Old Jack, Wendell, ungripping his hands, letting his fields finally go.

The phone rang in the nurses' quarters. It was the doctor, for me. He had just appraised all the latest readouts on the monitors. "Your son is essentially dead, Mr. Kesey. I'm very sorry."

And the sorrow rung absolutely honest. I said something. Zane picked up the extension and we watched each other while the voice explained the phenomena. We said we saw it also, and were not surprised. Thank you. . . .

Then the doctor asked a strange thing. He wanted to know what kind of kid Jed was. Zane and I both demanded what he meant. He said he was wondering how Jed would have felt about being an organ donor. Our hearts both jumped.

"He would love it! Jed's always been as generous as they come. Take whatever you can use!"

The doctor waited for our elation to ease down, then told us that to take the kidneys they had to take them before the life support was turned off. Did we understand? After a while we told him we did.

So Faye and I had to sign five copies apiece, on a cold formica countertop, while the machine pumped out the little "beep . . . beep . . . beep . . ." in the dim tangle of technology behind us. In all my life, waking and dreaming, I've never imagined anything harder.

Everybody went in and told him goodbye, kissed his broken nose, shook his hand, squeezed his big old hairy foot . . . headed down the corridor. Somebody said it might be a good idea to get a scrip for some kind of downers. We'd all been up for about forty hours, either in the chapel praying like maniacs, or at his bedside talking to him. We didn't know if we could sleep.

Chuck and I walked back to the intensive care ward to ask. All the doctors were there, bent over a long list, phoning numbers, matching blood types, ordering nurses . . . in such a hurry they hardly had time to offer sympathy. Busy, and justly so. But the nurses, the nurses bent over their clipboards, could barely see to fill out the forms.

They phoned the hotel about an hour later to tell us it was over, and that the kidneys were in perfect shape. That was about four in the morning. They phoned again a little after six to say that the kidneys were already in two young somebodies.

What a world.

We've heard since that they used twelve things out of him, including corneas. And the redwinged blackbirds sing in the budding greengage plumtree.

With love,
Ken

PS: When Jed's wallet was finally sorted out of the debris and confusion of the wreck it was discovered that he had already provided for such a situation. He had signed the place on his driver's license indicating that he wanted to be an organ donor in the event of etc., etc.

One man gathers what another man spills. . . .

kk

So, Stewart, we now have the beginning of our own graveyard—a big basalt headstone, an iron gate Page welded, poplar trees and honey locust that Zane and Joy Smith planted. It was simpler to do than anyone ever imagined. When the guy from the mortuary came to pick up our pine box he shook his head in awe. "Beautiful," he marveled, "and in only a day and a night. Beautiful." And when the county health inspector came out to okay the grave site that I pointed out, all he said was, "Looks just fine to me." Because they are just people—fathers, husbands, neighbors—and they respect what they see respected. They didn't take death away from us; we relinquished it.

Next is part of a letter I wrote to Senator Hatfield. He called the other day and asked if he could use it in the Senate appropriations debates going on back in Washington. I told him okay and asked if I could do the same, send it to seatbelt advocates in our state legislature and to antimilitary groups. He said fine. Since then I have read of stiffening resistance to Reagan's obscene military budget requests.

Dear Senator Hatfield:

. . . From the very first my response to this anguish has been nagged by a terrible teeth-grinding of blame, of blame un-laid. I tried to stanch it. Don't blame, I told myself. It just hurts people. There's been enough hurt already. Turn the other cheek, I kept telling myself.

But the nagging kept on: "What if the other cheek is somebody else's kid? In some other slapdash rig? On some other ill-fated underfunded trip next wrestling season? Or next debate season? Or next volleyball season? Moreover, what if this young blood has been spilled not merely to congregate people and their feelings, but also to *illuminate* a thing going wrong?"

So I want to try to apprise you, Senator, of just how my chain of blame is proceeding:

I could blame the Oregon coach or his assistants for driving a borrowed rig over a treacherous pass without snow studs, or seatbelts, or even doors that closed properly. But these guys are already doing the best they can to scrape together funds and transportation for a "minor" sport. I could blame my alma mater for not funding the activity better. I could blame the Pacific Athletic Conference for not protecting athletes en route to sanctioned events, or I could blame the whole National Collegiate Association for fostering a situation where more energy is devoted to monitoring the ethics of the few "stars" in the sports firmament than to the actual welfare of the untold thousands of unknown athletes traveling to their minor events all across the nation.

Faye and I have received more than a thousand letters from around the nation. Most are like yours—sweet, straight, supportive. Many are from people who have lost kids or grandkids on the highways, like Bob Straub and Len Casanova. But a lot of them are from teams, the kids and coaches of wrestling teams, high school and college. Or the parents of kids on teams. And most of these letters mention at least one near scrape. Some speak of worse, like the wreck of the wrestling bus in Montana that killed nine on the same day and in the same area. One member of the Washington State

College woman's crew team writes of returning from a rowing meet in Lewiston last year, over the same road that got Jed and Lorenzo. The girls couldn't even afford state vans. They were traveling in private cars. She said she came around a foggy corner and saw her sister's car mashed into the grill of a Greyhound. Her sister was dead. No one in the big bus was so much as bruised.

And every wrestling tournament we've attended since the accident (yeah, they still go on, and we still go; it's always been our family's fashion) has prompted a parent or coach or school administrator to come up and speak to us of their renewed anxieties—the midnight returns from Glide down foggy I-5; battling the chiptrucks along the Umpqua; picking their way across the January passes from Redmond and La Grande and Lakeview. In rigs without seatbelts, without CBs or trauma kits, usually driven by the coach or his wife. But what can they do? they ask. It's hard enough to pass a school budget in Oregon without asking for fancy protection. Just not enough money in the communities. Nobody wants to increase property taxes, not even for safer playgrounds, let alone for safer activity buses. Sure, the kids need to be defended against the treacheries of travel, but there's just not enough money. Where are the already-scrimping schools gonna come up with the revenue for that kind of defense?

Then, the other night, as I watched the national news, it came to me. We were lobbing those sixteen-inch shells into the hills of Lebanon. The Pentagon spokesman said he wasn't certain exactly which faction we were hitting, but he reassured us that we were certainly hitting *somebody*. Then he was asked what each of those shells costs. The price was something enormous. I can't remember. But the spokesman countered by saying that the price for national defense is always high, yet it must be paid.

And I began to get mad, Senator. I had finally found where the blame must be laid: that the money we are spending for national defense is not defending us from the villains real and near, the awful villains of ignorance, and cancer, and heart disease and highway death. How many school buses could be outfitted with seatbelts with the money spent for one of those sixteen-inch shells?

I know it's a radical notion, and I have no idea what to do about it. There are going to be a lot of lawsuits coming out of this tragedy; there will be no other way the Topliff family can afford a boy paralyzed from the neck down; there will be no other way to force new safety regulations. It's going to be a real tough battle for a lot of folks who are already badly wounded, and it's going to be messy. And I'm afraid the real villains will squirm away again.

Help deal with this, Senator. Please. Talk about it. Talk about bringing some of these umpteen billions back home, back into the vulnerable guts of this nation where our dollars can actually be used for our actual national defense. I intend to begin work on it, in whatever ways I can find. I may have to join those old long-haired peaceniks on the railroad tracks when the next White Train full of nuclear warheads rolls across our land. Just like in the sixties. I guess it's kind of old-fashioned, but it looks to me like it's the job God has dealt this hand around.

Thanks for listening to me ramble. I remain,

Sincerely,
Ken Kesey

Ken Kesey wrote about Jed once before in a Whole Earth publication. It was Spring of 1971, The Last Supplement to the Whole Earth Catalog, which Kesey was guest editing with Paul Krassner. He was reviewing The Bible ("All of it. All the rest of your life."). It was a three page review, with Jed at the pivot. . . .

Stewart Brand

It's about four years ago in my hometown of Springfield. Summer. Sundown. We've just had a family supper at my folks' house and I'm driving my mom's Bonneville over to my brother's creamery. In the car with me are my daughter Shannon, my youngest son Jed, and my dog Pretzels. The radio is playing and

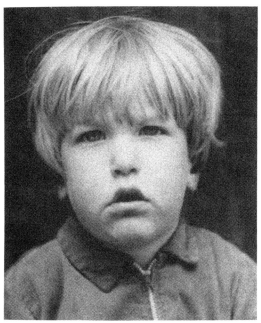

The Kesey Family

Jed, age two

Shannon is prattling plans and the windows are down to the full-ripened Oregon day. . . .

(I've told this tale a lot since, and each telling has drained a little from the event. I've tried to be judicious in my allotment of the tellings because of this depletion. I hope I can tell it this time for good and save what's left for my own lost times ahead.)

We're traveling on old West Q Street, which used to be the main artery to Eugene before the freeway came in. The house where my mother and father and brother and I lived all our school years until Chuck and I left to get married is just up ahead, dwarfed now by the freeway that came by a few years ago like a sudden river of cement and Chevies. This was the river that forced my folks to seek higher ground in the tract house where we just ate. I never lived in the tract house so the old house up ahead there on West Q is still what I consider home in my sentimental mind. I used to lie awake late across my bed with my front teeth resting on my windowsill until the sill was gnawed paintless. I could see past the raccoon cage, the blinking radio tower of KEED, and beyond that the friendly outline of the Couburg hills where a little logging train used to come from a few times a week at 11:45 P.M. and then fewer times and fewer times until, well, I guess it's been clear back in high school I can last remember hearing that whistle, lying there blinking out past the coon cage at my mysterious futures, thinking, "Someday I'll go someplace on that train . . ." but it stopped running and I grew up and now, here it is, ten feet away coming across the road and the Bonneville is already on the tracks and for once added power is important and I tromp at least the front half of the car across before that awful black noise running on a track red with rusted neglect ripped away everything from the backdoor back and sent the rest spinning on down West Q.

Shannon was crying and bloody. The Walkers, our old neighbors, were helping her from the mangled door. My head hurt but I felt whole. On the floor my little dog whimpered, her teeth through her lip. The train was stopping somewhere behind me. Where was Jed?

I picked him up and carried him into the Walkers'. He didn't look hurt anywhere but *oh* he was such desolate heaviness in my arms. I sat down in a chair, holding him. And he sighed, a curiously familiar sigh though I'd never heard another like it before, and I felt the life go out of him as though that soft sound were wings assigned to bear its essence gently away. My ear found no beating at his chest. I looked up. There I sat across the room in the Walkers' big dining-room mirror, holding my dead son in my arms. In the middle of my forehead a two-bit-sized bone plug had been punched neatly from my skull and hung on a piece of skin like an open trap door; the hole and the plug joined thus formed a bleeding figure eight. I blinked at my garish image and thought "if anything ever counts, this counts." Then I closed my eyes on my reflection and called aloud:

"O dear Lord, please don't let him die."

Then things became completely calm. Shannon was trying to hush her crying; the Walkers stopped rushing about and talking and waited . . . the frantic phoning paused (things will make a space) . . . then I knew what to do. Opening my eyes I leaned back to Jed and be-

gan to give him mouth-to-mouth resuscitation. The ambulance drivers came in but made no move to interrupt me, though one of them reached down and neatly popped the plug back in my forehead while I worked over Jed. Finally Jed sighed again, the same soft wings except this time they bore the life back into its sacred vessel.

I knew I had participated in a miracle and I was absolutely amazed. As the days went by and Jed drew out of danger in the hospital I found that it wasn't the miracle that had amazed me. That returning sigh will sound through all the rest of my life and I will be ever thankful. What amazed me, though, was that when the chips were down I knew *where* to call, and that I knew Who answered. I had interceded in my son's behalf, and talked the powers into letting us have him for a time more, Thank God.

THE COFFIN

George Walker

When I was asked to build Jed's coffin, my first thought was of regulations. I was expecting to have to meet some long, convoluted list of government requirements. Sealed, Inspected, & Approved, that sort of thing. Not so, I quickly discovered upon inquiring at the mortuary. I could not only build the coffin, I could even buy a kit! The Plain Pine Box, I believe it was called, and it was exactly that: a few straight rough pine boards cut to length, a handful of nails, and simple, easy instructions. It was OK, but not what I had in mind. I wanted to build something more personal, and with more class.

I didn't have a design to work from, but I had an idea how I wanted it to look. I drew a few rough sketches and we started from there. George Proddock, Kesey's stepfather Ed Jolley and I all worked together at building it, which helped get it done in time, and also made it more interesting as we tried to think our way through the many complex angles we had to cut and fit. This was to be no straight-sided rectangular box, but rather a complex tapered hexagonal shape. I thought of our trip to Egypt as we laid out the plan, trying to duplicate, as my mind's eye remembered, that exact proportion of the sarcophagi. After several attempts and erasures, I got a drawing that "looked right," and we laid it out full size and cut it from a sheet of ¾-inch plywood. This was to be the floor of the coffin; we would build up around it.

"Dang, it really looks *small*," everyone thought. Six feet six inches long and almost two feet wide at the shoulders, tapering in at both the head and the feet, it did indeed look undersized. We took turns lying down on it to convince ourselves it was adequate before going ahead with construction. We still didn't know exactly what we were going to build; we designed it as we went along. I don't really recommend this method of building, as opposed to having a complete plan, as it's easy to go astray. My experience in boat carpentry helped get us over the hard places, as boats are generally built without straight lines or right angles, and the pieces are hand fit.

We selected some clear white pine boards for the sides and top. Nice looking and easy to work with, pine is also traditional. In addition to tapering the sides in "toe-pincher" style, we angled them out wider at the top. This made the job of fitting the corners immensely more difficult, as every cut was a compound angle. It wasn't necessary to do it that way, but it looked better, and somehow that made it important.

> I made it on the bevel. . . . A body is not square like a crosstie. . . . The animal magnetism of a dead body makes the stress come slanting, so the seams and joints of a coffin are made on the bevel. . . . It makes a neater job.
>
> William Faulkner,
> *As I Lay Dying.*

It also makes a longer job. We worked well past midnight for two days, carefully fitting thin redwood trim strips around all the edges, dowelling and splining the seams in the top, handrubbing to finish . . . massaging, a work of love. Rope-work handles were added, again calling on skills learned in my years as a sailor. To complete the job, the interior was padded and lined with a fine old tapestry. All this in time to deliver to the mortuary, where the body had been prepared.

It was a very good coffin, as coffins go, very beautiful everybody said, and certainly a labor of love. But I don't really believe that is the point. The real value of that coffin was in the doing, in the building of it ourselves. Not in the coffin, as a thing, but in the act of creating it, as an event. It made us all feel better to do this ourselves, to take charge of things as much as we could, not just the coffin but the burial as well. Perhaps it's because, when we lose someone close, particularly someone young and in the prime of life, we feel more than a little burned that things have been jerked so irrevocably beyond our control. Anything we can do to regain our handle on events is gratifying.

Whatever the reason, all who kept themselves actively involved in getting Jed buried agreed: we all gained something through our efforts. We felt better about it than if we had just turned it all over to the professionals, and gone about our business of feeling bad. So, I would say to anybody who feels that they might want to give it a try when someone close dies, absolutely yes; build it yourself. Even if you can't do basic carpentry, you can nail together a kit. If you do have skills, you can make something that will make you feel good long after it's buried out of sight. It doesn't have to be fancy; simple and neat is just fine, but *do* make it strong. You'll be surprised by the weight.

HARRY AND LARRY
INGHAM

The Difference Between Writing and Building Racing Engines

*From the original introduction
(Summer 1984):*
Harry Ingham recently graduated
from the University of California
graduate writing program, and is
currently a freelance writer. Larry
Ingham had five engines in this
year's Indianapolis 500.

Jay Kinney

1. When you're writing, your last step is to throw away everything you don't like.

2. In writing, the small parts are always the same, but the large shapes change every time. Next time you will use the same letters and even the same words. In racing, the overall design usually stays the same, but the little stuff is different every time. If I raced books, instead of writing them, I'd have to start with a given book design, and then try to make it work better than anyone else had. I'd have to

work over the word *and* to make it fit just a little better, be a little lighter maybe. I'd have to make sure I got the best *and* to start with. Somewhere in between big and little is a place where the work on books and engines is similar.

3. Nobody calls you up and tells you that you have to do overtime because his old novel blew up and he has nothing to read.

4. The people who claim they can build better engines on LSD are relatively rare, although the number who claim they can do it better on uppers is about the same.

5. All engine-building is nonfiction.

6. Engine-building skills and experience are invisible, but the tools are visible.

7. Almost anyone can write a little.

8. At a party, if you say you are a racing mechanic, people will ask you about racing, while if you say you are a writer, people will tell you about writing.

9. In a collaboration, a racing mechanic is more help to a writer than a writer is to a racing mechanic.

10. A racing mechanic knows whether he's unemployed or not.

11. While he's at the peak of the day's momentum of work, the exact time when he is full of himself, and can make or unmake the work of the day, of the week, of his life—at that moment, the mechanic gets asked by the boss if he's busy. The writer relies on his loved ones to do this.

12. Racing mechanics sometimes get scalded, deafened, or stuck with tiny metal slivers. Writers are often driven to drink or screaming, but then so are engine builders.

13. There is an exact list of the people who will blame you if your engine blows. If your

novel inhales its valves, people will be pissed, but you'll never meet most of them.

14. Racing people get free T-shirts.

15. When asked a question that goes to the heart of his art, each one looks down and shrugs, but the engine man shrugs bigger shoulders.

16. A writer can bullshit himself and everyone right in the middle of his art form. For a mechanic, the bullshit, if he does it, has to be outside the work. There are agreed standards for racing engines: they should propel the car fast, and hold together. A writer can tell himself his slow, rickety work is good, and he may be right.

17. Burned-out racing mechanics fix Chevies at your corner gas station; burned-out writers quit art altogether.

18. There are almost no women racing mechanics, which is bad for racing. There are almost no racing mechanics on TV, which is good for racing.

19. There are no Indy-engine schools, but a good talent can find a way to work with a master. In writing, very few work with masters, but schools abound. Neither system of training works very well, and perhaps neither should.

20. Nobody publishes reviews of a mechanic.

21. A mechanic can have his tools stolen.

22. In racing, there is no being good by playing at being bad, there is no teasing.

23. There are people alive who have met the first racing mechanics. There are no racing engines chiseled in ancient obelisks.

24. Engine builders are divided between Republicans and Democrats.

25. Writers talk more, and sometimes better.

26. Writers like writing letters, sending angry notes, and sometimes even filling out questionnaires. A racing mechanic hates fixing his own car.

27. Writers, given their head, will talk about taxes, how to survive on a small variable income, and getting laid. Racing mechanics will talk about getting laid and smog devices. (They're for getting laid and against smog devices. They have good reasons for both, which you need to know.)

28. Writers who have an inspiration can get up in the middle of the night and write it down. Racing folk have to try to keep the golden moment until work tomorrow.

29. A real mechanic can drive to the market feeling his engine's concatenated explosions and steel twisting in grease. When a writer learns to do this it gets in his way; he can't read newspapers or talk to his kids without words forming into chunks and stopping his listening.

30. Perplexity takes the same amount of time, but when he's sure, a writer can go fast, and come back to clean up later. If he wants.

31. Nobody ever left a bundle of racing engines, with instructions to his family to destroy them when he died.

32. Racing engines make noise here and now.

33. Both go to the same bars after work, but some of the writers think they're slumming, or perhaps doing research.

34. You've already done the job well, but there's a deadline, and it's time to take the job one step higher. The way to decide which profession you want is to decide whether you would like to do that in a half-darkened shop or at home, growling at the kids to keep them away.

35. Some writers go to meetings.

36. Innovations in racing can be tested by asking, does the thing go faster?

37. When the competition makes a change, the writer has to avoid it, like the horns of the bull, holding in as close as he can. The racing mechanic has to decide whether to use it. Oscar Wilde thought it was all right for him to steal from others, because he improved their work. On the other hand, those who stole from him were criminals, because their work was inferior. No such conflict could exist in racing.

FREDDY BOSCO

Who Do
You Think
You Are?

*From the original introduction
(Fall 1984):*
A string of pearls fished out of the
Denver Public Library by Freddy
Bosco. It is made up entirely of book
titles taken from the card catalog,
with minimal editing.

Kevin Kelly

As sometimes happens with pieces in
COEVOLUTION QUARTERLY, we
dunno the first thing about who
Freddy Bosco is. It ends this book as
a kind of dedication to the CQ
reader.

Art Kleiner

You all want something. You Americans. You
among the stars. You are all sanpaku.

You are as young as your spine. You are born
to victory. You are earnestly requested to meet.
You are extraordinary. You are happy. You are
my friends.

You are never alone. You are not the target.
You are psychic. You are the jury. You are what
you eat.

You are younger than you think. You be the
judge. You better believe it. You broke my
dream.

You can always tell a fisherman. You can always tell a Harvard man. You can analyze
handwriting. You can be a better cook than
mama ever was. You can be a carpenter. You
can be a plumber. You can be a printer.

You can be happily married. You can be
healed. You can become the person you want
to be.

You can build your own sailboat. You can
catch fish. You can change the world. You can
change your career. You can communicate with
the unseen world.

You can conquer. You can cook for one. You
can cope. You can design. You can die
laughing.

You can do anything with crepes. You can do
it. You can do it from a wheelchair. You can
draw cartoons.

You can fight for your life. You can find God.
You can find uranium! You can fix it. You can
get it right. You can get so much justice.

You can get there from here. You can get what
you want if you find it within yourself. You
can get your real estate taxes reduced. You can
have what you say.

You can help your country win. You can hook rugs. You can improve your vision. You can increase your heart power. You can landscape it yourself. You can learn Russian.

You can learn to fly. You can live cheaply in the Canaries. You can live in an apartment. You can live longer than you think. You can make a bow.

You can make a Stradivarius violin. You can make an insect zoo. You can make money in the stock market. You can make the difference.

You can make your own gloves. You can master life. You can own a business. You can play par golf. You can predict your heart attack and prevent it.

You can prevent illness. You can profit from a monetary crisis. You can quit smoking in fourteen days. You can raise decent children. You can remake America. You can say that again, Sam.

You can see a lot standing under a flare in the Republic of Viet Nam. You can sleep well. You can speak again. You can start all over. You can stay well. You can stop.

You can survive any financial disaster. You can survive the outdoors. You can survive the bomb. You can take them with you. You can talk well.

You can teach music. You can train your cat. You can trust the Communists. You can vote.

You can whittle and carve. You can win. You can win a scholarship. You can wreck it. You can write. You can write Chinese.

You can't be an immigrant twice. You can't beat the hours. You can't buy a dog. You can't catch me.

You can't count on dying. You can't do business with Hitler. You can't do that. You can't eat magnolias.

You can't eat peanuts in church. You can't escape. You can't get there from here. You can't go home again. You can't have everything.

You can't have your kayak and heat it. You can't live your own life. You can't make me if I don't want to. You can't pet a possum. You can't print that!

You can't say what you think. You can't steal first base. You can't tell a man by the song he sings. You can't turn the clock back. You can't win.

You come, too. You could live if they let you. You could look it up. You don't have to be rich.

You don't have to exercise. You don't know what you like. You don't need an enemy. You don't say.

You fix them. You fly it. You go away.

You go your way. You got to live. You got to stay happy. You have a friend, Pietro. You have a point there.

You have heard of them. You have to pay the price. You haven't changed.

You know I can't hear you when the water's running. You know me Al. You know what people are. You know who. You learn by living. You live as you breathe.

You look ridiculous. You make America. You make your own luck.

You may cross examine! You may safely graze. You meet them in Mexico. You may as well live. You must break out sometimes.

You must go to Mexico. You must know everything. You must relax. You must see Canada. You mustn't weep, it's Yom Tev.

You need help, Charlie Brown. You need never walk alone. You never can tell. You never know with mama. You no longer count. You only have to get rich once.

You only live twice. You ought to patent that. You ought to see Herbert's house.

You pay and pay. You reach for your hat. You read to me, I'll read to you. You rolling river.

You sell with your voice. You shall be as gods. You shall know them. You should have been here an hour ago. You should have brought your mink.

You should start sooner. You still can't eat Mt. Rainier! You, the jury. You, the person you want to be. You think you got trouble? You, too, are a believer.

You, too, can make a speech. You touched me. You train your dog. You want to build a school? You wear the big shoe.

You were born again to be together. You were princess last time. You will die today! You will go to the moon. You will live under the sea. You will never be the same. You will survive your death.

STEWART BRAND

Afterword:
Outtro

Editing is reading. Semicolon. Actually it's a two-minded reading—one reading and one watching the reader read. "Little pause in confusion there, what's that about?" "Hm, you read that sentence twice with satisfaction, it must be a pull quote." "Still turning pages, eh, looks like a buy."

COEVOLUTION QUARTERLY was founded to see what would happen if an editor were totally unleashed. I would print anything that kept me turning its pages. I figured I had the requisite skills of an editor—I was a writer too lazy to write, a reader still curious about how the world might really work, and easily bored. I could say no. I could pick up the phone.

It took me a long time to catch on it was not me and my impeccable taste that was working, it was the formula: editor unleashed. Not only would anybody do, they would commonly do better. Art's editing of this book, for example; finer than I could do by a mile. In case you the reader are getting the itch to start a magazine at this point, I'll pass on for your benefit the lies I was told. It takes a million dollars to even think of starting a magazine. You've got to be able to identify your audience in detail in advance. You've got to find advertisers who want that audience. You must be prepared to lose money for three years minimum. All the niches are filled anyway.

I should warn you that Point Foundation is currently in an expansionist phase with its publications.

This book is an empty casket. COEVOLUTION is alive and well as *Whole Earth Review*, still quarterly but mass-distributed on newsstands. Still without ads, except of course ones like this: a *Whole Earth Review* subscription costs $18/year (4 issues) from 27 Gate Five Road, Sausalito, CA 94965. There are a few innovations, such as the subtitle, "Tools and Ideas for the Computer Age," which makes many readers wish to throw up.

Simultaneously we're reselling much of the same info in a weekly half-page newspaper column nationally syndicated by United Features, also frequently called "Whole Earth Review." Don't knock reselling. It's almost the only way you can make money off words. This book, for example.

In our tireless research to determine how much is too much computer stuff, we've done a second edition of the *Whole Earth Software Catalog*, published October 1985 by Doubleday. You could even say that our efforts to swallow all of computerdom have suffered a catastrophic reversal: we've been swallowed by them. We now publish *via* computer on a teleconferencing system we run for the San Francisco Bay Area called The WELL (Whole Earth 'Lectronic Link), unless the customary volatility of the computer biz has turned the whole project into something else, like ash. In any case, a new medium for us. Fresh meat.

COEVOLUTION was a name, and an excuse, to purvey the biological metaphor. Quick, recursivate. What's the evolutionary perspective on the dead but reborn COEVOLUTION? Three angles come to mind. One is what's called The Red Queen Hypothesis—running frantically to stay in one place; an explicitly coevolutionary current theory that says everyone's evolving all the time to keep up with the competition (and also the cooperation). True, true. Another is the Punctuated Evolution Hypothesis—a popular recent notion that most life evolves by fits and spurts, only when pressed by adversity or released by opportunity, and is otherwise conservative. That's us too. The third is my own theory of evolution: the way you can tell that evolution is going on is, you don't know, and can't know, what's going to happen next.

The last time I was in this position of reflective summing up was in August 1978. I had introduced over sixty CQ contributors in two afternoons at the Whole Earth Jamboree for their five-minute speeches (Anne Herbert's Jonah sermon on p. 136 was one). At the end I was exhausted and expected to Say Something. I said: "There's some kind of dialogue that goes on between grasp and reach. Ten years ago we reached for something with the *Whole Earth Catalog*. A lot of us reached for various things—some to stop the war in Vietnam, some to save various species, some to find a way to stay high. We have spent ten years refining our activ-

ities so that our grasp could catch up with that reach. . . . But each time the grasp catches up with the reach and we come to do something rather well—well enough that it's as if we could do it in our sleep—then probably we are doing it in our sleep. . . . I think all of us should have in mind to keep various hobbies going that might take off and become a line of work, and keep working at times for other kinds of people and in other kinds of jobs, so that our own diversity can increase and match the diversity we're trying to bring about everywhere." Red Queen says: You have to keep saying it. Punctuated Evolution says . . .
Semicolon;

ART KLEINER

Appendix: A History of CoEvolution Quarterly

Issue 1 (Spring 1974): After a two-year hiatus from publishing, Stewart Brand (who signs himself SB in the magazine) founds COEVOLUTION QUARTERLY simultaneously with editing the *Whole Earth Epilog*. "I had [originally wanted] to call it 'The Never Piss Against the Wind Newsletter' . . ." SB writes in the *Epilog*. "I did have a formula in mind: we would print long technical pieces on whatever interested us—the opposite of the predigested pap in, say, *Intellectual Digest*." The first issue is small (96 pages), and introduces an ongoing concern with forecasting environmental/energy/economic apocalypse in a regular section called "Apocalypse Juggernaut, Hello." Other sections carry forward from the *Whole Earth Catalog*: Understanding Whole Systems, Land Use, Soft Technology, Community, Communications, Learning, and Craft. Michelle Phillips, Richard Nilsen, and Rosemary Menninger begin their long associations with CQ as Land Use reviewer/evaluators.

Issue 2 (Summer 1974): Long (174 pages), perfect bound (making it look more like a book than a floppy magazine). Introduces young curmudgeon/naturalist Peter Warshall ("I daydream of the day when BOOK [field guides] die out and a strong spoken tradition revives.") Introduces J. Baldwin, the

source of COEVOLUTION's ongoing authoritativeness on soft technology (known to some people as alternative or appropriate technology). Introduces editor-to-be Stephanie Mills, writing on salons (see p. 10). One article describes the New Games tournament, which SB had invented the previous fall. The only dramatic play published in CQ, Michael McClure's *Gorf* (about a giant penis aloft in the apocalypse), appears this issue.

Issue 3 (Fall 1974): This issue is guest-edited by the Black Panther Party of Oakland, California, who design it to read and look like one of their newsletters.

Issue 4 (Winter 1974): Gregory Bateson, whose work and conversation will form a philosophic underpinning for the magazine, is first introduced to COEVOLUTION readers. (SB had published an interview with him in *Harper's* two years before.) J. D. Smith, "Whole Earth's resident cowboy," returns from Idaho to be a regular presence in the office and magazine for the next three years. CQ's original offices (on a pier in Sausalito, California) are threatened by development, so the magazine moves one mile north. "You've heard of industrial parks?" writes SB in the magazine's Gossip section. "We're in the longhair industrial dump at Gate 5 now, in a building called HARVEY'S LUNCHES and as unwelcoming to visitors as ever. Mail we love."

Issue 5 (Spring 1975): First of many appearances by Wendell Berry in the magazine. An article about Nitinol, a metal alloy that people thought could make mechanical engines powered from solar heat, will generate mail from curious would-be inventors for years. J. Baldwin writes "One Highly Evolved Toolbox," a description of his most-used tools; one of CQ's most popular articles, it will get updated five years later in the *Next Whole Earth Catalog*. Zentatsu Richard Baker-roshi, abbot of the San Francisco Zen Center, makes his first CQ appearance with a transcript of one of his lectures. Later, he joins the board of CQ's parent organization, the nonprofit Point Foundation.

Issue 6 (Summer 1975): First of many articles on

the Gaia hypothesis (see p. 15). Dan O'Neill, creator of "Odd Bodkins" in the 1960s, begins eight years of quarterly cartoons for COEVOLUTION. Young hacker Marc Le Brun inaugurates a section on personal computers—to my knowledge the first coverage of personal computing by any general-interest magazine. J. D. Smith brings volleyball (a *Whole Earth Catalog* office sport) to the CQ office—two games a day on paid time when the weather's nice. With the end of large sales of the *Whole Earth Catalog*, CQ begins "an austere period, its first since 1968." That austere period will last for the rest of CQ's history. SB introduces the uniform wage—everyone in the office gets $5/hour.

Issue 7 (Fall 1975): The cover announces "[Gerard] O'Neill's Space Colonies: practical, desirable, profitable, ready in fifteen years." This kicks off a debate between proponents and opponents of space colonies (thousands of people living years in totally man-made environments in space) that lasts four issues and introduces arguments between ecologists and technologists that will reverberate in various forms throughout the magazine's history. This issue also includes the first of five CQ interviews in the office of California governor Jerry Brown; SB introduces Gregory Bateson to the governor, and monitors the talk with a tape recorder. (The other such interviews will, respectively, be with Herman Kahn/Avory Lovins, Thomas Szasz, Marshall McLuhan, and Ken Kesey.) Editor-to-be Jay Kinney makes his first CQ appearance this issue as a cartoonist. To save money, SB limits this and most future issues to 144 pages.

Issue 8 (Winter 1975): J. D. Smith guest-edits an issue more hippie-oriented than usual, without any of the usual section headings; "having been around the heading Whole Systems for years," he writes, "and trying to fit things in and out of it, the categories get melted into one another." SB and J. Baldwin visit Marlon Brando and make tentative plans for a Whole Earth TV series—the series will not happen, but the interview is published.

Issue 9 (Spring 1976): Seventy-five pages of responses to Space Colonies. SB asks forty writers and thinkers to respond on the topic and prints the results, a technique used successfully several times during CQ's history. Storyteller/teacher Ron Jones's true story "Take As Directed," about a simulated Third Reich in high school, appears (and is later reprinted in the *Next Whole Earth Catalog*). Norman Lear will later make it into a made-for-TV movie. CQ publishes the first of many reports on The New Alchemy Institute, a group of biologists and inventors doing original research on energy technology. CQ business manager Andrew Fluegelman leaves to start his own publishing house, the Headlands Press; he will eventually become well-known in personal computer circles as the inventor of "shareware"—user-supported software. Meanwhile, CQ has its first subscription price-hike—from $6/year to $8—based partly on Fluegelman's last financial analysis ("Thank you for a quick pin in our balloon," Stewart replies in print).

Issue 10 (Summer 1976): Introduces Robert Horvitz (see p. 51), who will become CQ's "art editor," a liaison with conceptual artists. Wendell Berry and SB quarrel in print over space colonies. "How long is it going to take us to live down the Space Colony issue?" writes SB in Gossip. "Besides the Wendell Berry trauma, here's part of a letter from Andrea Sharp's mom. 'I noticed what your answer was, Andrea, on the last page of the CQ about Space Colonies' [which quizzed each CQ staff member about how they felt about them]. 'I was very glad you said no to them' (Andrea turns page, expecting moral lecture) . . . 'California's far enough.'"

Issue 11 (Fall 1976): CQ publishes its first special product, a map of World Biogeographical Provinces (see p. 68). An article by Herman Kahn prompts SB to change his first section heading to "NO Apocalypse?!" SB and Gregory Bateson hold a conference to address the pathology of Cartesian mind/body dualism, and SB prints some of the position papers in this issue. Architect Malcolm Wells advocates underground architecture ("I do it primarily because it is so beautiful"); his article will later become the basis for a book about same.

Issue 12 (Winter 1976): Peter Warshall guest-edits one of CQ's most popular issues, on watershed consciousness and politics. SB advertises for an "assistant editor, someone to help me expand my range"; writer Anne Herbert responds from Columbus, Ohio, gets hired, and makes her first appearance this issue. Her values, oriented to people and processes, will come to modify the magazine's printed sensibility. SB joins Governor Brown's staff as an ongoing part-time consultant. "Sacramento, to me, is Oz," he writes. "Munchkins, witches, wizards, the motley band with Dorothy, and all. There's dazzling magic. You gesture gracefully toward yonder wall, and PHOOM! spectacular goings-on. Gesture again: PHOOM! over on that side. Gesture again: nothing happens. Gesture repeatedly: nothing happens. Turn your back: PHOOM! As Jimmy Breslin said of politics, 'It's all done with mirrors and smoke.' What isn't?"

Issue 13 (Spring 1977): Introduces a regular section-heading on Politics. Introduces cartoonist Robert Crumb, who will appear regularly in CQ. Introduces C. Scott Van Strum, who will become Whole Earth's Learning editor. Introduces Medical editor Tom Ferguson, M.D., who will shortly thereafter start his own quarterly magazine, *Medical Self-Care*. SB reports in Gossip that Gregory Bateson has been appointed to the Board of Regents of the University of California ("the closest thing this state has to knighthood") and quotes his remarks: "There is at large among our students the medieval demon named *Accidie*—he's the one who whispers in your ear, 'It's not worth doing.' The students have lots of ideas, but they lack an underpinning of some sort which would let them feel that the universe makes sense. They don't know what entropy means, so they don't understand science. They don't know what a sacrament is, so they don't understand about religion."

Issue 14 (Summer 1977): Introduces fiction writer Will Baker with "Left Over in Your Heart," a humor story about Americans traveling in the Near East. Publishes Peter Warshall's interview with astronaut Rusty Schweikart, another CQ regular, on urination and defecation in space; the interview will be reprinted in the *Next Whole Earth Catalog*. Reprints a report from Stanford Research Institute called "Voluntary Simplicity," which says, "The fastest-growing sector of the market is people who don't want to buy much." Many CQ readers read into this study either vindication of their values or a frightening warning that the mass culture may co-opt them.

Issue 15 (Fall 1977): John Perlin and Ken Butti find evidence of solar power use in the early twentieth century, material that will eventually become a book (*A Golden Thread*). Reacting against attempts by the city of Sausalito to "sanitize" the waterfront area at the expense of its residents, SB begins writing about neighborhood preservation, an ongoing interest that will eventually crystallize into a series of articles in CQ on the practice of local politics. Jeanne Campbell, "longtime voice of CQ in all promotion and distribution matters," and "Godzilla on the volleyball court," leaves the staff. Penguin Books publishes the first of two CQ books, *Space Colonies*, a compendium of CQ's material on that subject.

Issue 16 (Winter 1977): Larry Lee and Scoop Nisker, news reporters and performers on KSAN, a radio station which "invented the progressive-rock format," guest-edit a special issue of CQ on broad-

cast. "How often does one get to edit one's favorite magazine?" they write. "It is doubtful that our second favorite, the *New Yorker*, is going to follow suit." Jerry Mander's article, "Four Arguments for the Elimination of Television," will later become a book with the same name. Patty Phelan and Dick Fugett join the CQ staff; Patty to do "projects," Dick to handle subscription complaints and eventually to write CQ's popular tongue-in-cheek renewal letters.

Issue 17 (Spring 1978): CQ unearths the scrambled fable "Ladle Rat Rotten Hut" and prints a popular article on using road kills for meat (both reprinted in the *Next Whole Earth Catalog*). SB organizes a benefit for R. Crumb, who owes the IRS $35,000 after being "shafted by crooked lawyers." Kathleen O'Neill, who will eventually design CQ's pages, joins the staff. An article called "In Defense of Sacred Measures" by an Englishman, John Michell, begins an ongoing argument against the introduction of the metric system into America. The cover article, about how language can cause or cure disease—based on the author's work with acne—ensures that this issue will forever be known around the office as "the pimple issue." The second Penguin/CQ book, a compilation of energy-and-tool-oriented articles and reviews called *Soft Tech*, appears. CQ attempts its first large-scale mailing-list rental and promotional mailing, which fails miserably. CQ's circulation reaches 30,000 with this issue, and henceforth will hold steady there.

Issue 18 (Summer 1978): Introduces the "Million Galaxies Poster," a computer photo-map of "the large-scale texture of the universe." SB announces the "Whole Earth Jamboree," a two-day tenth-anniversary festival for Whole Earth, held in August, organized by Patty Phelan. "The last time we had a party (The Demise Party in 1971), we gave away $20,000 in cash to the crowd," SB writes. "That won't happen this time. Other things will." In Gossip he adds, "Of the invited speakers for the event even those refusing have style—from the graceful [Ursula Le Guin: 'Woe. Alas. Phooey. Sob.'] to the cruel [Lewis Mumford: 'Thank you! But to escape the Whole Earth Jamboree I'd buy a one-way ticket on a spaceship to Saturn.']"

Issue 19 (Fall 1978): The "Poet's Issue." Guest-edited by beat poets Lawrence Ferlinghetti, Michael McClure, David Meltzer, and Gary Snyder, this issue is designed as a rebirth of a 1961 City Lights magazine called the *Journal for the Protection of All Beings*. The editors write, "We aimed at an issue centered on how to liberate mind & body and protect endangered species (including ourselves) from pathogenic industrial civilization." Partly because of its unfamiliar format, this becomes one of the most controversial (and worst-selling) issues CQ has published. Future guest-edited issues will usually involve at least one Whole Earth staffer as editor.

Issue 20 (Winter 1978): The "Jamboree Issue," quoting liberally from speeches at the Whole Earth Jamboree (Anne Herbert's Jonah story on page 136 is first published here; her reaction to the Jamboree on the next page also appears in this issue). Sheila Benson begins her regular film review column, "Good Movies," in CQ.

Issue 21 (Spring 1979): SB researches and writes "Genetic Toxicity" (p. 142): the cover announces, "New chemicals may have already done more damage to the human gene pool than nuclear energy ever will." In the same issue, "Used Magazines" queries CQ regulars on their favorite magazines. I appear for the first time, writing about the history of magazines. Dan O'Neill, protesting a $190,000 copyright infringement suit from Walt Disney for an underground comix parody he did of Mickey Mouse, draws a four-page "communiqué from the Mouse Liberation Front." It ends by announcing, "The preceding comic strip is a federal crime—contempt of the Supreme Court of the United States."

Issue 22 (Summer 1979): Introduces former *New Scientist* editor Peter Laurie with a regular column called "Pig Ignorant." A contributor to the "Broadcast Issue," Ira Einhorn, is "indicted for murder in Philadelphia. His girlfriend Holly disappeared in 1977 (it must have been shortly after he wrote [for CQ]). . . . This spring, after neighbors complained of stains on their ceiling and bad odors, Holly's dismembered remains were found in Einhorn's closet." Also, Disney responds to the Mouse Liberation Front by suing SB, Dan O'Neill, and Point Foundation for criminal and civil contempt of court (maximum fines: $10,000 each). SB publishes an open letter to Disney president Donn Tatum in *Variety,* saying: "I'm reserving equal space (four pages) in the Fall COEVOLUTION for Disney to reply to O'Neill or do whatever it wants. If Disney parodies us, I would not mind, or sue. Parody, as part of Free Speech, is a fragile right, all too susceptible to overzealous suing. . . . How would Mickey handle a situation like this? He'd come up with some goodhearted solution no doubt."

Issue 23 (Fall 1979): Guest-edited "Oceans Issue" by *Mariners' Catalog* editors Peter Spectre and George Putz, who visit from Maine for the occa-

sion. Patty Phelan leaves to manage Planetree, a San Francisco health resource library and information/advocacy service. Anne Herbert resigns as assistant editor to be replaced by Land Use evaluator Richard Nilsen. Disney offers to withdraw its charges if O'Neill and CQ promise never to draw or print Disney characters again, and to help stop other artists from parodying Disney characters. SB refuses ("I don't like seeing copyright law used to stifle criticism which is supposed to be protected by law") and prints four blank pages labeled "Walt Disney's reply to Dan O'Neill."

Issue 24 (Winter 1979): The "Swastika issue." CQ prints excerpts of a major poem by Antler, which will later become a City Lights Press book, *Factory.* Cover artist Robert Crumb, illustrating "Factory," draws a cartoon of a factory worker with swastikas in his eyes. Nine CQ staffers protest; Anne Herbert withdraws her writing from the issue. SB keeps the cover, prints her protest ("I think the cover is immoral") and his reply ("If CQ is marginally different from other publications, it is partly in our defense of the contributors' material from the depredations of insurance mentality or group-think"), and invites reader response. CQ prints three articles on New Wave and Punk music, and SB writes in Gossip: "The show violence of punk is good explosive theater, exposing a paradoxical sweetness to the night." James Lovelock's book *Gaia* is reviewed. "In the brutal/apologetic tones you would use asking someone to scrub the toilets," SB hires me to begin work coordinating the *Next Whole Earth Catalog.*

Issue 25 (Spring 1980): Several articles appear on Third World culture and politics, beginning an unplanned but prominent CQ preoccupation that will last the next four years. These include "Shramadana" by Joanna Rogers Macy, an article (that will also appear in the *Next Whole Earth Catalog*) on using community to tackle huge projects. In response to the swastika cover, CQ receives "ninety-one letters," reports SB. "Forty-one disliking or hating the cover (three canceled their subscriptions), thirty-one liking or loving the cover, and nineteen mixed, informative (swastikas aren't just Nazi, you know), peace-making, or indecipherable." The independent but allied Whole Earth Truck Store, almost out of business, is bought by the San Francisco Zen Center and becomes the Whole Earth Household Store. Disney settles with O'Neill and CQ, who agree to stop drawing or printing mice; Disney drops its previous $250,000 lawsuit. The staff swells to nearly twice its size to put out the

608-page *Catalog*. Stephanie Mills joins the staff as assistant editor, alternating with Richard Nilsen.

Issue 26 (Summer 1980): Introduces Ivan Illich as a regular CQ contributor, with a twenty-seven-page essay "on the fate of Vernacular Values during the last five hundred years of warfare that has been waged by the modern State against all forms of Subsistence." It will later become a book called *Vernacular Values*. Illich writes, "I guess that, in 1980, through no other journal I could reach a comparable motley readership of unusual critics." This issue also introduces economist/small businessman Paul Hawken, who will become CQ's most popular author and the most influential member of the Point Foundation board. Another article by Peter Nabokov and Margaret MacLean will later become a book: *Indian Running*. Meanwhile, the staff is consumed by work on the *Next Whole Earth Catalog*. "None of us have private lives or social lives left worth mentioning," writes SB. "For lack of a life, Anne notes, we've gone in for dressing weird—her tie, for example, sports a paper dollie with staples in its head."

Issue 27 (Fall 1980): Everyone is too exhausted to do an issue. Subscribers gleefully receive a copy of the *Next Whole Earth Catalog* instead. The *Catalog* is dedicated to Gregory Bateson, whose death on July 11 will be described by his daughter, Mary Catherine Bateson, in the following issue (see p. 170).

Issue 28 (Winter 1980): Guest-edited by Anne Herbert, this issue focuses on neighborhoods and includes articles by several previously unpublished (in CQ) staffers—David Burnor, Dick Fugett, Don Ryan, *Catalog* codesigner David Wills, proofreader Angela Gennino. CQ reviews take on a tone of update-to-the-*Catalog*, often specifically filling in niches that the *Catalog* didn't cover. Editor-to-be Kevin Kelly makes his first appearance with a page of haiku written while bicycling across America. An article by Orville Schell about antibiotics in meat will later become a book, *Modern Meat*. Another article by Wavy Gravy, about the Seva Foundation's work to end preventable blindness in Nepal, will later result in a $10,000 gift to Seva.

Issue 29 (Spring 1981): A compendium of computer slang, taken off the Arpanet computer network ("FLAME: To speak incessantly and/or rabidly on some relatively uninteresting subject or with a patently ridiculous attitude") will later become a book, edited by Guy Steele. Paul Hawken's article "Disintermediation" will later become the core of his book *The Next Economy*. Typesetter Evelyn El-

dridge-Diaz, who has worked for Whole Earth since the *Last Whole Earth Catalog*, resigns to take care of her new daughter, Maria Francesca. Office manager Andrea Sharp also has a daughter, Sarah, who spends the first year of her life watching her mother work in the CQ offices.

Issue 30 (Summer 1981): The "Local Politics Issue," formally opening up the practice of local politics as an ongoing topic of concern. This issue introduces Bryce and Margaret Muir, a toymaker and an anthropologist, who will take several CQ-published concepts—disintermediation, local politics—and test them in the real-world laboratory of their town in maritime Maine. A Betty Dodson illustration this issue of two women making love in Space, running with a short story called "The Day They Tested the Rec Room," will provoke a swarm of subscriber protest. Working on a *Next Whole Earth Catalog* revision, Joe Kane joins the CQ staff and introduces professional-level copy editing—a controversial move in a magazine that prides itself on never changing an author's words. The second edition also brings in proofreader Susan Erkel.

Issue 31 (Fall 1981): The Point Foundation loses some of what it made on the first edition of the *Next Whole Earth Catalog* by creating a second edition only a year later, which results in large returns of the first edition. The second edition never sells all of its overlarge first printing, 150,000 copies. Since the Point Foundation, not Random House, is the publisher (thus paying for the printing), that effectively ends income from the *Next Catalog* into CQ for at least the next several years. An article by Alia Johnson ("Stopping the Unthinkable") lists, for the first time in one place, groups organizing against nuclear war and foreshadows a new wave of peace-movement activity during the following year. In Gossip, after mentioning "the giddy life in California," SB quotes Wes Jackson of the Land Institute in Salina, Kansas: "California's too easy. Any fool can appreciate California. It takes subtlety and attention and character to appreciate Kansas."

Issue 32 (Winter 1981): Stephanie Mills and *Planet Drum* editor Peter Berg guest-edit an issue on Bioregions—"government by life," in the words of writer Jim Dodge; government by indigenous peoples, local cultures, and ecologically distinct communities, all influenced by the natural systems around them.

Issue 33 (Spring 1982): Stephanie Mills and I take on alternating editorship of CQ; SB changes his title to "publisher." Most of the major decisions about the magazine still belong to SB, but now other editors will begin to develop major voices in the direction of the magazine. Pat Califia's essay, "Feminism and Sadomasochism" (p. 206) appears; it will spark more protest than "Rec Room" did. On the following page, CQ prints letters defending "Rec Room." CQ begins a wave of major budget cuts, under the direction of financial advisor Paul Hawken. Included, for the first time in the magazine's history, is the selling of CQ's subscriber list. An anticipated wave of subscriber protest does not emerge. In Gossip, SB reports that the campaign for metrication, fought against repeatedly in CQ's pages, has lost both in England and in the United States. "Ronald Reagan, in his only known uncontested budget cut, is [dismantling] the U.S. Metric Board," he writes.

Issue 34 (Summer 1982): A cover story by Michael Phillips, "White America is Predominantly a Viking Culture," will prompt a series of reader rebuttals in future issues. By the time they're done, Vikings, Celts, Picts, Germanics, Slavs, Indo-Europeans, Greeks, and Romans will have been blamed and credited for the American Way of Life. SB unveils a new project, an adult school called "Uncommon Courtesy," with classes on "compassionate skills" like home care, first aid, creative philanthropy, and preventing street violence. It is intended to nurture a "school of thought" called the Peripheral Intelligence Agency—potentially a group of hand-picked people with the mission to "1. Do good. 2. Try stuff. 3. Follow through."

Issue 35 (Fall 1982): Three articles in this issue—Lewis Hyde's "The Gift Must Always Move," about the healthful practice among Indians of passing on gifts, Tom Parker's collection of "Rules of Thumb," and Ken Weaver's compendium of Lone Star State raunchiness, "Texas Crude"—will later become books. The *San Francisco Chronicle* begins a weekly column edited from CQ material by SB and Joe Kane, called the "Chronicle Whole Earth Catalog." Robert Fuller and associates unveil the Mo Tzu Project, for amateur peacemaking between disparate countries and peoples. Ongoing reports about Mo Tzu will appear henceforth in the magazine. SB proposes two editions of CQ: "Lite" for people offended by sexually explicit material, and "Bold" with full content. "I don't want to publish in fear of readers," he writes. "I do want there to be a magazine which can publish, potentially, anything. If that's to be truncated, I want it to be at least in part the choice and responsibility of the reader."

Issue 36 (Winter 1982): A guest-edited section by Conn Nugent, "When Things Go Wrong," about failure and misfortune. One essay in this section, "Poetry and Marriage" by Wendell Berry, will later become part of his book *Standing By Words*. Partly because of the flood of letters about the Bold/Lite idea (mostly protesting, some supporting), CQ opens its first regular letters column, called "Backscatter." SB writes, "The volume and forcefulness and ambiguity of the letters on the two-issue issue tells me to proceed full tilt, not hang back, till we find out what's at the bottom of that whirlpool."

Issue 37 (Spring 1983): This issue is concerned with agricultural diversity and includes articles on deforestation and on an agricultural patron saint, Kokopelli (p. 267). SB is given a computer to help him teach courses over a computer network, and begins investigating the world of personal computing. The first Bold section appears, with "More Texas Crude" and a two-page short story by a San Francisco poet named Pheno Barbidol. Anonymous author Szanto, a strategic planner for a larger multinational corporation, begins a regular column called "Real Intelligence," in which he writes, "The Europeans view the U.S./U.S.S.R. conflict as the competitive decadence of two empires, with the only real uncertainty being which one will decline faster." In Gossip, SB reports, "So far 190 people have requested CQ Lite versus 1900 people requesting CQ bold—10 percent. A much larger number haven't indicated which they want, and they get Bold. We won't know for a year if it'll pay off [in extra subscriptions], but it certainly isn't breaking us, and it's interesting to try."

Issue 38 (Summer 1983): Editor Stephanie Mills resigns; Jay Kinney takes her place. An article by Robert Gnaizda foreshadows the "simple tax" proposals of the following year. Regular contributor Sallie Tisdale makes her first appearance in this issue. The last CQ Bold section appears, a two-page article on Japanese "Love Hotels" by Michael Phillips; thereafter, no raunchy material shows up that's good enough to merit a special section. SB announces two new Whole Earth publications: a *Software Catalog*, to be published by Doubleday in fall 1984; and a quarterly *Software Review*, to begin publication fall 1983—"two publications evaluating the best personal computer software, hardware, suppliers, magazines, books, accessories, services, and promising directions to watch for. . . ." A $1.3 million advance from Doubleday provides initial funding for the project. Editors of the new publication are hired from a competitive computer-writing job market at substantially larger salaries than the normal CQ staff. Thus ends the equal-pay-for-all-staffers salary policy that had held constant since 1976. (In 1983, most CQ staffers were making $10/hour.) The change disrupts some of the CQ staff's longtime community feeling. The Software publications and CQ share production facilities and staff, who move to the new Software offices across the street from "Harvey's Lunches." CQ subscription prices rise to $18/year; at Paul Hawken's suggestion, this is done without a major announcement in the magazine.

Issue 39 (Fall 1983): Jay Kinney edits a special section on reconciling Politics and Religion, including Gary Snyder's essay "Good, Wild, Sacred" (p. 282). In Gossip, SB writes: "The *Whole Earth Catalog* and *CoEvolution Quarterly* are godchildren in part of Buckminster Fuller, who died a few weeks ago, followed a day later by his wife Anne. A few days after that another friend, the 300-pound "neo-Stoic" Herman Kahn, died untimely at 63. . . . Fuller and Kahn started conversations that I expect to keep having with them the rest of my life."

Issue 40 (Winter 1983): CQ runs articles on the political, financial, and sexual abuses of two prominent counterculture religious leaders. The first is an investigative probe into the affairs of Swami Muktananda of the Siddha Meditation movement. The second involves a former member of Point's own board: Zentatsu Baker-roshi of the San Francisco Zen Center (see p. 298), who will eventually be asked to resign by the Zen Center community. The change affects many Zen Center businesses, including the Whole Earth Household Store, which is now sold to a Bay Area retail chain originally inspired by the *Whole Earth Catalog*, a chain called the Whole Earth Access Company. Two months before the Zen Center article appears, Stewart Brand and Patty Phelan are married at the Zen Center's Green Gulch Farm. CQ publishes an Anne Herbert essay called, "It Is Easier to Stop a Slow-Moving Vehicle Than It Is a Runaway Horse. Safer, Too." It will eventually appear in her book *Random Kindness and Senseless Acts of Beauty*. James Donnelly, who will shortly become CQ's most consistently hilarious cartoonist, joins the staff as a typesetter.

Issue 41 (Spring 1984): The financial needs of the *Whole Earth Software Review* bring budget planning to the rest of Whole Earth. Uncommon Courtesy is suspended "until Point is fat enough to do interesting charity again." The CQ products are discontin-

ued, because they drain more money than they bring in; SB remarks that Products Manager Debbie Hopkins "diligently assisted the very analysis that ended her job." Product fulfillment is given to the Whole Earth Access Company. The CQ library (excess review copies and research books accumulated over the years) is sold. Meanwhile, the first issue of the *Whole Earth Software Review* appears—132 pocket-book-sized pages, full-color, no advertising—to mixed critical reception. A subsequent issue is better, but gathers far fewer subscribers than expected. After the second issue, editor Richard Dalton resigns.

Issue 42 (Summer 1984): I leave CQ to edit the *Whole Earth Software Review*. Kevin Kelly is hired from Athens, Georgia, to replace me. An article ("Nicaragua's Other War") by Bernard Nietschmann, on the battles between the Sandinista government and Nicaragua's Miskito Indians, will incite so much controversy that CQ will ultimately send Will Baker to Nicaragua to sort out the situation. The *Whole Earth Catalog* newspaper column begins to be syndicated nationally. The wedding of longtime CQ staffers Don Ryan (maps, photographs, paste-up) and Susan Erkel (proofreading, behind-the-scenes organization, unclassifieds) is reported in Gossip. Two other longtime employees—production liaison Jonathan Evelegh and librarian Ben Campbell, the unofficial conscience and all-around caretaker of the CQ office—leave the staff.

Issue 43 (Fall 1984): The LAST COEVOLUTION QUARTERLY. Says the cover: "Next issue is *Whole Earth Review*: livelier snake, new skin." Writes SB in Gossip: "The Point Foundation Board of Directors, doing its job, said [the *Software Review*] was pissing away what's left of the million-buck advance we got from Doubleday for the *Whole Earth Software Catalog*. . . . Gloom. Financial officer Paul Hawken brooded for a couple of weeks and then made the kind of suggestion we retain him for. 'Don't kill the *Software Review*. Blend the best of it into COEVOLUTION. Find a new title if need be. Use the money saved to make the new magazine be even better, and promote it properly.'" Coedited by Kevin Kelly and myself, the first issue of the *Whole Earth Review* appears in December 1984, with a fifty-four-page special section called "Computers as Poison," and a twenty-two-page section on "Computers as Tools," updating the *Whole Earth Software Catalog*.

Design by David Bullen
Typeset in Mergenthaler Garamond #3
with Aldus display
by Wilsted & Taylor
Printed by Maple-Vail
on acid-free paper